Culture and Personality

*THE DORSEY SERIES IN ANTHROPOLOGY
AND SOCIOLOGY*

EDITOR   ROBIN M. WILLIAMS, JR.   *Cornell University*

ANDERSON   *Sociological Essays and Research: Introductory Readings*
ANDERSON   *Toward a New Sociology: A Critical View*
BARNOUW   *Culture and Personality*   rev. ed.
BARNOUW   *An Introduction to Anthropology*
   Volume I.   *Physical Anthropology and Archaeology*
   Volume II.   *Ethnology*
BELL   *Marriage and Family Interaction*   3d ed.
BELL   *Social Deviance: A Substantive Analysis*
BELL & STUB (eds.)   *The Sociology of Education: A Sourcebook*   rev. ed.
BREER & LOCKE   *Task Experience as a Source of Attitudes*
GAMSON   *Power and Discontent*
GEORGES (ed.)   *Studies on Mythology*
GOODMAN   *The Individual and Culture*
GORDEN   *Interviewing: Strategy, Techniques, and Tactics*
GOTTLIEB & RAMSEY   *The American Adolescent*
HAGEN   *On the Theory of Social Change: How Economic Growth Begins*
HSU (ed.)   *Psychological Anthropology: Approaches to Culture and Personality*
JACOBS   *Pattern in Cultural Anthropology*
JOHNSON   *Crime, Correction, and Society*   rev. ed.
JOHNSON   *Social Problems of Urban Man*
JUHASZ   *Sexual Development and Behavior: Selected Readings*
KNUDTEN   *Crime in a Complex Society: An Introduction to Criminology*
KNUDTEN   *Crime, Criminology, and Contemporary Society*
KOHN   *Class and Conformity: A Study in Values*
LEMASTERS   *Parents in Modern America*
MARIS   *Social Forces in Urban Suicide*
SALISBURY   *Religion in American Culture: A Sociological Interpretation*
SHOSTAK (ed.)   *Sociology in Action: Case Studies in Social Problems and Directed
   Social Change*
WARRINER   *The Emergence of Society*
WILSON   *Sociology: Rules, Roles, and Relationships*   rev. ed.

Culture and Personality

VICTOR BARNOUW
Professor of Anthropology
University of Wisconsin—Milwaukee

REVISED EDITION • 1973
THE DORSEY PRESS *Homewood, Illinois 60430*
IRWIN-DORSEY LIMITED *Georgetown, Ontario*

Revised Edition

First Printing, January 1973

ISBN 0-256-01403-5
Library of Congress Catalog Card No. 72-86628
Printed in the United States of America

To A. IRVING HALLOWELL,
true scholar and teacher

Preface

The present edition of *Culture and Personality* has been revised to take account of developments in the field during the past ten years. Increased attention has been given to cognitive aspects of culture-and-personality. There has been a great increase in cross-cultural correlational studies making use of the Human Relations Area Files. In field methods there has been a new emphasis on the use of standardized questionnaires in cross-cultural studies, which may have been partly in response to another recent tendency, a decrease in the use of projective tests.

Cognitive aspects of culture-and-personality are now dealt with in Chapter 3, which incorporates some sections of former chapters 6 and 22.

In the first edition a chapter on cross-cultural correlational studies was included under a section on Methods. This chapter has been greatly expanded and has now been moved to Part III on Current Approaches.

Standardized questionnaires have been used in a few large-scale cross-cultural studies, notably the Six Cultures project, the Cornell-Aro psychiatric study of the Yoruba compared with Stirling County in Canada, the investigation of peasant "social character" in a Mexican village made by Erich Fromm and Michael Maccoby, and Robert B. Edgerton's study of four East African tribes. All four of these ambitious, well-conceived projects are important both for their findings and for innovations in field methods. Some of the ethnographic data of the Six Cultures project are discussed in Chapter 9. The field methods used are dealt with in Chapter 11. Erich Fromm's concepts of character orientation and social character are presented in the first two chapters. In Chapter 1 more attention than in the first edition has been given to different theoretical approaches to personality.

In the 1963 edition I tried to confine my survey of culture-and-personality research to studies made by anthropologists of non-Western societies and explained that this limitation involved omitting consideration of studies of the American scene by such observers as David Riesman, Erich Fromm, and others. This limitation now seems arbitrary. The views of Riesman, Fromm, and others about American culture and personality are now discussed in Chapter 17, which is greatly expanded from former Chapter 22.

An interesting development in the last 10 years or so is that many non-anthropologists have been entering the field of culture-and-personality, including economists such as Everett E. Hagen, political scientists such as Richard H. Solomon, and psychologists such as David C. McClelland, whose works are discussed in Chapter 17.

The present edition has a new chapter on National Character (Chapter 10), presenting some of the views of Francis L. K. Hsu and others, as well as work done in Japan by William Caudill, George De Vos, and others.

The new additions have required some deletions of earlier material. Most of former Chapter 2 on "Some Forerunners," former Chapter 8 on "Childhood Determinism and the Study of National Character," and former Chapter 9 on the Chippewa have been cut, although parts of these chapters have been transplanted to other sections of the book. Former Chapter 19 on the interpretation of art has been deleted, and so have Jim Mink's anecdotes in the chapter on life history material.

I would like to thank the following for their critical comments and suggestions concerning the revised version: Pertti Pelto, University of Connecticut, Storrs, Connecticut; Allen C. Fanger of Kutztown State College, Pennsylvania; Charles C. Harrington, Teachers College, Columbia University; James A. Clifton, University of Wisconsin at Green Bay, Wisconsin; and Robin Williams, consulting editor of The Dorsey Press.

Since 1965 I have given a seminar on Culture and Personality in the Honors Program at the University of Wisconsin-Milwaukee. I learned a lot from the alert, questioning students who attended it, and I express my appreciation to them.

As always, I am grateful to my wife Sachiko for her help and encouragement.

In the course of this book I have drawn upon some previously published pieces of mine, particularly *Acculturation and Personality among the Wisconsin Chippewa* (Memoir No. 72 of the American Anthropological Association, October 1950) ; "The Phantasy World of a Chippewa Woman," *Psychiatry*, Vol. 12, 1949, pp. 67–76; "Ruth Benedict: Apollonian and Dionysian," *University of Toronto Quarterly*, Vol. 18, 1949, pp. 241–53; "A Psychological Interpretation of a Chippewa Origin Legend," *Journal of American Folklore*, Vol. 68 (Part I, No. 267) , January–March 1955, pp. 73–87; (Part II, No. 268) April–June 1955, pp. 211–23; (Part III, No. 269) July–September 1955, pp. 341–55; "The Amiable Side of *Patterns of Culture*," *American Anthropologist*, Vol. 59, 1957, pp. 532–36; "Chippewa Social Atomism," *American Anthropologist*, Vol. 63, 1961, pp. 1006–13; and "Cross-Cultural Research with the House-Tree-Person Test," in John N. Buck and Emanuel F. Hammer (eds.) , *Advances in the House-Tree-Person Technique: Variations and Applications* (Los Angeles: Western Psychological Services, 1969) , pp. 417–47.

December 1972   VICTOR BARNOUW

048072

Contents

part I

BASIC CONCEPTS AND APPROACHES

Part I sets forth some basic concepts and approaches. Chapter 1 presents definitions of *culture* and *personality* and some contrasting views about personality. Chapter 2 introduces the concept of *social character,* with two illustrations, discussed at some length. In Chapter 3 there are definitions and illustrations of a series of concepts: world view, ethos, themes, postulates, values, prejudices, and self-concepts, and there is some discussion of the influence of language on cognition.

chapter *1*

An Introduction to the Field

Culture-and-personality is an area of research where anthropology and psychology come together—more particularly where the fields of cultural and social anthropology relate to the psychology of personality. Ethnologists, or cultural anthropologists, are students of culture—of the different ways of living that have developed in human societies in different parts of the world, while psychiatrists and (at least some) psychologists are analysts of human personality whose work involves an effort to understand why and how individuals differ from one another as they do. Serving as a bridge between ethnology and psychology, the field of culture-and-personality is concerned with the ways in which the culture of a society influences the persons who grow up within it.[1]

Sociology and social psychology are allied social sciences related to this field, although studies by sociologists and social psychologists have generally been made within the setting of modern Western

---

[1] Kluckhohn and Murray have expressed some dissatisfaction with the phrase "culture and personality," partly because of the dualism implied by it. They feel that "culture *in* personality" or "personality *in* culture" would serve as better conceptual models. The usual phrase ignores other determinants of personality beside culture. " 'Culture and personality' is as lopsided as 'biology and personality.' " (Clyde Kluckhohn and Henry A. Murray, *Personality in Nature, Society, and Culture* [New York: Alfred A. Knopf, Inc., 1948], p. 44.) Francis L. K. Hsu has suggested the term "psychological anthropology" to designate this field. The word "psychoethnography" has also been used, i.e., as a book review heading in the *American Anthropologist.* However, the most usual designation continues to be "culture and personality." I prefer to hyphenate this phrase to emphasize its unity.

3

culture. It is not always possible, or necessary, to draw boundary lines between these disciplines. The present work, however, focuses primarily on contributions made by anthropologists who have an interest in the psychology of personality. It is mainly concerned with cross-cultural studies; these have generally been pursued by anthropologists, although analyses of some of their data (e.g., Rorschach records) have often been made by specialists in other fields.

Ethnologists get most of their information from the observation of behavior and from interviews. The usual job of the ethnologist is to record and analyze ethnographic data; he studies the customs and social organization of a particular society. In addition to this, researchers in the field of culture-and-personality are concerned with observing behavior expressive of personality to see how culture and personality patterns are related in the society. In contrast to psychologists, ethnologists seldom make use of controlled experiments, although they have sometimes used doll play under controlled conditions. They do not usually give paper and pencil tests, for very often they work in nonliterate societies. Anthropologists have, however, made use of projective tests, such as the Rorschach and modified Thematic Apperception Tests which do not require literacy.

Despite their very different theoretical approaches, both Freudian psychoanalysts and behaviorists in psychology agree that the early childhood years are of crucial importance in the formation of personality. This suggests the importance of studying child development in different cultural contexts. One focus in anthropology is the study of *enculturation,* the process whereby a growing child acquires familiarity with his culture. An ethnologist observes child behavior in the course of fieldwork, noting how mothers treat their children and how children in turn respond. He may note such features as the length of the suckling period, weaning procedures, toilet training practices, attitudes toward children's sexual exploration, parental sanctions for good behavior, children's games, and other related topics. Cross-cultural data of this sort make one aware of the great range of variation in child-rearing practices in different parts of the world and of how these different practices prepare children to become different kinds of adults.

Much of our knowledge of human personality has come from the work of psychiatrists and psychoanalysts like Freud. Although this knowledge is of the greatest value, it has two limitations. First, it is necessarily derived from people who were unhappy enough to go to a psychiatrist for help. Although everyone has problems, this makes for a rather biased sample of human beings. The second limitation is that most psychiatric patients whose cases have been analyzed are Europeans or Americans. We need to study the lives of successful and relatively unneurotic persons as well as the emotionally disturbed, both in our own society and in others with contrasting cultures.

The anthropologist studies man in his natural sphere of action, not in a clinic or laboratory. He may spend several weeks or months with a particular family or group of families. These persons are not apt to pour out their troubles to him as a patient does to a psychiatrist, so the anthropologist probably takes much longer to learn something about them. But he sees them in the course of their daily lives, not in an artificial setting, and he sees them in a variety of activities and circumstances. This is not to say that the information thus acquired is more enlightening or of greater value than that provided by the psychologist or psychiatrist. It is open to the criticism of being less scientific than that of the psychologist, in that it is not based on controlled experimentation. But culture-and-personality research provides a valuable, alternative way of learning about human personality which can check and supplement the findings of psychology and psychiatry.

Unfortunately, the terms "culture" and "personality," which give the field its name, are hard to define in clear-cut unambiguous fashion. Both are associated in popular usage with older colloquial meanings which differ from those given in social science literature. ("He has a lot of culture," we might say, "but she's the one with the personality.") We must first consider these two terms in some detail.

THE DEFINITION OF CULTURE

E. B. Tylor, in 1871, was the first to use the word "culture" in English in the sense now accepted by anthropologists and sociologists.[2] Following the lead of some German writers who used *Kultur* in this sense, he named his pioneer work *Primitive Culture* and defined the term on page one as "that complex whole which includes

---

[2] A. L. Kroeber and Clyde Kluckhohn, "Culture: A Critical Review of Concepts and Definitions," *Papers of the Peabody Museum of American Archeology and Ethnology*, Vol. 47, No. 1 (Cambridge, Mass.: Harvard University, 1952), p. 9.

knowledge, belief, art, law, morals, custom, and any other capabilities and habits acquired by man as a member of society."[3]

This may be called an omnibus or sum-total definition, in that it lumps together a number of different categories which serve to make up the term defined. One weakness of such a definition is that it omits the element of integration found in every culture, although that is hinted at in the phrase "complex whole." Another weakness is that the list of categories cannot be complete. However, Tylor's definition was an important achievement in its time, for it set forth the subject matter of the then new science of cultural anthropology.

Under this view, culture could be studied as a sphere apart from psychology or biology, because cultural phenomena were believed to have their own laws.

Years later, Ralph Linton offered a definition of culture which stressed the factor of integration: "A culture is the configuration of learned behavior and results of behavior whose component elements are shared and transmitted by the members of a particular society."[4] Here some might object to the inclusion of "results of behavior" in the definition, for opinions are divided as to whether objects—"material culture," so called—are to be regarded as culture.[5] Note that Linton has defined *a* culture and not culture in general. The broader term is useful in clarifying how man's behavior differs from that of other animals, which do not have a language and which cannot, therefore, transmit culture in the human sense. But anthropologists more frequently speak of particular cultures—of "Blackfoot culture," for example, meaning the way of life characteristic of the Blackfoot Indians of Montana in the early 19th century.

Here is a definition which I think most anthropologists would accept: *A culture is the way of life of a group of people, the configuration of all of the more or less stereotyped patterns of learned behavior which are handed down from one generation to the next through the means of language and imitation.* The nub of this definition is the first clause: "the way of life of a group of people." This

---

[3] Edward B. Tylor, *Primitive Culture. Researches into the Development of Mythology, Philosophy, Religion, Language, Art, and Customs* (New York: Henry Holt & Co., 1877), Vol. I, p. 1.

[4] Ralph Linton, *The Cultural Background of Personality* (New York: Appleton-Century Co., 1945), p. 32.

[5] For statements by those who oppose including "material culture," see E. A. Hoebel, "The Nature of Culture," in Harry L. Shapiro (ed.), *Man, Culture and Society* (New York: Oxford University Press, 1956), p. 176; Walter W. Taylor, *A Study of Archeology* (American Anthropological Association Memoir No. 69, 1948), pp. 98–102; and Ralph L. Beals and Harry Hoijer, *An Introduction to Anthropology* (New York: Macmillan Co., 1961), p. 229.

way of life has some integration and cohesion to it—hence the term "configuration." It consists of patterns of learned behavior which are transmitted through language and imitation—not through instinct or any direct action of the genes. These patterns are only relatively fixed. For example, in our culture it has long been the custom for men to wear trousers and women to wear skirts. But this pattern is amenable to change and is only "more or less" stereotyped; for women often wear slacks, and some Scotsmen wear kilts. Culture, then, is marked by plasticity and change; although some societies have gone through centuries, even millennia, with very little change.

The culture of a society provides a number of ready-made answers to the problems of life. The child learns these as he grows up and comes to see the world through the particular spectacles of his culture. The culture provides him with means for coping with the world; mastery of these methods increases his sense of confidence. The culture also has a body of doctrines about the world—religious traditions and folklore—which give some orientation and reassurance to the individual. But the culture may also provide threatening influences such as beliefs in evil spirits, malevolent gods, sorcery, and so forth, which may structure a view of the world as dangerous.

From a logical point of view, it is surprising how seldom people come to question the tenets of the culture into which they are born. But usually they do not have the perspective to do so. In some ways cultural behavior is like that of persons under posthypnotic suggestion, who perform actions without realizing why they do so. Man would be lost without his culture—hardly different from the apes. But while he gains so much from culture, man is also brainwashed, to some extent, by the culture to which he is exposed from birth. Equipped with a collection of stereotypes with which to face the world, man is apt to lose sight of possible alternative modes of behavior and understanding.

THE DEFINITION OF PERSONALITY

The definition of "personality" is an even more vexed question than that of culture, and there are many types of definition to choose from.[6] For example, there are omnibus definitions, like this one from Morton Prince: "*Personality* is the sum-total of all the biologi-

---

[6] For a brief history of this term, from its beginnings in the Greek word *persona*, meaning mask, see Gordon W. Allport, *Personality, A Psychological Interpretation* (New York: Henry Holt, 1937).

cal innate dispositions, impulses, tendencies, appetites, and instincts of the individual, and the acquired dispositions and tendencies— *acquired* by experience."[7]

Such definitions are open to the same objection as is Tylor's definition of culture—the omission of an element of integration. Another type of definition puts the emphasis on just this factor—the integrative nature of personality, which gives some consistency to the behavior of the individual. Allport's definition may be cited as an example: "Personality is the dynamic organization within the individual of those psychophysical systems that determine his unique adjustments to his environment."[8]

Not all psychologists would accept such a definition. Those influenced by positivistic and behaviorist traditions might regard it as an unwarranted reification or even as an effort to reintroduce soul or psyche into psychology. Avoiding such dangers, Watson refers to personality as "the sum of activities that can be discovered by actual observation over a long enough period of time to give reliable information,"[9] while, for McClelland, personality is "the most adequate conceptualization of a person's behavior in all its detail that the scientist can give at a moment of time."[10]

Parallel problems appear in defining "culture" and "personality." As we have seen, each term has been given "sum-total" definitions and also definitions which emphasize configuration or integration. For both terms, some definitions include and some exclude behavior. McClelland's definition, which stresses that personality is an abstraction in the mind of the scientist, has its counterpart in Osgood's definition of culture: "Culture consists of all ideas of the manufactures, behavior, and ideas of the aggregate of human beings which have been directly observed or communicated to one's mind and of which one is conscious."[11]

One's definition of culture or personality, then, evidently reflects one's central assumptions. A behaviorist's definition of personality will differ from a psychoanalyst's. American academic psychology has been much influenced by the behaviorist viewpoint. However,

---

[7] Morton Prince, *The Unconscious* (rev. ed.; New York: Macmillan Co., 1929), p. 532.

[8] Allport, *Personality, A Psychological Interpretation,* p. 48.

[9] John B. Watson, *Behaviorism* (rev. ed.; New York: W.W. Norton & Co. Inc., 1930). Italics in original.

[10] D. C. McClelland, *Personality* (William Sloane Associates, 1951), p. 69.

[11] Cornelius Osgood, "Culture, Its Empirical and Non-Empirical Character," *Southwestern Journal of Anthropology,* Vol. 7 (1951), p. 208. Italics in original.

the American anthropologists who have done the most research in culture-and-personality have, for better or worse, been influenced more by psychological and psychiatric schools of European origin, such as the Gestalt and psychoanalytic schools; and they have tended, at least implicitly, to accept a view of personality which stresses its integrative, configurational character. I think that they have also tended to think of personality as something which influences behavior, rather than equating it with behavior itself.

A statement about personality with which I agree, though with some reservations, is one given by the authors of *The Authoritarian Personality:* ". . . personality is a more or less enduring organization of forces within the individual. These persisting forces of personality help to determine response in various situations, and it is thus largely to them that consistency of behavior—whether verbal or physical is attributable. But behavior, however consistent, is not the same thing as personality; personality lies *behind* behavior and *within* the individual. The forces of personality are not responses but *readinesses for response. . . .*"[12]

An objection that can be raised here is that consistency of behavior might be ascribed to culture or to the social role of the individual, rather than to personality. Consistency of verbal behavior, if we mean speaking English or Chinese, is certainly a matter of culture, not of personality. Consistency of physical behavior (sitting on chairs in our culture, or squatting in a primitive tribe) may also be more readily ascribed to culture. If a man is consistent in going to work every morning at a certain hour by subway and returning home at a predictable time in late afternoon, this consistency is the product of a particular sociocultural system and the man's role within it, although the performance of this dull routine may well require a particular kind of personality organization. But this is not what the authors of the statement in *The Authoritarian Personality* had in mind.

With the reservations noted, their view of personality is one which I share. Moreover, I believe that part of the consistency inherent in personality relates to the acquisition of values and attitudes by the individual. The analysis of a Thematic Apperception Test, for example, or of a life history document, brings to light the characteristic attitudes and values of the subject, and it is assumed

---

[12] T. W. Adorno, Else Frenkel-Brunswik, D. J. Levinson, and R. Nevitt Sanford, *The Authoritarian Personality* (New York: Harper, 1950), p. 5. Italics as in the original.

that there is some degree of stability in these patterns. Personality is also characterized by certain patterns of perception and cognition, as may be manifest in a subject's Rorschach protocol. In modifying the statement in *The Authoritarian Personality*, let me conclude with this suggested definition: *Personality is a more or less enduring organization of forces within the individual associated with a complex of fairly consistent attitudes, values, and modes of perception which account, in part, for the individual's consistency of behavior.*

CONSISTENCY IN PERSONALITY

Those who hold a view of personality along some such lines as these are apt to see everything that a person does, or the way in which he does it, as expressive of his personality to some degree. Experiments have shown that individuals have characteristic and consistent patterns of walking, gesturing, and even of sleeping.[13] We recognize that our friends have certain predictable styles of behavior and modes of expression—something well illustrated by the works of composers and painters. A music lover may correctly identify a piece of music as being by Mozart even if he hasn't heard that particular piece before, just as one can recognize a painting as the work of Rembrandt or van Gogh, or a passage of prose as being by Hemingway or Henry James on the basis of style. But is there a general consistency in such matters as posture, gait, vocal expression, and so forth? That is to say, did Mozart, for example, have a particularly Mozartian way of walking or writing? Did Hemingway put out a cigarette very differently from Henry James, and would that way of putting it out express something of the writer's inner nature?

Werner Wolff has approached this sort of problem through some ingenious matching experiments. He showed a group of 20 subjects three specimens of musical notations, one by Bach, one by Beethoven, and one by Mozart; and asked them to guess which musician wrote which (see Figure 1–1). Sixteen of the subjects made correct matchings, the four mistakes being made with the samples of Mozart and Bach.[14] While this experiment turned out successfully, it raises some questions. One wonders if Beethoven in his earlier years, when his music was more like Mozart's, had a more Mozartian calligraphy

---

[13] For references, see "Suggestions for Further Reading," at end of this chapter.

[14] Werner Wolff, *The Expression of Personality. Experimental Depth Psychology* (New York: Harper & Bros., 1943), pp. 20–21.

Figure 1–1. Musical notations to be matched to the Names of Three Composers: A., Bach; B., Beethoven; C., Mozart. Correct matchings: IB, IIC, IIIA. (From Werner Wolff, *The Expression of Personality. Experimental Depth Psychology.* New York: Harper & Bros., 1943, pp. 20-21)

and style of writing notations? And did Mozart, in his later years, when his music became more like Beethoven's, write in a more Beethovenish handwriting? Such second thoughts show how intricately culture and personality are interrelated. A particular literary or musical style may come to be imitated by people of very different personality characteristics. Yet, as one may see in the impressionist school of painting (or any other), individual differences still persist. All the children in a particular class may have learned how to write from the same teacher; nevertheless, each soon develops idiosyncratic peculiarities of style, a characteristic handwriting, which friends and relatives can recognize at once.

Wolff carried out various other matching experiments similar to the one just described. In one of these, 23 students were asked to write this sentence: "Good day, I wonder whether these experiments will yield any results." Each subject then spoke the same words into a sound recording device. At a later period the students received three specimens of handwriting and listened to three recordings of the sentence. Their task was to match the voice with the handwriting. The number of correct matchings in this case was from one and a half to two times the chance numbers.[15] Similar experiments in matching voice with other manifestations of behavior have been made by W. Huntley, G. W. Allport, and H. Cantril, with results much better than chance.

Gordon W. Allport and Philip E. Vernon carried out an extensive experiment with a group of 25 male subjects ranging in age from 18 to 50. For each of these subjects they studied matters such as speed of reading aloud; normal walking tempo; estimation of certain distances, weights, and sizes; drawings of circles, squares, rectangles, and other figures; strength of grip; speed of tapping with finger, hand, leg, and stylus; and degree of muscular tension. An analysis was made of each subject's handwriting, using instruments designed to test pressure. In discussing their results, the authors assert: "At least three quarters of the experiments have been unequivocal in their proof of the interconsistency of expressive movements."[16] In still another study of expressive movements, Philip Eisenberg found fairly consistent syndromes of behavior in dominant and nondominant subjects. This study was based on tests and interviews with a group of Columbia and Barnard students. Eisenberg concluded:

Dominant men draw squares and circles, and write normally and under conditions of maximum speed, faster than non-dominant men, but their speed of walking, relative to the length of legs, is slower under observation. Dominant men tend to cover more space on a page when writing than non-dominant men. . . . Dominant men exert greater point-pressure in both normal and maximum writing than non-dominant men. . . . Dominant men tend to come late for their appointments, and non-dominant tend to come early. These differences are statistically reliable, or nearly so.[17]

Individuals show consistency in dealing with certain cognitive tasks, for example in the speed with which they can find a hidden figure embedded in a picture. Herman A. Witkin and his associates termed those who are quick to discover the hidden figure "field-independent," while those who are slow to do so are "field-dependent." Field-independence, which represents a greater degree of psychological differentiation, increases with age. At the same time, the level of psychological differentiation is relatively stable during

---

[15] Ibid., p. 22.

[16] Gordon W. Allport and Philip E. Vernon, *Studies in Expressive Movement* (New York: Macmillan Co., 1933) , p. 120.

[17] Philip Eisenberg, "Expressive Movements Related to Feelings of Dominance," *Archives of Psychology*, No. 211 (1937) , p. 70.

development, so that a child who is more "field-dependent" than his age-mates will tend to have a similar position as a young adult. On the basis of a wide range of psychological tests, it has been claimed that field-dependent persons have a less differentiated body image than field-independent persons, tend to repress their impulses, to lack insight, and to be passive, readily giving in to feelings of inferiority.[18] Thus, in various ways, persons show consistency over time in certain cognitive and emotional patterns of behavior.

To affirm that personality is characterized by consistency is not to deny that a personality may have its internal conflicts and inconsistencies. A man given to swagger and boastfulness is not necessarily a person with a deep sense of confidence in himself; perhaps quite the contrary. A boy who feels himself to be physically inferior may develop overcompensating tendencies and "act tough"; but inconsistencies of this sort are not basic. Such a mechanism may be seen as part of the total personality. There are also apparent inconsistencies stemming from situational conditions of status and role; a boy may behave differently with his parents than with his friends at school. But the playing of different roles does not negate an underlying consistency of personality. We must grant that personality may change over time. Despite much carry-over, the adult is a different person from the child. Gordon Allport who has done so much to demonstrate the consistency of personality, has also emphasized the "functional autonomy" of adult life. According to him, adult motives may grow out of antecedent childhood systems, but are functionally independent of them.[19] Thus, there are both consistency and change in personality, just as there are both consistency and change in culture.

THE REALITY OF PERSONALITY

The experiments mentioned above of Wolff, Allport, Vernon, Eisenberg, Witkin, and others tend to support a view of personality which stresses its integration and internal consistency; personality

---

[18] H. A. Witkin et al., *Personality through Perception. An Experimental and Clinical Study* (New York: Harper & Bros., 1954) ; H. A. Witkin et al., *Psychological Differentiation. Studies of Development* (New York: John Wiley & Sons, Inc., 1962) ; Herman A. Witkin, Donald R. Goodenough, and Stephen A. Karp, "Stability of Cognitive Style from Childhood to Young Adulthood," *Journal of Personality and Social Psychology*, Vol. 7 (1967) , pp. 291–300.

[19] Gordon W. Allport, *Personality, A Psychological Interpretation* (New York: Henry Holt, 1937) , p. 194.

is seen as something very "real." On the other hand, Francis L. K. Hsu has recently warned against acceptance of a viewpoint of this kind. In order to bypass the embarrassments raised by the term "personality," Hsu proposes that we change the name "culture-and-personality" to "psychological anthropology."

    . . . the term "personality" possesses connotations that often lead the student to regard it as a complete entity in itself. Instead of seeing personality as a life-long process of interaction between the individual and his society and culture, he thinks of it as being some sort of reified end-product (of very early experiences according to orthodox Freudians, of somewhat later sociocultural forces according to many Neo-Freudians and social scientists) , which is ready to act in this or that direction regardless of the sociocultural fields in which it has to operate continuously. . . . [Given] the social scientist's individualist cultural heritage of hero and martyr worship, and a Judaeo-Christian theological background of absolute conversion and final salvation, the one-sided finished-product view of personality would seem too "natural." Such a view must be resisted and the beginning of such a step is to eliminate the word personality from the title of our subdiscipline.[20]

It is true that we must avoid the fallacy of misplaced concreteness. Both "culture" and "personality" are abstractions and refer more to processes than things. We may run the risk of reifying culture and de-emphasizing personality as Leslie White does in his "culturological" approach,[21] or we may run the risk of reifying personality, which Hsu warns against. I think, however, that there has been a tendency for social scientists to err more in the culturological direction, and that it would be well to counter this by emphasizing the reality of personality.

Personalities must have existed before culture came into being. Various anthropologists who have observed primate groups in the field have used the term "personality" to apply to apes and monkeys. In a brief survey of such literature, John O. Ellefson makes the

---

[20] Francis L. K. Hsu (ed.) , *Psychological Anthropology* (Cambridge, Mass.: Schenkman Publishing Company, 1972) , pp. 8–9. Hsu has renewed his opposition to the term "personality" "Psychosocial Homeostasis and *Jen:* Conceptual Tools for Advancing Psychological Anthropology," *American Anthropologist,* Vol. 73 (1971) , pp. 23–44. As a substitute for "personality" Hsu suggests the Chinese word *jen* which has reference to the individual's transactions with his fellow human beings.

[21] White speaks of culture as "a thing *sui generis.*" See Leslie A. White, "Ethnological Theory," in Sellars, McGill, and M. Farber (eds.) , *Philosophy for the Future* (New York: Macmillan Co., 1949) , p. 374. Recently White has repudiated the charge that he reifies culture, but he does so in a paradoxical and self-consistent way: "It is not we who have reified culture; the elements comprising culture, according to our definition, were things to start with." (Leslie A. White, "The Concept of Culture," *American Anthropologist,* Vol. 61 [1959], p. 239) .

suggestion that: "The modal or normative personalities of species have adaptive significance; that is, norms of personality are the result of an adaptive process, an interplay between natural selection and the genetic variation intrinsic to sexual reproduction and mutation through time in populations."[22]

"Personality" differences between primate species may represent adaptations to different environments. It has been suggested, for example, that the aggressive temperament of baboons is related to their adjustment to terrestrial life on the savannahs, where they are exposed to predators, while arboreal primates are under less pressure of that sort.

A contrast has often been noted between the calm, aloof behavior of the gorilla and the noisy sociable behavior of the chimpanzee. V. Reynolds has argued that these contrasts are related to differences in social organization and foraging patterns. The food supplies of the chimpanzees are more varied, located in different places at different times, and their social organization is looser, permitting groups to split up and later regroup. Their loud chorusing alerts chimpanzees to areas of plentiful food.[23]

While there seem to be differences in personality or temperament between such species as gorillas and chimpanzees, there are also individual differences within a species. George B. Schaller has written: "Free-living gorillas exhibit great individual variation in their affective behavior, and the spectrum of emotions exhibited by the members of the same group to my presence varied from excitement to seeming disinterest; in other words, there were nervous individuals and calm ones, aggressive individuals and shy ones."[24]

May one say, then, that gorillas have personalities? That would, of course, depend upon one's definition of personality. The definition given earlier refers to "a complex of fairly consistent attitudes, values, and modes of perception which account, in part, for the individual's consistency of behavior." If attitudes and values are derived from culture, involving the use of language, then nonhumans and human infants could not be said to have personalities,

---

[22] John O. Ellefson, "Personality and the Biological Nature of Man," in Edward Norbeck, Douglass Price-Williams, and William M. McCord (eds.), *The Study of Personality. An Interdisciplinary Appraisal* (New York: Holt, Rinehart & Winston, Inc., 1968), p. 137.

[23] V. Reynolds, "Some Behavioral Comparisons between the Chimpanzee and the Mountain Gorilla in the Wild," *American Anthropologist*, Vol. 67 (1965), pp. 691–706.

[24] George B. Schaller, *The Mountain Gorilla. Ecology and Behavior* (Chicago: University of Chicago Press, 1963), p. 80.

and personality could not antedate culture. But if some other definition of personality, such as Allport's, were used, there would be no logical inconsistency in saying that our earliest hominid forebears had personalities before speech or the use of tools were developed. Their personalities, indeed, may have tended more toward the chimpanzee model than a gorilla or other primate model, as Ellefson has suggested.[25]

While personality in the distant past must have existed without culture, culture can only be mediated through individual personalities. The reality of personality is indicated by the difficulty which psychotherapists encounter when they try to bring about character changes in their patients. It must be admitted that there is something tough and consistent about personality.

CONTRASTING VIEWS OF PERSONALITY

As the variety of definitions has implied, there are many different conceptions about the nature of personality. Different schools of thought present contrasting views. A useful way of grouping such schools is Salvatore R. Maddi's classification. Maddi, a professor of psychology at the University of Chicago, points out that most writers on personality make two kinds of generalizations. One is about the inherent nature of man, concerning those features common to all people which do not change much in the course of life. Such statements concern the *core* of personality. The other kind of generalization has to do with behavior which is generally learned, more circumscribed, and which differentiates people from one another. Maddi calls this sphere the *periphery* of personality. Theorists may be grouped according to their differing conceptions of the core of personality.

The Conflict Model

First of all, following Maddi's scheme, there are those who assume that a person is always caught in a clash between opposing forces, between which he must make compromises. Maddi calls this the conflict model. The outstanding representative of this approach is Sigmund Freud, the founder of psychoanalysis. For Freud the core tendency of man is to maximize instinctual gratification while mini-

---

[25] Ellefson, "Personality and the Biological Nature of Man," pp. 145–47.

mizing punishment and guilt. The selfish instincts of man inevitably come into conflict with the taboos of society. As Philip Rieff has phrased it, ". . . human culture is established through a series of renunciations. The sacrifice of self is the beginning of personality."[26] One way in which man protects himself against the inevitable frustrations of life and the attendant anxiety is to develop unconscious defenses such as repression, projection, reaction formation and sublimation, among others.[27] Many writers on personality, including Henry A. Murray and Harry Stack Sullivan, have followed a similar conflict model. Among anthropologists we can cite Weston La Barre and George Devereux.

The Fulfillment Model

The fulfillment model, on the other hand, assumes only one great force, located in the individual. Conflict may exist, but it is not held to be inevitable or continuous. Life is seen as an unfolding or realization of possibilities. Carl R. Rogers, for example, sees an actualizing tendency in all living things; in the case of man there is an attempt to actualize the self, involving the realization of a need for the approval of others and approval of one's self.

Other exponents of a fulfillment model include Gordon W. Allport and Abraham Maslow. Maddi classifies Erich Fromm in this group (correctly, I believe), although Fromm has been much influenced by Freudian theory. Few attempts have been made to explicitly apply a fulfillment approach to the field of culture-and-personality, but one example may be cited: Joel Aronoff has made use of Maslow's self-actualization theory in a culture-and-personality study of a community in the West Indies.[28]

The Consistency Model

Third is the consistency model. Here there is little emphasis on forces, whether in conflict or not. Life is seen as an effort to maintain consistency. There is less emphasis on an inherent human nature than in the other two models. "For consistency theorists, the

---

[26] Philip Rieff, *Freud: The Mind of the Moralist* (New York: The Viking Press, Inc., 1959), p. 197.

[27] Freudian theory is discussed further below, pp. 28–35.

[28] Joel Aronoff, *Psychological Needs and Cultural Systems. A Case Study* (Princeton, N.J.: D. Van Nostrand Co., Inc., 1967). See below, p. 268.

content of personality is largely learned, and represents the history of feedback resulting from interacting with the world."[29]

George A. Kelly, for example, believed that a person tries to predict and control events on the basis of personal constructs which he has built up in the past. When his constructs fail to adequately predict or control events, the individual experiences anxiety, which may lead to a modification of constructs.

Looking at efforts toward consistency in another way, everyone has some general notion of what sort of person he is or would like to be. Since he may feel anxiety when there is a discrepancy between his self-evaluation and the ideal model, he tries to behave in a reasonably consistent fashion. The term *cognitive dissonance* has been applied to a discrepancy between a person's concepts or between expectation and actual outcome. Leon Festinger and other social psychologists who have used this term assume that whenever cognitive dissonance is experienced, the individual acts to reduce it.[30]

Donald W. Fiske and Salvatore R. Maddi believe that the core tendency in an individual is to maintain the level of neuropsychological activation to which he has been accustomed.

There have been few attempts to explicitly apply a consistency model of personality in cross-cultural studies.[31] But it is likely that many anthropologists have sometimes assumed a consistency model of personality without formulating it as such. For example, in commenting on the displeasure occasioned by observing bad table manners, Franz Boas remarked: ". . . bad manners are always accompanied by rather intense feelings of displeasure, the psychological reason for which can be found only in the fact that the actions in question are contrary to those which have become habitual."[32]

---

[29] Salvatore R. Maddi, *Personality Theories. A Comparative Analysis* (Homewood, Ill.: The Dorsey Press, 1968), p. 110.

[30] For a review of literature on cognitive dissonance and allied theories, see Robert B. Zajonc, "Cognitive Theories in Social Psychology," in Gardner Lindzey and Elliot Aronson (eds.), *The Handbook of Social Psychology*, (2d ed.; Reading, Mass.: Addison-Wesley Publishing Co., Inc., 1968), Vol. I, pp. 488–567. For a massive reader on the subject, see Robert P. Abelson et al. (eds.), *Theories of Cognitive Consistency: A Sourcebook* (Chicago: Rand McNally & Co., 1968).

[31] For two attempts, see Harry C. Triandis and Martin Fishbein, "Cognitive Interaction in Person Perception," *Journal of Abnormal and Social Psychology*, Vol. 67 (1963), pp. 446–53; and Donald T. Campbell and Robert A. LeVine, "Ethnocentrism and Intergroup Relations," in Abelson et al., "Theories of Cognitive Consistency," pp. 551–64.

[32] Franz Boas, *Introduction to the Handbook of American Indian Languages*. I, Bureau of American Ethnology Bulletin 40, Part I, 1911. Reprinted by Georgetown University Press, Washington D.C., 1963, p. 57.

It could be argued that anthropologists who have used the concept of "world view" or "mazeway," assume a consistency model and that the personal constructs delineated by George A. Kelly could be compared with the cultural constructs which make up the world view of a particular society. Ruth Benedict's approach, discussed in Chapter 4, could be similarly categorized. Although Benedict did not use the term *cognitive dissonance,* she did discuss the difficulties experienced in discontinuities in the process of growing up, when expected adult patterns contrast with earlier learned childhood patterns of behavior, so that an individual must unlearn what he has previously learned. Little children, for example, do not have to be responsible, but adults do. Submissiveness and obedience may be expected of children, but when they become adults they may have to assume dominant attributes of behavior. There are also contrasts in sexual roles between the childhood and adult states. Some cultures allow for easier transitions in these areas than do others. There are often problems at puberty or adolescence when formerly consistent self-concepts are altered and new patterns of consistency assumed.[33]

In a consistency model of personality, the important elements in the determination of consistency are cognitions, such as attitudes and opinions. Some examples of aspects of cognition, such as world view, values, self-concepts, and mazeway are discussed in Chapter 3.

Maddi has made both rational and empirical analyses of the work in both core and peripheral areas of some of the theoreticians mentioned above. He comes to the conclusion that the conflict model is less fruitful than either the fulfillment or the consistency model, and he favors some combination of the fulfillment model and the Fiske and Maddi version of the consistency model.

It may be noted that these different models of personality imply somewhat different conceptions of the nature of culture. In the conflict model, culture is seen as inhibiting or repressive, a view epitomized in the title of Jules Henry's book, *Culture against Man.* Associated with this idea may be the Rousseauistic conclusion that cultural development has involved an increase of human frustration and that simpler cultures (like Samoa or Trobriand) are less conducive to neurosis than our complex one. This notion was expressed in Robert Redfield's folk-urban continuum, according to which folk societies are homogeneous and well integrated, while urban

---

[33] Ruth Benedict, "Continuities and Discontinuities in Cultural Conditioning," *Psychiatry,* Vol. 1 (1938), pp. 161–67.

cultures are diverse, impersonal, and socially disorganized. Implicit in Karen Horney's title *The Neurotic Personality of our Time* is the suggestion that maybe people were less neurotic in former times. We will return to this question in Chapter 16 on "Culture and Mental Disorders."

The fulfillment model involves a more beneficent view of culture, which may be seen as providing various channels for self-realization. This conception would be in keeping with Bronislaw Malinowski's functional view of culture, which he saw as fulfilling human needs. "The functional view of culture insists upon the principle that every type of civilization, every custom, material object, idea, and belief fulfills some vital function, has some task to accomplish, represents an indispensable part within a working whole."[34] Malinowski could hardly have used the phrase "Culture against Man." Rather, it is through culture that man's various needs are met and his goals attained.

This fulfillment approach of Malinowski's may have been part of the difficulty he experienced in trying to test the application of Freudian theory to Trobriand culture, a topic to be discussed in Chapter 5. Malinowski did not see why, given their assumptions, psychoanalysts should consider the Oedipus complex to be so harmful. "After all, to a psycho-analyst, the Oedipus complex is the beginning of religion, law, and morality."[35]

The consistency model seems to be more neutral in its assessment of culture than the two preceding ones. Presumably, any cultural routine which has become familiar will allay anxiety if it is adhered to.

A weakness of the consistency model, as Maddi has pointed out, is that it does not account for boredom. People do not always like familiar routines; some dissonance may be pleasurable. At the same time, it is true that a culture, in providing pattern and meaning, is a source of security. This becomes evident in the sense of disorientation known as "culture shock," when persons are exposed to an unfamiliar way of life. In Chapter 16, we will consider the relationship between migration and mental disorder; the mental breakdowns which attend migrations to foreign countries may often be related to the experience of culture shock.

---

[34] Bronislaw Malinowski, "Anthropology," *Encyclopædia Britannica*, first supplementary volume (1926), p. 132.

[35] Bronislaw Malinowski, *Sex and Repression in Savage Society* (New York: Meridian Books, 1955), p. 237. (Originally published in 1927.)

If they are consistent in their views of culture, adherents of a conflict model of personality should be more tempted to rebel against the system, while those who prefer a fulfillment model should be more conservative and aware of the advantages of tradition.

PRIMATE TRAITS

In seeking to understand core aspects of personality, an anthropologist is tempted to examine general primate characteristics before turning to man himself. Let us briefly review some general characteristics of primates, the order of mammals to which man belongs, along with the apes, monkeys, lemurs, and tarsiers. Primates are creatures with prehensile (grasping) five-digited hands and feet. These grasping hands and feet are useful in getting about in the arboreal habitat shared by most primates and also in exploring and manipulating objects. They are important for monkeys in infancy, since monkeys are born with a clinging reflex which enables them to hang onto the mother's fur, leaving her arms free when she climbs through the trees.

The mother-child relationship is closer and longer lasting among primates than in most other animal species. A general trait of mammals is that females suckle their young. This results in a continuing relationship, at least for a while, between mother and offspring in all mammals, but the relationship is longer lasting in primates than in the other orders of mammals, since the complex nervous system and brain development of the primates needs time to become co-ordinated. The young are born in a relatively helpless condition which increases dependence upon the mother. While a baby deer can walk about on the day of birth, a baby primate clings to its mother's body for the first weeks or months of life.

The importance of maternal care is illustrated by Jane van Lawick-Goodall's careful observations of the behavior of chimpanzees in Tanzania. Through great patience she got chimpanzees to become accustomed to her presence, so that she could watch them at close quarters. Van Lawick-Goodall recorded four cases of chimpanzee infants whose mothers died. Three of these orphans were three years of age. Since chimpanzees mature more rapidly than humans, this represents an older stage than that of a three-year-old human child. The chimpanzee orphans were carried about and looked after by older siblings and were not abandoned. Nevertheless, they showed signs of severe depression, and some subsequently developed abnormal behavior.[36]

A primate is always born into a social group which includes a male or males as well as a female or females. Some primate groups, like those of the gibbon, are small, consisting of only a male, female, and offspring, while others, like the baboons, have large bands with many males and females of different ages. Adult males in most primate groups are either tolerant or helpful toward the young.

Young primates spend a lot of time in rough and tumble play with one another, as their dependence on the mother decreases. Thus, a juvenile primate typically interacts with peers, older males, and older females.

While human beings share the general features of primates just reviewed, they have a still more developed brain and complex central nervous system than other primates, and consequently have an even longer period of dependency upon the mother. Every human being starts out as a helpless, dependent, and nonresponsible creature but must learn to become relatively competent, independent and responsible. This development toward maturity and competence, involving the actualization of inherent human potentialities, gives support to the fulfillment model for the core of personality. However, the same data we have reviewed also give some support to a conflict model, since the long period of dependence on the mother sets the stage for the Oedipus complex and other problems of incompatible dispositions, such as dependence-independence.

LANGUAGE AND CULTURE

Human beings differ from the other primates in their use of language, the distinctive basis for human culture. Since so much of our life is tied up with language, our world of experience must be very different from those of apes and monkeys, despite the common features just reviewed.

The first learning of language by a growing child marks an adaptation to a realm quite different from the visible environment; it is a new world of concepts. From this point on, the child is strongly influenced by the prevailing cultural conceptions of the society into

---

[36] Jane van Lawick-Goodall, *In the Shadow of Man* (Boston, Mass.: Houghton Mifflin Co., 1971), pp. 214–25. See the reference to Harry Harlow's work with maternally deprived rhesus monkeys below, p. 38.

which he is born. It is hard for us to imagine the direct contact with reality, without names for things, that children have before this point. Since it must be very different from our own structured picture of the world, it is probably nearly impossible to remember that earlier period.

In the second six months of life a child begins learning words. He may be speaking about 1,500 words by the time he is three and a half or four and he may understand more than twice that number. The child acquires not only a vocabulary of words but also (usually without being deliberately taught) a knowledge of syntax and word order, although he often leaves out some features of the adults' speech, such as articles, prepositions, and conjunctions.

Thus a child learns the names for things and how the adults construe the world about him. He learns what their values and attitudes are and will accept many of them as his own. The structuring of reality established by language and culture gives some support to the consistency model of the core of personality. A person feels comfortable with the patterns of behavior which he has acquired in the process of growing up; they are hard to unlearn.

OTHER APPROACHES TO PERSONALITY

Another way of dividing up contrasting views about personality is in terms of what are held to be the main factors which determine personality. The *physiological* approach puts the emphasis on physiological or constitutional factors. *Childhood determinism* stresses the importance of childhood experiences. The *situational* approach emphasizes current situational factors.

The Physiological Approach

Under the first heading, the physiological approach, belong studies which emphasize the hereditary endowments of the individual and the physiological functioning of the body. Roger J. Williams has drawn attention to the enormous range of variation among human beings in the functioning of different organs and organ systems. To give only one example, although the "standard" number of parathyroid glands in humans is 4, the number may range from 2 to 12.[37] Kinsey and his associates have similarly pointed

---

[37] Roger J. Williams, *Biochemical Individuality. The Basis for the Gerontotrophic Concept* (New York: John Wiley & Sons, Inc., 1956), p. 84.

out the apparently great variation in the strength of the sex drive in males.[38] Louis Berman, an early writer on the influence of the endocrines, believed that such glandular variations were the key to personality differences, and he delineated what he believed to be the adrenal type, the pituitary personality, the thyroid, thymocentric, and other types, all depending upon the over- or underfunctioning of particular endocrine glands.[39]

Related to such an approach is an emphasis on biochemical factors. It may be noted that some individuals suffer more readily than others from vitamin and other deficiencies. Niacin deficiency may produce profound psychoses, which disappear when the deficiency is remedied, and psychoneuroses may result from thiamin deficiency.[40] Calcium deficiency may lead to the development of hysteria (see p. 424); pellagric psychosis may develop from vitamin deficiency. It is well known that marked effects on consciousness are produced by such substances as LSD, amphetamine, and alcohol.

Attempts have been made to relate some mental disorders to chromosomal or genetic factors. In some cases the relationships are clear enough; in others there is uncertainty about causal factors. Some pathological disturbances result from the presence of too many or too few chromosomes; mongolism and Kleinfelder's and Turner's syndromes are examples. The latter two involve sexual aberrations related to an abnormal number of sex chromosomes.

Many studies have been made of the possible role of heredity in the genesis of schizophrenia. The most common research approach to this problem has been to study twins, sometimes twins who have been reared apart and thus exposed to different environmental conditions. Twin studies have been made with both monozygotic (identical) and dizygotic (fraternal) twins. The problem is to find the rate of *concordance* in pairs of twins; that is, whether, when one twin develops schizophrenia, the other does also, and whether the concordance rate for monozygotic twins is greater than that for dizygotic twins, which would presumably indicate the presence of a genetic factor. David Rosenthal has reviewed such twin studies and has made the following points: (1) the concordance rate for monozygotic twins is always less than 100 percent and sometimes

[38] Alfred C. Kinsey, Wardell B. Pomeroy, and Clyde E. Martin, *Sexual Behavior in the Human Male* (Philadelphia: W. B. Saunders Co., 1948).

[39] Louis Berman, *The Glands Regulating Personality* (rev. ed.; New York: Macmillan Co., 1928).

[40] Williams, *Biochemical Individuality*. pp. 203–4.

much less, suggesting that nongenetic factors may also play a role in the development of schizophrenia. (2) The concordance rate is always greater for monozygotic than for dizygotic twins, sometimes with a ratio of as much as six to one. (3) There is a wide range in the rates reported both for monozygotic and dizygotic pairs.[41]

In summarizing data from a number of studies, Bernard Rimland presents the following table to show that the likelihood that a per-

Table 1-1. INCIDENCE OF SCHIZOPHRENIA RELATED TO PRESENCE OF SCHIZOPHRENIA IN BLOOD RELATIVES

	Percent
No schizophrenic relatives	1
Grandparents, cousins, nephews, and nieces	3–4
One schizophrenic parent	16
Both parents schizophrenic	39–68
Half-siblings	7
Sibling	5–14
Fraternal twin	3–17
Identical twin	67–86

son will be schizophrenic is a function of the presence of schizophrenia in his blood relatives.[42]

It was noted above that concordance of schizophrenia in identical twins is always less than 100 percent. One identical twin may become schizophrenic while the other remains normal. It might be deduced from this that the ailment is caused by psychosocial factors, but Rimland points out that one of the twins in such a case might have suffered adverse biological effects in the uterus, at birth, or by postnatal infection, and that the schizophrenia might therefore have nothing to do with psychosocial experiences.[43]

Another approach to the possible genetic factor in schizophrenia is through adoption studies involving cases in which parents and children have been separated early in life, and when the incidence of schizophrenia in the children and their families has been studied. In reviewing studies of this kind, Rosenthal asserts that ". . . the evidence has turned up so consistently and so strongly in favor of

---

[41] David Rosenthal, *Genetics of Psychopathology* (New York: McGraw-Hill Book Co., 1971) , pp. 72–74.

[42] Bernard Rimland, "Psychogenesis versus Biogenesis: The Issues and the Evidence," in Stanley C. Plog and Robert B. Edgerton (eds.) , *Changing Perspectives in Mental Illness* (New York: Holt, Rinehart & Winston, Inc., 1969) , p. 730. The table is based on a table in Arnold H. Buss, *Psychopathology* (New York: John Wiley & Sons, Inc., 1966) , p. 319.

[43] Rimland, "Psychogenesis versus Biogenesis," p. 709.

the genetic hypothesis that this issue must now be considered closed. Genetic factors do contribute appreciably beyond any reasonable doubts to the development of schizophrenic illness."[44]

A claim has recently been made (May 1972) by two Detroit doctors, Jacques S. Gottlieb and Charles E. Frohman, that their research group has discovered an enzyme deficiency in the brains of schizophrenic patients which leads to an abnormal production of chemicals known to have mentally disturbing effects.

Biogenic factors have been alleged to cause the condition known as early infantile autism.[45]

While the case for a genetic basis for some forms of mental disorder seems to be good, this cannot be held to apply to mental disorders in general. As will be discussed in Chapter 16, there is a school of thought which holds that there is no such thing as mental illness and that the medical or "sickness" model of mental disorder is a false analogy. The various labels that exist for different types of "mental illness" may give a spurious impression of diagnostic specificity. In practice, psychiatrists often disagree as to whether or not a particular patient is schizophrenic.

Franz J. Kallman, who has contributed to the study of the genetic factors involved in schizophrenia, has also pointed to a chromosomal basis for some homosexual behavior,[46] but Rosenthal states that in the great majority of male homosexuals studied no hormonal or chromosomal abnormalities have been found.[47] Social and cultural conditions must be considered as possible determinants of homosexual behavior. This is suggested by the fact that there are societies like the Kiwai and Keraki of New Guinea where all males engage in homosexual behavior.[48]

Another school of thought, represented by E. Kretschmer and W. H. Sheldon, places the emphasis upon constitutional type. Kretschmer made physical measurements of 260 psychotic patients, sufferers from schizophrenia and manic-depression. In schizophrenia

---

[44] Rosenthal, *Genetics of Psychopathology*, p. 84.

[45] Bernard Rimland, *Infantile Autism. The Syndrome and Its Implications for a Neural Theory of Behavior* (New York: Appleton-Century-Crofts, 1964).

[46] Franz J. Kallman, "Comparative Twin Study of the Genetic Aspects of Male Homosexuality," *Journal of Nervous and Mental Disease*, Vol. 115 (1952), pp. 283–98.

[47] Rosenthal *Genetics of Psychopathology*, p. 144.

[48] For a brief discussion of these issues, see Victor Barnouw and John A. Stern, "Some Suggestions Concerning Social and Cultural Determinants of Human Sexual Behavior," in George Winokur et al., *Determinants of Human Sexual Behavior* (Springfield, Ill.: Charles C Thomas, Publisher, 1963), pp. 206–9.

there is a loss of emotional responsiveness to others and often a development of delusions and hallucinations; while in manic-depression there may be mood-swings ranging from violent manic excitement to apathetic, depressive lethargy. On the basis of his findings, Kretschmer claimed that there is an association between schizophrenia and body builds tending to be lanky, or (sometimes) athletic, while manic-depression he found to be associated with more plump physical types. Kretschmer believed that there is continuity between normal and abnormal states and that the different constitutional types have characteristic differences in temperament, the lean asthenics tending to be more schizoid—sensitive, inhibited, and cold; while more plump individuals tend to be moody and changeable, but more sociable and realistic than the asthenics.[49]

W. H. Sheldon, who has measured and tested Harvard students and other groups in the United States, has followed Kretschmer's lead but has developed different methods of measurement, classification, and terminology. According to Sheldon, thin individuals tend to be tense introverts, plagued by skin troubles, fatigue, and insomnia. Muscular athletic types tend to be energetic persons delighting in noise and adventure, exercise, and open air; while those who tend to be fat are apt to be comfortable extroverts, fond of food, company, and luxurious surroundings. Sheldon believes that there is a regular correlation of this sort between physique and temperament, although not in any one-to-one fashion.[50]

Allied to Sheldon's work is that of Carl C. Seltzer, who has tried to show the bearing of constitutional factors upon "masculine" tendencies in men,[51] while David M. Levy has explored the physiological basis for maternal behavior in women.[52]

Criminal behavior has had its interpretations along constitutional lines—E. A. Hooton believed that a correlation exists between constitutional type and the kind of antisocial behavior in which a per-

[49] E. Kretschmer, *Physique and Character*, trans. W. J. H. Sprott (New York: Harcourt Brace, 1925). See especially pp. 254–62.

[50] W. H. Sheldon, *The Varieties of Human Physique* (New York: Harper, 1940), pp. 235–37; W. H. Sheldon, *The Varieties of Temperament* (New York: Harper, 1942), pp. 247–79. At the risk of oversimplifying I have omitted the special terminologies used by Kretschmer and Sheldon, feeling that such terms as "pyknic," "ectomorph," "somatotonic," need not be forced on the reader.

[51] Carl C. Seltzer, "The Relationship between the Masculine Component and Personality," in Kluckhohn and Murray, *Personality in Nature, Society, and Culture*, pp. 84–96.

[52] David M. Levy, "Psychosomatic Studies of Some Aspects of Maternal Behavior," ibid., pp. 97–103. For a discussion of male-female differences, see Amram Scheinfeld, *Women and Men* (New York: Harcourt Brace, 1944).

son may engage. In a survey of American criminals he found, for example, that assault and sex offenses tend to be associated with short, heavy men but not with tall slender ones.[53]

Needless to say, there has been a good deal of criticism of these studies, as there has also been of the other approaches to be considered presently. My present purpose is not to pass judgment but merely to categorize some of the leading approaches to our subject.

Childhood Determinism

Under this heading may be grouped those approaches which consider personality to be largely fixed by the age of five or six, as the result of experiences undergone during the early years of life. Although the Freudians stress the biological basis for developments in this period, it would seem appropriate to classify them here. According to this school of thought, weaning, toilet training, and sexual disciplines significantly affect the personality of a growing child, and the Oedipus complex, the "primal scene" (the child's witnessing of its parents' intercourse), and real or imagined castration threats may establish attitudes and reactions of lifelong importance. Later influences on the individual, such as status and occupation, are seen as playing only a relatively minor role in the shaping of personality.

From a Freudian point of view a sociable disposition would not be accounted for by an individual's plump constitution (if he has one). Rather, such patterns would be traced to the "oral optimism" established in the subject's infancy through adequate suckling and maternal care. The reserved, cold individual, on the other hand, might be seen as an "anal pessimist" whose toilet training was too rigid. Character attitudes, according to Freud, represent compromises between instinctual impulses and the controlling forces of the ego.[54] "The permanent character traits," he wrote, "are either unchanged perpetuations of the original impulses, sublimations of them, or reaction formations against them."[55]

Freud believed that the individual passes through certain stages of libido development: first the *oral*, during the first year of life, when pleasurable sensations are centered around the mouth. Second

---

[53] E. A. Hooton, *Crime and the Man* (Cambridge, Mass.: Harvard University Press, 1939), p. 87.

[54] Otto Fenichel, *The Psychoanalytic Theory of Neurosis* (New York: W. W. Norton & Co., Inc., 1945), p. 470.

[55] S. Freud, *Character and Anal Erotism,* Collected Papers, II, (London: The Hogarth Press, 1950), p. 50.

is the *anal* stage, during the second year of life, when toilet training is initiated in some societies, although it may be started after six months in some American middle-class families. This may be the child's first encounter with outside interference with his instinctual impulses. Third is the *phallic* stage, from about the third through fifth years, when pleasurable sensations begin to be found in the genital areas and other erogenous zones. This is said to be followed by a latency period of sexual quiescence, until the coming of puberty. (As we shall see in Chapter 5, Bronislaw Malinowski claimed that the latency period is not a universal aspect of human development.) If the individual successfully passes through the pregenital stages of psychosexual development, the stage of genital primacy follows. If he meets with sufficient frustration at some point in this development, he may regress to an earlier level, thus becoming neurotic or psychotic. The type of neurosis or psychosis would be determined, not by constitutional type, but by the strength and nature of the frustration met with and the degree of security previously known.

Erik Homburger Erikson, a modified Freudian, has drawn up a sequence of Eight Ages of Man in which the first four stages correspond roughly with Freud's sequence, although there is less emphasis on biological factors. During the first year of life, in Erikson's scheme, the nature of the infant's experiences, especially in relation to his mother, establishes a sense of basic trust, or else of basic mistrust. If sufficient trust is acquired, the child moves with confidence to the next stage of Autonomy versus Shame and Doubt, which occupies the second year and corresponds with Freud's anal stage. When successfully traversed, this stage gives the child a sense of control over himself and his environment. He learns, both literally and figuratively, to stand on his own two feet, although he is still dependent on his parents, but lack of success at this stage may lead to feelings of shame, doubt, and inadequacy.

From three to five is a stage which Erikson labels Initiative versus Guilt. It is a period of rapid physical development and locomotion, and awareness of genital sensations: the period also of the Oedipus complex and its attendant problems (discussed further in Chapter 5). The successful outcome of this stage is a sense of initiative, purpose, lively imagination, and readiness to learn, while lack of success may lead to loss of spontaneity, jealousy, suspicion, and feelings of castration.

The fourth stage is the latency period, from about the age of 6 to

11. This may result, when adequately traversed, in a sense of duty, industry, and competence, while frustrations at this stage produce feelings of inferiority and futility.[56]

Erich Fromm has presented a theory of character orientations which, like Erikson's, is derived from Freud's but less linked to physiology. Later in this book (Chapters 11 and 17), we will examine Fromm's application of his concepts to the analysis of a Mexican peasant community and to Western Europe in general. Fromm defines character as the "(relatively permanent) form in which human energy is structuralized in the process of assimilation and socialization."[57] The core of a person's character consists of his characteristic orientations to the world. Fromm distinguishes between productive and nonproductive orientations. These correspond to Freud's genital and pregenital character types. Fromm's nonproductive orientations are: the *receptive* orientation (corresponding to Freud's oral-receptive type), the exploitative (corresponding to Freud's oral-sadistic), and the *hoarding* orientation (corresponding to Freud's anal personality type).

Table 1–2. FREUDIAN AND MODIFIED FREUDIAN STAGES OF DEVELOPMENT

Ages	Freud	Erikson	Fromm
First year	Oral stage	Basic trust vs. Basic mistrust	Receptive orientation Exploitative orientation
Second year	Anal stage	Autonomy vs. Shame and doubt	Hoarding orientation
Third through fifth years	Phallic stage	Initiative vs. Guilt	
Sixth to about eleventh year	Latency period	Industry vs. Inferiority	
Puberty and adolescence	Stage of genital primacy	Identity vs. Role confusion	Productive orientation
Young adulthood . .		Intimacy vs. Isolation	
Adulthood		Generativity vs. Stagnation	
Maturity		Ego integrity vs. Despair	

---

[56] We will not examine Erikson's four adult stages which make distinctions and differentiations within Freud's unitary genital stage. Their labels are given on Table 1–2. See Erik H. Erikson, *Childhood and Society* (2d ed., revised and enlarged; New York: W. W. Norton & Co., Inc., 1963), chap. 7.

[57] Erich Fromm and Michael Maccoby, *Social Character in a Mexican Village. A Sociopsychoanalytic Study* (Englewood Cliffs, N.J.: Prentice-Hall, Inc., 1970), p. 69.

These are ideal types. The personality of a given individual represents a blend of orientations. A virtue of Fromm's scheme is that he presents both the positive and negative aspects of each type of non-productive orientation. (Fromm has also discussed a *marketing* orientation related to modern industrialized commercial society; this is dealt with in Chapter 17.)

Table 1–30. POSITIVE AND NEGATIVE ASPECTS OF FROMM'S NONPRODUCTIVE ORIENTATIONS

RECEPTIVE ORIENTATION (*Accepting*)

Positive Aspect	Negative Aspect
accepting	passive, without initiative
responsive	opinionless, characterless
devoted	submissive
modest	without pride
charming	parasitical
adaptable	unprincipled
socially adjusted	servile, without self-confidence
idealistic	unrealistic
sensitive	cowardly
polite	spineless
optimistic	wishful thinking
trusting	guillible
tender	sentimental

EXPLOITATIVE ORIENTATION (*Taking*)

Positive Aspect	Negative Aspect
active	exploitative
able to take initiative	aggressive
able to make claims	egocentric
proud	conceited
impulsive	rash
self-confident	arrogant
captivating	seducing

HOARDING ORIENTATION (*Preserving*)

Positive Aspect	Negative Aspect
practical	unimaginative
economical	stingy
careful	suspicious
reserved	cold
patient	lethargic
cautious	anxious
steadfast, tenacious	stubborn
imperturbable	indolent
composed under stress	inert
orderly	pedantic
methodical	obsessional
loyal	possessive

Source: Erich Fromm and Michael Maccoby, *Social Character in a Mexican Village. A Sociopsychoanalytic Study* (Englewood Cliffs, N.J.: Prentice-Hall, Inc., 1970), p. 79. This table appeared earlier in Erich Fromm, *Man for Himself. An Inquiry into the Psychology of Ethics* (New York: Rinehart, 1947), where Fromm's theory of character orientations was first set forth.

While Fromm's views are related to Freud's, he is less of a childhood determinist. Being also influenced by Marxism, Fromm places importance on situational factors, and he has written that "The importance of childhood by no means excludes later changes in character."[58]

Returning to more orthodox Freudians, some "criminal" behavior, if not all, may be explained in Freudian terms. For example, Franz Alexander and Hugo Staub have described a type of "neurotic criminal" who compulsively acts out antisocial impulses which stem from an unresolved Oedipus complex. Punishment is no deterrent to criminals of this sort, for they have an unconscious desire for punishment.[59]

Childhood determinist approaches to the study of national character have been made by Geoffrey Gorer and Weston La Barre, among others; these will be discussed in a later chapter.

In 1943, Gorer wrote an article entitled "Themes in Japanese Culture,"[60] in which he pointed to the Japanese preoccupation with ritual, tidiness, and order, and compared it with the behavior of compulsive individuals who have suffered from severe early toilet training, leading to repressed unconscious feelings of aggression. A similar analysis was written at about the same time by Weston La Barre, although neither of the two authors had evidence that Japanese toilet training is actually severe. Later researches after World War II indicated that it is not particularly severe.[61]

The Freudian-influenced school of Linton, Kardiner, and Du Bois, to be discussed in Chapter 7, has an essentially childhood determinist approach, although taking many other factors into account.

A combination of psychoanalysis and behavioristic learning theory has been pursued by John W. M. Whiting and various associates in a number of publications making use of the Human Relations Area Files. In broad cross-cultural surveys which are subjected to statistical treatment, Whiting and his associates look for cor-

---

[58] Fromm and Maccoby, *Social Character in a Mexican Village,* p. 21.

[59] Franz Alexander and Hugo Staub, *The Criminal, the Judge, and the Public; A Psychological Analysis,* trans. from the German by Gregory Zilboorg (New York: Macmillan Co., 1931).

[60] *Transactions of the New York Academy of Sciences,* Series II, Vol. 5, 1943, pp. 106–24.

[61] See below, pp. 213–16. See also Weston La Barre, "Some Observations on Character Structure in the Orient: The Japanese," *Psychiatry,* Vol. 8 (1945), pp. 319–42.

relations between certain aspects of child rearing (such as post-partum sex taboo and mother-child sleeping arrangements) and certain cultural institutions (such as male initiation ceremonies at puberty). William N. Stephens has also made use of the Human Relations Area Files in a cross-cultural survey of data bearing on the presence or absence of the Oedipus complex. These and other studies of this genre are discussed in Chapter 8. Writers like Whiting and Stephens are childhood determinists with a vengeance, because they not only hold that childhood experiences determine personality patterns but, further, that certain childhood experiences bring about particular institutions in adult life, such as male initiation ceremonies, avoidance relationships, and menstrual taboos.

The Freudians are not the only childhood determinists. A number of writers have drawn attention to the importance of early mother-child relationships and to the damaging consequences of early maternal separation for the development of personality.[62]

William Goldfarb has compared early institutionalized children with children reared in foster homes, giving Stanford-Binet and Wechsler-Bellevue intelligence tests and collecting life history data. It is Goldfarb's conclusion that early maternal deprivation and institutionalization brings about defects in intellect and emotion, weakness of concept formation, difficulty in learning songs, rhymes, stories, grasping number concepts, and learning concepts of time and space. The institution-reared children studied by Goldfarb were hyperactive, disorganized, and often threw temper tantrums. They seemed to have an insatiable need for love without being able to love others in return.[63] Some other writers, however, claim that the dangers of maternal deprivation have been exaggerated. One study reports that "statements implying that children who experience institutionalization and similar forms of severe privation and deprivation in early life *commonly* develop psychopathic or af-

---

[62] John Bowlby, *Child Care and the Growth of Love,* abridged and edited by Margery Fry (London and Tonbridge: Penguin Books, 1953); Margaret Ribble, *The Rights of Infants: Early Psychological Needs and Their Satisfaction* (New York: Columbia University Press, 1943); René A. Spitz, "Hospitalism. An Inquiry into the Genesis of Psychiatric Conditions in Early Childhood," *The Psychoanalytic Study of the Child,* Vol. I (New York: International Universities Press, 1945); pp. 53–74; Jenny Roudinesco, "Severe Maternal Deprivation and Personality Development in Early Childhood," *Understanding the Child, A Magazine for Teachers,* Vol. 21 (1952), pp. 104–8.

[63] William Goldfarb, "Psychological Privation in Infancy and Subsequent Achievement," *American Journal of Orthopsychiatry,* Vol. 51 (1945), pp. 247–55.

fectionless characters are incorrect."[64] Other recent studies have reached similar conclusions.[65]

Differentiating factors to be considered are age of institutionalization, the nature of the institution, and the number and character of the caretakers. In the cases where psychological damage has occurred, there are different interpretations about the causal factors involved. For René Spitz the cause is maternal deprivation, lack of mother love. Another suggested cause is lack of stimulation, which is apt to occur in a large institution where there are not many caretakers to look after the children.

At the other extreme from maternal deprivation, David M. Levy has discussed the damaging consequences of maternal overprotection, which may also have lasting effects upon personality.[66]

Counter to the underlying assumptions of childhood determinists like Gorer and La Barre, some anthropologists have argued that child upbringing in certain societies (for example, the Hopi, Navaho, St. Thomas Negroes) may be ideal from a Freudian point of view, but the typical adult personality found in these groups may nevertheless be tense and anxious.[67] Dealing with a later age period, Martha Wolfenstein has described French childhood as a period of restriction and preparation for adult life, full of hard work; yet the French grow up with a great capacity for enjoyment of life. "It remains one of the puzzles of French culture how this effect is achieved: that the restraints to which children are subjected have only a temporary influence and do not encumber the adult with lasting inhibitions."[68] Here, again, we have a contrast between the childhood and adult picture.

[64] John Bowlby, Mary Ainsworth, Mary Boston, and Dina Rosenbluth, "The Effects of Mother-Child Separation: A Follow-up Study," *British Journal of Medical Psychology*, Vol. 29 (1956), p. 242.

[65] Hilda Lewis, *Deprived Children. The Mersham Experiment. A Social and Clinical Study* (London: Oxford University Press, 1954); J. W. B. Douglas and J. M. Blomfield, *Children under Five* (London: George Allen and Unwin, 1958).

[66] David M. Levy, *Maternal Overprotection* (New York: Columbia University Press, 1943).

[67] Dorothy Eggan, "The General Problem of Hopi Adjustment," *American Anthropologist*, Vol. 45 (1943), pp. 357–73; Esther S. Goldfrank, "Socialization, Personality, and the Structure of Pueblo Society," *American Anthropologist*, Vol. 47 (1945), pp. 516–39; Dorothea Leighton and Clyde Kluckhohn, *Children of the People* (Cambridge, Mass.: Harvard University Press, 1947), pp. 68, 111; A. Campbell, "St. Thomas Negroes. A Study of Personality and Culture," *Psychological Monographs*, Vol. 55, No. 5 (1943), pp. 43, 89.

[68] Martha Wolfenstein, "French Parents Take Their Children to the Park," in Margaret Mead and Martha Wolfenstein (eds.), *Childhood in Contemporary Cultures* (Chicago: University of Chicago Press, 1955), pp. 114–15.

Some psychologists such as G. H. Frank have explicitly denied the idea that early childhood experiences are major determinants in the development of psychopathology. "A review of the research of the past 40 years failed to support this assumption. No factors were found in the parent-child interaction of schizophrenics, neurotics, or those with behavior disorders which could be identified as unique to them or which could distinguish one group from the other, or any of the group from the families of the controls."[69]

The Situational Approach

In this group belong those who stress the more immediate contemporary scene in which the individual finds himself—the roles which he has learned to play, his "reference groups," his current interpersonal relationships. Although the individual may have been considerably shaped by past events, he is seen as having a good measure of "functional autonomy," in Allport's words. The neo-Freudians, Fromm and Horney, share this emphasis on the present situation; so do psychologists of the "field theory" school, and many sociologists and anthropologists. In discussing "the culture of poverty," Oscar Lewis has emphasized the conditioning factors of poverty, while David M. Potter has drawn attention to the influence of an economy of abundance upon American national character. Some of the psychological consequences of modern business organization are explored by William H. Whyte, Jr. The writings of Riesman and his associates about the changing American character may, I think, be characterized as "situational."[70] The abundant writings about the American class system by such sociologists as the Lynds and W. L. Warner also embody an implicit situational approach.

Studies of class and caste in the Deep South, like those of Dollard and of Davis and the Gardners, emphasize the influence of sociological factors, such as the maintenance of social distance.[71] This ap-

---

[69] G. H. Frank, "The Role of the Family in the Development of Psychopathology," *Psychological Bulletin*, Vol. 64 (1965), p. 191.

[70] Oscar Lewis, *La Vida. A Puerto Rican Family in the Culture of Poverty—San Juan and New York* (New York: Random House, Inc., 1965), Introduction; David M. Potter, *People of Plenty. Economic Abundance and the American Character* (Chicago: University of Chicago Press, 1954); William H. Whyte, Jr., *The Organization Man* (New York: Doubleday & Co., Inc., 1956); David Riesman, with Nathan Glazer and Reuel Denney, *The Lonely Crowd. A Study of the Changing American Character* (New York: Doubleday & Co., Inc., 1953).

[71] John Dollard, *Caste and Class in a Southern Town* (New York: Harpers, 1949); Allison Davis, Burleigh B. Gardner, and Mary R. Gardner, *Deep South; A Social Anthropological Study of Caste and Class* (Chicago: University of Chicago Press, 1941).

proach has also been applied in the study of American Indian groups; Bernard J. James, for example, interprets Ojibwa personality in terms of the "reservation situation" and the nature of the self-image developed by Indians through their contacts with whites.[72]

The assumption of a particular role may exert an influence upon personality and behavior. George A. Kelly, who was himself an officer in the Navy at one time, was struck by the effect upon individuals of assuming an officer's rank. He noted that men often assumed officerlike qualities much more successfully than their past record would have led one to suspect. "Even men who are literally on the borderline of feeble-mindedness make fairly convincing officers. Perhaps it is because they *construe* themselves as officers."[73]

But one does not always assume a role so easily. There may be a sense of incongruence between the self and the role to be enacted, or there may be a conflict between two or more roles which the individual enacts.[74]

Some writers have examined the effects that assuming a particular profession may have upon personality. Thus, Willard Waller has discussed what teaching does to teachers, and how experienced teachers differ from those just starting in the profession. Robert K. Merton has dealt with the influence of bureaucratic occupation upon personality, and William E. Henry has delineated the personality characteristics of the successful business executive.[75] In these studies reference is made to relatively late events in the individual's life and to the role of a profession or status in bringing about modification in character.

A boy living in the slums might develop antisocial behavior in somewhat the same way, through membership in a gang and exposure to its way of life. He comes to accept a criminal "culture," let us say, much as an Eskimo child assumes the patterns of Eskimo

---

[72] Bernard J. James, "Social-Psychological Dimensions of Ojibwa Acculturation," *American Anthropologist,* Vol. 63 (1961), pp. 721–46.

[73] George A. Kelly, *The Psychology of Personal Constructs.* Vol. I. *A Theory of Personality* (New York: W. W. Norton & Co., Inc., 1955), p. 367.

[74] On this point and other topics concerning roles, see Theodore R. Sarbin and Vernon L. Allen, "Role Theory," in Gardner Lindzey and Elliot Aronson (eds.), *The Handbook of Social Psychology,* (2d ed.; Reading, Mass.: Addison-Wesley Publishing Co., Inc., 1968), Vol. I, pp. 488–567.

[75] Willard Waller, *The Sociology of Teaching* (New York: John Wiley & Sons, Inc., 1932), pp. 381–436; Robert K. Merton, "Bureaucratic Structure and Personality," *Social Forces,* Vol. 18 (1940), pp. 560–68; William E. Henry, "The Business Executive: The Psychodynamics of a Social Role," *American Journal of Sociology,* Vol. 54 (1949), pp. 286–91.

culture. We need not assume that there is any inborn criminal streak in him or that he has been maimed by some early childhood trauma.

A situational approach to mental disorders has been made by Robert Faris and H. W. Dunham in their study of Chicago. The authors found that schizophrenic patients in Chicago generally come from the poor rooming-house districts in the center of the city, while patients suffering from manic-depression tend to come from more peripheral and higher rental residence areas. The authors interpret the high incidence of schizophrenia in central Chicago as being due to the absence of close, rewarding social relationships in the disorganized migrant population. Social isolation, they claim, makes for mental breakdown, although a different kind of etiology is seen in manic-depression.[76] A large-scale investigation of the relationship between social class and mental illness in New Haven has been made by A. B. Hollingshead and F. O. Redlich. These authors find a significant relationship between social class and the prevalence and nature of mental disorder. In general, the lower the class, the higher the rate of mental disorder. This is not due to a downward "drift" of the maladjusted, nor to any biological differences between rich and poor.[77]

R. Jay Turner and Morton O. Wagenfeld, in a study of schizophrenic males, found that a disproportionate number came from the lowest occupational category.[78] Braginsky, Braginsky, and Ring believe that many unhappy lower class persons welcome institutionalization, with its comparatively easy life, and contrive to stay in the "last resort" of the mental hospital as long as possible.[79]

Another situational factor affecting mental health is migration. Many studies have reported a high incidence of mental disorders for migrants. In some areas rapid culture change seems to be a source of mental disorder. These topics are dealt with in Chapter 16.

Some studies have tried to trace the psychological consequences of certain drastic experiences, such as slavery, concentration camp in-

[76] Robert L. K. Faris and H. Warren Dunham, *Mental Disorders in Urban Areas* (Chicago: University of Chicago Press, 1939).

[77] August B. Hollingshead and Fredrick C. Redlich, *Social Class and Mental Illness. A Community Study* (New York: John Wiley & Sons, Inc., 1958). For other studies with similar findings, see Chapter 16.

[78] R. Jay Turner and Morton O. Wagenfeld, "Occupational Mobility and Schizophrenia: An Assessment of the Social Causation and Social Selection Hypotheses," *American Sociological Review,* Vol. 32 (1967), pp. 104–13.

[79] Benjamin M. Braginsky, Dorothea D. Braginsky, and Kenneth Ring, *Methods of Madness. The Mental Hospital as a Last Resort* (New York: Holt, Rinehart & Winston, Inc., 1969).

ternment, and combat experience.[80] The term "situational" thus covers a wide variety of studies. Most contemporary work in the field of social psychology seems to be of a situational character.

The physiological and childhood determinist approaches would seem to be closer to the core area of personality, while the situational approach seems to be concerned with the periphery of personality.

INTERRELATIONS OF THE DETERMINANTS

The different approaches which have been reviewed—the physiological, the childhood determinist, and the situational—are not, of course, mutually exclusive. Hollingshead and Redlich, for instance, suggest some childhood determinist hypotheses in a study which I have labeled "situational,"—that is, that a loveless infancy is more likely to occur in the lowest socioeconomic class than in the upper middle class.[81]

Many combinations are possible. There seems to be no reason to rely upon any one of these approaches to the exclusion of the others. One approach may work best in one situation, another in another. Clearly, the sluggish personality traits of a cretin are most readily explained in terms of endocrine deficiency, but a physiological explanation would probably not be the best way to account for the fanaticism of a convinced Nazi.

It is often difficult to assess the relative significance of the various determinants of personality, since they are all constantly at work. A human being is always in a particular situation, but he sees that situation in a manner determined by his past experience. A person's physical makeup and his culture are always with him. Moreover, physiological functions are related in complex ways to early social relationships. This has been indicated by Harry Harlow's experiments with rhesus monkeys. Harlow has shown that monkeys deprived of their mothers and raised with surrogate cloth or wire "mothers" fail to develop normal patterns of heterosexual behavior in later years. Females brought up in this way and who have, despite their lack of interest, been impregnated by normal male monkeys, fail to develop maternal feelings toward their offspring.[82]

---

[80] Stanley Elkins, "Slavery and Personality" in Bert Kaplan (ed.), *Studying Personality Cross-Culturally* (Evanston, Ill.: Row, Peterson & Co., 1961), pp. 243–67; Elie A. Cohen, *Human Behavior in the Concentration Camp* (New York: W. W. Norton & Co., Inc., 1953); Roy Grinker and John Spiegel, *Men under Stress* (Philadelphia: Blakistan, 1945).

[81] Hollingshead and Redlich, *Social Class and Mental Illness*, p. 361.

[82] Harry Harlow, "The Heterosexual Affectional System in Monkeys," *American Psychologist*, Vol. 17 (1962), pp. 1–9.

It is difficult to relate Harlow's findings in any direct way to human beings, since, fortunately, people are never brought up in caged isolation from birth. However, a study by Spitz and Wolf has pointed to differences in autoerotic behavior among institutionalized infants and infants in homes with good maternal care, there being much more genital self-stimulation in the latter group.[83] Physiological and social determinants of personality seem to be closely interrelated, as may be seen in psychosomatic and hysterical disorders and in the development of a self-concept. One's self-image is compounded partly of one's own bodily consciousness and awareness of one's appearance; it is also influenced by the experiences that one has with other persons and by the attitudes manifested towards oneself.

Although physiological, social, and cultural determinants of personality are closely intermeshed, this book will not deal with the physiological or constitutional aspects of man. The reason for this limitation is that culture-and-personality studies have focused on social and cultural factors rather than on biological ones. There must be limits to any field of investigation. Let us at any rate see how far we can get in our understanding of personality by considering only its cultural and social determinants.

The field of culture-and-personality has come in for some severe criticism in recent years, much of it well deserved. It is necessary to correct past mistakes and to improve methods of research. Yet, while mistakes have been made, a great deal has been learned as well. The relationship between culture and personality is full of puzzles, but it is marked by regularities too. This is what makes it a suitable and challenging area of research.

SUGGESTIONS FOR FURTHER READING

For the reader who is unfamiliar with literature on the psychology of personality, Gordon W. Allport's book, *Personality, A Psychological Interpretation* (New York: Henry Holt, 1937), is suggested as a good place to begin. Also recommended is Gardner Murphy's *Personality* (New York: Harper & Bros., 1947). Three good, more recent texts are: Salvatore R. Maddi, *Personality Theories. A Comparative Analysis* (Homewood, Ill.: The Dorsey Press, 1972); Walter Mischel, *Introduction to Personality* (New York: Holt, Rinehart & Winston, Inc., 1971); and Irving L. Janis, George F. Mahl, Jerome Kagan, and Robert R. Holt,

---

[83] René A. Spitz and Katherine M. Wolf, "Autoerotism. Some Empirical Findings and Hypotheses on Three of its Manifestations in the First Year of Life," *The Psychoanalytic Study of the Child* (New York: International Universities Press, 1949), Vol. III–IV, pp. 85–120.

Personality: Dynamics, Development, and Assessment (New York: Harcourt, Brace & World, Inc., 1969). The latter book has a psychoanalytic orientation; Mischel's has a more behavioristic approach. There are four stimulating readers in culture-and-personality: Clyde Kluckhohn and Henry A. Murray (eds.), *Personality in Nature, Society and Culture* (New York: Alfred A. Knopf, Inc., 1948); Douglas G. Haring (ed.), *Personal Character and Cultural Milieu* (Syracuse, N.Y.: Syracuse University Press, 1956); Bert Kaplan (ed.), *Studying Personality Cross-Culturally* (Evanston, Ill.: Row, Peterson & Co., 1961); and Francis L. K. Hsu (ed.), *Psychological Anthropology* (Cambridge, Mass.: Schenkman Publishing Company, 1972).

It is stated on page 10 that experiments have shown that individuals have characteristic and consistent patterns of walking, gesturing, and even sleeping. For walking, see Werner Wolff, *The Expression of Personality*, pp. 88–100; for gesturing: M. H. Krout, "Autistic Gestures," *Psychological Monograph* 46, No. 208, (1935); for sleeping: H. M. Johnson and G. E. Weigand, "The Measurement of Sleep," *Pennsylvania Academy of Science, Proceedings*, II (1927–8), pp. 43–48. Experiments in matching voice with other manifestations of behavior, referred to on p. 10 are described in W. Huntley, "Judgments of Self Based upon Records of Expressive Behavior," *Journal of Abnormal and Social Psychology*, Vol. 35 (1940), pp. 398–427; and by G. W. Allport and H. Cantril, "Judging Personality from the Voice," *Journal of Social Psychology*, Vol. 5 (1934), pp. 37–55.

chapter 2

The Concept of "Social Character"

So far we have been considering personality primarily on an individual basis. We turn now to the question of whether there may be similarities in personality among people who share the same culture. It is this notion which underlies such concepts as "basic personality type," "national character," and "social character." Explaining the latter term, Erich Fromm writes: ". . . we are interested . . . not in the peculiarities by which these persons differ from each other, but in that part of their character structure that is common to most members of the group. We can call this character the *social character*."[1]

There are critics who do not believe that there is such a thing as "basic personality type" or "social character." The concept would seem to be more applicable to a small tribal or village group than to a large nation which has class stratification and an elaborate division of labor. It is partly for this reason that anthropologists interested in culture-and-personality problems have often worked in small, relatively undifferentiated societies.

Instead of discussing the question of social character in abstract, theoretical terms, let us now consider studies of two specific peasant societies: (1) Egyptian peasants in a village in Aswan Province, and (2) the Aymara Indians of Peru. This will quickly introduce the reader to some of the problems which face culture-and-personality research.

---

[1] Erich Fromm, *Escape from Freedom* (New York: Farrar and Rinehart, 1942), p. 277.

41

THE EGYPTIANS OF SILWA

The source for our first example is a single work, *Growing Up in an Egyptian Village* by Hamed Ammar.[2] It would of course be better to have reports by other observers on the same people—a requirement which is met in the case of the Aymara. But the Egyptian study has one signal, rather unusual advantage: its author was born and grew up in the village which he describes. Although Ammar left the community at the age of seven to go to school, he never lost contact with the village and spent his holidays there. For him there were none of the problems of learning an alien language and introducing himself to the villagers which face most ethnologists in their fieldwork. This point is important, since the author cannot be charged with having an outsider's bias. It might be argued, however, that the experience of encountering a freer way of life outside his native village led Ammar to become critical of it, so that he acquired a bias of a different sort, like that of Sinclair Lewis in writing about Babbitt and Main Street. Nevertheless, Ammar's account is written in a careful, objective manner.

Generalizing about the villagers of Silwa (and Ammar is writing only about them, not about "Egyptian national character"), the author remarks:

Hearty laughter is rare, and it usually occurs amongst adults in their sarcastic allusions to others, and in belittling their esteem, while apparently seeming to praise them. Suspicion of the evil intentions of others is institutionalized in the evil eye, seeing potential danger in practically everybody. The small family guards its private affairs with great caution, especially its misfortunes, for fear that others may exult or gloat at their expense. . . . The villagers mutually describe each other as greedy, envious, and malicious, and, as they usually put it, "people would distribute your property while you are alive. . . ."[3]

The author makes the point that this character should not be seen as something neurotic but as an understandable result of adjustment to a particular set of realities, experienced by each Silwa villager as he grows up. What are some of these realities?

Silwa is a small, rather isolated town in Aswan, the southern border province in Upper Egypt, having a population of nearly 3,500. Almost all the men are farmers, and land is the most valued possession. To sell land is calamitous; to buy land is a sign of God's

---

[2] Hamed Ammar, *Growing Up in an Egyptian Village* (London: Routledge & Kegan, Paul Ltd., 1966).

[3] Ibid., p. 230.

blessing. Descent is traced patrilineally, in the male line. There is no primogeniture; a dead man's property is divided among his children. During a man's lifetime his children have no legal right to own any of his property.

There is a definite sexual division of labor. Women's place is in the home; men work in the fields. A man who does not mix with other men is called "man of the oven." A woman who often leaves her house is called a "strayer." When walking in the street, men walk down the middle; women keep to the wall. When meeting a man in the street, a woman turns her head away or pulls her head covering across her face, while the man lowers his gaze. Women do not go to the mosque to worship. During the first year of marriage a wife does not eat with her husband. After they begin to eat together, she should eat later than he does.

Children are suckled for an average of between one year and a year and a half, sometimes for two or three years. They are never weaned before the end of the first year. According to the views of Freud and Erikson, we might expect this to establish feelings of basic trust and "oral optimism." But there is much finger sucking among children, which is encouraged by their mothers; and in later childhood years there is much concern about food, expressed in children's stories, conversations, reports of dreams, and responses to projective tests. There is a realistic basis for this concern, for Ammar gives evidence that in postweaning years the children of Aswan province are very undernourished when compared with children elsewhere. Little meat is eaten in Silwa, and the diet is deficient in proteins and fats. Adults are described as being secretive and careful with food.

There is no special stress on toilet training in Silwa. When a child learns to walk, it is taught to indicate when it wants to defecate. After the age of three or four this is usually done outside the house; but after the age of 12, girls defecate in a special room indoors. There is no disgust about feces and urine, for these people are peasants who often handle animal dung for fertilizer or fuel.

Scaring techniques are used as a sanction to cultivate submissiveness in children. Bogeys are invoked, including a huge animal that eats its young after suckling them, and a hairy beast which attacks children while they sleep.

Children must show their respect for elders. Until the age of four or five, a child touches an older person's hand with his lips and forehead.

There is much sibling rivalry in Silwa, although brothers are

taught that they must show strong solidarity. Sibling rivalry is deliberately encouraged, since it is believed to be healthy, especially
for boys, and helps the child to stand up to rivals. A mother may encourage such rivalry by saying to a child, "Eat this before your
brother takes it," or else she praises the other child. When a visitor
meets a boy, he asks, "Who is better, you or your brother?" Siblings
of different ages play in separate groups, especially after the age of
six or seven.

Boys are circumcized between the ages of three and six. Girls go
through an operation of clitoridectomy at around seven or eight
years of age. This is thought to reduce sensuality and prevents the
girl's future husband from suspecting that she is not a virgin. Girls
may be married by 12 or 13, but boys usually marry after 18, on
completing their military service.

Children start to work early and work hard. Since hired labor is
difficult to obtain, a father makes his sons help him in the fields. This
may lead to father-son conflict, and some boys run away from the
village, if they are overworked. But deference to the father is emphasized in the culture. Disobedience to parents is a major sin, according to the Koran, and is severely punished in the afterworld.

A boy walks behind his father, not abreast. A mature son is not
expected to sit beside his father in a gathering of men. If the father
is sitting on a bench, the son sits on the ground or on another
bench.

The oldest son is the father's representative and gives orders to
the younger sons. When walking to the fields, brothers do not walk
together but follow, one behind the other to avoid the evil eye.

It is interesting that in this society the evil eye is particularly
feared from relatives. There are many popular sayings which express tension among relatives, such as "Relatives are like scorpions,"
and "Who brings disaster but relatives?"

Ammar describes the adolescents of Silwa as being timid, apprehensive, and withdrawn, with little drive or self-assertion. Sex is
regarded with shame, embarrassment, and guilt. There seems, in
general, to be a constricted personality. For those who accept a fulfillment model of personality, Silwa would seem to be a community
which does not encourage much self-actualization but inhibits it.

The foregoing account, which attempts to summarize Ammar's
work, could be criticized on the grounds that it overemphasizes
negative features. After all, the villagers of Silwa must get enough
satisfaction from life, and they have to be people of a particular

kind in order to lead the kind of life they must lead. For Erich Fromm the function of the social character is to make men desire to act as they have to act.

This view suggests, though, that the Silwa villagers *want* to be submissive, hardworking toilers. Not all wish to do so, evidently, since some young men run away from the village. Such young men are in the minority, however; those who remain come to terms with the system for which they have been prepared throughout childhood. As Ammar puts it, "Adults continually wean their offspring from flights of imagination and spontaneity of action till they almost completely achieve their end by the time their offspring reach adolescence."[4] The adult scaring techniques employed in childhood, the segregation between the sexes and age levels, which emphasize prudery and respect for elders, all contribute to forming a personality in which submissiveness is combined with undercurrent feelings of fear, resentment, envy, and hostility, as suggested by the quotation from Ammar which introduced this discussion. The general picture may be overdrawn, but it does seem to give support to Fromm's concept of social character. Insofar as the personality traits in question are determined by common childhood experiences, support would also be given to the concept of "basic personality type" which will be discussed in Chapter 7.

THE AYMARA INDIANS

Let us now consider another group of people who have also been described in rather discouraging terms, the Aymara Indians of Bolivia and Peru, who live in the Andes Mountains around Lake Titicaca. Here we are dealing, not with a single village like Silwa, but with a population of over 700,000; so our two examples are not exactly comparable.

In presenting data on the Aymara, my purpose is, first of all, to provide some evidence that a rather consistent Aymara "social character" has been reported by several observers over a considerable period of time, although it may be undergoing some changes at present. The second purpose is to use the Aymara data as a vehicle for discussing various possible determinants of personality and to show how one could go about testing their relative importance. In this case, unlike the data for Silwa, we have no report by a native

---

[4] Ibid., p. 231.

Aymara inhabitant. The descriptions are by outsiders, which opens the door to possible ethnocentric bias.

Among the anthropologists who have worked among the Aymara are Harry Tschopik, Jr., Weston La Barre, William E. Carter, John M. Hickman, Dwight B. Heath, Hans C. Buechler and Judith-Maria Buechler. Some of the earlier travelers to this region have described the Aymara in very consistent terms. From many of their accounts we get a general picture of these Indians as being submissive, gloomy, anxious and mistrustful, dirty and slovenly in personal habits, quarrelsome and capable of cruelty and malice. The Aymara seem to have little in the way of aesthetic interests; and Tschopik has characterized them as "utilitarian," meaning by this that they stress the useful and practical, although the term does not imply any special resourcefulness or ingenuity on their part.[5] Tschopik tells us that the Aymara, brought up to be submissive to authority, are reluctant to assume leadership. Hostility is suppressed or repressed among them, but may break through in drunken acts of violence.[6] Above all, in Tschopik's view, the Aymara are an anxious people:

> . . . among the Aymara anxiety is so general and intense, so ever-present and all-pervading, that it has left its particular mark on virtually every individual and has colored the entire fabric of the culture. . . . Anxiety is, in fact, the keystone of Aymara "modal" personality, the central principle in terms of which other personality characteristics become intelligible. . . . Diffuse anxiety is revealed by their pessimistic outlook as well as by fits of depression and gloom for which they have a name. In addition, flight from anxiety is indicated by the inordinate use of alcohol and coca. On the cultural level the presence of anxiety is reflected in the elaborate pharmacopoeia, the vast number of omens, most of them boding ill, and the proliferation of divinatory techniques.[7]

If only one writer had described the Aymara in these terms, one might suspect exaggeration in this picture—at least some degree of personal projection or subjectivity. But many published accounts, while differently expressed, reflect the same state of affairs—and one apparently persisting over a period of time.

Thinking about the Aymara in these terms, one can't help but

---

[5] Harry Tschopik, Jr., *The Aymara of Chucuito, Peru: I. Magic* (Anthropological Papers of the American Museum of Natural History, Vol. 44, Part 2) (1951), p. 185. For quotations about the Aymara by early writers, see Tschopik, ibid., pp. 172–73; and Weston La Barre, *The Aymara Indians of the Lake Titicaca Plateau, Bolivia* (Memoir of the American Anthropological Association, Number 68) (1948), p. 39.

[6] Tschopik, *The Aymara of Chucuito, Peru*, pp. 182–83.

[7] Ibid., p. 174.

wonder why they have come to be such anxious, unhappy people. A number of possible reasons—indeed, a whole battery of them—appear in the accounts of Tschopik and La Barre. There is first the matter of adjustment to high altitudes. *Sorroche* is a native term for high altitude sickness, brought about by lack of oxygen. Among the symptoms are headache, nausea, a sense of oppression and fatigue, and sometimes even temporary psychosis. Commercial pilots who are often exposed to anoxemia are said to suffer from grouchiness, as an almost standard occupational disease.[8] Perhaps, then, high altitude is one of the contributing factors to the Aymara personality picture.

We learn from La Barre that intoxication at high altitudes has more drastic effects than at sea level, and that "The Aymara are a notoriously drunken group. . . . All travellers have remarked on the quantities of alcohol the Aymara can consume, and the states of intoxication to which they can attain, and I can only confirm that I have never anywhere seen American Indians more thoroughly intoxicated than at the usual Aymara fiesta."[9] Alcohol, then, must be another contributory factor, as well as being an indicator of the degree of anxiety among the Aymara.

In addition to liquor, the Aymara are widely addicted to the chewing of coca, from which the narcotic cocaine is derived. Frequent coca chewing, as medical experiments have shown, may lead to pallor and muscular weakness. Gutierrez and Von Hagen state that ". . . coca chewers present emotional dullness or apathy, indifference, lack of will power, and low capacity for attention. They are mistrustful, shy, unsociable, and indecisive."[10] Perhaps, then, this is the source, or one of the sources, of the observed Aymara traits.

Moreover, we learn from Tschopik that the houses of these highlanders give poor protection. They are crowded, unheated, dirty, and unhygienic. Their clothing is inadequate too, and men often walk without sandals in subfreezing weather. The children are poorly clad. According to a medical survey in Ichu, the diet of at least some Aymara groups is inadequate—low in fats, vitamins A and C, iron, and calcium, and energy-producing foods.[11]

Little wonder that there is a good deal of sickness, especially res-

---

[8] La Barre, *The Aymara Indians of the Lake Titicaca Plateau, Bolivia*, p. 174.
[9] Ibid., pp. 48, 65.
[10] Quoted by Tschopik, *The Aymara of Chucuito, Peru*, p. 187.
[11] Ibid., pp. 157–58.

piratory and heart ailments, but also skin diseases, smallpox, scarlet fever, typhus, and venereal disease, among others. The Aymara, indeed, are said to have the highest infant mortality rate in the New World—one in seven during the first year.[12]

We learn from the Buechlers that Aymara infants are tightly swaddled from birth to the fourth month. If one took a childhood determinist approach, one might attempt to derive some Aymara characteristics from this experience, as Gorer did for the Russians. According to the Buechlers' brief account, children seem to be treated indulgently. Children are suckled for an average period of two years and fed on demand. They are played with by their parents and siblings and not allowed to cry for long. As in Silwa, children begin to work early, starting to herd pigs at the age of four or five, and later, sheep. They also take care of young siblings and carry water.[13]

Childhood does not seem to be an especially difficult time, but the high rate of child mortality and sickness must be kept in mind.

High altitude, excessive drinking and coca chewing, combined with unsanitary homes, inadequate clothing, poor diet, and much sickness—is there any wonder that the Aymara are said to be unhappy? Yet these are not the only factors that may be responsible for their alleged character traits. There is also the historical background of these people and their social relationships with the Mestizos toward whom they play a submissive role.

During the Spanish colonial period, the Aymara were made to work in the mines at forced labor. The Spaniards treated them brutally, and it has been estimated that 8 million natives, the majority of them Aymara, died during this time.[14] The Aymara rebelled repeatedly, but with little success, and they have remained in a subordinate position for the past five centuries. Their present overlords, the Mestizos, now command all the important political offices, own the best farmlands and better houses, and are, in general, much better off than the Aymara, who tip their hats submissively to the Mestizos as they pass, and who kiss the hands or garments of the Mestizos in gratitude for favors conferred.[15]

Among the Aymara, to consider another aspect, there is a grow-

[12] La Barre, *The Aymara Indians of the Lake Titicaca Plateau, Bolivia*, pp. 47, 126.

[13] Hans C. Buechler and Judith-Maria Buechler, *The Bolivian Aymara* (New York: Holt, Rinehart & Winston, Inc., 1971), pp. 23–26.

[14] La Barre, *The Aymara Indians of the Lake Titicaca Plateau, Bolivia*, p. 31.

[15] Tschopik, *The Aymara of Chucuito, Peru*, p. 159.

ing shortage of land. Ideally, members of an extended family are expected to cooperate with one another, but the land shortage leads to individualistic self-assertive behavior and to conflicts within the extended family. According to Tschopik, this results in more uneasiness and anxiety. Moreover, there is a good deal of tension within the average family. Marriages are unstable, infidelity and divorce common. The children born to such families are given relatively little affection.[16]

There are, then, a multitude of possible causes for the alleged character traits of the Aymara—climatic, toxicological, historical, and sociological. Granted that all the factors cited have played a role in the shaping of Aymara personality, have they all been equally important? Have not some exerted a more telling influence than others? How could we weigh their relative importance?

How significant, for example, is the factor of high altitude? If the Aymara lived at lower levels, would they be different? Are all mountaineers and highlanders anxious and grouchy? We have no intensive personality study of the Nepalese or Tibetans, but judging from the accounts of travelers, the high-dwelling Himalayan peoples seem to be quite different from the Aymara, often being pictured as cheerful, cooperative, and self-reliant. For example, C. J. Morris has written:

The most striking element in the character of the Gurkhas [Nepalese] is their unfailing cheerfulness even in the most adverse circumstances; and this, more perhaps than any other single factor, distinguishes them so markedly from the peoples of India proper. This essential difference is very apparent to the foreign traveller who has the good fortune to be allowed to enter Nepal. There is at once a sense of something utterly different, but a sense so subtle that it is difficult to define in *words*. I think it is due to this pervading cheerfulness of the people more than to anything else; they are happy and contented—on good terms with life— and the stranger who is prepared to accept them as they are cannot help but feel the same. Their sense of humor and especially of the ridiculous is highly developed, and no Gurkha can remain for long without a joke, even though it be against himself.[17]

Yet some Nepalese live at even higher levels than the Aymara. Moreover, both La Barre and Tschopik claim that the depressing

---

[16] Ibid., pp. 162–63.

[17] Charles John Morris, "Some Aspects of Social Life in Nepal," *Journal of the Royal Central Asian Society*, Vol. 22 (1935), p. 437. See also Ella Maillart, *The Land of the Sherpas* (London: Hodder & Stoughton, 1955), p. 12.

personality picture of the Aymara which they present applies more specifically to the Aymara of towns and haciendas than to the more independent Indians who live in *ayllus,* the traditional social units of the highland region.[18] This is not a difference in altitude, but in the texture of social life. Social and cultural factors may therefore be the more important determinants in this respect.

The Aymara Reexamined

The foregoing account of the Aymara, with some minor changes, appeared in the first edition of this book. Since then, this negative picture of the Aymara has been criticized by some anthropologists who have recently worked in Peru, although others have supported it in part.

John M. Hickman spent 10 months doing fieldwork among the Aymara of Chinchera. In addition to getting a series of depth interviews, Hickman trained 50 Indian interviewers to give an extensive survey schedule to 1,810 Indian adults in six communities—four Aymara and two Quechua—to get information about values and attitudes concerning culture change. In 1964, Hickman wrote: "The quality of life is one of general 'amoral familism' that places the family as the only center of concern and effort. The degree of suspicion, insecurity, hostility, ambivalence, and alienation as a group is high, corresponding to reports of previous investigators."[19] On the other hand, Hickman also noted that the Indians were optimistic about the future and that an increase in their level of education now made them less dependent on the ruling class. An eagerness to learn among the younger Aymara was also noted by A. Bouroncle Carreón.[20] Some Aymara have now entered advanced professions: the law, medicine, education, priesthood, and aviation. They have also taken an active role in politics, including Bolivia's recent revolutions.[21]

In 1966 there appeared a paper by John F. Plummer in which he

---

[18] La Barre, *The Aymara Indians of the Lake Titicaca Plateau, Bolivia,* pp. 39, 40, 156; Tschopik, *The Aymara of Chucuito, Peru,* p. 173.

[19] John M. Hickman, "The Aymara of Chinchera, Peru: Persistence and Change in a Bicultural Context," *Dissertation Abstracts,* No. 7, XXIV, (Ann Arbor, Mich.: University Microfilms, Inc., 1964) , p. 3498.

[20] "Contribución al Estudio de los Aymaras," *América Indígena,* (Mexico) , Vol. 24 (1964) , pp. 129–69.

[21] Dwight B. Heath, "The Aymara Indians and Bolivia's Revolutions," *Inter-American Economic Affairs,* Vol. 19 (1966) , pp. 31–40.

took issue with the traditional negative view.[22] Plummer points out that most travelers in the Aymara region used Mestizo or white interpreters, who were hated by the Aymara. According to Tschopik, in Chucuito a person had to be either an Indian or a Mestizo, and the Tschopiks were perforce classed as Mestizos. Plummer also notes that most travelers in the region seldom stayed long in one place and had no opportunity to get to know the Indians well.[23] As for the accounts by Tschopik and La Barre, Plummer points out that both made various positive comments in their writings which serve to modify the dominantly negative impression. For example: "The Aymara does laugh and joke as do other human beings, and affection, love and friendship are far from non-existent in this society."[24] Plummer also quotes passages from Tschopik's unpublished diaries and letters which stress the friendliness of individual Aymara.[25]

In the same year as Plummer's paper, Weston La Barre published an analysis of a series of Aymara folktales, which seem to depict a dog-eat-dog universe. Themes of aggression and duplicity are recurrent, and there is an obsessive emphasis on food. La Barre had evidently not changed his views about the Aymara by this time, for he concluded:

If the Aymara, as evidenced in their folktales (and indeed throughout the rest of their culture), are apprehensive, crafty, suspicious, violent, treacherous, and hostile, one important reason for this may be that such a character structure is an understandable response to their having lived for perhaps as long as a millennium under rigidly hierarchic and absolutist economic, military, and religious controls.[26]

Perhaps one could accept this as a valid statement of the traditional Aymara world view and at the same time acknowledge the changes now occurring, reported by Hickman, Carreón, Heath, and Plummer.

[22] John F. Plummer, "Another Look at Aymara Personality," *Behavior Science Notes*, HRAF Quarterly Bulletin, Vol. 1 (1966), pp. 55–78.

[23] This seems to have been true in Plummer's case as well. He writes: "Unfortunately, we were never able to stay in one place for more than a few days at a time. It is true that the Aymara avoided us when we first appeared, but the longer we stayed, the more friendly they became." Ibid., p. 70.

[24] Tschopik, *The Aymara of Chuchuito, Peru*, p. 148.

[25] See also the criticisms of my review of the Aymara literature in William E. Carter, "Secular Reinforcement in Aymara Death Ritual," *American Anthropologist*, Vol. 70 (1968), p. 262.

[26] Weston La Barre, "The Aymara: History and Worldview," in Melville Jacobs and John Greenway (eds.), *The Anthropologist Looks at Myth* (Austin, Texas: University of Texas Press, 1966), p. 143.

The reader may have noted that, although the characterizations of the Aymara are more extreme, there are some similarities between the Aymara and the people of Silwa, Egypt. The latter do not drink or use drugs (at least, Ammar gives no information about such practices), but otherwise, there are many similarities. In both areas, we have peasants living under conditions of poverty and malnutrition, brought up to be submissive and fatalistic, and feeling much anxiety and suppressed resentment. These features seem to be characteristic of many peasant communities. Similar descriptions of Mexican peasants have been given by Erich Fromm and Michael Maccoby (see Chapter 17), of Rajput peasants in India (see Chapter 9), and of Italian peasants.[27] In his study of Tepoztlán, Mexico, Oscar Lewis described the Tepoztecans as being mutually suspicious, envious, unsmiling, and constricted.[28] The normal type of personality in Aritama, a peasant community in Colombia, is described as extremely controlled and rigid. "There is mistrust of all motivations in others, little submission, and never rebellion, but rather avoidance of all close relationships. . . . Gloominess and cynical self-accusations are frequent."[29] As will be seen in the following chapter, some writers have made generalizations about the world view of peasants.

What interests the antropologist, however, is not only the similarities which may be found in some peasant communities, but also the differences. Why are the peasants of Taira, Okinawa (discussed in Chapter 9) apparently more trusting and cooperative than those of Silwa? Why is alcoholism rife among the Aymara but rare among poor Italian and Sicilian peasants, despite their similarly dull rounds of experience?

CROSS-CULTURAL COMPARISONS

The heart of anthropology, including culture-and-personality research, is cross-cultural comparison. Cross-cultural comparisons and contrasts are necessary if one is to support any generalization about

---

[27] Edward C. Banfield, *The Moral Basis of a Backward Society* (Glencoe, Ill.: The Free Press, 1958).

[28] Oscar Lewis, *Life in a Mexican Village. Tepotzlán Restudied* (Urbana, Ill.: University of Illinois Press, 1951), chap. 14.

[29] Gerardo and Alicia Reichel-Dolmatoff, *The People of Aritama. The Cultural Personality of a Colombian Mestizo Village* (London: Routledge and Kegan Paul, 1961), p. 449.

a particular society. For example, if you allege that the Aymara are gloomy, you must be able to point to another group of people who are less gloomy; otherwise the statement has no meaning.

When the historian Jacob Burckhardt argued in 1860 that the Italian Renaissance was a period marked by great individualism, he drew contrasts between the earlier Middle Ages and the Renaissance and between northern Europe and Italy in such varied fields as forms of dress, incidence of crime, and fields of achievement.[30] Thus, to document the statement that the Aymara are gloomy or that the Italians of the Renaissance were individualistic, one must make contrasts with less gloomy or less individualistic societies and provide some indices for the extent of gloom or individualism in these societies.

Comparisons in different contexts may also help to elicit the significant determinants of personality patterns. If high altitude, for example, is said to account for some personality traits of the Aymara, one can compare Aymara who live at high altitudes with Aymara who live in low-lying jungle areas, as some of them do, and see if there are any significant differences between these groups. Or one can compare the high-altitude Aymara with other peoples, like the Nepalese, who live at high altitudes. If the Aymara are said to have suffered mainly from the oppression of Mestizos, one can compare the Aymara of towns and haciendas with the more independent Indians who live apart from white or Mestizo control, or make comparisons of Aymara before and after the Bolivian revolutions, before and after the acquisition of education.

I do not mean to suggest that anthropologists should descend upon the Aymara to carry out these investigations. The Aymara and the villagers of Silwa have served in this chapter, first to introduce the concept of "social character," and secondly to illustrate how comparisons and contrasts may be made between cultures to elicit the significant determinants of personality patterns.

SUGGESTIONS FOR FURTHER READING

For a discussion of the concept of social character, see Erich Fromm and Michael Maccoby, *Social Character in a Mexican Village. A Socio-psychoanalytic Study* (Englewood Cliffs, N.J.: Prentice-Hall, Inc., 1970),

---

[30] Jacob Burckhardt, *The Civilization of the Renaissance in Italy* (Oxford: Phaidon Press, 1945).

especially chapters 1 and 11. For a criticism of some of Fromm's views, see Reinhard Bendix, "Compliant Behavior and Individual Personality," *American Journal of Sociology,* Vol. 58 (1952), pp. 292–303.

The concepts of "basic personality structure" and "modal personality" are discussed in Chapter 7. National character studies are dealt with in Chapter 10.

chapter *3*

Cognition and Culture

This chapter deals with ways in which culture influences cognition and perception. It concerns such concepts as world view, ethos, themes, postulates, values, attitudes, prejudices, self-concepts, the influence of language upon cognition, and the influence of physical environment upon perception.

WORLD VIEW

Let us start with the broad, rather vague notion of world view. In the last chapter it was mentioned that some writers have made generalizations about the world view of peasants. A number of questions at once suggest themselves. What is a peasant? What is a world view? What features of world view, if any, are held to be characteristic of peasants in general? How would such a world view differ from those of nonpeasants?

One anthropoligist who has tackled some of these questions is Robert Redfield. Redfield applied the term "folk society" to societies which existed before the rise of cities and also to present-day societies which have been little affected by the world's great civilizations. "Peasant societies" are former "folk societies" which have made contact with the city. There were no peasants before the first cities. A mutual symbiosis exists between the peasant and the city or town, peasants providing grain and other produce and acquiring city-made goods in return.[1] Redfield believed that there is a special

---

[1] Robert Redfield, *The Primitive World and Its Transformations* (Ithaca, N.Y.: Cornell University Press, 1957) , pp. 30–34.

peasant "style of life," marked by a characteristic set of attitudes and values, to be found in peasant communities in different parts of the world. It is expressed, for example, in Hesiod's *Works and Days,* where we find:

> . . . a practical and utilitarian attitude toward nature, yet with such a positive valuation of work as sees it as not only materially productive but also a fulfillment of divine commands; a de-emphasis of emotion; a concern with security rather than adventure; a high valuation of procreation and children; a desire for wealth; and the joining of social justice with work as basic ethical notions.[2]

Redfield finds evidence of much the same "style of life" in Polish, Chinese, Kurdish, and Guatemalan peasants.

The peasant appears as a human type that is recognizable, widespread, and long enduring, brought about by the development of civilization. Presumably it is such a mode of existence as permits continuation of many of the adaptive characteristics of the folk society with the new necessities brought about by the city. The peasant society exists by virtue of the traditional moral solidarity to be found in any isolated folk society; kinship relationships are still of first importance; the ends of living are implicit and strongly felt. On the other hand the peasant makes certain elements of civilization a part of his life: a trading spirit, money, formal and impersonal controls, whether economic or political.[3]

The world view of a people, according to Redfield, is the way they regard the universe, their most comprehensive attitudes toward life, their conception of the structure of things.[4] A world view may be seen as stemming from the integration of a society's culture, its strain toward consistency. A child born into the society is likely to accept its prevalent world view along with the rest of the culture he absorbs.

Redfield suggested but did not clearly define the nature of a typical peasant world view. In another publication he made some attempts to generalize about "the peasant view of the good life." After citing some writers who have stressed the similarities of peasants in different parts of the world, Redfield mentioned being struck by the similarities of three peoples in particular: the sixth-century Boeotians described by Hesiod, the rural folk of Surrey described by George Sturt, and the Maya of Yucatán whom Redfield studied. But

---

[2] Ibid., p. 39. Redfield here cites E. K. L. Francis, "The Personality Type of the Peasant According to Hesiod's *Works and Days,*" *Rural Sociology,* Vol. 10 (September 1945), pp. 275–95.

[3] Ibid., p. 39.

[4] Ibid., pp. 85–86.

after making this comparison, Redfield acknowledged that many peasant groups provided exceptions to the patterns he noted.[5]

Another attempt to generalize about such matters has been made by George M. Foster, with his concept of "the image of limited good." Foster explains this concept as follows:

By "Image of Limited Good" I mean that broad areas of peasant behavior are patterned in such fashion as to suggest that peasants view their social, economic, and natural universes—their total environment—as one in which all of the desired things in life such as land, wealth, health, friendship and love, manliness and honor, respect and status, power and influence, security and safety, *exist in finite quantity* and *are always in short supply*, as far as the peasant is concerned. Not only do these and all other "good things" exist in finite and limited quantities, but in addition *there is no way directly within peasant power to increase the available quantities.* . . . If "Good" exists in limited amounts which cannot be expanded, and if the system is closed, it follows that *an individual or a family can improve a position only at the expense of others.*[6]

This picture can be supported by various field studies of peasant communities. For example, the Blums write of Greek villagers:

. . . it was said that when good things happen to a villager, the other villagers express their envy in gossip, criticism, and calumny. The villagers described their life altogether as an uneasy one, with each family feeling competitive and jealous toward any other that might achieve success or happiness.[7]

The notion of "limited good" has some basis in the realities of peasant life; most peasants are poor, land is in limited supply, and so are other goods. This state of affairs could easily be projected onto the world at large. Thus, Foster considers sibling rivalry to be influenced by the conception of a mother's love as being finite and directed mainly to the youngest child; hence the jealousy of older siblings. Foster notes the expectation of sibling rivalry and jealousy in Mexican villages as well as in Ammar's Egyptian village.

Foster remarks that peasant families can be relatively self-sufficient

---

[5] Robert Redfield, "The Peasant View of the Good Life," in Robert Redfield, *The Little Society and Peasant Society and Culture* (Chicago: University of Chicago Press, 1960) , pp. 60–79.

[6] George M. Foster, "Peasant Society and the Image of Limited Good," reproduced by permission of the American Anthropological Association from *American Anthropologist,* Vol. 67 (1965) , pp. 296–97. Italics as in the original.

[7] Richard Blum and Eva Blum, *Health and Healing in Rural Greece* (Stanford, Calif.: Stanford University Press, 1965) , p. 128. See also the account of Italian village life by F. G. Friedman, "The World of 'La Miseria,'" reprinted in Jack M. Potter, May N. Diaz, and George M. Foster (eds.) , *Peasant Society. A Reader* (Boston, Mass.: Little, Brown and Company, 1967) , pp. 324–36.

and individualistic; so each family sees itself in a competitive struggle with others for the scarce values of life. They do not compete for outward symbols of success or display; instead, everyone tries to be inconspicuous and to look like everyone else, in order to avoid evoking jealousy, envy, and criticism.

Much of this cognitive approach may be true of nonpeasant societies as well as of peasant societies. Also, there are peasant societies which do not fit the scheme very well. For example, the villagers of Niiike, Japan, are described as having little anxiety or aggression but with a high stress on achievement. There seems to be little tension compared to what has been described of Silwa or the Aymara.[8] The people of Niiike engage in much cooperative activity. Perhaps a crucial factor which distinguishes this Japanese village from the other peasant communities we have considered is that it is relatively prosperous.[9]

It would be wrong to generalize too broadly about peasants. Reinhold Löffler has described a type of peasant leader who is eager for change and modernization.[10] But there is value in hypotheses like Foster's which suggest the operation of cross-cultural regularities in societies which share a particular kind of economy.

Selective Borrowing and Other Keys to World View

How can one find out what a society's world view is—assuming that there is such a thing? One way is through the study of selective borrowing, by noting which patterns of culture a society accepts from its neighbors, which it rejects, and how borrowed items of culture are refashioned. Oswald Spengler was one of the first theoreticians to deal with the selective borrowing of culture traits. He showed that borrowed items of culture usually undergo some kind of transformation in the new setting and are tailored to fit the culture into which they have been introduced. Thus, when Buddhism diffused from India to China, it became a new, quite different religion.[11] The ways in which such borrowed items are modified tell us something about the prevalent values or attitudes of the in-

---

[8] George De Vos, "Social Values and Personal Attitudes in Primary Human Relations in Niiike," *Occasional Papers, Center for Japanese Studies* (Ann Arbor, Mich.: University of Michigan, 1965), pp. 53–91.

[9] Richard K. Beardsley, John W. Hall, and Robert E. Ward, *Village Japan* (Chicago: University of Chicago Press, 1959).

[10] Reinhold Löffler, "The Representative Mediator and the New Peasant," *American Anthropologist*, Vol. 73 (1971), pp. 1077–91.

[11] Oswald Spengler, *The Decline of the West*, trans. C. F. Atkinson (New York: Knopf, 1939), Vol. II, p. 57.

corporating society. The rejection of uncongenial culture traits is diagnostic in the same way. Thus, Spengler writes:

> Try to follow, element by element, the "influence" of Egyptian plastic upon early Greek, and you will find in the end that there is none at all, but that the Greek will-to-form took out of the older art-stock some few characteristics that it would in any case have discovered in some shape for itself. All round the Classical landscape there were working, or had worked, Egyptians, Cretans, Babylonians, Assyrians, Hittites, Persians, and Phoenicians, and the works of these peoples—their buildings, ornaments, art-works, cults, state-forms, scripts, and sciences—were known to the Greeks in profusion. But how much out of all this mass did the Classical soul extract as its own means of expression? I repeat, it is only the relations that are *accepted* that are observed. But what of those that were *not accepted?* Why, for example, do we fail to find in the former category the pyramid, pylon, and obelisk of Egypt, or hieroglyphic, or cuneiform?[12]

Behind such rejections and transformations Spengler saw the working of an underlying word view. In the chapter that follows it will be shown that Ruth Benedict followed a similar procedure in delineating the underlying set of attitudes and values shared by the Pueblo Indians of the American Southwest.

Another way of identifying the salient attitudes and values of a society is through linguistic analysis. The vocabulary of a society may have reference to concepts not present or less common in other languages. For example, in her book on Japanese culture and personality, Ruth Benedict discussed at length some of the various terms which Japanese have for feelings of obligation, while L. Takeo Doi has drawn attention to the Japanese word *amaeru,* referring to an attempt to establish a state of close dependency on another person.[13] Similarly Hu Hsien-Chin has analyzed Chinese terms for concepts of "face."[14]

Other ways of identifying attitudes and values in a particular society are through the use of interviews, questionnaires, or projective tests like the Thematic Apperception Test. A discussion of these techniques is reserved for Part IV of this book.

ETHOS

The Oxford English dictionary defines ethos as "the characteristic spirit, prevalent tone of sentiment of a people or community, the

---

[12] Ibid., Vol. II, p. 58.

[13] See below, p. 233.

[14] Hu Hsien-Chin, "The Chinese Concept of 'Face,'" *American Anthropologist,* Vol. 46 (1944), pp. 45–64.

'genius' of an institution or system." Gregory Bateson has clarified this concept as follows:

When a group of young intellectual English men or women are talking and joking together wittily and with a touch of light cynicism, there is established among them for the time being a definite tone of appropriate behavior. Such specific tones of behavior are in all cases indicative of an ethos. They are expressions of a standardised system of emotional attitudes. In this case the men have temporarily adopted a definite set of sentiments toward the rest of the world, a definite attitude towards reality, and they will joke about subjects which at another time they would treat with seriousness. If one of the men suddenly intrudes a sincere or realist remark it will be received with no enthusiasm—perhaps with a moment's silence and a slight feeling that the sincere person has committed a solecism. On another occasion the same group of persons may adopt a different ethos; they may talk realistically and sincerely. Then if a blunderer makes a flippant joke it will fall flat and feel like a solecism.

The point which I wish to stress in this example is that any group of people may establish among themselves an ethos, which as soon as it is established becomes a very real factor in determining their conduct. This ethos is expressed in the tone of their behavior. I have deliberately for my initial example chosen an instance of labile and temporary ethos in order to show that the process of development, far from being mysterious and rare, is an everyday phenomenon. . . . But if, instead of such a temporary conversation group, we examine some more formed and permanent group—say an army mess or a college high table—whose members continually meet under the same conditions, we find the ethological position much more stable.[15]

With the suggestion that this state of affairs might apply to whole societies, particularly small isolated ones, Bateson proceeds to examine the Iatmul from this point of view. Here he finds not one ethos but two—one for the men and one for the women. Iatmul men are occupied with dramatic activities centered in their ceremonial house, where they swagger about self-consciously, engaging in angry debates with violent gestures. Pride and exhibitionism characterize the men, whose dramatic shows are appreciatively watched by the more unobtrusive women. (Formerly the Iatmul were headhunters —an activity which gave full expression to the male ethos.)

Women have a humbler way of life centered in the home and concerned with the mundane business of food getting, cooking, and bringing up children. These are largely private rather than public activities. The women are described as being jolly and readily

---

[15] Gregory Bateson, *Naven* (2d ed; Stanford: Stanford University Press, 1958), pp. 119–20. (The first edition was published in 1936.)

cooperative, in contrast to the touchy self-assertive males who find it hard to cooperate. At times the women assume something of the male ethos, for on ceremonial occasions they elaborately dress up and display among their decorations some ornaments normally worn by the men. At these times the women march with "a fine proud bearing" quite different from their usual manner, and receive the admiration of both men and women in the audience.[16] In contrast, when men don women's clothes, in the ritual activities concerning their sisters' sons, they make themselves look ridiculous, thus indicating the superiority of the male ethos.

Another concept used by Bateson is that of *eidos*, which he defines as the standardization of the cognitive aspects of the personality of individuals within a society.[17] Bateson finds that Iatmul culture is characerized by a tendency to complexity, and that the Iatmul are stimulated to a degree of intellectual activity unusual among primitive peoples. This intellectual activity takes the form of memorizing thousands of names in connection with debates about totems. There is also a proneness to visual and kinesthetic imagery. The term *eidos* does not seem to have been used much by other anthropologists.

THEMES

Morris E. Opler has argued that it is rare to find cultures dominated by a single integrative principle, as is suggested in Ruth Benedict's *Patterns of Culture,* discussed in the next chapter. Opler has offered, instead, the concept of *themes*—"dynamic affirmations" which are found, in limited number, in every culture and which structure the nature of reality for its members. An example of a theme would be the high valuation of long life and old age among the Chiricahua Apache. Opler points out evidence for the significance of such a theme in various Chiricahua culture patterns. But there is another theme, "validation by participation," which limits the first. An old man is admired and respected as long as he is active and fit, but when he can't keep pace with younger men, his years and knowledge do not prevent his retirement. Themes, then, are not necessarily pervasive in a culture but interact with and balance one another.[18]

---

[16] Ibid., pp. 122–51.

[17] Ibid., p. 220.

[18] Morris E. Opler, "Themes as Dynamic Forces in Culture," *American Journal of Sociology,* Vol. 51 (1945) , pp. 198–206.

Opler has applied a themal analysis to the culture of North India, in which he distinguishes the following themes:

1. Divisiveness. (Family cleavages, subcaste divisions and factions.)
2. Hierarchy. (The grading of castes, of supernaturals, and of parts of the body.)
3. Concern for right action or *dharma.*
4. Concern for ritual purity and fear of pollution. (Untouchability, attitudes toward leather and other polluting substances, ideas about menstruation, food taboos, frequent bathing for ritual purification.)
5. Ascendancy of the male principle, with some fear and suspicion of the female principle. (Rites to ensure male offspring. More celebration if a child born is a boy. Purdah. Godlings of disease are always female.)
6. Familism. (The family takes precedence over the individual. Debts are family responsibilities. The family suffers outcasting for the sin of a member. Marriages are arranged by parents. Presence of ancestor worship.)
7. Balance, consensus, or harmony. (Efforts toward compromise, prevention of family friction. The Hindu view of sickness as resulting from imbalance.)
8. Nonviolence. (Vegetarianism. Fasting as a form of protest.)
9. High value of intellect, rationalism.
10. Transcendentalism. (Other wordly emphasis. The notion that the world is an illusion. The taking of vows and fasting.)
11. Conception of rhythm of existence. (Beliefs in cycles of time. Fatalism.)

Opler points out that some of these themes (such as Male ascendancy and Hierarchy) support each other, while some are at odds with each other (such as Familism versus Divisiveness). Some themes act as limitations or restraints on others. For example, Hierarchy would promote a sense of self-esteem and resentment of insult, but the emphases on harmony and nonviolence would tend to check the anger of an insulted person. Many of the themes tend to perpetuate the caste system (Concern for right action, Familism, Concern for ritual purity and fear of pollution, and Hierarchy).[19]

---

[19] Morris E. Opler, "The Themal Approach in Cultural Anthropology and Its Application to North Indian Data," *Southwestern Journal of Anthropology,* Vol. 24 (1968), pp. 215–27.

The themes distinguished by Opler do seem to be important guiding principles in North India and help one to conceptualize the system. In some later parts of this book there will be references to Indian data which seem consonant with Opler's analysis.[20]

POSTULATES

Similar to themes are basic propositions shared by members of a society which E. Adamson Hoebel has called *postulates*. Like themes, postulates may be at odds with one another. Hoebel suggests that the degree to which they are consistent and harmonious with one another in a particular society is a measure of the integration of its culture.[21] In his book on law, Hoebel used the concept of postulates in a cross-cultural study of legal institutions in a series of societies: Eskimo, Ifugao, Comanche, Kiowa, Cheyenne, Trobriand, and Ashanti. Later, in a work on the Cheyenne, Hoebel singled out 16 postulates which underlay Cheyenne culture in general.[22]

Francis L. K. Hsu has suggested the use of postulates as a way of comparing and contrasting the cultures of complex literate societies like China and the United States. The postulates would be underlying assumptions about the nature of things which carry with them various associated corollaries. The postulates and corollaries of a particular society may be inferred from a study of the society's literature, philosophies, ethical systems, laws, mores, and from studies on abnormality, crime, and other forms of breakdown.

Hsu has tried to compare and contrast China and the United States in this fashion, a topic to which we will return in later chapters of this book.[23] To give an idea of Hsu's suggested approach, here is Hsu's Postulate I on China: "An individual's most important duty and responsibility are toward his parents, which take precedence over any other interest, including self-interest. The essential expression of this is filial piety. Filial piety is the individual's way of repaying parents for giving him life and raising him."[24] Associated with this postulate are 15 corollaries. There are 14 postulates in all.

---

[20] See pp. 461–65.

[21] E. Adamson Hoebel, *The Law of Primitive Man. A Study in Comparative Legal Dynamics* (Cambridge, Mass.: Harvard University Press, 1954), pp. 13–14.

[22] E. Adamson Hoebel, *The Cheyennes. Indians of the Great Plains* (New York: Henry Holt & Co., 1960), pp. 98–99.

[23] See Chapters 15 and 17.

[24] Francis L. K. Hsu, *The Study of Literate Civilizations* (New York: Holt, Rinehart & Winston, Inc., 1969), p. 65.

We may contrast the first Chinese postulate with Hsu's Postulate I for the United States: "An individual's most important concern is his self-interest: self-expression, self-development, self-gratification, and independence. This takes precedence over all group interests."[25]

This postulate may be open to question; our income tax and draft laws do not seem to be in agreement with it. Like Chinese Postulate I, it is associated with a string of corollaries. It remains to be seen whether others will follow Hsu's lead in using this approach to the cross-cultural study of national character in complex societies.

VALUES

It would seem to be difficult to make cross-cultural studies of the dominant values held by people in different societies. The first question is how to go about it, whether to make use of a questionnaire or some other technique. A problem with questionnaires is that a person's answers may not necessarily express his actual values. Despite the various difficulties involved, a number of efforts have been made to deal with this subject.

Charles Morris of the University of Chicago has drawn up a document called "Ways to Live," in which 13 styles of life are described. Morris has affixed labels to these various ways, such as Apollonian, Dionysian, Promethean, Christian, Buddhist, Mohammedan, and Maitreyan. The subject is asked to read the descriptions of the 13 ways and to rate each of the ways on a seven-point scale as to how much he likes or dislikes it. This questionnaire formed the basis of Morris' cross-cultural investigation of the values of college students in the 1940s, although it was supplemented by interviews. The largest samples came from the United States (2,015 men, 831 women), China (523 men, 220 women), and India (724 men, 410 women). Smaller samples came from Japan, Norway, Canada, and some other countries. The responses were subjected to factor analysis, according to such factors as social restraint and self-control, enjoyment and progress in action, withdrawal and self-sufficiency, receptivity and sympathetic concern, and self-indulgence or sensuous enjoyment.

Morris found much similarity in the Indian, American, and Chinese ratings, although American students emphasized the values of flexibility and many-sidedness, Indian students stressed social

---

[25] Ibid., p. 78.

restraint and self-control, and Chinese students were more actively and socially oriented.[26]

James M. Gillespie and Gordon W. Allport made use of a questionnaire involving 50 items, designed to tap values. They also asked the subject to write an autobiography of the future, "From Now to 2000 A.D." The authors hoped to secure about 100 male and 100 female college students' sets of responses in 10 countries, but their final samples were sometimes smaller. The 10 countries were the United States, New Zealand, South Africa, Egypt, Mexico, France, Italy, Germany, Japan, and Israel. The materials were collected between 1949 and 1951.

Like Morris, the authors found much similarity among the different groups of students, which could be attributed to the fact that they are all liberal arts students exposed to a common international culture. Students in all nations, for example, favor permissive and affectionate parent-child relationships and express hope for more racial equality. There were also differences: more nationalism, for example, expressed by Afrikaners, Bantus, Egyptians, and Mexicans. American students in 1949 showed relatively little interest in social problems (no doubt changed by now). In agreement with Morris' findings, American students expressed a desire for a rich many-sided life. Associated with this was an attitude of "privatism" in contrast to more involvement in corporate loyalties among Egyptians, Bantus, Mexicans, and Japanese.[27]

In the 1950s, Mary Ellen Goodman asked children in four Japanese and eight American schools to write compositions on the topic "What I want to be when I grow up, and why." About 1,250 Japanese and 3,750 American children from grades one through eight responded.

One contrast between the national groups was in connection with military service; no interest was shown by Japanese boys, while seven or eight out of a hundred American boys looked forward to a military career. Japanese children showed much more interest in politics and holding public office than did the American children and also more interest in business pursuits. American children expressed more self-oriented individualism than did the Japanese.[28]

[26] Charles Morris, *Varieties of Human Value* (Chicago: University of Chicago Press, 1956).

[27] James M. Gillespie and Gordon W. Allport, *Youth's Outlook on the Future: A Cross-National Study* (New York: Doubleday & Co., Inc., 1955).

[28] Mary Ellen Goodman, "Values, Attitudes, and Social Concepts of Japanese and American Children," *American Anthropologist*, Vol. 59 (1957), pp. 979–99.

Probably the best cross-cultural study of values undertaken so far is Kluckhohn and Strodtbeck's *Variations in Value Orientations.*[29] Value orientations are defined by Kluckhohn as "complex but definitely patterned (rank-ordered) principles, resulting from the transactional interplay of three analytically distinguishable elements of the evaluative process—the cognitive, the affective, and the directive elements—which give order and direction to the ever-flowing stream of human acts and thoughts as these relate to the solution of 'common human' problems."[30]

The authors make the assumptions that: (1) All societies face a limited number of common human problems which must be solved; (2) The range of possible solutions is limited, neither random nor limitless; and (3) Although all alternative solutions are always present in all societies, some solutions to problems are differentially preferred. There is almost always a rank ordering of preferences.

Five basic problems are singled out:

1. What is the innate nature of man?
2. What is the relation of man to nature?
3. What is the nature of time orientation?
4. What is the modality of human activity?
5. What is the modality of man's relationships to others?

To each question a threefold set of possible answers or solutions is suggested. Human nature may be seen as (1) evil, (2) neutral or a mixture of good and evil, or (3) good. Man's relation to nature may be seen as (1) subjugated to nature, (2) in harmony with nature, or (3) dominating nature. The significant time orientation may be seen as directed to (1) past, (2) present, or (3) future. The significant activity orientation may be (1) being, (2) being-in-becoming, and (3) doing. The modality of human relationships may be (1) lineal, (2) collateral, or (3) individualistic.[31]

Most of these alternatives are self-explanatory or readily understood. There is some difficulty, though, with the distinction between lineality and collaterality. Both refer to group relationships. Lineality has to do with the continuity of a group through time, as in the

---

[29] Florence Rockwood Kluckhohn and Fred L. Strodtbeck, with the assistance of John M. Roberts, A. Kimball Romney, Clyde Kluckhohn, and Harry A. Scarr, *Variations in Value Orientations* (Evanston, Ill.: Row, Peterson and Company, 1961).

[30] Ibid., p. 4. This sentence is italicized in the original.

[31] Ibid., pp. 10–12.

case of a Chinese family line. In harking back to Hsu's postulates, we can see that Chinese Postulate I emphasizes lineality, while American Postulate I emphasizes individualism. Collaterality concerns ties with laterally extended groups; but since these may include the family, the distinction between lineality and collaterality is not always clear.

Kluckhohn considers the dominant U.S. orientations to be individualism, future time orientation, mastery over nature, and doing. (An evil-but-perfectable conception of human nature is a heritage from our Puritan forebears but is now changing.) In contrast, Spanish-Americans of the Southwest are seen to have emphases on lineality (now changing), present time orientation, subjugation to nature, and being.

Every person is said to have a rank order of value orientations as part of his personality. According to this theory, the nature of rank order is considerably influenced by the culture into which one is born.

Kluckhohn's theories were tested by the administration of a questionnaire schedule of 22 items in five communities within the same area of the American Southwest: Spanish-Americans, Texans, Mormons, Navaho, and Zuñi. Members of the research team made predictions in advance about the ranking of the value orientations in these five groups. They predicted that the Spanish-Americans would give priority to individualism (Ind) but with some stress on lineality (Lin) and preferences for present time orientation (Pres), subjugation to nature (Subj), and being. The Texans were predicted to give the following rankings: In relations: Ind > Coll > Lin. In time orientation: Fut > Pres > Past. In man-nature orientation: Over > Subj > With. In activity orientation, doing was given slightly more stress than being. The authors were more unsure about the Mormons but expected them to give about equal stress to collaterality and individualism. In time orientation: Fut > Pres > Past. In man-nature orientation: With > Over > Subj. The Mormons were expected to give priority to doing rather than being. The predictions for the Navaho were: in relations: Col > Lin > Ind. In time orientation: Pres > Past > Fut. In man-nature orientation it was predicted that priority would go to Harmony-with-Nature. These predictions were not made for the Zuñi. No predictions were made concerning the innate nature of man, since the questionnaire schedule did not cover that area. Nor was the being-in-becoming variant considered.

To give an idea of how value preferences were elicited, one of the 22 schedule items goes as follows:

A man had a crop failure, or, let us say, had lost most of his sheep or cattle. He and his family had to have help from someone if they were going to get through the winter. There are different ways of getting help. Which of these three ways would be best?

B   Would it be best if he depended mostly on his brothers and
(Coll) sisters or other relatives, all to help him out as much as each one could?

C   Would it be best for him to try to raise the money *on his own*
(Ind) outside the community (his own people) from people who are neither relatives nor employers?

A   Would it be best for him to go to a boss or to an older important
(Lin) relative who is used to managing things in his group, and ask him to help out until things get better?[32]

Each question had three alternative choices. The subject was asked to give his first choice and then his preference for the remaining alternatives. He could give equal weight to two or all three alternatives if he wished.

The questionnaire was given to between 20 and 25 adult subjects in each of the five communities, roughly divided between males and females. The sample size was partly determined by the size of the Spanish-American community, which had no more adults than that. Random samples were drawn from persons over 20 in the Texan, Mormon, and Navaho groups. Random samples were not drawn for the Zuñi because of probems concerning rapport, and persons who had been working with the ethnographer were chosen as subjects.

This interesting experiment produced results in consonance with Kluckhohn's theories. Statistical analyses of the responses showed that there were both significant within-culture regularities and between-culture differences. The Spanish-American data accorded remarkably with the predictions which had been made. There was also much correspondence between predictions and data for the Texans, except that there was more stress on present time orientation than had been expected. The Mormon predictions were generally borne out, but the Mormons gave priority to over-nature rather than to with-nature in contrast to the prediction. The Navaho findings also accorded well with the predictions, especially in regard to activity orientation. No predictions were made for the Zuñi, whose responses were also those which gave the least conclusive

---

[32] Ibid., pp. 83–84.

results. This seems to provide very good support for Kluckhohn's theories about value orientations.[33]

A further study of values in the southwestern groups has been made by John W. M. Whiting and associates. This study was directed to a comparison of child-rearing practices in three of the five groups and the ways in which the characteristic values of each group are fostered. When the mothers of the three groups, Zuñi, Mormon, and Texan, were rated on a scale measuring intolerance of aggression by children against peers, 77 percent of the Zuñi and 69 percent of the Mormon mothers scored above the median for the three groups, while only 6 percent of the Texan mothers scored as high. Since the main contrast here was between the nuclear Texan families and the extended Zuñi families, the researchers considered whether this represented a characteristic difference between nuclear and extended families. Perhaps crowded living conditions require an emphasis on harmony and control of aggression. A cross-cultural correlational survey supported this hypothesis. "Twenty-five of thirty cases, approximately 80 percent, confirm our expectation. . . . 92 percent of the extended families are above the median in the severity with which children's aggression is punished, whereas but 22 percent of the societies with nuclear family households are equally severe."[34]

Commenting on this study, Robert A. LeVine has suggested that in certain child-rearing practices the Texans may be roughly representative of northern Europe and the United States, while the Zuñi may be representative of folk and peasant populations of the New World, Asia, and Africa. The severe aggression training in such groups ". . . may be part of a larger tendency to make children orderly, obedient, and pacific, producing an inhibitedness that manifests itself in performance on cognitive tasks."[35] LeVine also makes

---

[33] A study making use of the same methods has been done in Japan with 619 subjects by William Caudill and Harry A. Scarr. On the basis of his knowledge of the Japanese, Caudill successfully made predictions about their rankings of value orientations. Particularly striking was the Japanese emphasis on collaterality, which remained strong in different generations, being emphasized even more by the young than by the old. See William A. Caudill and Harry A. Scarr, "Japanese Value Orientations and Culture Change," *Ethnology*, Vol. 1 (1962), pp. 53–91.

[34] John W. M. Whiting, Eleanor H. Chasdi, Helen F. Antonovsky, and Barbara C. Ayres, "The Learning of Values," in Evon Z. Vogt and Ethel M. Albert (eds.), *People of Rimrock. A Study of Values in Five Cultures* (Cambridge, Mass.: Harvard University Press, 1966), p. 113.

[35] Robert A. LeVine, "Cross-Cultural Study in Child Psychology," in Paul H. Mussen (ed.), *Carmichael's Manual of Child Psychology* (3d ed.; John Wiley & Sons, Inc., 1970), p. 594.

the suggestion that this restraint of aggression in traditional societies is apt to give way in the process of Westernization. "Western child-rearing values seem to entail tolerance of children's fighting and other aggressive encounters, and it looks as if Westernization among nonindustrial agricultural peoples involves relaxation of traditional constraints on childhood aggression."[36]

Another contrast in the three southwestern groups studied by Whiting and his colleagues was in the relative stress on need for achievement. This was tested by giving the Magic Man test to Zuñi, Mormon, and Texan children.

Once upon a time a magic man met a child and said, "I'm going to change you into something else. You can be any kind of person you like." If you were this child, what kind of person would you want to be?[37]

Each child was also asked: If he could be changed into a father, mother, sister, or brother, which would he want to be? If he could be any age, how old would he want to be?

Whiting and his colleagues found that achievement was expressed by 57 percent of the Texan children, 38 percent of the Mormon children, and 20 percent of the Zuñi children. No cross-sex choices were made by the Texans, but 10 percent of the Zuñi boys chose to be females, and 23 percent of the Mormon girls chose to be males. No Mormon boys or Zuñi girls made cross-sex choices. Valued ages were higher for Texans and Mormons than for Zuñi. These answers seem to reflect the high status of Mormon men and Zuñi women in their respective cultures, the relative equality of sexes among the Texans, and the value of growing up and need for achievement among the Texans.[38]

Whiting and his colleagues present some speculations about the historical backgrounds of the value systems in the three groups and the reasons for their having adopted certain child-rearing practices. In the case of the Texans, they trace the emphasis on the nuclear family to frontier conditions in the New World. After 1750 the kinds of advice given to parents on child-rearing practices in counseling literature in North America stressed measures of encouraging independence in children. "The child rearing practices of modern Texans conform strikingly to this advice; they wean early, value in-

---

[36] Ibid., p. 593.

[37] Whiting et al., "The Learning of Values," p. 106.

[38] Ibid., pp. 106–08.

dividualism and early independence, and are permissive with respect to aggression."[39]

There is a good deal of consistency in the findings of the southwestern values studies, those of Whiting and his associates and the earlier study by Kluckhohn and Strodtbeck. Also, as the reader will note later, there is correspondence with the analysis made by Whiting and Whiting of the Type A and Type B cultures in the Six Cultures project discussed in Chapter 9.

PASTORALISTS AND FARMERS

Pastoralists and farmers lead somewhat different ways of life, with pastoralists being more nomadic and often engaged in fighting and cattle raiding, while farmers are more sedentary, tied to the land. We might expect that, related to their different ways of life, contrasting sets of attitudes and values would characterize pastoralists and farmers. An investigation of this subject has been made by Robert B. Edgerton of the University of California at Los Angeles as part of a larger research project known as the Culture and Ecology in East Africa Project, organized by Walter Goldschmidt. The project involves a study of four East African tribes, the Hehe, Kamba, Pokot, and Sebei. These tribes engage in both pastoralism and farming. An effort was made to find groups in each tribe which were more limited to pastoralism or to farming. Eight communities were thus selected for investigation, with a pastoral and a farming group from each tribe.

With the help of native interpreters Edgerton gave a series of questionnaires and tests to samples from each group: 85 questions, the Rorschach Ink Blot Test, 9 "values pictures" showing scenes of native life to which the subjects were asked to respond, and 22 color slides.[40] Edgerton interviewed about 30 men and 30 women in each of the eight communities.

One of Edgerton's conclusions from an analysis of the subjects' responses is that there is a good deal of uniformity within a tribal group, so that a Pokot pastoralist is more like a Pokot farmer than like a pastoralist from another tribe. At the same time, there were clear differences between pastoralists and farmers in each tribe, too numerous to be expected by chance.[41] The farmers showed more

[39] Ibid., p. 116.

[40] Robert B. Edgerton, *The Individual in Cultural Adaptation. A Study of Four East African Peoples* (Berkeley, Calif.: University of California Press, 1971), p. 39.

[41] Ibid., p. 272.

anxiety, hostility, emotional restraint, indirection, and disrespect for authority, while the pastoralists were more open in their expression of feelings, and showed more independence, overt aggression, direct action, social cohesion, and respect for authority. These findings were in line with Edgerton's and Goldschmidt's expectations and with Edgerton's behavioral observations made in the course of fieldwork.

A plausible conclusion about the findings is that the farmer must repress or suppress his hostility, because he and his neighbors are tied to the land; they cannot move away. Pastoralists have more mobility and can separate if a quarrel breaks out. There is therefore less inhibition in pastoralists' expression of feelings. Resort to witchcraft would be more likely in a farming community, where hatred cannot be expressed as openly as in a pastoral society, a hypothesis for which Edgerton found partial confirmation.[42]

In an epilogue to Edgerton's work, Walter Goldschmidt notes that a pastoralist's way of life reinforces patterns of direct action and decision making. The pastoralist cares for large mammals which have wills of their own; he has to direct them, impose his own will, and at the same time meet their needs. The farmer's daily routine is more passive and involves more drudgery. The pastoralist is always on the move, leading his animals to pasture and water, and keeping alert for enemies, raiders, and wild animals.[43] The pastoral way of life involves a more striking division of labor between the sexes, emphasizing "masculinity" in the animal-tending, frequently warring males. Pastoralists would seem to have less reason than farmers to acquire an image of limited good, for an increase in one man's herd does not necessarily result in the decrease of another's.[44]

The consistent findings about farmers' hostility, anxiety, and emotional constraint in Edgerton's research are in keeping with the generalizations about peasant societies cited earlier. Edgerton's and Goldschmidt's speculations help one to understand why such a complex of traits has been reported so often for peasant communities.

PREJUDICES

Prejudiced attitudes toward particular groups, involving stereotyped prejudgments, may be considered as forms of cognition.

---

[42] Ibid., pp. 288–92.

[43] Ibid., p. 296.

[44] Ibid., pp. 17–18.

Value judgments are involved. Allport suggests as a definition of prejudice, "being down on something you're not up on." Ethnocentrism in some form may well be a universal feature of human life. But there is probably more prejudice in some societies than in others. Despite our traditions of democracy and Christianity, prejudice has a long history in the United States. "Racial segregation and an ideology of racial superiority have been part of the American culture for generations and in some sense every white American is implicated in this aspect of American life."[45]

White racial prejudice antedated the slave trade; perhaps, without such prejudice, the slave trade would never have been allowed to expand.[46] We thus have a long heritage of prejudice behind us from which it may be difficult to extricate ourselves, especially since much of it is on a more or less unconscious level.

Within the past 30 years a great deal of research has been done in the effort to understand prejudice and the personality of the prejudiced person. Prejudice may be seen either in terms of a consistency model of personality or in terms of a conflict model.

Prejudice is not a matter of personality alone, and there may be people who passively accept the prejudiced views of the culture in which they have grown up without experiencing any marked psychological sequelae as a result. But there is much evidence to indicate that, for many people, prejudice is a vital aspect of the personality, part of a defense system developed by an ego which is shaky and insecure.

The classic work on this subject is *The Authoritarian Personality* by T. W. Adorno et al. This massive study, based on the use of questionnaires, interviews, and projective tests, employed a psychoanalytic approach to delineate a complex of personality characteristics shared by persons holding right-wing authoritarian views. The authors suggest that such individuals come from relatively affectionless families in which the parents demand strict obedience to conventional modes of conduct. There is little opportunity for spontaneous development of the self. The expression of sex and aggression are tabooed. Children in such families develop compliant, submissive behavior and repress the hostility which cannot be directed toward the parents. Thus they develop a cleavage between the conscious and unconscious segments of the personality. Such individ-

---

[45] Angus Campbell and Howard Schuman, "Racial Attitudes in Fifteen American Cities," *Supplemental Studies for the National Advisory Committee on Civil Disorders* (New York: Frederick A. Praeger, Inc., 1968) , p. 62.

[46] Winthrop D. Jordan, *White over Black: American Attitudes toward the Negro, 1550–1812* (Chapel Hill, N.C.: University of North Carolina Press, 1968) pp. 6–8, 30.

uals come to see the world as dangerous and threatening; safety lies in conforming to the conventional patterns of behavior required of them.

Persons of this sort are prone to projection and the displacement of hostility. For such a personality structure, prejudices play a functional role in supporting the self-image and in providing targets for the hostility which seeks an outlet. The individual who, at bottom, feels weak and insecure, places a high value on power and toughness, despises weak out-groups and admires strong leaders. This, in brief, is the "authoritarian personality."[47] A discouraging implication of this picture is that as long as family conditions like those described continue to persist, prejudices will be hard to eliminate. Exhortation and propaganda for tolerance are not likely to have much influence on persons who desperately need to maintain their prejudices.

The Authoritarian Personality and succeeding volumes in the series edited by Max Horkheimer and Samuel J. Flowerman have been very influential and have stimulated much research along similar lines. A book of essays has been published which deals with *The Authoritarian Personality* and attempts to assess its contributions.[48] Herbert H. Hyman and Paul B. Sheatsley point to various methodological weaknesses in *The Authoritarian Personality,* such as inadequate sampling, over-generalization from this sample, failure to validate questionnaire data, and absence of control over the variable of formal education.[49] Edward A. Shils notes that the authors of *The Authoritarian Personality* never investigated the actual behavior and roles of their subjects in everyday life. Shils' principal criticism, however, is that the authors follow an outmoded assumption in placing right and left authoritarianism at opposite poles. They have ignored left-wing authoritarianism and dealt only with the right-wing authoritarian personality, not with the authoritarian personality per se.[50]

While these and other criticisms in the same volume suggest that Adorno and his colleagues may not have proven their case, I feel that

---

[47] T. W. Adorno, Else Frenkel-Brunswik, D. J. Levinson, and R. N. Sanford, *The Authoritarian Personality* (New York: Harper & Bros., 1950).

[48] Richard Christie and Marie Jahoda, *Studies in the Scope and Method of "The Authoritarian Personality." Continuities in Social Research* (Glencoe, Ill.: The Free Press, 1954).

[49] Herbert H. Hyman and Paul B. Sheatsley, " 'The Authoritarian Personality'— A Methodological Critique," *Ibid.,* pp. 50–122.

[50] Edward A. Shils, "Authoritarianism: 'Right' and 'Left,' " *Ibid.,* pp. 24–49.

there must be a core of truth in their picture of the nature and etiology of the right-wing authoritarian personality. This conviction is strengthened by the fact that many other studies have presented corroborative data.

Else Frenkel-Brunswik has shown that children raised in restrictive authoritarian households develop what she calls "intolerance of ambiguity." They become accustomed to disciplines demanding the quick learning of rigid externally imposed rules which they do not understand but dare not violate. Patterns of this sort influence the children's performance in test situations involving perception and the solution of problems. Frenkel-Brunswik has reported on some tests given to children who scored either extremely high or extremely low on scales designed to measure degree of prejudice. In one test children were shown pictures of a dog which, through a number of transitional stages, finally became the picture of a cat. At each stage the subjects were asked to identify the object depicted. The more prejudiced children tended to hang on longer to the original object and responded more slowly to the changes than did the unprejudiced children.[51]

In another test, persons in a dark room were shown a point of light which, although stationary, appears to move in such conditions. Persons who scored high on the Berkeley Ethnocentrism Scale tended to soon establish a norm for themselves and reported the light as moving in a constant direction for a constant number of inches, while those scoring lower on ethnocentrism took longer to establish such norms.[52]

Milton Rokeach has devised a number of experiments in which a mental set is established by having the subject solve a problem in a particular way. Rokeach then poses a problem which may be solved either by the former method or else by switching to a different, more direct technique. In these tests subjects rated as high on ethnocentrism tended to show difficulty in restructuring the field and persisted longer than did less-prejudiced individuals in maintaining the original set.[53]

---

[51] Else Frenkel-Brunswik, "Intolerance of Ambiguity as an Emotional and Perceptual Personality Variable," *Journal of Personality*, Vol. 18 (1949), pp. 108–43.

[52] Jack Block and Jeanne Block, "An Investigation of the Relationship between Intolerance of Ambiguity and Ethnocentrism," *Journal of Personality*, Vol. 19 (1951), pp. 303–11.

[53] Milton Rokeach, "Generalized Mental Rigidity as a Factor in Ethnocentrism," *Journal of Abnormal and Social Psychology*, Vol. 48 (1943), pp. 259–78; Milton Rokeach, *The Open and Closed Mind. Investigations into the Nature of Belief Systems and Personality Systems* (New York: Basic Books, 1960).

An important source of this kind of behavior is fear. People who cling to stereotypes are under pressure and seem to have a deeplying fear of the environment which restricts their range of perception. A person who acquires such fears in early childhood develops a rigidity which is apt to persist into adult life.

The role of fear in relation to prejudice in the United States has also been touched on by Francis L. K. Hsu, although without reference to childhood. Hsu believes that a stress on independence and self-reliance is a core value for Americans. In a constantly changing world, the isolated individual in a competitive system is bound to feel anxiety. While he looks upward for loopholes to advancement, he is also afraid of the groups beneath him. Fearing contamination from less successful inferior groups, he tries to maintain social distance from them, including manifestations of racial and religious prejudice.

Hsu claims that support for his thesis comes from the fact that there is less racial or religious prejudice in such traditional stratified Eastern societies as India, China, and Japan, where there is less need for competition and status seeking. Racial and religious prejudices, he argues, are most intense and widespread in the Protestant-dominated societies of the Western world.[54]

A weakness in this argument is that there is much prejudice in India on the part of higher castes toward lower castes, particularly toward the 65,000,000 or so Untouchables or Ex-Untouchables, as they have been called.[55] The writings of Isaacs, Berreman, De Vos, Wagatsuma, and others have shown not only how many parallels there are in prejudiced attitudes (and in the responses of discriminated against minorities) in India and the United States, but also that similar patterns appear in Japan, where the Eta, formerly a leatherworking "caste," are still discriminated against today, although they are racially indistinguishable from the rest of the population, and although many of the Eta no longer have any connection with leatherwork or other traditionally defiling occupations.[56]

A caste system may tend naturally toward the maintenance of prejudiced attitudes. The high-ranking castes adopt paternalistic

---

[54] Francis L. K. Hsu, "American Core Value and National Character," in Francis L. K. Hsu (ed.), *Psychological Anthropology. Approaches to Culture and Personality* (Homewood, Ill.: The Dorsey Press, 1961), pp. 222–25.

[55] Harold R. Isaacs, *India's Ex-Untouchables* (New York: The John Day Co., Inc., 1964).

[56] George De Vos and Hiroshi Wagatsuma, *Japan's Invisible Race. Caste in Culture and Personality* (Berkeley, Calif.: University of California Press, 1966).

attitudes of *noblesse oblige* toward the lower castes, approximating adult-child relations.[57] Fear of contamination from contact with lower caste members can be cited for India, Japan, and the United States.[58]

In India, Japan, and the United States there have been similar self-improvement and protest movements and demands for integration on the part of the discriminated against minorities. De Vos and Wagatsuma point out that Buraku (Eta) children score more poorly in IQ tests than do non-Buraku children, as do culturally underprivileged groups in the United States. In both cases they attribute this to early damage in social self-identity and self-respect. There is much truancy and delinquency among Buraku children. Thus there seem to be some cross-cultural regularities, not only in attitudes of prejudice but in responses to prejudice in India, Japan, and the United States. Of course, there are also differences in these respects.

The right-wing "authoritarian personality" is a product of Western culture. We cannot say to what extent prejudices in non-Western societies are associated with family backgrounds like those described by Adorno and his colleagues.

Bettelheim and Janowitz have suggested a relativistic view in relation to the etiology of anti-Semitism. "Although anti-Semitism has been present in slave societies, feudal societies, capitalist societies, and recently too in communist society, it appears in each case to have been a different social phenomenon."[59]

But this is a matter which requires some investigation. The studies by Isaacs, Berreman, De Vos, and Wagatsuma cited above suggest that there are some universally operative mechanisms associated with prejudice.

SELF-CONCEPTS

While the concept of world view refers to a person's set of beliefs about the surrounding world, there are also terms for the no-

---

[57] Gerald D. Berreman, "Concomitants of Caste Organization," in De Vos and Wagatsuma, *Japan's Invisible Race*, p. 309.

[58] For the United States, see Allison Davis, Burleigh B. Gardner, and Mary R. Gardner, *Deep South: A Social Anthropological Study of Class and Caste* (Chicago: University of Chicago Press, 1941), p. 16; see also John Dollard, *Class and Caste in a Southern Town* (2d ed.; New York: Harper & Bros., 1949); Gunnar Myrdal, with the assistance of Richard Sterne and Arnold Rose, *An American Dilemma: The Negro Problem and Modern Democracy* (New York: Harper & Bros., 1944).

[59] Bruno Bettelheim and Morris Janowitz, *Dynamics of Prejudice. A Psychological and Sociological Study of Veterans* (New York: Harper & Bros., 1950), p. 163.

tions that a person has about himself, such as identity or self-image. These ideas result from the individual's experiences in growing up, his interactions with others, and the identifications which he makes with other persons, such as mother, father, and older siblings.

An early acquired aspect of self-image is sex identity. With the acquisition of language, a child comes to realize that people are divided into men and women, mommies and daddies, boys and girls. Told that he is a boy, this idea becomes part of his self-image; in normal circumstances he tends to identify with his father, is encouraged to do so, and uses his father as a model for imitation. There are different theories about how this process operates. Freud believed that a boy's anxiety about his Oedipus complex becomes reduced when he identifies with his father; the identification is thus seen as a defense, if one accepts a conflict model of personality. But from the viewpoint of a fulfillment model, the process of identification could be seen as essentially rewarding for a growing boy and not a defensive reaction. Various other persons besides the father may serve as models for a child. Choice of a model seems to depend upon the nurturant qualities of the person, his power over the child and others, competence in various tasks, and acceptance by others.

The process of sex identification does not always work smoothly. In families where the father is absent and where the boy has no male model, he may develop a feminine identification. Indications that this happens have been shown in studies of doll play and fantasy of children from father-absent homes when compared with children from households having both parents.[60]

There is a theory that boys from father-absent homes who initially identify with the mother are likely to later engage in exaggeratedly masculine behavior as a way of undoing the cross-sex identity and asserting their masculinity. Writings by Walter D. Miller and Beatrice B. Whiting on this subject are discussed in Chapter 9. These analyses are related to John W. M. Whiting's theories about the functions of male initiation ceremonies discussed in Chapter 8.

Self-esteem is another aspect of self-image, a person's estimate of his own worth. This is affected by feedback in his encounters with the world. For example, reference was made in the preceding sec-

---

[60] G. R. Bach, "Father-fantasies and Father Typing in Father-separated Children," *Child Development,* Vol. 17 (1946), pp. 63–80; Robert P. Sears, M. H. Pintler, and P. S. Sears, "Effect of Father Separation on Preschool Children's Doll Play Aggression," *Child Development,* Vol. 17 (1946), pp. 219–43; David B. Lynn and William L. Sawrey, "The Effects of Father-Absence on Norwegian Boys and Girls," *Journal of Abnormal and Social Psychology,* Vol. 59 (1959), pp. 258–62.

tion to De Vos and Wagatsuma's suggestion that the poor performance on IQ tests by Eta children is attributable to early damage in social self-identity and self-respect.

Still another aspect of self-conception is that of body image. A person is aware of having a particular kind of body. Moreover, other people's responses to him are partly influenced by their reaction to his appearance. This subject is discussed in Chapter 14.

The set of ideas which a person has about himself may be very consistent. They may be reinforced by feedback from experience, but they may also persist despite contradictory, negative feedback, in keeping with a consistency model of personality.

One point at which there may be confusion about self-identity is at adolescence, when physiological changes take place, often with rapid body growth. At the same time, in the Western world, the adolescent may be faced with various alternative courses of action with regard to choice of profession, political, or religious affiliation, as well as sexual problems. In Erik H. Erikson's Eight Ages of Man, adolescence is the period characterized by conflict between Identity and Role Confusion. Attraction to cliques and ideologies is part of the adolescent's search for identity at this time.[61] Here is a point where world view and self-image may become importantly interlinked.

MAZEWAY

The term *mazeway* has been suggested by Anthony F. C. Wallace to refer to "the entire set of cognitive maps of positive and negative goals that an individual maintains at a given time. This set includes goals of self, others, and material objects, and of their possible dynamic interrelations."[62] Mazeway is more amorphous than either "world view" or "self-image," since it includes both, along with values, objects and techniques. "Mazeway is to the individual what culture is to the group."[63]

Mazeways may change, as cultures do. Wallace uses the term "mazeway resynthesis" to refer to a process which may take place at a time of crisis, helping to make sense of a world which has be-

---

[61] Erik H. Erikson, *Childhood and Society* (New York: W. W. Norton & Co., 1963), pp. 261–63.

[62] Anthony F. C. Wallace, *Culture and Personality* (2d ed., New York: Random House, Inc., 1970), p. 15.

[63] Ibid., p. 15.

come threatening to the individual. Through a transvaluation of values and change of beliefs, perhaps through conversion to a religious sect, mazeway resynthesis is effected, enabling the individual to cope in a new way with the world around him. Revitalization movements, discussed in Chapter 17, fulfill such functions, as Wallace has illustrated for the Seneca Handsome Lake Religion in his book, *The Death and Rebirth of the Seneca.*[64]

A difficulty with the concept of mazeway is that it includes so many varied categories. But Wallace defends the concept by stating that "From the standpoint of the individual mazeway-holder, however, all these phenomena normally constitute one integrated dynamic system of perceptual assemblages."[65]

THE INFLUENCE OF LANGUAGE ON COGNITION

There has been much debate among anthropologists and linguists about the influence of language on cognition. An early approach to this subject has become known as the Sapir-Whorf hypothesis. More recently, a branch of anthropological linguistics concerned with such matters has become known as ethnoscience or cognitive anthropology. Let us first consider the Sapir-Whorf hypothesis.

The Sapir-Whorf Hypothesis

A leading figure in the early days of culture-and-personality research was Edward Sapir (1884–1939), a linguist and ethnologist to whom, according to Clyde Kluckhohn, "more than to any other single person, must be traced the growth of psychiatric thinking in anthropology."[66] It was Sapir, together with John Dollard, who directed the first seminars on culture-and-personality at Yale in the early 1930s, which influenced such students as Ernest and Pearl Beaglehole, Weston La Barre, and Scudder Mekeel, all of whom subsequently did work in this new field.

Sapir was in some respects a configurationist interested in the

---

[64] Anthony F. C. Wallace, *The Death and Rebirth of the Seneca* (New York: Alfred A. Knopf, Inc., 1970).

[65] Wallace, *Culture and Personality*, p. 19.

[66] Clyde Kluckhohn, "The Influence of Psychiatry on Anthropology in America during the Past One Hundred Years," in J. K. Hall, G. Zilboorg, and H. A. Bunker (eds.), *One Hundred Years of American Psychiatry* (New York: Columbia University Press, 1944), p. 601. Reprinted in Douglas G. Haring (ed.), *Personal Character and Cultural Milieu,* (3d ed.; Syracuse, N.Y.: Syracuse University Press, 1956), p. 494

ways in which peoples' thought and behavior are patterned by language and culture. (He once wrote to Ruth Benedict that Spengler's *Decline of the West* struck him as "needlessly long and muddle-headed in places but fundamentally sound.") [67] At the same time Sapir always insisted on the significance of the individual personality and was dissatisfied with culturological accounts in which the individual was conceived of as a passive culture carrier. "Cultures as ordinarily dealt with," he wrote, "are merely abstracted configurations of idea and action patterns, which have endlessly different meanings for the various individuals in the group . . ." [68]

Nevertheless, there was a configurational cast to Sapir's thinking, especially in connection with his study of languages. Every language, from Sapir's point of view, structures the world in a particular way for its speakers. Thus, to learn an unfamiliar language is to enter a new realm of thought.

Human beings do not live in the objective world alone, nor alone in the world of social activity as ordinarily understood, but are very much at the mercy of the particular language which has become the medium of expression for their society. It is quite an illusion to imagine that one adjusts to reality essentially without the use of language and that language is merely an incidental means of solving specific problems of communication or reflection. The fact of the matter is that the "real" world is to a large extent unconsciously built up on the language habits of the group. No two languages are ever sufficiently similar to be considered as representing the same social reality. The worlds in which different societies live are distinct worlds, not merely the same world with different labels attached. [69]

We have here a relativistic view which is similar to Benedict's view of culture. Aberle has suggested that Sapir and Benedict followed a linguistic model in their writings about culture, and saw

---

[67] Margaret Mead, *An Anthropologist at Work. Writings of Ruth Benedict* (Boston: The Riverside Press; Cambridge, Mass.: Houghton Mifflin Co., 1959) p. 185.

[68] Edward Sapir, "The Emergence of the Concept of Personality in a Study of Cultures," *Journal of Social Psychology*, Vol. 5 (1934), p. 411. Reprinted in David G. Mandelbaum (ed.), *Selected Writings of Edward Sapir. In Language, Culture, and Personality* (Berkeley and Los Angeles: University of California Press, 1949), p. 593.

This viewpoint led Sapir to a criticism evidently directed at Benedict, in which he remarked: "We then discover that whole cultures or societies are paranoid or hysterical or obsessive! Such characterizations, however brilliantly presented, have the value of literary suggestiveness, not of close personality analysis."

"The Contributions of Psychiatry to an Understanding of Behavior in Society," *American Journal of Sociology*, Vol. 29 (1937), pp. 866–67.

[69] Mandelbaum, *Selected Writings of Edward Sapir*, p. 162. For an earlier adumbration of this viewpoint, see Franz Boas, "Introduction," *Handbook of American Indian Languages* (Washington, D.C., Smithsonian Institution, 1911), Part I, pp. 63, 70–71.

cultures as having some of the same characteristics as languages—being selective (choosing "a small number of actualizations from a large number of possibilities") ; exemplifying patterning, some of which is unconscious; representing unique configurations; undergoing changes through "drift"; being functionally equivalent, neither "superior" nor "inferior" to others; and being shared by the members of a given community.[70] A language, like the larger culture of a society, shapes its perceptions of the world. Aberle considers the linguistic model to have been unfortunate and misleading for culture-and-personality studies. This is not to deny, of course, that language and culture do have certain analogous features. Moreover, language and culture are inextricably interrelated. Systems of kinship terminology, for example, differ widely from one society to another, and in different societies people develop quite different conceptions of how they are related to one another.

Benjamin Lee Whorf, who has done more than anyone else to develop Sapir's line of thought along these lines, gave further examples of such patterning. Perhaps because of his training in the physical sciences and his broad interests in philosophy, Whorf particularly focused on conceptions of space and time implicit in different linguistic systems. From this point of view he contrasted Hopi and what he called SAE—"Standard Average European"—languages.[71] Whorf claimed, for example, that the Hopi language contains "no words, grammatical forms, constructions, or expressions that refer directly to what we call 'time,' or to past, present, or future, or to enduring or lasting, or to motion as kinematic rather than dynamic. . . ."[72]

The study of Hopi and other languages illuminated for Whorf some of the assumptions implicit in SAE languages.

In our language, that is SAE, plurality and cardinal numbers are applied in two ways: to real plurals and imaginary plurals . . . We say "ten men" and also "ten days." Ten men either are or could be objectively perceived. . . . But "ten days" cannot be objectively experienced. . . . Concepts of time lose contact with the subjective experience of "becoming later" and are objectified as counted QUANTITIES, especially as lengths, made up of units as a length can be visibly marked

---

[70] David F. Aberle, "The Influence of Linguistics on Early Culture and Personality Theory," in Gertrude E. Dole and Robert Carneiro (eds.), *Essays in Honor of Leslie A. White* (New York: Thomas Y. Crowell Co., 1960) , pp. 1–29.

[71] John B. Carroll (ed.), *Language, Thought, and Reality. Selected Writings of Benjamin Lee Whorf* (Boston: Technology Press of Massachusetts Institute of Technology, 1956) , pp. 57–64, 134–59.

[72] Ibid., p. 57.

off into inches. A "length of time" is envisoned as a row of similar units like a row of bottles.[73]

This facet of European languages is seen to have all sorts of far-reaching consequences. Here Whorf's writing takes on a Spenglerian tone. Our objectified time, he tells us,

. . . puts before imagination something like a ribbon or scroll marked off into equal blank spaces, suggesting that each be filled with an entry. Writing has no doubt helped toward our linguistic treatment of time, even as the linguistic treatment has guided the uses of writing. Through this give-and-take between language and the whole culture we get, for instance:
1. Records, diaries, bookkeeping, accounting, mathematics stimulated by accounting.
2. Interest in exact sequence, dating, calendars, chronology, clocks, time wages, time graphs, time as used in physics.
3. Annals, histories, the historical attitude, interest in the past, archaeology, attitudes of introjection toward past periods, e.g., classicism, romanticism.[74]

It may be noted that many of the above features have appeared in complex civilizations speaking non-SAE languages, such as that of China. The significance of language in their etiology is thus not clear. However, just as Whorf traces some of the consequences of SAE languages for European cultural development, so he points to a relationship between Hopi linguistic and cultural behavior, for instance, in "preparing" activities in Hopi life.

To us, for whom time is a motion on a space, unvarying repetition seems to scatter its force along a row of units of that space, and be wasted. To the Hopi, for whom time is not a motion, but a "getting later" of everything that has ever been done, unvarying repetition is not wasted but accumulated. It is storing up an invisible charge that holds over to later events.[75]

It is in these terms that Whorf considers such features of Hopi behavior as willing or praying and the repetitive steps of ceremonial dances.

Whorf's essays are difficult and technical, and because of their specialized nature are hard to evaluate. Indeed, when one has read them, one wonders whether, after all, Hopi and Western conceptions of

---

[73] Ibid., pp. 139–40. (Whorf's capitalization.)
[74] Ibid., p. 153.
[75] Ibid., p. 151.

space and time can really be so different. Just because we call a ship "she" does not mean that we actually think of the ship as being feminine. Languages are not always so tyrannical, nor is grammar necessarily an "invisible 'thought control' in our philosophical prison," as La Barre has put it.[76] Evidence of this lies in the fact that communication is, after all, possible, though often difficult, across language barriers. While the diffusion of culture patterns may be slowed up by difficulties in communication, it need not be blocked thereby—as witness the worldwide spread of modern technology since the industrial revolution.

Moreover, as Hoijer has pointed out, peoples very similar in the rest of their culture sometimes speak languages that are wholly unrelated, while closely related languages are often spoken by peoples whose cultures are otherwise very different. For example, the Hopi and the Hopi-Tewa (pueblo of Hano) have lived together on First Mesa since about 1700 and share the same general Puebloan culture, but they belong to different language stocks. The Hupa and Navaho speak closely related Athapaskan languages, but otherwise their cultures are quite different. The same applies to the Hopi and the Southern Paiute, who are both Shoshonean speaking.[77] This does not, of course, invalidate the Sapir-Whorf hypothesis. The latter may eventually prove to be very useful in the field of culture-and-personality, but at present this is only a potentiality. We still need to know more about how different languages structure the nature of interpersonal relationships and the general world view of their speakers.

John B. Carroll and Joseph B. Casagrande have devised some experimental methods for exploring this field.[78] Their experiments indicate that languages help to structure perception somewhat differently in different linguistic groups.[79]

---

[76] Weston La Barre, *The Human Animal* (Chicago: The University of Chicago Press, 1954), p. 200.

[77] Harry Hoijer, "The Sapir-Whorf Hypothesis," In Harry Hoijer (ed.), *Language in Culture. Proceedings of a Conference on the Interrelations of Language and Other Aspects of Culture* (American Anthropological Association, Vol. 56, No. 6, Part 2, Memoir No. 79 [December 1954], p. 102–4).

[78] John B. Carroll and Joseph B. Casagrande, "The Function of Language Classification in Behavior," in Eleanor E. Maccoby, Theodore M. Newcomb, and Eugene L. Hartley (eds.), *Readings in Social Psychology* (3d ed.; New York: Henry Holt Co., 1958), pp. 18–31.

[79] In connection with a subsequent chapter dealing with the Trobriand Islanders, the reader may be interested in reading a Whorflike analysis of Trobriand language by Dorothy D. Lee, "A Primitive System of Values," *Philosophy of Science,* Vol. 7 (1940), pp. 355–79.

Ethnoscience

Some anthropological linguists have specialized in the field of ethnoscience or cognitive anthropology, with the aim of understanding the taxonomic principles of particular languages. There is the assumption that if we can find out how the speakers of a language classify phenomena in the world around them, it should help us to understand how they perceive the world. Linguists who engage in this enterprise question informants in the native language to elicit taxonomic features, including the existence of particular *semantic domains*. A domain refers to a class of objects which share some characteristic feature or features which differentiate them from other domains. Furniture would be a semantic domain in English which includes chairs, sofas, desks, and tables, but not cows, chrysanthemums, crossword puzzles, and other features which are classified in other domains. Domains can be subdivided into narrower classifications; so that tables, for example, can be subdivided into end tables, dining tables, and so forth. Ethnoscientists investigate the principles of organization and classification in the languages they study. Among the topics which have been dealt with in this fashion are componential analyses of various kinship systems, color terminologies, and the plant and animal classifications of various peoples.[80]

The term *forced observation* has been used of some characteristics of language which direct attention to particular aspects of reality. The fact that English has separate words for orange and yellow may facilitate our perception of differences in these colors. The Zuñi language does not distinguish between these colors but has one word which includes both. Roger Brown and Eric H. Lenneberg report on an experiment in which color tests involving discrimination between orange and yellow were given to monolingual Zuñi-speaking subjects, monolingual English-speaking subjects, and bilingual Zuñi who spoke both Zuñi and English. The monolingual Zuñi frequently confused orange and yellow in the stimulus set; the English-speaking subjects never did, while the bilingual Zuñi fell in between the two monolingual groups in the frequency of errors.[81]

This implies a relativistic view of color perception. In contrast, Brent Berlin and Paul Kay have made a study which offers a chal-

---

[80] Stephen A. Tyler, "Introduction," in Stephen A. Tyler (ed.), *Cognitive Anthropology* (New York: Holt, Rinehart & Winston, Inc., 1969), pp. 1–23.

[81] Roger Brown and Eric H. Lenneberg, "A Study of Language and Cognition," *Journal of Abnormal and Social Psychology*, Vol. 49 (1954), pp. 454–62.

lenge to a relativistic view. In a study of color naming in 98 languages from a number of unrelated language families, Berlin and Kay conclude:

. . . although different languages encode in their vocabularies different *numbers* of basic color categories, a total universal inventory of exactly eleven basic color categories exists from which the eleven or fewer basic color terms of any given language are always drawn. The eleven basic color categories are *white, black, red, green, yellow, blue, brown, purple, pink, orange,* and *grey.*[82]

The analysis of language can be a useful key to some features of the world view of a particular people, as suggested by Ruth Benedict's discussion of Japanese terms for the sense of obligation.[83] But some authors have questioned the value of cognitive studies which involve formal semantic analysis. Robbins Burling asks:" . . . when an anthropologist undertakes a semantic analysis, is he discovering some 'psychological reality' which speakers are presumed to have or is he simply working out a set of rules which somehow take account of the observed phenomena?"[84] Is the anthropologist really getting at the cognitive system of the speakers of that language? Burling is skeptical about that.

As Oswald Werner has pointed out, a single language like English or Chinese is capable of expressing a great variety of world views. Moreover, some aspects of a world view may be found in many societies without any necessary relationship to language.[85] If, for example, there are recurrent patterns in peasant societies which conduce to the formation of a particular set of values and attitudes, this may have no necessary relationship to the languages spoken in those societies. The world views associated with Buddhism, Christianity, Islam, and modern science have influenced societies with different languages in many parts of the world, even though these views may have been locally modified in the process of absorption. These considerations would seem to limit the directive influence which language may have on cognition.

---

[82] Brent Berlin and Paul Kay, *Basic Color Terms: Their Universality and Evolution* (Berkeley, Calif.: University of California Press, 1969) , p. 2.

[83] See below, p. 231.

[84] Robbins Burling, "Cognition and Componential Analysis: God's Truth or Hocus-Pocus?" *American Anthropologist,* Vol. 66 (1964) , p. 27.

[85] Oswald Werner, "Cultural Knowledge, Language, and World View," in Paul I. Garvin (ed.) , *Cognition: A Multiple View* (New York: Spartan Books, Inc., 1970) , p. 157.

ENVIRONMENT AND PERCEPTION

Do people who live in flat, treeless plains develop different habits of perception than inhabitants of dense tropical jungles? Do city dwellers, accustomed to rectangular rooms, see things somewhat differently than do African natives who live in round houses? The possibility that such differences do occur has been shown by experiments with geometric designs like the Müller-Lyer figure (see Figure 3–1).

The Müller-Lyer illusion is that the figure to the left looks longer than the one on the right but is actually shorter.

Around the turn of the century the British anthropologist W. H. R. Rivers showed the Müller-Lyer figure and also a horizon-

Figure 3–1. The Müller-Lyer Illusion

tal-vertical figure to Papuan natives of Murray Island and later to Todas of the Nilgiri Hills in south India. He found that both groups were less susceptible to the Müller-Lyer illusion than were his English subjects, but they proved to be more susceptible to the horizontal-vertical illusion. Rivers' findings are thus said to be bidirectional; the two non-Western groups were more subject to one illusion, less subject to the other.

Rivers' experiments were done with rather small samples of subjects. A recent large-scale cross-cultural investigation of the same problem involved showing a series of geometrical figures, including those used by Rivers, to 1,878 persons in 14 non-European areas and in the United States. This work was done over a six-year period by a team of anthropologists and psychologists. The bulk of the non-Europeans tested were natives from different parts of Africa. Some of these, as in Dahomey and Fang, live in rather dense, compressed environments which do not provide extended vistas; while others (e.g., Senegal, Zulu) inhabit open savannahs. Two groups (Zulu and Bushmen) generally live in circular homes.

The findings of this ambitious and well-executed project were in agreement with Rivers' conclusions, with similar bidirectional results. The authors offer as explanations for their findings a set of hypotheses: that people who live in a "carpentered world" and who have an "experience with two-dimensional representation of reality" (as Western peoples do) are more susceptible to the Müller-Lyer illusion and the Sander parallelogram illusion than are non-Western peoples who have different kinds of visual environments and experiences. They also suggest that people who inhabit areas with broad horizontal vistas are likely to be more subject to the horizontal-vertical illusion than those living in restricted environments such as forests. The data provide a good fit for their hypotheses.[86]

But, according to Douglass R. Price-Williams, there are studies which fail to confirm the ecological hypothesis, while others partially confirm it and partially do not.[87] At any rate, it seems to have been shown that the nature of one's culture and experience influence some aspects of visual perception.

SUGGESTIONS FOR FURTHER READING

A review of anthropological studies related to perception and cognition is available in David French, "The Relationship of Anthropology to Studies in Perception and Cognition" in Sigmund Koch (ed.), *Psychology: A Study of a Science,* Vol. VI. *Investigations of Man as Socius: Their Place in Psychology and the Social Sciences* (New York: McGraw-Hill Book Co., 1963), pp. 388–428. For another survey, see Harry C. Triandis, "Cultural Influences upon Cognitive Processes," in Leonard Berkowitz (ed.), *Advances in Experimental Social Psychology,* Vol. I (New York: Academic Press, Inc., 1964), pp. 1–48.

Some treatments of ethos and world view are available in the following: John J. Honigmann, *Culture and Ethos of Kaska Society,* Yale University Publications in Anthropology, No. 40 (New Haven, Conn: Yale University Press, 1949); Francis L. K. Hsu, *Americans and Chinese: Two Ways of Life* (New York: Henry Schuman, 1953); Dorothy Lee, *Freedom and Culture* (Englewood Cliffs, N.J.: Prentice-Hall, Inc., 1959); A. Irving Hallowell, "Ojibwa Ontology, Behavior, and World

---

[86] Marshall H. Segall, Donald T. Campbell, and Melville J. Herskovits, *The Influence of Culture on Visual Perception* (Indianapolis, Ind.: The Bobbs-Merrill Co., 1966), pp. 212–13.

Another cross-cultural experiment in susceptibility to visual illusions is Gordon W. Allport and Thomas F. Pettigrew, "Cultural Influence on the Perception of Movement. The Trapezoidal Illusion among the Zulus," *Journal of Abnormal and Social Psychology,* Vol. 55 (1957), pp. 104–13.

[87] Douglass R. Price-Williams, "Ethnopsychology I: Comparative Psychological Processes," in James A. Clifton (ed.), *Introduction to Cultural Anthropology. Essays in the Scope and Methods of the Science of Man* (Boston, Mass.: Houghton Mifflin Co., 1968), p. 312. The author cites studies by G. Jahoda; A. J. Gregor and D. A. McPherson; and A. C. Mundy-Castle and G. K. Nelson.

View," in Stanley Diamond (ed.), *Culture in History. Essays in Honor of Paul A. Radin* (New York: Columbia University Press, 1960), pp. 19–52.

Hallowell has written about various aspects of the relationship between culture and cognition: world view, cultural factors in spatial and temporal orientation, and psychological aspects of measurement. See A. Irving Hallowell, *Culture and Experience* (Philadelphia: University of Pennsylvania Press, 1955).

For some cross-cultural studies of cognition in children along Piagetian lines, see Jerome S. Bruner et al., *Studies in Cognitive Growth* (New York: John Wiley & Sons, Inc., 1966), Chaps. 11–14. For a reader with many articles on cognition and perception in different cultures, see Ihsan Al-Issa and Wayne Dennis (eds.), *Cross-Cultural Studies of Behavior* (New York: Holt, Rinehart & Winston, 1970). See also Robert A. LeVine, "Cross-Cultural Study in Child Psychology," in Paul H. Mussen (ed.), *Carmichael's Manual of Child Psychology* (3d ed.; New York: John Wiley & Sons, Inc., 1970), pp. 559–612.

On values, see Ethel M. Albert, "The Classification of Values," *American Anthropologist,* Vol. 58 (1956), pp. 221–48; and Victor F. Ayoub, "The Study of Values," in James A. Clifton (ed.), *Introduction to Cultural Anthropology,* pp. 244–72.

On prejudice: For a balanced review and evaluation of different theories about prejudice, see Arnold M. Rose, "The Causes of Prejudice," in Francis E. Merrill (ed.), *Social Problems* (New York: Alfred A. Knopf, Inc., 1950), pp. 402–24. See also George Eaton Simpson and J. Milton Yinger, *Racial and Cultural Minorities. An Analysis of Prejudice and Discrimination* (New York: Harper & Bros., 1958), especially chap. 3. See also S. Reichard, "Rorschach Study of Prejudiced Personality," *American Journal of Orthopsychiatry,* Vol. 18 (1948), pp. 280–86; Nathan W. Ackerman and Marie Jahoda, *Anti-Semitism and Emotional Disorder. A Psychoanalytic Interpretation* (New York: Harper & Bros., 1950); D. B. Harris, H. G. Gough, W. E. Martin, "Children's Ethnic Attitudes: II, Relationship to Parental Beliefs Concerning Child Training," *Child Development,* Vol. 21 (1950), pp. 169–81; Gordon W. Allport, *The Nature of Prejudice* (Boston, Mass.: The Beacon Press, 1954).

On prejudice in India, see Gardner Murphy, *In the Minds of Men. The Study of Human Behavior and Social Tensions in India. Based on the UNESCO Studies by Social Scientists Conducted at the Request of the Government of India* (New York: Basic Books, 1953). For a fuller bibliography, which gives some references to studies of prejudice in non-Western countries, see Donald T. Campbell and Robert A. LeVine, "A Proposal for Cooperative Cross-Cultural Research on Ethnocentrism," *The Journal of Conflict Resolution,* Vol. 5 (1961), pp. 107–08.

On ethnoscience, see Stephen A. Tyler (ed.), *Cognitive Anthropology* (New York: Holt, Rinehart & Winston, Inc., 1969).

There is more on the influence of culture on perception, particularly in connection with the Rorschach Test, in Chapter 13 on "Projective Tests."

part *II*

PIONEER STUDIES

Part I served to introduce the general field of culture-and-personality, presenting some different approaches, schools of thought, and basic concepts. Proceeding in a roughly chronological order, Part II presents a historical review of work done in this field from the 1920s to 1940s.

It seems to me that a historical approach to a subject is a good way of coming to understand it and its problems. We can see at what point, and why, new methods, such as the use of projective techniques, were introduced. As will be seen, there has been a progressive increase in sophistication and thoroughness in the field methods used.

chapter 4

Ruth Benedict's Patterns of Culture

Patterns of Culture has been described by Margaret Mead as "one of the great books of the second quarter of the twentieth century."[1] Geoffrey Gorer paid a still greater tribute in these words: "I should choose 1895, the year of the publication of Freud and Breuer's *Studien Über Hysterie,* as the year in which the scientific study of individual psychology was born, and 1934, the year of the publication of Ruth Benedict's *Patterns of Culture,* as the birth year of the scientific study of national character."[2]

It is hard to evaluate a ground-breaking work. In recent years it has become evident that there are some weaknesses and errors in *Patterns of Culture.* Nevertheless, it has been an influential book with a great popular success as a paperback. One reason for this success is that the book is written with a sense of style, for Benedict was a poet as well as an anthropologist. She came to the study of anthropology when she was 32—"to have something really to do," as she put it,—first taking courses at the New School for Social Research (1919–21), then at Columbia University, where ultimately she became an assistant and colleague of Franz Boas.

Patterns of Culture was a compilation of some previously pub-

[1] Margaret Mead, "Ruth Fulton Benedict," *American Anthropologist,* September 1949, p. 460.

[2] Geoffrey Gorer, "The Concept of National Character," C. Kluckhohn, H. A. Murray, and D. Schneider (eds.), *Personality in Nature, Society, and Culture* (New York: Alfred A. Knopf, 1953), p. 247.

lished articles, combined with the descriptions of three primitive societies: Pueblo, Dobu, and Kwakiutl. In the following pages I will not deal with her description of the Dobu, which was based entirely upon the work of one anthropologist, Reo Fortune, who spent only six months among these islanders.[3] Her fullest discussion dealt with the Pueblo Indians of the Southwest, to which we turn first.

PUEBLO CULTURE

Ruth Benedict had at least one predecessor in this field. As early as 1916, H. K. Haeberlin had written an article which foreshadowed some of the themes in *Patterns of Culture,* called "The Idea of Fertilization in the Culture of the Pueblo Indians."[4] Haeberlin pointed out that many religious ceremonies and other aspects of culture could be found common to both the Hopi and Navaho Indians, but that there were differences of emphasis in these societies. A ceremony designed to heal the sick among the Navaho was directed toward securing fertility for the fields among the Pueblo Indians. The bull-roarer was used among the Hopi to produce rain, but among the Navaho it was applied to the body of a patient by the shaman as part of a cure. The myth of the Twin War Gods, while similar in the two groups, had different emphases and associations—with fertility among the Pueblos, with healing among the Navahos. A game associated with the buffalo among the Plains tribes was associated with crops among the Hopi. Haeberlin explained this local refashioning as due to a psychological orientation. In the case of the Pueblo Indians this orientation could be designated under the heuristic catchword of "the idea of fertilization."

In 1928, the same year in which Ruth Benedict first set forth her views about the Pueblo area in "Psychological Types in the Cultures of the Southwest,"[5] Benedict's friend Edward Sapir published an article entitled "The Meaning of Religion" in the September issue of *The American Mercury,* in which he contrasted Pueblo and Plains religion. Sapir pointed to the emphasis on ritual among the Pueblos

---

[3] R. F. Fortune, *Sorcerers of Dobu. The Social Anthropology of the Dobu Islanders of the Western Pacific* (London: Routledge & Sons, 1932). This is not intended to deny the merits of this monograph, which is highly praised by Malinowski in an introduction to the book.

[4] H. K. Haeberlin, "The Idea of Fertilization in the Culture of the Pueblo Indians," *American Anthropological Association Memoirs,* Vol. 3, No. 1 (1916).

[5] *Proceedings of the 23rd International Congress of Americanists, September 1928* (New York, 1930), pp. 570–81.

and their repudiation of anything orgiastic. Thus, Protestant revivalism might be taught to a Blackfoot Indian, but never to a Zuñi.

In 1930, Barbara Aitken published an article called "Temperament in Native American Religion,"[6] in which she showed, again, that there were different emphases between the religions of the Pueblos on the one hand and certain Woodland and Plains tribes on the other. Among the Winnebago and other tribes in the latter group there was an individual emphasis in the guardian spirit quest. Every man sought his own religious experience. The religion had a "Protestant" tone. Among the Hopi, however, everything was related to agriculture, and there was a stress on mutual confidence, cooperation, and "being happy." The guardian spirit search was absent. Here the religion had a more "Catholic" tone.

A few writers, then, had been attracted to this theme of contrasting the Pueblo with other Indian groups. Ruth Benedict, who had done field work among the Zuñi in 1924 and 1925, found in the writings of Nietzsche a key to this contrast:

The basic contrast between the Pueblos and the other cultures of North America is the contrast that is named and described by Nietzsche in his studies of Greek tragedy. He discusses two diametrically opposed ways of arriving at the values of existence. The Dionysian pursues them through "the annihilation of the ordinary bounds and limits of existence"; he seeks to attain in his most valued moments escape from the boundaries imposed upon him by his five senses, to break through into another order of experience. The desire of the Dionysian, in personal experience or in ritual, is to press through it toward a certain psychological state, to achieve excess. The closest analogy to the emotions he seeks is drunkenness, and he values the illuminations of frenzy. With Blake, he believes "the path of excess leads to the palace of wisdom." The Apollonian distrusts all this, and has often little idea of the nature of such experiences. He finds means to outlaw them from his conscious life. He "knows but one law, measure in the Hellenic sense." He keeps the middle of the road, stays within the known map, does not meddle with disruptive psychological states. In Nietzsche's fine phrase, even in the exaltation of the dance, he "remains what he is, and retains his civic name" . . . .

It is not possible to understand Pueblo attitudes towards life without some knowledge of the culture from which they have detached themselves: that of the rest of North America. It is by the force of the contrast that we can calculate the strength of their opposite drive and the resistances that have kept out of the Pueblos the most characteristic traits of the American aborigines. For the American Indians as a whole, and including those of Mexico, were passionately Dionysian. They valued all

---

[6] Barbara Aitken, "Temperament in Native American Religion," *Journal of the Royal Anthropological Institute,* Vol. 60 (1930), pp. 363–87.

violent experience, all means by which human beings may break through the usual sensory routine, and to all such experiences they attributed the highest value.[7]

Benedict then provided illustrations of this widespread Dionysian tendency, such as fasting and self-torture in the vision quest and the ceremonial use of drugs, peyote, and alcohol to induce religious intoxication. These patterns were uniformly rejected by the Pueblo Indians, she explained, because they ran counter to the Apollonian values cherished by these people. The Hopi and Zuñi had never brewed intoxicants or accepted drugs, although they were surrounded by Indian groups who did. Drinking was consequently no problem on Pueblo reservations. Self-torture was also incomprehensible to the Pueblos; and while whipping took place during the puberty ceremonies, this ordeal was merely a symbolic beating which drew no blood.

In a similar vein the author went on to delineate the rejection of the "Dionysian" Ghost Dance of the Great Plains, the shamanistic trance, the tradition of boasting, and other un-Apollonian patterns, such as competition for prestige, cruel punishment for adultery, frenzied lamentation at funerals, recourse to suicide, sense of sin, and dualism in cosmology.

This long list of items, so persuasively tied together, is cumulatively impressive. But there are some dubious assertions. It is hard to accept the statement that "the American Indians as a whole, and including those of Mexico, were passionately Dionysian." This would presumably link together such varied cultures as the hunting bands of Labrador, the fishing communities of the Northwest Coast, the caste societies of southeastern North America, and the complex civilization of the Aztecs. In labeling them all "Dionysian," Benedict seems to commit the error for which she castigates the armchair anthropologists of the 19th century, who made facile generalizations about "primitives" and who failed to recognize the tremendous diversity of nonliterate cultures. Writers like Frazer, Benedict tells us, ignore all the aspects of cultural integration.

Mating or death practices are illustrated by bits of behavior selected indiscriminately from the most different cultures, and the discussion

---

[7] Ruth Benedict, *Patterns of Culture* (New York: Penguin Books, 1946), pp. 72–73. Originally published by Houghton Mifflin Co., Boston, Mass., 1934. In this chapter I have drawn from two articles of mine: "Ruth Benedict: Apollonian and Dionysian," *University of Toronto Quarterly* (University of Toronto Press), Vol. 18, No. 3 (April 1949), pp. 241–53; and "The Amiable Side of *Patterns of Culture*," *American Anthropologist*, Vol. 59, No. 3 (June 1957), pp. 532–36.

builds up a kind of mechanical Frankenstein's monster with a right eye from Fiji, a left from Europe, one leg from Tierra del Fuego, and one from Tahiti, and all the fingers and toes from still different regions. Such a figure corresponds to no reality in the past or present. . . .[8]

Now how does this erroneous procedure differ from that which Benedict follows at this point? To demonstrate the "Dionysian" bent of the American Indians, she selects a pierced tongue from Mexico, a chopped off finger from the Plains, and a bitten off nose from the Apache. These she somehow pieces together to suggest the ethos of "the culture from which they [the Pueblos] have detached themselves."

A good case could be made for the "Apollonianness" of many American Indian cultures. Even if we take the Cheyennes, who provide some fine examples of Dionysian behavior—self-torture on the part of the young men, suicidal bravado in battle, and so forth— it will be seen that a firm set of Apollonian values was also present —as in the exemplary behavior expected of chiefs,[9] in the chastity required of unmarried girls (they wore chastity belts) , in the police control exercised by the military societies, and in the low rate of ingroup aggression.[10] Indian cultures were, of course, not uniform; and one could hardly assert that they were uniformly Dionysian.

At the same time, Benedict seems to have made Pueblo culture itself out to be more homogeneous than seems warranted. E. A. Hoebel has taken Benedict to task on this point:

The Western Pueblos (Hopi and Zuñi) are uxorilocal, matrilineal, and have strong clans. But it is wrong to leave the impression that this is a universal Pueblo characteristic. Among the several Keres-speaking Pueblos of Central New Mexico . . . clans, although matrilineal, are weak. Moieties, which are lacking in the west, are strong. Fraternal associations also play a correspondingly greater role. Among the Eastern Pueb-

---

[8] Ibid., p. 44.

[9] "In the Cheyenne view, the first duty of a chief. . . was that he should care for the widows and orphans; and the second that he should be a peace maker—should act as mediator between any in the camp who quarreled. The dignity of a chief did not permit him to take part in any quarrel; he might not take personal vengeance for an offense committed against himself; to do so would result in loss of influence. . . . A good chief gave his whole heart and his whole mind to the work of helping his people, and strove for their welfare with an earnestness and a devotion rarely equalled by other rulers of men." George Bird Grinnell, *The Cheyenne Indians* (New Haven, Conn.: Yale University Press, 1923) , Vol. I; pp. 336–37.

[10] For a discussion of Cheyenne control systems, see Karl N. Llewellyn and E. Adamson Hoebel, *The Cheyenne Way* (Norman, Okla.: University of Oklahoma Press, 1941) ; and E. Adamson Hoebel, *The Law of Primitive Man* (Cambridge, Mass.: Harvard University Press, 1954) , chap. 7.

los north of Santa Fe . . . clans are patrilineal and relatively important. Patrilineal moieties dominate social life. Houses are owned by the men, and residence is consequently virilocal.[11]

Although her chapter on the Pubelos is entitled "The Pueblos of New Mexico" and deals primarily with the Zuñi, Benedict included the Hopi under the general rubric of Pueblo, for she felt it necessary to argue that the Hopi snake dance is not really Dionysian.

Turning now to Benedict's items which illustrate the Apollonian nature of Pueblo culture, let us first consider what she says about Pueblo aversion to liquor:

This repugnance is so strong that it has even been sufficient to keep American alcohol from becoming an administrative problem. Everywhere else on Indian reservations in the United States alcohol is an inescapable issue. There are no government regulations that can cope with the Indian's passion for whiskey. But in the pueblos the problem has never been important. . . . It is not that the Pueblos have a religious tabu against drinking. It is deeper than that. Drunkenness is repulsive to them. In Zuñi after the early introduction of liquor, the old men voluntarily outlawed it and the rule was congenial enough to be honored.[12]

After we read this, it comes as a surprise to learn, in Smith and Roberts' report on Zuñi law, that by far the most common "crimes" at Zuñi are drunkenness and drunken driving. "In 1949 there were 57 arrests for drunkenness on the first night of the Shalako festival and 150 bottles of liquor were confiscated."[13] The anthropologist E. A. Hoebel informs us that "Field work among the Central Pueblos in 1945 to 1947 revealed the Pueblo governments almost helpless in the face of uncontrollable drunkenness and violence."[14] And Edmund Wilson, describing a visit to Zuñi in 1947, tells how his car was searched for liquor by the police when he entered the pueblo at the time of the Shalako festival. He adds: "This, I was later told, failed almost completely in its purpose, since the Zuñis,

---

[11] E. Adamson Hoebel, *Man in the Primitive World* (New York: McGraw-Hill Book Co., 1949) , p. 450. While Benedict says that her discussion of Northwest Coast culture is largely confined to the Kwakiutl, that section of her book is entitled "The Northwest Coast of America," which, again, would seem to slight cultural differences between such groups as the Haida, Tsimshian, and Coast Salish. See Helen Codere, *Fighting with Property: A Study of Kwakiutl Potlatching and Warfare 1792–1930* (Monographs of the American Ethnological Society, 18 [1950]) , p. 62.

[12] Benedict, *Patterns of Culture*, p. 82.

[13] Watson Smith and John M. Roberts, *Zuñi Law, A Field of Values.* Papers of the Peabody Museum, Vol. 43, No. 1 (Cambridge, Mass., 1954) , p. 58.

[14] Hoebel, *The Law of Primitive Man*, p. 452.

by way of their grapevine, would send the word back to Gallup for their bootleggers to come in around the hills."[15]

No doubt a strong disapproval of drinking exists, particularly among the older and more conservative members of many Pueblo communities. My colleague, Robert Black, was much impressed by the strength of these attitudes among the Hopi, among whom he has done fieldwork. Nevertheless, people do drink, particularly the younger men, and especially since World War II. But these tendencies are not necessarily new. Ruth Bunzel, with whom Ruth Benedict worked in Zuñi, wrote: "Long ago, before the drinking of whiskey was forbidden, the Zuñis suffered much from its effects. People sold all their goods to get liquor, got drunk, and fought with each other."[16] Matilda Coxe Stevenson, whose report on Zuñi was published in 1904, also described prevalent drinking, particularly around the time of the Shalako festival.[17] It seems that there must be a crack in the Apollonian structure, as far as drinking is concerned. The repugnance felt for liquor can apparently be overcome among these people.

Turning to another point, Benedict describes the Pueblos as being invariably mild people, averse to any show of violence or aggression. "In Zuñi," she writes, "whipping is never used as a corrective of children. The fact that white parents use it in punishment is a matter for unending amazement."[18] Here again Benedict has probably overstated the case. We know, at least, that whipping of children is familiar to the Hopi. Don Talayesva, the Hopi Indian whose autobiography is such a rich mine of information, writes:

My parents whipped me some and so did my grandfather, Homikniwa —at least twice. . . . My father's brother and clan brothers, called my fathers, could whip me whenever either of my parents asked them. My grandfathers, the husbands of my father's sisters and clan sisters, played rough jokes on me and scolded me some, but never flogged me. The relatives that a boy needs to watch closest are his mother's brothers and clan brothers. They have a right to punish an unruly lad severely and almost kill him.

There was a time when my father and mother said that I needed a spanking daily, but they could not make me behave. Since blows seemed

---

[15] Edmund Wilson, *Red, Black, Blond, and Olive* (London: Oxford University Press, 1956), p. 23.

[16] Ruth Bunzel, *Zuñi Texts,* Publications of the American Ethnological Society, Vol. 15 (1933), p. 44.

[17] Matilda Coxe Stevenson, *The Zuni Indians,* Bureau of American Ethnology, 23rd Annual Report, 1904, p. 253.

[18] Benedict, *Patterns of Culture,* p. 63.

useless, one day they put some coals in a broken dish, covered them with cedar boughs, and held me under a blanket in the smoke.[19]

Dorothy Eggan quotes a 42-year-old Hopi man on the same subject: "I was 'licked' when I was a kid, by my father, mother, mother's and father's brothers, and even by an older sister sometimes."[20] Clearly the whipping of children was not a matter of "unending amazement" to the Hopi.

Benedict admitted that whipping of children takes place at Pueblo puberty ceremonies. But she treated this lightly: "In the initiation children are supposed to be very frightened, and they are not shamed if they cry aloud. It makes the rite more valuable."[21] And again: "The Pueblo practice of beating with stripes is . . . without intent to torture. The lash does not draw blood. . . . The adults repudiate with distress the idea that the whips might raise welts. Whipping is 'to take off the bad happenings'. . . ."[22]

However, according to the observations of some other writers, these initiation whippings are not so mild. This is evident with regard to the Hopi, at any rate. H. R. Voth described the floggings at Oraibi as being "very severe," and added that "pandemonium reigns in the kiva during this exciting half-hour"—which doesn't sound Apollonian. In his autobiography Sun Chief confessed that he suffered permanent scars as the result of his initiation. Describing the blows, he wrote:

I stood them fairly well, without crying, and thought my suffering was past; but then the Ho Katcina struck me four more times and cut me to pieces. I struggled, yelled, and urinated. . . . Blood was running down over my body. . . . When they let me go, I wrapped the blanket around my painful body and sat down. I tried to stop sobbing, but continued to cry in my heart. . . . I was led home and put to bed on a sheepskin. The next morning when I awoke, the pelt had stuck fast to my body, so that when I tried to get up it came with me.[23]

Like the initiation ceremony, the Hopi snake dance might be interpreted as having Dionysian qualities.[24] But Benedict did not

---

[19] Leo W. Simmons (ed.), *Sun Chief, The Autobiography of a Hopi Indian* (New Haven, Conn.: Yale University Press, 1942), pp. 70–71.

[20] Dorothy Eggan, "The General Problem of Hopi Adjustment," Kluckhohn, Murray, and Schneider, (eds.), *Personality in Nature, Society, and Culture*, p. 285. See also the comments on child discipline in Li An-Che, "Zuñi. Some Observations and Queries," *American Anthropologist*, Vol. 39 (1937), pp. 62–76.

[21] Benedict, *Patterns of Culture*, p. 63.

[22] Ibid., p. 83.

[23] Simmons (ed.), *Sun Chief*, p. 83.

[24] See, for instance, the description by Fewkes, quoted in Walter Hough, *The Hopi Indians* (Iowa: Torch Press, 1915), p. 152.

see it this way, for she claimed that the Indians have little fear of snakes: ". . . our unreasoned repulsion is no part of their reaction. Nor are snakes especially feared for their attack. There are Indian folktales that end, 'that is why the rattlesnake is not dangerous.' "[25] However, Benedict went on to point out that the poison sacs of the snakes are removed before the dance. If such is the case, the Indians know quite well that the rattlesnake is dangerous; the practice would, however, help to account for their *sang-froid*.

There would certainly seem to be Dionysian elements in the practices followed by some Zuñi medicine societies of walking on red hot coals and swallowing swords. Benedict refers to these in passing, but without comment on their possible Apollonian or Dionysian significance.[26] Elsie Clews Parsons has observed: "The curing society is the part of Zuñi ceremonialism least known to recent observers who therefore underestimate, I think, the orgiastic potentiality of Zuñi character, also the hold of witchcraft belief."[27]

Turning to another point, Benedict says that the ideal man in Zuñi avoids office. "He may have it thrust upon him, but he does not seek it."[28] However, in a criticism of Benedict's analysis, Li An-Che, a Chinese anthropologist who did fieldwork in Zuñi, asserts that "not only do ordinary forms of struggle for individual supremacy exist, but violent forms also occur once in a while." He proceeds to give some examples.[29]

In general, Benedict seems to underplay the tension and conflict in Pueblo society. Much has been written about the clash of factions in the Pueblos, but one gets no hint of factionalism in Benedict's description, since the stress is all on the unity of the society and its cooperative spirit.

Ruth Bunzel has written that when she and Benedict first arrived at Zuñi the village was in one of its "periodic" states of upheaval in which anthropologists figured. "The 'progressive' faction, favorable to Americans and friendly to anthropologists, had been ousted after unsuccesful attempts by anthropologists to photograph the midwinter ceremonies, and its members were so discredited that any contact with them would have been disastrous."[30]

---

[25] Benedict, *Patterns of Culture,* pp. 86–87.

[26] Ibid., p. 65.

[27] Elsie Clews Parsons, *Pueblo Indian Religion* (Chicago: University of Chicago Press, 1939) , p. 879.

[28] Benedict, *Patterns of Culture,* p. 91.

[29] Li An-Che, "Zuñi. Some Observations and Queries," p. 69.

[30] Ruth Bunzel, *Chichicastenago, A Guatemalan Village,* Publications of the American Ethnological Society, No. 22 (1952) , p. xv.

One would never suspect such a state of affairs from reading *Patterns of Culture*. The Pueblo culture, as she describes it, seems somehow disembodied and unrelated to our historical world. This timeless quality may be related to Benedict's emphasis on the underlying ethos of the culture, which seems to be self-perpetuating and unchanging.

Benedict evidently saw Pueblo culture in a particular light. She was selective in what she responded to. To some extent, this is inevitable in fieldwork. John Bennett has shown that different ethnologists have responded very differently to Pueblo culture, and he has grouped them roughly into two divisions: (1) an "organic" school, which stresses the integration of the culture with its "sacred" values and its ideal type of the nonaggressive cooperative individual; (2) a "repressive" school, which stresses the covert tension, anxiety, and suspicion in everyday life. These two viewpoints are not, to be sure, incompatible, and Bennett observes that there are competent ethnographers in both groups, Ruth Benedict and Laura Thompson being classified under the first heading; Esther Goldfrank, Dorothy Eggan, and Mischa Titiev under the second.[31] Evidently, one's values and attitudes partially determine what one will see in the field and how one will describe what is seen. It is fortunate, therefore, that a number of different investigators have worked among the Pueblos.

KWAKIUTL CULTURE

Ruth Benedict's prime example of a Dionysian culture was that of the Kwakiutl Indians of the Northwest Coast of North America, the last of the three cultures which she described in her book. Benedict never did fieldwork among the Kwakiutl; her data came from Franz Boas, whose studies of Northwest Coast culture covered a period of over 40 years. She had access to Boas's published and unpublished material, both voluminous.

The idea of cultural configurations was apparently not antipathetic to Boas. Six years before the publication of *Patterns of Culture*, Boas had sketched out a theme which Benedict was to elaborate upon in her book:

---

[31] John W. Bennett, "The Interpretation of Pueblo Culture," *Southwestern Journal of Anthropology*, Vol. 24, No. 4 (1946), pp. 361–74. Reprinted in Douglas Haring (ed.), *Personal Character and Cultural Milieu* (Syracuse, N.Y.: Syracuse University Press, 1956), pp. 203–16.

Wherever there is a strong, dominant trend of mind that pervades the whole cultural life it may persist over long periods and survive changes in mode of life. This is most easily observed in one-sided cultures characterized by a single controlling idea. . . . On the North Pacific Coast the importance of hereditary social rank, to be maintained by the display and lavish distribution of wealth, determines the behavior of the individual. It is the ambition of every person to obtain high social standing for himself, his family, or for the chief of his family. Wealth is a necessary basis for social eminence and the general tone of life is determined by these ideas.[32]

Boas saw the stress on status, associated with wealth and property, as the integrating principle in this culture. Benedict added to this the Dionysian motif. After a very brief summary of the geographical environment and subsistence techniques on the Northwest Coast, Benedict plunged at once into an account of the dramatic religious ceremonials—an approach which places the emphasis on the Dionysian nature of the culture.

In their religious ceremonies, the final thing they strove for was ecstasy. The chief dancer, at least at the high point of his performance, should lose normal control of himself and be rapt into another state of existence. He should froth at the mouth, tremble violently and abnormally, do deeds which would be terrible in a normal state. . . . The Kwakiutl youth about to become a member of one of their religious societies was snatched away by the spirits, and remained in the woods in isolation for the period during which he was said to be held by the supernaturals. He fasted that he might appear emaciated, and he prepared himself for the demonstration of frenzy which he must give upon his return. The whole Winter Ceremonial, the great Kwakiutl series of religious rites, was given to "tame" the initiate who returned full of "the power that destroys man's reason" and whom it was necessary to bring back to the level of secular existence.

The initiation of the Cannibal Dancer was peculiarly calculated to express the Dionysian purport of Northwest Coast culture. Among the Kwakiutl the Cannibal Society outranked all others. Its members were given the seats of highest honour at the winter dances, and all others must hold back from the feast till the Cannibals had begun to eat. That which distinguished the Cannibal from the members of all other religious societies was his passion for human flesh. He fell upon the onlookers with his teeth and bit a mouthful of flesh from their arms. His dance was that of a frenzied addict enamoured of the "food" that was held before him, a prepared corpse carried on the outstretched arms of a woman. On great occasions the Cannibal ate the bodies of slaves who had been killed for this purpose. . . . During the time when the Cannibal initiate was secluded alone in the woods, he procured a corpse from a tree where it had

---

[32] Franz Boas, *Anthropology and Modern Life* (New York: W. W. Norton & Co., Inc., 1928), pp. 151–52.

been disposed. The skin had already been dried by exposure, and he especially prepared it for his "food" in the dance. . . . At last all the Cannibal Society by their combined frenzy roused the new initiate, who all of a sudden was heard upon the roof of the house. He was beside himself. He shoved aside the boards of the roof and jumped down among all the people. In vain they tried to surround him. He ran around the fire and out again by a secret door. . . . All the societies followed him toward the woods, and presently he was seen again. Three times he disappeared, and the fourth an old man went out ahead, "the bait" as he was called. The Cannibal rushed upon him, seized his arm, and bit it. The people caught him in the act and brought him to the house where the ceremonial was to be held. He was out of his senses and bit those whom he laid hold of. When they came to the ceremonial house he could not be made to enter. At last the woman co-initiate whose duty it was to carry the prepared body across her arms appeared naked with the corpse. She danced backward, facing the Cannibal, enticing him to enter the house. He still could not be prevailed upon, but at length he again climbed the roof and jumped down through the displaced boards. He danced wildly, not able to control himself, but quivering in all his muscles in the peculiar tremor which the Kwakiutl associate with frenzy.[33]

This certainly sounds Dionysian! But, in a discussion of this ceremony, Philip Drucker writes that it is highly improbable that corpses were actually used. The Kwakiutl had a remarkably developed interest in sleight-of-hand and stage effects—dramatic mock murders, decapitations with false heads, disappearances through trapdoors, wounded men gushing blood from concealed seal's bladders, and so on.[34] Drucker suggests that the carcass of a small black bear, fitted with a carved head, could easily resemble a human corpse, especially by the dim firelight.[35]

As for the biting of bystanders, this seems to have occurred, but it did not happen at random. People were contacted by the "cannibal" ahead of time. They would agree upon the biting beforehand, and later the victim would be compensated by special gifts.[36] This places the ceremony in a different light. It cannot have been so wild and Dionysian then. The "cannibal's" behavior was not so frenzied and uncontrolled, but rather carefully planned, at least to the extent that he did not dash about just biting anyone.

Charles Nowell, in the Kwakiutl autobiography, *Smoke from*

---

[33] Benedict, *Patterns of Culture*, pp. 162, 164, 166.

[34] For some striking examples of such staged effects, see C. S. Ford (ed.), *Smoke from Their Fires* (New Haven, Conn.: Yale University Press 1941), pp. 118–22.

[35] Philip Drucker, *Indians of the Northwest Coast* (New York: McGraw-Hill Book Co., 1955), pp. 151–52.

[36] Ibid.

Their Fires, explains that when he displayed aggressive ceremonial behavior in the bear's skin, going from house to house to smash dishes, he was accompanied by a man who kept track of everything he broke, so that the owner could be compensated later.[37] Dionysian? Yes, to some extent, but in a controlled setting. Benedict's picture ignores the elements of staging and planning, so important in these dramatic ceremonials. The enormous amount of time spent in food getting and in the production of standardized goods also shows that there must have been a strong "Apollonian" core in Kwakiutl society.[38] And when we examine the magnificent art products of the Northwest Coast, we are struck by the emphasis on form. This is not a wild expressionistic art; the elements of tension and the occasional strong colors are bound by strong forms and definite outlines.

Clellan S. Ford makes the interesting suggestion that the Kwakiutl ceremonies were violent, not because the Kwakiutl were habitually violent people, but quite the contrary—because the daily life of the Kwakiutl demanded so strict a control over aggression. And he asks: "Can it be that they derived pleasure from thus participating in acts of violence which they badly wanted to do yet dared not?"[39] One thinks in this connection of the extraordinary amount of violence in American films—in westerns, gangster films, and animated cartoons. Some might interpret the popularity of these films as an indication of the bloodiness and violence of American life; but a more likely explanation, it seems to me, would be in terms of Ford's hypothesis of repressed aggression and the tensions of everyday life.

At any rate, there were Apollonian features in Kwakiutl life, just as there were Dionysian ones in the Pueblos. Indeed, it would seem inevitable that there would be some mixture of these human tendencies. Dionysian peoples cannot very well be always Dionysian. Could a society exist in which everybody was engaged in pursuing ecstatic experiences, cutting off fingers, taking dope or hashish, getting drunk, and going into trances? Of course not. Some Apollonian

---

[37] C. S. Ford, *Smoke from Their Fires,* p. 117.

[38] See Helen Codere, *Fighting with Property: A Study of Kwakiutl Potlatching and Warfare 1792–1930,* Monographs of the American Ethnological Society, No. 18 (New York, 1950) , pp. 18–19. According to Codere, they were a peaceable people, who did not engage in much warfare. See p. 115.

[39] Ford., *Smoke from Their Fires,* p. 27. There are some passages in Ford's book which could, however, be cited as evidence for a Dionysian tendency in Kwakiutl culture. See the descriptions of children's games and Nowell's account of a rather bloody ceremony in which he participated, pp. 65 f., 115 f.

core of sobriety and responsibility must be found in any culture, or else it will fall apart. At the same time, Dionysian elements can usually be discovered in any culture, no matter how "middle of the road" it may be.

Meanwhile, how are we to characterize forms of integration which exist outside of the Apollonian-Dionysian polarity? Should we find a new catchword for each culture (Babbittian? Confucian? Nanookian?) with each label representing a different principle of integration? Obviously, this is an unsatisfactory stratagem, as Benedict admitted in an almost self-disparaging passage: "It would be absurd to cut every culture down to the Procrustean bed of some catchword characterization. The danger of lopping off important facts that do not illustrate the main proposition is grave enough even at best. . . . We do not need a plank of configuration written into the platform of an ethnological school."[40]

Although I have expressed some criticisms of Benedict's descriptions of Pueblo and Kwakiutl culture, I do not want to give the impression that I reject them outright, for I think that much of the analysis, in both cases, must be valid. A difficulty in both cases is Ruth Benedict's tendency to overstatement. For instance, there is her extravagant assertion that suicide is "too violent an act, even in its most casual forms, for the Pueblos to contemplate. They have no idea what it could be."[41] Here it is sufficient for Hoebel to cite three Pueblo suicides (all after 1939) to refute her.[42] But the easy refutation that is possible in this case should not blind us to the reality of a difference between the Pueblo and Plains tribes in their attitudes toward suicide and aggression. Benedict's overstatements tempt one to throw out the baby with the bath water. If she had written "Suicide is rare," no one would have objected.

Overstatements seem to abound in Benedict's description of the Kwakiutl, who are characterized as "megalomanic," "paranoid," and so on. Helen Codere has written an article in which she seeks to modify this harsh picture. "The Kwakiutl are more real, more complex, more human than they have been represented to be," Codere tells us.[43] This is a necessary corrective, and is in line with the less sensational emphasis in the accounts of Northwest Coast

[40] Benedict, *Patterns of Culture*, p. 211.

[41] Ibid., p. 107.

[42] Hoebel, *The Law of Primitive Man*, p. 452.

[43] Helen Codere, "The Amiable Side of Kwakiutl Life: The Potlatch and the Play Potlatch," *American Anthropologist*, Vol. 58 (1956), pp. 349–50.

culture written by Ford and Drucker, which seem more plausible than Benedict's highly colored one. However, in accepting this milder view there is a danger that we may develop a blind spot to the significance of Boas's rich material. Boas, after all, was closer in time to the living culture than later workers in this area, and the amount of work he did was prodigious. Moreover, we should not let our notions of plausibility influence us too far in this connection. Those who have lived through the era of the Nazi regime have some vivid evidence of the extreme forms which cultures may assume. If we had simply read about the Nazis in an anthropologist's account of a remote people, we might well reject the whole report as exaggerated.

With regard to the Northwest Coast, there is abundant evidence that the culture was characterized by a set of values and attitudes which permeated the whole life of the people. Boas is not the only one who provided evidence for this. We find similar impressions in Aurel Krause's work on the Tlingit, first published in German in 1885:

The Tlingit has a highly developed sense of ownership. He not only has his own clothes, weapons, and utensils, he also has his own hunting grounds, his own trade trails which no one else may use without his permission or without paying damages. Generally everyone's property rights are respected by his tribesmen, less from a sense of justice than from fear of revenge. . . . Even in his relationship with his friends and his nearest relatives the Tlingit shows great selfishness. For every service he renders, for every gift he gives, he expects a return. . . . Vanity is one of the leading traits of Tlingit character. Nothing can hurt him more than injury to his self esteem. Jealously he is on guard to see that all his prerogatives and rights are recognized, and he looks with disdain on anyone who has lost an advantage. . . . The Indian cannot stand a peaceful, quiet existence. His great sensitivity and his strong sense of property rights are constant cause of resentment. For every bodily injury, for any damage to his goods and property, for any infringement by strangers on his hunting or trading territory, full compensation is demanded or extracted by force.[44]

It seems to me that a revised picture of Northwest Coast culture, although incorporating modifications suggested by the work of Codere, Ford, and others, should retain some of the insights of this sort made by Krause, Boas, and Benedict. For Benedict and Boas may have been on the track of something valid. I feel, for example, that Benedict convincingly showed that the motifs of rivalry and

[44] Aurel Krause, *The Tlingit Indians. Results of a Trip to the Northwest Coast of America and the Bering Straits,* trans. Erna Gunther (Seattle: American Ethnological Society, 1956) , pp. 115–16, 169.

self-glorification appear not only in the potlatch, but also in connection with marriage and shamanism.[45] And surely the boastful speeches of Kwakiutl chiefs quoted by Benedict are striking evidence for the attitudes she describes.

SOME GENERAL CONSIDERATIONS

One important problem which Benedict did not pursue in *Patterns of Culture* concerns the means by which individuals are "Apollonianized." In other words, how do the Hopi manage to become such submissive, gentle people? And how were "Dionysian" attitudes cultivated among the Blackfoot in each new generation? In this book Benedict seemed to assume that the whole thing works by contagion. Thus, an individual born into an "Apollonian" culture and exposed to it long enough automatically becomes an "Apollonian" person, just as an Eskimo baby naturally learns to speak Eskimo rather than another language and eventually "takes over" Eskimo culture.

An implicit consistency model of personality is suggested here, although a fulfillment model is also possible. At any rate, Benedict explicitly rejects a conflict model, stating several times that there can be no inherent antagonism between society and the individual.[46] There is no conflict because human nature is so malleable.

Most people are shaped to the form of their culture because of the enormous malleability of their endowment. They are plastic to the moulding force of the society into which they are born. It does not matter whether, with the Northwest Coast, it requires delusions of self-reference, or with our own civilization the amassing of possessions. In any case the great mass of individuals take quite readily the form that is presented to them.[47]

This was in the days before Ruth Benedict had become interested in problems of child-rearing—a matter to which she turned her attention in later works. There is a passing reference in *Patterns of Culture* to the probable absence of the Oedipus complex among Zuñi. Beyond this, there is not much evidence of psychoanalytic orientation in this work, although Clyde Kluckhohn has written concerning "Psychological Types in the Cultures of the Southwest" and "Configurations of Culture in North America" that "every page

---

[45] Benedict, *Patterns of Culture,* pp. 187–98.

[46] Ibid., pp. 232–34.

[47] Ibid., p. 235.

is colored by an attitude that can only be called 'psychiatric' and which must be traced eventually from the influence of psychiatry."[48]

Be that as it may, *Patterns of Culture* seems to have had some influence in furthering the formation of a new school of psycho-analytic thought. Karen Horney paid her respects to the anthropologists (including Benedict) in *The Neurotic Personality of Our Time,* asserting that cultural factors had been understressed by Freud in his studies of the etiology of neuroses. Accordingly, Horney emphasized cultural conditions at the expense of the orthodox libidinal drives and infantile experiences. In the course of her remarks, Karen Horney touched on Ruth Benedict's Apollonian-Dionysian duality, describing the Dionysian tendency as a desire to lose the self.

In our culture we are more aware of the opposite attitude toward the self, the attitude that emphasizes and highly values the particularities and uniqueness of individuality. Man in our culture feels strongly that his own self is a separate unity, distinguished from or opposite to the world outside. Not only does he insist on this individuality but he derives a great deal of satisfaction from it; he finds happiness in developing his special potentialities, mastering himself and the world in active conquest, being constructive and doing creative work.

But the opposite tendency that we have discussed—the tendency to break through the shell of individuality and be rid of its limitations and isolation—is an equally deep-rooted human attitude, and is also pregnant with potential satisfaction. Neither of these tendencies is in itself pathological; both the preservation and development of individuality and the sacrifice of individuality are legitimate goals in the solution of human problems.[49]

This seems like a curious conclusion. But perhaps it is in keeping with the Spengler-Benedict tradition of cultural relativism. For one cannot pass value judgments (can one?) upon the incommensurable metaphysical assumptions and attitudes which underlie the destinies of cultures. Which is "better"—to be Apollonian or Dionysian?—or (to use Spengler's terms) to be Classical, Magian, or Faustian? This is like asking if it is better to be an oak tree or a cow. There may be an answer, but one hardly knows where to begin.

Yet there is a catch in this relativist position, at least for "re-

---

[48] Clyde Kluckhohn, "The Influence of Psychiatry on Anthropology in America During the Past One Hundred Years," J. K. Hall, G. Zilboorg, and H. A. Bunker (eds.), *One Hundred Years of American Psychiatry* (New York: Columbia University Press, 1944), p. 597.

[49] Karen Horney, *The Neurotic Personality of Our Time* (New York: W. W. Norton & Co., Inc., 1937), pp. 273–74.

formers" like Benedict and Horney. Spengler was more consistent in his Olympian view, jeering sarcastically at "world improvers" from his privileged position beyond space and time. But Ruth Benedict, whose books and pamphlets urgently combated racial prejudice, was a "world improver" caught up in the issues of her day, passing value judgments right and left upon the culture of her world.

Could we not say that in some societies people seem to be "happier" than in others, or that there are fewer mental and emotional disturbances in society A than in society B? From reading *Patterns of Culture,* one receives the very definite impression that the Pueblo tribes are "happier" than the Dobu. "Life in Dobu fosters the extreme forms of animosity and malignancy which most societies have minimized by their institutions," Benedict tells us,[50] while Pueblo culture is described as "a civilization whose forms are dictated by the typical choices of the Apollonian, all of whose delight is in formality and whose way of life is the way of measure and sobriety."[51]

In which society would you rather live? Or does it make no difference? One would think that Ruth Benedict would rather be a Zuñi than a Dobu or a Kwakiutl. Yet in the final paragraph of her book she speaks of the "coexisting and equally valid patterns of life which mankind has created for itself from the raw materials of existence."[52] At the same time, at other points in *Patterns of Culture* she seems to approach absolute criteria for the evaluation of social systems. "It is possible," she suggests, "to scrutinize different institutions and cast up their cost in terms of social capital, in terms of the less desirable behavior traits they stimulate, and in terms of human suffering and frustration."[53]

Elgin Williams has discussed the internal contradictions and inconsistencies in Ruth Benedict's work. "Formally she sticks to relativism," he observes. "Her pragmatism is not so much at the tip of her tongue as bred in the bone. Try as she may to maintain the pose of relativism, the test of consequences intrudes."[54] He is aware that Benedict's concern for tolerance was expressed in her cultural relativism, but he inquires whether this relativism, if carried to a logical

---

[50] Benedict, *Patterns of Culture,* p. 159.

[51] Ibid., p. 119.

[52] Ibid., p. 257.

[53] Ibid., p. 229.

[54] Elgin Williams, "Anthropology for the Common Man," *American Anthropologist,* January-March 1947, p. 88.

conclusion, would not lead to an acceptance of Jim Crowism in the South and other manifestations of intolerance.

However, one aspect of Benedict's view of culture should be congenial to the assumptions of a "world improver." I refer to the absence of any cyclical fatalism like that of Spengler, or of any constitutional determinism like that of Sheldon. Nor was she a "childhood determinist" in *Patterns of Culture*. It may seem paradoxical in the light of Leslie White's polemics against the "Boas school," but Benedict was something of a culturologist, at least in *Patterns of Culture*. Her emphasis was always on the culture rather than on the individual. There is no study of individuals in Benedict's book and no life histories. What Benedict analyzes is Pueblo *culture*, especially its ideal form. The only determinism which Benedict stressed in this work was a cultural determinism, but with the saving implication that man may develop some culture consciousness and insight into the mold of his own culture and thereby change or transcend it in some way. In this respect, perhaps, her viewpoint was close to that of her teacher, Boas, who once wrote: ". . . my whole outlook upon social life is determined by the question: how can we recognize the shackles that tradition has laid upon us? For when we recognize them, we are also able to break them."[55]

SUGGESTIONS FOR FURTHER READING

Among Benedict's numerous contributions to culture-and-personality, two can be singled out as of special interest: "Continuities and Discontinuities in Cultural Conditioning," *Psychiatry*, Vol. 1 (1938), pp. 161–67; and *The Chrysanthemum and the Sword, Patterns of Japanese Culture* (Boston: Houghton Mifflin Co., 1946). Biographical data about Benedict may be found in Margaret Mead's *An Anthropologist at Work. Writings of Ruth Benedict* (Boston: Houghton Mifflin, 1959).

Since *Patterns of Culture* was written, some writers have continued to discuss the contrast between the Pueblo religion and those of the hunting-gathering tribes of North America and have tended to see this contrast in a cultural evolutionary context. The shift to agriculture may be seen as involving a conversion to a less mobile and individualistic way of life and to the development of more rigid control over the individual. The following sources are relevant to such a view: Ruth Underhill, *Ceremonial Patterns in the Greater Southwest*, American Ethnological Society Monograph, No. XIII (New York: J. J. Augustin, 1948), pp. vii–62; Robert E. Ritzenthaler, *Chippewa Preoccupation with Health. Change*

---

[55] Franz Boas, "An Anthropologist's Credo," *The Nation*, August 27, 1938, pp. 201–2.

in a Traditional Attitude Resulting from Modern Health Problems, Milwaukee Public Museum Bulletin No. 19, Vol. 4 (Milwaukee, 1953), pp. 175–258; Joseph Campbell, *The Masks of God: Primitive Mythology* (New York: The Viking Press, Inc., 1959), pp. 229–42; Herbert Barry III, Irvin L. Child, and Margaret K. Bacon, "Relation of Child Training to Subsistence Economy," *American Anthropologist,* Vol. 61 (1959), pp. 51–63; Roy G. D'Andrade, "Anthropological Studies of Dreams," in Francis L. K. Hsu (ed.), *Psychological Anthropology,* pp, 325–26; Peter B. Field, "A New Cross-cultural Study of Drunkenness," in David J. Pittman and Charles R. Snyder (eds.), *Society, Culture, and Drinking Patterns* (New York: John Wiley & Sons, 1962), pp. 48–74. See below, pp. 173–74.

An explicit attempt to see the Dionysian-Apollonian polarity in a cultural evolutionary context has been made by Alvin W. Gouldner and Richard A. Peterson, who, on the basis of a factor analysis of data drawn from 71 primitive societies described in the Yale cross-cultural files, assert that Apollonianness or impulse control has increased with the development of technology and civilization. (Alvin W. Gouldner and Richard A. Peterson, *Notes on Technology and the Moral Order* [Indianapolis: The Bobbs-Merrill Co., Inc., 1962]).

chapter 5

Malinowski's Criticism of Freudian Theory

In dealing with the writings of Benedict, we were not concerned with the effects of childhood experiences upon personality, but this will be our theme in this and in many subsequent chapters. A pioneer work in the cross-cultural study of this subject was Bronislaw Malinowski's *Sex and Repression in Savage Society*, first published in 1927,[1] the first part of which appeared as a pair of articles in *Psyche* in 1924.[2] Some conclusions in these articles were challenged by Ernest Jones,[3] the psychoanalyst who later became Freud's biographer. In the second half of *Sex and Repression*, Malinowski dealt with the criticisms of Jones and other Freudians. The present chapter will set forth Malinowski's argument, the data he presented, and an evaluation of this work.

Bronislaw Malinowski (1884–1942) was one of the leading figures in modern anthropology. He was born and educated in Poland and received a Ph.D. degree in physics and mathematics at Cracow in 1908. Later, however, after a period of illness, Malinowski became so interested in anthropology (through reading Frazer's *The Golden Bough* in convalescence) that he went to study under C. G. Selig-

---

[1] Bronislaw Malinowski, *Sex and Repression in Savage Society* (London: Routledge and Kegan Paul, 1953).

[2] Bronislaw Malinowski, "Psychoanalysis and Anthropology," *Psyche*, Vol. 4 (April 1924), pp. 293–332.

[3] Ernest Jones, "Mother-Right and the Sexual Ignorance of Savages," *International Journal of Psycho-Analysis*, Vol. 6, Part 2 (1925), pp. 109–30.

man and others in England. In 1914, he traveled to Melanesia and lived for two years in the Trobriand Islands, where he learned the native language and intimately observed the life of the people. This crucial experience provided him with the material for a series of books which made both him and the Trobriand Islands famous.[4] Like Joseph Conrad, Malinowski was a Pole who preferred to write in English and did so with the greatest skill. He made the Trobriand scene vivid and immediate to the reader. In this chapter we will be concerned with only one corner of his work, his criticism of Freudian theory. The reader should keep in mind that there is much more to be found in Malinowski's survey of Trobriand life— the study of economic institutions, law, magic and religion, all of which, as a true "functionalist," Malinowski saw as being intricately interrelated.

In *Sex and Repression in Savage Society,* Malinowski examined Freud's concept of the Oedipus complex. He asked the telling question: Is the Oedipus complex as described by Freud to be considered a universal human phenomenon found in all cultures, or is it the product of a particular type of family system? Freud clearly considered the Oedipus complex to be a universal, inevitable aspect of human life, since it is rooted in biology and in the processes of growing up. The child, suckling at the mother's breast, receives not only nourishment but its first erotic sensations, localized around the mouth, the first channel of its contacts with the outer world. Later in the child's development, erotic feelings become connected with the anal zone, and ultimately with the genitals. The mother, through the act of suckling, is the first love object of the child and remains such for the little boy, while the girl comes to transfer her attachment to the father.

. . . it is easy to see [wrote Freud] that the little man wants his mother all to himself, finds his father in the way, becomes restive when the latter takes upon himself to caress her, and shows his satisfaction when the father goes away or is absent. He often expresses his feelings directly in words and promises his mother to marry her. . . . When the little boy shows the most open sexual curiosity about his mother, wants to sleep with her at night, insists on being in the room while she is dressing, or even attempts physical acts of seduction, as the mother so often observes

---

[4] Bronislaw Malinowski, *Argonauts of the Western Pacific* (London, 1922) ; *Crime and Custom in Savage Society* (London, 1926) ; *The Sexual Life of Savages in North-Western Melanesia* (New York, 1929) ; *Coral Gardens and Their Magic* (2 vols.) (New York, 1935) ; and *Magic, Science and Religion and Other Essays* (New York, 1948) .

and laughingly relates, the erotic nature of this attachment to her is established without a doubt.[5]

That is why, according to Freud, modern civilized men, even today, are moved by Sophocles' *Oedipus Rex,* for this play represents the enactment of a forbidden wish—the desire to murder the father and marry the mother. This wish, although repressed, is seen to lurk in the subconscious of every man, but is particularly pressing and insistent among neurotics and psychotics who have failed to successfully "resolve" the Oedipus complex.

For a son, the task consists in releasing his libidinal desires from his mother, in order to employ them in the quest of an external love-object in reality; and in reconciling himself with his father if he has remained antagonistic to him, or in freeing himself from his domination if, in the reaction to the infantile revolt, he has lapsed into subservience to him. These tasks are laid down for every man.[6]

Malinowski asked whether this was really so. He pointed out that the composition of the family varies in different societies. Would an Oedipus complex be apt to appear in a society having a matrilineal type of family?

Malinowski was in a position to throw light on this question, for the Trobriand Islanders among whom he lived for so long have matrilineal descent. Moreover, as he went on to show, the role of the father in Trobriand society is quite different from that in the Western world.

In the first half of *Sex and Repression,* Malinowski described the Trobriand family situation as follows: Descent is traced in the female line. At birth one becomes a member of one's mother's clan.

From a woman's point of view, residence after marriage is virilocal; that is, the bride goes to live in her husband's community. But the term *avunculocal* residence is more appropriate, for at the time of marriage, or shortly thereafter, the husband leaves his father's village, where he was born, and goes to live in the village owned by his mother's subclan, where his mother's brother lives. Except for chiefs, who may have many wives, marriages are monogamous.

Every man and woman in the Trobriands settles down eventually to matrimony, after a period of sexual play in childhood, followed by general license in adolescence, and later by a time when the lovers live to-

[5] Sigmund Freud, *A General Introduction to Psychoanalysis,* Joan Riviere, trans. (New York: Permabooks, 1956) , pp. 341–42. (First published 1920.)

[6] Ibid., p. 346.

gether in a more permanent intrigue, sharing with two or three other couples a communal "bachelor's house."[7] [As we shall see later, this is not all strictly true for "every man and woman."]

The Trobriand Islanders recognize no relationship between sexual intercourse and pregnancy. They believe that a child is inserted in the mother's womb by a dead female relative of hers. The male head of the household, therefore, is not considered to be a progenitor of the child, who is regarded as solely a product of the mother, related to her family, not his.[8] However, the "father" does take an active, indulgent interest in "his" children, and spends much more time playing with them than the usual European or American father does.

Since this is a matrilineal society, a Trobriand boy does not inherit property from his "father" but from his mother's brother, whom he looks up to as the principal family authority. The father's role in the Trobriands also differs in that he is not the traditional food provider or breadwinner for his family, as with us. Instead, every man turns over most of his garden produce to his sister, even though he usually lives in a different village, sometimes as much as six or eight miles away. The "father" is not a disciplinarian; he exerts no special authority over the children. It is the maternal uncle who disciplines the boy when he is old enough—at around seven—to go and work in his uncle's village and to learn from him the techniques of agriculture and the traditions of his clan.

Within the family circle, Trobriand children never see their mother brutalized or in abject dependence upon her husband. "They never feel his heavy hand on themselves; he is not their kinsman, nor their owner, nor their benefactor. He has no rights or prerogatives."[9] Here Malinowski exaggerates somewhat, forgetting for the moment that residence is virilocal. (He writes elsewhere: ". . . the man is considered to be the master, for he is in his own vil-

---

[7] Malinowski, *Sex and Repression in Savage Society*, p. 9.

[8] Various writers have expressed skepticism about the Trobrianders' nescience of the facts of life. The same lack of knowledge has been attributed to the Australian aborigines, whose "spiritual" conception of conception is somewhat similar to that of the Trobriand Islanders. However, Géza Roheim, William Lloyd Warner and others have reported that Australian groups whom they have studied really do understand the male role in procreation. This topic has been discussed at length in M. F. Ashley-Montagu's *Coming into Being among the Australian Aborigines* (London: George Routledge & Sons, 1937). However, one cannot generalize from the Australian to the Melanesian scene. As far as I know, no one has disproved Malinowski's account of Trobriand beliefs concerning conception.

[9] Malinowski, *Sex and Repression in Savage Society*, p. 31.

lage and the house belongs to him . . .")[10] However, the status of the Trobriand woman is high. She has her own possessions; her brother supplies the family with food, and next to him she is the legal head of the family.

Trobriand children grow up with much freedom to do as they like, freedom which includes the sphere of sex. Children play sexual games in imitation of adult copulation, which is regarded with amused tolerance by their elders. But there is one important taboo which governs sexual behavior, an incest taboo proscribing any intimacy between brother and sister. A kind of avoidance relationship is consequently established between them at the approach of puberty. To a lesser degree this taboo extends to clan "sisters" as well. According to Malinowski, there is no latency period among Trobriand children. They maintain an interest in sex throughout childhood during the period which Freud described as marked by diminution of such interest.

During adolescence, boys live in bachelors' houses to which they bring their girl friends. After a few years of casual affairs with different partners, they finally get married, thus assuming full adult status. At puberty, ideally, the boy leaves his father's community to live in the village of his mother's brother.

This is the village associated with his clan, where he will inherit property, and which he will ultimately come to regard as his own village, rather than the village of his father, where his father's clan members may even regard him as a sort of outsider.[11] However, the move to the uncle's village may not be made until between 18 and 22 years of age.[12]

While living at the bachelors' house, the boy continues to have meals at his parents' home.[13] He brings his bride there, while his own dwelling is being built, and they spend a "protracted honeymoon" under his parents' roof.[14] In some cases, as with the sons of chiefs, no shift in residence takes place. Once a couple is married, fidelity is expected of both partners, and a rather stiff propriety replaces the earlier free and easy license. Husband and wife never

---

[10] Bronislaw Malinowski, *The Sexual Life of Savages in North-Western Melanesia* (New York: Harcourt Brace, 1929), p. 18.

[11] Ibid. p. 7.

[12] Malinowski, *Coral Gardens and Their Magic*, Vol. I, p. 205. See also his *Crime and Custom in Savage Society* (Totawa, N.J.: Littlefield, Adams, & Co., 1959), pp. 108–10.

[13] Malinowski, *The Sexual Life of Savages*, p. 75.

[14] Ibid, pp. 91, 109. See also pp. 86–88.

hold hands or otherwise touch one another in public and do not exchange amorous glances or smiles while others are present. Nevertheless, most married couples are said to be on excellent terms with one another.

It was Malinowski's impression that the Trobrianders were a very well-adjusted people, lacking in neuroses or perversions. "In the Trobriands, though I knew scores of natives intimately and had a nodding acquaintance with many more, I could not name a single man or woman who was hysterical or even neurasthenic. Nervous tics, compulsory actions or obsessive ideas were not to be found."[15] Nor was there any evidence of homosexuality, except among boys and girls who had been penned up in the Mission Station.

What of the Oedipus complex? Was there any evidence for repressed longings for the mother? Obviously, this is not an easy thing to find out. Malinowski tried to get accounts of dreams from his Trobriand friends but discovered they dream very little. This supports the Freudian view of the function of dreams—to relieve suppressed tensions—if we accept the assertion that the Trobrianders are well adjusted. Malinowski learned that sex dreams occurred and asked his informants if they ever dreamed in this way about their mothers. There were shocked denials to this, but there were admissions of sexual dreams about sisters. No Oedipus legends occur in Trobriand folklore; on the other hand, brother-sister incest forms an important motif in their mythology. Malinowski could not unearth a single case of mother-son incest, but did find some involving brother and sister.

Were there reports of hostility felt toward the father? Here again, findings were negative. Sons seemed to entertain warm feelings toward their fathers, but sometimes expressed hostility for maternal uncles. No cases of parricide were reported. Malinowski's conclusion was as follows:

In the Trobriands there is no friction between father and son, and all the infantile craving of the child for its mother is allowed gradually to spend itself in a natural, spontaneous manner. The ambivalent attitude of veneration and dislike is felt between a man and his mother's brother, while the repressed sexual attitude of incestuous temptation can be formed only towards his sister. Applying to each society a terse, though somewhat crude formula, we might say that in the Oedipus complex there is the repressed desire to kill the father and marry the mother, while

---

[15] Malinowski, *Sex and Repression,* p. 87.

in the matrilineal society of the Trobriands the wish is to marry the sister and to kill the maternal uncle.[16]

Malinowski thought that this Trobriand complex might apply to other matrilineal societies as well, for he claimed that myths of incest between brother and sister are often found among matrilineal peoples, especially in the Pacific, while stories of hostility between a man and his maternal uncle are also widespread.[17]

The prinicipal conclusion in the first part of Malinowski's *Sex and Repression* is that we are "not to assume the universal existence of the Oedipus complex, but in studying every type of civilization, to establish the special complex which pertains to it."[18] This is a clear-cut position, but in the second half of his book Malinowski surrenders much of it. During the first half of the book we are led to believe that Malinowski rejects the universality of the Oedipus complex.[19] In the second half, although continuing to criticize aspects of Freudian theory, such as the dubious myth of the primal parricide, Malinowski retreats from his original stand and affirms agreement with his Freudian critic, Ernest Jones, on some crucial points.

Jones insists upon the presence of the Oedipus complex in the Trobriands. The father is hated here, he says, as elsewhere; this hatred, in fact, is the "reason" for the Trobriander's denial of the male role in procreation. But hatred for the father in his society is deflected toward the maternal uncle. Thus we have a "decomposition of the primal father into a kind and lenient actual father on the one hand and a stern and moral uncle on the other."[20] Malinowski observes: "For Dr. Jones, then, the Oedipus complex is fundamental; and the 'matrilineal system with its avunculate complex arose, . . . as a mode of defense against the primordial Oedipus tendencies.'" Malinowski's next sentence comes as a considerable surprise: "All these views will strike the readers of the first two

---

[16] Ibid., p. 80. Malinowski usually writes as though a boy had only one sister and one uncle. We do not know whether, if a boy had several uncles, he would hate all of them or only one or two—perhaps those with most authority.

[17] Ibid., p. 134.

[18] Ibid., p. 82.

[19] ". . . this complex is assumed to exist in every savage or barbarous society. This certainly cannot be correct . . . they cannot reach correct results when they try to trace the Oedipus complex, essentially patriarchal in character, in a matrilineal society . . . ." Ibid., pp. 5–6.

[20] Ibid., p. 138.

parts of this book as not altogether unfamiliar, and sound in all the essentials."[21] He expresses agreement with the idea that "hate is removed from the father and placed upon the maternal uncle."[22]

But this means to concede the presence of an Oedipus complex among the Trobrianders, for why should there by any hatred for the father in the first place? In the early part of his book Malinowski gives the impression that where such hatred is found in Europe it is apt to stem more from resentment at the authoritarian role of the European father than from any sexual rivalry.[23] It would be consistent with this view that in the Trobriands no hostility is reported as being felt for the father (who is not a disciplinarian), while there is hostility expressed toward the maternal uncles, who are authority figures. Malinowski's point, comparable to one of Erich Fromm's,[24] would seem to be that sexual rivalry need not be invoked to account for the hostility which sons may feel for their fathers. Indeed, Malinowski writes in a footnote: "The statement that 'a young organism reacts sexually to close bodily contact with the mother' appears to me now absurd. I am glad that I may use this strong word, having written the absurd statement myself."[25] Why, then, should there be any hatred for the Trobriand father, with whom children have such a good relationship? Such hatred must presumably exist if it is to be "removed from the father and placed upon the maternal uncle." While appearing to criticize Freud, Malinowski, in effect, concedes the basic Freudian premise.

Géza Roheim, an orthodox Freudian analyst who has done ethnological field work in Melanesia and Australia, asserts, as does Jones, that the Oedipus complex is present among the Trobrianders. He points out that the composition of the Trobriand family is essentially like ours, consisting of husband, wife, and children. The mother's brother does not play an intimate part in the life of this family, for he generally lives in another village. In Freudian doctrine, the crucial events concerning the Oedipus complex are believed to occur before the age of seven, but it is not until then that the boy goes to work in his uncle's village. The uncle, therefore,

---

[21] Ibid.

[22] Ibid., p. 139; see also p. 170.

[23] Ibid., pp. 27–29.

[24] Erich Fromm, *Escape from Freedom* (New York: Rinehart, 1941), p. 178.

[25] Malinowski, *Sex and Repression*, p. 241, fn. 5. (New York: Meridian, 1955 edition).

does not become an important figure in the boy's life until after that time. Roheim also claims that the Trobrianders have Oedipal legends in their mythology.[26]

Malinowski tells us that Trobriand children witness much of their parents' sexual behavior, and that no special precautions are taken to prevent their watching.[27] Since it is Freud's view that such "primal scenes" (often interpreted by the child as the father's aggressive attack upon the mother) implant resentment in the son, the conditions for an Oedipus complex would seem to be present in Trobriand society, if one accepts the Freudian premise. As we shall see later, Trobriand lovemaking is characterized by some sado-masochistic behavior, which would heighten the impression of an aggressive attack, although, as it happens, it is the male who is on the receiving end of most of the sadism.

To be sure, the free sexual behavior of children and adolescents would, at the same time, seem to obviate the building-up of tensions. But this raises another point. Judging from Malinowski's data, the free sex life he describes is not open to everyone, although in *Sex and Repression* we get the impression that it is. In *The Sexual Life of Savages,* however, we discover that patrilateral cross-cousin marriage is often practiced, that is, the marriage of a man to his father's sister's daughter. Such marriages are arranged by parents when their children are infants and are considered binding. "The betrothed are spoken of as husband and wife, and thus address one another."[28] A girl so betrothed may not sleep with other men or go on girls' sexual expeditions to other villages. At the same time, the boy's father tries to control his son's behavior in these respects. Betrothed couples are not expected to have affairs.[29]

Cross-cousin marriages are popular in the families of chiefs, village headmen, and men of rank, wealth, and power. Unfortunately, Malinowski does not tell us what percentage of marriages

[26] Géza Roheim, *Psychoanalysis and Anthropology, Culture, Personality, and the Unconscious* (New York: International Universities Press, 1950), pp. 167, 191. Oedipal motifs seem to be widespread in Oceania. William A. Lessa believes that this is largely due to diffusion and that such stories may be told in societies where there would seem to be little likelihood for an actual Oedipus complex to develop. See William A. Lessa, "Oedipus-Type Tales in Oceania," *Journal of American Folklore,* Vol. 69 (1956), pp. 63–73.

[27] Malinowski, *The Sexual Life of Savages,* p. 54.

[28] Ibid., p. 105.

[29] Ibid., pp. 106–7.

conforms to this pattern, although he writes, "Wherever there is a possibility of it, a cross-cousin marriage will be arranged . . ."[30] Malinowski believes that cross-cousin marriage (which results in matrilocal or uxorilocal residence in this culture) represents a compromise between the conflicting principles of mother-right and father-love,[31] but this is an unlikely idea, at least as a general principle, since cross-cousin marriage is found in so many different kinds of societies, including patrilineal ones.

There are other individuals beside those betrothed in infancy who do not experience the traditional Trobriand sexual freedom. Chiefs and other men of high rank may have plural wives. A chief takes a wife from each subclan in the villages of his territory, his wealth stemming from the fact that all of his brothers-in-law contribute to his store of yams. The chief of Kiriwina, for example, had 60 wives and received from 300 to 350 tons of yams a year.[32] At the death of such a wife, her community of origin provides a substitute. These are among the prettiest girls in the village, for "the chief simply indicates which of the girls pleases him best, and, irrespective of her previous attachments, she is given to him."[33] These girls, then, are also removed from the life of the *bukumatula,* the bachelors' house, and from the girls' erotic expeditions to other villages. While intrigues occur among the younger wives of chiefs and their boyfriends, they may be punishable by death.[34] Not everyone, therefore, has an unrestricted sex life in childhood and adolescence in the Trobriand Islands. Those betrothed in infancy and the many wives of chiefs do not take part in the casual liaisons described by Malinowski. We do not know what percentage of the population was thus restricted. If a free sex life is given as a reason for the well-adjusted character of the Trobriands, what are we to say of those who do not experience it?

This brings us back to Malinowski's generalizations about the absence of neuroses and perversions among these people. These generalizations, it must be said, are based largely on impressions. Malinowski had no extensive psychiatric background, administered no psychological tests, employed no "depth interviews," and was not

---

[30] Ibid., p. 98. In the context of this passage it is not certain whether the statement is meant to apply only to chiefs or to others as well.

[31] Ibid., p. 101.

[32] Ibid., p. 132.

[33] Ibid., p. 137.

[34] Ibid., p. 140.

equipped to give the sort of medical or psychiatric examinations which might have revealed neurotic trends. Even though Malinowski lived a relatively long time among the Trobrianders, learned their language, and was a keenly perceptive person, he was probably not qualified to speak as a psychiatrist about the incidence of neurotic tendencies among them.

In *The Sexual Life of Savages* there are various indications of sadomasochistic behavior. Malinowski tells us that girls in the Trobriand Islands generally inflict a good deal of pain in their lovers by scratching, beating, or stabbing them before engaging in lovemaking. Apparently the young men do not object to this treatment but welcome it as evidence of love and temperament in their girl friends. Malinowski once had to dress the wound of a Trobriand boy who had received a deep cut beneath his shoulder blades. The girl, who had struck harder than she realized, was very concerned about the wound, but the young man did not seem to mind, although he was obviously in pain. Malinowski was told that the boy received his reward that same evening.[35] Apparently, women inflict more lacerations on men than the men do on women. Malinowski saw larger telltale scratches and wounds on men than on women.

Malinowski describes an erotic festival which was said to have been formerly celebrated in the Trobriands but suppressed in more recent years. It had not been held in about 20 years, at the time of the anthropologist's visit. However, Malinowski believes in the accuracy of the accounts given him. According to these reports, the women at this festival used to attack men and boys with shells, bamboo knives, pieces of obsidian, and small sharp axes. Again, the men do not seem to have objected to being cut up in this fashion; it was a sign of manliness and popularity to receive many gashes. A woman's aim, on this occasion, was to slash as many men as she could. A man's aim was to receive wounds from the more attractive women, from whom he would seek his reward. Malinowski tells us that sexual intercourse took place openly in public on this occasion.[36]

Even if this alleged festival were only a fantasy of Malinowski's informants, the nature of the fantasy is instructive. There are also Trobriand traditions, or fantasies, about gangs of sexually ravenous women in distant villages who attack men, passing strangers, and

---

[35] Ibid., p. 257.
[36] Ibid.

subject them to violent sexual indignities.[37] It is women, incidentally, who are feared as witches in this society.[38]

In Malinowski's description of Trobriand lovemaking, he refers to biting and scratching as part of the erotic techniques employed. As mentioned above, it is the woman who inflicts the greater wounds. The man, however, bites off the woman's eyelashes during intercourse. Malinowski says that this is done "tenderly"; so perhaps there is nothing sadistic about this practice.[39] Malinowski does acknowledge that there may be some sadistic and masochistic elements in the erotic behavior of the Trobriand Islanders; but he says that flagellation as an erotic practice is unknown and that he does not consider the Trobriand lovemaking practices to be perversions. Here agreement or disagreement with Malinowski would depend upon one's definition of "sadism" and "perversion."[40]

It may be noted that a recurrent motif in the folktales presented by Malinowski is the cutting off of a woman's clitoris.[41] There are also stories of self-castration by men.[42] Why should such motifs appear in a society of genitally adequate people who lack neurotic traits? If stories of this sort were generally found in all, or most, human cultures, their presence might not seem unusual. But according to Clyde Kluckhohn, who made a survey of the mythology of 50 cultures with a widely scattered distribution, following Murdock's six major cultural regions, there were only four cases from all the material he surveyed where actual castration was mentioned. One of these was the Trobriand self-inflicted castration.[43]

---

[37] Ibid., pp. 274–79, 422–25.

[38] Ibid., pp. 45–46. See also Malinowski, *Magic, Science and Religion and Other Essays*, pp. 152–53.

[39] Ibid., *The Sexual Life of Savages*, p. 475.

[40] It is interesting to note, incidentally, that the Normanby Islanders, a matrilineal people who live near the Trobrianders and who have a similar culture, are reported by Roheim to have strong sadomasochistic patterns. "Coitus itself is openly sadistic and masochistic. Both parties bite, scratch, and hit each other. This is done before and during the sexual act, but they will avoid it when somebody is in the house and they do not want to make a noise. We have here one of the most significant facts in understanding the psychology of these people, *they pretend to be so mild and they are so violent.* Cruelty is an outstanding character trait. Prisoners of war were made to walk up and down between two fires until they were gradually roasted. Their own kinsfolk who had the *rara* disease were buried alive. They would never bother to kill a turtle before getting it out of its shell or to kill a goat before skinning it." Roheim, *Psychoanalysis and Anthropology, Culture, Personality, and the Unconscious*, p. 175. (Roheim's italics).

[41] Ibid., pp. 406, 407, 408.

[42] Ibid., pp. 412, 415.

[43] Clyde Kluckhohn, "Recurrent Themes in Myths and Mythmaking," in Henry A. Murray (ed.), *Myth and Mythmaking* (New York: George Braziller, 1960), p. 52. See also William N. Stephens, *The Oedipus Complex. Cross-Cultural Evidence* (Glencoe, Ill.: The Free Press of Glencoe, 1962), p. 116.

To my mind, *The Sexual Life of Savages* presents data which show that the picture of Trobriand life presented in *Sex and Repression* is oversimplified. I also feel that the handling of the central question concerning the Oedipus complex is unsatisfactory and leaves the problem still unsettled.

It must be admitted, however, that Malinowski did demonstrate the point that sex may be differently regarded and expressed in other cultures, and that there may be variations in the structuring of the family romance. Anthropologists have since provided further illustrations of these themes. For example, among the Hopi there is a sexually tinged joking relationship between a boy and his "father's sisters," the female members of his father's clan. The husbands of such women affect to feel (or perhaps do feel) resentment and jealousy of the boy and may threaten to castrate him. Some examples of such behavior are given in Don Talayesva's autobiography.[44]

Curiously enough, there is also a sexual joking relationship between a boy and his father's sister among the Trobriand Islanders. Malinowski states that sexual intercourse would be permitted in this case, but it is not common because of the difference in age. (Nothing is said about the jealousy of the husband.) A paternal aunt's daughter, however, is a preferred sexual and marriage partner. Among the Trobrianders a man should not simultaneously be in the presence of both a sister and a paternal aunt, since the first is an inhibiting relationship and the second a relaxing one.[45]

In the writings of A. R. Radcliffe-Brown and Claude Lévi-Strauss, we find some suggested structural explanations for attitudes toward mother's brother and father's sister. In an essay on "The Mother's Brother in South Africa," Radcliffe-Brown pointed out that in different societies there may be two antithetical kinds of attitudes toward a mother's brother. In the one case, the mother's brother represents family authority and is feared and respected. In the second case, the nephew treats his maternal uncle with familiarity and may take liberties with him.[46] The first type is associated with matrilineal descent, the second with patrilineal descent. "In groups

---

[44] Leo W. Simmons (ed.), *Sun Chief. The Autobiography of a Hopi Indian* (New Haven, Conn.: Yale University Press, 1942), pp. 38–40, 76, 108.

[45] Malinowski, *The Sexual Life of Savages*, pp. 534–35. Here, again, Malinowski writes as though a boy had only one father's sister, just as he seems to have only one sister and one mother's brother.

[46] A. R. Radcliffe-Brown, "The Mother's Brother in South Africa," in A. R. Radcliffe-Brown, *Structure and Function in Primitive Society. Essays and Addresses* (Glencoe, Ill.: The Free Press, 1952), pp. 15–31.

where familiarity characterizes the relationship between father and son, the relationship between maternal uncle and nephew is one of respect; and where the father stands as the austere representative of family authority, it is the uncle who is treated with familiarity."[47]

In patrilineal societies, the mother's brother may be considered a "male mother" and is sometimes called by such a term. A young man in such a society may expect more indulgence from his mother than from his father, and this feeling may be extended to other members of her family and lineage, including the mother's brother. Similarly, the father's sister may be regarded as a kind of "female father" and must accordingly be regarded with deference and respect in a patrilineal society.[48] But in a matrilineal society, where the maternal uncle is head of the family, a more familiar, friendly attitude may be taken toward the father, and this attitude of indulgence may in turn be extended to his sister. This might account for the parallel attitudes toward the father's sister among the matrilineal Hopi and Trobriand Islanders. However, the Hopi do not seem to have the same kinds of attitudes toward the mother's brother as the Trobriand Islanders do, and they have matrilocal rather than avunculocal residence.

Another difference between these two matrilineal societies is that the Hopi do not have brother-sister avoidance, which is such an important feature of Trobriand social life. In this respect the Hopi seem to be atypical of matrilineal societies. Of 15 matrilineal societies studied by David M. Schneider, Kathleen Gough, and their associates, 12 are known to have taboos affecting brother-sister relationships, apart from the incest taboo. The main exceptions are the Hopi and the Ashanti of West Africa. Gough offers as a possible partial explanation for this the fact that among the Hopi and Ashanti brothers-in-law seldom co-reside. Brother-sister taboos seem to be strictest among the Minangkabau of Indonesia and the Nayars of central Kerala, India, where brothers share a joint household with their sisters and often have contact with their sisters' husbands. In both cases, brothers are not allowed to enter their sisters' rooms.[49]

There seem to be many variations as well as parallels among matrilineal societies. They do not all share the features which

---

[47] Claude Lévi-Strauss, *Structural Anthropology,* trans. from the French by Claire Jacobson and Brooke Grundfest Schoepf (New York: Doubleday & Co., 1967) , p. 39.

[48] Radcliffe-Brown, "The Mother's Brother in South Africa," pp. 19–20.

[49] Kathleen Gough, "Variation in Interpersonal Kinship Relationships," in David M. Schneider and Kathleen Gough (eds.) , *Matrilineal Kinship* (Berkeley, Calif.: University of California Press, 1961) , pp. 598–99.

Malinowski described for the Trobriand Islanders. The role of the mother's brother varies in different matrilineal societies. It appears to be strong among the Ashanti, the Nayars, and to some extent among the Plateau Tonga, but the maternal uncle does not seem to figure prominently in the everyday life of the Navaho Indians.[50] Thus the "matrilineal complex" proposed by Malinowski cannot apply generally to matrilineal societies, although they often do have brother-sister avoidance and other parallel features.

Sex and Repression was the first important study to test Freudian propositions in a nonliterate non-Western society. Moreover, Malinowski pointed to some possible areas of culture-and-personality research for the future. He claimed that the Amphlett Islanders differed from the neighboring Trobrianders in some respects. "Though matrilineal," he remarked of the former group, "they have a much more developed patriarchal authority and this, combined with the sexual repressiveness, establishes a picture of childhood more similar to our own."[51]

In yet another group, the patrilineal Mailu, there was a still greater strictness and the presence of people whom Malinowski classed as neurasthenic. Recognition of such variations led Malinowski to formulate an imaginative proposal of research:

The problem would . . . be: to study a number of matrilineal and patriarchal communities of the same level of culture, to register the variation of sexual repression and of the family constitution, and to note the correlation between the amount of sexual and family repression and the prevalence of hysteria and compulsion neurosis. The conditions in Melanesia, where side by side we find communities living under entirely different conditions, are like a naturally arranged experiment for this purpose.[52]

Malinowski had a remarkable knack for asking significant questions. Here he foreshadowed, to some extent, the Linton-Kardiner concept of "basic personality structure."[53]

---

[50] Schneider and Gough, *Matrilineal Kinship*, pp. 84, 169–70, 291.

[51] Malinowski, *Sex and Repression*, p. 86.

[52] Ibid., p. 89.

[53] It is unfortunate that Malinowski's picture of Trobriand life has sometimes been assumed to be characteristic of matrilineal peoples in general, as if the Trobriand Islanders represented a stage in man's cultural evolution, before the development of a sexually repressive stage of patriliny. Misleading notions of this sort are expressed in the writings of Wilhelm Reich and Erich Fromm. See Wilhelm Reich, *Character-Analysis*, Theodore P. Wolfe, trans. (3d enlarged ed.; New York: Orgone Institute Press, 1949), p. xxiv; and *The Mass Psychology of Fascism* (3d ed.; New York: Orgone Institute Press, 1946), p. 73 ff; Erich Fromm, *The Sane Society* (New York: Rinehart, 1955), p. 44 ff.; "The Oedipus Complex and the Oedipus Myth" in Ruth Nanda Ans-

SUGGESTIONS FOR FURTHER READING

The Oedipus complex will be discussed further in Chapter 8. For the titles of Malinowski's other works on the Trobriands, see footnote 4 of this chapter. A brief general description of Trobriand culture may be found in Elman R. Service, *A Profile of Primitive Culture* (New York: Harper & Bros., 1958), pp. 222–42.

For more on the problem of the universality of the Oedipus complex and local variations thereof, see Anne Parsons, "Is the Oedipus Complex Universal? The Jones-Malinowski Debate Revisited," in Anne Parsons, *Belief, Magic, and Anomie. Essays in Psychosocial Anthropology* (New York: The Free Press, 1969), pp. 3–66.

Twenty-five years after his death, a diary kept by Malinowski during his Trobriand fieldwork was published: Bronislaw Malinowski, *A Diary in the Strict Sense of the Term* (New York: Harcourt, Brace, & World, 1967). It is of interest because it shows that Malinowski surprisingly enough, had intolerant, prejudiced attitudes toward the natives. It might also be deduced that Malinowski had something of an Oedipus complex, judging from some of the entries: "At last I begin to feel a deep, strong longing for [Mother] in my innermost being." (p. 22); "Main interests in life: Kipling, occasionally strong yearning for Mother—really, if I could keep in communication with Mother I would not mind anything and my low spirits would have no deep foundation." (p. 41); "Mother is the only person I care for really and am truly worried about." (p. 52). But the biggest surprise in this diary, perhaps, is to learn that Malinowski hated doing fieldwork. "As for ethnology: I see the life of the natives as utterly devoid of interest or importance, something as remote from me as the life of a dog." (p. 167) "Ethnographical problems don't preoccupy me at all. At bottom I am living outside of Kiriwina, although strongly hating the *niggers*." (p. 264)

The reader of Malinowski's voluminous ethnographic works would never infer such attitudes on the author's part. It is a tribute to his determination and hard work that Malinowski was able to accomplish so much in spite of his depression and malaise. For an interesting review of this diary, see Clifford Geertz, "Under the Mosquito Net," *The New York Review*, September 14, 1967, pp. 12–13. For some rejoinders to Geertz by loyal students of Malinowski who protest that the diary gives a misleading impression of the man, see letters to *The New York Review* by Hortense Powdermaker and Ashley Montagu, November 9, 1967, pp. 36–37.

---

hen, (ed.), *The Family; Its Function and Destiny* (rev. ed., New York: Harper & Bros., 1959), pp. 420–48; and *The Forgotten Language, An Introduction to the Understanding of Dreams, Fairy Tales, and Myths* (New York: Rinehart, 1951), chap. 7.

The dour Dobu are matrilineal. So were the Ashanti of West Africa, who insisted upon virginity in their brides, severely punished adultery, and inflicted the death penalty for various sexual offenses. The Nuer of the Upper Nile River, on the other hand, are patrilineal, but allow a good deal of experimental lovemaking before marriage, and there are many patrilineal peoples in northeastern India which take an indulgent view of premarital relations between boys and girls. The Todas of South India, famous for their lax sexual mores, are also patrilineal.

chapter *6*

Margaret Mead's
From the South Seas

Margaret Mead has been one of the most influential and widely read contributors to the field of culture-and-personality. Her three best known works, the subject of this chapter, have been brought out together in one volume under the title *From the South Seas*. This trilogy comprises *Coming of Age in Samoa* (1928), *Growing Up in New Guinea* (1930), and *Sex and Temperament in Three Primitive Societies* (1935).[1] With these books Mead introduced a new pattern into American anthropology—fieldwork centered about a problem. The traditional fieldwork of the Boas school in which Mead received her training had been all encompassing, with the ethnographer noting down everything that he could about the culture he was studying. Franz Boas, realizing that primitive cultures in different parts of the world were giving way under the impact of modern Western civilization, wanted anthropologists to get out and record as much as possible about them while there was still time. While Mead has published some ethnographic reports in this tradition, her best known works have been directed to questions which have some relevance to our own life.

COMING OF AGE IN SAMOA

Boas himself deserves some credit for this deviation from his own approach, for he helped to suggest and to discuss Mead's research

---

[1] Margaret Mead, *From the South Seas. Studies of Adolescence and Sex in Primitive Societies* (New York: William Morrow & Co., 1939).

129

problems with her before she went to Samoa on her first field trip. In a letter of 1925, Boas wrote:

One question that interests me very much is how the young girls react to the restraints of custom. We find very often among ourselves during the period of adolescence a strong rebellious spirit that may be expressed in sullenness or in sudden outbursts. In other individuals there is a weak submission which is accompanied, however, by a suppressed rebellion that may make itself felt in peculiar ways, perhaps in a desire for solitude which is really an expression of desire for freedom, or otherwise in forced participation in social affairs in order to drown the mental troubles. I am not at all clear in my mind in how far similar conditions may occur in primitive society and in how far the desire for independence may be simply due to our modern conditions and to a more strongly developed individualism.[2]

Coming of Age in Samoa was concerned with this relationship between adolescence and culture. In it, Mead asked the question: "Are the disturbances which vex our adolescents due to the nature of adolescence itself or to the civilization?"[3] We tend to think of adolescence as a time of emotional conflict and rebellion against authority. Is such a state of affairs due to the physiological changes occurring at puberty, or is it largely brought about by certain social and cultural conditions in our society? If the former alternative is true, adolescence should present similar characteristics in all cultures. If it does not do so, the social and cultural conditions would seem to be the more significant determinants.

To answer these questions, Mead lived for nine months in Samoa, studying 50 girls in three small neighboring villages. She found, in brief, that adolescence was not a difficult period for Samoan girls. This was partly because of the generally casual nature of the society. Among these people, according to Mead, there is a lack of deep feeling or involvement. Children grow up in family units where there are many adult figures, and their emotional relations to others become diffuse and relatively shallow. Premarital sexual relationships are accepted naturally, but with little emotional investment in the partner. The facts of life—birth, sex, and death—are learned at an early age and are not hedged about with secrecy. Samoan life, moreover, lacks the confusing alternatives found in the United States, where an adolescent must choose between a host of ideologies, political doctrines, religious tenets, standards of morality,

---

[2] Margaret Mead, *An Anthropologist at Work. Writings of Ruth Benedict* (Boston: Houghton Mifflin Co., 1959), p. 289.

[3] Mead, *Coming of Age in Samoa* (in *From the South Seas*), p. 11.

and occupational choices. Thus adolescence in Samoa is not characterized by tension, emotional conflict, or rebellion. The source of such characteristics in American youth must therefore lie in the social institutions and traditions of the Western world.

Coming of Age in Samoa in some ways recalls Malinowski's work. There is the same sense of problem, together with a literary skill which makes an exotic culture become vivid to the reader. One wonders, however, whether it was necessary, in dealing with the problem of physiological versus sociocultural factors affecting adolescence, to go to Samoa for an answer. Couldn't one simply have studied some adolescents in the United States instead? There must be some young people in this country who are relatively well adjusted and for whom adolescence involves no great upheaval. Such a group could be contrasted with a more maladjusted one, and an attempt made to see what significant sociocultural factors were involved in differentiating the two groups. Difficulties of learning a new language and establishing rapport in a strange culture would be obviated by an investigation of this sort, and it would be easier to study boys as well as girls. (For Mead's conclusions can have reference only to girls.) However, this is a minor quibble. Margaret Mead was an anthropologist, and anthropologists are expected to go to "primitive" cultures.

A more crucial question may also be raised. In Chapter XI Mead describes a few girls whom she calls "deviants" who did show evident conflicts. One wonders whether some of the other girls, although outwardly placid, might not have similarly harbored internal stresses and strains. Day-to-day interaction with these girls, even over a period of months, might not necessarily disclose emotional tensions. We have no Rorschach or Thematic Apperception Test records for them, for this study was made in the days before these tests became popular.

We do, however, have such projective tests for two rather similar cultures—Truk and Ifaluk in Micronesia. In Truk there is the same absence, as in Samoa, of Western socioeconomic complexity and division of labor. There is the same casualness and acceptance of sex, and there are also many similarities in the nature of family life and childhood experiences. Yet, according to Seymour B. Sarason, the Rorschach and Thematic Apperception Test records express a great deal of conflict over sex—more than one would find in a Western society.[4] This seems surprising in a society with premarital

---

[4] Thomas Gladwin and Seymour B. Sarason, *Truk: Man in Paradise* (New York: Viking Fund Publications in Anthropology, No. 20, 1953), p. 449.

sexual freedom. At any rate, it shows that such freedom does not obviate tension; nor does the simplicity of the socioeconomic order.

The same may be said of Ifaluk, as described by Melford E. Spiro. Here, again, premarital sexual activity is sanctioned, and life is leisurely and placid; there is little economic specialization, the climate is quite pleasant, and there is little need for long or strenuous work.

Ifaluk social structure seems to evoke as little conflict or anxiety as its physical setting. Absent from its economic system are important inequalities in, and social classes based on, wealth. . . . Absent, too, is economic competition, either for subsistence or for prestige goals.[5]

The Ifaluk ethos stresses kindliness, cooperation, generosity, and peaceful behavior. Nevertheless, according to Spiro, there are indications of tension and hostility in Ifaluk, manifest in the concepts about ghosts, in legends, in the content of dreams collected by Spiro, in Thematic Apperception Test protocols, and in various aspects of Ifaluk behavior. Spiro describes three cases of apparently psychogenic mental illness, in which the underlying tensions of Ifaluk culture are most clearly expressed.

The data from Truk and Ifaluk show that in an easygoing "simple" culture there may still be stresses and strains, not always readily discernible, but manifest in certain areas. The use of projective tests helps to indicate their presence in these two studies. The point made here is that a similar condition may have been true of Mead's community in Manu'a.

Incidentally, based on her observations of chimpanzee behavior, Jane van Lawick-Goodall has written that "Adolescence is a difficult and frustrating time for some chimpanzees just as it is for some humans. Possibly it is worse for males, in both species."[6] Older, more mature male chimpanzees are quick to punish signs of insubordination in adolescents. Van Lawick-Goodall writes that nearly all the adolescent males she had known spent long periods of hours or even days away from the rest of the group.

In an appendix to *Coming of Age in Samoa*, Dr. Mead listed all the cases she learned of in Manu'a of mentally defective and mentally ill people. From these figures Ellen Winston has estimated the rate of mental disorder to be 100 per 100,000 population. Winston esti-

---

[5] Melford E. Spiro, "Cultural Heritage, Personal Tensions, and Mental Illness in a South Sea Culture;" in Marvin K. Opler, (ed.), *Culture and Mental Health. Cross Cultural Studies* (New York: Macmillan Co., 1959), p. 144.

[6] Jane van Lawick-Goodall, *In the Shadow of Man* (Boston, Mass.: Houghton Mifflin Co., 1971), p. 173.

mates the rate in rural areas in the United States to be about the same.[7] In view of these estimates, one wonders whether the picture of a tension-free Samoa may not, to some extent, be a projection or wish-image.[8]

Another kind of question is also suggested by *Coming of Age in Samoa.* In most of Mead's account we get the impression that she is describing a traditional and relatively unchanging "primitive" culture. Christianity has been taken over, to be sure, together with some other trappings of Western civilization, but these have been rather minor in their effects, mainly having the consequence of making the lives of the people more comfortable.[9] Yet in some passages, principally in an appendix, Mead presents evidence of far-reaching cultural changes in this area. We learn that, formerly, household heads had life and death powers over their family members and that girls could be punished for sexual lapses by being severely beaten or having their heads shaved. Upon the marriage of girls of high rank a defloration ceremony was performed to test the bride's chastity. The authority of household heads has since been broken by the American legal system and missionary teachings; beatings and head shavings have been discouraged, and the defloration ceremony is now forbidden by law.[10]

There have been sweeping changes in other areas of Samoan life as well. Formerly all young men were tattooed, an important *rite de passage,* before which a youth was not considered an adult and could not marry or go to war.[11] Warfare was an important activity for young men, a source of power and prestige—and status considerations were of great importance in Samoa. This warfare was characterized by some rather curious formal behavior—courtesy rituals between opposing armies before the affray—, but the fighting was real

---

[7] Ellen Winston, "The Alleged Lack of Mental Diseases among Primitive Groups," *American Anthropologist,* Vol. 36 (1934), pp. 236–37.

[8] A newspaper item informs us that ulcers are very common in Samoa. According to Dr. Lawrence Winter, who spent two years as director of medical services in American Samoa, ulcers are one of the most common reasons for surgery there. However, this may be due to diet rather than to psychosomatic factors. *The Milwaukee Journal,* March 13, 1961.

[9] Mead, *Coming of Age in Samoa,* p. 277.

[10] Ibid., pp. 98, 273–74. However, Holmes cites the description of such a ceremony which took place as late as 1952. See Lowell D. Holmes, *Ta'u. Stability and Change in a Samoan Village* (Wellington, New Zealand: Reprint of the Polynesian Society, No. 7, 1958), p. 53.

[11] George Turner, *Samoa a Hundred Years Ago and Long Before* (London: Macmillan Co., Ltd., 1884), p. 88; William Green, "Living Conditions among Samoans," *Journal of Applied Sociology,* Vol. 9 (1924), p. 39.

and earnest enough.[12] Ritual tattooing and warfare have by now been put down by the white authorities. This may make Samoan living conditions more "comfortable," but it does involve a profound change in the way of life of these people. Many former sources of prestige and excitement for young men have been disallowed. The former class of master craftsmen has vanished through the introduction of modern technology. Long sea voyages by canoe have been given up and large canoes are no longer made. Much of the old social and ritual life has disappeared. Keesing wrote, as of 1930:

> The *taupo* system, by which the ceremonial life of each community revolves around the person of a village virgin, is passing: chiefs who are entitled by tradition to the honor of having a *taupo* find the entertainments connected with the position too costly; again, due to the breakdown of the old order, the marriage of such maidens has lost its former value in securing political alliances and economic and ceremonial advantages; the missions have discouraged the custom as heathen, preferring the unmarried and unattached women who formed in the old days the *taupo's* entourage (*aualuma*) and slept together in her house, to live at home or in the pastor's house; the old women find guarding and caring for her a burden.[13]

The social world of both men and women, then, has greatly changed from "aboriginal" Samoan conditions. The navy, the missions, and the schools have largely brought about these changes. In 1911 school attendance was made compulsory for all children between the ages of 6 and 13.[14]

Niels W. Braroe, from whose paper the references to Turner, Brown, and Keesing have been drawn, has suggested that the Samoan personality, as depicted by Margaret Mead, shows the effects of these culture changes. A kind of apathy, he believes, has resulted from the processes of acculturation. "If we define apathy as 'want of feeling or affect' and indifference, then the materials presented by Mead indicate that we may characterize Samoan personality and behavior in these terms."[15] As evidence for a condition of apathy Braroe points to Mead's reports that Samoans do not engage in strong friendships or in any social ties which generate deep emotions.[16] As

---

[12] George Brown, *Melanesians and Polynesians, Their Life-Histories Described and Compared* (London: Macmillan Co., Ltd., 1910), pp. 164–76. See also Turner, *Samoa, a Hundred Years Ago and Long Before*, p. 192 ff.

[13] Felix M. Keesing, *Modern Samoa* (Stanford, Calif.: Stanford University Press, 1934), p. 142. See also Mead, *Coming of Age in Samoa*, p. 77.

[14] Holmes, *Ta'u*, p. 72.

[15] Niels W. Braroe, "Acculturation and Personality in Samoa," Typescript ms., p. 7.

[16] On this point, see the supporting statements in Holmes, *Ta'u*, p. 45.

has been noted, there is a casual attitude toward life; no one plays for high stakes or fights for any convictions or particular goals. Mead has also described the Samoans as being very submissive to the aggression of others.[17] These characteristics do not seem to have been applicable to the precontact culture.

While Braroe's characterization of some of the above-mentioned traits as "apathetic" may be open to question. I think that his suggestion is worth considering. We know that some Polynesian peoples have been profoundly upset emotionally by the disappearance of their old way of life. The Marquesans, Linton tells us, now refuse to breed. "This was a perfectly deliberate measure, the people preferring extinction to subjection. I visited many villages populated entirely by persons of early middle age to old age with not a single child in the group. On Tahuata, the island next to the one on which I was living, there were over two hundred deaths for every birth."[18] For Samoa, itself, William Green has observed, "A prevalent lethargy seems to have taken the place of the old wars. The games partly supply the need, but doubtless, life has less zest today than in days gone by."[19]

Thus, the shallow emotional relationships reported by Mead may be related to the collapse of an old way of life. The premarital sexual freedom of former days may have had a somewhat different character from that described by Mead. Robert W. Williamson has suggested that immorality was not so general in Samoa as some writers have made it out to be. He believes that some "retrogression" may have taken place in Samoan sexual mores.[20] Keesing also speaks of ". . . a general loosening up as regards the sexual conduct of young folk," and adds that "The old village system with its segregation of the young and unattached people (the *aualuma,* and the corresponding groups of youths and men, called *aumanga)* apparently put certain constraints upon the mingling of the sexes that are now gone." [21]

---

[17] See Mead, *Coming of Age in Samoa,* chap. ix, "The Attitude toward Personality," pp. 122–30.

[18] Ralph Linton, "Marquesan Culture," in Abram Kardiner, *The Individual and His Society, The Psychodynamics of Primitive Social Organization* (New York: Columbia University Press, 1939), pp. 137–38.

[19] William Green, "Social Traits of Samoans," *Journal of Applied Sociology,* Vol. 9 (1925), p. 134.

[20] Robert W. Williamson, *Essays in Polynesian Ethnology,* ed. by Ralph Piddington (Cambridge: Cambridge University Press, 1939), pp. 157, 186.

[21] Felix M. Keesing, "The System of Samoa, A Study of Institutional Change," *Oceania,* Vol. 8 (1937), p. 8.

Mead has herself suggested that young female sex delinquents had a harder time of it in aboriginal Samoa.[22]

The point made here, then, is that the picture of adolescent behavior presented in *Coming of Age in Samoa* should be seen in a particular historical context. Mead was aware of this context, but felt that the historical changes in the recent past were irrelevant for her purposes.[23] Hence a consideration of them was left to the Appendix.

GROWING UP IN NEW GUINEA

Growing Up in New Guinea has the subtitle, *A Comparative Study of Primitive Education.* It deals with the upbringing of children among the Manus of the Admiralty Islands north of New Guinea. At the time of Mead's 1928 field trip, the Manus whom she studied were living in houses raised on stilts above the waters of a lagoon. They lived primarily by fishing and trading and had a kind of Protestant ethic—valuing property, hard work, and financial success.

Switching to the "ethnographic present," this is a society with a high infant mortality rate, but the children who survive are healthy, self-confident, and alert. They learn to swim at the age of three and soon thereafter are paddling about in little canoes. This freedom and mobility makes them relatively independent of adults. One rule is instilled at an early age: respect for property. Otherwise, children are left to their own devices. They eat, play, and sleep when they wish and do no work. Girls begin to perform some household chores after they are 11 or 12, but boys do hardly any work until they are married. Little deference is shown to parents or other adults.

According to Mead, Manus husband-wife relations are usually difficult and strained. Marriages are arranged by parents and entered upon with reluctance. Residence is virilocal, the bride being a stranger in her husband's home. When a child is born or adopted, the father at once takes a proprietary interest in it, and a closer bond develops between him and his child than between mother and child.

Manus children, however, live largely in a world of their age-mates. They spend their time in energetic play.

The adults give the children no story-telling pattern, no guessing games, riddles, puzzles. The idea that children would like to hear legends seems quite fantastic to a Manus adult. . . . Where we fill our children's

---

[22] Mead, *Coming of Age in Samoa,* p. 273.
[23] Ibid.

minds with a rich folklore, songs which personalize the sun, the moon, and the stars, riddles and fairy tales and myths, the Manus do nothing of the sort.[24]

Hence Manus children do not develop animistic concepts. A naturalistic view of the universe, says Mead, is as congenial to a child as a supernatural one. He accepts the view provided by his elders. Hence there is little imagination in Manus play. And since there are no children without playmates, there are no imaginary playmates. The children believe in spirits but ignore them.

Mead's conclusion is: "If the children's imaginations are to flourish, they must be given food. Although the exceptional child may create something of his own, the great majority of children will not even imagine bears under the bed unless the adult provides the bear."[25] Mead thus drew attention to the enriching qualities of cultural tradition. In Manus there is little interest in the arts, the emphasis of the culture being on practical success. Little contact exists, in any case, between adults and children. With marriage, the adult world finally begins to bear down upon the individual, and the carefree life of childhood is over.

In Growing up in New Guinea, Margaret Mead's unusual gifts—imagination, acute observation, and literary flair—find their fullest expression.[26]

SEX AND TEMPERAMENT

Sex and Temperament in Three Primitive Societies, the third in Mead's trilogy, deals with the influence of culture upon sex roles

---

[24] Mead, *Growing Up in New Guinea,* pp. 125, 130.

[25] Ibid., p. 258.
Wayne Dennis has taken issue with Margaret Mead's conclusion about the absence of animistic thinking in Manus children, arguing that the various tests given to the children to gauge animistic responses were inadequate for the purpose and did not make use of the methods developed by Jean Piaget to elicit animistic concepts in children. Dennis, who has given tests for animistic thinking among children in a number of different cultural settings, believes that animistic notions among children are probably worldwide. "It is likely that they develop out of universal experiences, such as the experiences of self-movement, of visual movement, of frustration and success, of sleeping and waking—experiences which are common to the children of all societies." Wayne Dennis, "Animism and Related Tendencies in Hopi Children," *Journal of Abnormal and Social Psychology,* Vol. 38 (1943), p. 33.

[26] In 1953 Mead revisited the Manus—25 years later. She found the culture extraordinarily changed. The Manus no longer live on the lagoon but have moved ashore. The people now wear clothing of European type. The old religion has entirely disappeared. This is described and discussed by Mead in *New Lives for Old. Cultural Transformations—1928–1953* (New York: William Morrow & Co., 1956). The reader interested in the Manus is also advised to consult Reo F. Fortune's interesting work, *Manus Religion* (Memoirs of the American Philosophical Association, Vol. III, 1935).

and attitudes. In the preface of a 1950 paperback reprint, Mead remarks that this is her most misunderstood book. Part of the misunderstanding seems to hinge on the central theme of the book. In the original 1935 Introduction, Mead wrote:

This study is not concerned with whether there are or are not actual and universal differences between the sexes either quantitative or qualitative.[27]

To the average reader, however, this seems to be just what the book is about. At any rate, in a concluding section of the book entitled "The Implication of These Results," Mead presents some generalizations:

The material suggests that we may say that many, if not all, of the personality traits which we have called masculine or feminine are as lightly linked to sex as are the clothing, the manners, and the form of head-dress that a society at a given period assigns to either sex.[28]

Again:

We are forced to conclude that human nature is almost unbelievably malleable, responding accurately and contrastingly to contrasting cultural conditions. The differences between individuals who are members of different cultures, like the differences between individuals within a culture, are almost entirely to be laid to differences in conditioning, especially during early childhood, and the form of this conditioning is culturally determined. Standardized personality differences between the sexes are of this order, cultural creations to which each generation, male and female, is trained to conform.[29]

Our conceptions of what constitute masculine or feminine characteristics, therefore, are the product of particular historical, cultural traditions, rather than of any innate biological differences between the sexes.[30]

Mead's conclusions about sex and temperament were based upon fieldwork done in three New Guinea tribes—the Arapesh, Mundugumor, and Tchambuli—all of whom live within a hundred mile area and yet show remarkable differences in culture and temperament. Among the Arapesh, Mead found that both men and women act in a mild, maternal, cooperative manner, behaving as we expect

[27] Mead, *Sex and Temperament in Three Primitive Societies,* p. viii,

[28] Ibid., p. 280.

[29] Ibid.

[30] However, in a reply to a review of *Sex and Temperament* Mead wrote ". . . nowhere do I suggest that I have found any material which disproves the existence of sex differences." Margaret Mead, "A Reply to a Review of *Sex and Temperament in Three Primitive Societies,*" *American Anthropologist,* Vol. 39 (1937), p. 559.

women to behave. Mundugumor men and women, on the other hand, are fierce and aggressive, behaving as we expect men to behave. Neither of these two cultures harbors assumptions about the existence of sex differences in temperament. But in the third tribe, the Tchambuli, there are clear-cut differences between men and women; only here we have a kind of parody in reverse of the situation in the United States. Tchambuli women, who are the food-providers, are described as being hearty, efficient, and comradely among themselves. "Solid, preoccupied, powerful, with shaven unadorned heads, they sit in groups and laugh together . . ."[31] The men, however, are principally concerned with art, with their hairdos, and their relationships with women.

About half the book deals with the Arapesh. Of the three, this was the culture in which Mead and Reo F. Fortune worked the longest and got to know best. Fortune paid a return visit in 1936. A number of publications by Fortune and by Mead about the Arapesh are available, so we have more to go on here than with the other two tribes.

In one of Mead's publications, there is an excellent account of the field methods employed in their work.[32] Although Mead has often been accused of subjective impressionism, it is evident that her standards of fieldwork are high; her dedication to the job, as revealed in this monograph, is certainly impressive. Nevertheless, as we shall see, there are weaknesses in her descriptions of the three tribes. Let us start with the Arapesh.

Mead tells us in *Sex and Temperament* that the Arapesh ". . . see all life as an adventure in growing things," and that "the duty of every man and women is to observe the rules, so that the children and the food upon which the children depend will grow. Men are as wholly committed to this cherishing adventure as are women. It may be said that the rôle of men, like the rôle of women, is maternal." As a chapter heading tells us, this is a Co-operative Society. Nine-tenths of a man's time is spent in responding to other people's appeals for assistance.[33]

---

[31] Mead, *Sex and Temperament,* p. 257.

[32] *The Mountain Arapesh, II. Supernaturalism* (Anthropological Papers of the American Museum of Natural History, Vol. 37, 1940, pp. 326–38).

[33] Ibid., pp. 14, 22. In a later publication, Mead wrote that the Arapesh should be characterized as "helpful" rather than as "cooperative," cooperation being defined as the sharing of a common end, in which the end is the essential goal, while helpfulness involves the activity of two or more persons toward an end conceived as belonging to only part of the group whom the others help. See Margaret Mead, *The Mountain*

Mead writes that warfare is practically unknown among the Arapesh. Their feelings toward a murderer and toward a man who kills in battle are not essentially different. No cult of military bravery exists. There are occasional brawls between villages over women who have been abducted, but ". . . abductions of women are really the result of marital disagreements and the formation of new personal attachments, and are not unfriendly acts on the part of the next community."[34]

This seems contradictory, especially since the same passage also refers to abductions as "unfriendly acts" which must be avenged.

In a brief paper Reo F. Fortune observes that warfare has been kept down since before 1914 by the colonial (originally German) administration. Thus, the absence of fighting does not necessarily express a peaceful maternal nature on the part of the men, since peace has been externally imposed. "A census of the war records of individual grey-headed old men revealed the fact that approximately 50% of them claimed one or more war homicides each to his credit."[35]

An externally imposed peace has also affected Mundugumor and Tchambuli life. In her description of the Mundugumor, Mead preferred to describe the life as it had been lived up to three years before she came to that area. The contrast between Arapesh and Mundugumor is therefore heightened by the fact that the Arapesh are described as of the postcolonial peace period, while the Mundugumor are described as of the precolonial period.[36]

In his article, "Arapesh Warfare," Fortune expresses doubt that the Arapesh expect a similar temperament in men and women. He cites a proverb, "Men's hearts are different; women's hearts are different," and mentions the existence of a class of men called *arama-gowem*—"women male," or effeminate men. "The class of *arama-*

Arapesh III. Socioeconomic Life, American Museum of Natural History Anthropological Papers, Vol. 40, Part 3, 1947, p. 205.

Mead has written elsewhere: "In only a very few instances is there genuine cooperation and these are mostly in the interests of the Tamberan cult." Margaret Mead, "The Arapesh of New Guinea," in *Cooperation and Competition among Primitive Peoples* M. Mead (ed.), (New York: McGraw-Hill Book Co., 1937), p. 36.

[34] Mead, *Sex and Temperament,* p. 23.

[35] Reo F. Fortune, "Arapesh Warfare," *American Anthropologist,* Vol. 41 (1939), p. 28.

[36] At the same time, the Pax Britannica must be credited with a large share in affecting the roles of men and women in Tchambuli life, since Tchambuli men have been deprived of some formerly traditional male pursuits. This should be kept in mind when considering Mead's description of the Tchambuli.

gowem is a definitely assigned class, with definite functions, given inferior food at feasts and special subordinate place."[37]

There is no socially organized class of masculine women, but there are stories about individual women who had taken part in warfare, one of whom was buried by the men's secret society with a warrior's honors.

Mead herself presents evidence that different expectations are held about the behavior of men and women. Boys are preferred to girls. If there are already a number of girls in a family, a newly born daughter may be killed. (Note that it is the *father* who makes this decision.) [38] Girls learn to control their fits of rage much earlier than little boys, who may still have temper tantrums at 15 without a sense of shame. (One wonders, incidentally, why the children of such maternal parents would have temper tantrums. Temper tantrums among the children in Alor, as we shall see later, are attributed by Kardiner and Du Bois to maternal neglect.) "Furthermore," observes Mead, "as it is considered appropriate for big men to simulate anger and defiance in their public speeches, to wield a spear, stamp their feet, and shout, the little boy has a model of violent expression before him that the little girl lacks . . ."[39] The men are described as being more restless than the women and given to traveling about on visits to relatives—a source of jesting reproach by the women.

Girls are described as having less curiosity than boys.

A habit of intellectual passivity falls upon them, a more pronounced lack of intellectual interest than that which characterizes their brothers' minds. All that is strange, that is uncharted and unnamed—unfamiliar sounds, unfamiliar shapes—these are forbidden to women, whose duty it is to guard their reproductivity closely and tenderly. This prohibition cuts them off from speculative thought and likewise from art.[40]

When Mead showed them a brown life-sized doll, the women shrank away from it in fright, thinking it a corpse, but the men recognized the doll as a mere representation.

Mead writes: "The whole organization of society is based upon the analogy between children and wives as representing a group who are younger, less responsible than the men, and therefore to be

---

[37] Fortune, "Arapesh Warfare," p. 36.
[38] Mead, *Sex and Temperament,* p. 32.
[39] Ibid., pp. 51–52.
[40] Ibid., p. 70.

guided."[41] This sounds like a very important assertion of different expectations concerning the sexes in this society.

Mead mentions several cases of men beating their wives, but only one of a woman beating a man. It is men who fight over women and capture women from other communities, not vice versa. Polygyny, not polyandry, is practiced.

In a critical review of *Sex and Temperament*, R. Thurnwald wrote:

The author tries to picture Arapesh society as an idyll of "no violent, no possessive individuals, a people incapable of developing the ego" (73, 141–2, 310). The true Arapesh society seems, however, to be a bit different, according to the author's own report. We hear of screaming boys and violent children (50, 143, 145), of the drama of sex relations (112–4), of quarrels over women (79), of temper fits (153), man and wife attacking each other with axes (161), of violent half-brothers (153), of men beating their wives (147, 151, 153), of a woman beating her husband (149), of a quarrel which followed the abduction of a woman (137–8), of a mother trying to strangle her baby and stepping on the head of another (151), and of a brother trying to use force upon his sister (150). After the description of a quarrel the author says: "this gives a fair picture of the violent, unreasonable rages to which persons like Agilapwe (a man) were subject" (160).[42]

Much of the behavior cited by Thurnwald is drawn from a chapter on those who "deviate" from the Arapesh ideal. But as Thurnwald points out, their percentage is not recorded. This is the same problem that comes up in *Coming of Age in Samoa,* where exceptions to Mead's generalizations are dealt with in a chapter on "deviants." Mead does not hide or skirt seemingly contradictory information. By tagging it with the label of "deviancy" she brings it under control. To what extent, however, are the tensions manifest by "deviants" shared by other members of the society?

Mead's answer to Thurnwald on the question of percentages is that under conditions of cultural breakdown, ". . . practically every individual of a given age and sex may become in his own mind, and in the opinion of the community, a deviant."[43] Deviants are people who fail to exhibit the approved personality of the culture. If the majority fails to manifest it, then the majority is deviant.[44] Questions

[41] Ibid., p. 81.

[42] R. Thurnwald, Review of *Sex and Temperament in Three Primitive Societies,* in *American Anthropologist,* Vol. 38 (1936), pp. 558–61.

[43] Margaret Mead, "A Reply to a Review of *Sex and Temperament in Three Primitive Societies,*" *American Anthropologist,* Vol. 39 (1937), p. 558.

[44] See Margaret Mead, *The Changing Culture of an Indian Tribe* (Columbia University Contributions to Anthropology, Vol. XV, New York, 1932), p. 93.

of percentage are therefore irrelevant, since deviants do not have to be a minority group. Besides, Mead asserts, "Researches which depend upon statistical validation cannot be carried out among primitive peoples under the existing conditions of work."[45]

Apparently Mead's way of studying a culture involves finding out the rules of the game, then looking to see whether these rules are broken. Thus, she is able to write of some Arapesh as follows:

These aberrants' own misunderstanding of their culture was further aggravated by the existence of very stupid people among themselves—such as Menala, who further complicated Wabe's life by accusing him of a willful act of violence that had actually been carried out in strict accord with the rules of the culture, in which he had co-operated with her brothers in breaking up a marriage of which they disapproved.[46]

Again:

Persons like Wabe and Agilapwe, Amitoa and Temos, by their conspicuous aberrancy serve to distort for growing children the picture of Arapesh life. . . . The picture of a gentle community in which all men are loving relatives is not quite so vivid to the little boy who has just seen his mother bind up Yaluahaip's wound. The quiet responsive non-initiatory nature of men and women is blurred by those who watch Amitoa take an ax to Baimal, or Wabe beat both his wives and declare that he wishes he was rid of the pair of them.[47]

Mead evidently has a Platonic ideal conception of the culture as it should be. Although some members of the society evidently do not understand their own culture and thus confuse matters, Mead is able to make out its true form through the distortions of actual life. This Platonism is paradoxical in an ethnographer who has such a keen eye for immediate realities.

The Mundugumor, the next tribe discussed by Mead, are described as being violent, aggressive, and mistrustful cannibals. Unlike the situation in many parts of New Guinea, there is no village with a central plaza and men's clubhouse; there is no real community. Family groups, some polygynous, live in palisaded compounds, whose location the members try to keep secret. These isolated family units are rife with tension, since there is traditional hatred between brothers and between fathers and sons. "Between brothers," Mead tells us, "there is only one possible form of close contact; they can fight each other and abuse each other publicly."[48]

---

[45] Mead, "A Reply to a Review . . . ," p. 559.

[46] Mead, *Sex and Temperament,* p. 154.

[47] Ibid., pp. 160–61.

[48] Ibid., p. 177.

A man is supposed to get a wife through brother-sister exchange—by giving his sister to someone in exchange for the other's sister. But a man may also trade off his daughter for an additional wife for himself. Anxious mothers keep warning their sons that the father may thus deprive the boy of a future wife. According to Mead, the pattern of hostility between brothers and between father and son is repeated in every family group in varying degrees.[49]

However, Mead cites a Mundugumor saying, "He was not strong, he had no brothers," and tells us that the phrase "a man who has brothers" often occurs in their remarks, "and this means a man who, by a stroke of luck, has some weak-willed docile brothers who will follow his lead, and instead of disputing his progress will form a more or less permanent constellation about him in his middle age."[50] So apparently there is sometimes cooperation between brothers, although Mead labels such cooperative individuals as deviants. At any rate, perhaps there should be some modification in the statement that "between brothers there is only one possible form of close contact; they can fight each other and abuse each other publicly."

Mead says that a wife who has become pregnant hurts a man at his most vulnerable spot: ". . . she has taken the first step toward his downfall by possibly conceiving a son. And for herself, she has shifted her husband's active sexual interest into angry frustrated resentment—for what? Possibly to bear a daughter, who will be her husband's, not hers."[51]

But Mead tells us that a man desires a daughter, the woman a son. And we learn that adoption is a very common practice, with girls being adopted more often than boys. In such cases "the wife is compensated for this by the better relationship to her husband."[52]

The practice of adoption indicates at least some interest in children. "Even women who have never borne children are able in a few weeks, by placing the child constantly at the breast and by drinking plenty of coconut milk, to produce enough or nearly enough milk to rear the child, which is suckled by other women for the first few weeks after adoption."[53]

Could one say, then, that these people show strong maternal ten-

---

[49] Ibid., p. 180.
[50] Ibid., pp. 191, 225.
[51] Ibid., p. 191.
[52] Ibid., p. 193.
[53] Ibid., p. 193.

dencies? Apparently not, for Mead goes on, in the next few pages, to describe a frustrated, loveless childhood, and makes some contrasts with the Arapesh: "if an Arapesh child that has been weaned for several years is screaming wth pain or fright, the mother will offer her slack, dry breast to comfort it; the Mundugumor mother will not even offer a still suckling child her full one."[54] The weaning process is accompanied by cross words and blows.

However, the picture is not all black, for we learn that there are some adults who are fond of children. "Within every child's circle of kin there are likely to be one or two of these persons, a mild unassuming paternal uncle, or some remarried widow who lives a quiet, unaggressive life, not competing with her co-wives or thinking it worthwhile to be disagreeable to their children."[55] If relationships between the parents and such kind persons are strained, the child may not be allowed to visit them. But perhaps these kind persons have children? At any rate, if every child knows one or two such people, there must be a fair number of well-disposed deviants in this society, although not enough, evidently, to modify Mead's grim picture.

Because of Margaret Mead's way with words, her books are much more readable than the standard ethnographic monograph. But her literary approach carries certain dangers. Like an official guided tour, it leads the reader to view the culture in a particular way. This is most evident in Mead's description of the Tchambuli.

Here Mead does not give us the news straight; she editorializes throughout, with her conclusions being constantly imbedded in the ethnographic description. For example:

All that remains to the individual Tchambuli man, with his delicately arranged curls, his handsome pubic covering of a flying fox-skin highly ornamented with shells, his mincing step and self-conscious mien, is the sense of himself as an actor, playing a series of charming parts—this and his relationships to the women.

. . . each man sits daintily in his own place and observes his companions narrowly.

. . . the men moving self-consciously, abashed to eat, among the crowds of smiling, unadorned, efficient women.

. . . in a group of men there is always strain, watchfulness, a catty remark here, a *double entendre* there.[56]

---

54 Ibid., p. 196.
55 Ibid., p. 200.
56 Ibid., pp. 248, 239, 241, 253.

Of course, it is hard to be objective in the description of behavior. What one observer characterizes as "mincing" might be differently interpreted or phrased by another.

Jessie Bernard has raised some pertinent questions about this account of the Tchambuli:

> Would everyone who saw what Miss Mead saw agree with the observations upon which she based these conclusions? . . . would everyone agree that women who devoted themselves cheerfully, happily, and efficiently to feeding and nursing children, growing and cooking food, to plaiting mosquito nets, women whose attitudes toward men were kindly, tolerant, and appreciative (p. 255), were masculine? I for one found myself constantly confused between the facts Miss Mead reported and the interpretations she made of them. I would not consider Tchambuli men effeminate on the basis of the data she presents, nor do the women she describes seem masculine. . . . even accepting Miss Mead's observations as valid, one can come to exactly opposite conclusions to those she arrives at. For example, Miss Mead concludes that temperament is not sex-linked (pp. 164, 280, 282 *passim*) but that it is overwhelmingly cultural. A skeptic, accepting her data, might argue to the contrary: that the reversion of cultural roles among the Tchambuli violated the natural masculine temperament to such a degree that the men were prone to neuroticism. For, as she informs us, Tchambuli "men are the conspicuous maladjusts, subject to neurasthenia, and maniacal outbursts" (p. 275). She found more neurotic males than in any other primitive culture she has studied.[57]

It is probably because of such criticisms by Bernard and by Thurnwald that Mead referred to *Sex and Temperament* as her most misunderstood book. To some critics, the three cultures seemed to provide ready-made demonstrations for a point of view which Mead must have held in the first place. In her 1950 preface, Mead rejected such suspicions and claimed that "the seemingly 'too good to be true' pattern is actually a reflection of the form which lay in these cultures themselves."[58] More fieldwork in these tribes by other anthropologists—if it is not too late—would seem to be the only way to settle this problem.

Sex and Temperament, one can see in retrospect, reflected and also contributed to the environmentalist ideology characteristic of the 1930s. This was the period in which Marxism attracted many intellectuals and in which neo-Freudians like Horney and Fromm were emphasizing the importance of social and cultural factors af-

---

[57] Jessie Bernard, "Observation and Generalization in Cultural Anthropology," *American Journal of Sociology,* Vol. 50 (1945), pp. 285, 289. Copyright 1945 by the University of Chicago.

[58] Margaret Mead, *Sex and Temperament* (New York: Mentor Books, 1950), preface.

fecting personality. This stress on the cultural environment was part of the liberal tradition, influenced, among other currents, by the philosophy of John Dewey. Related to this tradition was the repudiation of racism, as manifest in the South's Jim Crowism and in Hitler's Nazi movement. This was a period, too, in which women were attaining more freedom and recognition in many fields; indeed a feminist stance is not hard to detect in the writings of Benedict and Mead.[59]

The three works which make up *From the South Seas* were beginnings in a new kind of undertaking. They were vigorous, imaginative, and influential books. If there were shortcomings in them, Mead was herself aware of the fact, for in the preface to the combined volume, she wrote:

They are pioneer studies made by a method which I myself shall not use again; my future work, like my past three years' work in Bali and among the Iatmul of New Guinea . . . will be cooperative, in which at least two, and sometimes as many as six observers, armed with modern methods of recording, typewriters, or stenotypes, miniature cameras and motion-picture cameras, will bring a battery of observation to bear upon the behavior of native children or native mothers.[60]

In later parts of this book we will deal with some of Mead's more recent work.[61]

SUGGESTIONS FOR FURTHER READING

Mead's bibliography is enormous and runs on for pages. Only a few books will be mentioned here: *The Changing Culture of an Indian Tribe* (1932) ; *And Keep Your Powder Dry* (New York: William Morrow & Co., 1942) ; *Male and Female* (New York: William Morrow & Co., 1949) ; *New Lives for Old, Cultural Transformation—Manus, 1928–1953* (1956) . For a fuller list see the Haring reader, Douglas G. Haring (ed.) , *Personal Character and Cultural Milieu. A Collection of Readings* (Syracuse, N.Y.: Syracuse University Press, 1949) , pp. 810–12.

For a retrospective review of her own work, see Margaret Mead, "Retrospects and Prospects," in Thomas Gladwin and William C. Sturtevant (eds.) , *Anthropology and Human Behavior* (Washington, D.C.: The Anthropological Society of Washington, 1962) , pp. 115–49.

---

[59] See Richard Chase, "Ruth Benedict: The Woman as Anthropologist," *Columbia University Forum,* Vol. 2, No. 3 (Spring 1959) , p. 21.

[60] Mead, *From the South Seas,* p. vii.

[61] See Chapters 11, 17.

chapter 7

The School of Linton, Kardiner, and Du Bois

By the late 1930s an increased interest in Freudian and Gestalt viewpoints could be noted in the United States. This was furthered by the influx of refugees from Nazi Germany. Neo-Freudians like Karen Horney, Erich Fromm, Franz Alexander, and Erik Homburger Erikson, and Gestaltists like Wertheimer, Koffka, Köhler, and others took up residence in this country. Their writings, perhaps especially those of Horney and Fromm, received a wide circulation. In this new intellectual atmosphere, the time was ready for revised theoretical approaches and improvements in methodology in the field of culture-and-personality. Some new approaches along these lines began to be threshed out in a seminar on culture-and-personality conducted by the psychiatrist Abram Kardiner in conjunction with a group of anthropologists. In 1936 and 1937, Kardiner and Cora Du Bois held a seminar at the New York Psychoanalytic Institute, at which Edward Sapir, Ruth Benedict, and Ruth Bunzel were guest lecturers.

After Ralph Linton came to Columbia University in 1937, he joined forces with Kardiner and the two held a joint seminar at the university which continued for several years. At these seminars it was the practice for some anthropologist to describe a culture in which he had done fieldwork, after which Kardiner would present an analytic interpretation which would then be discussed by the group. The first product of this seminar was an exploratory work, *The Individual and His Society* (1939), followed in 1945 by *The*

148

Psychological Frontiers of Society, in which Linton, Du Bois, and James West collaborated with Kardiner. Meanwhile Cora Du Bois published *The People of Alor* in 1944.

BASIC PERSONALITY STRUCTURE

A concept central to the whole investigation is that of "basic personality structure," which Kardiner defines as "the effective adaptive tools of the individual which are common to every individual in the society."[1] The concept applies only to particular societies, such as the Trobriand Islanders; its nature differs from one society to another.

Since Kardiner is a Freudian, albeit a modified one, he believes that the earliest years of life are crucial in forming the personality of an individual. Techniques of child-rearing, suckling, toilet training, sexual and other disciplines all profoundly influence the growing child in one direction or another. Now these techniques of raising children tend to be fairly standardized within a particular society. While there may be individual differences in various respects, by and large, women tend to suckle their children for about the same length of time as their neighbors do, feed them the same foods, and apply the same kinds of discipline. Therefore the children who grow up within a particular society pass through the same general gamut of childhood experiences. They are apt to react to such experiences in much the same ways and therefore develop many personality traits in common. As Linton has put it, "The *basic personality type for any society* is that personality configuration which is shared by the bulk of the society's members as a result of the early experiences which they have in common."[2]

One possible weakness in this formula is that, even if all the children of a society have the same kinds of early experiences, they would not necessarily all react to them in the same ways. There are constitutional differences among children, present at birth, and children also differ in their positions in the birth order of the family. These differentiating factors would have to be seen as subordinate by supporters of the basic personality approach.

---

[1] Abram Kardiner, with a Foreword and two Ethnological Reports by Ralph Linton, *The Individual and His Society, The Psychodynamics of Primitive Social Organization* (New York: Columbia University Press, 1939), p. 237.

[2] Abram Kardiner, with the collaboration of Ralph Linton, Cora Du Bois, and James West, *The Psychological Frontiers of Society* (New York: Columbia University Press, 1945), p. viii.

This approach is essentially a form of childhood determinism. Economic factors are taken into consideration, but primarily as they affect the family and childhood upbringing. Attention is directed to such matters as weaning, toilet training, and sexual disciplines. "If the character of the human mind is integrative, then it follows that the earliest constellations are basic, and if they prove expedient they will form the groundwork of all subsequent integrations, because they become a part of the individual's appreciation of reality."[3]

"PRIMARY" AND "SECONDARY" INSTITUTIONS

Another term used by Kardiner is "institution." He does not use this term as Malinowski has sometimes used it,[4] or as some other social scientists have done. Kardiner defines an institution as "any fixed mode of thought or behavior held by a group of individuals (i.e., a society) which can be communicated, which enjoys common acceptance, and infringement of or deviation from which creates some disturbance in the individual or in the group."[5]

In *The Individual and His Society*, Kardiner distinguishes between "primary" and "secondary" institutions. The first group includes such features as "family organization, in-group formation, basic disciplines, feeding, weaning, institutionalized care or neglect of children, anal training, and sexual taboos including aim, object, or both, subsistence techniques, etc."[6] This somewhat heterogeneous assemblage is held to be older and more stable than the "secondary institutions" and less apt to be affected by changes in climate or economy. These primary institutions are accepted as natural by the members of a society, "as self-evident as breathing."[7] Childhood disciplines may, however, be harsh in their effects, and the individual must accommodate himself to them in some way. These primary institutions are instrumental in shaping the basic personality structure of a society. The personality thus formed may, in turn, exert an influence upon the culture by creating certain "secondary institutions." The latter refer primarily to folklore and religious beliefs, concepts about deities, attitudes toward them, and

---

[3] Kardiner, *The Individual and His Society*, p. 484.

[4] As, for example, in "The Group and the Individual in Functional Analysis," *American Journal of Sociology*, Vol. 44 (1939), pp. 938–64.

[5] Kardiner, *The Individual and His Society*, p. 7. I have omitted the italics in which this phrase appears in the original.

[6] Ibid., p. 471.

[7] Ibid.

techniques used in dealing with them. These are fashioned through projection, conceptions about the gods being modeled after the child's relationships with its parents.

Freud dealt with this theme in *The Future of an Illusion,* in which he wrote:

> Now when the child grows up and finds that he is destined to remain a child for ever, and that he can never do without protection against unknown and mighty powers, he invests these with the traits of the father-figure; he creates for himself the gods, of whom he is afraid, whom he seeks to propitiate, and to whom he nevertheless entrusts the task of protecting him."[8]

Kardiner carried these observations further by examining the characteristic features of the religions in the societies he studied and by noting their relationships to the form of the family and parent-child relations. An example of this will later be given in the discussion of Alor.

The principal tenets set forth in *The Individual and His Society* are the concept of basic personality structure, the notion that the basic personality structure of a given society is shaped by its primary institutions, and the idea that the basic personality structure, through "projective systems," fashions its secondary institutions.

While the same general approach is continued in *The Psychological Frontiers of Society,* the terminology is a bit different, and we hear less about primary and secondary institutions. This is partly because the study of Alor showed that some practices (for example, maternal neglect of children) are not institutionalized but may have important consequences for personality formation. More important, however, it proved to be difficult to classify many institutions as either primary or secondary.[9]

Although they were close collaborators, Linton did not agree with Kardiner about primary and secondary institutions and pointed out that all societies have a long history, with most of the cultural content being borrowed from outside.[10]

In his books Kardiner occasionally writes in a general theoretical vein, sometimes taking issue with other analysts. He criticizes Freud, Reik, and Roheim for assuming that repressions always fall in the

---

[8] Sigmund Freud, *The Future of an Illusion* (New York: Doubleday 1957), pp. 39–40. (First published in 1927.)

[9] Kardiner, *The Psychological Frontiers of Society,* p. 25. See also p. 97.

[10] Francis L. K. Hsu (ed.), *Aspects of Culture and Personality* (New York: Abelard-Schuman, 1954), pp. 270–71.

same place in all cultures.[11] He is critical of the libido theory. Some internal contradictions, however, have been noted by Inkeles and Levinson in their discussion of Kardiner's work:

. . . although he rejects the Freudian theory of psychosexual development, he speaks of "oral" and "anal" adult character types and seeks their origins in corresponding periods of childhood development. The conceptual status of these presumably de-instinctivized terms remains unclear.[12]

Kardiner is generally categorized as a Neo-Freudian, but he has been critical of others who are so classified, and has written:

The so-called culturalist schools of psychodynamics represented by such writers as Harry Stack Sullivan, Karen Horney, and Erich Fromm, have not produced any enduring contributions to the social sciences.[13]

APPLICATIONS

The value of concepts such as those set forth by Kardiner must be tested by their application to ethnological data. In this respect some weaknesses appear in these two books, particularly in *The Individual and His Society*. It should be kept in mind, however, that Kardiner warns in a preface that the emphasis of the book must fall on the method; the conclusions must remain provisional.[14]

In *The Individual and His Society* there is a brief discussion of five cultures: Trobriand, Kwakiutl, Zuñi, Chukchee, and Eskimo, and a longer treatment of two cultures described by Ralph Linton— the Marquesas and the Tanala of Madagascar. In *The Psychological Frontiers of Society* three more cultures are discussed—Comanche (Linton), Alor, and Plainville, U.S.A. (James West).

There are some drawbacks in Linton's accounts of the Marquesas and Comanche. He was originally sent to Marquesas to study the local archaeology and material culture. Linton was not at that time interested in personality studies and had no knowledge of psychoanalysis.[15] It is true that he made friends with various natives and came to know them closely during a year's stay. But Linton tells us

---

[11] Kardiner, *The Individual and His Society*, p. 387.

[12] Alex Inkeles and Daniel J. Levinson, "National Character: The Study of Modal Personality and Sociocultural Systems," in Gardner Lindzey (ed.), *Handbook of Social Psychology* (Reading, Mass.: Addison-Wesley, 1954), Vol. II p. 986.

[13] Abram Kardiner and Edward Preble, *They Studied Man* (New York: World Publishing Co., 1961), p. 243.

[14] Kardiner, *The Individual and His Society*, p. xxii.

[15] Ibid., p. xvii.

that at the time of his visit Marquesan culture was already a broken one, although it was possible to reconstruct a picture of the old days from the reminiscences of old men still living in the islands.[16]

Linton's picture, therefore, is largely a reconstruction. The same is true of the Comanche study. While the psychological inferences made about these people may be correct, they would certainly be hard to check or verify. Projective tests could not very well be used, and Linton presented no life histories. If one wishes to make generalizations about the personality characteristics of a group, there should be adequate documentation for them, and in this respect the descriptions of Marquesas, Tanala, and Comanche are insufficient. James West's study of Plainville is fuller, but it does not provide a sufficient basis for the sweeping generalizations which Kardiner makes about the personality characteristics of Western man. We learn, for example, that the basic personality structure of our society is essentially the same for all economic classes, and that this basic personality structure has been common to all of the Western world since the time of Job.[17]

When we come to the study of Alor, however, we find much better groundwork. Here is the account of a living culture presented by a competent anthropologist with some psychiatric training, who collected life histories and gave projective tests in the field.

THE CONCEPT OF "MODAL PERSONALITY"

The People of Alor is the outstanding research study to come from the Kardiner-Linton-Du Bois group. Let us therefore consider this work in more detail. The first thing to note is a difference in terminology. Instead of "basic personality structure," Du Bois uses the term "modal personality," which involves a more statistical concept. Du Bois notes that in Alor both the test material and her own impressions indicate a wide range of variation. "Ranges, however, are measured on a common base line. On such a base line, data will show central tendencies that constitute the modal personality

---

[16] Ibid., p. 137.

[17] Kardiner, *The Psychological Frontiers of Society*, pp. 337–38, 365, 432–34. In view of this assertion, it comes as a surprise to discover, in a later work by Kardiner and Lionel Ovesey, that the American Negro has a basic personality structure different from that of the rest of the American people. See Abram Kardiner and Lionel Ovesey, *The Mark of Oppression: A Psychological Study of the American Negro* (New York: W. W. Norton & Co., Inc., 1951) , p. 317.

for any particular culture."[18] The term "modal personality" or "modal personality structure" has recently been used by a number of other writers and may well gain wider acceptance than "basic personality structure."[19]

THE PEOPLE OF ALOR

The People of Alor is a study of the village complex of Atimelang on the island of Alor in Indonesia, where Cora Du Bois worked for about 18 months in 1938–39. In order to work with the Alorese, Du Bois learned Dutch, Malay, and also the native tongue, which had not been studied before, and which she named Abui. Autobiographical material was not recorded until after Du Bois had been at Atimelang for a year, by which time she could translate directly into English as informants gave their life histories. In addition to writing a general ethnography and getting eight rather lengthy biographies, Du Bois administered the Rorschach test to 37 subjects, a word association test to 36 subjects, and the Porteus maze test to 55 subjects; she also collected children's drawings from 33 boys and 22 girls. She set up a daily clinic, treating wounds, infections, and fevers, thereby establishing communication and rapport with the villagers.

Du Bois states that the autobiographies do not represent the ideal or "type" person of Atimelang. The more successful Alorese were too busy with their affairs to take time off to tell their life histories and were not sufficiently attracted by either the money or prestige involved in working with the anthropologist. Autobiographical interviews were limited to one hour each morning before the informant began his day's work. The informant was encouraged to tell his dreams and to discuss them. The autobiographical material makes up about half the book. Each life history is analyzed by Abram Kardiner, who also presents some general conclusions to the autobiographical data.

---

[18] Cora Du Bois, *The People of Alor. A Social-Psychological Study of an East Indian Island,* with Analyses by Abram Kardiner and Emil Oberholzer (Minneapolis: University of Minnesota Press, 1944), pp. 4–5.

[19] A. F. C. Wallace, *The Modal Personality Structure of the Tuscarora Indians as Recorded by the Rorschach Test,* Bulletin No. 150, Bureau of American Ethnology (1952); Louise Spindler and George Spindler, "A Modal Personality Technique in the Study of Menomini Acculturation," in Bert Kaplan (ed.), *Studying Personality Cross-Culturally* (Evanston, Ill.: Row, Peterson, & Co., 1961), pp. 479–92; Alex Inkeles, Eugenia Hanfmann, and Helen Beier, "Modal Personality and Adjustment to the Soviet Socio-Political System," in Bert Kaplan (ed.), *Studying Personality Cross-Culturally* (Evanston, Ill.: Row, Peterson & Co., 1961), pp. 201–26.

The Rorschach tests were submitted to Dr. Emil Oberholzer, a Rorschach expert, for a "blind" analysis. He knew nothing of Kardiner's conclusions, drawn from the life history material, nor did Kardiner know of his. Each worked independently. Oberholzer's analysis (pp. 588–650 in *The People of Alor*) is brilliant and presents many striking correspondences to Kardiner's.

The same procedure was used with the children's drawings, submitted for "blind" analysis to Dr. Trude Schmidl-Waehner. Here, again, the agreement with the findings of Kardiner and Oberholzer is noteworthy.[20] These correspondences strengthen the likelihood that each analyst has been on the right track and has correctly identified some general tendencies in Alorese personality. Through this technique the possibility of bias and subjective impressionism in the ethnographer are minimized. This innovation in methodology, together with the outstanding fieldwork, makes *The People of Alor* a milestone in culture-and-personality research.

Let us now turn to some of the data presented by Du Bois. As among the Iatmul and Tchambuli, the women in Alor are the principal food producers, concerned with the cultivation and collection of vegetable foods. The men are occupied with financial transactions involving the exchange of pigs, gongs, and kettledrums. This sexual division of labor has an important consequence for Alorese personality development in infancy, for the mother usually returns to regular agricultural work from 10 days to two weeks after the birth of her child. She does not take the baby with her to the fields, but leaves it in the care of its father, brother, sister, or grandparent. The child may be nursed by other women than the mother, but these substitutes are not consistently available. Consequently, children suffer from oral deprivation, although the mother nurses and fondles the child upon her return from the field in late afternoon and whenever she is at home and not too busy. One substitute for offering the breast is to massage the child's genitals. There is no stress on toilet training during the prewalking period, and no efforts are made to teach the child either to talk or to walk during infancy. But walking begins at about the same time as in the Western world—from the 12th to the 18th month. Weaning rarely occurs before this time.

The period from the age of first walking to about five or six is considered by Du Bois to be probably the time of greatest stress for the

---

[20] Du Bois, *The People of Alor*, pp. 584–87.

child. The oral frustration continues, and by now the child is no longer carried about much in the carrying shawl, and thus loses the constant skin contacts and support of the previous period. When the mother goes off to work, the child is left from about eight in the morning to about five in the afternoon. It is fed irregularly by older siblings and others, but often, presumably, goes hungry. If a younger sibling is born during this time, the weaning process is hastened. Children are generally weaned and toilet trained by the age of three.

Teasing of the child is sometimes resorted to, similar to that described by Mead and Bateson for Bali.[21] That is, the mother may deliberately stimulate jealousy in her baby by showing preference for some other child. Oddly enough, there is not much finger sucking among Alorese children. Sexual disciplines are lenient. Children may masturbate freely in public, and knowledge about sexual matters is common by age five. If a child is the last born, it may continue to sleep with its mother until the age of seven or eight; if displaced by a younger sibling, it sleeps with an older one or with some adult.

Children are often frightened by their elders. "Constant threats, accompanied by the brandishing of a knife, are made to cut off children's ears or hands. The adult is playful in his intentions, but some children are seriously frightened by this form of teasing."[22] Shame sanctions are used in dealing with children, to ensure conformity. But children may also be consoled with gifts, usually gifts of food.

A striking aspect of Alorese childhood is the temper tantrums. "Rages are so consistent, so widespread, and of such long duration among young children that they were one of my first and most striking observations."[23] A common precipitating cause of this behavior is the mother's morning departure for the fields. Du Bois describes a particular child whose paroxysms sometimes lasted as long as 20 minutes. "He would begin by pursuing his mother; then as she outstripped him he would throw himself on the ground, roll back and forth, and often beat his head on the earth."[24]

Temper tantrums begin to cease at about age five or six, when the child starts to wear the loincloth, a first step toward adult status. During the day, children—more particularly boys—roam about in groups, foraging for food. (They can expect meals at home at around

---

[21] Gregory Bateson and Margaret Mead, *Balinese Character: A Photographic Analysis.* Special Publications of the New York Academy of Sciences, Vol. II (New York, 1942).

[22] Du Bois, *The People of Alor,* p. 48.

[23] Ibid., p. 81.

[24] Ibid., p. 51.

7 A.M. and 7 P.M.) Adults don't object to minor raiding, but may punish children if they catch them stealing food. During this period the lives of boys and girls become differentiated. Boys have more mobility and may attach themselves to young men whom they serve as fags, or they may take part in work groups in the fields, pulling out weeds. Girls, however, stay closer to their mothers, have less time to play, and learn to weave, sew, make bark cloth, and engage in agricultural work. Both boys and girls may be saddled with the care of younger siblings.

Girls are tattooed between 10 to 14 years of age—a sort of indication of adult status. Boys are sometimes tattooed as well, but their symbolic mark of adulthood is letting their hair grow long.

When boys begin to let their hair grow long, they also begin borrowing or acquiring male accouterments. These are dwelt upon in loving detail in many myths and consist of a sword, a front shield, a back shield, a parrying shield, a bow, a wide belt of woven rattan that serves as a quiver, an areca basket with bells, and the tubular, areca-bark hair cylinder with the accompanying combs and head plumes. Naturally, a young man rarely succeeds in borrowing or acquiring all these articles at first, but he gets as many as he can and struts about in them, often followed by the half-admiring, half-derisive comments of older women and girls.[25]

During adolescence boys and girls go through a process of having their teeth blackened, an occasion which provides a kind of picnic, during which some sexual license takes place. Women often take the initiative in courtship.

A man seems to look for a mother in the woman he marries. This was expressed in a statement by Du Bois's interpreter, Fantan:

Wives are like our mothers. When we were small, our mothers fed us. When we are grown, our wives cook for us. If there is something good, they keep it in the pot until we come home. When we were small, we slept with our mothers; when we are grown, we sleep with our wives. Sometimes when we are grown we wake in the night and call our wives "mother."[26]

Marriage involves many financial transactions, but, although the masculine-controlled finance acts to stabilize marriage, Atimelangers average about two divorces apiece. There seems to be much tension between men and women. This tension is interpreted by Kardiner and Du Bois as being due to the ambivalent attitudes developed toward the mother in childhood and to the continuing search in the

---

[25] Ibid., p. 81.

[26] Ibid., p. 96.

man for a nurturing mother. The average Atimelang woman cannot meet these needs and thus continues to be a frustrating figure for the man. Much jealousy is in evidence, largely on the part of the men. Feeling unsure of themselves, men find an avenue to self-importance through the elaborate financial exchanges in which they engage.

According to Kardiner, Alorese childhood experiences are such that parental figures are not idealized, and suger-ego formation is weak. "So slight is the tendency to idealize the parental imago that effigies are made in the most careless and slipshod manner, are used in the most perfunctory way, and are forthwith discarded. There is little emphasis on giving the spirits permanent housing or idealized form."[27] There is also an absence of artistic creation and of interest in the outer world—a lack which must also, ultimately, be traced to the maternal frustrations of childhood.

Much of this analysis seems convincing, and there is much supporting evidence in the autobiographical data and in Oberholzer's Rorschach analysis. For instance, in discussing the Alorese black-color responses, which generally manifest "black-color shock," Oberholzer writes:

From this we assume that the Alorese are suspicious and distrustful; they are so not only toward everything that is unknown and new to them, such as foreigners, for instance, but also among themselves. No one will trust another. Moreover, they are fearful and timid in their heart of hearts, feeling uneasy and insecure.[28]

Oberholzer also finds evidence of deep passivity:

They are indifferent and listless; they let things slide and get dilapidated, where we would feel the necessity of making repairs . . . . The organization of conscience and its dynamic expression is not developed, or is inadequately developed. . . . Outlets offered by a capacity for long-lasting enthusiasm and self-sacrifice, for sublimation, contemplation, and creative power—all of these are ruled out. . . . There must be emotional outbursts and tempers, anger and rage, sometimes resulting in violent actions. . . . The Alorese must be lacking in individual personal contact, living beside one another but not with one another. . . . Either there are no friendships and relationships or there are none that are deeply rooted.[29]

The interested reader should examine Oberholzer's impressive analysis in full, for these brief quotations do not do it justice. Al-

----

[27] Ibid., p. 190.

[28] Ibid., p. 596.

[29] Ibid., pp. 598–600.

though it may contain a few discrepancies with the views of Kardiner and Du Bois, the most striking thing is the close correspondence. The same may be said of Dr. Trude Schmidl-Waehner's drawing analysis, in which she speaks of the children's "feeling of aloneness," their poverty-stricken relationships, and absence of creativity.[30]

Perhaps the main question raised by Du Bois's study is whether the personality traits singled out by Kardiner, Oberholzer, Du Bois, and Schmidl-Waehner are primarily due to the maternal neglect in infancy. There are other possible etiologies; Du Bois touches on at least one in referring to the prevalence of dysentery, respiratory infections, malaria, and yaws. "The possible effect on personality of these debilitating diseases, often suffered in acute form during childhood, is worth bearing in mind."[31] Might not lack of ambition, for example, be traced to such a cause? How could one decide which factors were the crucial ones?

In a review of this book, Hortense Powdermaker observed: "We are not sure that this absence of the mother, which is common among all horticultural people in Melanesia, would necessarily lead to the mother being an object of frustration. My field work in New Ireland, where the pattern of childhood feeding was identical to that of Alor, did not give me the impression that it led to feelings of frustration."[32] Powdermaker suggests that too much emphasis may have been placed on prohibitory factors in Kardiner's analysis and not enough on the permissive, restitutive ones mentioned in the ethnography.[33]

Roheim comments on the Alor study as follows:

The mothers could take the children along with them into the fields, but they don't do it. Other primitive mothers carry their children all day; if these mothers don't, it is evident that they resent either the children or the fact that they have to do all the field work (or nearly all) and also take care of the children. . . . We are driven to the conclusion that the mothers leave the infants at home simply because they have a lot of hostility toward them.[34]

---

[30] Ibid., pp. 584–85.

[31] Ibid., p. 81.

[32] Hortense Powdermaker, "Review of *The People of Alor*", *American Anthropologist*, Vol. 47 (1945), p. 160.

[33] For an example of the latter: "Everyone seems entranced by small babies and many people will ask to hold and fondle them." Du Bois, *The People of Alor*, pp. 33–34.

[34] Géza Roheim, *Psychoanalysis and Anthropology. Culture, Personality, and the Unconscious* (New York: International Universities Press, 1950), p. 261.

Such hostility, if it exists, might be more significant than the temporary absences of the mother, although in either case the mother would come to be seen as frustrating by the child.

What is the more significant factor affecting personality in Alorese children: food deprivation or maternal rejection? In a paper on the Gurage of Ethiopia, D. N. Shack claims that nutritional depriva- tion is cross-culturally associated with such personality character- istics as selfishness, unrelatedness, emotional detachment, passivity, dependency, and feelings of worthlessness.[35] Ronald P. Rohner, on the other hand, asserts that parental neglect is a more significant determinant of personality. He argues that parental rejection causes feelings of anxiety, frustration, aggression, and a lowered sense of self-esteem. The child comes to feel that he is not worthy of love; he is also apt to become more dependent than an accepted child. As a result of the frustrating experiences in childhood, the individual tends to generalize his feelings so as to see the world as hostile and unfriendly. Rohner expects that as adults such persons would find it hard to form close emotional relationships and would, in turn, be likely to reject their own children. They would also find it hard to tolerate stress and would be less emotionally stable than persons who had been accepted in childhood. In a cross-cultural statistical study, Rohner tested the foregoing hypotheses about the effects of parental rejection as against Shack's hypotheses about the effects of food deprivation and found lack of confirmation for the latter but support for the former.[36]

Parental rejection is probably a more crucial determinant of per- sonality in Alor than food deprivation per se. Rohner's findings seem to fit in well with the conclusions of the Alor study.

Although there is consistency in these conclusions, and although the general picture carries conviction, there are still points where questions and criticisms of the Alor study may be raised. One point which may be noted is that Kardiner's analysis of Alorese infancy and its sequelae seems to be based on the wet season births. If birth takes place during the dry season, when there is less agricultural work, the mother spends more time with her child. The seasons seem to be about equally long. Oberholzer was struck by the great

---

[35] D. N. Shack, "Nutritional Processes and Personality Development among the Gurage of Ethiopia," *Ethnology*, Vol. 8 (1969), pp. 292–300.

[36] Ronald P. Rohner, "Parental Rejection, Food Deprivation, and Personality De- velopment: Tests of Alternative Hypotheses," *Ethnology*, Vol. 9 (1970), pp. 414–27.

variability manifest in the Alorese Rorschachs, and this was attributed to the variations in maternal and paternal care. But if there are such great variations, is it safe to make generalizations about the personality tendencies of this society? Eight biographies and 37 Rorschachs are the principal sources from which generalizations are made about modal personality characteristics in a population of about 600, although the latter number represents only a small part of the total Alorese population. Moreover, Du Bois tells us that the life histories are drawn from some of the less successful members of the society.

Even within the small group of biographies there seems to be a great range of variation in personality patterns. Anthony F. C. Wallace has drawn attention to Kardiner's difficulties in finding a basis for making generalizations. Kardiner wrote at first: "It is difficult to decide how typical Mangma is. I would venture to say that if he were typical the society could not continue to exist."[37] But later Kardiner wrote, "Mangma is the most typical, and his character corresponds to the basic personality structure."[38] Kardiner also wrote that Malelaka was difficult to evaluate but that, nevertheless, his life history was in every way typical. Wallace comments: "This is remarkable, because Malelaka was a notorious prophet who attempted to launch a religious revival. On the other hand he is said to be similar to Rilpada, another seer, who in turn was described as 'atypical.' And to complicate things still further, the analyst says that 'characters such as Mangma, Rilpada and Fantan can be found in any society.' "[39]

While it is right to question the adequacy of the sampling in this study, historical perspective must remind us that no one had previously collected so much psychological data of this sort in culture-and-personality research. Moreover, Cora Du Bois has herself been conscious of these problems; for in answer to the question "If you were doing Alor again, how would you go about it?" she replied, in part:

I would be far more precise in sampling (if the Alorese would lend themselves to it). Quantifications would be a more salient concern and would cover *inter alia* sample observations and systematic interviewing,

---

[37] Du Bois, *The People of Alor,* p. 227.

[38] Ibid., p. 549.

[39] Anthony F. C. Wallace, *Culture and Personality* (2d. ed.; New York: Random House, Inc., 1970), p. 125.

including probably sentence completion and multiple choice schedules developed in the field. . . ."[40]

The methods developed by the Linton-Kardiner group were applied in many subsequent studies. One of these may be singled out here: *Truk: Man in Paradise* by Thomas Gladwin and Seymour B. Sarason.

TRUK: MAN IN PARADISE

This work shows the influence of *The People of Alor,* but in some respects marks an advance over the latter. More care is given to sampling. Gladwin, the anthropologist, wanted to select informants manifesting a wide range of personality type. At the beginning of his work he devised a sort of popularity poll to guide him in this selection. Five men and five women were drawn by lot from all the adolescents and adults on the island. They were asked to rate all other persons on the island on a four-point scale of like and dislike. It was felt that if a person was consistently said to be liked or disliked, there was something distinctive about him in one way or another.

With the ratings completed, the men and women of the island were ranked separately from highest to lowest. The six most "liked" and the six most "disliked" of each sex were set apart, and three were selected by chance out of each such group for intensive study; there were thus six persons of each sex in our sample who were putatively "unusual." Of those remaining in the middle range five of each sex were again selected by chance for inclusion in the sample, making a total of eleven men and eleven women.[41]

To this number a Trukese assistant of Gladwin's was added, giving a total of 12 men.

Each of the 23 subjects was given the Rorschach and Thematic Apperception Test by Gladwin and was asked to tell his or her life history. The Thematic Apperception Test was a modified one, adapted to the Trukese scene, and consisting of a series of ink line drawings. The projective test protocols were later submitted for

---

[40] Cora Du Bois, "Two Decades Later," 1960 edition of *The People of Alor* (Cambridge, Mass.: Harvard University Press, 1960), p. xxiv.

[41] Thomas Gladwin and Seymour B. Sarason, *Truk: Man in Paradise,* Viking Fund Publications in Anthropology, No. 20 (New York, 1953), p. 211. Gladwin has written that the method of sampling was intended only to establish putatively "normal" and "deviant" samples. No validity was assumed for the poll as a measure of actual popularity (personal communication to author).

"blind" analysis to Seymour B. Sarason, the psychologist. Sarason was not told anything about the culture, and great care was taken to prevent any leakage from Gladwin to him, although a certain amount of information was necessary for the evaluation of certain Rorschach responses.

Thus if a person had said he saw a canoe ornament, for example, it was my responsibility to judge whether the resemblance of the blot as seen was sufficiently close to the appearance of such an ornament in actuality, a judgment which Sarason, not having been to Truk, was not competent to make. I did not, however, offer any other information on the individuals or the Trukese culture until Sarason's analysis of the Rorschachs and Thematics was completed.[42]

As in the Alorese study, there turned out to be a remarkable degree of congruence between Sarason's analyses and the general impressions of the anthropologist—a congruence which considerably outweighs the occasional discrepancies. It might have been better, however, if different specialists had been asked to interpret the Rorschach and Thematic Apperception Tests, for impressions gained from the Rorschachs may in this case have colored Sarason's evaluations of the TAT stories. However, this is a minor quibble, for *Truk: Man in Paradise* is a first-rate study. Each life history is presented, together with the Rorschach, TAT, and Sarason's analysis of each, thus enabling the reader to see how Sarason arrived at his results.

SUGGESTIONS FOR FURTHER READING

The concept of "basic personality structure" is discussed by Abram Kardiner in "The Concept of Basic Personality Structure as an Operational Tool in the Social Sciences," in Douglas G. Haring (ed.), *Personal Character and Cultural Milieu. A Collection of Readings* (Syracuse, N.Y.: Syracuse University Press, 1949), pp. 469–83. Also in the Haring volume (pp. 241–53) is a brief account of Alor, "Attitudes toward Food and Hunger in Alor," by Cora Du Bois, pp. 241–53. For an analysis of American Negro personality, see Abram Kardiner and Lionel Ovesey, *The Mark of Oppression: A Psychological Study of the American Negro* (New York: W. W. Norton & Co., Inc., 1951). For a general discussion, see Ralph Linton, *The Cultural Background of Personality* (New York: D. Appleton-Century, 1945).

---

[42] Ibid., p. 214.

part *III*

CURRENT APPROACHES

Part III is a continuation of Part II, dealing mainly with work done in the 1950s and 1960s. Most of the cross-cultural correlational studies reviewed in Chapter 8 were published during these two decades. The field research of the Six Cultures Project was undertaken in the 1950s, with the resulting publications appearing in the 1960s. The situation is different with studies of national character. These fell out of favor after 1960, but in Chapter 10 we will consider Francis L. K. Hsu's suggestions for new approaches to this field. Chapter 10 also includes a survey of studies of Japanese national character, including recent works by William Caudill, George De Vos, Ezra Vogel, and others.

chapter 8

Cross-Cultural Surveys

While the basic personality approach was being advanced at Columbia University, a rather different approach was under way at Yale, where George P. Murdock and John W. M. Whiting were leading figures in the launching and development of Yale's Cross-Cultural Survey, which later became known as the Human Relations Area Files (HRAF). In contrast to the intensive investigation of a single culture, such as Du Bois's study of Alor, researchers making use of HRAF sources try to make generalizations from a large number of societies, usually selected from different culture areas of the world. These studies usually set forth some specific hypotheses which are made to either stand or fall on the basis of statistical evaluations.

The HRAF is an extensive filing system containing ethnological data about a few hundred societies from different culture areas. The material is so classified and sorted that it is easy for anyone familiar with the coding system to rapidly find whatever he is looking for. If a student, let us say, wants information about fishing techniques among the Yurok, Tikopia, and Ainu, he simply finds the files for these three groups and draws out the cards dealing with fishing. This is much simpler than going through a lot of library references. Moreover, the files facilitate the discovery of recurring correlations, associated features between institutions, or what E. B. Tylor, in an early cross-cultural survey called "adhesions."[1]

---

[1] E. B. Tylor, "On a Method of Investigating the Development of Institutions; Applied to Laws of Marriage and Descent," *Journal of the Royal Anthropological Institute of Great Britain and Ireland,* Vol. 18 (1889), pp. 245–69.

Those who are attracted to cross-cultural surveys making use of the files tend to believe that human behavior is characterized by a good deal of regularity, which makes it possible to make predictions about what sorts of institutions are apt to go together. Thus hypotheses can be stated and tested. One proponent of cross-cultural studies, Yehudi A. Cohen, suggests that two main principles form a basis for such research. The first is the principle of limited possibilities, "that there are a finite number of forms which any institution, belief, or custom can take."[2] In other words, there is a limited number of solutions to particular problems. The second principle is "the psychic unity of mankind," the notion that despite racial and cultural differences all men have essentially the same basic thought processes and feelings.

A cultural relativist like Ruth Benedict would not be apt to find research with the HRAF files congenial. What facilitates such research, as Cohen puts it, is a "clearly defined point of view about the ways in which sociocultural systems operate."[3] The views of Murdock, Whiting, and others at Yale were congenial to this approach, since they had some rather definite notions about the nature of personality and of cultural institutions. Although they shared with the Linton-Kardiner school the influence of psychoanalytic theory, they differed in also having a behaviorist orientation.

With their stress on the importance of culture, which involves learned behavior, many anthropologists have been attracted to behaviorism, since this school of psychology de-emphasizes the role of instincts or inborn qualities. Behaviorist psychology also places emphasis on the observation of behavior, which is in line with the traditions of anthropological fieldwork. Clark L. Hull taught learning theory at Yale, where he influenced psychologists such as O. H. Mowrer, John Dollard, and Neal Miller, but also such anthropologists as Murdock and Whiting. Both Murdock and Whiting have tried to apply learning theory to cross-cultural data. They have also tried to express psychoanalytic concepts in the terminology of learning theory.[4]

---

[2] Yehudi A. Cohen, "Macroethnology: Large-Scale Comparative Studies," in James A. Clifton (ed.), *Introduction to Cultural Anthropology. Essays in the Scope and Methods of the Science of Man* (Boston, Mass.: Hougton Mifflin Co., 1968), p. 405. This principle was first set forth by Alexander Goldenweiser; see his *History, Psychology, and Culture* (New York: Alfred A. Knopf, 1933), pp. 45–49.

[3] Cohen, "Macroethnology," p. 403.

[4] On the influence of behaviorism in psychological anthropology, see Robert A. LeVine, "Behaviorism in Psychological Anthropology," in Joseph M. Wepman and Ralph W. Heine (eds.), *Concepts of Personality* (Chicago: Aldine Publishing Company, 1963), pp. 361–84.

In this chapter we will deal with cross-cultural studies which concern the field of culture-and-personality. The HRAF files have been used for other kinds of studies as well, for example in relation to cultural evolution. As will be seen later, there are some disadvantages as well as advantages in cross-cultural surveys. But before attempting an evaluation of the method, let us first consider a series of examples of such research.

SORCERY AND SOCIAL CONTROL

Let us start with *Paiute Sorcery* by Beatrice B. Whiting, an interesting monograph which combines the investigation of a particular society with the cross-cultural survey approach. Beatrice Whiting did field research among the Harney Valley Paiute in Burns, Oregon, in the summers of 1936, 1937, and 1938. Most of her work concerns the Paiute, and it is only in a concluding chapter that the cross-cultural approach is employed.

Paiute bands were small in number, fluctuating in size with the seasons, and the individual families which constituted the essential economic units often lived alone. Few economic activities involved the cooperation of more than one extended family. There were no true chiefs, no council of elders, and no police force. How, then, was social control achieved? Whiting suggests, as Hallowell has done for the Saulteaux or Canadian Chippewa, that fear of sorcery was a crucial factor. "Within the band, the most important mechanisms of social control were retaliation and the fear of sorcery and accusations of sorcery."[5]

Control of aggression within the individual family was very strict, for the solidarity of the family unit was essential. Children were promptly punished for aggressive behavior.

> Probably more important than this direct punishment is the fear of aggression which they acquire by observing their parents and hearing them discuss sorcery and fighting. . . . They observe that their parents are afraid to express aggression overtly for fear of being accused of sorcery. They are admonished never to laugh or make fun of other people lest they be attacked. They are warned always to be polite, to speak to people and to speak pleasantly. They hear much gossip about sorcerers and how dangerous such individuals are.[6]

Despite this control, intrafamily aggression sometimes did break loose, particularly in the case of men attacking their wives. Aggres-

---

[5] Beatrice Blyth Whiting, *Paiute Sorcery*, Viking Fund Publications in Anthropology, No. 15 (New York, 1950), p. 13.

[6] Ibid., p. 69.

sion was also turned inward, and Whiting tells us that the suicide rate was high. Within the memory of her informants there had been as many as 23 suicides in a population of between 200 and 300.

It occurred to Whiting that some of the functional relationships which she found among the Paiute might appear in other societies as well. Much of her picture accords closely with that of the

Table 8–1. RELATIONSHIP BETWEEN IMPORTANCE OF SORCERY AND PRESENCE OR ABSENCE OF SUPERORDINATE CONTROL

$$24 \ (48\%) \qquad 11 (22\%)$$
$$1 \ (\ 2\%) \qquad 14 \ (28\%)$$
$$R = .85 \text{ (reliable at .60)}$$

	No Superordinate Justice (coordinate control)			*Superordinate Justice*	
Sorcery important	Arunta	Apache	Barama Caribs	Ashanti	Hill Maria Gonds
	Buka	Chuckchee	Delaware	Azande	Kwakiutl
	Dieri	Copper Eskimo	Jivaro	Chagga	Lamba
	Dobu	Ifugao	Witoto	Fiji	Sanpoil
	Kiwai	Kutchin		Kamilaroi	
	Kwoma	Mala		Tiv	
	Lesu	Maori		Venda	
	Murngin	Paiute			
	Orokaiva	Yurok			
	Trobriands	Zuñi			
Sorcery unimportant	Lango			Bali	Cayapa
				Japan	Cheyenne
				Kazak	Crow
				Lepcha	Samoa
				Masai	Tikopia
				Ontong Java	Tonga
				Riff	
				Tanala	

Source: Reprinted from Beatrice Blyth Whiting, *Paiute Sorcery*, Viking Fund Publications in Anthropology, No. 15 (New York, 1950), p. 85. Copyright 1950 by the Wenner-Gren Foundation for Anthropological Research Inc., New York.

Chippewa, although these groups did not belong to the same culture area, geographic environment, or linguistic stock. Whiting's cross-cultural study shows that similar patterns appear in still other "atomistic" societies. Whiting does not, however, use this term. She speaks of societies as having either *coordinate* or *superordinate* systems of social control.

In societies with superordinate control persons are delegated authority to settle disputes and exact punishment. These persons have high status, either ascribed or acquired. Societies with coordinate control lack such individuals or groups, and offenses are dealt with by retaliation on the part of the kin or local group. The Paiute are an example of the latter type; in their case fear of sorcery is functionally related to coordinate control.

Whiting classified societies described in the Cross-Cultural Survey as having either coordinate or superordinate control on the basis of how murders were dealt with in the society. She also rated these societies with regard to the importance of sorcery as an explanation for sickness, establishing two groups: Sorcery Important and Sorcery Unimportant. Four tables with tetrachoric correlations are presented in her monograph, together with statistical evaluations. These tend to support the hypothesis of a functional association between sorcery and coordinate control.

Whiting's Table 8–1 is reproduced to illustrate the approach of many such studies.

THE FUNCTIONS OF ALCOHOL

Another cross-cultural study is Donald Horton's investigation into the functions of alcohol in primitive societies. Part of this study is related to the work of Beatrice Whiting just cited. Horton asserts that the primary function of liquor consumption is reduction of anxiety, although counteranxiety may also develop as a result of drinking—through punishment for acts committed under intoxication, hangovers, and so forth. Horton suggests some "theorems" which he proposes to test:

1. The drinking of alcohol tends to be accompanied by the release of sexual and aggressive impulses.
2. The strength of the drinking response in any society tends to vary directly with the level of anxiety in that society.
3. The strength of the drinking response tends to vary inversely with the strength of the counteranxiety elicited by painful experiences during and after drinking.[7]

Horton considers various sources of anxiety, including subsistence insecurity and acculturation. Societies described in the Yale files, for whom there were descriptions of drinking behavior, were classified into those having "high," "moderate," or "low subsistence insecurity." They were also grouped under the headings "strong insobriety" and "moderate or slight insobriety." Subsistence insecurity was found to be positively and significantly associated with male

---

[7] Donald Horton, "The Functions of Alcohol in Primitive Societies: A Cross-Cultural Study," *Quarterly Journal of Studies on Alcohol,* Vol. 4 (1943), p. 230.

insobriety. This association was held to substantiate the posited relationship between the level of anxiety and strength of the drinking habit.[8]

The same applies to acculturation, which also tended to be associated with strong insobriety. Less clear-cut relationships were found between warfare and insobriety and between sorcery and insobriety. Nor was the type of beverage directly related to the strength of the drinking response. "Where anxiety is low, people will remain relatively sober with distilled liquor; where anxiety is high, they will try to become intoxicated with beer or wine."[9]

Horton notes that for many societies a similar sequence of behavior occurs during drinking. In the early stages there is laughter and friendly conversation, but in the later stages of intoxication quarrelling and fighting often break out among the men. Women do not seem to engage in drunken aggression, as the men do, and in many societies women hide the men's weapons or otherwise try to forestall their outbursts. Drunken aggression was reported for 36 of 37 societies in the files whose drinking behavior was described. It is evident that normally inhibited aggression is released under intoxication.

Horton suggests that sorcery may be used as a measure of the level of inhibited aggression. "It was predicted that strong aggression and an active belief in sorcery would tend to occur together, and medium or slight aggression would tend to occur where the belief in sorcery is not important."[10] This prediction is supported statistically in a series of tables.

Horton cites Whiting's association between sorcery and coordinate control and points out that in societies having coordinate control there is no central authority or police force to restrain drunken aggression. Such outbreaks would therefore probably be dealt with less effectively than in a superordinate society.

Another cross-cultural study of drinking behavior is that of Peter B. Field, who takes issue with some of Horton's findings. He points out that an anxiety theory of excessive drinking is inadequate, because it does not explain why other anxiety-reducing mechanisms are not resorted to, instead of drinking. Moreover, while acculturation may sometimes increase anxiety, it may in some cases decrease it

---

[8] Ibid., p. 268. Horton says that the "nuclear data" of this study concerns 56 societies, each with a culture significantly different from the others (p. 236).

[9] Ibid., p. 279.

[10] Ibid., p. 286.

by diminishing supernatural fears or by providing new rational solutions to old problems. Field's own cross-cultural examination leads him to conclude that excessive drinking is related to an informal type of social organization in which there is a good deal of personal autonomy and an absence of institutional constraints. This would generally apply to nomadic hunting-gathering societies, which are rated high on drunkenness. Where stability and permanence are characteristic of a society, and where there are corporate kin groups having collective ownership of property, there is less evidence of excessive drinking. Such institutions as patrilocal residence and the bride price are also associated with relative sobriety. Sociological factors such as these, rather than the level of anxiety, are for Field the significant factors accounting for the extent of drinking behavior.[11]

The most comprehensive cross-cultural study of drinking is that of Bacon, Barry, and Child, in which data are drawn from 139 societies, mostly nonliterate, incorporating the 57 societies used by Horton. The authors' correlations support the conclusions of Horton but not those of Field, finding little relationship between drinking behavior and egalitarian or informal social order. A prediction tested in this study is that drinking and drunkenness should tend to be frequent in societies that produce much conflict about dependence and independence. In a correlational analysis the authors find that drinking is associated with low indulgence in infancy and childhood, with pressure for responsibility in childhood, and a low degree of indulgence of dependence or nurturance in adult life. These findings would support, or at least do not contradict, the hypothesis that drinking is partially motivated by a need to relieve frustrated or conflicted needs for dependency.[12]

"Apollonianism": Some Correlations

Although Field's interpretation was not supported by the work of Barry, Bacon, and Child, his type of explanation might help to account for the relative "Apollonianism" of the Pueblos, when compared with formerly hunting-gathering tribes like the Chippewa.

---

[11] Peter B. Field, "A New Cross-Cultural Study of Drunkenness," in David J. Pittman and Charles R. Snyder (eds.), *Society, Culture, and Drinking Patterns* (New York: John Wiley & Sons, Inc., 1962), pp. 48–74.

[12] Margaret K. Bacon, Herbert Barry III, and Irvin L. Child, "A Cross-Cultural Study of Drinking: II. Relations to Other Features of Culture," *Quarterly Journal of Studies on Alcohol,* Supplement No. 3 (1965), p. 46.

Two other cross-cultural studies are of interest in this connection. Barry, Child, and Bacon have argued that in pastoral and agricultural societies a future food supply is best assured by faithful adherence to routine. There is a fear of innovation, and child training emphasizes conformity and obedience. In hunting and fishing societies, on the other hand, individual initiative is at a premium. There is less fear of innovation; child training emphasizes initative and self-reliance. The authors find evidence for these patterns in a cross-cultural survey of child training patterns.[13]

D'Andrade has followed up these findings with a further cross-cultural survey on dreams. His hypothesis is that hunting and fishing societies will be more apt to use dreams to acquire supernatural power than agricultural ones. D'Andrade reasons that anxiety about being isolated and under pressure to be self-reliant might lead to the development of fantasies and dreams about magical helpers. He has found statistical support for the postulated relationship between type of economy and use of dreams. Approximately 80 percent of the hunting and fishing societies in his sample used dreams to acquire supernatural power, in contrast to 20 percent of the societies having agriculture and animal husbandry.[14] It might be argued that it was the shift to agriculture and the development of a corporate society that led to the appearance of those Apollonian features in Pueblo life which Benedict described, such as strong disapproval of drinking, emphasis on conformity, and absence of the guardian spirit quest. At least, these cross-cultural studies seem to suggest such a conclusion, which would also be supported by the findings of the cross-cultural survey by Gouldner and Peterson, in which the authors conclude that Apollonian impulse-control has increased with the development of technology.[15]

CHILD TRAINING AND PERSONALITY

The first major culture-and-personality work to make use of the Human Relations Area Files is *Child Training and Personality: A Cross-Cultural Study* by John W. M. Whiting and Irvin L. Child.

---

[13] Herbert Barry III, Irvin L. Child, and Margaret K. Bacon, "Relation of Child Training to Subsistence Economy," *American Anthropologist,* Vol. 61 (1959), pp. 51–63.

[14] Roy G. D'Andrade, "Anthropological Studies of Dreams," in Francis L. K. Hsu (ed.), *Psychological Anthropology* (Homewood, Ill.: The Dorsey Press, 1961), pp. 325–56.

[15] Alvin W. Gouldner and Richard A. Peterson, *Notes on Technology and the Moral Order* (Indianapolis, Ind.: The Bobbs-Merrill 1962).

This work is concerned with the mutual interplay of culture and personality and with the integration of culture through the mediation of personality. It focuses upon one particular aspect of culture —customs relating to illness. One reason for this choice is that in primitive societies such practices are apt to be fashioned by projection and to be retained because of their compatability with personality tendencies. Whiting and Child are interested in seeing how early childhood experiences in a particular society predispose to the development of certain medical practices.

The authors make use of the concept of fixation, but without endorsing the whole psychoanalytic canon surrounding this term. They point out that psychoanalysts have derived fixation from two quite different experiences—on the one hand from excessive gratification, and on the other hand from excessive frustrations at a given level. Whiting and Child suggest that fixation which results from a high degree of gratification be called *positive fixation,* while fixation which results from severe socialization be called *negative fixation.*

The authors wish to determine how severity or lenience in particular childhood disciplines are related to curing practices and explanations of sickness. For example, does early oral gratification lead to "oral" forms of curing?

Whiting and Child propound a hypothesis of negative fixation as follows: "In any society, the greater the custom potential of socialization anxiety for a system of behavior, the greater will be the custom potential of explanations of illness which attribute illness to events associated with that system."[16]

The systems of behavior to which the authors refer are oral, anal, sexual, dependence, and aggression. Their hypotheses of negative fixation and the other hypotheses which follow are tested with reference to data from 65 societies described in the Cross-Cultural Files, plus 10 more societies for which relevant information was available. Three judges were selected to make ratings on various aspects of child experience. In relation to "socialization anxiety," for example, they had to evaluate for each society "the brevity of the transition from freedom of indulgence of the initial habit to the requirement of complete acceptance of childhood or adult inhibitions."[17]

---

[16] John W. M. Whiting and Irvin L. Child, *Child Training and Personality: A Cross-Cultural Study* (New Haven, Conn.: Yale University Press, 1953), p. 149. Italicized in the original.

[17] Ibid., p. 53.

They also had to evaluate the severity of punishment, frequency of punishment, and signs of emotional disturbance in the children. The judges were required, moreover, to indicate how confident they felt about their judgments by labeling them either *confident* or *doubtful*. The judges did not always agree in their evaluations; hence their pooled judgments were used. Whiting and Child were satisfied with the degree of consistency or reliability characterizing the confident judgments of their judges.

Two of the judges were also given the task of deciding whether "oral," "anal," or other explanations for illness were present in the various cultures under review. This was done for each of the systems of behavior specified above—oral, anal, sexual, dependence, and aggression. The authors set forth their criteria for determining such judgments. Some of these criteria are open to question and will be discussed in the concluding section of this chapter.

It is to be noted that Whiting and Child did not make the various judgments themselves, lest their bias influence the results. An evident advantage in having judges who are unfamiliar with the hypotheses to be tested is that contamination and bias are avoided.

From their investigation the authors conclude that for every system of behavior there is evidence to support the hypothesis of negative fixation, but especially in the case of oral, dependent, and aggressive behavior; less so for anal and sexual behavior.

The authors also propound a hypothesis of positive fixation: "In any society, the greater the custom potential of initial satisfaction in any system of behavior, the greater will be the custom potential of therapeutic practices which involve the performance of responses in that system."[18]

This hypothesis did not receive much confirmation. Other hypotheses were also tested with the cross-cultural data, but with inconclusive results. If this procedure constitutes verification, therefore, the main hypothesis verified in this work is the one concerning negative fixation.

In a final chapter, the authors present some conclusions to the effect that child training practices are influenced by the "maintenance system," that is, the economic, political, and social organizations of the society. They give the following diagram, which is reminiscent of Kardiner: maintenance systems → child training practices → personality variables → projective systems.[19]

---

[18] Ibid., p. 192. Italicized in the original.
[19] Ibid., p. 310.

This brief summary of *Child Training and Personality* may seem rather arid and abstract, but in the course of the book much interesting information is revealed about ranges in lenience and severity in the child socialization practices of different societies. What adds to the interest is that modern American child training practices are compared with those of the primitive societies. The American sample was drawn from two works by W. A. Davis and R. J. Havighurst: "Social Class and Color Differences in Child Rearing" and *Father of the Man*.[20] The representativeness of this sample may be questioned. However, Whiting and Child say that this was the best source that they could find for their purposes. The scores used in comparisons with primitive societies are relevant only to the white middle-class group in the Davis and Havighurst studies.

Some of the conclusions based on these comparisons are as follows:

1. Oral indulgence is much more restricted in white middle-class American society than in the other societies studied. The nursing period is short, and there are rigid schedules of feeding, limited in time and amount. The authors state that such an interference with free indulgence of oral satisfaction is unknown among the other societies in their sample.

2. Anal training is much more severe in white middle-class American society than in the other societies studied, with the exception of the Tanala and the Chagga. Slightly over half of the primitive societies begin toilet training somewhere between the ages of one and a half and two and a half. The American middle-class group is judged to start toilet training when the child is a little over six months old.

3. Concerning indulgence of the child's sexual self-stimulation, the American middle-class group was given a rating which fell just below the least indulgent of the primitive societies, "but still not extremely low on the basis of the absolute estimate of the judges."[21] The American group was judged to be rather extreme in the severity with which children were punished for masturbation, and was given the same rating as the most extreme of the primitive societies. However, in overall severity of sexual socialization, it fell halfway between the median and the upper extreme of the primitive societies.

This information is of value in giving Americans some perspective

---

[20] W. A. Davis and R. J. Havighurst, "Social Class and Color Differences in Child Rearing," *American Sociological Review*, Vol. II (1946), pp. 698–710, and *Father of the Man* (Boston: Houghton Mifflin Co., 1947).

[21] Ibid., p. 79.

on their child training practices. Of course, there have been some changes in these practices in recent years, and there is evidence that the present-day American middle class tends to be more lenient in the various disciplines than was the middle class of the early 1940s.[22]

Later in this chapter we will return to some further considerations of the Whiting and Child book. Despite the criticisms that may be made of it, it was clearly an imaginative pioneering work, which stimulated various other cross-cultural surveys along similar lines.

THE FUNCTIONS OF INITIATION RITES

Whiting, in collaboration with others, has made further investigations that make use of the cross-cultural files. One paper, written in collaboration with Richard Kluckhohn and Albert Anthony, concerns the function of male initiation ceremonies. The authors set forth this hypothesis:

> Societies which have sleeping arrangements in which the mother and baby share the same bed for at least a year to the exclusion of the father and societies which have a taboo restricting the mother's sexual behavior for at least a year after childbirth will be more likely to have a ceremony of transition from boyhood to manhood than those societies where these conditions do not occur (or occur for briefer periods).[23]

The reasoning behind this proposition is that the mother-son sleeping arrangements must establish strong dependent relations on the part of a boy toward his mother. This may also involve attitudes of hostility toward the father, especially after the latter resumes sexual relations with his wife and displaces the son. It is necessary, with the advance of puberty, to sever the boy's emotional dependency, to remove the dangers of incest and father-son rivalry. Hence the features which are so widespread in initiation ceremonies among primitive societies—seemingly sadistic hazing of the boys, their separation from the women, and exposure to tests of endurance and genital operations.[24]

The hypothesis linking mother-son sleeping arrangements and postpartum sex taboos with the presence of initiation ceremonies

---

[22] See Daniel R. Miller and Guy E. Swanson, *The Changing American Parent. A Study in the Detroit Area* (New York: John Wiley & Sons, 1958).

[23] John W. M. Whiting, Richard Kluckhohn, and Albert Anthony, "The Function of Male Initiation Ceremonies at Puberty," in Eleanor E. Maccoby, Theodore M. Newcomb, and Eugene L. Hartley (eds.), *Readings in Social Psychology* (3d ed.; New York: Holt, Rinehart & Winston, Inc., 1958), p. 364. Italicized in the original.

[24] A similar argument appears in Theodor Reik, *Ritual. Psychoanalytic Studies* (New York: International Universities Press, 1958), p. 99 ff.

was tested for 56 societies representing 45 of the 60 culture areas designated by George P. Murdock in his "World Ethnographic Sample."[25] Of 20 societies where both the antecedent variables were found, 14 had initiation ceremonies and only 6 did not. Where both of the antecedent variables were absent, only 2 of the 25 societies had the ceremonies. There were of course some mixed cases, but over 80 percent of the cases corresponded with the prediction. Moreover, the authors were able to present some plausible explanations for the cases which did not jibe with their expectations.[26]

However, Whiting has since made some modifications of the theories set forth in this paper. He no longer attributes importance to the Oedipal rivalry posited earlier. Exclusive mother-son sleeping arrangements have a high correlation with polygyny. The father usually has access to another wife or wives and thus is not apt to regard his son as much of a rival. Moreover, he does not replace his son in his wife's bed, for in more than half of the societies of this sort investigated by Whiting, the man never *sleeps* with his wife.[27]

Whiting now believes that one consequence of exclusive mother-child sleeping arrangements is a boy's cross-sex identification with his mother. He also suggests that since the mother is deprived of normal sexual gratification during the long taboo period, she may find some sexual satisfaction from the close relationship with her son, especially in nursing. This adds to the dangers of incest, which the male initiation rites serve to counteract. It is reported that there are relationships between the prolonged postpartum sex taboo and such practices as mother-in-law avoidance (for a man), father-in-law avoidance (for a woman), and brother-sister avoidance, and it is suggested that "these avoidances result from sexual conflict produced by the seductive and incestuous relationship between mother and infant consequent upon the prolonged postpartum sex taboo."[28]

---

[25] George P. Murdock, "World Ethnographic Sample," *American Anthropologist,* Vol. 59 (1957), pp. 664–87.

[26] For a criticism of this paper and an alternative hypothesis, more along the lines of the classic views of Arnold van Gennep, see Edward Norbeck, Donald E. Walker, and Mimi Cohen, "The Interpretation of Data: Puberty Rites," *American Anthropologist,* Vol. 64 (1962), pp. 463–85.

[27] John W. M. Whiting, "Socialization Process and Personality," in Francis L. K. Hsu (ed.), *Psychological Anthropology,* 1961, p. 361. See also Roger V. Burton and John W. M. Whiting, "The Absent Father and Cross-Sex Identity," *Merrill-Palmer Quarterly of Behavior and Development,* Vol. 7 (1961), pp. 85–95.

[28] John W. M. Whiting, "Socialization Process and Personality," p. 364.

This topic has been further pursued by William N. Stephens in his book *The Oedipus Complex. Cross-Cultural Evidence.*[29] Again making use of the cross-cultural files, Stephens reports a series of correlations between certain institutions, leading to the conclusion that an Oedipus complex is intensified by a long postpartum sex taboo. This results in lasting sexual fears, castration anxiety (manifest in the extensiveness of menstrual taboos, according to Stephens), and severity of avoidance rules. In agreement with the Whiting, Kluckhohn, and Anthony study, Stephens believes that the occurrence of initiations for boys is partly determined by the intensity of father-son rivalry.

Frank W. Young has proposed an alternative explanation for the occurrence of male initiation ceremonies, making use of the same cross-cultural methodology and data used by Whiting, Kluckhohn, and Anthony. His assumptions are more sociological and less psychoanalytic. Young claims that initiation ceremonies serve primarily to dramatize and reinforce the social solidarity of adult males. Male solidarity is particularly emphasized in what he calls "middle-level" societies, "where the variety of food exploitation patterns is limited and where the resources may be exploited by cooperative groups. Moreover, it is among such societies that intergroup hostilities conducive to male solidarity are possible."[30]

But what about the reported association of mother-child sleeping arrangements and postpartum sex taboos with male initiation rites? Young interprets these as being common traits in polygynous societies characterized by male solidarity. Young claims that when male social solidarity is controlled in his cross-tabulations, "no relation remains between the typology of child-care items and the presence of initiation ceremonies."[31]

Still another cross-cultural analysis (although not making use of the HRAF) is one by Yehudi A. Cohen, presented in two publications.[32] Cohen argues that while Whiting and his students have

---

[29] William N. Stephens, *The Oedipus Complex. Cross-Cultural Evidence* (Glencoe, Ill.: The Free Press, 1962).

[30] Frank W. Young, "The Function of Male Initiation Ceremonies: A Cross-Cultural Test of an Alternative Hypothesis," *American Journal of Sociology*, Vol. 67 (1962), p. 380; Frank W. Young, *Initiation Ceremonies. A Cross-Cultural Study of Status Dramatization* (Indianapolis, Ind.: Bobbs-Merrill Co., 1965.)

[31] Ibid., p. 383.

[32] Yehudi A. Cohen, *The Transition from Childhood to Adolescence. Cross-Cultural Studies of Initiation Ceremonies, Legal Systems, and Incest Taboos* (Chicago: Aldine Publishing Company, 1964); and "The Establishment of Identity in a Social Nexus: The Special Case of Initiation Ceremonies and Their Relation to Value and Legal Systems," *American Anthropologist*, Vol. 66 (1964), pp. 529–52.

claimed that initiation ceremonies function to resolve conflict in sex identity, they have not been able to show that such a conflict actually exists.

Cohen believes that there are two stages of puberty. The first, from about 8 to 10 years of age, the "latency" period, does not have observable changes in sex characteristics as does the succeeding second stage, although biochemical hormonal changes are already occurring in the earlier stage. During the first period it is common for people in different societies to weaken the child's ties with its family by instituting two practices. One is *extrusion,* the dislodgment of the boy from his home, so that he sleeps elsewhere, as in a men's house, dormitory, or the home of another relative. The second custom is brother-sister avoidance.

According to Cohen, initiation ceremonies usually take place during the second stage of puberty and are less drastic in their effects than the comparable experiences of the first stage. They are found in fewer societies than the customs of extrusion and brother-sister avoidance, which are also longer lasting. Cohen agrees with Young about the social functions of initiation rites in dramatizing male solidarity, and he suggests that initiation ceremonies tend to occur in societies which emphasize the importance of the wider kin group. Cohen's argument is complicated, with many ramifying side issues.[33]

More complexities are presented in considering the significance of the genital operations which sometimes take place in male initiations. There are three types: circumcision, supercision, and subincision. Writers who have speculated about the underlying motives for these operations usually consider them to be equivalent. Despite their different views, both Whiting and Young see the operations as accentuating the sexual differences between males and females. Bruno Bettelheim, on the other hand, sees them as making for sexual nondifferentiation, for through these operations the males want to make themselves like women, to have vulvas and to menstruate.[34]

Charles Harrington has pointed out that Bettelheim's theory was based primarily on cases of supercision and subincision and that he then extended his interpretation to apply to circumcision as well. Harrington argues that since the effects of supercision and cir-

---

[33] See the review by Melvin Ember, *American Anthropologist,* Vol. 67 (1965), pp. 1039–40.

[34] Bruno Bettelheim, *Symbolic Wounds: Puberty Rites and the Envious Male* (Glencoe, Ill.: The Free Press, 1954).

cumcision are quite different, they should be considered separately. Harrington's cross-cultural sample consisted of 21 societies having circumcision, 6 with supercision, and 81 with neither operation. His hypothesis is that in societies practicing circumcision at adolescence there will be a high degree of sexual differentiation in socialization practices, boys and girls being treated differently. But sexual differentiation should not be emphasized in societies which practice supercision. These predictions were supported by the statistical analysis.[35]

Whiting has pointed out that circumcision is more common in tropical than in temperate regions, and he has launched into wide-ranging speculations about the relationships between such factors as warm weather, people sleeping apart to stay cool, mother-child sleeping arrangements, and a long suckling period related to protein deficiency in rainy tropical areas. This chain of reasoning serves to explain why male initiation rites involving circumcision are often found in tropical regions.[36] Here, again, Yehudi A. Cohen has offered an alternative explanation. From his point of view, the customs of extrusion, brother-sister avoidance, and initiation ceremonies at puberty are all related to kin-group solidarity, which tends to be found, although not exclusively, in horticultural and agricultural societies. Since warm climate is a precondition for such socioeconomic systems, initiation ceremonies tend to be found in warm (Cohen does not say tropical) climates.[37]

While the literature on male initiation ceremonies has been full of conflicting opinions, there has also been controversy about female initiation ceremonies and allied features. In his book *Initiation Ceremonies,* Frank W. Young applies the solidarity hypothesis to girls' initiations and parenthood ceremonies,[38] while in another cross-cultural study Judith K. Brown concludes that female initiation rites occur in societies in which the girl does not leave her parents' home after marriage. Since the girl remains in the same social setting, such a ceremony serves to give notice of her changed status to adulthood. No such ceremony is performed in societies

[35] Charles Harrington, "Sexual Differentiation in Socialization and Some Male Genital Mutilations," *American Anthropologist,* Vol. 70 (1968), pp. 951–56.

[36] John W. M. Whiting, "Effects of Climate on Certain Cultural Practices," in Ward H. Goodenough (ed.), *Explorations in Cultural Anthropology. Essays in Honor of George Peter Murdock* (New York: McGraw-Hill Book Co., 1964), pp. 511–44.

[37] Yehudi A. Cohen, "On Alternative Views of the Individual in Culture-and-Personality Studies," *American Anthropologist,* Vol. 68 (1966), pp. 355–61.

[38] Frank W. Young, *Initiation Ceremonies,* pp. 105–121.

where girls leave home upon marriage, since the mere act of leaving home marks this change. Brown also notes that female initiation rites are found in societies in which women make a notable contribution to subsistence.[39]

Societies differ greatly in the attention given to first menstruation and subsequent menstrual periods, sometimes having such practices as secluding girls in separate huts and having them observe various taboos. William N. Stephens finds the origin of such customs in male castration anxiety, evidenced in a roundabout way in certain cultural institutions.[40] Frank W. Young and Albert Bacdayan, on the other hand, find menstrual taboos to be associated with male dominance and social rigidity, thus offering a sociogenic as opposed to Stephens' psychogenic explanation.[41]

OTHER CORRELATIONAL STUDIES

Landauer and Whiting conclude from a cross-cultural survey that in societies where infants are exposed to such practices as piercing of nose, lips, or ears, stretching of arms or legs, exposure to extreme heat or cold, abrasions, massage, or painful swaddling, there is an increase in adult male stature, when compared with societies that do not have such practices. The authors point to experiments in the stimulation of infant rats and mice, which show a more rapid rate of development than do nonstimulated unstressed rats and mice, suggesting that early exposure to stress has stimulating effects on the endocrine system and growth.[42]

Yehudi A. Cohen suggests an alternative explanation for the correlations found by Landauer and Whiting, hypothesizing that infants and children subjected to stress will eat more as a way of coping with anxiety, thus gaining in stature.[43] Whiting, however, rejects the idea that nutrition is a primary determinant of normal growth.[44]

---

[39] Judith K. Brown, "A Cross-Cultural Study of Female Initiation Rites," *American Anthropologist,* Vol. 65 (1963), pp. 837–53.

[40] William N. Stephens, "A Cross-Cultural Study of Menstrual Taboos," *Genetic Psychology Monographs,* Vol. 64 (1961), pp. 385–416.

[41] Frank W. Young and Albert Bacdayan, "Menstrual Taboos and Social Rigidity," *Ethnology,* Vol. 4 (1965), pp. 225–41.

[42] Thomas K. Landauer and John W. M. Whiting, "Infantile Stimulation and Adult Stature of Human Males," *American Anthropologist,* Vol. 66 (1964), pp. 1007–28.

[43] Cohen, "On Alternative Views. . . ", pp. 355–56.

[44] John W. M. Whiting, "Methods and Problems in Cross-Cultural Research," in Gardner Lindzey and Elliot Aronson (eds.), *The Handbook of Social Psychology* (2d

On the subject of food, or food sharing, Cohen has produced another cross-cultural study, arguing that in societies where young children are generously fed on demand there will be practices of food sharing among adults.[45] This article is paired with a cross-cultural study of friendship, both making use of the same sample of 65 societies. In the second study Cohen finds different forms of friendship to predominate in differently structured types of societies.[46]

Dorrian Apple Sweetser has examined the kinds of social situations in which avoidance relationships occur and argues that ". . . men will avoid their parents-in-law when unilineal affiliation is an important basis on which social relationships are organized, and yet residential family groups are fragmented and impermanent. Their wives will avoid their parents-in-law under the same conditions and when also the mother's brother has no special role to play; they tend not to avoid when such a special role exists."[47] In his avoidance behavior the person is saying, in effect, "I am affiliated with these people by marriage, not by blood. . . ." He also shows by such behavior that he is not disposed to sexual relations and thus respects the principle of family authority.

The foregoing survey of cross-cultural studies by no means exhausts the list. There are many more correlational studies which relate to culture-and-personality problems, but enough examples have now been given to illustrate the possibilities of the method.

ADVANTAGES AND DRAWBACKS

We may now discuss some of the advantages and drawbacks of the cross-cultural survey method. It must be said that the proponents of this method are quite aware of the criticisms that have been made of it; indeed, some of the best discussions of its difficulties appear in their works.[48]

ed.; Reading, Mass.: Addison-Wesley Publishing Co., Inc., 1968), Vol. II, p. 718. For some comments by anthropologists on the Landauer and Whiting thesis, see the brief communications by Edward E. Hunt, Jr. and C. I. Jackson, *American Anthropologist,* Vol. 67 (1965), pp. 997–1000.

[45] Yehudi A. Cohen, "Food and Its Vicissitudes: A Cross-Cultural Study of Sharing and Nonsharing," in Yehudi A. Cohen, *Social Structure and Personality. A Casebook* (New York: Holt, Rinehart & Winston, Inc., 1961), pp. 312–50.

[46] "Patterns of Friendship," ibid., pp. 351–86.

[47] Dorrian Apple Sweetser, "Avoidance, Social Affiliation, and the Incest Taboo," *Ethnology,* Vol. 5 (1966), p. 304.

[48] See, for example, John W. M. Whiting, "The Cross-Cultural Method," in Gardner Lindzey (ed.), *Handbook of Social Psychology,* Vol. I (Reading, Mass.: Addison-Wesley Publishing Company, 1954), pp. 523–31, and Donald T. Campbell, "The Mutual Methodological Relevance of Anthropology and Psychology," in Francis L. K. Hsu (ed.), *Psychological Anthropology,* (Homewood, Ill.: Dorsey Press, 1961) pp. 333–52.

First among the advantages of the cross-cultural correlational study is that this method encourages the formulation of hypotheses and the attempt to test them. The only question is how successfully they are tested in this way.

Another advantage of the cross-cultural correlational method is that it permits a cumulative building on previous studies. "The analysis of a sample drawn from these files will be available for the next study based on the same or an overlapping sample. This is particularly valuable if the analysis includes scalar judgments done with due care for independence and reliability."[49]

Turning to the question of how successfully hypotheses are tested by this method, we have seen that different solutions to a problem were presented by Whiting *et al.* and by Frank W. Young on the basis of the same data. Correlations do not speak for themselves. When one tries to present a causal explanation, various alternatives are possible. The mere appearance of a correlation, moreover, does not necessarily prove anything, even when it is in the "predicted direction." If two items are associated in a number of different cultures, this may be due to a number of different causes. We need not assume that the same complex of factors led to the association in each case.

Morris Cohen once expressed a perhaps extreme skepticism about the value of establishing correlations, or drawing conclusions from them. We need not follow him all the way, but his dissenting words are worth keeping in mind:

. . . correlations are often mere coincidences that do not indicate any significant connection, or any reason for expecting such correlation to continue. I have on several occasions referred to the high correlation of 87% for 13 years between the death-rate in the State of Hyderabad and the membership in the International (American) Machinists Union. If there are not many instances of this sort, it is because we do not, as a rule, look for them. We generally begin with a hunch or a suspicion of a causal relation between certain facts and seek for correlation to confirm it. But to regard such confirmation as proof is to commit the fallacy of arguing from the affirmation of the consequent. A number of diverse hypotheses, notably theologic ones, find their teachings confirmed by everything that happens, but this will not verify any one of them. For verification involves not only confirmation but the exclusion or disproof of alternative hypotheses.[50]

This is one aspect of the problem. But there are other difficulties inherent in the cross-cultural survey method. One of its disadvan-

---

[49] Whiting, "The Cross-Cultural Method," p. 530.

[50] Morris Cohen, "Causation and Its Application to History," *Journal of the History of Ideas*, Vol. 3, No. 1 (January 1942), p. 16.

tages is that there are so many steps in the procedure at which error can enter in: (1) on the part of the ethnographer reporting a piece of behavior, (2) on the part of the judge who has to classify or evaluate this behavior, and (3) on the part of the writer who makes an interpretation based on the judge's rating.

At step number 2, in the classification or rating of behavior, errors are easily possible. Norbeck, Walker and Cohen point out that in a discussion of the length of postpartum sex taboos in *Patterns of Sexual Behavior,* Clellan S. Ford and Frank A. Beach classify as short (from six weeks to 10 months) four societies that Whiting classifies as long (over one year).[51]

A more confused case is Arnold R. Pilling's criticism of Beatrice Whiting's analysis of Paiute sorcery. While noting that an anthropologist may misclassify his data before applying statistical methods and thus make the statistical operation meaningless, Pilling charged that Beatrice Whiting made some errors in classifying societies as having coordinate or superordinate control. The Paiute, Aranda, Trobrianders, and Zuñi were, according to him, wrongly classified.[52] But in this case Whiting has been supported by M. M. Bax and A. J. F. Köbben. In a check on Whiting's classifications, Bax concluded that her judgments were, after all, correct.[53] Such disagreements, however, make one doubtful about the procedures involved. And this is only one stage at which mistakes in judgment may be made.

Another difficulty is that the authors of cross-cultural studies sometimes have to find an indirect index for something they want to measure. The amount of inhibited aggression in a society cannot be measured directly. Horton therefore takes sorcery as an index of it; societies are rated as having either strong or weak belief in sorcery, and this is supposed to indicate which societies have much or little inhibited aggression. Murdock and Horton have both used premarital sexual freedom as an indirect measure of sexual anxiety. That is to say, they asume that societies which permit premarital sexual behavior have less sexual anxiety than those which restrict or taboo such behavior.[54] But while this seems reasonable enough, the

---

[51] Norbeck, Walker, and Cohen, "The Interpretation of Data: Puberty Rites," *American Anthropologist,* Vol. 64 (1962), p. 481.

[52] Arnold R. Pilling, "Statistics, Sorcery, and Justice," *American Anthropologist,* Vol. 64 (1962), pp. 1057–59.

[53] A. J. F. Köbben, "Why Exceptions? The Logic of Cross-Cultural Analysis," *Current Anthropology,* Vol. 8 (1967), p. 6.

[54] Horton, "The Functions of Alcohol in Primitive Societies," pp. 275–76.

case of Truk shows that premarital sexual freedom may be associated with considerable sexual anxiety.

In an interesting and almost convincing cross-cultural survey on the genesis of narcissistic personality, Slater and Slater frankly state the tenuous basis for their study. ". . . (*a*) it treats cross-cultural correlations as essentially identical with cross-individual correlations; (*b*) it allows a structural pattern to serve operationally for an interpersonal process; and (*c*) it argues for causation, albeit of a circular kind, on the grounds of correlation alone."[55] The authors add that these limitations are typical of cross-cultural studies having to do with socialization or personality.

Indirect indices of traits often seem unconvincing.

To get indices of negative fixation as expressed in beliefs about illness, Whiting and Child had judges determine whether "oral," "anal," or other explanations for illness were present in the cultures under review. Criteria were established to determine the necessary judgments, but the adequacy of some of these criteria may be questioned. For example, under "Oral Explanations" we find: "Verbal spells and incantations performed by other people are the material responsible for illness. This was selected as the one item which indicated concern about specifically oral activity in other people."[56] But under "Anal Explanations" we find: "The use of charms, curses, spells or incantations in ritual is responsible for illness."[57]

How is a conscientious judge to decide whether to label a spell oral or anal under these conditions? For both items the authors have psychoanalytic explanations. A verbal spell is related to the mouth—hence oral. A spell is related to compulsiveness, to ritual, and this "is a common outgrowth of severe toilet training";[58] so it is anal. Here, incidentally, the authors use psychoanalytic criteria in the process of testing some psychoanalytic hypotheses. Whether this is justifiable or not, it is certainly an involved procedure. Indeed, the complexity of the Whiting and Child demonstration sometimes takes on the dimensions of a Rube Goldberg machine.

Many of the cross-cultural studies have to do with the influence of early childhood experiences. The earlier studies suffered from

[55] Philip E. Slater and Dori A. Slater, "Maternal Ambivalence and Narcissism: A Cross-Cultural Study," *Merrill Palmer Quarterly of Behavior and Development,* Vol. 11 (1965), p. 241.

[56] Whiting and Child, *Child Training and Personality,* p. 150.

[57] Ibid., p. 151.

[58] Ibid.

the fact that there were not many careful descriptions of child training and children's behavior in the ethnographic literature. When
Whiting and Child report that their study is based on data from
75 societies, that sounds impressive, but for many of these societies
little information is available on the relevant topics. The authors
tell us that the material given to a judge for rating varied from
about one printed page to several hundred.[59]

In the appendix the authors give the "confident" ratings for their
75 societies, omitting those classed as "doubtful." A review of these
columns gives some idea of what the data are like. The following
societies have either a high or full complement of confident ratings:
Alor, Arapesh, Balinese, Chagga, Chiricahua, Dahomey, Hopi, Lep-
cha, Lesu, Manus, Marquesans, Navaho, Ontong-Javanese, Papago,
Samoans, Siriono, Tanala, Tenino, Teton, Western Apache, and
Wogeo. For these societies, then, good information about childhood
seems to be available. But the following societies have fewer than 6
confident ratings out of 17: Abipone, Chewa, Jivaro, Kazak, Kiwai,
Lapp, Omaha, Palaung, Riffians, Taos, Tiv, Wapisiana, Warrau,
Yukaghir, Yungar, Zuñi. Of these societies the Kazak received no
confident ratings at all, the Riffians only one, and the Zuñi two. If
the conclusions of the Whiting and Child book are based mainly
on the confident ratings, these conclusions are drawn from a relatively small number of societies.

As more ethnographic work of good quality is done, and as the
files improve, these problems will become less serious. Meanwhile
there is the question of the reliability or completeness of data in the
HRAF sources.[60]

A common criticism of cross-cultural surveys is that the method
involves pulling items of behavior out of context and forcing them
into pigeonholes for purposes of quantification. One may sometimes
question the degree of identity of institutions and patterns of behavior in different cultures which are classified together.

Another point often made about cross-cultural studies is that the
influence of diffusion tends to be ignored. Each society is counted as
a separate entity. Both the Hopi and Zuñi are listed by Whiting and

---

[59] Ibid., p. 49.

[60] Raoul Naroll has devoted a whole book to these problems as they affect the study
of culture stress: Raoul Naroll, *Data Quality Control—A New Research Technique.
Prolegomena to a Cross-Cultural Study of Culture Stress* (New York: The Free Press
of Glencoe, 1962).

Child, although they share the same general cultural tradition. In statistical assessments these societies should probably count as one, not two. But what about the Papago and the Navaho, who are also listed? These societies have been influenced by Pueblo culture and are not sealed off cultural islands.

The problem of diffusion was raised by Francis Galton at the meeting of the Royal Anthropological Institute in 1889, when Edward B. Tylor presented the first cross-cultural survey, suggesting relationships between particular descent systems and kin avoidance practices.[61] Avoidance relationships may have developed independently at many times and places, but they may also diffuse from one society to another. Harold E. Driver has, in fact, shown that this must have been the case in aboriginal North America. On the basis of a detailed survey, Driver remarked, ". . . one can predict whether an unspecified society will have kin avoidance from knowledge of its culture area and language family membership with greater accuracy than from knowledge of its residence, descent, or kinship terminology. Geographical-historical factors are more powerful than these functional ones."[62] The problem is how to control for diffusion in correlational cross-cultural studies. Various attempts have been made to cope with this difficulty.

Beatrice Whiting retested her hypothesis of the relationship between sorcery and coordinate control with a smaller number of societies (26) which she held to be distinct. This second test revealed significant correlations, as did the first. Whiting and Child retested their hypothesis of negative fixation separately for each of five major culture areas of the world: (1) Africa, including Madagascar, (2) Asia, including Japan, the Andaman Islands, and Lapland, (3) North America, (4) South America, (5) Oceania, including Australia, Indonesia, the Philippines, and Pacific islands. They found their hypothesis confirmed in these separate tests. The authors argue that this indicates "that the association between child training practices and explanations of illness is not simply spread by joint diffusion but is dependent upon some more or less universal functional relationship between them which creates the association anew within sets of societies living in any single region of the world."[63]

---

[61] See footnote 1, p. 167.

[62] Harold E. Driver, "Geographical-historical *versus* Psycho-functional Explanations of Kin Avoidances," *Current Anthropology*, Vol. 7 (1966), p. 148.

[63] Whiting and Child, *Child Training and Personality*, p. 187.

Raoul Naroll has been active in suggesting various techniques for solving "Galton's problem," to control for diffusion.[64] He has also been concerned with the related problem of defining the cultural units to be used in cross-cultural comparisons. What are we to compare—communities, tribes, nations, linguistic groups? Naroll coined a new term for his proposed unit: the *cultunit,* which he defined as "a group of territorially contiguous people who not only are domestic speakers of mutually intelligible dialects but also belong to the same state or contact group."[65] Naroll objected to the use of the local community as a unit in cross-cultural research. Whiting, Young, and Murdock, however, all consider the local community to be the most appropriate unit for such investigations.[66]

George P. Murdock and Douglas White have proposed a Standard Sample of well-described cultures to be used in cross-cultural studies. Each society is pinpointed to a specific date and locality. This becomes a necessary precaution when communities change in the course of time and are described by ethnographers at different periods. Formerly, each scholar who made cross-cultural studies chose his own particular sample of societies, and there was usually little overlap between samples. Murdock and White believe that there is need for a large world sample which could henceforth be used in many different studies, so that the results of each study may be intercorrelated with others. Hence the proposed Standard Sample, which includes 186 societies, divided as follows: 28 from Sub-Saharan Africa; 28 from the Circum-Mediterranean area; 34 from Eastern Eurasia; 31 from the Insular Pacific; 33 from North America; and 32 from South and Central America. In addition some past civilizations are included: Babylonia at the end of Hammurabi's reign; the Hebrews at the time of the Code of Deuteronomy; and the Romans of the early imperial period. Not all of these cultures are now represented in the HRAF files, which included 120 of the societies, or 64 percent, at the time of Murdock and White's publication.[67] It seems likely that many future studies will make use of the proposed Standard Sample.

[64] Raoul Naroll, "Two Solutions to Galton's Problem," *Philosophy of Science,* Vol. 28 (1961), pp. 15–39; Raoul Naroll and Roy G. D'Andrade, "Two Further Solutions to Galton's Problem," *American Anthropologist,* Vol. 65 (1963), pp. 1053–67; Raoul Naroll, "A Fifth Solution to Galton's Problem," *American Anthropologist,* Vol. 66 (1964), pp. 863–67.

[65] Raoul Naroll, "On Ethnic Unit Classification," *Current Anthropology,* Vol. 5 (1964), p. 286.

[66] John W. M. Whiting, "Methods and Problems in Cross-Cultural Research," p. 698.

[67] George P. Murdock and Douglas White, "Standard Cross-Cultural Sample," *Ethnology,* Vol. 8 (1969), pp. 329–69.

CONCLUDING COMMENTS

The kind of research described in this chapter is very different from most of the studies dealt with in preceding chapters. Malinowski, for example, made an intensive investigation of a single culture, trying to see it in all its complexity and to learn how its interrelated institutions impinge upon the members of the society. Malinowski's effort to "get inside the native's skin" and to see the world as a Trobriander sees it has been called an "emic" approach to the study of culture, in contrast to an "etic" approach, which Marvin Harris has defined as follows: "Etic statements depend upon phenomenal distinctions judged appropriate by the community of scientific observers."[68]

Like Malinowski, Franz Boas and many of his students had an emic approach. Marian W. Smith wrote that "Boas conceived of his main task as the adoption of an informant's mode of thought while retaining full use of his own critical faculties."[69]

From Boas's point of view, broad cross-cultural comparisons of institutions run into the difficulty that culture elements classified under the same rubric by an anthropologist might not be the same from the viewpoints of the peoples concerned. "If we choose to apply our classification to alien cultures we may combine forms that do not belong together. The very rigidity of definition may lead to a misunderstanding of the essential problems involved. . . ."[70]

The term "idiographic" is applied to the detailed study and understanding of a particular, unique entity, such as the personality of a particular individual, in contrast to the term "nomothetic" which refers to the search for general laws or principles, such as generalizations which would apply to all personalities. Boas's approach to culture was idiographic and relativistic, in contrast to the nomothetic and etic approach of Whiting, Murdock, and others who make studies using the Human Relations Area Files.

While Boas's reservations should be kept in mind, it seems to me that there need be no essential conflict between emic and etic approaches; we can learn from both approaches, and they may supplement one another. Moreover, what is learned from the intensive study of a single culture may be further investigated in cross-

---

[68] Marvin Harris, *The Rise of Anthropological Theory. A History of Theories of Culture* (New York: Thomas Y. Crowell Co., 1968), p. 575.

[69] Marian W. Smith, "Boas' 'Natural History' Approach to Field Method," in Walter Goldschmidt (ed.), *The Anthropology of Franz Boas*, Memoir 89 (Washington, D.C.: American Anthropological Association, 1959), p. 58.

[70] Franz Boas, "Recent Anthropology," *Science*, Vol. 98 (1943), p. 314.

cultural surveys. For example, Cora Du Bois described child rearing in Alor and ascribed to typical Alorese childhood experiences the characteristics of Alorese personality discussed in Chapter 7. As we have seen, D. N. Schack suggested that food deprivation could account for some of these traits, often found in societies with poor nutrition, while Ronald P. Rohner argued that parental neglect was the more significant determinant. In a cross-cultural survey Rohner found that his own hypothesis received support, while Schack's did not. In the chapter that follows we will see that a generalization about concern with "toughness" among lower middle-class males in our own society has been considered in the light of cross-cultural survey data. There are bound to be more extensions of this sort, checking on generalizations arrived at in one society through cross-cultural survey studies of others. The first example of a cross-cultural survey in this chapter, Beatrice B. Whiting's study of Paiute sorcery, followed this pattern.

There has been a remarkable increase in cross-cultural correlational studies in the past 10 years. In 1961, Donald T. Campbell complained about the neglect and rejection of this technique by anthropologists.[71] There seems to be no such neglect today, although Whiting has indicated that psychologists are using the cross-cultural method more than anthropologists are.[72] The list of suggested readings that follows, although far from complete, shows how much work has been done in this field in recent years.

Despite the criticisms that have been made here and elsewhere, cross-cultural surveys do seem to have been a stimulating addition to the field of culture-and-personality. They serve as a useful supplement to the intensive study of particular cultures. Moreover, the hypotheses put forward in these studies will give field workers a host of issues to check on in future field researches.

SUGGESTIONS FOR FURTHER READING

There is a comprehensive bibliography on cross-cultural research in Timothy J. O'Leary, "A Preliminary Bibliography of Cross-Cultural Studies," *Behavior Science Notes*, Vol. 4 (1969), pp. 95–115. See also the massive compilation in Robert B. Textor, *A Cross-cultural Summary* (New Haven, Conn.: HRAF, 1967). A review of what has been learned

---

[71] Donald T. Campbell, "The Mutual Relevance of Anthropology and Psychology," p. 346.

[72] John W. M. Whiting, "Methods and Problems. . . ." p. 693.

from cross-cultural studies is provided by Raoul Naroll, "What Have We Learned from Cross-Cultural Surveys?" *American Anthropologist,* Vol. 72 (1970), pp. 1227–88. See also John W. M. Whiting, "Methods and Problems in Cross-Cultural Research," in Gardner Lindzey and Elliot Aronson (eds.), *The Handbook of Social Psychology* (2d ed.; Reading, Mass.: Addison-Wesley Publishing Co., 1968), Vol. II, pp. 693–728.

For a recent review of some work in this field, emphasizing socialization, see Charles Harrington and John W. M. Whiting, "Socialization Process and Personality," in Francis L. K. Hsu (ed.), *Psychological Anthropology* (Cambridge, Mass.: Schenkman Publishing Co., Inc., 1972), pp. 469–507.

A few outstanding works which make use of this method deserve mention here, although they do not deal mainly with culture-and-personality problems.

George Peter Murdock's *Social Structure* (New York: Macmillan Co., 1949) bears the influence of Albert G. Keller's sociology, the anthropological approach of Franz Boas, behavioristic psychology, and psychoanalysis. It applies statistical analyses to data on social organization in 250 societies. Chapter 10, which presents an analysis of incest taboos and their extensions, is the section of the book most nearly related to culture-and-personality research. Otherwise the book is not primarily concerned with culture-and-personality but, as the title suggests, with social structure; hence it has not been dealt with here. Another study making use of the HRAF files is Guy E. Swanson's *The Birth of the Gods. The Origin of Primitive Beliefs* (Ann Arbor, Mich.: University of Michigan Press, 1960). Again, this work touches only peripherally on the field of culture-and-personality. It is a cross-cultural study of religious beliefs in 50 societies. Such beliefs as monotheism, polytheism, reincarnation, and witchcraft are explored by seeing how they are correlated with certain institutions in these societies. To give two examples: (1) there is a correlation between monotheistic beliefs and societies having the most stable sources of food, namely grain agriculture with settled residence; (2) societies with social classes are significantly more likely than others to possess a belief in superior gods.

Another work peripherally related to culture-and-personality is George C. Homans and David M. Schneider, *Marriage, Authority, and Final Causes: A Study of Cross-Cousin Marriage* (Glencoe; Ill.: The Free Press, 1955).

There have been some cross-cultural studies of suicide and homicide, including: Herbert H. Krauss and Beatrice J. Krauss, "Cross-Cultural Study of the Thwarting-disorientation Theory of Suicide," *Journal of Abnormal Psychology,* Vol. 73 (1968), pp. 353–57; and Herbert H. Krauss, "Social Development and Suicide," *Journal of Cross-Cultural Psychology,* Vol. 1 (1970), pp. 159–67; and David Lester, "Suicide, Homicide, and the Effects of Socialization," *Journal of Personality and Social Psychology* Vol. 5 (1967), pp. 466–68. See also Raoul Naroll, "Cultural Determinants and the Concept of the Sick Society," in Robert B. Edgerton and Stanley C. Plog (eds.), *Changing Perspectives in Mental Illness*

(New York: Holt, Rinehart & Winston, Inc., 1969), pp. 128–55; and Stuart Palmer, "Murder and Suicide in Forty Nonliterate Societies," *Journal of Criminal Law, Criminology and Police Science,* Vol. 56 (1965), pp. 320–24.

For a cross-cultural study of crime, see Margaret K. Bacon, Irvin L. Child, and Herbert Barry III, "A Cross-cultural Study of Correlates of Crime," *Journal of Abnormal and Social Psychology,* Vol. 66 (1963), pp. 241–300.

On the subject of romantic love, see Paul C. Rosenblatt, "A Cross-cultural Study of Child Rearing and Romantic Love," *Journal of Personality and Social Psychology,* Vol. 4 (1966), pp. 336–38; and "Marital Residence and the Functions of Romantic Love," *Ethnology,* Vol. 6 (1967), pp. 471–79. See also Robert M. Coppinger and Paul C. Rosenblatt, "Romantic Love and Subsistence Dependence of Spouses," *Southwestern Journal of Anthropology,* Vol. 24 (1968), pp. 310–19.

There are various studies which seek to relate patterns of early child training to concepts of the supernatural, attempting to find some cross-cultural statistical validation for the idea that religions are projective systems. One is "A Cross-Cultural Study of Some Supernatural Beliefs," by Melford E. Spiro and Roy G. D'Andrade, *American Anthropologist,* Vol. 60 (1958), pp. 456–66. A second is W. W. Lambert, Leigh Triandis, and Margery Wolf, "Some Correlates of Beliefs in the Malevolence and Benevolence of Supernatural Beings: A Cross-Societal Study," *Journal of Abnormal and Social Psychology,* Vol. 58 (1959), pp. 162–68. A third is another study by John W. M. Whiting entitled "Sorcery, Sin, and the Superego: A Cross-Cultural Study of Some Mechanisms of Social Control," in Marshall R. Jones (ed.), *Nebraska Symposium on Motivation* (Lincoln, Neb.: University of Nebraska Press, 1959). Each of these studies, in one way or another, tends to find confirmation for the projection hypothesis.

chapter 9

The Six Cultures Project

An important outgrowth of the work of John W. M. Whiting and his associates was the Six Cultures Project. Whiting recognized that there were deficiencies in the Whiting and Child volume, *Child Training and Personality,* discussed in the previous chapter. The ethnographic data available in the Yale files in 1953 had often been collected by anthropologists who were not particularly interested in child-rearing and reported on such matters only incidentally. The coverage of many aspects of childhood experience was not sufficient.

Some conferences were held among scholars from Cornell, Harvard, and Yale in 1953 and 1954 to plan a more extensive and intensive study of child-rearing in a few different societies. One product of these efforts was a handbook for fieldworkers written by Whiting and his associates, *Field Guide for a Study of Socialization in Five Societies.*[1]

In 1954 and 1955, six research teams were in the field, each making use of the field guide. Each team chose a community of between 50 and 100 families which became their unit of study. Special attention was given to 24 mothers in each society who had children between the ages of 3 and 10. These mothers were interviewed on a standard schedule, and their interaction with their children was systematically observed. It had been decided to rely on behavioral observation and interviews rather than use projective tests, although

---

[1] Originally mimeographed, later published as Volume I in the Six Cultures Series (New York: John Wiley & Sons, 1966).

some Child Thematic Apperception Tests were given. In observation and interviewing, particular attention was given to nine behavioral systems: succorance, nurturance, self-reliance, achievement, responsibility, obedience, dominance, sociability, and aggression. Each research team spent between 6 and 14 months in the field. Efforts were made toward comparability of data, and the reports were drawn up along similar lines. Part I of each report, called The Ethnographic Background, starts off with a description of the local environment, village plan, house types, basic economy, social organization, family type, religion, recreation, and other aspects of the adult world into which the child is born and to which he must adjust. Part II, called Child Training, deals with pregnancy and childbirth, infancy, weaning, early and late childhood.

These reports were published together first in one volume, *Six Cultures. Studies of Child Rearing,* edited by Beatrice B. Whiting,[2] and later, along with Whiting's *Field Guide* in a series of seven separate volumes. A later study, applying factorial analyses to the interviews with mothers in these reports, was *Mothers of Six Cultures. Antecedents of Child Rearing* by Leigh Minturn and William Lambert.[3] The present chapter presents a brief review of some of the data in these studies. The New Englanders of Orchard Town, described by John and Ann Fischer, will be omitted in this chapter.[4]

THE GUSII

The Gusii of Nyansongo, East Africa, differ from the other societies in having polygynous marriage as an important institution. Mother-child households and mother-child sleeping arrangements occur, since the husband rotates in visiting the houses of his different wives. This should lead to what William N. Stephens has called "diluted marriage," in which husband and wife are not emotionally close to one another. There may also be coolness between husband and wife due to the fact that a Gusii man was apt to take a wife from a clan with which his own clan has been at war. They have a proverb, "Those whom we marry are those whom we fight." Considerable hostility is shown to a Gusii bride at her wedding by

---

[2] Beatrice B. Whiting (ed.), *Six Cultures. Studies of Child Rearing* (New York: John Wiley & Sons, Inc., 1963).

[3] Leigh Minturn and William Lambert, *Mothers of Six Cultures. Antecedents of Child Rearing* (New York: John Wiley & Sons, Inc., 1964).

[4] John L. Fischer and Ann Fischer, *The New Englanders of Orchard Town, U.S.A.,* Six Cultures Series, Vol. IV (New York: John Wiley & Sons, 1966).

the groom's relatives who shout insults at her. We are told that Gusii girls feel very ambivalent about the prospect of marriage. (Residence is patrilocal.) The stage would thus seem to be set for emotional distance between husband and wife, which would be accentuated by quarrels between co-wives. There is a special Gusii word which means "hatred between co-wives."

The Gusii are unusual in having a kind of avoidance relationship between father and son. Father and son should not bathe together, see each other naked, or discuss sexual matters in one another's presence. A father must never enter the house of a married son. A son is expected to be obedient and deferential toward his father, who tends to be feared in childhood.

In addition to avoidance behavior between father and son, there is also some avoidance between a mother and her adult son, who may not go behind the partition in her house but is served food in the foyer or outside. Feelings of sexual shame are strongest of all between father and daughter. Avoidance rules are extended to classificatory fathers but are less stringent.

Although no formal postpartum sex taboo is reported, most of the other elements cited by Stephens as fostering an Oedipus complex seem to be present among the Gusii. On the basis of cross-cultural studies, Stephens claims that peoples with a "diluted marriage complex" are unusually phobic and taboo-ridden, particularly about matters involving sex.[5] Severity of avoidance relations would be related to this syndrome, which fits the Gusii case well. It is also in keeping with the theories of Whiting and Stephens that male (and also female) initiation ceremonies involving genital operations take place at puberty. However, one point does not jibe with Stephens' generalizations. There is no fear of menstrual blood among the Gusii, which would be expected by Stephens as an outcome of presumed male castration anxiety.

Despite the "diluted marriage complex," Gusii mothers do not seem to pour out their emotional feelings on their sons, as one might expect. The LeVines report that it is rare to see a mother kissing, cuddling, or hugging a child, although this may be done by grandmothers, child nurses, or other caretakers. Nevertheless, it is the mother rather than someone else that a frightened child runs to for comfort. The LeVines describe the Nyansongo child emerging from infancy as being fearful and dependent.

---

[5] William N. Stephens, *The Oedipus Complex. Cross-Cultural Evidence* (Glencoe, Ill.: The Free Press, 1962), p. 13.

Weaning, which often occurs at around the 19th month, is described as being very upsetting to the child, and this may be aggravated by the birth of a younger sibling, leading to temper tantrums. Fear is an important sanction in controlling children's behavior, including threats and warnings of bogeymen. Caning and other physical punishments are used. There seems to be no severity in toilet training, but attitudes toward sex are strict. Masturbation is strongly disapproved of, and children are beaten for it.

Among adults, sex seems to be associated with tension. A bride is expected to put up a fierce resistance to her husband's first sexual advances, while it is a matter for boasting on his part as to how many times he has been able to have intercourse the first night. An explicit purpose in this is to hurt the bride, so that the man can make her cry or have difficulty in walking the next day. These attitudes are not limited to the first night but continue to be important in later marital relations.

It is striking that the Gusii have a remarkably high rate of rape and also a fairly high rate of homicide. Drinking beer, a leading form of recreation for the men, often leads to quarreling and aggression. The Gusii are also outstanding for their litigiousness and readiness to accuse others of offenses.[6]

THE RAJPUTS OF KHALAPUR

Khalapur, about 90 miles north of Delhi, seems to be a typical north Indian village in which the Rajputs are the dominant land-owning caste. Although they are very different in culture and historical traditions, the following similarities may be noted between the Rajputs and the Gusii: both are agriculturists with military traditions, both have patrilineal descent, patrilocal residence, and live in joint family households; both have mother-child sleeping arrangements, with the Rajputs also having a postpartum sex taboo. Both have long suckling periods. If the Rajput sacred thread ceremony may be so considered, both have initiation ceremonies for boys. Both have some respect-avoidance relationships, especially affecting father-in-law and daughter-in-law. Both have ancestor cults.

As for differences, the Rajputs do not have polygyny or genital operations at puberty. Their marriages are arranged, whereas Gusii can choose their own mates. Gusii mothers, more than Rajput

---

[6] Robert A. LeVine and Barbara B. LeVine, *Nyansongo: A Gusii Community in Kenya,* Six Cultures Series, Vol. II (New York: John Wiley & Sons, 1966).

mothers, punish their children for aggression against themselves. In *Mothers of Six Cultures* they were rated as highest of the six cultures on this item. Rajput children were not reported to be upset by weaning as were the Gusii children. They have fewer chores to perform than Gusii children and were rated lowest of the six cultures in this respect. Girls in particular are given little work to do, for they are regarded as "guests" in their homes, which they must leave after marriage.

The Rajput and Mixtecan mothers were rated the least warm among the six samples.

Two important institutions in Khalapur are the caste system and the custom of purdah, or segregation of women. Both institutions serve to maintain social distance. Purdah, in particular, keeps women confined to their courtyards. A woman pulls her sari across her face in the presence of her husband or older men. She must always show respect to her mother-in-law, father-in-law, and other members of her husband's family. A man and his wife should not talk to one another in the presence of older members of his family. Minturn and Hitchcock say that since the mother-in-law is always around, and since the young wife cannot leave the courtyard, the only time they can whisper together is at night. But husband and wife do not sleep together. Men sleep in a separate men's house, sometimes visiting their wives briefly for sexual relations.

Men and women also eat separately. A woman takes her food to her own room or a corner of the courtyard. There is no family meal. Children are fed when they ask for food.

The confined life of the courtyard leads to occasional flaring up of temper among the women, quarrels, and sometimes divisions of the joint family. The Rajputs of Khalapur are described as being suspicious and mistrustful of the motives of other persons.[7]

A concern on the part of male Rajputs is to preserve their semen, which is thought to lead to vitality and spiritual strength. Sexual intercourse is therefore seen as weakening.[8]

A surprising aspect of Rajput childhood in Khalapur is the reported rarity of sibling rivalry. Minturn and Hitchcock explain this partly by noting that adults are not very affectionate with

---

[7] This is also reported by G. Morris Carstairs in *The Twice-Born. A Study of a Community of High-Caste Hindus* (Bloomington, Ind.: The Indiana University Press, pp. 39–62. The community he describes is a Rajput-dominated town in Rajasthan, North India.

[8] This topic, briefly mentioned by Minturn and Hitchcock, is discussed at greater length in Carstairs, *The Twice-Born*.

children, and infants are not given special attention, cuddled, or played with. Older children do not feel excluded or displaced. There are also many other older persons in a joint family household who can replace the mother in looking after a child. Temper tantrums seldom occur.

The explanations offered for the absence of sibling rivalry do not seem to explain it very well. If the mother does not give much love, one might expect the child to be demanding for the little love available and to compete for it. Some writers about childhood believe sibling rivalry to be an inevitable development. If so, its apparent absence must be due to suppression or repression, which in turn might lead to psychosomatic complaints like skin rashes and asthma, or to nightmares, bed-wetting, and feelings of anxiety, but we cannot say whether or not these are present in Khalapur.

In many ways the culture of Khalapur is similar to that of Silwa, Egypt, discussed in Chapter 2. In both of these peasant communities, there is sexual segregation, purdahlike behavior among the women, and an emphasis on deference toward older persons. One difference is the encouragement of sibling rivalry in Silwa and its apparently successful discouragement in Khalapur.

In Khalapur, we seem to have another case of "diluted marriage." Marriages are arranged. Men and women eat and sleep separately. But development of an Oedipus complex may be inhibited by the fact that the Rajput mother, like the Gusii mother, does not demonstrate much affection and does not cuddle or play with her children much. The child training process would seem to foster passive, dependent tendencies, which would be in keeping with joint family household life, arranged marriages, and the fact that occupation and clientele are largely determined by birth in a particular caste.[9]

TAIRA, OKINAWA

It was noted in Chapter 2 that in peasant communities like Silwa, Khalapur, and Tepoztlán there is often a good deal of mutual suspicion and mistrust. Although Taira is a peasant community, it seems to be more cooperative and characterized by friendlier interpersonal relations than the communities just mentioned. People seem to be quite willing to work for other families in a rotation system, which appears to function effectively. Formal cooperatives have been suc-

[9] Leigh Minturn and John T. Hitchcock, *The Rājpūts of Khalapur, India,* Six Cultures Series, Vol. III (New York: John Wiley & Sons, 1966) .

cessfully introduced. There are also mutual finance groups formed to extend credit for building construction, buying livestock, or other purposes. Taira seems to be relatively egalitarian. There is no caste system like that of Khalapur, nor any marked separation of the sexes as in both Khalapur and Silwa. Taira seems to be more progressive and modern in spirit than these other peasant communities. There is much more emphasis on education, much better schooling, and the involvement of parents in a PTA. Women have relatively high status. Some women are priestesses in the local religious cult. Although there are a few cases of polygyny, most marriages are monogamous. Courtship occurs, but there are more arranged marriages. One rather surprising item is that in a high percentage of marriages the wife is older than her husband. Few women marry before the age of 20. There is no postpartum sex taboo, and sexual intercourse is resumed about a week after birth. Husband, wife, and child sleep together; so there is no evidence of diluted marriage, and there is no exclusive mother-child sleeping arrangement.

The Taira mothers were rated highest of the six cultures on "warmth." They were also rated less hostile than any other group. Children are indulged in Taira and are considered to be not responsible until six years of age. A child is carried about most of the time during its first two years or so. There is no crawling stage for children. There is a belief that the habit of crying is formed in the first four months of life. Therefore a child is comforted, cuddled, and nursed until he stops crying. The early period of indulgence is gradually withdrawn by the mother as she returns to the work of gathering firewood in the mountains, which keeps her away from home most of the day. The period after weaning is very frustrating for the child. It is then looked after by child caretakers who are less indulgent than the mother. Although mothers are indulgent, they have some severe punishments, particularly the application of moxa, burning powder on the skin. A child's hands and feet may also be tied as a punishment. Striking, slapping, and pinching are also engaged in. However, these are all relatively rare, and praise and other positive sanctions are often used. Mothers are the main socializers. Fathers do not spend much time with their children, being gone most of the day, at work in the fields or hills.

A child is held to become responsible and teachable at seven. Children who die before this age are given unceremonious burials, but they have adult funerals after seven. This is the time of entrance into first grade at school, and also the time of assuming various chores, such as caring for younger children, cooking, cleaning, and bringing water. According to the Maretzkis, Taira children are often eager to assume such new responsibilities. Four- and five-year-olds ask if they may carry younger siblings. Such nurturant behavior is encouraged by the custom of children carrying dolls on their backs.

In contrast to the Gusii and Rajputs, there are no avoidance relationships, and there is nothing like purdah. There is no initiation ceremony, as among the Gusii, unless admission to the first grade be so considered. There are no genital operations. There seem to be no avoidance customs relating to menstruation. In these respects Stephens' generalizations seem to be supported, since the people of Taira have no postpartum sex taboo or mother-child sleeping arrangements, and they do not seem to have "diluted" marriages.

Despite the period of frustration after weaning and birth of a younger sibling, children are not aggressive toward younger siblings but are quite nurturant. There does not seem to be much sibling rivalry. Grandmothers may make up for some of the frustration the children suffer from their mothers' frequent absence from the home when they are at work. There seems to be some general tension between boys and girls during the latency period while they are attending school. Boys tease and bully girls, and there is sexual segregation, which often occurs at this age in societies in different parts of the world.

Children have a lot of independent play with much freedom to roam about the village. They usually play in groups of more than two; solitary play is discouraged. The people of Taira seem to be sociable and hard working but able to enjoy themselves in their free time. Although the community is relatively isolated, they are quite progressive in their adoption of new patterns, involvement in self-government and community responsibilities.[10]

THE MIXTECAN INDIANS OF JUXTLAHUACA, MEXICO

The Mixtecan community is a subgroup within a larger community. While the Rajputs are a dominant caste in Khalapur, the Mixtecans of Santo Domingo barrio form a sort of lower caste group looked down upon by the people of the main part of town. Between

---

[10] Thomas W. Maretzki and Hatsumi Maretzki, *Taira: An Okinawan Village*, Six Cultures Series, Vol. VII (New York: John Wiley & Sons, 1966).

the Mixtecan Indians and the townsmen there are differences in speech and dress and in food habits. They are divided by a geographical barrier, a *barranca* or ravine between the barrio and el Centro, the center of town. Hostility is shown to the Mixtecans by townsfolk. Indian children go to school there, but the town children may throw stones at them and insult them. The Mixtecan children have been trained not to fight back. The authors say that this cleavage serves to emphasize barrio solidarity. Indeed, there is much cooperative behavior within the barrio. There is very little ingroup aggression even under intoxication, in contrast to the Gusii; and there is no fear of sorcery *within* the barrio.

Like the Rajputs, people live in compounds in extended family groups, such as two brothers and their families. Residence is patrilocal. But there are some differences from the Rajputs in the direction of more independence for the nuclear family. Each nuclear family has separate sleeping quarters and cooking facilities and eats apart from the others. The food used by a particular woman is kept separate from that of all other women in the compound. Unlike Khalapur, the community is endogamous. Unlike the situation in India, there is no head of the extended family. Adult males still in the prime of life have more or less equal status, and an older brother does not have authority over the younger. Cousins are equated with siblings, the same kinship terms being used for both. Cousins may act as caretakers as often as siblings. The same sort of behavior is shown toward cousins as toward siblings; no special distinctions are made. But a child gets food from its parents and sleeps in their house; and a child's father and mother are closer than its uncles and aunts. However, a father does not usually interact much with his children except for boys aged 12 and over who work with him in the fields. The mother spends most of her time with her youngest child and oldest daughter. She attends the nursing child and gives instruction to the oldest daughter. The authors say that neither men nor women play much with children. Between infancy and young adulthood the children spend their days apart from adults. A child sleeps with its mother in infancy. Weaning, initiated abruptly at age one or two, marks the end of the time when a child is carried in a shawl. It is now turned over to caretakers. From this point on the child has considerable separation from the mother. Before about two years of age children are considered to be "senseless," but after that become "children who know." (There is a much longer period in Okinawa for the time when a child is held to be without understanding.) At six or seven children are held to be teachable. Before that they are given few chores; they work more thereafter.

In *Mothers of Six Cultures,* the Mixtecan mothers were rated among the least warm, along with the Rajput mothers, who were rated still lower on the scale. The mothers rank fifth in the amount of time they spend with children. The Mixtecan mothers demand a good deal of work from their children, but they seldom praise them for work well done.

In *Mothers of Six Cultures,* Minturn and Lambert suggest a reason for the low ratings of Mixtecan mothers on maternal warmth. As in Khalapur, a woman lives in a compound shared with her husband's brothers' wives. Adult ties are more intimate than in Khalapur, however, for Juxtlahuaca is an endogamous community, and most mothers are related to their sisters-in-law by blood as well as by marriage. Those who favor their own children over their cousins would risk disrupting family ties. It would therefore be bad for a mother to take sides with her own children in disputes. "Treating all children with some emotional distance and strongly discouraging fights among the children are highly functional socialization practices in this type of community."[11] The Mixtecan mothers were rated highest on punishment for aggression against peers. Since the adults themselves are unaggressive, the children have peaceful models with whom to identify. They are seldom beaten by their parents. The Romneys did not once see a parent strike a child.

Play groups in both early and late childhood are usually composed exclusively of closely related children. Unlike the situation in Okinawa, where mothers want their children to play with others, the Mixtecan mothers want their children to play alone—mainly to avoid getting into fights. This training against aggression seems to work. Although men drink a great deal at fiestas, they seldom fight. Children even avoided giving aggressive themes in Thematic Apperception Test Stories. The Mixtecans think that anger and aggression may cause sickness or even death.

After the age of 12, boys work in the fields and assume adult tasks. School education is a recent development; not much emphasis is placed on it by parents. Many children do not go to school, or skip attendance. Discipline at school is described as being almost chaotic.

---

[11] Minturn and Lambert, *Mothers of Six Cultures,* p. 207.

There is little stress on achievement motivation, which might conflict with the barrio solidarity which the people value so highly.[12]

ILOCOS BARRIO, TARONG, PHILIPPINES

In *Mothers of Six Cultures,* the Tarong mothers were rated second in maternal warmth after the mothers of Okinawa and last in emotional instability. Like the Mixtecan mothers, the mothers of Tarong rate high in the proportion of time in which a nonparental adult takes care of the children. The Philippine mothers do not live in extended family compounds as the Mixtecans do; they have nuclear family households. But the homes that compose a *sitio* are crowded close together. Siblings, cousins, and other close relatives may live close by. Women seem very willing to look after other women's children. Minturn and Lambert write: "More than most mothers they tend to rear their children as a group. . . . Women sometimes nurse each other's children, a custom seldom found in other groups."[13] Another woman is asked to suckle a child before its mother's milk comes.

The Tarong mother does not have to leave her home for work or marketing, as the Okinawan or Mixtecan mother must do. For the first month or so after childbirth the mother and child are confined to the house, resting on a special, inclined bed, where the mother is supposed to undergo therapeutic "roasting" for two or three weeks, together with massage. The closeness between mother and child continues after the first month. The child sleeps between the parents until the next child is born, perhaps when he is two or three years old. The general picture is one of great indulgence and nurturance. There is some teasing of children, however. Grownups pretend that they are going to take away something the child values. When the child cries, the onlookers laugh. This kidding seems to be in line with the shaming techniques which help to bring about obedient, submissive personalities in this culture.

There is a long suckling period, although supplementary foods are given from four months on. Weaning takes place between one and four years of age. Two or two and a half is considered to be the ideal age. There is no preparation for this event, and weaning is

---

[12] Kimball Romney and Romaine Romney, *The Mixtecans of Juxtlahuaca, Mexico,* Six Cultures Series, Vol. IV (New York: John Wiley & Sons, 1966).

[13] Minturn and Lambert, *Mothers of Six Children,* p. 212.

abrupt and apparently quite traumatic for the child, who may throw temper tantrums. These are dealt with leniently by the parents, since they recognize that this is a difficult period, but later displays of anger or aggression are punished. If a child has been displaced by a younger one, it is said that his hostility is not directed toward the younger sibling but toward his mother. Lightening the blow of weaning is the fact that there are usually several substitute care-takers available who will show an interest in the child and look after it. Also, the child has a new autonomy to replace his former relative lack of freedom. He becomes part of a children's group; play seems seldom to be solitary.

A mother need not worry about her child's straying from home; for all grownups in the community have a sense of responsibility for the children. While this gives a child security, it also means that he may be disciplined by any adult, not only his parents.

Training in responsibility begins early. Children of three are given chores to perform. By five, boys and girls carry water, feed stove fires, and help look after the baby. Older children run errands and learn to cook—boys as well as girls. Assignment of tasks by sex is not as rigid as in some other cultures. Children are praised if they undertake work associated with a higher age level.

One sanction in inducing good behavior is scaring techniques. Children are frightened by being told about evil spirits and other dangerous creatures. One bogeyman is a witchlike creature imper-sonated once or twice a year by a woman dressed up in a black cloak.

As seen by the people of Tarong, the world is divided into what is close, familiar, and trustworthy and what is foreign, uncertain, and dangerous. Quarrels within the *sitio* are kept under control, and efforts are made to smooth them over and forget about them. Interbarrio quarrels are more long-lasting. Outsiders and strangers may be feared and suspected of sorcery.

Children grow up playing mainly with siblings, cousins, and close relatives. By the age of eight or nine, they usually have a best friend of the same sex from whom they are inseparable.

School education is fairly recent, having begun only about 40 years ago, but education is valued. Almost all children attend the Tarong school for the first four years. Those who can afford it try to have their children graduate from sixth grade, and some go even further in education. Friendships at school seem to remain within *sitio* lines. The close friendships of the *sitio* group make possible the continued functioning of the men's cooperative work-exchange groups, an important aspect of the local economy.[14]

SOME INTERPRETATIONS

Some interesting speculations about the six cultures data have been presented by Beatrice B. Whiting. She makes use of the data to explore a hypothesis of Walter D. Miller's about lower-class American males' concern with "toughness," especially among street corner gangs. Miller points out that "a significant proportion of lower-class males are reared in a predominantly female household and lack a consistently present male figure with whom to identify and from whom to learn essential components of a 'male' role. Since women serve as a primary object of identification during pre-adolescent years, the almost obsessive lower class concern with 'masculinity' probably resembles a type of compulsive reaction-formation."[15]

Whiting points to a cross-cultural survey of correlates of crime made by Margaret K. Bacon, Irvin L. Child, and Herbert Barry III,[16] in which it was shown that both thefts and personal crimes such as assault, rape, suicide, sorcery, and murder are more common in societies having polygynous families and mother-child households than in societies with monogamous nuclear households. Whiting does not mention Stephens' concept of "diluted marriage," but she has the same assumptions about the relatively weak role of the father in polygynous societies with mother-child households. She refers to the papers by John W. M. Whiting and his associates on the relationship of this complex to male initiations at puberty, designed to break the mother-son bond and counteract the boy's cross-sex identity. As was noted in the previous chapter, some such ritual or its equivalent was held to be needed in a society in which the father plays a weak role in relation to the child during early childhood but in which males are more dominant and important than women

[14] William F. Nydegger and Corinne Nydegger, *Tarong: An Ilocos Barrio in the Philippines,* Six Cultures Series, Vol. VI (New York: John Wiley & Sons, 1966).

[15] Walter D. Miller, "Lower Class Culture as a Generating Milieu of Gang Delinquency," in Marvin E. Wolfgang, Leonard Savitz, and Norman Johnston (eds.), *The Sociology of Crime and Delinquency* (New York: John Wiley & Sons, 1958), p. 270.

[16] Margaret K. Bacon, Irvin L. Child, and Herbert Barry III, "A Cross-Cultural Study of Correlates of Crime," *Journal of Abnormal and Social Psychology,* Vol. 66 (1963), pp. 291–300.

in adult life. Feminine identification for a boy need not be a problem in a society in which men and women have roughly equal
status. In such a case, there should be no need for masculine protest.

Turning to the Six Cultures data, Whiting notes that there is
much more assault, homicide, and litigation reported for the Gusii
and the Rajputs of Khalapur than for the other four societies. These
are the two societies with the most diluted marriage, in which the
husbands neither regularly sleep with nor eat with their wives. Nor
do they work together with them. In Taira, Tarong, Juxtlahuaca,
and Orchard Town, on the other hand, there are family meals, the
father is home more often, and there is more shared activity, both
in work and recreation, between men and women. Of the six cultures, then, it is in Nyansongo and Khalapur that we would expect
to find "protest masculinity" and physical violence, in keeping with
Miller's hypothesis and the cross-cultural findings of Bacon, Child,
and Barry.[17]

This is a stimulating paper, but, as usual, other interpretations of
the same data are possible. In contrast to the other four societies,
the Gusii and Rajputs share traditions of cattle raiding and fighting,
traditions which have their own momentum, with no necessary relationship to diluted marriage. One might expect to find violence
and homicide in a society which emphasizes military virtues and
masculine pride.

We are also brought back to the problem of which units are to
be compared in cross-cultural comparisons. Following the recom-
mendations of John W. M. Whiting, Murdock, and Young, the
practice in Beatrice B. Whiting's paper has been to compare and
contrast local communities. But Orchard Town is not an isolated
social unit. It is part of a larger society in which there is a great
deal of violence and homicide.

John W. M. Whiting and Beatrice B. Whiting have continued to
analyze the data from the Six Cultures project. Their concluding
volume, not yet published, is tentatively entitled *Behavior of Children in Six Cultures*. The Whitings were kind enough to let me
read part of the manuscript on which they have been working. In
the following paragraphs I will summarize some of their findings.

The Whitings' analysis is based on the observations of children's

---

[17] Beatrice B. Whiting, "Sex Identity Conflict and Physical Violence: A Comparative
Study," *American Anthropologist*, Vol. 67 (1965), Special Publication: Laura Nader
(ed.), *The Ethnography of Law*, pp. 123–40. Some support for the views of Miller and
Whiting is provided in Charles C. Harrington's *Errors in Sex-Role Behavior in Teen-
Age Boys* (New York: Teachers College Press, 1970).

behavior made by the ethnographic teams in the six cultures. The methods employed in these behavioral observations are described in Chapter 11. The behavior that was observed and recorded involved social interaction, not solitary behavior, and generally covered a five-minute period for each sample of observation. The behavioral data were mailed to Cambridge, where they were coded according to 12 categories: *acts sociably, symbolic aggression, offers help, reprimands, offers support, seeks dominance, seeks help, seeks attention, suggests responsibly, assaults sociably, touches, assaults.*

When this material was quantified, the Whitings found that the six cultures fell into two distinct groups:

Type A: Nyansongo, Juxtlahuaca, Tarong
Type B: Taira, Khalapur, Orchard Town

At first glance, this grouping is puzzling. Attention was drawn above to the similarities between Nyansongo and Khalapur, which are here grouped separately. Attention was also drawn to similarities between Khalapur and Juxtlahuaca, which both have extended family compounds. One might therefore have expected a division like this:

Type A: Nyansongo, Khalapur, Juxtlahuaca
Type B: Taira, Tarong, Orchard Town

However, as the Whitings present their data and the inductive reasoning applied to them, their A and B types soon come to make sense and carry conviction.

Children of the three groups which make up Type A (Nyansongo, Juxtlahuaca, and Tarong) *offer support* significantly more, and *seek help* and *seek dominance* significantly less than the children in Type B. Children of Type A also *offer help* and *suggest responsibly* more than do children of Type B. It was hypothesized that the Type A cultures stress the importance of the group, while the Type B cultures are more individualistic.

Extended families share a courtyard in the three Type A cultures, but this is also true of Khalapur in Type B. It was decided that a more significant factor in differentiating the two types is degree of cultural complexity. The Type A cultures are all characterized by subsistence farming with little economic specialization and settlements composed mainly of dwellings, with few specialized buildings. The Type B cultures have more division of labor, a cash economy, some class or caste stratification, a centralized political and legal system, and communities containing specialized buildings of various sorts. Orchard Town and Khalapur also have an organized priesthood.

It seems reasonable to conclude that in the Type A cultures, children's contributions to the family work load are valued, and children are trained to be helpful and responsible. Chores such as bringing firewood and water, housecleaning, taking care of animals, farm work, running errands, carrying things, and looking after younger siblings are more often required of children in the Type A cultures than in the Type B cultures, and these chores are assumed at an earlier age than chores are assumed in the Type B cultures. The daily performance of such tasks, which represent real contributions, must give the child feelings of worth, responsibility, competence, and concern with the family welfare.

The tasks assigned to children in the more complex cultures may seem more arbitrary to the child, less self-evidently contributory to the welfare of the family or of the child himself. At the same time, school education plays a more prominent role in the Type B cultures and emphasizes individual achievement and egoism rather than concern for others. In the Type B cultures, children have to be trained for specialized roles for which they may have to compete. In this context, a stress on *seeking attention* and *seeking dominance* is understandable.

Punishment for disobedience or nonfulfillment of tasks was judged to be much more severe in the Type A than in the Type B cultures. This recalls Robert A. LeVine's comment, cited in Chapter 3, that the severe aggression training found in folk and peasant societies may be part of a general tendency to make children orderly, obedient, and pacific. The contrasts between the Type A and Type B cultures are also in keeping with the findings of John W. M. Whiting et al. in the Rimrock study discussed in Chapter 3 concerning the greater emphasis upon individualism and need for achievement among the Texans than among the Zuñi. There seems to be an evolutionary progression from Type A to Type B cultures, reminiscent of the change described by David Riesman from tradition-direction to inner-direction discussed in Chapter 17.

The ethnographic reports in the Six Cultures project which have been summarized in this chapter are among the best studies in the field of culture-and-personality. They gain in significance from the follow-up volumes, *Mothers of Six Cultures,* and the prospective publication, *Behavior of Children in Six Cultures,* with the analysis just discussed. Since Whiting's *Field Guide* has been used by other ethnologists in organizing their fieldwork,[18] more comparable accounts are being added to the original six, and it will soon be possible to judge how well the generalizations about the Type A and Type B cultures are supported when more societies are taken into consideration.

SUGGESTIONS FOR FURTHER READING

A work which made use of Whiting's *Field Guide* and is thus comparable to the reports described in this chapter is Thomas Rhys Williams, *A Borneo Childhood: Enculturation in Dusun Society* (New York: Holt, Rinehart & Winston, Inc., 1969).

Robert A. LeVine has published several articles on the Gusii. One which deserves mention is "Gusii Sex Offenses. A Study in Social Control," *American Anthropologist,* Vol. 61 (1959), pp. 965–90.

The work by Carstairs cited in this chapter makes good supplementary reading to the Minturn and Hitchcock report on the Rajputs. It contains some interesting life history material and Rorschach data.

A suggested reading in connection with the report on the Mixtecans is John Gillin, *The Culture of Security in San Carlos,* Middle American Research Institute, Tulane University of Louisiana, Publication No. 16, 1951. Gillin distinguishes between the ethos of the dominant and aggressive Ladino "caste" and the submissive Indian "caste" in a Guatemalan community. The nonaggressive Indians he describes are reminiscent of the Mixtecans in Juxtlahuaca.

A picture of Philippine life somewhat similar to that of the Nydeggers is Ethel Nurge's *Life in a Leyte Village* (Seattle: University of Washington Press, 1965). Nurge made use of the same *Field Guide* that was used by the investigators in the Six Cultures project. Another description of Philippine childhood is available in F. Landa Jocano, *Growing Up in a Philippine Barrio* (New York: Holt, Rinehart & Winston, 1969). There is a review of Philippine culture-and-personality studies by Robert Lawless, "The Foundation of Culture-and-Personality Research in the Philippines," *Asian Studies,* Vol. 5 (1967), pp. 101–36. The author gives a bibliography of 128 items. In general, he takes a dim view of Philippine culture-and-personality studies, which he says have been characterized by "inadequate methodology, unreliable operations, and unjustifiable conclusions." (p. 128). Lawless cites the Nydegger and Nurge studies and says that ". . . this is probably some of the best writing on Philippine culture-and-personality, and certainly the best on child rearing." (p. 112). But he doubts that their findings can be generalized for the Philippine rural population, or that generalizations can be made about the "lowland Filipino," since there are so many regional differences in the

---

[18] Some titles are mentioned in the "Suggestions for Further Reading."

Philippines. For a different view, see George M. Guthrie and Pepita Jimenez Jacobs, *Child Rearing and Personality Development in the Philippines* (University Park, Pa.: Pennsylvania State University Press, 1966).

Film: John T. Hitchcock has made a film about the Rajputs of Khalapur entitled *North Indian Village,* International Film Bureau, color, 32 minutes.

chapter 10

Studies of National Character

HISTORICAL REVIEW

During World War II many anthropologists were drawn into government agencies of one kind or another. Among the culture-and-personality specialists, Gregory Bateson joined the Office of Strategic Services, and Margaret Mead lectured in England for the Office of War Information. Geoffrey Gorer, Alexander Leighton, Clyde Kluckhohn, and Ruth Benedict all worked for the Office of War Information, with Gorer later shifting to the British Embassy wartime staff. During this time Mead, Gorer, Bateson, and Benedict were trying to delineate the "national character" of various countries, such as Rumania, Thailand, and Japan.

One difficulty in such an enterprise was that a war was going on, and travel to Japan was impossible. Neither Gorer nor Benedict had ever been to that country. What they did was to interview Japanese living in the United States and to read and analyze Japanese books, magazines, and films. They studied Japanese history and tried to see the world as the Japanese saw it.

As mentioned in Chapter 1, Gorer's long-distance conclusion was that Japanese national character has a compulsive tendency, showing a preoccupation with ritual, tidiness, and order, stemming from severe early toilet training which results in repressed unconscious feelings of aggression.[1]

---

[1] Geoffrey Gorer, *Transactions of the New York Academy of Sciences,* Series II, Vol. V, pp. 106–24. Reprinted in Douglas G. Haring (ed.) , *Personal Character and Cultural Milieu. A Collection of Readings* (Syracuse, N.Y.: Syracuse University Press, 1949) , pp. 273–90.

But do the Japanese have very severe toilet training? Here Gorer's information was limited to the following brief comment:

After four months the child is held out over the balcony or road at frequent intervals, either when it cries, or when its guardian considers the time is ripe; any lapse from cleanliness is punished by severe scolding, the mother's voice expressing horror and disgust, and often also by shaking or other physical punishment. The training is meant to be complete by the time the child can toddle on to the balcony and all informants agree that this ideal is obtained.[2]

A similar interpretation of Japanese character was written at about the same time by Weston La Barre, who had been Community Analyst with the War Relocation Authority at a Japanese civilian internment camp at Topaz, Utah, and had thus had some contact with Japanese and Japanese-Americans. He had already written the bulk of his paper when he came across a summary of Gorer's findings in *Time,* August 7, 1944.

The Japanese, [wrote La Barre] are probably the most compulsive people in the world ethnological museum. The evidence is, I believe, conclusive that they are even more compulsive than the north Germans. . . . The analytic psychiatrists describe the individual compulsive character in a manner which is in almost one-to-one correspondence with the ethnographer's description of typical Japanese character structure.[3]

La Barre listed these compulsive traits as follows:

. . . secretiveness, hiding of emotions and attitudes; perseveration and persistency; conscientiousness; self-righteousness; a tendency to project attitudes; fanaticism; arrogance; "touchiness"; precision and perfectionism; neatness and ritualistic cleanliness; ceremoniousness; conformity to rule; sadomasochistic behavior; hypochondriasis; suspiciousness; jealousy and enviousness; pedantry; sentimentality; love of scatological obscenity and anal sexuality.[4]

In the rest of his paper La Barre went on to document the presence of these characteristics among the Japanese. Like Gorer, he assumed that the traits in question stemmed from severe toilet training in early childhood. However, since neither he nor Gorer had made observations on family life in Japan, their conclusions, although quite consistent, were open to question. Would not life in a war relocation camp, with all its attendant indignities, foster in

---

[2] Gorer, in Haring, *Personal Character and Cultural Milieu,* p. 278.

[3] Weston La Barre, "Some Observations on Character Structure in the Orient: The Japanese," *Psychiatry,* Vol. 8 (1945), p. 326.

[4] Ibid.

many individuals of different nationality such traits as secretiveness, hiding of emotions and attitudes, self-righteousness, a tendency to project attitudes, fanaticism, arrogance, touchiness, conformity to rule, sadomasochistic behavior, hypochondriasis, suspiciousness, jealousy, enviousness, and sentimentality? Interviews with people in such a setting and observations of their behavior would not necessarily give the same picture that one would receive in peacetime Japan. On the positive side, however, was the fact that both Gorer and La Barre were able to document their interpretations with a number of examples of Japanese behavior which do strike an American reader as seeming "compulsive."

After the war Ruth Benedict published her book on Japan, *The Chrysanthemum and the Sword*. Here she echoed Gorer's view about early toilet training:

> Everyone agrees that a baby in Japan, as in China too, is trained very early. . . . He experiences only an inescapable routine implacably insisted upon. Besides, the mother has to hold the baby away from her body, and her grip must be firm. What the baby learns from the implacable training prepares him to accept in adulthood the subtler compulsions of Japanese culture.[5]

However, this is not a major theme in Benedict's book, and the link with obsessive-compulsive behavior is not made.

In 1947 Hermann M. Spitzer published an article entitled "Psychoanalytic Approaches to the Japanese Character,"[6] in which he wrote that "the whole Japanese civilization presents the pattern of a compulsion neurosis."[7] This point of view, therefore, had a number of proponents. Unfortunately, none of them seems to have been to Japan. The linkage of the alleged personality traits with severe toilet training suggested by Gorer and La Barre had the advantage of being consistent with Freudian doctrine, but the empirical problem remained—whether or not toilet training in Japan actually is severe.

In the 1948 and 1949 editions of Haring's reader, *Personal Character and Cultural Milieu*, there is an article by Mildred Sikkema, omitted in the third edition, entitled "Observations on Japanese Early Child Training."[8] The observations in question

---

[5] Benedict, *The Chrysanthemum and the Sword, Patterns of Japanese Culture* (Boston: Houghton Mifflin Co., 1946), pp. 258–59.

[6] In Géza Roheim (ed.), *Psychoanalysis and the Social Sciences* (New York: International Universities Press, 1947), Vol. I, pp. 131–56.

[7] Ibid., p. 139.

[8] In Haring, *Personal Character and Cultural Milieu*, pp. 590–99.

were made, not in Japan itself, but among Issei and Nisei families in Hawaii. The author noted in the parents of these families an absence of emotional involvement in toilet training practices. According to her, there was little early disciplinary training; urination and defecation were not tinged with the same emotional tone for the Japanese as for Westerners.[9]

Three articles in Haring's third edition touch on the same matter. By the time this volume appeared in 1956, peace and the Japanese occupation had made it possible for Americans to do research in Japan itself. Reporting on eight months' fieldwork in a Japanese fishing community, Edward and Margaret Norbeck describe a toilet training regime which does not seem at all harsh.[10]

In another article in the Haring volume, Betty B. Lanham presents the findings of a questionnaire filled out by parents in the city of Kainan (449 respondents). Each household was asked to complete three forms, one dealing with the children of the household, one concerning the father's, and one concerning the mother's childhood. Concerning toilet training, Lanham observes:

> The wide range and distribution of practices with respect to toilet training could hardly be interpreted as meaning that in Japan punishment or completion occur at an unduly early age. In a like manner, the forms of punishment administered are not indicative of severity. . . . Toilet training may not be too different from what occurs in the United States.[11]

In another essay in the same volume, Douglas G. Haring argues that most of the allegedly compulsive traits of the Japanese can best be explained by the existence of a police state which exerted a close supervision over the individual for three centuries.

To say this does not refute psychoanalytic interpretations, for relentless police supervision modifies the human psyche profoundly. Psychological explanations, however, should be oriented to the facts of inescapable absolutism and sumptuary control of individuals. The psychological tensions habitual in parents outweigh details of specific practices such as

---

[9] Ibid., pp. 591, 599. However, J. C. Moloney has claimed that La Barre ". . discredited the Sikkema effort by pointing out that a statistically important percentage of the so-called 'Hawaian Japanese' are really Okinawans." J. Clark Moloney, "Discussion," in Milton J. E. Senn (ed.), *Problems of Infancy and Childhood* (New York: Josiah Macy Jr. Foundation, 1951), p. 35.

[10] Edward Norbeck and Margaret Norbeck, "Child Training in a Japanese Fishing Community," Haring, *Personal Character and Cultural Milieu* (3d ed., 1956), pp. 657–58.

[11] Betty B. Lanham, "Aspects of Child Care in Japan: Preliminary Report," in Haring, *Personal Character and Cultural Milieu*, p. 581.

toilet training. Police controls impose strains on individuals—strains that multiply and become more rigorous as adulthood is reached.[12]

Haring suggests two checks on this hypothesis: (1) If police controls were relaxed, would a change in character take place? (2) Are there "places not reached by Tokugawa discipline, where pre-Tokugawa customs survive . . ."?[13] Haring answers both questions in the affirmative. Having returned to Japan after the war, he has been struck by a marked change in the Japanese. "People now go where they wish, choose friends and write letters as they please, speak their minds with apparent freedom. The complex language of social status is falling into disuse."[14]

Haring goes on to describe the people of Amami Ōshima, an island situated between Kyushu and Okinawa. Tokugawa legislation never affected these islanders, and according to Haring their customs preserve traces of pre-Tokugawa Japan.

The picture of the neurotic "compulsive personality" does not fit Amami Ōshima. Local physicians deny the occurrence of neuroses; I saw a few apparently neurotic individuals, all of whom had been educated in Japan or in the United States. The taut repressions of the prewar Japanese do not appear in Amamians; they are not secretive, do not conceal emotions, are not unduly persistent, are free from self-righteousness and exaggerated conscientiousness, and, to put it mildly, hold their passion for ritual cleanliness within bounds.[15]

The author concludes, then, that police coercion has been a more significant factor in molding Japanese national character than toilet training. The point seems well taken. The only difficulty is that Haring's conclusions about the differences between prewar and postwar Japanese and between Japanese and Amamians are largely impressionistic. He has, however, presented a convincing thesis.

More recently Robert N. Bellah has, like Haring, drawn attention to the Tokugawa period as an important period in the shaping of Japanese national character. Bellah finds that the samurai code of values was spread, at that time, through some of the merchant and farmer classes by certain popular religious movements. This resulted

[12] Douglas G. Haring, "Japanese National Character: Cultural Anthropology, Psychoanalysis, and History," in Haring, *Personal Character and Cultural Milieu*, p. 432. Originally published in *The Yale Review,* copyright by Yale University Press.
[13] Ibid.
[14] Ibid., p. 433.
[15] Ibid., p. 437.

in something analogous to the "Protestant ethic" of hard work and self-denial.[16]

After World War II the anthropologists who had been engaged in government work continued their investigations of national character. Ruth Benedict established a project called Columbia University Research in Contemporary Culture, under a grant from the Office of Naval Research. A series of cultures was studied: those of China, Czechoslovakia, East European Jews, France, Poland, Russia, Syria, and Germany. Some of this work was continued in successor projects—Studies in Soviet Culture and Studies in Contemporary Cultures. Thus, between 1947 and 1953, a group of more than 120 people, representing 16 nationalities, were engaged in a collaborative investigation of national character. Some of the leading figures involved, beside Ruth Benedict and Margaret Mead, were Conrad Arensberg, Geoffrey Gorer, Sula Benet, Ruth Bunzel, David Rodnick, Martha Wolfenstein, and Rhoda Metraux.[17]

One of the leading projects of the Columbia group concerned Russian national character. Ruth Benedict invited Geoffrey Gorer to participate in the Columbia University project, particularly to develop hypotheses concerning Russia. Following the policy of interviewing Russian emigrés in New York and studying Russian novels, films, and cultural data, Gorer soon found a key to the Great Russian character: the institution of swaddling.[18] Gorer's swaddling hypothesis was discussed at some length in the first edition of this book, but it now seems too farfetched and inadequate to merit further attention here.[19]

A better organized investigation of Russian national character was carried out by a team of researchers in the Harvard Project on the Soviet Social System. They employed questionnaires, tests, and interviews with former Soviet citizens who decided not to return to the U.S.S.R. after World War II. Almost 3,000 subjects completed a long written questionnaire; 329 were interviewed for life history data, and from the latter group 51 were chosen for further

[16] Robert N. Bellah, *Tokugawa Religion, The Values of Pre-Industrial Japan* (Glencoe, Ill.: The Free Press, 1957).

[17] Margaret Mead and Rhoda Metraux (eds.), *The Study of Culture at a Distance* (Chicago: University of Chicago Press, 1953), pp. v, 6.

[18] Geoffrey Gorer and John Rickman, *The People of Great Russia. A Psychological Study* (New York: Chanticleer Press, 1950). (First published by The Cresset Press, London, England, 1949.)

[19] For an exposition of Gorer's views and criticisms of them, notably by Bertram D. Wolfe, see pp. 128–33 of the 1963 edition.

clinical study. Each of the Russian subjects in the latter group was given the Rorschach, TAT, a sentence completion test, and other personality tests. The Russians were compared with a "control" group of Americans matched with the Russian sample with regard to age, sex, occupation, and education.[20]

While this study was not done in the Soviet Union itself, it was certainly less "at a distance" than Gorer's. A possible weakness is that the subjects were refugees who chose not to return to the Soviet Union and thus might have been atypical in some respects. The clinical group was "disproportionately male, young, well educated, well placed occupationally and politically, and 'active' in defecting."[21]

The authors found the most salient trait of the Russian personality to be their need for affiliation, involving close personal relationships. A need for dependence was also manifest. In contrast to the American subjects, there was little stress on the need for achievement. The Russians showed awareness of their own impulses and tended to accept them as natural and to live them out. They readily expressed emotions and also criticized themselves and others freely. They showed fewer defensive reactions than the American subjects and seemed to have secure self-esteem, although they were also capable of lapsing into depression.[22]

It is hard to say how "modal" these traits might be for Russians in general. As refugees, the subjects were in atypical situational circumstances, which may have influenced the kinds of responses they made to interview questions and testing. But the authors' generalizations seem to have more secure foundations than Gorer's.

It may be that exaggerated formulations of national character like Gorer's led to desertion of this field of investigation. In 1962 David M. Potter noted that, while a philosopher may be described as a blind man in a dark room looking for a black cat that isn't there, a student of national character is in similar straits but is looking for a black cat which cultural anthropologists insist *is* there.[23] But, more recently, they have not been insisting on that. In a 1967 review of such literature, E. Adamson Hoebel noted that

---

[20] Alex Inkeles, Eugenia Hanfmann, and Helen Beier, "Modal Personality and Adjustment to the Soviet Socio-Political System," in Bert Kaplan (ed.), *Studying Personality Cross-Culturally* (Evanston, Ill.: Row, Peterson & Co., 1961), pp. 201–24.

[21] Ibid., p. 203.

[22] Ibid., pp. 205–12.

[23] David M. Potter, "The Quest for the National Character," in John Higham (ed.), *The Reconstruction of American History* (New York: Humanities Press, 1962), p. 210.

between 1942 and 1953, 10 or more books by anthropologists about national character were published, but since 1960 there have been only 2: Jules Henry's *Culture against Man,* and Francis L. K. Hsu's *Clan, Caste, and Club.*[24] In a 1967 review of psychological anthropology, Pertti J. Pelto concludes that the heyday of national character studies is over, at least for the present.[25]

It is easy to see why anthropologists are reluctant to generalize about national character. A modern nation is so large, with so many subunits, classes, professions, and differences in status, that it would be hard to find a basic or modal personality structure applicable to the whole population, or to most of it. Moreover, cultures change, and modal personality may change too; Elizabethan Englishmen seem to have been different from Victorians.

THE WORK OF FRANCIS L. K. HSU

In current anthropology, the most active proponent of national character studies is Francis L. K. Hsu, who has not been deterred by the slackening of his colleagues' interest in this field. Hsu grew up in China, graduated from the University of Shanghai, received a Ph.D. from the University of London in 1940, and then returned to China to do ethnological research in a Chinese community. Since 1947, Hsu has been in the Department of Anthropology at Northwestern University. The experience of having lived and worked in both China and the United States sharpened Hsu's sense of culture consciousness and his interest in the comparative study of national character. One of his books is *Americans and Chinese: Two Ways of Life*[26]. This cross-cultural investigation was carried a step further in Hsu's *Clan, Caste, and Club,* in which India was brought into

---

[24] E. Adamson Hoebel, "Anthropological Perspectives on National Character," *The Annals of the American Academy of Political and Social Science* (Philadelphia), Vol. 370 (1967), pp. 1–7.

Jules Henry describes his own book as "a passionate ethnography"; it is an arraignment of American culture, which suffers from the fact that it does not contrast the American way of life with that of any other nation, such as England, France, the Soviet Union, or Japan. (Jules Henry, *Culture against Man* [New York: Random House, Inc., 1963].) Francis L. K. Hsu's work on national character is discussed in the next few pages. (Francis L. K. Hsu, *Clan, Caste, and Club* [Princeton, N.J.: D. Van Nostrand Co., Inc., 1963].)

[25] Pertti J. Pelto, "Psychological Anthropology" in Bernard J. Siegel and Alan R. Beals (eds.), *Biennial Review of Anthropology* (Stanford, Calif.: Stanford University Press, 1967), p. 151.

[26] Francis L. K. Hsu, *American and Chinese: Two Ways of Life* (New York: Henry Schuman, 1953).

the picture. Here Hsu presented the argument that Hindus are supernatural-centered, Chinese are situation-centered, and Americans are individual-centered. Self-reliance is the key to the American character, while the importance of the family or clan is the key to Chinese character. Hsu has done ethnological fieldwork in Japan as well as in China and India. Accordingly, a Japanese edition of *Clan, Caste, and Club* includes an analysis of Japanese character as well, and Hsu is preparing a book on Japan for publication in English.

In 1969, Hsu published *The Study of Literate Civilizations,* in which he discussed the difficulties of making comparative studies of large complex nations. Hsu offered two solutions: one was the use of postulates in the manner of E. Adamson Hoebel, a technique discussed in Chapter 3. A second solution was the analysis of kinship, not only its structure but also what Hsu calls its content, which concerns the quality or character of interpersonal relations.

Hsu makes use of the term *dyad,* a two-person link such as father-son or husband-wife. Hsu believes that in a family system one dyad usually takes precedence over the others; he calls this the dominant dyad. Hsu offers the following hypothesis: "The dominant attributes of the dominant dyad in a given kinship system tend to determine the attitudes and action patterns which the individual in such a system develops toward other dyads in this system as well as toward his relationships outside of the system."[27]

According to Hsu, the Chinese kinship system is dominated by the father-son dyad, while the American system is dominated by the husband-wife dyad. Various consequences follow from the dominance of a particular dyad.

Hsu's hypothesis was further explored in a conference of anthropologists who discussed its applicability in a number of different societies. One difficulty is how to determine which is the dominant dyad in a particular kinship system. For example, Hsu suggested that Japan is a father-son dominated society, but a Japanese member of the conference, Takao Sofue, disagreed with this conclusion and pointed to the strong (covert but more emotional) mother-son relationship.[28] In another paper in the symposium, Marion J. Levy,

---

[27] Francis L. K. Hsu, *The Study of Literate Civilizations* (New York: Holt, Rinehart & Winston, 1969), p. 86.

[28] Takao Sofue, "Some Questions about Hsu's Hypothesis: Seen through Japanese Data," in Francis L. K. Hsu (ed.), *Kinship and Culture* (Chicago: Ill.: Aldine Publishing Company, 1971), pp. 284–87.

Jr. stated that "The mother-son relationship clearly cannot be the dominant one in any save matrilineal situations. . . ."[29] In analyzing family life in a Mexican village, Robert C. Hunt concluded that the father-son and mother-son relationships are equally dominant.[30] A good deal of confusion thus seems to attend the testing of these hypotheses. Hsu will no doubt pursue these questions further in forthcoming publications.

STUDIES OF JAPANESE NATIONAL CHARACTER

By this time the reader may have become impatient with the subject of national character. But let us stick with it a little longer. There still remains the problem of group differences. There must be at least some basis for the national stereotypes which are reflected in jokes about Englishmen, Scotchmen, Frenchmen, Germans, and other national groups. Let us take as a more detailed illustration the investigation of Japanese national character. It happens that some of the best work in culture-and-personality research since World War II has been done in Japan. Much of this work has focused on child training practices (not simply toilet training), and the review that follows will thus emphasize childhood experiences.

One justification for attempting generalizations about Japan is that its people long shared a relatively homogeneous culture. As Richard K. Beardsley put it: "Few areas of comparable population anywhere in the world have had such culturally homogeneous people who were so long isolated from other peoples. . . . In isolation, the Japanese missed what most peoples have experienced, a constant rubbing of elbows with outsiders. . . ."[31]

One of the best community studies in anthropological literature, which incidentally involves research in culture-personality relations, is the study of the village of Niiike in the southwestern part of the island of Honshu.[32] In their Foreword the authors note that even in

---

[29] Ibid., p. 39.

[30] Robert C. Hunt, "Components of Relationship in the Family: A Mexican Village," Ibid., pp. 106–43.

[31] Richard K. Beardsley, "Personality Psychology," in John Whitney Hall and Richard K. Beardsley, *Twelve Doors to Japan* (New York: McGraw-Hill Book Co., 1965), p. 360.

[32] Richard K. Beardsley, John W. Hall, and Robert E. Ward, *Village Japan* (Chicago: University of Chicago Press, 1959).

1959 almost half the Japanese population was rural, living in small rice-growing communities like Niiike. Moreover, a large proportion of city dwellers are recent migrants from such villages, which to some extent represent "the traditional cultural foundation of all modern Japan."[33]

The case for Japan's cultural homogeneity may be overstated here, but a consideration in its favor to which Nyozekan Hasegawa has drawn attention is that while other ancient Eurasian civilizations developed from walled cities, the civilization of Japan grew up in unwalled communities open to the outer world. To be sure, there was much fighting in the feudal Japanese period, and the *daimyo,* or feudal overlords, did have walled, fortified castles, but there were no walled cities like those of Europe and China.[34] In the survey that follows, data from both urban and rural communities (including Niiike) will be presented.

Sleeping Arrangements

One way in which Japanese families differ from American and European families is in their characteristic sleeping arrangements, the subject of a study by William Caudill and David W. Plath.[35] Caudill and Plath interviewed parents about the sleeping arrangements in their families. They have data on 332 households, 198 in Tokyo, 99 in Kyoto, and 26 in Matsumoto. The sample had an average of 4.8 persons per household. There were no one-person or two-person households. The sample was close to the 1960 census which found an average of 4.8 persons per household for all urban areas. No important differences in sleeping arrangements were found for different social classes. (This seems surprising, for one would expect more crowding in the lower classes.) Almost all the rooms counted had *tatami* mat covering, with people sleeping on quilts (*futon*) which are spread out each evening and removed in the morning after the people get up. Only 10 percent of the people used beds of Western style.

It was found that children sleep with parents to a much older age than is usually done in the United States. ". . . the sharpest break

---

[33] Ibid., p. viii.

[34] Nyozekan Hasegawa, *The Japanese Character. A Cultural Profile,* trans. John Bester, (Tokyo, Japan: Kodansha International Ltd., 1966), p. 37.

[35] William Caudill and David W. Plath, "Who Sleeps by Whom? Parent-Child Involvement in Urban Japanese Families," *Psychiatry,* Vol. 29 (1966), pp. 344–66.

in sleeping arrangements comes between the children who are 11 to 15 years old and those who are 16 to 20 years old. The former have a 50 percent chance of co-sleeping in a two-generation group (with a parent or extended kin member), whereas the latter have only a 17 percent chance of so doing."[36] The authors believe that the onset of puberty for a boy and of menstruation for a girl set the stage for withdrawal from co-sleeping with older persons. On the basis of their tables the authors state that a child can expect to co-sleep with an adult until he is 10 years old. The period from 11 to 15 years is one of transition. "After the age of 16, a child is more likely to co-sleep with a sibling or to be alone, but there always remains a fair chance (at about the 20 percent level) that he will co-sleep with a parent."[37] After 16, daughters are more apt than sons to co-sleep with a parent. Sons are more likely to sleep alone. Caudill and Plath conclude that: ". . . sleeping arrangements in Japanese families tend to blur the distinctions between generations and between the sexes, to emphasize the interdependence more than the separateness of individuals, and to underplay (or largely ignore) the potentiality for the growth of conjugal intimacy between husband and wife in sexual and others matters in favor of a more general familial cohesion."[38]

The authors point out that age periods when people commonly sleep alone coincide with age periods when suicide rates are high, as in adolescence and old age. They do not suggest that sleeping alone causes suicide but indicate that it may add to the sense of isolation for a person who has been used to co-sleeping patterns for most of the rest of his life. Where causal factors are concerned, much of the stress during adolescence in Japan seems to be related to the competitiveness of academic life and the struggle to be admitted into good schools and colleges. (This will be discussed later.) The physical isolation of the lone sleeper may add to his or her anxiety and depression.

One consequence of the Japanese sleeping arrangements seems to be some inhibition of sexual activity. In a study of a rural agricultural community in northern Shikoku, Robert J. Smith reports that sexual relations are engaged in as quickly as possible after a married couple's children have gone to sleep; neither partner disrobes fully,

---

[36] Ibid., pp. 352–53.

[37] Ibid., p. 353.

[38] Ibid., p. 363.

and there is almost no foreplay.[39] A similar picture is given of marital relations in the village of Niiike,[40] and in Ezra F. Vogel's study of middle-class Tokyo suburban families. Vogel claims that married couples in the suburban community called Mamachi have intercourse less frequently than American couples and have less foreplay. He gives comparative figures for frequency of intercourse per week for different age brackets in the United States and Japan, with the American figures coming from the Kinsey report on *Sexual Behavior in the Human Female* (1953) and the Japanese figures being drawn from a study by Nobuo Shinozaki, "Report on Sexual Life of Japanese" (1957), based on a sample of 635 persons in or near Tokyo. In the Japanese sample, 38.9 percent reported no foreplay before intercourse, while all of the American sample reported foreplay. The American frequencies for intercourse were higher for each age bracket than the Japanese.[41]

Statistical assessments like these may be open to question, but the findings seem to be consistent. According to Vogel, sexual repression makes it difficult for young wives to enjoy sexual relations soon after marriage.

Japanese and American Infants: Some Contrasts

Some different patterns in the early infancy of Japanese and American babies from middle-class homes have been noted by William Caudill and Helen Weinstein. The authors made observations in the home on 30 Japanese and 30 American firstborn normal three- to four-months-old infants and their families. All the families were judged to be middle class on the basis of occupation and level of education. The Japanese mothers in the sample were a little older than the American mothers and more frequently breast-fed their babies. Eighteen of the Japanese, but only five of the American mothers, were breast-feeding at the time of the observations.

The authors used a time-sampling procedure for about four hours on each of two days. "In this method, one observation of approximately one second in duration is made every fifteenth second in terms of a set of predetermined variables concerning the behavior

---

[39] Robert J. Smith, "The Life Cycle," in Bernard S. Silberman (ed.), *Japanese Character and Culture. A Book of Selected Readings* (Tucson, Ariz.: University of Arizona Press, 1962), p. 188.

[40] Beardsley, Hall, and Ward, *Village Japan*, p. 333.

[41] Ezra F. Vogel, *Japan's New Middle Class. The Salary Man and His Family in a Tokyo Suburb* (Berkeley, Calif.: University of California Press, 1963), p. 220.

of the infant and of the caretaker."[42] Four observations were made each minute; 40 in a 10-minute period. Eighteen hundred observations were available for each case for two days. On the first day, observations were made from 9:30 A.M. until noon; on the second day from 1:30 P.M. until 4:00 P.M.

The two samples, of course, are very small; it is questionable how representative they may be of Japanese and American middle-class mothers and infants. The study is still in progress. Meanwhile, some of the results have suggested that there may be considerable differences in the behavior of Japanese and American babies as early as three or four months of age. The American infants, for example, were more active than the Japanese babies. The American children played more with objects and gave more "happy" vocalizations. The Japanese infants were quieter, more passive, with more "unhappy" vocalization. The American infants were left alone more.

Differences were also noted in the behavior of the respective caretakers. The American mothers talked more to their babies, while the Japanese mothers rocked and lulled them more. The American mother seems to be trying to stimulate her baby, whereas the Japanese mother seems to have a more soothing effect, trying to keep the baby quiet and contented.[43]

Patterns of Bathing and Carrying

The closeness of Japanese mother and child is reflected in bathing customs. Middle-class Japanese families have private wooden bathtubs, usually heated by gas. They are narrower and deeper than American bathtubs. The bather crouches in it, knees drawn up, up to his neck in very hot water. Soaping and washing are done beforehand, outside the bath. Pleasure is derived from sitting and soaking in the tub. The washing must be done beforehand, since the water must stay clean for all the family members. Father, the head of the household, usually goes first, followed by sons in order of age, and then by the female members. If the mother is cleaning the dishes, she may take her bath last. The mother takes her young baby into the bath with her, in contrast to the bathing situation in the middle-

---

[42] William Caudill and Helen Weinstein, "Maternal Care and Infant Behavior in Japan and America," *Psychiatry*, Vol. 32 (1969), p. 19.

[43] Ibid., pp. 28–31. See also William Caudill and Helen Weinstein, "Maternal Care and Infant Behavior in Japanese and American Urban Middle Class Families," in Reuben Hill and Rene König (eds.), *Families in East and West* (The Hague, Neth.: Mouton, 1970), pp. 39–71.

class American home, where the mother stands outside the bath and bathes her baby.

Poorer families and those who have no private bath go to public baths, where there are usually separate baths for men and women. Boys below two or three years of age are taken by the mother to the women's side, but boys older than that are taken by the father to the men's bath.

Close contact with the mother is also represented by carrying techniques. For the first year or two of life the baby is carried on the mother's back with a special strap. In wintertime, when she goes out, the mother may wear a coat which covers both herself and the child. Babies being carried this way generally look quite contented. If the baby cries, the mother may jiggle it. According to Ruth Benedict, this form of carrying is conducive to passivity in the child and develops a capacity (which Benedict attributes to the Japanese) of being able to fall asleep anywhere, anyhow.[44]

One reason why the child is so constantly carried during the first year of life is that there are some dangers during the crawling period, particularly in the open floor-level toilet, into which the child might fall. The places for cooking and heating are also dangerous for children. Moreover, parents do not want their children to poke fingers through the sliding paper doors.[45]

Early Oral, Anal, and Sexual Disciplines

In the responses to Betty B. Lanham's questionnaire on child care in the city of Kainan, the lowest ages for completion of weaning were between nine months and one year and two months; the highest was six years, eight months. Weaning generally takes place after the first year.[46] This would support Benedict's statement that children are usually weaned after they can understand what is said to them. A mother teases a child who wants to continue suckling, comparing him unfavorably with a younger child who has already been weaned.[47]

Despite the claims by Gorer and La Barre, most reports suggest

---

[44] Benedict, *The Chrysanthemum and the Sword*, p. 257.

[45] Smith, "The Life Cycle," p. 192; Beardsley, Hall, and Ward, *Village Japan*, p. 293.

[46] Lanham, "Aspects of Child Care in Japan," p. 567. Mamachi middle-class women also continue breast-feeding for more than one year. (Vogel, *Japan's New Middle Class*, p. 231).

[47] Benedict, *The Chrysanthemum and the Sword*, p. 261.

that toilet training is not severe. The conclusions of the Norbecks, Lanham, and Haring were cited earlier in this connection. Smith writes that children are expected to have control over elimination processes by the age of two, "but because toilets in rural Japan are so dangerous, most parents do not permit the child actually to use the toilet alone until he is three or four years old."[48]

The Japanese do not have a puritanical rejecting attitude toward sex. Both Ruth Benedict and Robert J. Smith write that Japanese do not condemn childish sexuality or regard masturbation as dangerous.[49]

Methods of Achieving Compliance

Children, then, seem to be treated with much permissiveness and indulgence. With regard to the frequency of punishment, however, there are conflicting reports in the literature. Beardsley, Hall, and Ward write that "Loud-voiced commands, repetitions, and detailed instruction, scolding or tongue-lashing, and physical beating are relatively rare and disapproved in Niiike homes.[50] The same point is made by Vogel in his description of Mamachi parent-child relations; mothers seldom yell at, scold, or spank their children. "Several Japanese mothers, visiting the United States, have expressed their shock at the cruelty and crudity of American mothers who spank and yell at their children in public places such as supermarkets."[51]

However, Betty B. Lanham's questionnaires did elicit high percentages of reports of slapping and spanking used by parents to enforce compliance in children. Lanham estimated the frequency of slapping to be quite similar to what might be expected in the United States.[52] These conflicting findings may reflect subcultural differences.

The literature also contains conflicting conclusions about "spoiled" behavior in children. Some writers, including John F. Embree, Ruth Benedict, and Geoffrey Gorer, claim that Japanese children are spoiled and that boys are rude and aggressive to their mothers. In his work on Suye Mura, the only important community

---

[48] Smith, "The Life Cycle," p. 190.

[49] Benedict, *The Chrysanthemum and the Sword*, p. 270; Smith, "The Life Cycle," p. 193.

[50] Beardsley, Hall, and Ward, *Village Japan*, p. 296.

[51] Vogel, *Japan's New Middle Class*, p. 244.

[52] Lanham, "Aspects of Child Care in Japan," p. 578.

study made in Japan before World War II, Embree wrote that Suye Mura children ". . . can and do strike their mothers in a rage and call them the favorite Japanese epithet of *baka* (fool). Anything a child asks for or cries for long enough he gets."[53] Benedict echoed Embree's statement that the little boy may strike his mother with his fists. Such tantrums ". . . in both villages and upper-class homes . . . are looked upon as an ordinary part of child life between three and six. The baby pommels his mother, screams, and, as his final violence, tears down her precious hair-do. His mother is a woman and even at three years he is securely male. He can gratify even his aggressions."[54] But on the basis of her questionnaires, Betty B. Lanham denies that mothers generally acquiesce to such abuse from their sons. Two of her tables show ". . . that in a majority of families the mother as well as (or instead of) the father, is used as a threat to enforce proper behavior on the part of her young son. In slightly under half the families reporting, the mother punishes by slapping the boy."[55] In these areas, then, there is evidently much variation.

Besides slapping, other methods of achieving compliance are used. Threats and scaring techniques are employed, frightening the child by saying that he will be punished by god, or harmed by devils, the thunder god, goblins, the dead, and various animal spirits. Policemen, beggars, neighbors, or teachers may be invoked as threatening figures.

In Lanham's questionnaire, 17 percent of the parents reported the use of moxa cautery, which involves burning a cone of moxa powder on the child's skin, leaving a scar. This is done not only as a punishment but as a therapeutic technique, which may lessen its traumatic effect on the child. "He has at least some chance of perceiving moxa treatment as an act of love, however painful it may be."[56] Shaming, scolding, and ridicule are also used an sanctions for good behavior.

Vogel presents a very interesting account of how Mamachi middle-class mothers achieve obedience and compliance in their children. Part of the secret is that the mother teaches only when her child is in a cooperative mood. She wants to establish such a close relationship with him that he will automatically go along with her sug-

---

[53] John F. Embree, *Suye Mura. A Japanese Village* (Chicago: University of Chicago Press, 1964), pp. 184–85.

[54] Benedict, *The Chrysanthemum and the Sword*, p. 264. See also Gorer in Silberman (ed.), *Japanese Character and Culture*, p. 315.

[55] Lanham, "Aspects of Child Care in Japan," p. 581.

[56] Beardsley, Hall, and Ward, *Village Japan*, p. 294.

gestions. The mother avoids situations where she must force the child to do something against his will. She tries to anticipate difficulties and to resolve them before they develop. On shopping trips she carries a supply of candies to dispense if the child starts to get restless. Flattery and praise are given for good behavior. In addition to these positive sanctions, which do not always work, Mamachi mothers also make use of threats, shaming, and ridicule.[57]

Another technique used by Japanese mothers, according to George De Vos, on the basis of an analysis of Thematic Apperception Tests given in Niiike (discussed further below), is the assumption of quiet suffering. The mother reproaches herself if her children behave badly or fail to become successful.[58] This somewhat masochistic response is encouraged by popular literature directed toward Japanese women. "Among the favorite themes of movies, television, drama, and magazine fiction is that of the quiet suffering of a girl, young wife, or elderly mother whose self-sacrifice makes her a lovable person and wins copious tears from the responsive female audience."[59] A person who fails in life, and who has thereby hurt his mother, may feel guilt in consequence.

School Education

The pressure to achieve begins when children start going to school. Japanese children are required by law to complete nine years of schooling. Once admitted to school, no student is failed. While this may diminish the pressure somewhat, Japanese students work hard at their home assignments. Examinations are required for entrance to schools and colleges. According to Vogel, there are special schools in Tokyo to prepare three-and-four-year olds for their kindergarten entrance examinations. Great anxiety attends all school examinations, not only on the part of the child but also on that of the mother, often resulting in sleeplessness on nights before examinations.[60]

Mamachi middle-class mothers help their children with their homework. "In a sense, parents become assistant teachers, checking frequently with the regular teachers about the work the parents

---

[57] Vogel, *Japan's New Middle Class,* pp. 243–51.

[58] George De Vos, "The Relation of Guilt toward Parents to Achievement and Arranged Marriage among the Japanese," *Psychiatry,* Vol. 23 (1960), pp. 287–301.

[59] Beardsley, "Personality Psychology", p. 375.

[60] Vogel, *Japan's New Middle Class,* pp. 46–51.

should be doing to help educate and train their children. Therefore to a large extent the parent-child relationship is the relationship of teacher and student."[61]

The child's performance in school reflects on his family. If he does badly, he lets them down. According to both Ruth Benedict and Geoffrey Gorer, when a teacher sends in a bad report about the child, the family turns against the child.[62]

The Sense of Obligation

Ruth Benedict devotes four chapters of her book to discussing the Japanese emphasis on payment of obligations, for which the Japanese have a special vocabulary. Two words in particular are emphasized in her account: *on* and *giri*. Benedict defines *on* as a load, an indebtedness, or burden which one must repay. One receives *on* from the Emperor, from one's parents, and from one's teacher or superiors. Somehow one must make a return for the benefits received from these sources. *Giri* is another term for obligation, such as repayment for a kindness. Benedict speaks of *"giri* to one's name," which involves keeping the family reputation unsullied. This emphasis may lead to such features as stoicism, dignified comportment and living up to one's commitments in life.[63]

Notions of obligation were emphasized by both Buddhist and Confucian teachings, particularly among members of the warrior class of samurai during the Tokugawa period (1600–1867).[64] While such notions are still part of the Japanese tradition, Benedict probably exaggerated their importance in relation to Japan of the 1940s. One of the criticisms made by Japanese scholars who read *The Chrysanthemum and the Sword* after the war was that it seemed too much like a description of Japan during the feudal period.[65]

Achievement Motivation

Several writers have drawn attention to the stress on achievement motivation in Japan. We find evidence of this stress not only in

---

[61] Ibid., p. 65.

[62] Benedict, *The Chrysanthemum and the Sword*, pp. 273–74.

[63] Ibid., chaps. 5–8.

[64] See below, pp. 469–70.

[65] John W. Bennett and Michio Nagai, "Echoes: Reactions to American Anthropology: Japanese Critique of Benedict's "Chrysanthemum and the Sword," *American Anthropologist,* Vol. 55 (1953), pp. 404–11.

middle-class suburban Mamachi but also in rural Niiike, as manifest in Thematic Apperception Test stories told by the villagers. In analyzing Niiike TAT stories, George De Vos identifies four types: (1) self-motivated achievement, (2) encouraged or inspired achievement, (3) achievement as repayment, and (4) achievement as expiation. In the first category, there is an emphasis on persistence and success at all costs, which De Vos believes to be characteristic of the Japanese in comparison with other cultures. In the second category, the father is usually the source of inspiration, an example to his son. The third category involves *on* relationships; since parents undergo hardships to raise and educate their children, the children must succeed as a way of repaying them. The same theme occurs in the fourth category; a person who has let down his parents and thus incurred guilt tries to make amends by hard work and dedication.

One source of guilt in many of the Niiike TAT stories is the choice of a love marriage in opposition to one's parents. Guilt is not expressed for sexual transgressions; rather, the main transgression is rebellion against the parents. The worst eventuality is seen to be excommunication from the family or community.

It is rather surprising to find such an emphasis on achievement motivation in a farming village. De Vos draws attention to a contrast with characteristic American middle-class achievement stories, in which a young man leaves home to strike out for himself. In the Niiike stories the protagonist does not want to leave home, and if he does leave to study and work elsewhere, the story often ends with his return home.[66]

Some Generalizations on Personality

Let us now review some aspects of child development as described in the foregoing pages and see what effects they may have in personality formation. Perhaps the most striking feature is the very close mother-child relationship manifest in sleeping arrangements, bathing, carrying, suckling, and education. One consequence of these patterns may be some sexual inhibition. Caudill writes that the close mother-child relationship results in a strong attachment to the mother and a sense of trust in others but also in ". . . a chronic mild depression and nostalgia in later life concerning the loss of child-

---

[66] George De Vos, "Social Values and Personal Attitudes in Primary Human Relations in Niiike," *Occasional Papers,* Center for Japanese Studies, University of Michigan, 1965, pp. 53–91.

hood gratification," which he says is expressed in Japanese plays, movies, and songs.[67]

L. Takeo Doi thinks it significant that the Japanese have a term *amaeru,* for which there is no English equivalent. It refers to an attempt, usually on the part of a child, to get into a state of close dependence on another person. Doi writes that the desire to *amaeru* affects people in adult life and becomes manifest in therapeutic sessions. He cites a number of other Japanese terms related to the concept of *amaeru* for which, again, there are no English equivalents, although the feelings and attitudes to which they refer are universally recognizable. Doi mentions that Japanese do not say that an infant does *amaeru* until he is about one year old. This suggests that by that time the child has come to realize that his wish to *amaeru* may be frustrated.[68]

The closeness of early familial ties combined with some inevitable suppression and renunciation must lead to a certain constraint in personality. In a work on the psychology of the Japanese, Hiroshi Minami notes that the Japanese seldom express happiness, for which there are relatively few words in the Japanese language, although there are many Japanese words for unhappiness.[69] In looking up words for happiness in Obunsha's *Essential English-Japanese Dictionary* (revised edition), to check on this generalization, I found that there are, after all, quite a few Japanese words for happiness, but these do not refer to the more extreme ranges suggested by such English terms as gaiety, exhiliration, exuberance, rapture, and ecstasy.

As for unhappiness, Hiroshi Minami notes that it is a common theme in postwar popular songs which often deal with loneliness, helplessness, parting and "giving up."[70] However, this may mainly reflect the confusion of the postwar period. Despite such themes of

---

[67] William Caudill, "Anthropology and Psychoanalysis: Some Theoretical Issues," in Thomas Gladwin and William C. Sturtevant (eds.), *Anthropology and Human Behavior* (Washington D.C.: The Anthropological Society of Washington, 1962), p. 206.

[68] L. Takeo Doi, "*Amae:* A Key Concept for Understanding Japanese Personality Structure," in Robert J. Smith and Richard Beardsley (eds.), *Japanese Culture. Its Development and Characteristics* (Chicago: Aldine Publishing Company, 1962), pp. 132–39.

[69] Edward Norbeck and George De Vos, "Japan," in Francis L. K. Hsu (ed.), *Psychological Anthropology. Approaches to Culture and Personality* (Homewood, Ill.: The Dorsey Press, 1961), p. 24.

[70] Hiroshi Minami and members of the Institute of Social Psychology, "A Content Analysis of Post-War Japanese Popular Songs," in Hidetoshi Kato (ed. and trans.), *Japanese Popular Culture. Studies in Mass Communication and Cultural Change* (Rutland, Vt.: Charles E. Tuttle Co., 1959), pp. 109–23.

sadness, there seems to be no overt expression of sadness in every-day life. The people of Niiike are described as living in an atmo-sphere of quiet tranquility, which comes ". . . in good part from the restraint put on all expression of emotion. Exuberance is repressed; so is every form of violence. The people smile readily and often; they laugh not infrequently, but gently, never in boisterous guf-faws."[71] Also writing of Niiike, De Vos refers to the muted quality of emotional expression; ". . . few opportunities exist for the ex-pression of feelings with any vehemence or abandon. . . . Both happy and disturbed feelings generally remain muted and sup-pressed."[72] In Ruth Benedict's terms, the Japanese seem to be more Apollonian than Dionysian. This is suggested by a passage in Nyoze-kan Hasegawa's *The Japanese Character*. The emotional outlook of the Japanese, he tells us, ". . . is less subjective than objective, less romantic than realistic, less extreme than middle-of-the-way, less grandiloquent than concise, less pretentious than unassuming, less out-of-the-way than commonplace, less heroic than sensible."[73]

With the strong sense of responsibility, obligation, and need for achievement discussed earlier, there must be a concomitant sense of tension. William Caudill believes that there is an underlying ex-citability among the Japanese which is held in check by compulsive orderliness.[74]

Fortunately, Japanese culture has developed many institutions for relaxing tension and adding to the enjoyment of life: the family meal, the daily hot bath, *sake* parties, bars and geisha houses for the men, massage houses, and such refinements as the tea ceremony and the enjoyment of gardens. Ruth Benedict even includes sleeping as "one of the most accomplished arts of the Japanese. They sleep with complete relaxation, in any position. . . ."[75] Tensions, in any case, are handled and reduced in various ways.

The foregoing composite sketch of "Japanese national character" which I have drawn from various sources—the writings of Benedict, Caudill, De Vos, Beardsley, Hall, Ward, Lanham, Smith, Vogel, and others—seems to present a consistent picture. It should be taken with a grain of salt, all the same, since subjective factors enter into

---

[71] Beardsley, Hall, and Ward, *Village Japan*, p. 66.

[72] De Vos, "Social Values and Personal Attitudes . . .," p. 55.

[73] Hasegawa, *The Japanese Character*, p. 10.

[74] William Caudill, "The Study of Japanese Personality and Behavior", in Edward Norbeck and Susan Parman (eds.), *The Study of Japan in the Behavioral Sciences* (Houston, Texas: Rice University Press, 1970), Vol. 56, p. 42.

[75] Benedict, *The Chrysanthemum and the Sword*, p. 180.

any assessment of national character. This is evidenced by the fact that wartime American analyses of Japanese national character emphasized negative features—compulsiveness, anality, and fanaticism, while postwar American assessments have been much more positive and favorable, stressing collaterality, good maternal care, and the Japanese need for achievement. Toward the end of one essay on Japanese national character, Douglas G. Haring remarked, "The writer 'learned all the answers' in his first year in Japan. The next six years taught him that practically all of those answers were misleading or false."[76]

SUGGESTIONS FOR FURTHER READING

For a review of national character studies, see Alex Inkeles and Daniel J. Levinson, "National Character. The Study of Modal Personality and Sociocultural Systems," in Gardner Lindzey and Elliot Aronson (eds.), *The Handbook of Social Psychology* (2d ed.; Reading, Mass.: Addison-Wesley, Publishing Co., Inc., 1968), Vol. IV, pp. 418–506.

For methods used in the study of culture-at-a-distance, see Margaret Mead and Rhoda Metraux (eds.), *The Study of Culture at a Distance* (Chicago: University of Chicago Press, 1963).

For an investigation of German national character, see Bertram Schaffner, *Father Land. A Study of Authoritarianism in the German Family* (New York: Columbia University Press, 1948).

For surveys of work done in Japan related to culture-and-personality, see Takao Sofue, "Japanese Studies by American Anthropologists. Review and Evaluation," *American Anthropologist,* Vol. 62 (1960), pp. 306–17; and Edward Norbeck and George De Vos, "Japan," in Francis L. K. Hsu (ed.), *Psychological Anthropology. Approaches to Culture and Personality* (Homewood, Ill.: The Dorsey Press, 1961), pp. 19–47. See also William Caudill, "The Study of Japanese Personality and Behavior," in Edward Norbeck and Susan Parman (eds.), *The Study of Japan in the Behavioral Sciences* (Houston, Texas: Rice University Press, 1970), Vol. LVI, pp. 37–52.

More studies related to the topic of national character are discussed in Chapter 17 on "Culture, Personality, and Culture Change," where writings by Fromm, Riesman, and Bronfenbrenner, among others, are discussed.

---

[76] Douglas G. Haring, "Aspects of Personal Character in Japan," in Haring, *Personal Character and Cultural Milieu,* p. 421.

part IV

METHODS IN CULTURE-AND-PERSONALITY RESEARCH

In the preceding parts of this book there have been many references to methods used in fieldwork in culture-and-personality research. Part IV deals with these methods in more detail, considering their respective advantages and disadvantages. The main basis of culture-and-personality research lies in behavioral observation and interviewing; pioneer studies like Benedict's relied on that alone. Participant observation and unstructured interviewing used to be the commonest procedures, but recently there has been an increased use of standardized questionnaires.

The Rorschach Test began to be applied in cross-cultural studies in the 1930s and played an important part in the studies of Alor, Truk, Chippewa and Menomini Indians, among others. For reasons to be discussed below, the Rorschach Test has now lost favor, but modified Thematic Apperception Tests are still being used, and there has been some increase of interest in drawing analysis. Life histories, which once seemed to be a very promising approach to understanding personality in different cultural settings, have not been collected much in recent years.

The loss of interest in projective testing and the failure to realize the potentialities of life history material result in the primacy of behavioral observation and interviewing in most current culture-and-personality research.

Since the average person reading these pages is not likely to be planning to go out and do field research, the five chapters that follow may strike him as being rather remote from the problems of the contemporary world; it may seem that culture-and-personality is mainly a field for academic speculation with little or no relation to the practical issues of life. I think that such a conclusion is wrong and that culture-and-personality research does have important contributions to make to an understanding of current problems and issues. This is shown, I think, in Part V, which deals, among other topics, with the cross-cultural study of mental disorders and with the question of why economic development has proceeded more rapidly in some societies than in others. Clearly, these are serious practical issues. Culture-and-personality research can throw some light on them. But it can only do so if adequate research methods are used. Hence the discussion of field methods in the chapters that follow.

chapter *11*

Observation of Behavior
and Interviews

Cultural anthropologists get most of their information by watching what people do, and from conversations and interviews. The traditional purpose of their observation is to develop a picture of the culture under review. In this chapter, however, we will consider the observation of behavior more from the standpoint of the assessment of personality. The fieldworker in culture-and-personality is concerned both with distinguishing culture patterns and with noting manifestations of personality, which places an undue burden upon him as observer and recorder. For this reason, I think it is preferable for culture-and-personality studies to be carried out in societies where the ethnography has already been done, particularly if projective tests and life histories are to be collected. If the anthropologist is part of a team, that simplifies matters, although group research has its own complications, too.[1]

A distinction may be made between two types of observation. In one case, a person simply observes what is going on, without limiting his observations to any particular categorized items of behavior. In the second case, or in what has been called "directed observation," a previously prepared schedule focuses the observer's attention on certain selected acts. Other matters, irrelevant to these categories, are ignored.[2] Psychologists have done a good deal of work

---

[1] See Richard N. Adams and Jack J. Preiss (eds.), *Human Organization Research, Field Relations and Techniques* (Homewood, Ill.: The Dorsey Press, 1960), chaps. 1–3.

[2] See Percival M. Symonds, *Diagnosing Personality and Conduct* (New York: Century Co., 1931), pp. 30–31.

239

in the field of directed observation, which involves the rating or categorizing of items to be observed.[3] Some applied anthropologists and industrial sociologists have also made use of this approach,[4] and Elliot Chapple, an anthropologist, has developed techniques for recording rates of social interaction. Elements of this method can sometimes be noted in the field procedures of ethnologists. For example, there is something akin to directed observation in Clyde Kluckhohn's quantitative study of Navaho ceremonialism—recording the number of days on which singers participated in ceremonies over a six-month period, and various other indices to the extent of ceremonial behavior.[5] But for the most part, anthropologists have not used this directed approach in their fieldwork; instead, their observations have been of the more general wide-ranging order.

What can one learn about people, simply from watching them? A good deal, sometimes. Martha Wolfenstein, for example, observed French children at play in various parks in France. She noted that they generally stay with the mother (or other adult) rather than mix indiscriminately with other children, so that the park seems to be populated by small family enclaves, with the adults keeping careful watch over their possessions (toys, buckets, and so forth) which are apparently felt to belong to the parent rather than to the child. Wolfenstein also noted that French children show a great readiness to play with children younger than themselves, in contrast to the American child's consciousness of age grades. (She suggests that this willingness may stem from the requirement of remaining within the family circle, or in the circle of children whose parents know one another.) She noted, too, that French children are not taught to fight their own battles, or to stick up for their rights, as Americans would put it. Instead, grownups intervene and scold the aggressor in a conflict. Aggression is inhibited, with verbal disputes developing in substitution. Wolfenstein was amazed at how long French children can sit still.

A typical position of a child in the park is squatting at his mother's feet, playing in the sand. His hands are busy, but his total body position

---

[3] For a review of this literature, see Roger W. Heyns and Ronald Lippitt, "Systematic Observational Techniques," in Gardner Lindzey (ed.), *Handbook of Social Psychology*, Vol. I (Reading, Mass.: Addison-Wesley Publishing Co., 1954), p. 372 f.

[4] See Robert H. Guest, "Categories of Events in Field Observations," in Adams and Preiss, *Human Organization Research . . .*, pp. 225–39.

[5] Clyde Kluckhohn, "Participation in Ceremonials in a Navaho Community," *American Anthropologist*, Vol. 40 (1938), pp. 359–69; reprinted in Douglas G. Haring (ed.), *Personal Character and Cultural Milieu* (3d ed.; Syracuse, N.Y.: Syracuse University Press, 1956), pp. 67–77.

remains constant. Children are often brought to the park in quite elegant (and unwashable) clothes, and they do not get dirty. The squatting child keeps his bottom poised within an inch of the ground but never touching, only his hands getting dirty; activity and getting dirty are both restricted to the hands. While sand play is generally permissible and children are provided with equipment for it, they seem subject to intermittent uncertainty whether it is all right for their hands to be dirty. From time to time a child shows his dirty hands to his mother, and she wipes them off. . . . The requirement of keeping clean and the inhibition on physical aggression contribute to the restriction of motor activity, and so does the distrustful feeling about alien space, outside the family circle.[6]

In these few selections one can see that a variety of observations have been made in this study: observations on the composition of groups involved, on the nature of social interaction, on attitudes toward possessions, and on bodily postures. Of course, a number of questions can be raised about Wolfenstein's observations—how representative they may be and how widely one may generalize from them. But they serve here as an example of observation—rather sharp-eyed observation at that—of the sort that may be made in the field.

PSYCHOLOGICAL ECOLOGY

The observation of behavior is an approach that has been particularly emphasized by some social psychologists. For example, Roger G. Barker and Herbert F. Wright, veritable arch-observers, have presented a detailed account of one day in the life of a seven-year-old boy in a midwestern American town. We find entries such as these:

7:03:   He pulled on his right sock.
        He picked up his left tennis shoe and put it on.
        He laced his left shoe with slow deliberation,
            looking intently at the shoe as he worked
            steadily until he had it all laced.
7:04:   He put on his right shoe.[7]

Eight observers (all but one of whom were familiar adults to the boy) took turns during the day in watching Raymond, carefully noting all his actions and remarks. Thus 14 consecutive hours of ob-

---

[6] Martha Wolfenstein, "French Parents Take Their Children to the Park," in Margaret Mead and Martha Wolfenstein (eds.), *Childhood in Contemporary Cultures* (Chicago: University of Chicago Press, © 1955), pp. 106–7.

[7] Roger G. Barker and Herbert F. Wright, *One Boy's Day. A Specific Record of Behavior* (New York: Harper & Bros., 1951), p. 17.

servation were recorded, each observer in turn dictating into a sound recorder as he trailed the boy, and indicating the passage of time at one-minute intervals.[8]

The authors have extended this approach (although not always so intensively) to a general study of children in Raymond's town,[9] and Roger G. Barker and Louise Shedd Barker have made a comparative study in which they contrast the "psychological ecology" of children in Midwest, Kansas, with that of children in Yoredale, Yorkshire, England.[10] Observations in both areas were made in relation to what the authors call "behavior settings"—restaurants, stores, school classes, and so forth. They point to some features which "behavior settings" have in common: that is, each involves a characteristic pattern of behavior which is relatively independent of the presence of any particular person, and each has a particular spatial framework and boundary, so that a person knows when he is inside or outside the setting.[11]

Some of the conclusions based on this comparative study are rather surprising and of much interest. The authors find that "More of Midwest's than of Yoredale's settings are unsegregated; they are inhabited by persons of all ages, both sexes, and all social classes. The lesser segregation on the basis of age is especially marked in Midwest."[12] (Here we may note a possible conflict with Martha Wolfenstein's comments on the rigid age grade play groups in the United States.) The Barkers assert that the average person in Midwest is more than three times as frequently in responsible settings as his counterpart in the Yorkshire town.

The average citizen of Midwest is busier in essential jobs in community behavior settings (as secretary, president, teacher, soloist, clerk, trustee, etc.) and does a larger share of the town's public work than is true of Yoredale citizens. People, including children and adolescents, are in greater demand and in shorter supply. Midwest has fewer replacements; the average person is functionally more important.

Children are not exceptions. Sixty-four (11%) of Midwest's settings would have to shut up shop for lack of *operating* personnel if children

[8] Ibid., pp. 6–8.

[9] Roger G. Barker and Herbert F. Wright, *Midwest and Its Children, The Psychological Ecology of an American Town* (Evanston, Ill.: Row, Peterson & Co., 1955).

[10] Roger G. Barker and Louise Shedd Barker, "Behavior Units for the Comparative Study of Cultures," in Bert Kaplan (ed.), *Studying Personality Cross-Culturally* (Evanston, Ill.: Row, Peterson & Co., 1961), pp. 457–76.

[11] The authors discuss several other characteristic properties of "behavior settings," Ibid., pp. 465–69.

[12] Ibid., p. 470.

and adolescents were removed from the town; 14 (3%) of Yoredale's settings would have to close under these circumstances.[13]

The authors give further evidence for the importance of children and adolescents in various spheres of activity in Midwest—the local newspaper, sports settings, concerts, programs, and so forth—and they point to the relative lack of participation in corresponding areas by the children and adolescents of Yoredale. The greater involvement of young people in community life in Midwest results in a greater sense of their importance than in the case of Yoredale young people. There are more areas for self-expression and achievement (and also more possibilities of failure). There is a more familiar, often first-name relationship between children and adults in contrast to the situation in the Yorkshire town, where a greater social distance prevails between the young and the mature.[14]

Comparative studies like these bring into sharper focus the significance of observed behavior.

METHODS IN THE SIX CULTURES PROJECT

Since comparability of data was emphasized in the Six Cultures project, a standard approach to the recording of behavior was recommended to the six teams of field workers by Whiting et al. in their *Field Guide for a Study of Socialization*. The authors use the term *setting,* although in a different sense from the Barkers' usage. By settings they mean activities specified as to time and place in which the child spends a typical day, such as breakfast at home or playing in the schoolyard after school. By *situations* they mean conditions which instigate behavior, and by *responses* they refer to the child's reactions.

The authors recommend that three steps be taken in the observation of children's behavior. The first is to find out what the typical settings are in a child's day. "If possible, the child's waking day should be divided into hours and the record should be written in the form of a timetable, indicating where the child is, who is present, and what he is doing."[15] The second step is to find out the frequency with which certain situations are met with in typical settings. For this purpose it is recommended that the fieldworker make 12 five-

[13] Ibid. Italics as in the original.

[14] Ibid., pp. 472–74.

[15] John W. M. Whiting et al., *Field Guide for a Study of Socialization,* Six Cultures Series, Vol. I (New York: John Wiley & Sons, 1966), p. 93.

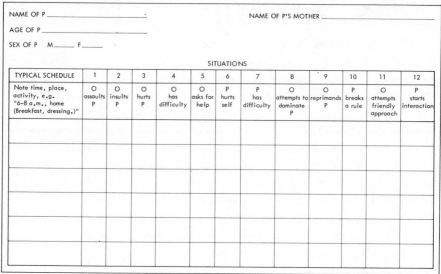

NAME OF P _____						NAME OF P'S MOTHER _____					

AGE OF P _____

SEX OF P   M_____ F_____

SITUATIONS

TYPICAL SCHEDULE	1	2	3	4	5	6	7	8	9	10	11	12
Note time, place, activity, e.g. "6–8 a.m., home (Breakfast, dressing.)"	O assaults P	O insults P	O hurts P	O has difficulty	O asks for help	P hurts self	P has difficulty	O attempts to dominate P	O reprimands P	P breaks a rule	O attempts friendly approach	P starts interaction

Figure 11–1.   Chart for Behavioral Observation. (From John W. M. Whiting et al., *Field Guide for a Study of Socialization*, Six Cultures Series, Vol. I, New York: John Wiley & Sons, 1966, p. 96.)

minute observations on each child. The third step is to draw up a protocol of P's behavior. (P stands for the particular child who is being observed, while O stands for a person with whom he interacts.) Finally, a record chart is kept for each child, with protocol numbers and dates recorded in the appropriate cells.

Difficulties were experienced when the fieldworkers tried to comply with some of these suggestions, and modifications were made, particularly in step three. The authors recommend that in future studies of child-rearing a variety of behavior observations be used. Besides recording a child's daily routine, efforts should be made to systematically sample and record the interaction of important dyads such as mother-child, father-child, and sibling-sibling.

FAMILY STUDIES

A pioneer in the field of family studies is Oscar Lewis, who presents a nine-page chart detailing the activities of each member of a particular peasant family in Tepoztlán, Mexico, from 6:00 A.M., March 28 to 9:30 P.M., March 31, 1944.[16]

---

[16] Oscar, Lewis, *Life in a Mexican Village: Tepoztlán Restudied* (Urbana, Ill.: University of Illinois Press, 1951), pp. 63–72.

In this case the purpose was primarily to illustrate work patterns and the family division of labor, but Lewis's detailed family studies are also relevant to culture-and-personality research. In *Five Families,* Lewis gives extensive accounts of one day in the lives of five Mexican families. He tells us that in four of the five days the family conversations were recorded stenographically by an assistant. In two cases the assistant was a relative of the family; in a third, a close friend.[17]

Lewis has taken some liberties with his material which may cause some raised eyebrows, but which probably contribute to the literary effectiveness of his accounts. For instance, the presence of the observer is never alluded to. Each family's day is described as if the observer were not there at all. Moreover, Lewis does not hesitate to present the thoughts and feelings of his subjects, along with their words and actions. Much material is presented in the form of flashbacks, to give something of the broader setting of the family life.

A brief selection will give something of the book's flavor:

> It was still dark on this July morning when Esperanza opened her eyes. The house was quiet and no sounds came from the street. Esperanza got out of the hard bed in which she and Pedro slept, smoothed her dress, and wrapped a thin dark blue cotton shawl about her head and shoulders to ward off the morning chill. She walked barefoot across the dirt floor, found the big clay water jug, and dashed some cold water on her face; then she dried herself with the edge of her shawl.
>
> Kneeling at the hearth, Esperanza uncovered the ashes of last night's fire and fanned some still glowing chunks of charcoal into flames. She didn't want to use a match to light the fire for a box of matches cost five centavos and was still a luxury. Now the big clock in the plaza struck four. It was a half-hour earlier than she had thought. Well, her daughter Machrina could sleep a little longer.[18]

From these family accounts one gets a general picture of the greater importance of the mother in the lower class Mexican home than of the father. The mothers tend to be devoted to their children. The fathers are more distant and authoritarian and spend a good deal of time away from home. Still, in most of the families the children feel respect and affection for their fathers. Lewis believes that the younger generation in these five families has known more family stability than the parent generation experienced, an observa-

---

[17] Oscar Lewis, *Five Families: Mexican Case Studies in the Culture of Poverty* (New York: Basic Books, 1959) , p. 6.
[18] Ibid., p. 25.

tion which somewhat lessens the prevailingly grim picture of the "culture of poverty" presented in this book.

STRUCTURED SITUATIONS

Two further categories may be distinguished in connection with the observation of behavior. In one category are studies, like those just cited, in which individuals are observed in the course of every-day life. A second category involves the observation of people in situations structured by the investigator. This approach may be more revealing for purposes of personality assessment, but fieldwork conditions do not usually lend themselves to it.

To give an example of the second category: during World War II members of the OSS assessment staff used to assign a candidate two helpers whom he had to direct in the building of a frame structure within a 10-minute period. The "helpers" were really trained stooges, one of whom acted in a sluggish passive way, while the other behaved in an aggressive and critical manner toward the candidate. While they did not disobey direct orders, these men did whatever they could to slow things up. The assessment officers meanwhile watched how the candidate handled this problem.[19]

Such stress situations can be most revealing, but, as has been indicated, anthropologists are not usually in a position to try this sort of thing. Perhaps a particularly well-endowed fieldworker could employ the techniques popularized by Allen Funt in "Candid Camera" —training concealed cameras and microphones on unsuspecting subjects who are inveigled into an exchange with the investigator. (In one example Funt posed as a watchmaker and "fixed" a customer's clock by smashing it to pieces.) Funt does this for purposes of entertainment rather than science, but it would seem to be a possible technique for the investigation of personality—not the smashing of watches, necessarily, but some use of the general approach. This would not be very different from some attempts by psychologists to study such matters as the nature of children's fears— for instance by exposing them to a strange room or awesome-looking objects, and noting their reactions.[20]

---

[19] The OSS Assessment Staff, *Assessment of Men. Selection of Personnel for the Office of Strategic Services* (New York: Rinehart, 1948), pp. 102–12.

[20] Jean M. Arsenian, "Young Children in an Insecure Situation," *Journal of Abnormal and Social Psychology*, Vol. 38 (1943), pp. 225–49. See also Arthur T. Jersild and Frances B. Holmes, *Children's Fears* (New York: Teacher's College Press, 1935).

DOLL PLAY

Perhaps the nearest approach made by anthropologists to the use of structured situations has been in studies of doll play. By watching how children play with dolls representing family members, anthropologists have found evidence for such patterns as sibling rivalry in cultures other than our own.[21] From the play of Normanby Island children, Géza Roheim deduced the presence in that group of such Freudian items as the Oedipus complex, the phallic significance of the snake, and enactments of the primal scene.[22]

The most extensive investigation of doll play made in a non-Western culture so far is the Henry Pilagá study. The principal play material used were a mother doll, a father doll, and several "child" dolls. The father doll was an "amputation doll," of a type used in David M. Levy's sibling rivalry experiments, with jointed and detachable arms and legs. The Pilagá children were also given scissors, a ball of plastilene, and a mechanical turtle. When a child was handed the dolls, each one was named after a member of the child's immediate family. Pilagá children often made breasts or genitalia of plastilene and stuck them on the dolls to differentiate the sexes. If a child did not make breasts and place them on the mother doll, the examiner suggested that he do so.[23]

It was hard to segregate individual children for observation in this study, since the Henrys' hut was invaded by swarms of children during the day and privacy was hardly possible. The observers therefore took notes on the activities of groups of children playing simultaneously.

The study of Pilagá doll play shows that sibling rivalry is present among these people as among ourselves. However, in contrast to David M. Levy's sibling rivalry experiments, Jules and Zunia Henry found that self-punishment on this account does not occur. A sense of guilt is not emphasized in Pilagá culture, as evidenced by the absence of confessionals, penitent speeches, self-flagellation, and traditions of suicide. There are no special rewards for love of a sibling and little punishment for injury to one. Hence Pilagá chil-

---

[21] David M. Levy, "Sibling Rivalry Studies in Children of Primitive Groups," *American Journal of Orthopsychiatry,* Vol. 9 (1939), pp. 205–14; Jules Henry and Zunia Henry, *Doll Play of Pilagá Indian Children. An Experimental and Field Analysis of the Behavior of the Pilagá Indian Children,* Research Monograph No. 4 (New York: American Orthopsychiatric Association, 1944).

[22] Géza Roheim, "Play Analysis with Normanby Island Children," *American Journal of Orthopsychiatry,* Vol. 11 (1941), pp. 524–49.

[23] Jules and Zunia Henry, *Doll Play of Pilagá Indian Children,* pp. 30–31.

dren openly detest their younger brothers and sisters and feel no guilt for doing so.

The problem of interpreting doll play is raised by David Landy, who expresses dissatisfaction with this approach to the study of children's personality patterns. Landy selected 18 families in a Puerto Rican village as representative of the largely lower class cane-workers there. A study was made of four sessions of doll play for one child from each family (10 boys and 8 girls between four and seven years of age). The dolls, representing mother, father, boy, girl, and baby, were made of pipe cleaners, cotton, and cloth. Play materials also included a roofless "house," furnishings, and outhouse.

Landy's approach involved directed observation. He had a scoring system for certain categories of acts: aggression, dependency, identification, nurturance, and noninteraction. Each child was brought alone to the doll play situation, with a Puerto Rican assistant being present. Landy scored and recorded each act performed by the child. He notes that much of the resultant doll play was routine and repetitive. These children were not encouraged in everyday life to act freely in the presence of adults and were not used to the sort of permissive behavior which Landy displayed. Landy found it difficult to interpret the doll play of his Puerto Rican subjects, and found it hard to determine when the technique elicited projective responses and when it reflected real-life situations.[24] Partly because of uncertainty over the extent to which children's play is projection, and also because the observation and recording of doll play is very time consuming, Landy concludes that he would not use doll play in another field situation and adds that he has obtained more data from child interviews in a later study among the Tuscarora.[25]

Jane Ritchie made use of doll play in a study of Maori children in Rakau, New Zealand. Her study is hard to compare or contrast with those of Landy and the Henrys, since the three investigations made use of different kinds of dolls and followed different procedures. In this case 12 dolls, dressed to represent a large family group, were presented to the child subjects. There was no pattern here, as in the Henry study, of adding bits of plastilene; bodily parts do not seem to have been removable.

---

[24] David Landy, "Methodological Problems of Free Doll Play as an Ethnographic Field Technique," in Anthony F. C. Wallace (ed.), *Men and Cultures,* Selected Papers of the Fifth International Congress of Anthropological and Ethnological Sciences (Philadelphia: University of Pennsylvania Press, 1960), pp. 162–63.

[25] Ibid., pp. 166–67.

Landy's question of what the doll play represents poses no problem to Ritchie:

Provided no extraneous stimulus material is introduced it seems that doll play directly echoes real life for the children and that they freely engage in projective activity without the mysteries, inhibitions, repressions and other subtleties which shroud such processes in adults. When a Rakau child said a doll was Mother he was speaking of his own mother.[26]

The author limits this generalization to the doll play of her Maori child subjects and does not mean to extend it beyond that area. Even here, however, one may note some exceptions to the notion that doll play reflects real life. In doll play, for example, the baby doll is rejected by the girls, but this does not take place overtly in real life. As the author puts it, "The doll behavior is a fulfillment of a wish which cannot be granted in real life. . . ."[27]

Among these Maori children there was no boisterous sexual behavior like that of the Pilagá children, but only oblique sexual references, which were slightly more prominent among the boys than among the girls. The boys showed over twice as much aggression as the girls, while the girls showed a much greater need for love. In their doll play, moreover, there was much more concern with the arrangement of dolls and the maintenance of order. The girls' rejecting behavior was assessed as four times that of the boys. It is Ritchie's interpretation that the boys typically have affectionate relationships with more family members than do the girls, and they are not tied by obligations to the home. Hence the boys' needs for love are less intense.

The principal doll rejected by the girls (and boys as well) was the baby, indicating jealousy of the younger sibling. Ritchie observes:

It is significant that the children do not often allocate themselves to other children or to parents, nor do they often allocate other family members to themselves. . . . The Rakau child in the present material does not see himself in any natural relationship with the mother or the home. Instead, he sees the home as including bonds of relationship between other members of the family, but not between himself and other members.[28]

---

[26] Jane Ritchie, *Childhood in Rakau, The First Five Years of Life*, Victoria University Publications in Psychology No. 10 (Monographs on Maori Social Life and Personality, No. 3), Department of Psychology, Victoria University, Wellington, New Zealand, 1957, pp. 107–8.

[27] Ibid., p. 148.

[28] Ibid., p. 113.

The baby doll accounts for 70 percent of the allocations and is thus seen by the children to be the most important figure in the home. A boy may openly express hostility for the baby, but the girls show more ambivalence, for they may attempt to "buy" parental love by caring for the baby. "In order to get love she must continue in association with the cause of her rejection."[29] (One wonders, in this connection, whether the doll play of youngest children differs from that of older siblings.)

It might facilitate researches in this field if some generally agreed-upon procedures could be adopted by those who make cross-cultural studies in doll play—that is, in the number and types of dolls to be used, methods of recording data, and so forth. Despite Landy's pessimism, productive material does seem to have come from doll play studies, and while it is true enough that there are difficulties in the interpretation of such material, the same applies to all techniques used in the field—to the Rorschach, TAT, and interview materials as well. Moreover, they all take up much of the fieldworker's time.

POSTURE AND GESTURE

In connection with the Wolfenstein article on French children's play, it was noted that the author made different kinds of observations. Let us characterize these as observations on rates of social interaction, verbal exchanges, posture, gesture, and facial expression. It is important to note not only what people say but how they say it. Consider John Dollard's remarks on his methods of research in a southern town:

In general two kinds of observation were made, first as to what people said, and second as to what they did and seemed to feel. . . . One could notice at what point in a conversation people became excited and what they did; one could see the sequence of behavior at a Negro picnic or revival meeting, or note the reception of a Yankee in a social group of white people. . . . An important aspect of the method is to watch the feeling tone of the statements people make and the acts they do. This is often more definitive than the words uttered or the external character of the act. People can say *no,* for example, in such a way that it means *yes,* or vice versa. The feeling tone indicated in giving a permission may indicate that if it is acted on, the recipient can count on terminating his effective contact with the grantor.[30]

---

[29] Ibid., p. 114.

[30] John Dollard, *Class and Caste in a Southern Town* (3d. ed.; New York: Doubleday Anchor Books, 1957) , pp. 19–20.

Dollard's comments indicate the importance of noting facial expression, posture, and gesture as clues to underlying attitudes and personality patterns. There is a good deal of literature on the question of how successfully one may gauge emotions or personality traits from facial expression or bodily stance.[31] Most of the work done in this field has involved subjects making interpretations of drawings, photographs, or films. The anthropological fieldworker, however, has a much greater range of clues to work with. He lives with a group of people over a period of time, sees them in a variety of circumstances, and knows something of the context in which observed events take place. Hence he has a great advantage over someone who is asked to interpret a collection of frozen split-second facial expressions in photographs of strangers. We have noted Bateson's vivid portrait of the swaggering posture of Iatmul men in the men's house and the "fine proud bearing" of Iatmul women when they dress up in men's regalia. These are psychologically significant observations. The ways in which people carry themselves, walk, and sit may tell us a good deal about them. As the studies of Werner Wolff, Allport and Vernon, M. H. Krout and others, cited in Chapter 1, have shown, individuals seem to have characteristic ways of walking and gesturing which remain as stable patterns over time.

Posture, of course, is much influenced by cultural tradition, as may be seen in Gordon W. Hewes' mapping of world distributions of postural habits.[32] Cultural traditions may even modify sleeping postures.[33] Gesture and facial expressions are also considerably channeled by cultural tradition. La Barre has persuasively argued that there is no "natural" language of emotional gesture.[34]

These considerations, of course, complicate the psychological interpretation of posture, gesture, and facial expression. A distinction may be made, however, between culturally standardized gestures,

---

[31] For a review of such literature, see Jerome S. Bruner and Renato Tagiuri, "The Perception of People," in Gardner Lindzey (ed.), *Handbook of Social Psychology*, Vol. II, *Special Fields and Applications* (Reading, Mass.: Addison-Wesley Publishing Co., 1954), pp. 634–38.

[32] Gordon W. Hewes, "World Distribution of Postural Habits," *American Anthropologist*, Vol. 57 (1955), pp. 231–44.

[33] To cite a rather extreme example, Prince Peter of Greece and Denmark has noted that, in order to keep warm, Tibetan caravaners sometimes sleep by kneeling together side by side, with shoulders and hips touching and their faces resting on the upturned palms of their hands placed on the ground before them. He also describes a seated posture in which Tibetans sometimes sleep. H.R.H. Prince Peter of Greece and Denmark, "Peculiar Sleeping Postures of the Tibetans," *Man*, Vol. 53 (1953), p. 145.

[34] Weston La Barre, "The Cultural Basis of Emotions and Gestures," *Journal of Personality*, Vol. 16 (1947), pp. 49–68.

like the handshake and the military salute, and more personal gestural behavior, such as nose picking or ear pulling, which Krout calls "autistic gesture."[35] The latter may be more significant psychologically than the former type of gesture. Even so, it may be of relevance to personality whether a particular individual, let us say, goes in for a good deal of handshaking.[36]

Not much attention has been paid to the cross-cultural study of posture and gesture, and what work has been done so far has been largely descriptive, with little attempt to relate characteristic postural or gestural features to personality patterns. These descriptions remain as valuable data, however, in which someone may yet find significant patterns.

Flora L. Bailey has written an article on Navaho motor habits. She tells us that a striking difference between Navaho and white American movements is the greater smoothness and flowing quality of Navaho motor behavior, while white American movements are seen as being more angular and staccato. Eating is performed daintily and slowly by the Navaho; walking is done with long strides, legs swinging freely from the hips, arms hanging loosely. The Navaho handshake is a limp clasp release, with no grip or up and down motion.[37] The author does not speculate on any possible connection between these motor habits and Navaho personality characteristics.

W. D. Brewer has discussed the gesture language of the Levantine Arabs, who, like other Mediterranean peoples, are said to have a more "obvious" or "rotund and fluid" type of gesture than Americans. Brewer gives a list of symbolic and pictorial gestures and makes one observation of psychological relevance: "It is at least interesting that so many of the common Arab gestures described above imply injured innocence, unwillingness to assume responsibility or a mere desire not to be included with the group as a whole."[38]

The most large-scale and methodologically rigorous cross-cultural investigation of gesture is David Efron's *Gesture and Environment*, the product of a two-year study of the gestural behavior of eastern European Jews and southern Italians in New York City. These subjects never knew that they were under scrutiny. On-the-spot observa-

---

[35] M. H. Krout, *Autistic Gestures*, Psychological Monograph 46, No. 208, 1935.

[36] For an example of this, see Jane Belo, *Trance in Bali* (New York: Columbia University Press, 1960), p. 129. The case referred to is discussed further on in this chapter.

[37] Flora L. Bailey, "Navaho Motor Habits," *American Anthropologist,* Vol. 44 (1942), pp. 210–16.

[38] W. D. Brewer, "Patterns of Gesture among the Levantine Arabs," *American Anthropologist,* Vol. 53 (1951), p. 237.

tions were made; 5,000 feet of film were taken, shot from hidden points of vantage (sometimes from adjacent buildings with a tele-photo lens), and the artist Stuyvessant van Veen made sketches drawn from life. A great deal of data was thus amassed; 1,500 subjects were studied by direct observation, 600 in sketches, and about 750 in film: a total of about 2,810 in all.

Ingenious methods were developed to record and represent gestural motions:

> . . . the film, taken at speeds varying from sixteen to sixty-four frames per second, was projected frame by frame upon coordinate paper. The position of motile bodily parts, such as wrist, elbow, and head, was marked in successive frame projections. When joined, these sequential positions give a precise representation of the fluent gestural movement.[39]

Efron found that the gestures of the "traditional," or unassimilated Eastern European Jews, were more confined in radius than those of "traditional" southern Italians, much of their gestural motion taking place close to the chest and face, in contrast to the Italians, who might make gestures of full arms' length.

> In the ghetto Jew the upper-arm participates seldom in the movement, and often is more or less rigid and attached to the side of the body. . . . The axis of gestural motion is often centered at the elbow.[40]

There was a good deal of head movement among the traditional Jews, little among the Italians. Jewish gestures were made sequentially, not simultaneously with both hands or arms as among the Italians. Efron noted an irregularity of tempo and abruptness in Jewish gestures, while there was a more even flow in the Italian. The traditional Jew often touched the body of his conversational partner, and conversational groups were often closely massed. These features were not noted among the Italians. There was also a difference in the body planes at which gesturing characteristically took place.

> The Eastern ghetto Jew exhibits a tendency to gesticulate chiefly in the vertical and frontal planes of his body. . . . In contrast to the "traditional" Italian, who is more likely to execute his gestural motions in a latero-transversal space-segment, i.e., at either side of his body, the Jew appears to direct most of his movements either in an up-and-down direction or in a direction toward the interlocutor . . .[41]

---

[39] David Efron, *Gesture and Environment* (New York: King's Crown Press, 1941), p. 41.

[40] Ibid., p. 43.

[41] Ibid., p. 54.

Efron found, finally, that assimilated southern Italians and assimilated eastern Jews in New York City differed from their respective traditional groups and appeared to resemble each other in gestural behavior.[42]

Efron does not attempt in this work to relate the type of gesturing to different personality tendencies in these two groups. His purpose seems to have been just to show that there are differences in gestural patterns in the two groups and that these patterns are culturally derived. Jurgen Ruesch and Weldon Kees have made some attempts at interpretation in this area and have discussed differences in posture and gesture in European national groups. For instance, concerning the Italians, the authors state: "The basic philosophy of this Mediterranean country is epitomized by a desire to express bodily and emotional needs in elaborate and somewhat outspoken terms while at the same time maintaining warm interpersonal contact."[43] Unfortunately, the observations of these writers are loose and impressionistic and offered with little supporting evidence.

INTERPRETATIONS OF BALINESE POSTURAL HABITS

The culture where most has been done to relate posture and gesture to personality patterns, and, further, to account for the genesis of the ascribed personality traits, has been that of Bali. Since these efforts are almost unique in the literature of culture-and-personality, they will be dealt with here in some detail. Observations on Balinese posture and gesture have been made by Jane Belo, Margaret Mead, and Gregory Bateson in a number of publications. Jane Belo has drawn attention to the "absolute poise and balance" of the Balinese in their movements and gestures, which, however, is combined with a sort of carefulness of bearing, as if they were afraid to disturb a delicate equilibrium. Belo discusses, as Bateson and Mead also do, the sense of spatial and social orientation which is always part of the Balinese consciousness: the sense of one's relationship to the points of the compass, to up and down, and to the social

---

[42] Ibid., pp. 56–136.

[43] Jurgen Ruesch and Weldon Kees, *Nonverbal Communication, Notes on the Visual Perception of Human Relations* (Los Angeles: University of California Press, 1956), p. 23.

standing of people of higher or lower caste.[44] She also touches on the tempo of activity.

The individual Balinese moves slowly, with deliberation. Westerners, seeing for the first time films representing the Balinese at their daily tasks, are immediately struck by the slow tempo of their actions. If a man seated in one pavilion of his house-court suddenly wishes to show something which is in another pavilion, he will rise to his feet and saunter across the intervening space, quite as if he were going for a casual stroll. He will never hurry, as we would, eager to grasp the object which has come to mind.[45]

This slowness of movement may be associated with the low tonus of Balinese children noted by Mead and Macgregor.[46]

There is a passivity in Balinese children which Mead traces to certain childhood experiences. Balinese children are carried about during most of their waking hours until they are from 15 to 18 months old.[47] They have no crawling stage comparable to that of Western children because of the Balinese disapproval of crawling, and so do not show as much activity as American children of the same age.[48] Children learn to adjust passively to the movements of the mother's body as they are carried about. The child's limbs are manipulated to teach it gestures and hand-dancing before he learns to walk. Both walking and dancing may be taught by holding the child from behind, so that he learns kinesthetically as well as from watching and a small amount of verbal instruction.[49]

Another aspect of Balinese posture noted by Bateson and Mead is an economy of movement which they see as involving a kind of dissociation.

Where an American or a New Guinea native will involve almost every muscle in his body to pick up a pin, the Balinese merely use the muscles immediately relevant to the act, leaving the rest of the body undisturbed.

Total involvement in any activity occurs in trance and in children's

[44] Jane Belo, "The Balinese Temper," *Character and Personality*, Vol. 4 (1935), p. 121. Reprinted in Douglas G. Haring (ed.), *Personal Character and Cultural Milieu* (3d ed.; Syracuse, N.Y.: Syracuse University Press, 1956), p. 158. See also Gregory Bateson and Margaret Mead, *Balinese Character. A Photographic Analysis* (New York: Special Publications of the New York Academy of Sciences, 1942), pp. 75–83, 88–89.

[45] Jane Belo, in Haring, *Personal Character and Cultural Milieu,* p. 158.

[46] Margaret Mead and Francis Cooke Macgregor, *Growth and Culture. A Photographic Study of Balinese Childhood* (New York: G. P. Putnam's & Sons, 1951), pp. 138–39.

[47] Ibid., p. 43.

[48] Ibid., p. 181.

[49] Ibid., p. 47. See also Bateson and Mead, *Balinese Character*, pp. 15, 84–87.

tantrums, but for the rest, an act is *not* performed by the whole body. The involved muscle does not draw all the others into a unified act, but smoothly and simply, a few units are moved—the fingers alone, the hand and forearm alone, or the eyes alone, as in the characteristic Balinese habit of slewing the eyes to one side without turning the head.[50]

This dissociation is seen to be particularly evident in the hands, in which the fingers at rest rarely lie in seriated flexion, but may stick out at different angles. When a Balinese watches two cocks fighting, there may sometimes be noted a twitching of the different hands, symbolically identified with the two birds.[51] Interestingly enough, Belo describes the case of a man whose hand was put into trance, while the rest of the man remained quite conscious.[52]

Bateson and Mead have also drawn attention to Balinese postures of withdrawal, illustrated in three photographs on pp. 132–33 of their work—a bent-over sitting position with the head held down over the knees. The implication of these postural details, from their viewpoint, is that there is a tendency toward narcissistic, schizoid withdrawal in the Balinese character. Bateson and Mead think that this tendency derives from early childhood frustrations. Children are overstimulated and unrewardingly teased by their mothers, who may, for instance, borrow some one else's baby and offer it the breast to rouse the child's jealousy. Or they may hold the borrowed baby over the child's head—a symbolically insulting gesture in Bali. As a result of repeated rebuffs of this sort, children learn, between the ages of three and six, to become aloof from the mother and other adults and turn in upon themselves.[53]

In contrast to the general mildness and passivity of everyday life in Bali, some very active and aggressive manifestations take place during trance, which in some villages is often induced on ritual occasions. At these times young men, and sometimes women as well, drive the points of their krises (daggers) against their chests, while leaning backward in an intense, straining manner. They finally fall down, exhausted, in convulsions, and are subsequently brought out of trance. Normally, they do not cut or hurt themselves. This may be at least partially explained by Dr. van Wulfften Palthe's statement that during trance the pectoral muscles are in rigid contraction.[54]

---

[50] Bateson and Mead, *Balinese Character*, p. 17.

[51] Ibid., p. 18, Photos illustrating use of the hands appear on pp. 96–105 of *Balinese Character*.

[52] Jane Belo, *Trance in Bali* (New York: Columbia University Press, 1960) , pp. 203–4.

[53] Bateson and Mead, *Balinese Character*, pp. 26, 32–33, 152–53, 204–5.

[54] Jane Belo, *Trance in Bali*, p. 62.

This trance activity is prominent in the classic Balinese drama, *Tjalonarang*, which involves a fearsome witch known as Rangda (*rangda* means widow).[55] Somewhat akin to the Hindu goddess Kali-Durga, from whom, as Belo suggests, she may be derived, Rangda, the Queen of the Witches, has long tusks and fingernails, staring eyes, and pendulous hairy breasts. In the play she is opposed by Barong, a Chinese dragonlike deity. Barong's followers, young men armed with krises, rush upon Rangda and try to stab her. She is limp, offers no resistance, but merely waves her cloth, a baby-carrying sling. At this, the men fall to the ground. When they get up again in a trance state they subsequently turn their krises upon themselves. Following a theory of projection like that of Abram Kardiner, Bateson and Mead identify Rangda as a maternal figure and Barong as a father image. Of the young men's inward-turning aggression, they remark, "Thus symbolically they complete the cycle of the childhood trauma—the approach to the mother, the rejection, and the turn-in upon the self."[56]

Some men, it may be noted, are more violent than others in these attacks upon the self. Jane Belo describes one such case in which she employs a wealth of observations on facial expression, posture, and gesture. Rawa, the man in question, was particularly aggressive and exhibitionistic in trance. Reporting on his own sensations at such times, he said that demons want to attack his body. His chest itches as if it were being burned, and he feels a powerful desire to stab himself in the chest. "As for me, it is as if there were someone ordering me to stab. When it's like that, if I don't get hold of a kris, I should die, so strong is my anger."[57] But after the self-stabbing, Rawa says that he feels extremely content, like a hungry man who has had a good meal of rice. Asked if desire for the kris were like desire for a woman, Rawa said that the former is stronger; he has had plenty of women.[58]

Rawa's behavior in normal life showed some contrasting features. Belo says that Rawa had a soft "almost wooing" manner with Westerners and was given to repeatedly shaking hands with them. "I have seen him seat himself beside a Westerner whom he hardly knew, lay his hand upon the man's knee and lean and fawn upon him for an

---

[55] Jane Belo, *Bali; Rangda and Barong*, American Ethnological Society, Monograph No. XVI (New York: J. J. Augustin, 1949), p. 18.

[56] Bateson and Mead, *Balinese Character*, p. 35.

[57] Belo, *Trance in Bali*, p. 128.

[58] Ibid., p. 128.

extended period of time, without receiving any encouragement from the object of his attentions."[59] Belo noted, however, that although Balinese often go around in pairs, with arms around each other's necks, she never saw Rawa with another Balinese in this fashion, and she guessed that perhaps he clung to Westerners because he was not on good terms with his own people.

Further fieldwork supported this inference. Rawa was not a native of the village in which he lived and was regarded by the local people as a sort of stranger. He was not liked, and Belo gives an extensive account of one occasion when another man in trance violently expressed this generally antagonistic feeling toward Rawa.[60] Such situational pressures may help to explain the particularly aggressive and exhibitionistic behavior which Rawa showed in trance, although its ultimate origin may also lie in the kind of childhood frustrations described by Bateson and Mead.

THE RECORDING OF BEHAVIOR

Since there is so much more going on in even the most lethargic society and so much to observe, there is a problem of how to record behavioral observations. The most usual method is the notebook. Margaret Mead, a particularly keen-eyed observer, followed the custom of recording bits of discrete data on slips of paper on the spot, with some reference category on each slip.[61] Verbal behavior can be jotted down or recorded on tape. Without a camera it is hard to record details of facial expression, posture, and gesture, although systems of annotation are given in Efron's *Gesture and Environment* and in Ray Birdwhistell's *Introduction to Kinesics*.[62] If a group is doing fieldwork together, different kinds of observations may be assigned to different members, and Mead has suggested this parceling-out process for certain occasions, with one worker covering ceremonial behavior, another recording verbatim conversations, and so on.[63] If possible, notes should be written up in full form while still in the field, for one is apt to forget many things.

---

[59] Ibid., p. 129.

[60] Ibid., p. 131 ff.

[61] Margaret Mead, *The Mountain Arapesh*. II. *Supernaturalism*, Anthropological Papers of the American Museum of Natural History, No. XXXVII, Part III (New York, 1940) , p. 326 f.

[62] Ray Birdwhistell, *Introduction to Kinesics* (Washington, D.C.: Department of State, Foreign Service Institute, 1952) .

[63] Mead, *The Mountain Arapesh*, p. 328.

Mechanical methods for recording data have sometimes been used, such as Chapple's interaction chronograph, the stenotype, and tape recorders.[64] Particularly valuable in the recording and presentation of field data are moving picture film and still photography. Certainly, no technique can match sound film in conveying the quality of another culture, but unfortunately, it is too expensive for the average fieldworker.

Bateson and Mead have been particularly enterprising in the use of photography and film. During their two years in Bali they took about 25,000 Leica stills and about 22,000 feet of 16-mm. film. Apparently they met with little objection to this constant photographing from the Balinese, and they assert that it is almost impossible for subjects to retain camera consciousness after the first dozen shots. They recommend that at least two workers collaborate, for a photographic sequence is of no value without a running account of what is going on, and one can't both take notes and handle a camera at the same time. Since they had to economize on film, Bateson and Mead saved the motion-picture camera for more active and interesting moments and stills for slower and less significant ones.[65]

Mead has discussed some of the uses of still photography for culture-and-personality research. While there is, of course, the value of graphically transmitting knowledge about another culture, there are other uses too, such as the possibility of checking new hypotheses not developed in the field.[66] Future fieldwork will no doubt see an increase in the use of photography and film.

PITFALLS IN OBSERVATION

There are some difficulties inherent in the process of assessing personality from observation of behavior. These difficulties are apt to be particularly pronounced in ethnological fieldwork. The anthropologist, of course, is not invisible. His presence affects, to some extent, the scene which he observes. This is true of any observational study, unless one uses a one-way screen. But not only is the anthropologist visible, he is apt to stick out like a sore thumb. The people he observes are usually very conscious of the stranger's presence,

---

[64] For a review of such machines see R. W. Heyns and R. Lippitt, "Systematic Observational Techniques," in Gardner Lindzey (ed.), *Handbook of Social Psychology,* Vol. I; p. 395 f.

[65] Bateson and Mead, *Balinese Character,* pp. 49–50.

[66] Margaret Mead, "Some Uses of Still Photography in Culture and Personality Studies," in Haring, *Personal Character and Cultural Milieu,* pp. 79–105.

especially at first, before they have become used to having him around.

People have to find some explanation for an anthropologist's appearance in their community. The interpretation at which they arrive will, of course, influence their behavior in his presence. When Benjamin Paul and his wife first arrived in a Guatemalan Indian village, the villagers crowded their doors, peered through the windows, fingered their clothes, and inquired the price of each item. What later clarified this behavior for the Pauls was the explanation that the Indians thought that they were merchants, about to set up shop.

We were not wholly wrong in judging the Indians to be curious about prices . . . but the avidity with which they crowded around to feel and look at everything made better sense in retrospect when we learned that our private residence was assumed to be a public shop. We had to revise our initial exaggerated estimate of their bold inquisitiveness.[67]

What an anthropologist sees, then, may be colored by his own presence and by the attitudes of the people toward him.

Another kind of difficulty which may affect the process of observation concerns the nature of the observer. An observer may project; he may have blind spots to certain aspects of behavior and be unduly attentive or sensitive to others. What he sees may be influenced by his mood or by his attitudes and values. This difficulty, again, may affect any observational study but applies particularly to ethnological fieldwork. The ethnologist finds himself in an unfamiliar setting. His mood, as he works, may be influenced by any number of things —the nature of his living quarters, the response he has met with in the community. He may feel somewhat homesick and ambivalent about fieldwork. He may fall ill. Any of these factors, or others, may bring about distortions in what he observes and records. As some have put it, a culture may be seen as a sort of huge Rorschach blot, in which different ethnologists with different personality tendencies, may detect different patterns. While this is an overstatement, there is some truth in it, and that is why it is good to have descriptions of a particular culture made by a number of anthropologists, not just one or two. I don't mean to suggest that one must be skeptical of what anthropologists report. But we are dealing here with the as-

---

[67] Benjamin D. Paul, "Interview Techniques and Field Relationships," in A. L. Kroeber (ed.), *Anthropology Today* (Chicago: University of Chicago Press, 1953), p. 433.

sessment of personality from observation—a tricky undertaking, in which opportunities for projection abound.

INTERVIEWS AND QUESTIONNAIRES

Interviews, in ethnological fieldwork, supplement what one learns by observation. They may provide clarification of what one has seen. At the same time, an interview involves observation too, for the ethnologist not only writes down what the informant tells him (or makes a mental note of what to write down later) ; but he also watches how the informant behaves, talks, and gestures—his blocks, pauses, and hesitations.

Interviews may be structured, loose, or "open ended," directive or nondirective, but most interviewing in the field is of the open-ended type. An ethnologist may have many brief exchanges with people which are not exactly interviews. He may engage in "participant observation"—take part in community affairs and to some extent involve himself or identify himself with the people. In that case he will have many contacts with individuals which are not interviews but which may be informative.[68]

When the purpose is to get some insight into personality characteristics, the ethnologist must gain the acquaintance of some members of the community and somehow get them to serve as informants. Moreover, he must retain the goodwill of these people, so they will go on working with him and not back out. The problem facing the culture-and-personality ethnologist is that he wants to get the sort of information that a psychiatrist acquires from his patients, while he does not have the psychiatrist's role. A patient turns to a psychiatrist for help—even pays him large sums to listen to his troubles. Since the patient wants to get well, he has a strong motivation to give an account of himself. The ethnologist, on the other hand, has to seek out informants; he may have to pay them to talk to him, and they may be slow to open up, for there is no special reason, after all, why they should talk about their hidden secrets, their difficulties with marital partners, or their feelings about their parents. The ethnologist has to work warily, lest he lose the interest and friendship of his informants.

On the other hand, if it is true that people may talk more freely to a stranger than to a friend or acquaintance, the ethnologist has a

---

[68] Ibid. This article has a good discussion of participant observation in field work, its advantages, disadvantages, and limits as well as very good material on interviewing.

certain advantage.[69] Oscar Lewis, for example, found that the people of Tepoztlán were distant to one another but willing to open up to him and his coworkers.[70] In the chapter dealing with life histories, some examples will be given of individuals who turned with gratitude to the ethnologist and were glad to confide in him.

Reference may be made, parenthetically, to another kind of interview, which has to do with linguistic data; this is the ethnoscience approach in eliciting folk taxonomies mentioned in Chapter 3.

Standardized questionnaires have sometimes been given in culture-and-personality studies, one example being in the Six Cultures project, in which Whiting's *Field Guide for a Study of Socialization* provided the English version of an interview to be used with the 24 mothers in each society. For example, the mother was asked what she did when her child cried, with follow-up questions such as:

a)   How quickly would you try to tend to him?
b)   How about when you were busy?
c)   How about at night?
d)   How did other members of the household feel about his crying?[71]

A wide range of questions was asked covering various areas of discipline and interaction between the mother and child. These questions had to be translated into the local speech with the help of bilingual assistants, and they were sometimes altered to suit local conditions. The completed interviews were later read by coders who rated the mothers according to such factors as maternal warmth, maternal instability, mother's responsibility for baby and for child care, responsibility training, and aggression training (for both mother-directed and peer-directed aggression). Some of the findings of these ratings were cited in Chapter 8. For example, it was mentioned that the Mixtecan and Khalapur mothers were rated the least warm of the six groups.

One can get some idea of why coders might rate the Rajput mothers low on this dimension if the following example, taken from the Appendix of *Mothers of Six Cultures* is representative of the questionnaire responses:

---

[69] Eleanor E. Maccoby and Nathan Maccoby, "The Interview: A Tool of Social Science," in Gardner Lindzey, *Handbook of Social Psychology*, Vol. I, p. 463.

[70] Oscar Lewis, *Life in a Mexican Village: Tepoztlán Restudied* (Urbana, Ill.: University of Illinois Press, 1951), p. xvii.

[71] Leigh Minturn and William W. Lambert, *Mothers of Six Cultures. Antecedents of Child Rearing* (New York: John Wiley & Sons, 1964), p. 306.

Q. When Mahender was a baby and crying at night, how quickly would you try to tend to him?

A. It is not in my hands. If a person is bent on crying, he will go on crying. When he is crying I pick him up and nurse him and if he is hungry, I give him something to eat.

Q. Do you feel that children should express their feelings? How about laughing?

A. When the child is laughing useless with no reason, I have to scold him.

Q. Tell me about the last time he learned to do something by himself.

A. He has not learned anything; he is mad. He does not know anything. . . . Those children who are clever, they do work but he is mad.

Q. What do you do when Mahender does not obey you immediately?

A. I beat him. I have no patience. I beat him with a stick. . . . Mahender is a shameless boy. I have to tell him a thing four times and then he does it. Other children do it when you ask them once and you feel so happy.

Q. What do you do when he tries to get his own way with you?

A. I beat him.

Q. How about when he tries to get his own way with other children?

A. Then I have to beat and scold.[72]

The interview continues along these lines. These responses may be compared or contrasted with the questionnaire answers of some of the mothers of the other cultures who were rated higher on maternal warmth, such as the mothers of Okinawa or the Philippines.

The use of a standard questionnaire makes cross-cultural comparisons possible. In view of the differences of opinion about projective tests, it may be that the leaders of the Six Cultures project chose wisely in emphasizing behavioral observation and interviews.[73]

In the East African study discussed in Chapter 3, Robert B. Edgerton used a questionnaire to elicit values and attitudes in each of the pastoral and farming groups of the four tribes he studied. To give a few examples of the questions asked: "Would the (Hehe, etc.) prefer to have sons or daughters? Why? What is the most important thing for parents to teach a toddler? . . . What is the most important thing for a young man to know before he gets married? . . . What is the best thing that can happen to a man?"[74] The answers

---

[72] Ibid., pp. 312–13.

[73] Interviews with children were also attempted in the Six Cultures project but worked out less successfully, partly because the number of interviews was insufficient and partly because of the lack of comparability of the situations. (Whiting et al., *Field Guide for a Study of Socialization*, pp. 118–23.)

[74] Robert B. Edgerton, *The Individual in Cultural Adaptation. A Study of Four East African Peoples* (Berkeley, Calif.: University of California Press, 1971), p. 310.

were coded and subjected to statistical analyses, providing basic data for the contrasts made by Edgerton between the farmers and pastoralists.

A psychiatric questionnaire was used in the 1961 Cornell-Aro Mental Health Research Project among the Yoruba of Nigeria by Alexander H. Leighton and his associates. The questionnaire was given to an adult male and female in each selected household, chosen according to sampling principles, in a group of 15 villages. The interviews, lasting about one and a half to two hours each, were given to 326 subjects. Comparisons were made with a mental health survey in Stirling County, Canada, in which Alexander and Dorothea Leighton also took part. The Stirling County form contributed to the construction of the Yoruba questionnaire, parts of it being modified to fit the Yoruba setting. Seventy-three questions were asked of the Yoruba subjects, including (to give a few examples) "Do you drink alcohol?" "Do you chew kola nuts?" "Do your hands ever tremble enough to bother you?" "Do you ever hear or see spirits or other things?" "Do you think you are troubled by witchcraft?"

In addition to this questionnaire, a cross-check questionnaire was given, usually to a village headman, for additional information about the respondent. Finally, a social data questionnaire was administered to 152 subjects with 109 questions covering a wide range of topics, such as amount of education, number of the respondent's marriages, languages spoken, and religion practiced. In most communities the subjects who were given the questionnaire made up half, or almost half, of the respondents to the psychiatric questionnaire, chosen as far as possible on a random basis. Four full-time and two part-time psychiatrists and three social scientists made up the research team, along with various interpreters, assistants, and a medical team. Two of the psychiatrists, T. Adeoye Lambo and Tolani Asuni, were members of the Yoruba tribe.

An attempt was made, both in the Stirling County study and in the Yoruba study, to select communities showing low and high levels of sociocultural integration and to see whether they are characterized by a higher or lower prevalence of mental disorder. The authors found the similarities between their two large samples, Yoruba and Stirling County, more striking than the differences with regard to both pattern quality, such as anxiety and depression, and prevalence in most of the categories tabulated. These similarities surprised the authors, since the cultures are so different; it led them to wonder whether the emphasis on cultural differences has been overdone.[75]

Where differences are concerned, the rural Yorubas seem to have a lower prevalence rate of impairing psychiatric disorders than their counterparts in Stirling County, while the prevalence rate among the urban Yorubas seems to be higher and closer to the North American level. In both areas the best mental health seems to be found in the best integrated communities.[76] It may be questioned how well the actual incidence of mental disorder is gauged from answers to questionnaires. However, this seems to be only the beginning of an extensive project, and meanwhile the method has provided a mass of relevant information.

An "interpretative questionnaire" provided the main basis for the analysis of social character in a Mexican peasant community studied by Erich Fromm and Michael Maccoby. This was a series of open-ended questions that differed from most other questionnaires in that the answers were analyzed for their unintended unconscious meaning. The questionnaire was given to 406 adult villagers (200 men and 206 women), or 95 percent of the adult population.

After such routine questions as for the subject's name, age, place of birth, extent of education, whether parents were living, and so forth, questions such as the following were asked: "How frequently do you see your mother now?" "For what reasons, if any, have you consulted her during the last year?" "Would you act against her wishes?" "On what occasions have you done so?"

The subject was asked to give a brief description of his mother and of his father and to describe his idea of a good mother. He was asked if he beats his children and if children should fear their parents. The subject was asked what work he did, what he likes most and least about his work, what he does for recreation, and what he most enjoys in life. How often does he get drunk? How does liquor affect him? What does he think of *machismo?* What

---

[75] Alexander Leighton et al., *Psychiatric Disorder among the Yoruba. A Report from the Cornell-Aro Mental Health Research Project in the Western Region, Nigeria* (Ithaca, N.Y.: Cornell University Press, 1963), p. 274.

[76] Alexander H. Leighton, "A Comparative Study of Psychiatric Disorder in Nigeria and Rural North America," in Stanley C. Plog and Robert B. Edgerton (eds.), *Changing Perspectives in Mental Illness* (New York: Holt, Rinehart & Winston, 1969), pp. 179–99.

persons does he most admire? What should a man do when his wife is unfaithful? Should women have the same rights as men? What is his concept of love?

There is a special set of questions for parents only, about their ways of dealing with children. Finally, there is a set of six story questions, of which the first may serve as an example: "A mother is ill and sends her son out to buy the food for the whole family. Because he stops to play, the boy loses the money and cannot buy the food. What do you think the mother did?"[77]

The authors are aware of problems concerning questionnaires, such as the fact that answers to many questions may be stereotyped answers which do not really express the views of the subject, but they express faith in their method. Certainly, the questionnaire elicits a rich mine of information.

The villagers' questionnaires were scored according to the dominant character orientation evidenced by the subject's responses—receptive, exploitative, hoarding, or productive.[78] They were also scored on such *modes of relatedness* as sadism, masochism, narcissism, love, indulgence, and conditional love, and *sociopolitical relatedness:* authoritarian orientation, orientation of traditional authority, democratic orientation, revolutionary orientation, submissiveness, active rebelliousness, and passive rebelliousness. They were scored on fixation to the mother and to the father and on the traits of enterprise-energy and depression.

In analyzing the tabulations of scores, it was concluded that the unproductive-receptive and (moderately) productive-hoarding types were the most frequent among the men. More men than women were narcissistic, while women were more masochistic. Most villagers of both sexes were fixated on the mother; only 4 percent were not, and 47 percent were scored as being "intensely fixated" on the mother.

As the result of a factor analysis, it was found that the most authoritarian and exploitative individuals were also the most narcissistic, and that the women tended to have more hoarding orientation than the men. A minority group of productive-exploitative villagers are the modern entrepreneurs who have been able to take advantage of new capitalistic opportunities, while the majority re-

---

[77] Erich Fromm and Michael Maccoby, *Social Character in a Mexican Village. A Sociopsychoanalytic Study* (Englewood Cliffs, N.J.: Prentice-Hall, Inc., 1970), pp. 239–43.

[78] See the discussion of Fromm's theory of character orientations above, pp. 30–31.

tain a helpless receptive orientation.[79] Fromm and Maccoby found the latter type of orientation to be particularly associated with landowners who raised sugar cane. Cane brings much lower profits than rice or garden crops, but it requires much less work, and the refinery offers inducements to farmers who raise it, such as free medical care, life insurance, and scholarships for children, which appeal to those with a passive, receptive outlook on life. Cane growing was also found to be significantly correlated with exclusive attachment to the mother.[80]

The authors found a significant agreement between their findings on the questionnaire and those from the Rorschach Test and Thematic Apperception Test.[81] The detailed and convincing picture which Fromm and Maccoby have been able to draw of the social character of these Mexican villagers, based largely on the analysis of questionnaire data, shows, again, that questionnaires can be a useful instrument in culture-and-personality research.

A similar kind of standardized test potentially useful in cross-cultural studies is a Sentence Completion Test (SCT). Its use is advocated by Herbert P. Phillips.[82] Combined with behavioral observation, Phillips' SCT was the main source of data from which he drew conclusions about Thai peasant personality. The SCT was designed to elicit attitudes toward authority through such incompleted sentences as "When the [big man] told him to do it, he . . ." "When he is in the presence of a [big man] he feels . . ." "When his superior gave him an order which he knew was wrong, he . . ." "When placed in a position of power, he . . ." "The best way to treat a subordinate, is . . ."

Other kinds of attitudes were elicited by incompleted sentences such as the following: "When he thinks of his mother, he thinks of . . ." "A real close friend is one who . . ." "When he found that his best friend spoke against him, he . . ." "People who never show their feelings are . . ." "His greatest problem was . . ." "The most important thing in life is . . ."

Phillips' SCT was given to 111 individuals representing an 11 percent stratified sample of the adult population of Bang Chan. Percentages of different types of responses are given for each SCT

---

[79] Ibid., chap. 5, pp. 83–125.

[80] Ibid., pp. 130–33.

[81] Ibid., pp. 284–91.

[82] Herbert P. Phillips, *Thai Peasant Personality. The Patterns of Interpersonal Behavior in the Village of Bang Chan* (Berkeley, Calif.: University of California Press, 1965).

completion, but it is difficult to assess the significance of these percentages, since Phillips cites no comparable study using the same incomplete sentences.[83]

If the same test gets to be used in other cultures, the special characteristics of the Thai completions, if there are any, will emerge.

Another person who has used a sentence completion test in cross-cultural research is Joel Aronoff, in a study of cane cutters and fishermen in the West Indies. Aronoff's incomplete sentences were different from Phillips', including "Money is . . ." "I am proud . . ." "I feel happy when . . ." "When somebody dies I . . ." This SCT was combined with a male interview, questions being asked about occupation, home, and personal data, and a female interview, including questions such as "What is a father supposed to do for the children?" "What is a mother supposed to do for the children?" and "Would you rather have boy or girl babies?"

Aronoff contrasts the SCT responses of the fishermen with those of the cane cutters, showing that the latter are more concerned about physiological and safety needs than the former, and show less evidence of self-actualization. These contrasts are related by the author to different environmental and sociocultural conditions in the two groups.[84] This study has the advantage of being able to make comparisons between two groups tested with the same instruments.

Standardized questionnaires were not usually used very much by anthropologists formerly, but if efforts are made toward comparability between groups, as in the case of the Six Cultures project, questionnaires become a useful device, especially in view of the decreasing use of projective tests. However, Robert A. LeVine has complained about "noncomparability" when the "same" questionnaires have been used, as in the Six Cultures study, in Puerto Rico by Landy, in Lebanon by Prothro, and in the Philippines by Guthrie and Jacobs. ". . . each investigator had so altered the interview schedule or manner of reporting results that there were no comparable findings across the full range of published studies."[85]

---

[83] For some criticisms of the Phillips study, see Pertti J. Pelto, "Psychological Anthropology," in Bernard J. Siegel and Alan R. Beals (eds.), *Biennial Review of Anthropology* (Stanford, Calif.: Stanford University Press, 1967), pp. 153–55.

[84] Joel Aronoff, *Psychological Needs and Cultural Systems. A Case Study* (Princeton, N.J.: D. Van Nostrand Co., Inc. 1967).

[85] Robert A. LeVine, "Cross-Cultural Study in Child Psychology," in Paul H. Mussen (ed.), *Carmichael's Manual of Child Psychology* (3d ed.; New York: John Wiley & Sons, 1970), p. 590.

As the Phillips' Thai study shows, there is not much point in giving standardized tests or questionnaires unless they are used in more than one cultural setting. But as LeVine's comment indicates, the administration of the same questionnaire in different cultural settings presents many problems, something easier said than done. The same difficulty occurs with respect to structured situations such as doll play, although here the lack of comparability is greater, since in the studies done so far, different kinds of dolls have been used and different instructions given.

In this respect, use of the Rorschach Test has some advantages, despite the other problems that attend it. Since every person taking the Rorschach Test sees the same set of inkblots presented in the same order, here, at least, is one situation that has been fairly well standardized.

Perhaps one should not expect too much of efforts toward standardization of questionnaires and test procedures and comparability of data from different groups, for not only is every field situation different from every other, but ever fieldworker is different from every other fieldworker. Anthropologists vary in their interests, values, abilities in different spheres, and alertness to different aspects of the world around them. Even when administering the same tests or questionnaires, some will do so somewhat differently from others. Besides, in different cultures the questions will be asked in different languages, which may sometimes result in slight differences of meaning. For example, how could one replicate in another culture Fromm and Maccoby's questions about *machismo?* Equivalent terms in other languages, such as "manliness" or "masculinity" may not have quite the same connotations.

These questions are not raised to discredit the use of standardized interview schedules or questionnaires. This chapter has reviewed cases where their usefulness is well attested. But all research methods have their limitations, and it is best to be aware of them.

SUGGESTIONS FOR FURTHER READING

Karl E. Weick, "Systematic Observational Methods," in Gardner Lindzey and Elliot Aronson (eds.), *The Handbook of Social Psychology* (2d ed.; Reading, Mass.: Addison-Wesley Publishing Co., 1969), Vol. II, pp. 357–451; and Charles F. Cannell and Robert L. Kahn, "Interviewing," Ibid., pp. 526–95.

Traditional fieldwork methods in anthropology are well described in the Introduction of Bronislaw Malinowski's *Argonauts of the Western*

Pacific (New York: E. P. Dutton & Co., Inc., 1961), pp. 4–25; first published in 1922.

On the uses of photography in culture-and-personality studies, see Margaret Mead, "Some Uses of Still Photography in Culture and Personality Studies," in Douglas G. Haring (ed.), *Personal Character and Cultural Milieu* (3d ed.; Syracuse, N.Y.: Syracuse University Press, 1956), pp. 79–105.

Films: The following films (black and white) made by Margaret Mead and Gregory Bateson are available at New York University Film Library (all have relevance to the field of culture-and-personality): *Childhood Rivalry in Bali and New Guinea* (17 minutes); *A Balinese Family* (17 minutes); *Trance and Dance in Bali* (20 minutes). Margaret Mead is commentator in a film about family life in four societies: *Four Families,* black and white, McGraw-Hill (60 minutes).

chapter *12*

The Analysis of Life History Material

BIOGRAPHICAL DATA

For the authors of that sociological classic, *The Polish Peasant,* personal life records, as complete as possible, constituted "the *perfect* type of sociological material."[1] Franz Boas, on the other hand, was skeptical of the value of life histories, which he regarded as little more than essays in retrospective falsification.[2] However, Boas also believed that anthropologists should study individuals, in addition to compiling broader ethnographic accounts; and some students of Boas were pioneers in the collection of biographies from members of nonliterate societies.[3] In the 1930s and 1940s, a growing interest in life histories was fostered by the influence of psychoanalytic doctrine, with its focus on the individual. Within a five-year period, three books were published which are still the fullest autobiographies we have by American Indians: *Son of Old Man Hat. A Navaho Autobiography,* recorded by Walter Dyk (1938); *Smoke from Their Fires. The Life of a Kwakiutl Chief,* edited by Clellan S. Ford (1941); and *Sun Chief. The Autobiography of a Hopi Indian,* edited by Leo W. Simmons (1942). Meanwhile, particularly after the appearance of a critique of *The Polish Peasant*

---

[1] William I. Thomas and Florian Znaniecki, *The Polish Peasant in Europe and America* (New York: Dover Publications, 1958), Vol. II, p. 1832. Italics as in the original. (Originally published in 1917–18).

[2] Franz Boas, "Recent Anthropology," *Science,* n.s. (1943), pp. 311–14, 334–47.

[3] For references, see "Suggestions for Further Reading" at the end of this chapter

by H. Blumer, efforts were made by some investigators in the social sciences to set up criteria by which life history documents could be judged and analyzed.[4]

Life histories have figured prominently in culture-and-personality studies, such as those of Alor and Truk, Carstairs' study of high-caste Hindus in a Rajasthan community, and many others. In the United States, American Negro life histories have been analyzed for recurrent sociopsychological patterns in *Children of Bondage* by Allison Davis and John Dollard (1940), and in *The Mark of Oppression* by Abram Kardiner and Lionel Ovesey (1951).

An innovation that deserves notice is the "family autobiography." In *The Children of Sánchez,* Oscar Lewis presented the story of a lower class family in Mexico City, as told by each of its members. Independent versions of the same episodes by the different individuals involved provide a check on the reliability and validity of some of the data. Moreover, one sees the same occurrence through different eyes, noting how it affects each individual differently. A dramatic incident, for example, is the early, unexpected death of Jesús Sánchez' wife, Lenore. Jesús tells this story; so do each of the children who remember the event vividly. Other episodes are similarly repeated, like recurrent motifs, in the individual autobiographies. In the process the reader gets to learn how the various members of the family feel about, and react toward, one another. This material was recorded by tape recorder, translated and edited by Lewis.[5]

In *La Vida* Lewis gave an extensive account of a poor Puerto Rican family consisting of five households. He described the Ríos family members as having "an almost complete absence of internal conflict and of a sense of guilt. . . . The leading characters in *The Children of Sánchez* seem mild, repressed, and almost middle-class by comparison."[6] Lewis has made more use of biographical material than any other anthropologist, but he has presented the material as raw data, without much analysis of particular personalities.

Edward H. Winter collected life history material from an Amba man, his two wives, and another Amba male informant in Uganda. As in Lewis' studies, we get a vivid picture of the dynamics of family

---

[4] For references see "Suggestions for Further Reading."

[5] Oscar Lewis, *The Children of Sánchez. Autobiography of a Mexican Family* (New York: Random House, 1961).

[6] Oscar Lewis, *La Vida. A Puerto Rican Family in the Culture of Poverty—San Juan and New York* (New York: Random House, 1968), p. xxvi.

living from these autobiographies. In addition, the husband of the two wives was persuaded to keep a diary. He gives frank day-by-day accounts of his wives' quarrels and other matters. No projective tests were given to these subjects, but they are hardly necessary since the life histories are so revealing.[7]

At their best, life histories are fascinating documents. The main difficulty lies in knowing what to do with them. How are they to be interpreted? Some collectors of such data have simply presented their narratives as raw material, leaving them to speak for themselves. In culture-and-personality studies, however, it seems preferable to make some effort at interpretation—not always an easy matter. There are other problems as well: questions of sampling, methods of procedure in recording data, and methods of presentation.

Most published life histories are either accounts of famous men or case histories by psychiatrists of their maladjusted patients. The "average man" is not apt to be represented, being neither successful enough nor sick enough to attract attention. In cross-cultural studies it often happens that informants are drawn from the ranks of the less successful. In the discussion of Alor, for example, it was mentioned that Du Bois' biographies were given by some of the less-successful members of the society.

Clyde Kluckhohn has suggested that American Indians who give autobiographies are apt to be drawn from the more maladjusted individuals in the group.[8] There must, after all, be a fairly strong motive to talk, when an informant works with an ethnographer for many sessions. Well-adjusted subjects may be motivated only by financial rewards and may thus not give so sincerely personal an account. Don Talayesva, the narrator of *Sun Chief*, seems to have been a tormented person, ill at ease in his own society, who turned with gratitude to the white anthropologists who showed a friendly interest in him. John Chavafambira, the Manyika medicine man whose autobiography is presented by Wulf Sachs in *Black Anger* (1947), was also an unhappy man, and Sachs, a psychoanalyst, got his story through a number of analytic sessions. Lewis' Sánchez family members are painfully tormented people. Charles Nowell,

[7] Edward H. Winter, *Beyond the Mountains of the Moon, The Lives of Four Africans* (Urbana, Ill.: University of Illinois Press, 1959).

[8] Clyde Kluckhohn, "The Personal Document in Anthropological Science," in Lewis Gottschalk, Clyde Kluckhohn, and Robert Angell, *The Use of Personal Documents in History, Anthropology, and Sociology*, Social Science Research Council Bulletin 53 (New York, 1945), pp. 99, 118.

the subject of *Smoke from Their Fires,* on the other hand, seems to have been a rather successful nonneurotic man; his autobiography is also relatively colorless and nonpersonal when compared with those of Don Talayesva, John Chavafambira, and the Sánchez family.

For a balanced picture of the society being studied, of course, one should try to get material from the more successful and well-adjusted members of the group as well as from those less well adjusted. Gladwin handled the sampling problem ingeniously, as described in Chapter 7.[9] Ideally one should have biographical data from young subjects as well as old, and of both sexes and of different status levels. Carstairs, who collected life history data from high-caste Hindus in a Rajasthan village, describes his own research design as follows:

> In drawing up plans for this research, my intention was to try to obtain prolonged interviews with twenty-seven informants, nine from each caste [i.e., Rajput, Brahman, and Bania]. In each case, three were to be relatively eminent and highly-regarded members of their community, three average, and three unquestionably low in their caste-fellows' esteem. Further, my ambition was to try to find one elderly, one middle-aged and one young man in each group of three.[10]

This design was not exactly achieved in practice, although the number of informants was increased from 27 to 37. A few of the pigeonholes were not filled. Carstairs also tried to keep a balance between the number of informants who were eldest sons and those who were younger sons.[11] The sampling procedures of Gladwin and Carstairs show a great advance over earlier work in culture-and-personality in which there was often little or no concern with this problem.

Robert W. White has made a pioneer effort to record and analyze biographical material of normal persons in the United States. Three case histories are described in his book *Lives in Progress.* The procedures followed could be used in cross-cultural studies where communities are revisited after an interval of time. Each subject was interviewed on two occasions several years apart. In addition to giving an autobiography, each subject was given the Rorschach Test, Thematic Apperception Test, Wechsler-Bellevue Adult In-

---

[9] See Thomas Gladwin and Seymour B. Sarason, *Truk: Man in Paradise,* Viking Fund Publications in Anthropology, No. 20 (New York, 1953), p. 211.

[10] G. Morris Carstairs, *The Twice-Born. A Study of a Community of High-Caste Hindus* (Bloomington, Ill.: Indiana University Press, 1958), p. 37.

[11] Ibid., p. 38.

telligence Test, some self-rating scales, and other tests. The analyses of the personalities of the three subjects seem to be more successful and convincing than in most such efforts. They show that life history material can have much value for the understanding of individual personalities and their development over time.[12]

Some of the best life history documents are those which show the least prodding on the part of the ethnographer. During his Rajasthan fieldwork, Carstairs was fortunate in acquiring the already written autobiography, or journal, of a young man of a Bania family. The value of this document lies in its utter frankness and naïveté. Here is a man searching his heart, weighing his own assets and liabilities, complaining about his wife, father, and other members of the joint family, and expressing his longings and ambitions. This document is only about 40 printed pages in length, but it gives a remarkably full picture of a human personality.

Autobiographies recorded by ethnographers are not apt to be so spontaneous or so honest. The informant often lapses into silence, or finds refuge in giving cultural data which have no personal significance. My Chippewa informant, Jim Mink, for example, used to launch into tedious explanations of how traps are made and other details of material culture. In such a case the ethnographer may direct the interview and ask questions or specify the kind of information he wants. Where prodding of this sort occurs, it should be indicated in the published version. This is one deficiency in the otherwise splendid document, *Sun Chief*. We never know when a particular piece of information was spontaneously volunteered by Don Talayesva and when it was elicited through cross-examination by Simmons. This criticism applies as well to Ford's *Smoke from Their Fires* and to *The Children of Sánchez* by Lewis.

The general question of editing is involved here. Kluckhohn believed that *Sun Chief* suffered from too much editing and condensation. (Only one fifth of the original data was published.)[13] The material is presented in orderly chronological sequence and not as Don Talayesva told it. A different method was followed by

---

[12] Robert W. White, *Lives in Progress. A Study of the Natural Growth of Personality* (New York: Holt, Rinehart & Winston, Inc., 1952).

For another good analysis along similar lines, see the case study of Morris Brown in Irving L. Janis, George F. Mahl, Jerome Kagan, and Robert R. Holt, *Personality. Dynamics, Development, and Assessment* (New York: Harcourt, Brace, & World, Inc., 1969), chaps. 36, 38, 39, and 40. Analysis of life history material is combined with interpretation of Rorschach, Thematic Apperception Test, and various other tests.

[13] Kluckhohn, "The Personal Document in Anthropological Science," p. 97.

Cora Du Bois, who presented the Alorese autobiographies as they were taken down, with no attempt at rearrangement. This method has the advantage of preserving chains of association. On the other hand, the Alorese life histories are hard to read or comprehend when compared with *Sun Chief* and some other edited biographies. The ethnographer must decide which method of presentation does most justice to his material.

Do not life history informants sometimes falsify and improvise? Of course they do, but this need not destroy their value as psychological documents. It was obvious to me that my Chippewa informant Julia Badger made up much of her information. She tended, for example, toward a dubious overspecificity; the numbers 56 and 57 kept coming up in her accounts. There were 56 people at a Winnebago peyote meeting she attended; her dormitory room at school had 57 beds. There were 357 boys and girls at one school she went to, which had 156 cows and where 856 loaves of bread were baked every day. But at another school that Julia attended there were 357 students, and 456 loaves of bread were baked every day. Many of Julia's anecdotes were evidently fantasies; all the same, they do provide psychologically revealing information, as will be shown later in this chapter.

Life histories are not always informative. Gladwin felt that the Trukese biographies told less about his subjects than the psychological tests which he used. Gladwin's informants were not able to remember much about their early years, and since Trukese men are not given to introspection, their accounts "tend to consist in a series of flat statements about happenings and perfunctory and conventional expressions of their reactions to them. . ."[14] In a review of *The People of Alor,* Jules Henry expressed a similar disappointment in the Alorese life histories. He suggests that autobiography is a phase of the historical perspective associated with Western culture. One need not expect to find this interest in self-revelation in all cultures.[15]

However, as *Sun Chief* testifies, rich life histories have been obtained from non-Western informants. To be sure, Don Talayesva is an acculturated individual, and Carstairs' introspective Bania diarist may also have been influenced by Western European traditions. Nevertheless, these men both belong to cultures which are still sig-

---

[14] Gladwin and Sarason, *Truk: Man in Paradise,* p. 215.

[15] Jules Henry, "Review of *The People of Alor,*" *American Journal of Orthopsychiatry,* Vol. 15 (1945), p. 372.

nificantly different from that of the Western world. The same certainly applies to Winter's Amba subjects and to John Chavafambira.

For the purposes of culture-and-personality research it is not necessary for life histories to be literarily satisfying. We hope to find clues in such material to the values and attitudes of the individual and to get some idea, if possible, as to why he has become the sort of person he is. For these purposes a fairly brief document may sometimes be sufficient. It is not always necessary to meet the demanding criteria which Dollard proposed for the life history. A life history can never be complete in any case. Even the fullest autobiography can be no more than a pale reflection of an individual's life in all its complexity. In analyzing a life history document, one looks for what the informant chooses to tell about himself and what values and attitudes he expresses, rather than attempt to reconstruct the whole sequence of his life.

THE INTERPRETATION OF DREAMS, VISIONS, AND FANTASIES

G. P. Murdock lists "dream interpretation" as a universal aspect of culture.[16] Not only does dreaming seem to be a universal human characteristic, but, if Murdock is right, an interest in dreams and an effort to understand them are found in all cultures. However, societies do vary considerably in the interest given to dreams. Among many American Indian tribes, where dreams were regarded as an avenue to supernatural power, this interest was intense, while among the Trobriand Islanders, according to Malinowski, there is little concern with dreams; people seldom tell their dreams spontaneously, and have no system of symbolic explanation.[17]

Dreams are very personal productions of the individual. The person who creates a dream is on his own; the setting, the cast, and the events of a dream are somehow of his own making. Due to their personal and intimate nature, the interpretation of dreams provides valuable clues to the personality of the individual. Because of the universality of dreaming, the study of dreams may be carried on cross-culturally.

---

[16] George P. Murdock, "The Common Denominator of Cultures," in Ralph Linton (ed.), *The Science of Man in the World Crisis* (New York: Columbia University Press, 1945), p. 124.

[17] Bronislaw Malinowski, *Sex and Repression in Savage Society* (New York: Meridian Books, 1955), p. 89.

It is evident that dreams reflect the culture in which one lives. Freud has discussed some "typical" dreams, "dreams which almost everyone has dreamed in the same manner," and to which Freud says he has usually failed to obtain clarifying associations from the dreamer.[18] One of these dreams is "the embarrassment-dream of nakedness." Such a dream, familiar enough in the Western world, can have no exact parallel among unacculturated Australian aborigines or other people who wear no clothing. Another "typical" dream cited by Freud is the examination-dream, which is also obviously the product of a particular type of culture characterized by formal schooling with competitive examinations.[19]

Griffith, Miyagi, and Tago discuss the "typical" dream of finding money, which is said to be usually in the form of coins rather than bills.[20] Whatever the denomination or form of currency, however, dreams of this sort can only appear in a society having some such medium of exchange. The dream of being chased by cows appears to be a "typical" dream in western Ghana, perhaps especially among disturbed individuals.[21] Culture, then, intimately influences the dreaming process.

Let us consider two general ways of studying dreams. First, one may collect dreams from a large number of individuals in a particular society and then look for characteristic features in this sample. Because of its group basis, such an investigation must be mainly concerned with the manifest content of dreams. Let us call this the *collective* approach. A second approach involves recording dreams in conjunction with life history material and other data concerning the individual, such as projective tests. In this case, especially if one can obtain free associations to the dream material, one may perhaps determine the "latent" content. Let us call this the *individual* approach. If one's sample of life history informants is large enough, these approaches could be combined.

---

[18] Sigmund Freud, "The Interpretation of Dreams," in *The Basic Writings of Sigmund Freud*, A. A. Brill trans. and ed. (New York: Modern Library, 1938), p. 292.

[19] Seligman reports this dream for ancient China, where competitive examinations were an avenue to political power. See C. G. Seligman, "Anthropology and Psychology," *Journal of the Royal Anthropological Institute of Great Britain and Ireland*, Vol. 54 (1924), p. 40.

[20] Richard M. Griffith, Otoya Miyagi, and Akira Tago, "The Universality of Typical Dreams: Japanese vs. Americans," *American Anthropologist*, Vol. 60 (1958), p. 1174.

[21] M. J. Field, *Search for Security. An Ethno-Psychiatric Study of Rural Ghana* (Evanston, Ill.: Northwestern University Press, 1960), pp. 155, 157, 163, 164, 172–73, 176, 180, 195, 250, 285, 298, 310, 311, 368, 414, 427, 434.

THE COLLECTIVE APPROACH

Dorothy Eggan has collected dreams from over 20 Hopi Indians over a fairly extended period of time.[22] One of her informants was Don Talayesva, the narrator of *Sun Chief,* for whom she has over 230 dreams, 15 of which are discussed in a stimulating article.[23] Her approach has therefore been both collective and individual. One of Eggan's conclusions, on a collective basis, is that:

. . . among the Hopi, the strength of tribal attitudes toward cooperative obligations to the tribe, frequently masked by surface changes, is well illustrated in dreams, as is also the superficiality of Hopi conversion to Christianity. A survey may show that 30% of a village is Christian in that they attend a missionary church; but their dreams indicate that the majority of the old Hopi who list themselves as Christian have as much respect for Masau'u, and many other Hopi deities, as they ever had.[24]

A particularly interesting collective study of dreams is a detailed investigation of Zulu dreams by S. G. Lee, which contains assessments of the latent content of the dreams. Lee asked 600 Zulu subjects, "How much do you dream?" and "What do you dream about?" In addition to recording their answers, Lee asked some 120 women the same questions, in each case following this up with further inquiries. These subjects were asked to describe two recent dreams in detail. Lee found that stereotyped typical dreams were very common—a circumstance which allowed quantitative comparisons to be made between groups, that is, between men and women, and between women of different ages and marital status. Because of their frequently stereotyped nature, all the dreams collected could be classified under less than 50 main content headings.

Women reported more dream activity than men, and more women dreamed of frightening objects, such as monsters, than did men. The men reported enjoying their dreams more than did the women. Men dreamed much more about cattle than did the women. Lee's explanation for this contrast is ingenious. Work with cattle used to be an exclusively male prerogative in the 19th century; and

---

[22] Dorothy Eggan, "Dream Analysis," in Bert Kaplan (ed.), *Studying Personality Cross-Culturally* (Evanston, Ill.: Row, Peterson & Co., 1961), pp. 567–68.

[23] Dorothy Eggan, "The Significance of Dreams for Anthropological Research," *American Anthropologist,* Vol. 51 (1949), pp. 177–98. See also Dorothy Eggan, "The Personal Use of Myth in Dreams," *Journal of American Folklore,* Vol. 68 (1955), pp. 67–75.

[24] Dorothy Eggan, "The Manifest Content of Dreams: A Challenge to Social Science," *American Anthropologist,* Vol. 54 (1952), p. 479.

there was then a taboo on women handling cattle. Nowadays, however, women must take care of the cattle, since the men are often away from home under present work conditions. The cattle dreams reflect the sexual division of labor that existed 50 to 100 years ago but not the present situation. Lee argues that superego patterns are early instilled, and that dream content also tends to be derived from this early period. Hence the "conservatism" of the dream content. If Lee is right, this might explain the similarly conservative pattern of Hopi dreaming just noted.

When women do dream of cattle, their dreams have a different character from those of men. Women may dream of being pursued and gored by an ox or bull,[25] while the men have pleasant wish-fulfillment dreams of owning large herds.

More frequently than men, women dream of flooded rivers, water, snakes, and a priapic creature called Tokoloshe, who lives in rivers and assaults women sexually. Thirty-two percent of the women reported water dreams; only 5 percent of the men did so; 17 percent of the women dreamed of snakes as against 3 percent of the men; 16 percent of the women reported dreams of flooded rivers; while only 6 percent of the men did so. Tokoloshe dreams were reported by 7 percent of the women and 2 percent of the men.

The local interpretation of Zulu diviners is that "To dream of flooded rivers means that you will give birth to a baby." Lee points to the interesting parallel with orthodox Freudian symbolic interpretation here.

The author goes on to examine the different age and marital status groups in which dreams are reported.

Snakes, *tokoloshe,* and flooded river dreams were practically limited to women under the age of fifty—while dreams of "a baby" and children were reported by women of ages when childbearing might be considered very probable, between 18 and 35. Dreams of "a wedding" were found in an even younger group, mostly unmarried. "Fighting,"a comparatively common dream in men, was a dream of a few unmarried women under 22. Overt aggression, after marriage, is forbidden the Zulu woman by her culture.[26]

Those who dreamed of a baby had the worst record of married infertility. Their dreams, evidently, represent simple wish-fulfillment. Those who dreamed of still water were more apt to be women

---

[25] Compare the "typical" Ghana dream of being chased by cows, referred to in footnote 21.

[26] S. G. Lee, "Social Influences in Zulu Dreaming," *Journal of Social Psychology,* Vol. 47 (1958), pp. 278–89.

who had borne no children, and also married and widowed women who had born relatively few. Flooded river dreams were mostly reported by married women with a very low rate of complete married infertility, but who were older than the "baby" dreamers. Such women have borne many more children than either of the other two "birth dream" groups and have a fear of further childbirth—a disinclination which is in conflict with social pressures to keep on bearing children.

If we are to make cross-cultural comparisons of the patterning of dreams, it would be useful to have data on the prevailing characteristics of dreams in the United States. Fortunately, abundant information on this has been made possible by Calvin S. Hall's collection of 10,000 dreams and by his generalizations about them. Hall's generalizations must be taken to apply to American dreams, not to dreams universally. Let us consider some of his findings. Hall claims that dreams generally concern the personal life of the dreamer and seldom have to do with current events, presidential elections, wars and other happenings reported in the newspapers. Nor does a person normally dream about his work or business activities. In 10 out of every 100 dreams, the dreamer is walking along a road; in about 15 out of 100, he is in some kind of conveyance. One out of three dreams occurs in a dwelling which is usually not the dreamer's own house. Family members and friends are commonly dreamed of, but about 4 of every 10 characters in our dreams are strangers. Strenuous activity is not generally characteristic of dreams; eating and drinking occur very infrequently, but swimming, dancing, and playing games are common.[27] Unpleasant dreams are more numerous than pleasant ones; this ratio increases as one gets older. About one dream in three has color in it.[28] Domesticated animals appear more frequently than wild animals, with the three most common being horses, dogs, and cats—in that order. Horses appear about twice as often in the dreams of women as in those of men.[29]

Another essay in the collective approach to the study of dreams is that by Griffith, Miyagi, and Tago, who made a comparison of

[27] Calvin S. Hall, *The Meaning of Dreams* (New York: Dell, 1959), pp. 19, 29–31, 37, 41.

[28] Ibid., p. 52. This seems a surprisingly high percentage. Schachtel refers to a Japanese study by Tatibana, in which it is stated that of 100 subjects questioned, only 25 reported having seen color in their dreams; 60 percent of these 25 recalled only a single instance of having seen a color in their dreams. E. G. Schachtel, "On Color and Affect," in Murray H. Sherman (ed.), *A Rorschach Reader* (New York: International Universities Press, 1960), p. 350.

[29] Hall, *The Meaning of Dreams*, pp. 62–63.

American and Japanese college students' dreams. In this case, instead of recording dreams, a dream questionnaire was used. Through the questionnaire Griffith collected figures on the occurrence of "typical" dreams and common dream contents from 250 American college students in Kentucky (134 males, 116 females), while his Japanese colleagues, using the same questionnaire, got similar data from 223 Tokyo college students (132 males, 91 females). The authors found that American and Japanese college students tended to have very similar types of dreams. Some differences, however, were noted in connection with aggressive dreams, and here the authors also seem to contradict one of the points made by Hall. Hall observes that aggressive dreams are common but outright murder rare. According to one report dealing with Hall's work, only 2 percent of the hostile dreams involved actual homicide.[30] On this point one gets a different impression from the findings of Griffith, Miyagi, and Tago, whose analysis also brings out an interesting point of sex difference in the two national groups studied.

To the question "Have you ever killed someone in your dreams?" 26 percent of the Americans responded "yes," versus 28 percent of the Japanese; of all the males combined, 29 percent reported the dream, versus 24 percent of the combined females. However, within the American culture, the males had the dream in proportion three to one over the females; the situation was completely reversed in the Japanese culture, where twice as many females as males reported the dream.[31]

Two other differences noted in this study were: (1) the rarity of nudity dreams in Japan, and (2) the greater frequency of dreams of fire in that country.

Robert A. LeVine has carried out a complicated but well-conceived and well-executed study of dreams of English-speaking Nigerian boys attending secondary schools. His purpose was to find evidence of differences in the strength of the need for achievement (*n*-Achievement) in three ethnic groups: Hausa, Yoruba, and Ibo. A number of writers have commented impressionistically on the drive and enterprise of the Ibo, contrasting them with the more conservative Hausa. LeVine believes that the high achievement motivation of the Ibo is related to a greater degree of status mobility among them than in the other two ethnic groups.

In measuring achievement motivation the most usual method

---

[30] Leonard Wallace Robinson, "What We Dream—And Why," *New York Times -Magazine,* February 15, 1959, p. 57.

[31] Griffith et al., "The Universality of Typical Dreams," p. 1176.

followed by David C. McClelland and his colleagues has been to use the Thematic Apperception Test (TAT).[32] But LeVine did not think that this method would work well with his three Nigerian groups, which differ greatly in styles of clothing and other aspects of culture. Accordingly, LeVine obtained dream reports instead. Each student in a classroom was asked to write in English an account of a dream he had had more than once. Some of the reported dreams were probably daydreams, but LeVine and his colleagues made no distinction between such types, considering all the reports to be fantasies produced in response to an ambiguous stimulus.

LeVine's hypothesis was that the Ibo dream reports would show the most evidence of *n*-Achievement and the Hausa the least, with the Yoruba falling in between. The testing sample consisted of 342 male secondary students: 65 Hausa, 139 Yoruba, and 138 Ibo.

The students' dream reports were typed, disguised to obviate clues to ethnic identity, and scored for *n*-Achievement along the lines followed by McClelland. The scorers had no knowledge of LeVine's hypothesis or the ethnic groups. The results turned out to be in keeping with LeVine's hypotheses. The frequency of achievement themes was greatest for the Ibo, followed by the Yoruba and Hausa in that order.

The Nigerian students were also asked to write essays on "What is a successful man?" and "How does a boy become a successful man?" Here the *n*-Achievement scores were not in the expected direction of Ibo-Yoruba-Hausa but, instead: Yoruba-Hausa-Ibo. However, differences between the groups were too small to be considered statistically significant. Another set of scores did accord with expectations. This time the essays were scored for the frequency of obedience and social compliance value themes, which proved to be highest for the conservative Hausa and lowest for the Ibo. LeVine cites similar findings in a nationwide public survey of Nigerian adults.[33]

THE INDIVIDUAL APPROACH

The individual approach to the study of dreams is possible when one has life history material to which the dream can be related.

---

[32] McClelland's work is discussed briefly in both Chapter 13 and Chapter 17.

[33] Robert A. LeVine, with the assistance of Eugene Strangman and Leonard Unterberger, *Dreams and Deeds: Achievement Motivation in Nigeria* (Chicago: University of Chicago Press, 1966). Further reference to this study will be made in Chapter 17.

Ideally, one should have the dreamer's associations to his dream. The Alorese study provides an example of this approach. Cora Du Bois began each day's work with her informants by asking for dreams of the previous night. She admits, however, that attempts to get associations to significant words in the dream were not very successful.[34] Wulf Sachs persuaded John Chavafambira and his wife to associate to their dreams, apparently with more success.[35]

Once a dream or dream series has been recorded, either with or without associations, the problem of interpretation arises. A given dream may, of course, be interpreted in a number of different ways. Books on dreams, like those of Wolff, Hadfield, and Boss,[36] draw attention to contrasting systems of interpretation based upon different assumptions about dreams. Hadfield presents a dream and its analysis as it might be interpreted by (1) a Freudian, (2) an Adlerian, and (3) a Jungian.[37] He also interprets some of Freud's dreams in a manner at variance with Freud's own analysis.[38] Boss[39] offers an interpretation of a recurrent dream which plagued the poet Rosegger—an interpretation which also contrasts with Freud's analysis of the same dream.[40] Wolff, too, analyzes some dreams of Freud's which Freud had interpreted quite differently.[41] Dream interpretations are therefore not self-evident. Each depends upon a particular set of assumptions.

In the case of conflicting views, how can one decide which is the most justified? Calvin S. Hall has suggested some criteria in this connection. Somewhat condensed, these involve: (1) *agreement between individuals;* for example, two or more persons formulate explanations independently of one another and compare them; (2) *internal consistency;* that is, "The more facts that can be explained by a theory, the stronger is the presumption that the theory is correct"; (3) *external consistency;* for example, comparison with other data, such as Rorschach or TAT interpretation; (4) *prediction;*

---

[34] Du Bois, *The People of Alor* (Minneapolis: University of Minnesota Press, 1944), pp. 191–92.

[35] Sachs, *Black Anger,* pp. 179, 291.

[36] Werner Wolff, *The Dream: Mirror of Conscience* (New York: Grune and Stratton, 1952); J. A. Hadfield, *Dreams and Nightmares* (New York: Penguin, 1954); Medard Boss, *The Analysis of Dreams* (New York: Philosophical Library, 1958).

[37] Hadfield, *Dreams and Nightmares,* pp. 85–87.

[38] Ibid., pp. 26–27, 52–58.

[39] Boss, *The Analysis of Dreams,* p. 41.

[40] Freud, "The Intrepretation of Dreams," pp. 444–45.

[41] Wolff, *The Dream,* pp. 131–55.

(5) *postdiction,* the reconstruction of past events. Since these may be verified, this method has an advantage over prediction, for which one must await the outcome.[42]

Comments may be made on two of these criteria. In the case of *agreement between individuals,* it would not be surprising if two or more Freudians arrive at the same interpretation of a dream, but we can't say that this agreement would necessarily constitute corroboration. In connection with *external consistency,* a word of caution may be suggested. Hiram L. Gordon has made a comparison of the dreams and TAT stories of a group of 29 psychiatric patients (24 men and 5 women). He found that his subjects' dreams, as compared with their TAT stories, expressed more aggression, tension, and fear, and less depression and self-blame. The central character in dreams was more passive and inadequate than in the subject's TAT stories. Gordon's conclusion is that in dreams the subject "is less concerned with maintaining his idealized self-concept of adequacy and maturity and more concerned with escaping threats to his safety," while in the TAT stories he is more concerned with defending and enhancing an idealized concept of the self.[43]

SYMBOLISM

The problem of symbolism is, of course, involved in the interpretation of dreams. Freud believed that most dreams of adults give expression to erotic wishes. To evade the "dream censor" these wishes may have to be disguised in symbolic form; hence the familiar equations of the male genital organ with snakes, swords, sticks, and so forth, and of the vagina with containers, vases, boxes, and bags.

Though much influenced by Freudian theory, Calvin S. Hall doubts this concept of symbolic disguise. His reasons for skepticism on this point seem cogent:

Having read hundreds of dream series in the past few years, I noticed that within the same series outspoken dreams occurred along with "symbolized" dreams. It is fairly common for one to dream of sexual activities in the frankest terms one night and in disguised terms the next. Open incest dreams alternate with camouflaged incest dreams. Patricide and fraticide are sometimes overt, sometimes concealed. I wondered what was

---

[42] Calvin S. Hall, "Diagnosing Personality by the Analysis of Dreams," *Journal of Abnormal and Social Psychology,* Vol. 42 (1947), pp. 73–79.

[43] Hiram L. Gordon, "A Comparative Study of Dreams and Responses to The Thematic Apperception Test. I. A Need-Press Analysis," *Journal of Personality,* Vol. 22 (1953), pp. 252–53.

the sense of preparing an elaborate deception in one dream when it was discarded in a subsequent dream.[44]

Hall also notes that many dream symbols for penis, vagina, and coitus are identical with slang terms given in Partridge's A *Dictionary of Slang and Unconventional English,* many of which terms are centuries old. They would therefore not be very effective disguises.

Freud gave another reason for symbolism in dreams—regard for representability. Thoughts, feelings, attitudes, and impulses are more vividly conveyed in pictorial form in dreams. The dream speaks in parables—not to confuse but to convey information. Hall prefers this view of symbolism to the disguise theory which he thinks is diametrically opposed to the former. Whichever view of symbolism one accepts, however, the problem of interpreting symbols remains. Are we safe in translating sword or snake as penis, or handbag as vagina? May not such symbols have different overtones and associations in other cultures? The snake is certainly a symbol for penis in various cultures beside our own, but in some areas it symbolizes a variety of other things as well, for example, healing, immortality, wisdom, the rainy season, the rainbow, and the afterworld. In such cases one should investigate both the local cultural concepts about the symbolic referent and the dreamer's own associations as well.

The attitude of culture-and-personality anthropologists toward the question of symbolism has been ambivalent, for they have been influenced both by Freudian theory and by the cultural relativism of Franz Boas. A word must be said about these conflicting attitudes. According to the more orthodox Freudian and Jungian analysts, some symbols have a universal significance. They are "permanent or constant translations"[45] and may be found in all societies because (for Freud) they are rooted in man's physiological functioning, common experiences, and associations,[46] or (for Jung) because they exist in the collective unconscious.[47] Most anthropologists, as far as

---

[44] Calvin S. Hall, "A Cognitive Theory of Dream Symbols," *Journal of General Psychology,* Vol. 48 (1953), pp. 172–73.

[45] Sigmund Freud, *A General Introduction to Psychoanalysis,* Stanley Hall, trans. (New York: Boni & Liveright, 1920), p. 123.

[46] Freud also considered the possibility of transmission through a sort of collective unconscious: "symbolism, a mode of expression which has never been individually acquired, may claim to be regarded as a racial heritage." (Ibid., p. 210).

[47] A rather extreme example of the Jungian view is Frances Wickes' discussion of a mandala drawn by a patient which "appeared to her as if painted on her own wall, a picture like those painted in Thibet thousands of years ago." Wickes writes, "phantasy

I can judge, take a more culturalist and relativist view of symbolism. A relativist approach stresses the differing cultural contexts in which a symbol may appear and which may alter the meaning of the symbol. This can be illustrated in Boas' treatment of design symbols.

Boas asserted that symbols, like all other aspects of culture, have a historical background. The form of a symbol, he argued, may diffuse from one society to another; but its associated meaning may or may not diffuse with it. As an example, Boas cited the design motif consisting of an isosceles triangle with short straight lines coming down from the base. This design is found in the decorative art of many North American Indian tribes, among whom it must have diffused from one group to another. Symbolic meanings are generally given to the design, but these vary from tribe to tribe. For one group it represents a bear's paw with long claws, for another a tent with tent poles, doorway, and pegs. Among the Pueblo Indians, concerned with rain and fertility, the design is interpreted as a cloud with falling rain, while another tribe sees it as a mountain with springs at its foot.[48] The design, therefore, does not have a fixed symbolic significance for all tribes but assumes, rather, the character of a semistructured inkblot into which varying interpretations may be projected.

Ruth Bunzel has similarly pointed out that many American Indian tribes use the cross in their decorative art. "To the Zuñi," she writes "it symbolizes the four quarters of the world; to the Arapaho, the morning star; to the Huichol it represents corn or peyote or a spark."[49] Thus, certain meanings for a symbol may become standardized within a given tribe. Yet within the group itself there may be differences of interpretation; the same individual, even, may give different explanations for a particular symbol at different times.

It must be noted, however, that the universal and relativist points of view need not be mutually exclusive. Perhaps the associations to

---

is not a personal creation. The images arise from levels far deeper than our own personal unconscious. They are archetypal in nature. When studied, these images are seen to embody ancient ideas, old symbols that have contained psychic energy from archaic times." (*The Inner World of Man* [New York: Henry Holt & Co., 1938], pp. 234, 237.) In the Jungian scheme these generalizations do not apply to all symbols, but only to the so-called archetypes. A more relativistic view is taken in other cases. See Ira Progoff *Jung's Psychology and Its Social Meaning* (London: Routledge, Kegan Paul, 1953), p. 138.

[48] Franz Boas, *Primitive Art* (New York: Dover, 1955), p. 120.

[49] Ruth Bunzel, "Art," in Franz Boas (ed.), *General Anthropology* (New York: Heath, 1938), p. 584.

design forms recorded by anthropologists represent only superficial, rational responses. It might be argued that on a deeper, more unconscious level some symbols may prove to have universal significance.[50]

But to demonstrate the existence of true universal symbols, one must rule out the influence of cultural diffusion. Most of Freud's evidence for symbolic meanings is drawn from the folklore, mythology, and proverbs of Western Europe. Even if we range further afield to India and China, we are still dealing with cultures in which the diffusion of folklore and beliefs has operated over long periods of time. To show true universality in symbolic associations one should examine the evidence from widely separated, historically unrelated culture areas.

Let us consider these problems with regard to snake symbolism. Ernest Jones considers the snake to be a good example of universal symbolism.

The idea of a snake, which is never consciously associated with that of the phallus, is regularly so in dreams, being one of the most constant and invariable symbols; in primitive religions the two ideas are obviously interchangeable, so that it is often hard to distinguish phallic from ophitic worship.

This association is attributed by Jones to the objective attributes common to both snake and penis: "shape, erectibility, habits—of emitting poison and of creeping into holes," as well as to certain attitudes of horror and disgust which may sometimes be present, as in the case of prudish virgins.[51]

Now can we say that phallic associations and attributes of fear and disgust concerning the snake are universal? If we mean by this all peoples of the world, the answer would seem to be negative, for there are some regions, in parts of northern Europe and Asia, the

---

[50] Erich Fromm, who has so often mediated between psychoanalytic and sociological traditions, has suggested a distinction between *accidental* (entirely personal) , *conventional* (restricted to a group sharing the same tradition) , and *universal* symbols. "The universal symbol," he writes, "is one in which there is an intrinsic relationship between the symbol and that which it represents. . . . The universal symbol is rooted in the properties of our body, our senses, and our mind, which are common to all men and, therefore, not restricted to individuals or to specific groups." (*The Forgotten Language, An Introduction to the Study of Dreams, Fairy Tales, and Myths* [New York: Rinehart, 1951], pp. 15, 18) . Unfortunately, Fromm's discussion of universal symbolism is rather weak. He gives two examples—fire and water—but offers so many "intrinsic" meanings of these properties that their symbolic significance remains unclear.

[51] Ernest Jones, *Papers on Psychoanalysis* (Baltimore: Williams & Wilkins, 1948) , pp. 101, 123.

Arctic, and some oceanic islands, where snakes are not found. It is interesting to note, however, that in some of these areas traditions about serpents may persist in folklore and legend. Some Eskimo groups, at least—perhaps the most southern ones—have folktales about snakes,[52] and the Chukchee of eastern Siberia, where there are no snakes, have traditions about snakelike creatures which may be survivals of a period before the northward migration of the ancestors of the present Chukchee.[53] The tenacity of such traditions is remarkable. Even so, there are probably societies in snakeless regions where no such traditions exist. Moreover, it must be conceded that there are differences in attitudes toward snakes in different cultural areas. For example, among many African tribes, according to Hambly, the python is revered as "a god of wisdom, earthly bliss and benefaction." Here there seems to be no attitude of horror; however, Hambly also says that there are phallic associations to the snake among these tribes,[54] also suggested, if not demonstrated, by Lee's material on Zulu dreams.[55]

Evidence for phallic associations to the snake is sometimes provided by linguistic clues. In Semitic languages, according to Howey, the same root signifies serpent and phallus.[56] In India "nāgalatā or climbing serpent, serpent-creeper, is one of the Hindoo names of the phallos."[57] A Chippewa term for penis, *kinébigustigwàn*, translated literally, means "snake head."[58]

Popular customs may also indicate such symbolic linkages. Rivet-Carnac has discussed some phallic implications of the Nāgpanchamī festival, as observed in Nāgpur, India, in the 1870s. At this time, he says,

. . . more than the usual license is indulged in. . . . Rough pictures of snakes, in all sorts of shapes and positions, are sold and distributed, something after the manner of Valentines. . . . In the ones I have seen, in days gone by, the positions of the women with the snakes were of the

---

[52] Heinrich Johannes Rink, *Tales and Traditions of the Eskimo* (William Blackwood, 1875), pp. 186–88.

[53] Waldemar Bogoras, *The Chukchee*, Memoir of the American Museum of Natural History, Jesup North Polar Expedition, 1909, p. 13.

[54] Wilfrid D. Hambly, *Serpent Worship in Africa*, Field Museum of Natural History, Publication No. 289 (Chicago, 1931), pp. 11, 23, 75.

[55] Lee, "Social Influences in Zulu Dreaming," p. 277.

[56] M. Oldfield Howey, *The Encircled Serpent* (London: Rider, 1949), p. 127.

[57] Angelo de Gubernatis, *Zoological Mythology* (New York: Macmillan Co., 1872), Vol. II, p. 399.

[58] A. I. Hallowell, personal communication.

most indecent description and left no doubt that, so far as the idea represented in these sketches was concerned, the cobra was regarded as the phallus.[59]

According to Ronald M. Berndt, the natives of northeast Arnhem Land frankly and consciously associate the penis with the snake.[60]

An almost universal theme in folklore is the snake-lover motif, that is, stories in which a girl is penetrated by or has sexual relations with a snake. In going through folklore literature I have found this motif reported for Italy, France, Portugal, Germany, South and Central India, Melanesia, Australia, and also in such American Indian tribes as the Hopi, Zuñi, Chippewa, Assineboine, Seneca, Sauk, Creek, and others. This motif would tend to strengthen the likelihood of a phallic association with the snake among these people. The evidence just presented does not, of course, demonstrate the universality of a phallic significance for the snake, but it does indicate the likelihood that such symbolism is not limited to Europe and the United States but obtains in many cultures in different parts of the world.

The same possibility may apply to other Freudian linkages: for example, the equation of feces and wealth. As suggested earlier, a dream involving coins or other currency can only appear in a society having some sort of monetary system. An equivalent may appear, of course, in societies like the Yurok, where cowrie shells serve as a kind of currency.[61]

J. S. Lincoln has presented some of the evidence for a symbolic equation of feces and wealth in cultures other than our own—such as Seligman's example of a psychotic Melanesian who "when remonstrated with for defaecating on the verandah, replied, 'It is not faeces, but money.' "; the Ashanti explanation that a dream of falling into a latrine means that you are going to get money; the Siamese interpretation that to dream of excrement promises riches; the belief in Tangier that if you dream your clothes are full of excrement it means wealth; and a number of other such examples.[62]

---

[59] J. R. Rivet-Carnac, "The Snake Symbol in India," *Journal of the Royal Asiatic Society of Bengal,* Vol. 48 (1879), p. 26.

[60] Ronald M. Berndt, *Kunapipi* (New York: International Universities Press, 1951), p. 21.

[61] See S. H. Posinsky, "Yurok Shell Money and 'Pains': A Freudian Interpretation," *The Psychiatric Quarterly,* Vol. 30 (1956), pp. 598–632.

[62] Jackson Steward Lincoln, *The Dream in Primitive Cultures* (Baltimore: Wilkins & Wilkins, 1935), pp. 107–8.

Alan Dundes has given some further examples, notably that the Nahuatl term for gold literally means "excrement of the gods."[63]

One consideration that should be kept in mind in assessing the significance of such symbolism is that in some peasant societies, like those of India and China, manure has a real economic significance, either for fuel, as in northern India, or for fertilizer, as in rural China. Hence, when a human figure modeled of cow dung is constructed at the Gobardhan festival in northern India, and a man exclaims "Long live Grandfather Cowdung Wealth!"[64] this need not be invested with any special Freudian overtones, for cow dung *is* a form of wealth to the Indian villagers.

JULIA BADGER'S FANTASIES

To illustrate some of the issues that have been discussed, as applied to a particular case, I will present some fantasy material from my Chippewa informant, Julia Badger. These fantasies are not dreams (although part of their origin may be in dreams), but the basic problems involved are the same.

When I collected this material in the summer of 1944 at Lac du Flambeau, Julia Badger was a 34-year-old woman married to Tom Badger, a conservative Mide priest in his seventies.[65] Julia was a very bulky woman, "wall-eyed," and somewhat schizoid. During her childhood she had had periods of temporary blindness and paralysis, and had worn a brace on her leg for several years. These ailments enforced absence from school for long periods of time and resulted in Julia's exposure to the gamut of conservative Chippewa curing practices: conjuring lodge, sucking doctor, bleeding, cedar bough medications, War Dance, Medicine Dance, and so forth. Eleven years of schooling could not erase this early impress of traditional Chippewa culture. Julia's parents seem to have rejected her in childhood, and she was brought up by grandparents, later going to school away from the reservation. After her return Julia had a brief marriage to a much older man, a Winnebago peyotist, by whom she became pregnant. This marriage was broken up by her relatives,

[63] Alan Dundes, "Earth-Diver: Creation of the Mythopoeic Male," *American Anthropologist,* Vol. 64 (1962), p. 1041.

[64] McKim Marriott, "Little Communities in an Indigenous Civilization," in McKim Marriott (ed.), *Village India,* American Anthropological Association Memoir No. 83 (1955), p. 200.

[65] The following pages draw upon my article "The Phantasy World of a Chippewa Woman," *Psychiatry,* Vol. 12 (1949), pp. 67–76.

who arranged a marriage with a Chippewa of whom they approved, but this man died not long after the birth of her child. Subsequently Julia married Tom Badger, who left his wife to live with her. When I worked with this couple in 1944, Tom and Julia had been husband and wife for 15 years, but there seemed to be a good deal of friction between them, partly because of Julia's refusal to perform the traditional chores of the Chippewa housewife. She preferred to lounge about and daydream. Tom, who was normally a mild and patient person, used to beat her when he was drunk.

On the first day of my work with Tom Badger (with Julia as interpreter) Tom told me about his encounter with a little man called Bebukowe, with whom he went sliding on the ice just before he (Tom) was born. Tom said that before he was born he was walking toward the sun, when he looked down and saw something shining. As he approached it, this turned out to be a river, frozen over. Behind him was the little man, Bebukowe. "When I was right next to that river, the man behind me spoke to me. We had reached a bend in that river, and this man said, 'Let's slide across to the bend there.' We slid along the ice. When I reached the bend, I was born."

When Tom had finished this story, Julia said that she too had seen Bebukowe. This happened when she was two months old. Julia had fallen very ill because a woman in mourning had stepped on her bonnet. This brought on paralysis and temporary blindness. A medicine man built a shaking tent to consult the spirits and took Julia into the tent with him, but meanwhile her spirit had already set out on the road to the other world. In the distance she could see the otter that stands beside the road. Julia heard a noise like jingling tin behind her. This was Bebukowe, who had come to take her back to her people. "He said, 'It isn't time for you yet.' Then he grabbed me by the waist and twisted and turned me around."

When she got back to the shaking tent, her parents were crying loudly. Bebukowe started to perform a dance. Julia said,

Bebukowe looks a lot like a man—except that his face is different. His face is a little like a grasshopper's face around the nose. [Tom Badger nodded in agreement to this description.] Bebukowe's face is handsome, though. And when he hollers, he's got a voice on him like any man's. He's dressed up in fine clothes, covered with bells. He likes to dance when he enters. He grabbed me around the waist like this. (Demonstrated) Then he said, "You're going to play around with a lot of men like this. You can't go now." He said, "I'm a handsome man. You'll see a lot of men like me. You'll play with us too.". . . He took my bonnet and whirled it around in the air. You could just see that cotton flying around.

He made like a wind when he did that. The bells started to go, and the wigwam was tipped way over. . . . It was like feathers flying around. That was the dirt from the floor that that woman had got into it . . . the woman who made me sick. [During this account Mrs. Badger also described some other spirits who she said were present in the lodge—an old woman and two whitehaired old men.]

In examining these fantasies, the first thing which struck my attention was the modification of the traditional picture of Bebukowe which appears in these accounts. Considering the respect and affection which Tom and Julia both felt for Bebukowe, it is curious to discover that Bebukowe does not at all play a kindly or beneficent role in Chippewa folklore. On the contrary, he is depicted as a villainous old fellow, an ugly hunchback with evil powers of sorcery. "He looks awful," said one informant, "He's humped way over. And he's everlastingly got the dirtiest nose. His snot hangs way down." In one story Bebukowe kills a handsome young hunter by shoving a heated stick down his throat. Then he changes bodies with the dead man, becoming a handsome fellow himself, and visits the dead man's girl in this guise; finally nemesis catches up with him, and Bebukowe is transformed back into his former ugly shape.

It might be suggested that Julia Badger's reinterpretation of this mythical character betrays a lack of contact with Chippewa tradition; but this does not seem to be an adequate explanation, because she is really very conversant with Chippewa folklore. Some characters in Chippewa folklore appear to be vague and flexible enough to admit of varying interpretations, for even *windigòg* (cannibal giants) can be friendly creatures in some anecdotes. Tom Badger also modifies the prevailing conception of Bebukowe, though in a much less dramatic fashion. Nevertheless, their conceptions of this figure do deviate markedly from the traditional patterns.

Such individual reinterpretations of local folklore provide a suggestive index of personality. In Julia's case we might say that her transformation of Bebukowe is typical of her approach to reality. She represses the painful aspects of her unhappy childhood, and in their place constructs a fantasy of happiness, gaiety, and affection. Bebukowe is an appropriate symbol for such a transformation. He is an ugly old fellow, crippled like herself, who temporarily takes on a handsome figure and masquerades under false pretenses.

Julia has seen fit to accept the temporary, handsome incarnation of Bebukowe, his false front, behind which the ugly reality lies hidden. Julia refuses to acknowledge the ugly reality; and so her picture of Bebukowe departs from that of others, just as her own version of reality is a private fantasy-tinged conception which others cannot share.

But Julia's Bebukowe has retained at least one characteristic of the original (in addition to the peculiarity of his nose) ; this is his libidinal quality. The traditional Bebukowe, although a villain, is at least aggressive in fulfilling his desires. While Julia's Bebukowe is lacking in villainy, he retains some of this erotic flavor. Perhaps one may say that in Julia's version Bebukowe has become a general incarnation of the life-affirming qualities, of the Eros principle, so to speak.

Bebukowe rescues Julia from death and restores her to her parents, whose lamentations demonstrate that they really loved her after all. Perhaps the circumstances surrounding Julia's narration of this story account for the compelling and emotional quality of her recital. For earlier that same day Julia had believed that Tom had deserted her, and the world looked black indeed for a while. But Tom had returned. He cared for her after all.

It may be said that the only positive figures in the foregoing story are the spirits of the supernatural world. Human beings are depicted as being rather helpless and incapable of solving their own problems without outside assistance. Julia's father calls upon his parents for help when his daughter falls sick, and exclaims, "They say I'm going to lose my first baby, if I don't get busy and do something for her." Then the medicine man decides to summon the spirits, weeping as he does so, with the remark, "I'll try to do all I can. A lot of people never believe me."

Here, I think, is a general Chippewa attitude rather than a purely individual one. Hallowell describes a similar emphasis in Chippewa mythology:

Among them *anicinábek* (men) are always the "receivers"; the *pawaganak* or *manitok* are always the ones who give help and "bless" human beings. They pity men and take cognizance of their needs, especially in misfortune. Human beings are conceived as being in constant need of help from birth to death. So essential is such help that no performance of any kind is due to an individual's own abilities or efforts. Leadership, too, always is the result of bestowed blessings. Furthermore, in neither myth, tale nor tradition is there evidence of a human being who left his mark upon the world, who made any discovery, or who invented anything.[66]

---

[66] A. I. Hallowell, "Myth, Culture, and Personality," *American Anthropologist,* Vol. 49 (1947), p. 554.

JULIA BADGER'S VISION

On a later occasion Julia told me about a vision which she had had. It struck me that there were some thematic similarities in the visionary experience and in the Bebukowe fantasy. Julia said that the third time she went through the Midewiwin (Medicine Dance) it was because of a vision. One day when she was alone and feeling unhappy, she asked aloud, "What is there that I didn't do right?" Then she had a vision of walking along a narrow trail on a bright sunny day. She could hear a tinkling sound in the distance. "As I came nearer to the sound, I saw four men sitting around something that was round. [A drum. The four men represent the four directions, as she later made clear.] Above their heads was something across the sky like a rainbow. One of these men called me his grand-child."

These grandfather figures, the four directions, gave Julia advice and promised that she would live to old age if she heeded them and offered them tobacco now and then. When Julia returned along the trail, she met a large snake, who raised his head about four feet from the ground. He told her not to be afraid but to tell Tom what she had seen. The snake said, "I want to come into that place. [He meant her home, Julia later explained.] I like that place. It makes no difference how it looks. I'm coming there just the same."

After this, Julia made preparations for going through the Mide-wiwin, because a snake hide is given to a candidate who joins the Midewiwin for the third time. One afternoon, when Julia was alone at home, an unexpected visitor came in, saying, "I have come at last." He told Julia to look after him carefully and to wear her prettiest dress. Then he became a snake and went out.

SYMBOLISM OF THE SNAKE

In this vision-fantasy sequence, the snake plays a role similar to that of Bebukowe in the earlier account, and Julia's private inter-pretation of the serpent is similarly at variance with the common conception. Snakes are generally feared by the Chippewa, since they are associated with the practices of medicine men and sorcery. Some medicine men were believed to obtain supernatural power by cut-ting off some of the flesh of giant serpents who inhabit swampy regions. According to Jenness, serpents were not only held to be guardian spirits and agents of sorcerers, but were feared as the chief enemies of both man and the thunderbirds. They could travel underground unseen and steal away men's souls. Children were warned never to accept the serpent as a guardian spirit in a fasting dream, for their lives might be ruined by the association.[67] According to Hallowell, the animals feared most by the Saulteaux are snakes, toads, and frogs, although these are actually among the most harmless animals in their environment. A small variety of garter is the only snake present.[68]

As she did with Bebukowe, Julia Badger seems to have effected a Nietzschean "transvaluation of values" in regard to her attitude toward the snake. However, the extent of Julia's personal reinterpretation need not be exaggerated. There are various instances in Chippewa folklore where the snake plays a beneficent role. In many Chippewa tales a serpent safely transports innocent people across a stream away from danger, and is respectfully addressed by his benefactors as "grandfather." The same serpent drowns malevolent people who ask him for a ferry ride across the river.[69] As we learn from Julia's account, those who join the Medicine Dance for the third time receive a snakeskin hide and obtain some sort of supernatural bond with the serpent *manido*.

The snake is therefore not altogether evil in Chippewa conception; he has some beneficent associations as well. This element of ambiguity somewhat reduces the deviant character of Julia's conception of the serpent. But even when these qualifications have been made, it must be admitted that Julia's personal evaluation of the snake is most unusual in the general setting of Chippewa belief. Once again, we note Julia's tendency to construct a world of private meanings and to transform the ugly aspects of "reality."

Like Julia's Bebukowe, the snake-man seems to symbolize life, health, and love. There is certainly an erotic element in her references to this "visitor," with his expressed desire to enter into her home and be near to her. Julia, of course, associates the snake with the Medicine Dance and with the third degree of initiation; but the serpent very likely possesses a deeper symbolic significance at the same time. In this case the Freudian conception of the snake as

---

[67] Diamond Jenness, *The Ojibwa Indians of Parry Island, Their Social and Religious Life,* Canada Department of Mines, National Museum of Canada, Bulletin No. 78 (1935), p. 35.

[68] A. I. Hallowell, "Fear and Anxiety as Cultural and Individual Variables in a Primitive Society," *Journal of Social Psychology,* Vol. 9 (1938), p. 28.

[69] These stories are reminiscent of the snake-log in the afterworld, concerning which see chapter 15, p. 388.

phallic symbol seems to be appropriate, particularly in view of the Chippewa term, *kinébigustigwàn* ("snake-head") for penis.

PHALLIC HUNCHBACKS

Since publishing the article from which I have quoted above, I have been struck by the phallic properties attributed to hunchback dwarf figures in aboriginal American folklore, which leads me to think that the parallel between Bebukowe and the snake may be stronger than I realized. In the Southwest of the United States there were stories about a humpbacked flute player with a long penis called Kokopelli, who seduced young girls.[70] (Bebukowe, incidentally, is also a flute player). A curious similarity between Kokopelli and Bebukowe is that Kokopelli is considered by Elsie Clews Parsons to have been an insect, perhaps a locust,[71] while Julia Badger described Bebukowe as looking like a grasshopper around the nose and referred to him as "the grasshopper man."

Ernest Jones has pointed out that the conception of the male organ as a "little man" is extremely widespread. He refers to stories of dwarfs, gnomes, and goblins—deformed, ugly and wicked men, yet sometimes friendly and able to perform magical feats and "winning their way in spite of their obvious disadvantages."[72] The character of Punch, with his long hooked nose, projecting hump, and pointed cap, is cited as an example of such a phallic figure.[73]

Notice the similarity between Punch and Bebukowe, not only in the hump but in the prominent nose, which Freudian literature has often designated as a phallic symbol. It is the only other protrusion, beside the penis, in the midline of the body. The snot-dripping quality of Bebukowe's nose seems to emphasize its phallic character. At any rate, the parallels between Punch, Bebukowe, and Kokopelli are rather remarkable and strengthen Jones' case. One might also point to the *tokoloshe* figures discussed by Lee in his paper on Zulu dreams, the priapic hairy creatures who come from rivers to attack women sexually. Laubscher has pictured *tokoloshe* as follows: "He

---

[70] Florence Hawley, "Kokopelli, of the Prehistoric Southwestern Pueblo Pantheon," *American Anthropologist*, Vol. 39 (1937), pp. 644–46; Elsie Clews Parsons, "The Humpbacked Flute Player of the Southwest," *American Anthropologist*, Vol. 40 (1938), pp. 337–78; Mischa Titiev, "The Story of Kokopele," *American Anthropologist*, Vol. 41 (1939), pp. 91–98.

[71] Parsons, "The Humpbacked Flute Player of the Southwest," pp. 337–38.

[72] Jones, *Papers on Psychoanalysis*, p. 93.

[73] Ibid., p. 94.

is described as a dwarf-like little man with short limbs and a powerful thick-set body. He wears a sheepskin wrapped round his shoulders. One of his outstanding physical characteristics is his huge
penis."[74]

Julia Badger's two fantasies, then, both appear to have an erotic
character. However, this does not seem to be their only significance.
As has been noted, Julia was very sickly, and her marital relationship with Tom was not a happy one. Julia had her moments of deep
depression. Perhaps her "vision," therefore, represented a compensatory wish-fulfillment, which assumed the function of reviving the
thwarted life-affirming qualities in Julia's psyche, enabling her to
face life once more—just as Bebukowe rescued Julia from death in
childhood and restored her to her parents.

The Four Directions serve somewhat the same function and give
"direction" to her life. These grandfather figures repeat the moral
instructions which Julia's own grandfather used to give her in childhood. They explain why she has gone wrong in the past, they encourage Julia to be more faithful about ritual observances in the
future, and they promise long life and health thereafter. Once again,
Julia played a purely passive role in relation to them and promised
to obey, although she did not always live up to such obligations
afterwards.

In her dependent and introversive tendencies Julia Badger exhibited to a heightened degree some general Chippewa characteristics. Remember that this was a society in which, not so long ago,
great emphasis was placed on dreams. At an early age children were
regularly sent out to fast for a dream or vision of a guardian spirit.
A fasting child was supposed to be addressed by such a spirit with
the words, "My grandchild, I come to pity (cherish) you." It would
not be surprising if a young child, denied food and sent out into
the woods, might actually dream of such a nurturing figure. The
stereotyped expected dream would be compatible with the needs of
a child who has met with parental rejection and hunger.

The emphasis on the inner world of dreams in Chippewa culture
is in keeping with the Rorschach characteristics to be discussed in
the following chapter—the greater stress on human movement responses (of a passive quality) than on color, which is generally
avoided.

To be sure, Julia cannot be considered to be a "typical" Chip-

---

[74] B. J. F. Laubscher, *Sex, Custom, and Psychopathology: A Study of South African
Pagan Natives* (London: Routledge and Kegan Paul, Ltd., 1937), p. 8.

pewa woman. Dr. Bruno Klopfer was properly cautious in his Rorschach evaluation of Julia when he observed, *"In our culture* she would be called schizoid."* But it should be noted that Julia was generally regarded as "queer" in her own community as well.

Are the collection and interpretation of dreams worthwhile in culture-and-personality studies? My general feeling is that although dreams are always interesting, they do not always tell a great deal about personality patterns. I know that others see the matter differently. In referring to his Walapai studies, Kroeber said, "I had the impression that the dreams revealed more personality than the life histories . . . . a dream is bound to be personal, while a life history can be heavily depersonalized."[75] Dorothy Eggan has also stressed the value of dream analysis.

My own view is that although Lee's study of Zulu dreams is impressive and interesting, it does not seem to reveal much about the personality characteristics of the Zulus; nor do we learn much about Hopi personality from Dorothy Eggan's collection of Hopi dreams. The Rorschach and TAT are more economical and effective techniques for such purposes. Dreams are, however, valuable ingredients in life history studies, especially if one knows something about the setting in which the dream has occurred, and if associations to elements in the dream can be obtained. A dream must be seen in its context in the life history of the individual.

SUGGESTIONS FOR FURTHER READING

Efforts to establish criteria by which life history materials can be judged and analyzed include the following:

H. Blumer, "An Appraisal of Thomas and Znaniecki's The Polish Peasant in Europe and America," Critique of Research in Social Sciences, No. 1, Social Science Research Council (1939), pp. xv, 210.

John Dollard, *Criteria for the Life History, With an Analysis of Six Notable Documents* (New York: P. Smith, 1935).

Gordon W. Allport, *The Use of Personal Documents in Psychological Science*, Social Science Research Council Bulletin No. 49 (1942).

Lewis Gottschalk, Clyde Kluckhohn, and Robert Angell, *The Use of Personal Documents in History, Anthropology, and Sociology*, Social Science Research Council Bulletin No. 53 (1945).

Two attempts to interpret individual life histories may be noted: Alexander H. Leighton and Dorothea C. Leighton, *Gregorio, the Hand Trembler. A Psychobiological Personality Study of a Navaho Indian*, Papers

---

[75] Quoted by Dorothy Eggan in "Dream Analysis," p. 552.

of the Peabody Museum of American Archaeology and Ethnology Vol. XL, No. 1 (1949).

David F. Aberle, *The Psychosocial Analysis of a Hopi Life History,* Comparative Psychology Monographs, Serial No. 107, Vol. 21, No. 1 (1951).

For a review, see L. L. Langness, *The Life History in Anthropological Science* (New York: Holt, Rinehart & Winston, 1965).

For psychoanalytic analyses of two famous charismatic men, see Erik H. Erikson, *Young Man Luther. A Study in Psychoanalysis and History* (New York: W. W. Norton & Co., 1958); and Erik H. Erikson, *Gandhi's Truth. On the Origins of Militant Nonviolence* (New York: W. W. Norton & Co., 1969). The analyses of life history material, combined with the analyses of personality tests such as the Rorschach and Thematic Apperception Test are well carried out in Robert W. White's *Lives in Progress* and in Irving L. Janis et al., *Personality, Dynamics, Development, and Assessment,* referenced in Footnote 12.

The best general works on dreams that I know are those, mentioned above, by Freud, Wolff, Hadfield, Boss, and Hall.

Articles on dreams by George Devereux, Weston La Barre, Dorothy Eggan (on Hopi dreams), and A. Irving Hallowell (on Ojibwa dreams), along with many others may be found in G. E. von Grunebaum and Roger Callois (eds.), *The Dream and Human Societies* (Berkeley, Calif.: University of California Press, 1966).

chapter *13*

Projective Tests

The Rorschach (inkblot) and the Thematic Apperception Test (TAT), among others, are known as projective tests. The term *projection* has been given some different meanings. Freud first defined projection as a defensive process whereby the ego ascribes its own drives and feelings to other persons or objects, and is thus able to remain consciously unaware of them.[1]

In *Totem and Taboo,* however, Freud suggested another meaning for this term:

> But projection is not specially created for the purpose of defence, it also comes into being when there are no conflicts. The projection of inner perceptions to the outside is a primitive mechanism which, for instance, also influences our sense-perceptions, so that it normally has the greatest share in shaping our outer world. Under conditions that have not yet been sufficiently determined even inner perceptions of ideational and emotional processes are projected outwardly, like sense perceptions, and are used to shape the outer world, whereas they ought to remain in the inner world.[2]

Leopold Bellak, who distinguishes between various types of apperceptive distortion, believes that a person's past perceptions of his father influences his perception of father figures in the Thematic

---

[1] Leopold Bellak, "On the Problems of the Concept of Projection. A Theory of Apperceptive Distortion," in Lawrence E. Abt and Leopold Bellak, *Projective Psychology, Clinical Approaches to the Total Personality* (New York: Grove Press, 1959), p. 8.

[2] Sigmund Freud, *Totem and Taboo,* in A. A. Brill (ed.), *Basic Writings of Sigmund Freud* (New York: Modern Library, 1938), p. 857.

Apperception Test and that "this constitutes a valid and reliable sample of his usual perceptions of father figures."[3] Bellak goes on to argue that all perception is influenced by past perception and that every person distorts apperceptively to some extent. This is also true of what one remembers of the past.[4]

Such assumptions underlie the use of the Rorschach Test, Thematic Apperception Test, drawing analysis, and other projective techniques.[5]

THE RORSCHACH TEST

The Rorschach Test was devised by Hermann Rorschach, a Swiss psychiatrist who died at the age of 37 in 1922, a few months after the publication of his book, *Psychodiagnostik,* in which the test was first described and discussed. The 10 Rorschach cards were originally published as part of this work. They represent a series of bilaterally symmetrical inkblots, half achromatic and half with some color. Rorschach experimented with thousands of different inkblots before finally choosing the 10 cards which are still used today.

The same 10 cards are shown, always in the same order, to every person who takes the test. The subject must tell what he sees in the blots, and the tester records his responses, also noting how long it takes him to respond. After the subject has completed all 10 cards, the tester usually goes through his responses with him, to make sure that he knows which parts of the blots have been used by the subject and, as far as possible, how the responses have been perceived, that is, whether a bat reported by the subject was seen to be flying or not, or whether the dark color of the blot contributed to the conception of the bat.

What the Rorschach analyst does is to examine the subject's responses for clues to his personality structure. His conclusions are based not so much on the content of the responses, but more on the manner of perception, accuracy of form discrimination, the nature

---

[3] Bellak, "On the Problems of the Concept of Projection," p. 10.

[4] Frederick C. Bartlett, *Remembering. A Study in Experimental and Social Psychology* (Cambridge: The University Press, 1932).

[5] My survey of methods is not intended to be exhaustive. A number of projective tests which have been used cross-culturally are not discussed here, for instance, word association tests, the Picture-Frustration Test, the Szondi Test, the Bender Gestalt Test, the Lowenfeld Mosaic Test, and others. The Rorschach and Thematic Apperception Test seem to be the two most widely and successfully employed in cross cultural studies; hence they receive the fullest treatment here.

of the determinants of responses given (such as movement, color, and texture) ; whether responses are given to the blot as a whole, to large details or small details, and so forth.

Human Movement and Color Responses

In this chapter frequent references will be made to human movement and to color responses. Since these are perhaps the most important "determinants" in the Rorschach Test, some preliminary discussion of them seems necessary.

Let us first consider movement responses. These are scored differently by different authorities. Rorschach scored as *M,* responses in which human movement was perceived; he excluded animal movement. His method of scoring has been followed by Samuel J. Beck, but Klopfer and Kelley have added two new categories: *FM* (animal movement) and *m* (inanimate movement) .[6] I shall follow the Klopfer and Kelley scoring system in this book, since that is the one I learned and used myself.

Human movement responses *(M)* generally tend to be interpreted as indications of inner control, ego strength, intellectual capacity, imagination, introversiveness, and capacity for empathy. *M* responses are rarely found in young children, subjects with organic brain damage, or with rigid constriction. The presence of such responses suggests some capacity for the enjoyment of inner life and may be an index of how much at home a person is with himself.[7]

The way in which a subject handles color in the Rorschach Test is supposed to tell something about his characteristic response to outside emotional stimuli. Compulsion neurotics and people who are very depressed are said to give few or no color responses, while persons characterized by affective lability give many. According to Rorschach, the more stable the emotions, the better the form visualization. Thus, people who lack control over their emotions may give the "explosive" or formless color responses designated as *C.* If some form is vaguely associated with the color response, but not very clearly, the response is designated as *CF.* When there is better

---

[6] Bruno Klopfer and Douglas McGlashan Kelley, *The Rorschach Technique. A Manual for a Projective Method of Personality Diagnosis* (Yonkers-on-Hudson: World Book Co., 1942) .

[7] Ibid., pp. 276–67; Bruno Klopfer, Mary D. Ainsworth, Walter G. Klopfer, and Robert R. Holt, *Developments in the Rorschach Test,* Vol. I, *Technique and Theory* (Yonkers on Hudson: World Book Co., 1954) , pp. 254–64.

control, expressed by a conjunction of definite form and color, the response is labeled *FC*.

Unfortunately, we do not know why color means what it is supposed to mean on the Rorschach Test, or why it is related to emotionality. Beck has remarked that "we know next to nothing about color as a psychologic stimulus."[8] An association between color and emotion is implied by many phrases in our language, such as "seeing red," "rose-colored glasses," "feeling blue," and so forth, but why such associations have been made is not very clear.

Ernest G. Schachtel has made an attempt to explain this linkage. Color and emotional experiences have, he tells us, two things in common: "the *passivity* of the subject and the *immediacy* of the relation object-subject."[9] One is visually assailed by a bright red color, so to speak, just as one is "seized" by a strong emotion. The subject in both cases plays a passive role. Views similar to Schachtel's appear in David C. McClelland's work, *The Achieving Society*, in which the hypothesis is put forth that the person with a high need for achievement "might prefer colors like blue and green which he can 'act on,' as background, so to speak, as contrasted with reds and yellows that act on him."[10]

The inner-directed "achiever" would presumably tend to avoid bright color, in contrast to the more other-directed extrovert, who, as Schachtel puts it, takes on the color of his environment.[11]

Despite such insights, the relationship between emotion and color still seems rather mysterious. However, this relationship has some experimental support, and there is further evidence of a linkage between color and emotionality in the field of drawing analysis also.[12]

A full discussion of the Rorschach should examine the other determinants in the test, but the purpose here has been only to set forth some of the key concepts used in Rorschach interpretation.

---

[8] Samuel J. Beck, "The Experimental Validation of the Rorschach Test. IV. Discussion and Critical Evaluation," *American Journal of Orthopsychiatry*, Vol. 22 (1955), p. 775.

[9] E. G. Schachtel, "On Color and Affect," *Psychiatry*, Vol. 6 (1943), pp. 393–409.

[10] David C. McClelland, *The Achieving Society* (Princeton, N. J.: D. Van Nostrand Co., 1961), p. 309.

[11] Schachtel, "On Color and Affect."

[12] See J. Ruesch and J. E. Finesinger, "The Relation of the Rorschach Color Response to the Use of Color in Drawings," *Psychosomatic Medicine*, Vol. 3 (1941), pp. 370–88. See also Rose H. Alschuler and La Berta Weiss Hattwick, *Painting and Personality, A Study of Young Children* (Chicago: University of Chicago Press, 1947), Vol. I, pp. 15–50; and see the discussion of Chippewa children's drawings in Chapter 14 below.

There is much more to Rorschach analysis than the interpretation of movement and color responses, but these are of special importance and hence they have been briefly dealt with here.

Figure 13–1. Rorschach Card I, reproduced at one sixth of the original size

To give some illustrations, let us consider some responses to the first card of the Rorschach Test given by three persons. Each was asked to tell what the blot might represent, what he could see in it. This is an achromatic card. All three subjects (two Chippewa Indians and one white man) looked at the same card, and yet they saw quite different things in it.

John Thunderbird (a pseudonym), a 54-year-old Chippewa Indian to whom I gave the test,[13] gave a single response. "Some kind of hawk, some kind of large bird. Indians years back would draw pictures of them. You see them on those poles there." The bird is sitting on a tree. This response made use of the blot as a whole. John Thunderbird pointed out the bird's eye, beak, feet, tail, and wings. The central portion was seen as the tree. "Must be a limb here, sticking out, that he's sitting on. An old tree top. The tree broke off up here. Probably the wind blew it off in a storm. It's an old stump."

To see this blot, or part of it, as a bird is quite a common response. John Thunderbird also projected into the blot the idea of an old stump, part of which has been broken off, blown away in a storm.

Another Chippewa subject, Julia Badger (aged 34), whose fantasies were discussed in Chapter 12, did not make use of the blot as a whole. Indeed, a characteristic feature of her Rorschach record was the extremely small percentage of Whole responses and the

---

[13] John Thunderbird's autobiography, as told to me, is in the Appendix of my *Acculturation and Personality among the Wisconsin Chippewa,* Memoir Number 72 of the American Anthropological Association (1950), pp. 89–112.

preference for small details. Mrs. Badger's first response was "Two snakes," which she later added were just heads sticking out, with their mouths open. (These are two small projections near the center of the top part of the blot.) It is interesting that snakes make an appearance here, as in her fantasies discussed earlier. Their mouths are open, suggesting Fromm's receptive orientation or oral character.

Julia Badger next saw a big hill on the left side of the blot with a valley and two large white rocks (the white space areas). This was an airplane view.

In parts of the interior of the right-hand side of the blot Mrs. Badger saw a man's face.

Our third subject is Amos Hale (a pseudonym), a 45-year-old white male bachelor school teacher. He gave 24 responses to Card I. The first four responses were Whole responses. "(1) *Os inominatum*. The ass. (2) Nose bone of nose. (3) Halloween false face. (4) A bat."

He next gave some responses to the central area of the blot: "(5) A toad. (6) A woman's thing. What do you call it?" (V.B.: "The vagina?") "Yes, that's what I mean." The line running down the center of the blot was next seen as (7) a road, a highway; and the small light area in the center was seen as (8) a diamond.

Two Whole responses followed: (9) "Clouds. (10) Entrance to caves." Then a small detail: (11) "A face." Then five Whole responses: (12) "Scattering of spots—ink. (13) Shell. (14) Butterfly. (15) Kindergarten cut paper. (16) Map, physiological map." Then a very small detail: (17) "Blemish on a face."

The last seven responses, most of which made use of irregular details, were: (18) "Broken glass. (19) Bottom of a bowl. (20) A cross. (21) Piles—coming out of the ass. (22) A coastline. (23) A child's paintbox. The whole thing. Just looks messy the way a child's paintbox looks when it's opened. (24) A long bug."

Notable in this series of responses to Card I is the depressing, negative content. Amos Hale sees thing that are scattered, broken, or messy. (In the second card he saw "smashed umbrellas.") He sees, in sequence, a bat, a toad, and a "woman's thing" (which, in the context, does not seem to be positively regarded.) Later, he sees a blemish on a face and a long bug. The anal responses (1, 21) suggest a hoarding orientation or anal personality. The subject gave similar anal responses to other cards, which were also characterized by depressing content.

The responses given by our three subjects show how much variation there is in the way different people perceive the same inkblot. They differed in the number of responses given (1 for John Thunderbird, 3 for Julia Badger, and 24 for Amos Hale). They differed in their use of the whole or part of the card. (A Whole response for John Thunderbird; none for Julia Badger, who used small details; while both Wholes and small detail responses were given by Amos Hale.) They also differed in the content of what they saw. It may be noted that in their responses to Card I none of our three subjects gave a human movement response.

The Cross-cultural Application of the Rorschach Test

The main issue that concerns us with regard to the Rorschach Test is its cross-cultural application. Why has the Rorschach Test been used so often by anthropologists? One reason is that the Rorschach does not require literacy, as some other personality tests do. Moreover, it is not culture-bound, for the blots do not represent anything in particular. Another advantage of the Rorschach Test is that it can be given to people of different age levels.

There are, however, some difficulties facing the use of the Rorschach in a non-Western culture. One is the language problem; another is the question of rapport between tester and subject.

If an ethnologist can become fluent in the language of the society he is studying, the Rorschach Test can be recorded in the native tongue, as was done by Jules Henry in the Pilagá records he obtained.[14] Ethnologists are not always such good linguists, however. Reliance upon partial knowledge of a language is less satisfactory than use of a good interpreter. Hallowell had recourse to an interpreter for some of his Berens River subjects and found no particular differences between the other protocols and those in which the interpreter was used.[15] All the same, the possibility of distortion of a subject's responses through translation would seem to be present when an interpreter is used. Horace Miner found an ingenious solution to this problem, however. In his study of Algerians, Miner wire recorded the Rorschach inquiry, so that the informants' responses in Arabic and the French translations could later be played back for another interpreter. Differences in translation could then be noted and followed up.

---

[14] Jules Henry, "Rorschach Technique in Primitive Cultures," *American Journal of Orthopsychiatry*, Vol. 11 (1941), pp. 230–34.

[15] A. I. Hallowell, "The Rorschach Method as an Aid in the Study of Personalities in Primitive Societies," *Character and Personality*, Vol. 9 (1941), p. 240.

Actually, Miner found few such differences. This method, however, would provide a check.[16]

In giving the Rorschach Test in Lebanon, Herbert H. Williams and Judith R. Williams found some positive advantages in working with an interepreter. It gave them more time to record motor and verbal behavior, and their subjects often made revealing side remarks to the interpreter which might not have been made to them.[17]

In order to get satisfactorily rich material from a Rorschach subject, the individual being tested should feel relaxed and at ease.[18] In the nature of things, this desideratum is often hard to arrange in ethnological fieldwork. The anthropologist is a stranger in the community he is studying; his Rorschach blots are queer things, and his explanation of why he wants responses to them may not make much sense to the informant. Honigmann found that administration of the Rorschach Test was irksome for his Kaska subjects. "The situation often grew so painful that it was necessary to beg the subjects to remain for a few more minutes."[19] Some of Spindler's Menomini subjects were very reluctant to take the test, suspecting him, in some cases, of being a Communist, a federal investigator, or an agent of the superintendent. Or else, they feared that the Rorschach Test might be some new technique for working sorcery.[20] Kaplan's Zuñi informants showed much fear of the test. They were afraid that Kaplan was prying into their religion or testing them for possible war service: "the writer saw menace and hostility in every Zuñi who looked his way."[21]

These are hardly ideal conditions for Rorschach administration. Of course, many excellent Rorschach protocols have been collected by anthropologists, but the situational factors affecting the test may result in an impoverishment of many Rorschach records. Compared

[16] Horace M. Miner and George De Vos, *Oasis and Casbah: Algerian Culture and Personality in Change,* Anthropological Papers, Museum of Anthropology, University of Michigan, No. 15 (1960), p. 13.

[17] Herbert H. Williams and Judith R. Williams, "The Definition of the Rorschach Test Situation: A Cross-Cultural Illustration," in Melford E. Spiro (ed.), *Context and Meaning in Cultural Anthropology* (New York: The Free Press, Inc., 1965), pp. 342–43.

[18] Klopfer and Kelley, *The Rorschach Technique,* p. 27.

[19] John J. Honigmann, *Culture and Ethos of Kaska Society,* Yale University Publications in Anthropology, No. 40 (New Haven, Conn.: Yale University Press, 1949), p. 240.

[20] George D. Spindler, *Sociocultural and Psychological Processes in Menomini Acculturation,* University of California Publications in Culture and Society, No. V (Berkeley: University of California Press, 1955), p. 61.

[21] Bert Kaplan, *A Study of Rorschach Responses in Four Cultures,* Papers of the Peabody Museum of American Archeology and Ethnology, Harvard University, Vol. 42, No. 2 (1954), p. 5.

with Western protocols, those from other cultures often seem rather barren. The total number of responses may be low, and there may be few movement or color responses. Two examples of this state of affairs may be given, in both of which the authors discuss the situational context and its possible effect on the subjects' responses. The first is a study of Northwest Coast Alaskan Eskimos by Caroline E. Preston. Preston's Eskimo Rorschachs had relatively few responses, with few movement, color, or texture responses. The Eskimo TAT's were characterized by prevailingly "unhappy" situations or feelings. Preston remarks that more than two thirds of her Eskimo subjects seemed anxious, angry, or inhibited in taking the tests, which she suggests as one explanation for the impoverishment of the records.[22] The other example is the Lebanese study by the Williamses which was mentioned above. The number of Lebanese villagers' responses was very low, with a group mean of 12.4, and the records were very unproductive, lacking in movement, color, and texture responses, as in the case of the Alaskan Eskimos. The Williamses point out that tests of any kind are unknown to the villagers; being shown the inkblots and asked to give responses was a frightening experience for them.[23] Erich Fromm and Michael Maccoby consider this to be a general peasant reaction to such testing,[24] while Frank Riessman and S. M. Miller hold it to be typical of lower class American subjects.[25] The test, as Ernest G. Schachtel has indicated, is for many people something strange and fantastic. Their response to the test may be characteristic of their response to unfamiliar aspects of life in general. There are no rules for prescribing how one must respond in such a novel situation. In that sense, the impoverished Rorschach record of a frightened or constricted subject may express an important aspect of his personality. But one should try to minimize the dysphoric aspects of the test situation.[26]

Ideally, a Rorschach session should involve the isolation of the

---

[22] Caroline E. Preston, "Psychological Testing with Northwest Coast Alaskan Eskimos," *Genetic Psychology Monographs,* Vol. 69 (1964) , pp. 323–419.

[23] Williams and Williams, "The Definition of the Rorschach Test Situation," pp. 338–54.

[24] Erich Fromm and Michael Maccoby, *Social Character in a Mexican Village. A Sociopsychoanalytic Study* (Englewood Cliffs, N.J.: Prentice-Hall, Inc., 1970) , p. 275.

[25] Frank Riessman and S. M. Miller, "Social Class and Projective Tests," *Journal of Projective Techniques,* Vol. 22 (1958) , pp. 432–39.

[26] On the effects of the Rorschach testing situation, see Ethelyn Henry Klatskin, "An Analysis of the Effect of the Test Situation upon the Rorschach Record: Formal Characteristics," *Journal of Projective Techniques,* Vol. 16 (1952) , pp. 193–99; and Ernest G. Schachtel, "The Interpersonal Meaning of the Rorschach-Test Situation," in Ernest G. Schachtel, *Experimental Foundations of Rorschach's Test* (New York: Basic Books, 1966) , chap. 12, pp. 268–328.

subject with the tester. Again, these conditions are often hard to arrange in the field. Jules Henry has observed that in most primitive cultures people are never alone but are apt to be surrounded by relatives. Privacy may be suspect. Moreover, curiosity about the ethnologist's work will attract crowds.[27]

In the case of the Lebanese villagers, the Williamses did succeed in getting each subject to take the test alone, but this only added to the frightening and unfamiliar nature of the experience. To be sure, matters are not always so difficult, and often the subject may be very relaxed. But ideal test conditions are not to be expected in the field.

The crucial question is sometimes raised of whether a test developed in our own culture, with Western-based norms, can be meaningfully applied in another culture. In a study by A. I. Rabin and Josefina Limuaco, the point was made that the connotative meanings of the Rorschach blots may differ from culture to culture. More specifically, the authors point to differences in this respect in the Rorschach responses of American and Filipino college students.[28] This led them to question the justifiability of the application of the test cross-culturally.

Some of the difficulties involved here can be illustrated in a Rorschach study of Samoan young men made by P. H. Cook. Cook gave the test to a group of 50 high school "boys" (aged 16–27), 30 of whom came from families of chiefs. These students were all training to become pastors. They are thus not representative of the population as a whole.

One feature of these Samoan Rorschach records is a high percentage of white space (S) responses, which make use of white space areas within the blots. These are rather rare in Western records; when they occur they are usually interpreted as signs of oppositional tendencies. But almost three fourths of Cook's subjects gave S responses. Should this be interpreted in the traditional way? Perhaps not, for Cook mentions that 31 of the 50 young men reported white (regarded as symbolic of purity) as their favorite color.

The Samoans gave few texture responses. The interpretation of texture responses varies with the general configuration of the response, but they are usually seen to indicate sensitivity, sensuality, or

[27] Henry, "Rorschach Technique in Primitive Cultures," p. 231.

[28] A. I. Rabin and Josefina Limuaco, "A Comparison of the Connotative Meaning of Rorschach's Inkblots for American and Filipino College Students," *Journal of Social Psychology*, Vol. 72 (1967), pp. 197–203.

a desire for contact. Such responses are often associated with animal skins or rugs, particularly seen in cards IV and VI. But furs and rugs are not generally known in Samoa; this response was not given once in Cook's sample. How, then, are we to interpret the low percentage of texture responses?

Cook's subjects gave many pure color (*C*) responses, in which no form was involved. As indicated in a preceding section, this would usually be held to express emotional impulsiveness. Cook tells us that the Samoans have not developed abstract names for colors. Their color words all have an object reference. For example, their word for red (*mumu*) means literally "like fire, flame." The idea of blood is also associated with this. The Samoan word for blue or green may mean either sky-colored or deep-sea-colored. Their color vocabulary is thus a limited one. Cook says that there is practically no artwork in this area except for crude designs in black and brown pigments stenciled on bark cloth. The culture offers little to foster any sensitivity to color nuances. Can Samoan color responses then be interpreted in the same way as Western European or American color responses?[29]

Some Rorschach responses can only be made in cultures which have been exposed to Western influence. This applies at least to *k* responses, in which a blot, or part of it, is seen as an X-ray, although there could be an equivalent in which objects are seen through water. At any rate, considerations such as these, and the questions raised by Cook's Samoan protocols, have led some anthropologists and psychologists to deny the applicability of Western-based Rorschach norms to protocols from other cultures. Since interpretation becomes so difficult under these circumstances, the cross-cultural use of the Rorschach Test has been called into question.

The main argument on the positive side, however, is that use of the Rorschach Test has often proven to be very revealing and to yield information in close agreement with that drawn from other sources. Doubts about the cross-cultural applicability of the Rorschach Test assailed Emil Oberholzer, when he was asked to interpret the Alorese protocols.

Not only was I confronted for the first time with the tests of individuals other than Europeans and Americans, but I did not know the norms of these people and had no way of working them out. I did not know the average of the numerical values for the various experimental factors.

---

[29] P. H. Cook, "The Application of the Rorschach Test to a Samoan Group," *Rorschach Research Exchange,* Vol. 6 (1942), pp. 52–60.

They must be widely different from ours, since there are even striking differences between the findings in the population groups of various sections of Switzerland. . . . Among the Alorese, I do not know, for example, what is an original and what is a popular answer; I do not know the border line between a normal and a small detail, since I do not know with certainty what constitutes with them normal and small details. I even have no reliable basis for qualifying a form. I do not know with certainty what form answer is to be scored as *good* or *bad*. In working out the norms it may turn out that a form answer which I consider poor according to my experience is good in the Alorese, and vice versa. Or, to put it briefly, I lack the statistical basis that underlies our scoring of European material.[30]

As it happened, Oberholzer went on to interpret the Alorese protocols, despite his misgivings, and the results were most impressive. In Chapter 7 we noted the marked agreement between his conclusions, based on the Rorschach data, with other analyses drawn from the interpretation of life histories, children's drawings, and so forth. The Rorschach Test often seems to work; at least in a number of studies it has presented similar corroborative evidence. This is the best answer that can be given to objections about the cross-cultural use of the Rorschach Test. The Truk study can be cited, along with that of Alor, in this regard.

Another example of "blind" analysis presenting similar agreement with the ethnologist's observations is the study of Algerians made by Miner and De Vos. Miner's Algerian Rorschachs were submitted to Professor Max Hunt for blind analysis.

An attempt was made to test the validity of Hutt's psychological ratings by comparing them with evaluations based on personal acquaintance with the individuals concerned. Taking the seven Arabs best known to the field worker and the five psychological traits [*Fn:* Maturity, cathexis, anality, anxiety, and overt hostility] which he felt he could evaluate, fifteen ratings were made. They represented, therefore, the judgments about which he was the most sure. Of the fifteen ratings, thirteen were in conformity with those of Hutt, which is comfortably within the limits of statistical significance.[31]

Still another procedure for validating Rorschach data has been used in the Rakau Maori study. On the basis of observation James E. Ritchie drew up a series of generalizations about Maori personality development. From this picture he next drew up a series of predictions as to what the Rorschach records of the Maori would be

[30] Du Bois, *The People of Alor* (Minneapolis: University of Minnesota Press, 1944), p. 588.

[31] Miner and De Vos, *Oasis and Casbah*, p. 108.

like. A similar set of predictions was made by a psychologist who was familiar with Ritchie's generalizations about Maori personality development. The Rorschach Test, given to 41 male and 37 female Maori subjects, was then interpreted independently by Ritchie and by another analyst. The final step was to see how much agreement appeared between the two predictions and the two analyses. These proved to be very closely correleated.[32]

The success of these various experiments lends considerable support to the cross-cultural applicability of the Rorschach Test. However, not everyone has been impressed by the successes of blind analysis. Ivan N. Mensh and Jules Henry have suggested that the similarity of the Rorschach Test results with the anthropologist's impressions may be due to "contamination."

> That is to say that the anthropologist biased the test results in favor of his own findings. This danger is obvious when the anthropologist does his own interpretation of the tests, but it is equally present when someone else interprets the results for the anthropologist. This is because the anthropologist consulted with his interpreting psychologist, and there are very few cases in which the anthropologist did not tell the psychologist much about the culture before, during, and after the process of interpretation of the test results.[33]

This objection may apply to some culture-and-personality studies, but in many it would not hold. This circumstance may, in part, be due to publication of the Mensh and Henry criticisms and a subsequent concern to avoid contamination in more recent studies. At any rate, as we have seen in Chapter 7, special pains were taken to rule out contamination in Gladwin and Sarason's work on Truk. Other cases where leakage from anthropologist to the psychologist seems improbable would include the Miner and De Vos Algerian study, a study by Kluckhohn and Rosenzweig,[34] and one by Clifton and Levine.[35]

If one wishes to be skeptical, another question could be raised concerning the correspondence of Rorschach results with other data.

---

[32] James E. Ritchie, *Basic Personality in Rakau*, Victoria University College Publications in Psychology, No. 8; Monographs on Maori Social Life and Personality, No. 1, Department of Psychology, Victoria University College, Wellington, New Zealand, 1956.

[33] Ivan N. Mensh and Jules Henry, "Direct Observation and Psychological Tests in Anthropological Field Work," *American Anthropologist*, Vol. 55 (1953), p. 469.

[34] Clyde Kluckhohn and Janine Chappat Rosenzweig, "Two Navaho Children over a Five-Year Period," *American Journal of Orthopsychiatry*, Vol. 19 (1949), pp. 266–78.

[35] James A. Clifton and David Levine, *Klamath Personalities, Ten Rorschach Case Studies*. Printed at the University of Oregon Press for private distribution by the authors, Eugene, Oregon, 1961.

Might not the correspondences be largely due to chance? In cases where the anthropologist and the Rorschach interpreter found themselves in agreement, they would be eager to publish the results of their study, but less so in cases where there was little similarity in their findings. In the latter case they might feel that the experiment had not been a success, and they might therefore fail to press for publication. If this is so, studies in which correspondences were found between Rorschach and other data would tend to be published and to become better known than those where little agreement had appeared.

While this is a logical possibility, I don't think that skepticism should carry us so far. There are, after all, orderly processes governing the interpretation of Rorschach records. In some of the fuller publications the original records are given, and it is possible to check the data and to see how the analyst arrived at the results. In their analyses of the records from Alor and Truk, Oberholzer and Sarason make quite clear to the reader how they developed their interpretations from the test materials.

Criticisms of the Rorschach Test

Interest in projective tests, including the Rorschach, has slackened in recent years, both among psychologists and anthropologists. In 1954, Joseph Zubin raised a series of criticisms of the Rorschach Test, claiming that it failed to provide an objective scoring system, lacked reliability, failed to provide sufficient evidence for clinical validity, and had little predictive power.[36]

In the following year, 1955, there was a symposium on projective testing in anthropology, in which Jules Henry, one of the first anthropologists to apply the test in a non-Western culture, stated that he would not use the Rorschach if he were going into the field again.

Although there was, at the same time, much support of projective testing by both psychologists and anthropologists, criticism has continued to mount, particularly from behaviorist, or neo-behaviorist psychologists. Some of this criticism is damaging. Consider this passage from Walter Mischel, a psychologist at Stanford University:

Clinicians have often suggested that the combination and integration of clinical techniques, rather than the use of single instruments in isolation, is important for effective assessment. A recent study (Golden, 1964) in-

---

[36] Joseph Zubin, "Failures of the Rorschach Technique," *Journal of Projective Techniques,* Vol. 18 (1954) , pp. 303–15.

vestigated the incremental effects of combining the Rorschach, TAT, and MMPI [Minnesota Multiphasic Personality Inventory] tests as opposed to using them singly. Neither the reliability nor the validity of clinical inferences increased as a function of the number of tests, nor were there any differences among tests or pairs of tests. Again the clinicians were experienced, having interpreted a median number of 200 MMPIs, 250 Rorschachs, and 200 TATs. The range of experience extended from about 40 to 2,500 administrations for each of these tests.

Similar findings come from a study by Soskin (1959) with different criteria, different judges, and additional data sources. None of the test information improved predictions beyond the level attained from biographical data alone.[37]

Since there has been so much criticism of this sort, it is understandable that in 1970, on the occasion of being given an award for her work in projective testing, Marguerite R. Hertz gave an address with the title "Projective Techniques in Crisis."[38] To be sure, Dr. Hertz ended her address on a note of optimism, pointing out that psychology had passed through many fads and cycles and predicted that projective techniques would weather the storm.

Anthropologists seem to have been influenced by the current disenchantment among psychologists about the use of projective tests, for in a biennial review of psychological anthropology published in 1967, Pertti J. Pelto pointed out that the use of both the Rorschach and the TAT had declined in recent cross-cultural studies, particularly the Rorschach.[39] Time will tell whether projective testing is undergoing a temporary recession or the beginning of the end. But if projective tests are rejected for use in cross-cultural studies, some other devices for gauging personality will have to be found, unless we must depend upon behavioral observation and interviewing alone. The latter alternative would mean that the anthropologist would have no cross-checking devices; his description of the people he studies would be open to the criticism of subjectivity. In giving Rorschachs to Alorese subjects and sub-

---

[37] Walter Mischel, *Personality and Assessment* (New York: John Wiley & Sons, 1968), p. 120. The references cited in this passage are: M. Golden, "Some Effects of Combining Psychological Tests on Clinical Inferences," *Journal of Consulting Psychology*, Vol. 28 (1964), pp. 440–46; and W. F. Soskin, "Influence of Four Types of Data on Diagnostic Conceptualization in Psychological Testing," *Journal of Abnormal and Social Psychology*, Vol. 58 (1959), pp. 69–78.

[38] Marguerite R. Hertz, "Projective Techniques in Crisis," *Journal of Projective Techniques and Personality Assessment*, Vol. 34 (1970), pp. 449–67.

[39] Pertti J. Pelto, "Psychological Anthropology," in Bernard J. Siegel and Alan R. Beals (eds.), *Biennial Review of Anthropology* (Stanford, Calif.: Stanford University Press, 1967), pp. 143–44.

mitting the protocols to a blind analysis, Cora Du Bois was able to diminish that difficulty.

An argument on behalf of use of the Rorschach Test in culture-and-personality studies is that different societies have different Rorschach patterns. The Pilagá Indian children tested by the Henrys give neither color nor movement responses (either animal or human). As we shall see, the Chippewa give movement responses but very little color. The Alorese give color, but little human movement. The Samoans, Algerians,[40] and the Tuscarora give many Whole responses, while Zuñi children give very few, but emphasize small details. These group variations must mean something, although it is not always evident just what they do mean. But they would seem to strengthen the hypothesis that different societies are characterized by different modal personality types.

If the varied cultures of the world did not selectively influence perception and response to the Rorschach blots, we would expect that in different parts of the world people would all give pretty much the same kinds of Rorschach responses; but they do not. A. Irving Hallowell made an early study of the distribution of so-called popular responses—responses very commonly given to the blots in our culture. In examining Rorschach protocols from six American Indian cultures, Hallowell found that three categories of popular responses could be distinguished: one which did seem to be universal in the six American Indian cultures, a second group of populars which were found in some but not all of the six cultures, and a third group of "unique" populars found only within a single culture.[41]

Bert Kaplan and Richard Lawless have examined the Rorschach records of adults from 11 cultures drawn from four main geographical world areas: American Indian, West Indies, Western Pacific, and South Asia (India, Pakistan). Kaplan and Lawless did find that there were differences in the characteristic responses of these groups, sometimes of quite a puzzling nature. "For example, both men and women in the Palau group give the response Bat to card I, 40% of the time, but no Ifaluk or New Ireland individuals do at all; or on

---

[40] According to an early Rorschach study by the Bleulers, Moroccans are low on Whole responses and emphasize small details. (M. Bleuler and R. Bleuler, "Rorschach Ink-Blot Test and Racial Psychology; Mental Peculiarities of Moroccans," *Character and Personality*, Vol. 4 [1935], pp. 97–114.) De Vos, however, found a relatively high *W* percent in Miner's Algerian records. (Miner and De Vos, *Oasis and Casbah*, pp. 125, 132.)

[41] A. Irving Hallowell, "Popular Responses and Cultural References: An Analysis Based on Frequencies in a Group of American Indian Subjects," *Rorschach Research Exchange*, Vol. 9 (1945), pp. 153–68.

card II, almost 50% of Menomini men give the response Bear to the whole card, a response which is found with substantial frequency in only one other group, the Hindus."[42] This shows that there are problems in understanding the multifarious ways in which peoples of different cultures respond to a series of 10 inkblots. Let us now consider in more detail the Rorschach characteristics of some particular groups.

THE ANALYSIS OF GROUPS

Although studies of a single Rorschach Test,[43] of two subjects,[44] or of a small group have been made, Rorschach studies in the field of culture-and-personality more often involve the analysis of a fairly large sample of protocols drawn from a particular society. Sometimes comparisons are made between the Rorschach characteristics of two or more societies. In order to arrive at group generalizations and to make cross-cultural comparisons, some workers in this field have subjected their data to statistical treatment. What, for example, is the percentage of color responses in the group of subjects from Society X and how does this compare with the C percent in Society Y? Similiar comparisons may be made with regard to other Rorschach categories.

Hallowell's Three Chippewa Groups

Before presenting Hallowell's Rorschach findings, it will be useful to have a brief ethnographic account of the Chippewa or Ojibwa, about whom data will also be presented later in connection with the Thematic Apperception Test, drawing analysis, and folklore motifs.

The Chippewa, an Algonkian-speaking Woodland people who lived in the region of the Great Lakes, were primarily dependent on hunting, fishing, and gathering as a basis of subsistence, although they raised small crops of corn and squash in summer, harvested wild rice in the fall, and tapped maple trees for sugar in the spring. Chippewa groups were first encountered by Europeans near Sault

---

[42] Bert Kaplan and Richard Lawless, "Culture and Visual Imagery. A Comparison of Rorschach Responses in Eleven Societies," in Spiro (ed.) *Context and Meaning in Cultural Anthropology,* p. 310.

[43] Margaret Mead, *The Mountain Arapesh. V. The Record of Unabelin, With Rorschach Analysis,* Anthropological Papers of the American Museum of Natural History, 1949.

[44] Kluckhohn and Rosenzweig, "Two Navaho Children over a Five-Year Period."

Ste. Marie (hence the name Saulteaux or Saulteurs), but largely through the influence of the fur trade and the pressure of tribes like the Iroquois, these Indians have since moved westward, so that Chippewa are now to be found in Michigan, Wisconsin, Minnesota, North Dakota, Montana, and the Canadian provinces of Ontario, Manitoba, and Saskatchewan.

They are one of the largest American Indian groups in population. The Chippewa cannot, however, be said to constitute a tribe, or even a collection of tribes. Their social order has been described as "atomistic." An atomistic society is one in which it is not difficult for the component units to break away and exist apart from the larger society of which they are a part; political authority is weak, and there are not many mechanisms for reinforcing larger-group social solidarity.

The Chippewa, especially before 1870, lived in small scattered bands. The time of greatest social interaction was in summer, when small villages, consisting of about a dozen families, were able to take advantage of relatively favorable food supplies—fish and agricultural crops, in addition to game. These village units, however, broke up in the fall, with families moving to shallow lakes where wild rice was harvested. After that, separate family groups occupied different hunting areas, to take maximum advantage of the sparse winter food resources. This dispersal appears to have been a deliberate policy, "a precaution which seems necessary to their very existence," as Peter Grant wrote in 1804.[45]

In the spring, families moved to maple groves to tap trees and make sugar. Then the village life of summer was resumed. People generally returned to the same village, but there was much fluctuation. Landes says that such a village was not stable in numbers or location over any considerable period of time. "Almost any circumstance may cause people to drift to a given village or to leave it."[46] Landes cites various reasons for such shifts of residence—visits to in-laws, hostilities, the abandonment of a site for sanitary or supernatural reasons, and so on.

In the Chippewa social order one notes a marked contrast with the more integrated social organization of Plains tribes, like the Cheyenne. In the latter a strong sense of social solidarity was mani-

---

[45] Peter Grant, "The Sauteux Indians: About 1804," in R. L. Masson (ed.), *Les Bourgeois de la Compagnie du Nord-Ouest* (Quebec: Cote et Cie, 1890), pp. 326–27.

[46] Ruth Landes, *Ojibwa Sociology,* Columbia University Contributions to Anthropology, Vol. 29 (1937), p. 3.

fest in the orderly camp circle, the communal buffalo hunt, the highly developed political organization with its council of chiefs and the soldier societies which served as police force. The Chippewa lacked such institutions; they had no organized council of chiefs, no policing system, no regularly constituted military societies, and no symbols of group unity like the "Medicine Arrows" or "Sacred Hat" of the Cheyenne. There was no communal hunting comparable to that of the Cheyenne, and there was little economic cooperation outside the family unit. Even the major religious ceremonies were not conducted for the benefit of the group as a whole, as they generally were among the Cheyenne.[47]

The Midewiwin, the Chippewa Medicine Dance, was limited to members and required initiation payments. Perhaps the outstanding feature of their religion was the individual guardian spirit quest, which began at the age of four or five in this society. The powers of medicine men were supposedly derived from contact with guardian spirits who appeared in a dream or vision. There were no societies of medicine men.

The Chippewa had patrilineal clans, but almost their sole function was the regulation of marriage. They had little or no religious or political significance, as did the clans of some Central Algonkian tribes. This was particularly true of the more northerly Chippewa; for the southern groups there are indications of a formerly more developed clan system. Dunning believes that the hunting economy prohibited the development of larger groupings and the social elaboration of the clan system in the north.[48]

The Chippewa practical bilateral cross-cousin marriage, which is reflected in their kinship terminology. The levirate and sororate were observed but often flouted.[49]

The foregoing description has been phrased in the past tense, for

---

[47] The picture presented here of Chippewa social organization has been questioned by Harold Hickerson in two papers: "The Feast of the Dead among the Seventeenth Century Algonkians of the Upper Great Lakes," *American Anthropologist,* Vol. 62 (1960), pp. 81–107, and *The Southwestern Chippewa: An Ethno-Historical Study* (American Anthropological Association Memoir No. 92, 1962). I have replied to Hickerson's first paper in "Chippewa Social Atomism," *American Anthropologist,* Vol. 63 (1961), pp. 1006–13. In his second paper Hickerson tries to prove that the southern Chippewa had military societies. To my mind, the evidence for this is flimsy. More recent publications by Hickerson are mentioned in the "Suggestions for Further Reading" at the end of this chapter.

[48] R. W. Dunning, *Social and Economic Change among the Northern Ojibwa* (Toronto: University of Toronto Press, 1959), p. 82.

[49] Ruth Landes, *The Ojibwa Woman* (New York: Columbia University Press, 1938), p. 81.

much of it no longer applies to many groups, such as the Wisconsin Chippewa. Landes, who worked in 1932, 1933, and 1935 among Ontario Ojibwa, described a contemporary culture which retained much of the old way of life. The same is true of the Saulteaux studied by Hallowell in the 1930s. Even the Wisconsin Chippewa, however, are not far removed in time from the ethnographic picture just presented. My older Chippewa informants in 1944 and 1946 remembered and described this way of life. Some of them had lived in wigwams, traveled in birchbark canoes, and had worn breech-clouts, leggings, and other traditional Indian clothing. They had fasted for guardian spirits in childhood, and they generally still believed in the thunderbirds, in Wenebojo, the culture-hero-trickster, in the dangers of sorcery, in the efficacy of the Midewiwin and in the sucking doctor's cure.

Acculturation among these Indians can be adjudged to be either very old or very recent, depending upon the aspects of culture selected for emphasis. Dunning writes that, from the 17th century on, it would not be true to consider the Chippewa an aboriginal population.

Perhaps because of their strategic location at the Sault rapids on the main western trade route and their early contact with Europeans they became thoroughly identified with the development of European interests. Suffice it to say that they alone of the western lakes peoples cooperated with the explorers and fur traders. The Sioux, Cree, and Assineboine withdrew under the pressure of increasing economic development.[50]

However, the nature of the Chippewas' contact with the fur traders was such as to perpetuate an aboriginal way of life based on hunting. New aspects of material culture were introduced—guns, traps, cloth, flour, tea, liquor, and so forth—but many groups do not seem to have had significant concomitant changes in other spheres, such as religion and kinship organization, until quite recent times. The precontact social order seems to have been atomistic, as defined above; the fur trade perpetuated and probably further emphasized this atomistic tendency. Many Chippewa bands lived in remote areas, having little contact with the outer world. As Hallowell has written, "not only was their subsistence economy retained, but the seasonal movements, institutions, attitudes, and beliefs that were closely integrated with it."[51]

---

[50] Dunning, *Social and Economic Change among the Northern Ojibwa,* p. 4.

[51] A. Irving Hallowell, *Culture and Experience* (Philadelphia: University of Pennsylvania Press, 1955), p. 119.

In his Rorschach study of these Indians, Hallowell made use of mean frequencies in a comparison of three Chippewa groups representing different levels of acculturation. Two are Berens River groups in Canada, the more conservative and unacculturated being termed Inland (with 44 Rorschach subjects) and the more acculturated group named Lakeside (58 Rorschach subjects). The third Chippewa population, at Lac du Flambeau, Wisconsin (represented by 115 Rorschach subjects), has experienced a still greater degree of acculturation. Hallowell presents a table giving the means of responses for various Rorschach determinants, locations, types of content, and certain percentage scores for each of the three groups.[52]

This approach provides a composite group profile, comparable to the superimposition of a number of photographs of faces, one on top of the other, leaving a final picture which represents no one individual face but which does show something of the general features of the group in question. This group portrait can then be compared with those of other groups. Perhaps the comparison would be more apt if the procedure were described as one of finding the mean nose breadth, the mean distance between the eyes, and so on, of the members of the group, as a way of building up the composite picture.

Hallowell finds both similarities and differences in his three Chippewa groups. In all three there is a very low percentage of color responses and a low percentage of answers to the last three cards (which are all chromatic). In each of Hallowell's three groups, the mean for the sum of the color responses is very low: 0.5 for Inland, 1.7 for Lakeside, and 1 for Flambeau. By contrast, a sample American group cited by Hallowell (157 Rorschach subjects) has a mean of 3.11.[53]

The low incidence of color responses would suggest that the Chippewa individual expects very little from others and is not apt to develop close emotional ties with them. The same rarity of color responses may be noted in Rorschachs collected by other investigators in the Chippewa area—Robert Ritzenthaler, Ernestine Friedl, Blanche Watrous, myself, and others. It seems to be a characteristic feature of Chippewa protocols.

The latter are also rather high in M. The mean for Hallowell's two Berens River groups is 4 for Inland and 3 for Lakeside.[54] The

---

[52] Hallowell, *Culture and Experience,* p. 350.

[53] A. I. Hallowell, "The Rorschach Technique in Personality and Culture Studies," in Bruno Klopfer, Ainsworth, et al., *Developments in the Rorschach Test,* Vol. II, *Fields of Application,* 1956, p. 527.

[54] Hallowell, *Culture and Experience,* p. 350.

implication of this M percentage, combined with the low color percentage, is that traditional Chippewa personality is characterized by introversiveness, with fantasy playing an important role. The character of Chippewa M responses is also of interest. Most of them are passive in nature—people seen as sitting, standing, lying down, or watching. Hallowell says that 82.3 percent of the M's of his adult subjects in the Inland group were of this type. At Lac du Flambeau the mean for M drops to 1—an indication of the disruptive effect of acculturation.

All three of Hallowell's groups have a mean of 3 for FM, or animal movement. Animal movement responses are believed by Klopfer and Kelley to represent the most instinctive layers in the personality.[55] In a normal record the number of M should generally exceed that of FM; the reverse is believed to indicate emotional immaturity, as would an excess of CF or C over FC. In the Chippewa records M and FM are generally on a par, except at Flambeau, where FM is higher. The relative increase in FM and the decline of M in the most acculturated group, together with some other Rorschach features, are seen by Hallowell to indicate a weakening of the rigid control characteristic of the traditional Chippewa personality, but without any new compensating factors in evidence. An apathetic type of personality has apparently developed at Lac du Flambeau, functioning with "a great paucity of inner resources."[56]

Chippewa Children's Rorschachs

Hallowell's Rorschach studies of the Chippewa have been supplemented by Blanche G. Watrous, who has analyzed 102 records of children from Lac du Flambeau and compared them with 49 Berens River children's protocols. The children were grouped into 2 age groups; there were 54 children from Flambeau and 25 from Berens River aged 6 years to 10 years, 11 months; 48 from Flambeau and 24 from Berens River aged 11 years to 15 years, 11 months. No distinction was made in this study between the Inland and Lakeside groups. As in the Hallowell study, mean scores were computed and compared.

In general, the Flambeau children's records conformed to the traditional Chippewa picture. Both the Flambeau and Berens River children gave M responses at an early age— mostly passive M's, often seen in unusual tiny detail areas. Both groups produced fewer FC

---

[55] Klopfer and Kelley, *The Rorschach Technique*, p. 278.

[56] Hallowell, *Culture and Experience*, pp. 351–52.

responses than has been reported for white children in the literature; *CF* responses exceeded the more controlled *FC*. Both Chippewa groups gave relatively few Whole responses, with more attention being paid to details, indicating a more practical than theoretical orientation. There was a high percentage of tiny details at Flambeau. Both groups show the introversive pattern characteristic of the traditional Chippewa; but it is interesting to note that the older children at Flambeau seem to be more "Indian" than the younger children. This is evidenced by a reduction in the total number of responses and a decrease in color responses.

More cards were rejected by the older children. At Flambeau there was an overemphasis on human and animal details in relation to whole human and animal responses. The Flambeau children, moreover, gave more *FM* responses and saw more active animal movement in the blots than did the Berens River children, which is interpreted to indicate a greater degree of emotional aggression. There is also a possible indication of greater anxiety in the larger number of texture responses at Flambeau. Blanche Watrous describes these children as having "oversensitive, hypercritical, fearful attitudes toward people, emotional aggression, underlying psychic conflicts, and an unsatisfactory rapport with their surroundings."[57]

It will be seen in a later section of this chapter that a similar picture emerges from an analysis of Chippewa children's Thematic Apperception Test records.

The Menomini

A very detailed Rorschach study has been made by George and Louise Spindler of the Menomini, neighbors of the Wisconsin Chippewa, who shared with them the same general kind of Woodland Indian culture of former times, and who, like the Chippewa, speak an Algonkian language. Here again, a statistical approach was used, except that Spindler used the median, rather than the mean, as an expresssion of central tendency.[58] Menomini males were studied first. Spindler divided his 68 male subjects into five segments representing different levels of adaption to Western culture: (1) a *native-oriented* group, followers of the Medicine Dance, Dream Dance, and other traditional Indian patterns, (2) *Peyote cult members*, (3) a

[57] Blanche G. Watrous, "A Personality Study of Ojibwa Children," Ph.D. Thesis, Department of Anthropology, Northwestern University, Evanston, Illinois, 1949, p. 205.

[58] George D. Spindler, *Sociocultural and Psychological Processes in Menomini Acculturation,* University of California Publications in Culture and Society, No. V, 1955.

transitional group which is not clearly identified with either the native or Western-oriented groups, (4) a *lower status acculturated* group, and (5) an *elite acculturated* middle-class higher status group.

The native-oriented group is very similar, in its Rorschach patterns, to the traditional Chippewa.[59] There is the same paucity of color responses. The Menomini, however, show more *FM* (animal movement) in relation to *M* than do Hallowell's Inland group.[60] The "elite" group closely resembles a control group of local white subjects in their Rorschach patterns, showing a more controlled extroversion than the other Indian groups. The native-oriented group and the "elite" seem to represent polar points in a continuum, in which the intermediate groups show more emotional responsiveness to others than do the native-oriented subjects, but have less emotional control than the "elite." Nothing comparable to the latter's psychological shift has been found in the Chippewa groups studied so far, a circumstance which may perhaps be attributed to the relatively favorable economic situation on the Menomini reservation, where the Indians own and operate their own sawmill.[61] It may be, however, that Chippewa who have left the reservation to live in cities like Milwaukee and Chicago, and who were not available for testing on the reservation, approximate more closely to the Menomini elite acculturated group.

Louise and George Spindler have also made a Rorschach study of Menomini women, in which they found that they appeared to be more homogeneous psychologically than the men, despite the fact that they were differentiated socioculturally in the same ways as the men. Menomini men must adapt psychologically to the conditions of acculturation, while the women are able to retain more of the native-oriented personality structure at each level of acculturation. The women are more conservative than the men in personality tendencies and less tense and anxious.[62] Similar observations have been made before for other American Indian groups, including the Chippewa.[63]

[59] Ibid., pp. 131, 137–38, 207.

[60] Ibid., p. 138.

[61] A. I. Hallowell, "The Rorschach Technique in Personality and Culture Studies," in Klopfer, Ainsworth, et al., *Developments in the Rorschach Test*, pp. 531–32.

[62] Louise Spindler and George Spindler, "A Modal Personality Technique in the Study of Menomini Acculturation," in Bert Kaplan (ed.), *Studying Personality Cross-Culturally*, pp. 479–91.

[63] A. I. Hallowell, "Acculturative Processes and Personality Changes as Indicated by the Rorschach Technique," *Rorschach Research Exchange*, Vol. 6 (1942), pp. 42–50; William Caudill, "Psychological Characteristics of Acculturated Wisconsin Ojibwa

The Kaska

A personality picture similar to that of the less acculturated Chippewa and Menomini has been described for the Kaska, who live a considerable distance away but who had a similar aboriginal economy. John J. Honigmann collected 28 Rorschach records from these Athapaskan-speaking Indians, who live in British Columbia, Canada, west of the Rocky Mountains. Honigmann presents mean scores, in the Hallowell manner.[64] He finds a very low percentage of color responses, as among the Chippewa, but a lower *M* percentage than among the latter. The picture is similar to that of the Chippewa, but more constricted. Honigmann's careful discussion of Kaska personality traits is not based on the Rorschach alone but on extensive field observations. Honigmann suggests:

> . . . a relatively homogeneous personality can be discerned in the vast coniferous forest zone extending from northeastern Canada to western Alaska. Briefly, such a personality is marked by strong emotional constraint and the inhibition of strong emotions in interpersonal relations. Emotional indifference is maintained through avoiding investing any great emotion in anything.[65]

This personality picture is associated with an atomistic social structure, a relatively isolated social world, and a predominantly hunting-gathering economy. The culture in each of these American Indian groups was one which emphasized a certain fearfulness and mistrust in others. Belief in sorcery was strong. The consistency of these findings in the Chippewa, Menomini, and Kaska materials is striking.

While acknowledging the various problems posed by administration of the Rorschach Test, especially in non-Western societies, I have tried to show that a good case can be made for its use in culture-and-personality research.

An encouraging aspect of the Rorschach Test is that Rorschach analysts continue to find new clues to interpretation. George De Vos, for example, has examined the Rorschach protocols of both Arabs and Japanese living in traditional and acculturated settings, and he has found that while Arabs and Japanese differ in many ways in their "overall Rorschach configurations," there seem to be some

---

Children," *American Anthropologist*, Vol. 51 (1949), p. 425; Victor Barnouw, *Acculturation and Personality among the Wisconsin Chippewa*, Memoir No. 72, American Anthropological Association, 1950, pp. 20–21, fn.

[64] John J. Honigmann, *Culture and Ethos of Kaska Society*, Yale University Publications in Anthropology, No. 40 (1949), pp. 240–43.

[65] John J. Honigmann, *Culture and Personality* (New York: Harper Bros., 1954), p. 334.

cross-cultural regularities operating in the acculturated groups. That is to say, both among the Arabs and among the Japanese there is an increase in body-content material in Rorschach responses among the more acculturated groups and an increase in specific forms of hostile symbolism. De Vos finds evidence of this tendency among still other groups undergoing the pressures of acculturation.[66]

A new development which may perhaps reanimate the cross-cultural use of projective techniques is the development of the Holtzman Inkblot Technique (HIT), devised by Wayne H. Holtzman and his associates. Instead of the 10 standard Rorschach blots, the Holtzman test has 2 parallel forms. A and B, each consisting of 45 inkblots, with 2 practice blots, making up a total of 92 blots. These blots are more varied in color, form, and shading than the Rorschach blots; they are not all bilaterally symmetrical. The subject gives only one response per card instead of as many as he wishes in the Rorschach Test. This test was designed to meet some psychologists' objections to the Rorschach Test, such as lack of test-retest reliability for many scores, and the widely varying number of responses given to individual Rorschach cards. Holtzman believes that his test provides a more reliable scoring system.[67] The test has been used cross-culturally, principally in Mexico. Reportedly universal "popular" responses to the HIT have been recorded for five areas: Denmark, Germany, Hong Kong, Mexico, and the United States.[68]

THE THEMATIC APPERCEPTION TEST

The Thematic Apperception Test (TAT) involves showing the subject a series of pictures, for each of which, in turn, he is required to make up a story. The subject is asked to tell what led up to the scene depicted, describing the thoughts and feelings of the individuals involved, and to tell what the outcome of the episode will be. The test, designed by C. D. Morgan and Henry A. Murray,[69]

---

[66] George De Vos, "Symbolic Analysis in the Cross-Cultural Study of Personality," in Bert Kaplan (ed.), *Studying Personality Cross-Culturally*, pp. 599–634.

[67] Wayne H. Holtzman, Joseph S. Thorpe, Jon D. Swartz, and E. Wayne Herron, *Inkblot Perception and Personality. Holtzman Inkblot Technique* (Austin, Tex.: University of Texas Press, 1961).

[68] Wayne H. Holtzman, "Holtzman Inkblot Technique," in A. I. Rabin (ed.), *Projective Techniques in Personality Assessment. A Modern Introduction* (New York: Springer Publishing Company, 1968), pp. 160–62.

[69] C. D. Morgan and H. A. Murray, "A Method for Investigating Phantasies: the Thematic Apperception Test," *Archives of Neurology and Psychiatry*, Vol. 34 (1935), pp. 289–306.

contains some pictures which are shown only to male subjects, some only to females, some used only with children, while some are shown to all subjects. There is a standard order of presentation, although this has been varied in some studies. A few of the pictures are re-productions of paintings; some look like magazine illustrations; one is a blank white card. The traditional practice is to show 20 pictures to a subject and have him tell a story for each; many testers, however, do not give the full range of TAT pictures but select a few which they feel to be particularly productive.

The cards are designed to tap different areas in human life and interpersonal relationships; there are pictures eliciting stories about a man's relationship with a mother figure, with a father figure, with a girl friend, pictures which may elicit stories of ambition, tragedy, and so forth. These narratives are analyzed for recurrent or unusual themes and for what they reveal of the individual's underlying as-sumptions and attitudes. Attention is paid to figures and objects not depicted in the picture but introduced in the story, and also to items which may be prominent or significant in the picture but omitted in the story. It is noted whether the outcomes of the narratives tend to be successful or unsuccessful. Does everything end in failure? Are realistic methods employed to resolve a conflict, or is a *deus ex machina* solution improvised? Many points of this sort enter into the process of interpretation. Saul Rosenzweig and Edith E. Fleming have pointed to some interesting minor variations in TAT protocols. For instance, in Card I, which represents a young boy contemplating a violin, some subjects may see the violin string as broken or else per-ceive the violin as otherwise damaged. This occurred only 8 times in a sample of 100 normal inviduals whose TATs they investigated. But in a sample of 100 mental patients there were 23 such instances.[70]

A number of different scoring systems have been devised for the TAT, but these will not concern us here. Our interest lies in the cross-cultural application of the Thematic Apperception Test. An inspection of the Murray pictures will soon make it clear that this series would not lend itself well to administration in a culture which differs considerably from that of the Western world. In some of the pictures middle-class American interiors are depicted which would have little meaning to members of "primitive" societies. Facial fea-tures are "Caucasian," clothing of American type.

---

[70] Saul Rosenzweig and Edith E. Fleming, "Apperceptive Norms for the Thematic Apperception Test, II. An Empirical Investigation," *Journal of Personality,* Vol. 17 (1948–49) , p. 502.

There are two solutions to this problem. One is to select a limited number of standard TAT cards which do not reflect Western cultural patterns so markedly. This approach can be followed when the society in question has undergone a good deal of acculturation and where the physical features are not particularly different from those of Europeans. This was the method William Caudill used in his study of Lac du Flambeau Chippewa children.[71] In a study of adolescents in an acculturated Maori community in New Zealand, D. G. Mulligan made use of the full TAT series.[72] The standard cards seem to have done the job successfully both at Lac du Flambeau and in the Maori group. The traditional Murray cards, then, may be shown, in whole or in part, when the group is sufficiently acculturated.

Modified TATs

With less acculturated groups a second alternative may be followed. This is to draw up a parallel series of cards in which the geographical setting, house types, clothing, and physical features correspond to the culture in question. In other words, an artist is commissioned to make a "modified" TAT series which will be meaningful to members of that society. This method has been used in the study of Hopi and Navaho children, in Gladwin and Sarason's work on Truk, in Lessa and Spiegelman's investigation of Ulithian personality, and in studies of various African groups.[73] A modified TAT, designed to elicit attitudes toward authority, the emperor, military service, and certain areas of interpersonal relations, has been given to Japanese subjects.[74] For use in Japanese rural areas De Vos and

---

[71] William Caudill, "Psychological Characteristics of Acculturated Wisconsin Ojibwa Children," *American Anthropologist,* Vol. 51 (1949), pp. 409–27.

[72] D. G. Mulligan, "Maori Adolescence in Rakau. A Thematic Apperception Test Study," Victoria University College Publications in Psychology, No. 9, Monographs on Maori Social Life and Personality, No. 2, Department of Psychology, Victoria University College (Wellington, New Zealand, 1957).

[73] William E. Henry, *The Thematic Apperception Technique in the Study of Culture-Personality Relations,* Genetic Psychology Monographs, No. 35 (1947), pp. 3–135; William A. Lessa and Marvin Spiegelman, "Ulithian Personality as Seen Through Ethnological Materials and Thematic Test Analysis," University of California Publications in Culture and Society, Vol. 2, No. 5 (1954), pp. 243–301; S. G. Lee, *Manual of a Thematic Apperception Test for African Subjects* (Pietermaritzburg: University of Natal Press, 1953).

[74] Jean Stoetzel, *Without the Chrysanthemum and the Sword. A Study of the Attitudes of Youth in Post-War Japan* (London, Paris: William Heinemann, UNESCO, 1955), Appendix II.

Wagatsuma have employed a modified TAT which closely resembles the original Murray series.[75]

One drawback in such tests is that a "modified" TAT is not the same test as the original series, although efforts have usually been made to parallel the Murray cards in a general way. William E. Henry has set forth some criteria for what a modified test should include. There should be mother-child and father-child scenes; a person alone; a heterosexual scene, a group scene, an authority scene, a typical environmental setting, and scenes of some characteristic economic activity. There should be one or two pictures of an "illogical arrangement of reality events," and one or two representing unreal or bizarre events. Henry suggests that there should also be some scenes characteristic of the culture in question, designed to touch on problems of local concern (for instance, caste groups in India).[76] Such a modified series will, of course, differ in many respects from the Murray sequence and from modified tests in other areas. This is unintentionally illustrated in three plates reproduced in the Henry article just cited. In each of these, two young men are being addressed by an older, authoritative male. The first plate represents an American Indian group, the second a Mexican, and the third a South-West African group. Inspection of these drawings shows that they are not exactly equivalent. The ages of the younger males seem to differ, particularly in the Mexican and African plates. The Mexican adult is taller than the younger males, but the older adult is not equally so in the American Indian and African drawings. Facial expressions also differ slightly. Differences in responses to these drawings in the three groups might be due to differences in the plates rather than to differences in group personality tendencies.

Most modified TATs, like the ones used in Truk and Ulithi, do not try to imitate the style of the original Murray reproductions, but consist of line drawings which lack the shading and chiaroscuro of the original plates. This stylistic factor might make a difference. Caudill has noted that the Ojibwa children whom he tested told

---

[75] George De Vos and Hiroshi Wagatsuma, "Value Attitudes toward Role Behavior of Women in Two Japanese Villages," *American Anthropologist,* Vol. 63 (1961), pp. 1204–30.

[76] William E. Henry, "The Thematic Apperception Technique in the Study of Group and Cultural Problems," in Harold H. Anderson and Gladys L. Anderson (eds.), *An Introduction to Projective Techniques and Other Devices for Understanding the Dynamics of Human Behavior* (Englewood Cliffs, N.J.: Prentice-Hall, 1951), pp. 263–64.

much longer stories than did the Hopi and Navaho children.[77] Might not this disparity be a function of the nature of the plates in use, rather than a reflection of different group personality tendencies? For Caudill used the standard Murray pictures, while the modified TAT was used with the other groups. Perhaps experiments should be made to determine whether line drawings provide as productive results in TATs as do pictures with chiaroscuro.

Edward T. Sherwood, who like Lee has devised a modified TAT for African subjects, has a series which bears somewhat more resemblance in style to the original TAT than do the Hopi, Navaho, and Micronesian TATs. Sherwood believes that the pictures should offer a good deal of variety to maintain the interest of the subject. Some should be close-up views, some seen at a distance; some should be dark in tone, some light. Some pictures should be in shade and highlight, others relatively monotone; and different graphic techniques should be employed in different cards.[78]

In any event, it is clear that modified TATs do not lend themselves to the same sort of cross-cultural comparisons that the Rorschach Test allows. In the Rorschach Test every subject sees the same 10 blots in the same order, whether he be an Eskimo, a Bushman, or a Yale undergraduate. With modified TATs, however, we have a number of different tests providing different series of stimuli. This does not mean that modified TATs are not useful and productive. As we shall see, such tests have proven to be very informative. If the purpose is simply to produce fantasy material, a modified TAT will do what is required of it. But it cannot be used so successfully in global cross-cultural comparisons.

Some other drawbacks may be noted. With relatively "primitive" groups there may be a lack of familiarity with pictures and some consequent difficulty in seeing perspective depicted in the plates. This may affect the test results and produce some seemingly bizarre responses. One Ulithian, for example, interpreted large ocean waves illustrated in one card as being pigs.[79] Some Micronesian subjects who were shown the same modified TATs by Melford Spiro were unable to interpret some of the objects represented in the pictures and could not identify certain depictions of fire, smoke, and tree

[77] Caudill, "Psychological Characteristics of Acculturated Wisconsin Ojibwa Children," p. 414.

[78] Edward T. Sherwood, "On the Designing of TAT Pictures, With Special Reference to a Set for an African People Assimilating Western Culture," *Journal of Social Psychology*, Vol. 45 (1957), pp. 182–83.

[79] Lessa and Spiegelman, "Ulithian Personality . . ." p. 280.

trunks. Perspective was not always understood. "Objects drawn above one another were seen as being above one another and not in spatially receding planes. A canoe, represented by the artist as being *in* a native canoe house, was seen as being *carried* by men standing in the foreground *outside* the house."[80]

S. Biesheuvel found a similar lack of comprehension of perspective in some African subjects taking a modified TAT.

A group of industrial operatives, presented with a picture of cattle grazing in a field, correctly identified those in the foreground, whilst those in the background, drawn smaller to simulate distance, were sometimes seen as hyenas or similar animals. A workman, standing on a box obscured by fellow-workers whom he was haranguing, against a background of factory buildings and chimney stacks, was seen by some as a giant catching the smoke that emanated from the stacks. Many did not perceive the latter as aspects of factory buildings at all, and the attempt to evoke attitudes concerning the work situation thus failed to come off. Conventional graphic details in the postural or facial representations frequently suggested mutilation or blindness.[81]

Group Studies

In the analysis of group protocols, different procedures have been followed by analysts, sometimes making use of statistical techniques along different lines. In their study of Ulithian personality, Lessa and Spiegelman make use of a quantitative approach involving certain categories set forth by Reuben Fine.[82] The Ulithian records were scored according to these categories, and the interpretation (made "blind") was based on the resultant quantitative findings rather than drawn from analyses of the TAT stories themselves.[83] D. G. Mulligan's analysis of Maori TATs follows a similar quantitative approach based on Reuben Fine's method and makes use of the mean frequencies of certain types of responses.[84] The "blind" analysis of the Ulithian material yielded results with which the ethnographer agreed. There is also close agreement between Mulligan's

---

[80] A. I. Hallowell, *Culture and Experience,* p. 45.

[81] S. Biesheuvel, "Methodology in the Study of Attitudes of Africans," *Journal of Social Psychology,* Vol. 47 (1958), p. 176.

[82] Reuben Fine, "TAT Scoring Sheet for Verbal Projective Techniques," mimeographed ms. See also Reuben Fine, Chapter 8 in Edwin Shneidman (ed.), *Thematic Test Analysis* (New York: Grune and Stratton, 1951), pp. 64–82.

[83] Lessa and Spiegelman, "Ulithian Personality . . ." p. 268.

[84] Mulligan, "Maori Adolescence in Rakau," p. 50.

TAT findings, observational data, and Rorschach conclusions in the Rakau study.

Most TAT analyses have followed a more informal procedure of simply looking for recurrent patterns in the protocols. This seems, for instance, to have been the method followed by Sarason in his "blind" analysis of the Trukese TATs, which also proved to be in close agreement with the ethnographer's impressions of the people.

Let us now consider in more detail some of the TAT analyses which have been mentioned.

Hopi and Navaho Children

One of the first cross-cultural applications of the TAT was in connection with the study of Hopi and Navaho children, aged 6–18, equally divided as to sex. There were 102 Hopi and 104 Navaho subjects who took a modified TAT consisting of 12 line drawings drawn by an Indian artist. On the basis of their TATs, Henry found that, among the Hopi, the mother is the principal authority.

There is considerable unconscious hostility to her although it is seldom expressed in direct form. . . . The dominance of the adult female in the fantasies of the children is so marked as to support the suggestion that their authority extends through the culture to all adult females rather than just to the mother-child relation. . . . The position of the father is one of far less importance than that of the mother. . . . In no case does there appear the hostility to him so characteristic of descriptions of the mother.[85]

In the large extended family setting, diffuse emotional attachments prevail. It would seem that a child can more easily move from one family unit to another than could a child in the white American middle class. Control of emotions is stressed and personal desires de-emphasized. Individuality is suppressed in the interests of the group, but this is accompanied by a sense of anxiety in the individual. A frequent Hopi motif is "I want to rebel, but I know I can't." Henry makes the suggestion that "this is a society whose restrained, non-aggressive front, and rigorous system of social controls represent a system of defense against two kinds of events: the real or imagined threat to the psychological integrity and maintenance of the culture and the presence of intra-group hostilities."[86]

---

[85] William E. Henry, *The Thematic Apperception Technique in the Study of Culture-Personality Relations*, Genetic Psychology Monograph, No. 35 (1947), p. 91.

[86] Ibid., p. 93.

The TAT evidence further suggests to Henry that the following channels of release may be resorted to: malicious gossip, indirectly expressed sibling jealousy, petty delinquencies such as stealing and acts of destruction, running away from home or school, and committing acts of cruelty to animals.[87] Reference to the section on the Pueblos in Chapter 4 on Ruth Benedict will show that many observational studies are in agreement with this general picture, such as those of Dorothy Eggan, Esther Goldfrank, and others. Hostility toward the mother might not have been expected, however, at least not to the extent suggested by Henry's analysis.

As for the Navaho, life seems easier than for the Hopi. There is less weight of personal responsibility, and the environment is less threatening. At least, there is no anxiety about food. There is greater freedom and spontaneity in emotional life. More respect is shown for individuality within the family. Family relations are easier and less characterized by ambivalence. Sibling rivalry does not have the force of such rivalry among the Hopi, and there is greater impartiality in the treatment of children. In contrast to the Hopi, there is an absence of guilt feelings concerning infractions of rules. The mental approach is practical and matter of fact, but individuality and imagination are expressed in the arts and crafts, in clothes and jewelry.

This interpretation, again, coincides with impressions of those who have worked with these Indians. Henry quotes a statement made by Clyde Kluckhohn, one of the foremost authorities on the Navaho:

> I hope you will emphasize . . . the independence of the convergent views [of the two reports]. Last winter in Chicago, which was the first time I heard [your report on the Navaho], I was astonished and pleased at how in many details your results seemed to parallel almost identically things which already stood in this manuscript [*The People and Their Children*]—the psychological parts of which have not been substantially altered since then.[88]

A quantitative assessment of the test's validity was also attempted. Among 16 Navaho cases studied, 451 interpretations were made. "When these 451 points were compared with all other sources of data, 375, or 83.1 per cent of them, were found to be substantiated

---

[87] Ibid., p. 95.
[88] Ibid., p. 114, fn.

and only 10, or 2.2 percent, were found to be incorrect statements."[89] This is a careful, well-executed study.

Chippewa Children

William Caudill's analysis of Ojibwa children's records from Lac du Flambeau provides more psychological insights into this community and should be considered in relation to the Rorschach evidence and the life history materials that have been presented in previous sections. Caudill notes, as an outstanding feature of these TAT records, the tendency to catalogue the contents of a picture, picking out small details.

Both details of the natural environment and human details are treated equally as if all were inanimate objects. There is little more, if any, warmth or involvement with a human detail than with an inanimate detail. . . . Another quality of this detailed approach is that the stories fail to relate one detail to another. More importantly, the human details are also seen with very little relationship to each other.[90]

The stories display little emotional feeling of any kind. This is true even when stories deal with physical aggression and drunkenness— perhaps, as Caudill suggests, because these are accepted as part of everyday life. Two examples are given:

F10, card 8 (4) There's a man and his wife. They're dancing. After they danced, the lady's husband wanted to fight and his wife was holding him back, and after they got through fighting they went home and that girl cooked her dinner, and after dinner, they were sitting around and they went for a walk and they came to a nice big building and the man wanted to fight again but the lady held him back, and they went home and went to bed.

M13, card 3 (12F) They're looking at their brother. He's drunk. He's drunk or something or go mad. His older brother went after him in a tavern. Brought him home. They're staring at him. They sent the younger brother after the father and the father and the younger brother put him to bed. The father had been uptown after some groceries. After that they had a late lunch and the brother sobered up and went back to bed again. That's all.[91]

---

[89] Henry in Anderson and Anderson, *An Introduction to Projective Techniques* . . . , p. 260.

[90] Caudill, "Psychological Characteristics of Acculturated Wisconsin Ojibwa Children," p. 414.

[91] Ibid., p. 415.

Most endings of stories have a neutral quality. If a story ends unhappily, the unhappiness is stated without emotion. Caudill notes three types of deficiency in these records:

(1) There is little indication of any emotional interpersonal relationships, and what there is involves hostility rather than warmth; (2) there is a total lack of any indication of ambition—no desire for education, for a better job, to be a good farmer or hunter; and (3) there are almost no remarks concerning moral or value judgments. Thus, going to jail simply happens, it is an ordinary part of life which is morally neither good nor bad.[92]

From a total of 88 children's records, 41 show definite psychological maladjustment. A number show drastic personality damage in the direction of schizophrenia. There are constant references to hunger and eating. Caudill believes that the impact of Western culture cannot be the sole source of these psychological patterns, but that they must in part be traced back to aboriginal conditions. Needless to say, there is much correspondence with the work done by Hallowell, Watrous, and others who have worked among the Chippewa.

Japanese-Americans

Caudill has also made a study of Japanese-Americans in Chicago, utilizing the standard Murray series. This study shows the usefulness of certain key cards in eliciting material—for instance, 6BM and 7BM in tapping attitudes toward parental figures. 6BM shows an elderly woman looking somewhat vacantly out of a window, while a tall young man in the foreground looks down with a perplexed expression on his face. 7BM shows the faces of an older and a younger man. The features in these pictures are "Caucasian," but the Japanese-Americans do not seem to have had any difficulty in identifying with these figures.

Consider some of the answers to 6BM:

1. This boy failed in school and he's asking his mother for forgiveness. After a long lecture from his mother he realizes his mistake and vows to try again and his mother forgives him.
2. This is a picture of a mother and her son. Her son has disappointed her. The son knows that the cause of the disappointment is his fault. He's probably a weak character, and will probably continue to disappoint his mother. This man is a weakling and the poignancy of the mother who apparently, or is becoming to lose a lot of, or all, her faith in her son. [*Sic*]
3. This is her son. He is suffering because he wants to get married but

---

[92] Ibid., pp. 420–21.

his mother doesn't like his sweetheart. In the end he leaves the house. He suffers, but because his mother won't listen, there's nothing he can do about it.

4. This looks like a son that's trying to explain to his mother the wrong he did, but the mother doesn't pay any attention to him. He feels sorry and wants his mother's forgiveness, but I guess she won't give it to him. [What has he done that was wrong?] Something like wanting to marry a girl he shouldn't and not the one his mother wants him to.

5. This is a mother and son. He has a sad face. They are separating, and he is off to school. The mother doesn't want him to go, and she has a strange, stupid [*bonyari*] expression on her face. This is difficult. The boy wonders, "Should I go or shouldn't I?" He finally decides to stay and take care of her.

6. This I understand also. This is mama and this is son. He did something bad and came back from jail, I think. She wants to teach him. Can't embrace and kiss him. He's a bad person and came back from the law.[93]

In all the stories the mother is a very strong person. She may be very punitive toward the son; he is submissive. When rejected by her, the son feels a sense of failure and guilt. The mother may interfere with his own personal desires, especially in connection with marriage; and her voice seems to be decisive in such cases. The mother may support the attitude of the community or the law, if the young man has broken a rule. In general, the son is compliant, suppresses his feelings, and continues to feel a sense of obligation toward his mother.

The most common adaptive mechanism utilized by Issei and Nisei is always to ask for parental advice and approval on any problem in order to avoid anxiety and guilt. This adaptive mechanism is extended by Japanese-Americans beyond the familial area and becomes one of constantly seeking advice on any important decision from older, and hence wiser, people. There is no defense against parental rejection, which usually results in feelings of masochistic guilt and personal failure.[94]

The stories told to Card 7BM, which reflect father-son relationships, are also revealing. Other cards tap themes of ambition and illustrate the high aspiration levels of Japanese-Americans. In sum, this is an interesting study which throws light on the similarities and differences between Japanese-Americans and white Americans of lower and middle class.[95]

---

[93] William Caudill, *Japanese-American Personality and Acculturation*, Genetic Psychology Monograph 45 (1952), pp. 39–42.

[94] Ibid., p. 65.

[95] For studies involving Rorschach findings on acculturating Japanese-Americans, see George A. De Vos, "A Quantitative Rorschach Assessment of Maladjustment and

Micronesian Studies

Two studies of Micronesian TAT's have been published. Both make use of the same modified series of cards. One study forms part of the Gladwin-Sarason monograph on Truk; the other is the Lessa-Spiegelman work on Ulithi, to which reference had been made. In both cases TAT analyses were made "blind" and the results compared with the ethnographer's observations, although with some differences in method, as has been noted.[96] Of the two studies, the analysis of Truk is more detailed and gives a more specific and complex picture of personality patterns, perhaps because Sarason worked more closely with the TAT stories themselves, while the psychologist in the Ulithian study based his analysis primarily on statistical breakdowns of categorized items. Sarason, moreover, had an additional source of information, for he had completed the group Rorschach interpretation before beginning his analysis of the TAT stories. Both psychologists had an added possible source of data on the culture— the pictures themselves, which might give some cues, as Lessa and Spiegelman imply.[97]

Some of Sarason's generalizations, based on the Truk TAT stories, are as follows: [98] Trukese parents treat their children inconsistently, sometimes kindly, at other times punishing and rejecting. This generalization would seem to be applicable to almost any parents, but Sarason goes on to underline the negative side of the picture. Parents, particularly the mother, are seen as fearsome, rejecting, and punishing figures against whom retaliation is best not attempted. Trukese children, moreover, experience severe oral frustrations. Indeed, anxiety over food is a common motif in the TAT stories. Sarason suggests that one would expect the Trukese to have little difficulty in "receiving" from others but much difficulty in giving of themselves. Many of the stories indicate the presence of a separation anxiety which seems to persist throughout life. Hostility and other strong feelings are suppressed and cloaked by overt conformity. Sarason sees little evidence of interests aside from food and sex, but a rather pas-

Rigidity in Acculturating Japanese-Americans," Genetic Psychology Monographs, No. 52 (1955), pp. 51–87; and William Caudill and George De Vos, "Achievement, Culture and Personality: the Case of the Japanese-Americans," *American Anthropologist,* Vol. 58 (1956), pp. 1102–26.

[96] Melford E. Spiro and Francis Mahoney have also given the TAT in Micronesia, but as far as I know, their results have not been published.

[97] Lessa and Spiegelman, "Ulithian Personality . . ." p. 300.

[98] Thomas Gladwin and Seymour B. Sarason, *Truk: Man in Paradise,* Viking Fund Publications in Anthropology, No. 20 (New York, 1953), pp. 232–46.

sive, lazy way of life. "It is surprising how in so many of their stories people are 'relaxing,' 'playing,' 'eating,' 'strolling,' 'bathing,' etc."[99]

Sarason's deductions about male-female relations are subtle and discerning. He believes that this is a society in which sexual activity plays a central role.

In the case of the male the chief motivation for his strong sexual drive appears to be the need to prove himself as a masculine figure. To conquer women sexually is to be assertive and has the effect of reducing the strength of feelings of inadequacy, satisfying strong dependency needs, and lessening the unpleasant effects of anticipations of rejection. However, because women are undependable, rejecting, and subtly domineering, the effect of sexual activity as a reducer of tension and conflict is probably only temporary. It appears that both men and women view or approach sexual activity in a rather self-centered (narcissistic) way in which the pleasures that might accrue to the partner are somewhat incidental.

It was said above that women are subtly aggressive toward, and assertive over, men. More from the stories of the men than of the women can one conclude that the latter take advantage of the former's needs for masculine status and (unconscious) dependency strivings to dominate the relationship. It is the Trukese male who devotes much thought and effort to trying to figure out how he can maintain the woman's attention. He gives her material things as a sort of bribe. But the stronger his dependency needs become the more hostility comes to the fore.[100]

The Trukese man is very jealous, but directs his hostility more to the woman in question than toward his rivals. Sarason hypothesizes that Trukese women are somewhat exhibitionistic—more so than the men. In general, social relations are superficial and unstable, one possible exception being the somewhat mutually supporting relationship between young "brothers." Women, on the other hand, do not seem to have such close relations with one another.

Gladwin, the ethnographer, expresses agreement on almost all of these points, and his description of the culture provides abundant documentation for them. But he does make some emendations. For example, Sarason stresses the men's concern with their genital adequacy, but Gladwin says that the women have the same kind of concern. There is a Trukese notion that a woman's vagina should be full of "little things"—prominent clitoris, labia minora, and so forth —which are believed to assure many lovers. Quarrels between women may lead to insults about each other's having inadequate vaginas, and this, in turn, may lead to mutual self-exposure of the genitals,

---

[99] Ibid., p. 237.
[100] Ibid., p. 233.

whose relative merits are then assessed by bystanders. A woman who is proved inferior is greatly shamed.[101] In general, however, Gladwin is in close agreement with Sarason's interpretations based on the TAT stories.

The analysis of the Ulithian TATs, as noted above, is less detailed than Sarason's. Moreover, many of the psychologist's generalizations are of a cultural rather than psychological order. For example:

> Although cooperation is higher among males than females, the latter exceed the males a little on the category of Group Activity. One hypothesis to explain this difference is that the men are the main ones to gather food and that they do this in a cooperative way with other men, whereas the women may prepare and cook the food alone. The females' concern with group activity may be largely in connection with the goal of Amusement (*e.g.,* dancing).[102]

Here are some of the more psychological TAT deductions concerning the Ulithians: These people are cooperative, basically optimistic people. Suicide and insanity are seldom mentioned in the stories and are probably rare. There is much concern with food and with work to attain it. Sexuality and menstruation do not seem to pose particular problems. Amusements are highly valued. Despite the basic optimism, there are many expressions of dysphoria in the stories. Feelings of anger and sadness are expressed, especially among adult males.

> They [the Ulithians] experience a full variety of emotions, but their general concreteness is evidenced here, as well, for their dysphoric emotions are confined to specific situations, are not extremely intense, and have no traumatic consequences. . . . Their concreteness and overwhelmingly group-oriented approach make for a lack of friction, but at the expense of abstract thought and individual differences.[103]

The ethnographer is in general agreement with these points. Incidentally, Sarason also speaks of "concreteness" in discussing the mental approach of the Trukese, but derives this from the Rorschach protocols rather than from the TAT stories.[104]

The foregoing examples seem to me to show that the TAT is a useful projective technique in cross-cultural studies. But there are those who disagree. In a book on projective techniques which emphasizes the TAT, Bernard I. Murstein concludes that projective

---

[101] Ibid., pp. 110, 244.

[102] Lessa and Spiegelman, "Ulithian Personality . . . ," p. 286.

[103] Ibid., p. 298.

[104] Gladwin and Sarason, *Truk: Man in Paradise,* pp. 225–26.

tests, including the TAT, have not demonstrated their usefulness in cross-cultural studies. However, he reports on only a few such studies and seems to draw his negative conclusion largely from a summary by Gardner Lindzey on the generally poor quality of this research.[105]

The anthropologists who have used the TAT generally seem to feel that it is a good technique; some believe it to be preferable to the Rorschach. This is Gladwin's view:

Interpretation of the Rorschach in any setting necessarily requires more inference than the TAT because the Rorschach presents a less structured stimulus, and its interpretation rests on a larger series of assumptions about unconscious psychological processes derived from our own culture than does the TAT.[106]

Bert Kaplan has expressed a similar preference for the TAT over the Rorschach.[107] Sarason has discussed the different contributions made by the two tests in the Truk study. The rigid "concrete" mental approach of the Trukese was more evident in the Rorschach than in the TAT, but the Rorschach gave no evidence about food anxiety.[108]

From the Rorschach we were able to detect a sexual concern but from the TAT we were able to elaborate on the context of such concern. The Rorschach enabled us to see how the Trukese were likely to handle aggressive conflicts by avoidance and suppressive mechanisms, but the TAT tells us more about the situational contexts in which these conflicts arise.[109]

This suggests (as Sarason recommends) that both tests should be used in the field.

It may be pointed out that various special picture tests with limited objectives have been used by anthropologists in ways similar to the TAT, although for somewhat different purposes. Walter Goldschmidt and Robert B. Edgerton have used a picture technique in studying the value systems of Menomini Indians. Edgerton made use of a series of drawings in his study of farming and pastoral tribes in East Africa. William Caudill showed a series of drawings to Japanese

---

[105] Bernard I. Murstein, *Theory and Research in Projectives (Emphasizing the TAT)* (New York: John Wiley & Sons, 1963), pp. 346–50.

[106] L. L. Langness and Thomas Gladwin, "Oceania," in F. L. K. Hsu (ed.), *Psychological Anthropology* (Cambridge, Mass.: Schenkman Publishing Co., 1972), p. 179.

[107] Kaplan, in Hsu (ed.), ibid.

[108] Gladwin and Sarason, *Truk: Man in Paradise,* p. 220.

[109] Ibid., p. 454.

subjects as a way of eliciting prevalent emotional themes and values. Seymour Parker employed pictures as a stimulus to reveal attitudes toward ethnic identity among Eskimo villagers, and George and Louise Spindler have used a set of drawings to find out attitudes toward various activities and occupations among the Blood Indians of Alberta, Canada. Richard H. Solomon has shown a series of modified TAT-like pictures to Chinese subjects in order to elicit attitudes toward authority. In each of these cases, drawings were made appropriate to a special cultural setting and designed to elicit particular kinds of responses.[110]

SUGGESTIONS FOR FURTHER READING

A recent review of projective techniques is A. I. Rabin (ed.), *Projective Techniques in Personality Assessment. A Modern Introduction* (New York: Springer Publishing Co., Inc., 1968). See also Bernard I. Murstein, *Handbook of Projective Techniques* (New York: Basic Books, Inc., 1965). For the cross-cultural application of projective techniques, see Gardner Lindzey, *Projective Techniques and Cross-Cultural Research* (New York: Appleton-Century-Crofts, 1961).

Some cross-cultural studies which were discussed in the first edition of this book but omitted in this edition because of space limitations are: Bert Kaplan, *A Study of Rorschach Responses in Four Cultures*, Papers of the Peabody Museum of American Archeology and Ethnology, Harvard University, Vol. 42, No. 2 (1954); Anthony F. C. Wallace, *The Modal Personality of the Tuscarora Indians as Revealed by the Rorschach Test*, Smithsonian Institution, Bureau of American Ethnology, Bulletin 150 (Washington D.C.: U.S. Government Printing Office, 1952); and D. G. Mulligan, "Maori Adolescence in Rakau. A Thematic Apperception Test Study," Victoria University College Publications in Psychology, No. 9, *Monographs on Maori Social Life and Personality*, No. 2, Department of Psychology, Victoria University College (Wellington, New Zealand, 1957).

An interesting application of the Thematic Apperception Test to the study of bilingualism is available in Susan M. Ervin, "Language and

---

[110] Walter Goldschmidt and Robert B. Edgerton, "A Picture Technique for the Study of Values," *American Anthropologist*, Vol. 63 (1961), pp. 26–47; Robert B. Edgerton, *The Individual in Cultural Adaptation. A Study of Four East African Peoples* (Berkeley, Calif.: University of California Press, 1971); William Caudill, "Patterns of Emotion in Modern Japan," in Robert J. Smith and Richard K. Beardsley (eds.), *Japanese Culture: Its Development and Characteristics* (Chicago: Aldine Publishing Co., 1962), pp. 115–31; Seymour Parker, "Ethnic Identity and Acculturation in Two Eskimo Villages," *American Anthropologist*, Vol. 66 (1964), pp. 325–40; George Spindler and Louise Spindler, "Researching the Perception of Cultural Alternatives: The Instrumental Activities Inventory," in Spiro (ed.), *Context and Meaning in Cultural Anthropology*, pp. 312–27; Richard H. Solomon, *Mao's Political Revolution and the Chinese Political Culture* (Berkeley, Calif.: University of California Press, 1971).

TAT Content in Bilinguals," *Journal of Abnormal Psychology,* Vol. 68 (1964), pp. 500–07.

Hallowell's essays on the Chippewa, including his Rorschach studies, are available in his *Culture and Experience* (Philadelphia: University of Pennsylvania Press, 1955).

Since most of the chapter on the Chippewa (Ojibwa) Indians which appeared in the 1963 edition of *Culture and Personality* has been omitted in this edition, let me take this opportunity to give some of the references in it. Ruth Landes is the author of the following works: "The Personality of the Ojibwa," *Character and Personality,* Vol. 6 (1937), pp. 51–60; *Ojibwa Sociology,* Columbia University Contributions to Anthropology, Vol. XXIX 1937; *The Ojibwa Woman* (New York: Columbia University Press, 1938); "The Ojibwa of Canada," in Margaret Mead (ed.), *Cooperation and Competition among Primitive Peoples* (New York: McGraw-Hill Book Co., 1937); and a more recent publication, *Ojibwa Religion and the Midéwiwin* (Madison, Wis.: University of Wisconsin Press, 1968).

Bernard J. James is the author of "Some Critical Observations Concerning Analyses of Chippewa 'Atomism' and Chippewa Personality," *American Anthropologist,* Vol. 56 (1954), pp. 283–86; and "Social-Psychological Dimensions of Ojibwa Acculturation," *American Anthropologist,* Vol. 63 (1961), pp. 721–46. See also Ernestine Friedl, "Persistence in Chippewa Culture and Personality," *American Anthropologist,* Vol. 58 (1956), pp. 814–25; and Stephen T. Boggs, "Culture Change and the Personality of Ojibwa Children," *American Anthropologist,* Vol. 60 (1958), pp. 47–58.

An attack on some of the culture-and-personality studies of the Chippewa is launched in Harold Hickerson, "Some Implications of the Theory of Particularity or 'Atomism' of Northern Algonkians," *Current Anthropology,* Vol. 8 (1967), pp. 313–43. For an ethnohistoric account of the Chippewa, see Harold Hickerson, *The Chippewa and Their Neighbors: A Study in Ethnohistory* (New York: Holt, Rinehart & Winston, 1970).

chapter *14*

Drawing Analysis

Much less use has been made of drawing analysis than of the Rorschach Test or TAT in culture-and-personality studies. Many anthropologists have collected drawings in the course of fieldwork, but few have done anything with them. This has been largely due to a general feeling that while there might be something in drawing analysis, it appears to be too intuitive and impressionistic a technique to have much validity, a feeling reinforced by the strong criticisms which some psychologists have made of interpretations of the Machover Draw-a-Person Test.[1] However, drawing analysis has been widely used in clinical practice in conjunction with the Rorschach and TAT. The approach would seem to have advantages for culture-and-personality studies. Drawings are relatively easy to collect in the field, are not time consuming, and do not require much equipment—mainly paper, pencils and crayons. Problems of verbal communication and translation are at a minimum. The technique is particularly useful with children, with shy subjects, and with people who, for one reason or another, find it difficult to communicate verbally. Drawings provide a permanent expression of personality. Hammer believes that this expression is less influenced by the administrator than in the case of the Rorschach or TAT. He also considers it to be a more direct manifestation of personality:

---

[1] Richard H. Blum, "The Validity of the Machover DAP Technique," *Journal of Clinical Psychology,* Vol. 10 (1954) , pp. 120–25; C. Swenson, "Empirical Evaluations of Human Figure Drawings," *Psychological Bulletin,* Vol. 54 (1957) , pp. 431–66.

"The subject's Rorschach percepts must, first, be translated into, and second, be communicated in, verbal language. In drawings, on the other hand, the subject expresses himself on a more primitive, concrete, motor level."[2]

Against the use of drawing analysis in cross-cultural studies is the argument that a subject's drawings reflect cultural traditions, local art styles and mannerisms, a point which has been demonstrated by many studies.[3] Both Jane Belo's Balinese subjects and Cora Du Bois' Alorese were unfamiliar with pencil and paper and had not drawn before. The Balinese children's drawings, however, were vigorous and complex, while the drawings of the Alorese children were weak and infantile. Perhaps the reason for this contrast is that Bali has a rich art tradition, while Alor has not. Balinese children's drawings, moreover, are patterned after the classical Balinese style, while drawings of Alorese children have little or no relation to the adult art.[4]

Wayne Dennis, who expresses some skepticism of the Machover test's validity, tells us that when Bedouins are asked to draw a person, they make very small drawings, averaging only two inches high and consisting largely of straight lines and darkened surfaces. Dennis ascribes these traits to the fact that what little art is known to the Bedouins consists largely of small geometric decorations.[5] On the other hand, Orotchen children and young people in Siberia who had never previously handled pencil and paper before and who had no traditions of figurative art made very good drawings,[6] and I have seen drawings by Naskapi Indian children, also previously unfamiliar with pencil and paper and lacking rich art traditions, which

---

[2] E. F. Hammer, *The Clinical Application of Projective Drawings* (Springfield, Ill.: Charles C Thomas, 1958) , pp. 600–601, 607.

[3] For example, A. C. Haddon, "Drawings of Natives of British New Guinea," *Man*, Vol. 4 (1904) , pp. 33–36; Anne Anastasi and John P. Foley, Jr., "A Study of Animal Drawings by Indian Children of the North Pacific Coast," *Journal of Social Psychology*, Vol. 9 (1938) , pp. 363–74; William Stephens Taylor, "A Note on Cultural Determination of Free Drawings," *Character and Personality*, Vol. 13 (1944) , pp. 30–36; Jane Belo, "Balinese Children's Drawings," in Margaret Mead and Martha Wolfenstein (eds.) , *Childhood in Contemporary Cultures* (Chicago: University of Chicago Press, 1955) , pp. 62–69. Copyright 1955, University of Chicago Press.

[4] Cora Du Bois, *The People of Alor. A Social Psychological Study of an East Indian Island*, with Analyses by Abram Kardiner and Emil Oberholzer (Minneapolis, Minn.: University of Minnesota Press, 1944) , p. 566.

[5] Wayne Dennis, "The Human Figure Drawings of Bedouins," *Journal of Social Psychology*, Vol. 52 (1960) , pp. 209–19.

[6] Anna Schubert, "Drawings of Orotchen Children and Young People," *Journal of Genetic Psychology*, Vol. 37 (1930) , pp. 232–44.

showed very good draftsmanship. Moreover, while both Manus and Alor lack strong art traditions, Manus and Alorese children do not draw in the same way.

The problems involved here are complex and merge with the question of whether or not one can analyze the art of a people for clues to their personality tendencies. Does the character of Bedouin art itself in some way reflect the Bedouin personality? The interpretation of art will be explored in Chapter 15. In the present chapter I will present some interpretations that have been made of Alorese and Chippewa children's drawings, to which will be added a discussion of the techniques developed by Machover, Dennis, Buck and others. I will also summarize some of my own research involving Buck's House-Tree-Person drawing test.

Alorese Children's Drawings

Alorese children were given paper and pencil and asked to draw whatever they wished. Drawings were obtained from 33 boys and 22 girls. Some differences were noted in subject matter: boys showed more interest in foreign and ceremonial objects, while girls showed a predominance of tattoo designs. (They were nearing the age when tattooing takes place.) Plants formed the largest content category for both sexes, followed by animals for boys and tools for girls. Buildings came third for both groups. Human beings were drawn with relative infrequency—7 percent of the subjects portrayed for boys and only about 1 percent of those portrayed by the girls. This provides a contrast to patterns found in the drawings of Western children. Ruth Griffiths, in a study of English children's drawings, found the favorite subject of children's drawings to be the human figure; houses came next; then trees and flowers.[7] Helga Eng similarly found the human figure to be the most commonly drawn, followed by the house.[8]

When human figures were drawn by the Alorese children, sexual organs were often omitted, despite the Alorese children's familiarity with sex. Figures with the male organ were sometimes identified as female. An interesting phenomenon was noted: house forms and

---

[7] Ruth Griffiths, *A Study of Imagination in Early Childhood* (London: Kegan Paul, Trench, Trubner, & Co., 1935), pp. 199, 219, 222.

[8] Helga Eng, *The Psychology of Children's Drawings* (London: Kegan Paul, Ltd., 1954).

human figures often seem to be combined or merged, which was also true of human figures and trees, with hands and feet resembling branches and roots. In view of some assumptions associated with the House-Tree-Person Test, these identifications are noteworthy.[9] The Alorese children made no attempt to portray groups and showed practically no sense of composition or design. There were only four cases in which two objects were brought into some relationship—all drawn by boys. Du Bois noted no improvement in drawing over a month's time.

Dr. Schmidl-Waehner's "blind" analysis of this material is as follows:

They have a feeling of aloneness as evinced by the lack of strong pressure in the lines and by the neatness of the line itself. . . . They look like children who have good abilities but are apart from each other. There are good units but there is never unity. . . . Their relationships are poverty-stricken, as evinced by the fact that each figure is lost among others. . . . The absence of free curves suggests an inability to bring themselves affectively into contact with others. . . . They lack a creative approach, as evinced by the smallness of the forms, by the fact that they do not have large conceptions taking up a single sheet, that there is no formal unity, that there are very few free-flowing curves, and that there is a lack of variation in pressure and of spontaneous detail in the lines. Also, they lack the "differentiated curve" and the "differentiated rhythm" which are indexes of creativeness. . . . They realistically estimate bounds, as evinced by the way they stay well within margins and do not begin to draw objects which will spill over the edge of the paper. . . . They probably have some manual dexterity.[10]

As was noted in an earlier chapter, these findings closely agree with "blind" analyses based on other data—Rorschachs and life histories, which were independently interpreted by different specialists. Schmidl-Waehner made the prediction that these subjects would lack movement responses in the Rorschach Test—which was borne out.

A problematic question concerns the omission of sexual organs. Du Bois remarks that, in the light of the children's knowledge of anatomy, this omission should indicate either strong castration fears

---

[9] An identification of house with person appears in the drawing of a female American patient anticipating surgery. She drew a rather anthropomorphic house with arms and small feet. See Bernard C. Meyer, Fred Brown, and Abraham Levine, "Observations on the House-Tree-Person Drawing Tests before and after Surgery," *Psychosomatic Medicine*, Vol. 17 (1955), p. 442.

[10] Du Bois, *The People of Alor*, pp. 584–85.

or their opposite—a lack of concern about sex. The latter alternative was considered more likely.[11] This is a point on which Géza Roheim strongly disagreed; in fact, he claimed that fear of castration was *the* outstanding factor in the make-up of the Alorese.[12] We need not become involved in this controversy. Either way, it seems that Schmidl-Waehner's pioneer "blind" analysis was a very successful one.

Chippewa Children's Drawings

Aside from Schmidl-Waehner's Alorese interpretation, the best study that I know of in the "blind" analysis of a collection of drawings is by Michal S. Lowenfels. The drawings in question were 267 spontaneous drawings made by 78 Chippewa children (44 boys, 34 girls) collected by Ruy Coelho at Lac du Flambeau in 1946 as part of A. I. Hallowell's group study. (The age range was from below 6 to 16 years of age). Lowenfels assayed a group characterization based upon a "blind" analysis of these drawings.

The writer did not have access to either the Rorschach or TAT data until she had completed her analysis of the drawings and had written the group interpretations, nor did she study the recent work of Dr. Hallowell and others on the psychological characteristics of the Ojibwa. The writer made no systematic study of Ojibwa ethnology.[13]

The drawings were scored according to a system combining the criteria of formal analysis devised by Elkisch and Schmidl-Waehner, with more weighting given to the latter's system. Drawings of human figures were analyzed according to Machover's method, by and large, "such as profile as an indicator of evasiveness in personal relationships, and the significance of arms and arm placement for indication of the quality of contact with the environment."[14]

Statistical methods of interpretation were not used. "It was felt that the total pattern of characteristics a child manifested were more important than the presence or absence of a single trait. The crucial question in group personality derivation is the way in which certain

---

[11] Ibid., p. 586.

[12] Géza Roheim, *Psychoanalysis and Anthropology. Culture, Personality, and the Unconscious* (New York: International Universities Press, 1950), p. 264.

[13] Michal S. Lowenfels, "Free Drawings as a Projective Test in Cross-Cultural Investigations" (unpublished master's thesis, The University of Pennsylvania, 1950), p. 31.

[14] Ibid., p. 43.

traits tend to cluster together."[15] The children were, however, rated for 64 personality traits, such as rigidity, constriction, and so forth.

Some of the author's conclusions are as follows:

Approximately two-thirds (63%) of the children approach the world in an essentially constricted, rigid fashion. In general this group tends to be overcontrolled and to manifest strong compulsive tendencies. Within this framework of inflexibility and a need to control the situation at all times, we find that 30% are in addition markedly introversive, passive and withdrawn.

The other major grouping represents the remaining third (37%) of the children and differs more in degree than in quality. This group, while also manifesting constriction and overcontrol, tends to show less compulsivity and less of inflexible static approach.[16]

In general, there is evidence of an avoidance of emotional involvement with others; evasive, stereotyped, and superficial relationships prevail. Lowenfels illustrates this by the treatment of human figures. Of the 47 percent of children who drew some human form, 37 percent drew only heads; 68 percent drew figures in profile—an indication of evasiveness, according to Machover.[17] If two human figures were drawn on the same page, they tended to be drawn back to back or front to back. Only one child drew a group of interacting human figures. There is a lack of emotional drive, a sense of defeat and resignation, combined with a good deal of anxiety and depression.

"Twenty-five percent of the total group used no color and an additional ten percent used only one or two colors. The children using more color tended to use either a pale or a dark color scale. The children who used less than three colors, or used a pale or dark color scale, usually coupled this with the violent and aggressive use of red."[18] There was little evidence of spontaneity, except for aggressive outbursts. "In child after child there was expression of affect hunger, of frustrated passive-dependency needs coupled with a fear of affective involvement."[19] Lowenfels hypothesizes that this must stem from parental rejection, since parents probably have the same kind of personality as the children—aloof and insecure.

This assessment agrees strikingly with interpretations based on

---

[15] Ibid., p. 45.

[16] Ibid., pp. 47–48.

[17] The drawing of heads rather than full figures is paralleled by the emphasis on human detail responses in the Lac du Flambeau Rorschachs.

[18] Ibid., p. 50.

[19] Ibid., p. 52.

other data concerning the Chippewa—life histories, Rorschachs, and TATs, as has been noted in previous chapters.

Lowenfels goes on to note some differences between boys and girls. The latter show more rigidity, constriction, and stereotypy, but also more emotional control than the boys. They manifest a preoccupation with glamor and sex. However, they portray the male figure as "weak, ineffectual, and smaller than the female."[20] Many of the girls show tendencies toward sexual delinquency, which may stem from the need to satisfy affect hunger.

Boys are more withdrawn, introversive, and passive. There is more repression but also less emotional control, with outbursts of aggression manifest. The girls behave in a more conventional and socially approved manner than the boys. The author presents a series of individual cases, accompanied by photostats of some drawings and the associated scoring charts. These analyses seem unstrained and convincing, at least to me.

We have, then, two cases of "blind" analysis of drawings—Alor and Chippewa. In both, considerable agreement appeared in relation to interpretations based on projective tests, life history material, and observational data. In both cases the children were free to draw whatever they liked—not required to draw a person, house, or tree, for instance. Both analyses were based primarily upon formal criteria —largely those suggested by Schmidl-Waehner. The success of these two experiments suggests that drawing analysis can be profitably pursued cross-culturally. But I think that future studies in this field should not depend on formal criteria alone, but should draw upon the symbolism of content. This can best be done, I believe, by using Buck's House-Tree-Person (H-T-P) Test. Within the latter, Machover's Draw-a-Person (DAP) Test can be incorporated. The DAP Test has been applied cross-culturally, although with some negative results.[21] Let me describe the administration of the Machover and Buck tests and discuss some of the assumptions associated with them.

THE DRAW-A-PERSON (DAP) TEST

In the Machover test the subject is given a medium-soft pencil with an eraser on it and a blank sheet of $8\frac{1}{2} \times 11$ inch paper. He is

---

[20] Ibid., p. 56.

[21] John J. Honigmann and Richard N. Carrera, "Cross-Cultural Use of Machover's Figure Drawing Test," *American Anthropologist,* Vol. 59 (1957) , pp. 650–54.

asked to draw a person. These purposefully vague instructions leave
the sex of the person drawn to the subject's choice. Once the first
drawing is completed, the subject is given a second blank sheet and
asked to draw a female, if he has drawn a man first, or a male, if he
has drawn a woman. The words "female" and "male" are used instead of "woman" or "man" because the subject may prefer to draw
a boy or girl instead of an adult.[22]

After the second drawing, the subject may be interrogated about
the figures he has drawn and asked to describe them or to make up
a story about them. However, this part of the test is optional.

Machover assumes that the drawings made by a person are projections, to some extent, of his own *body image*. This important, if
somewhat vague, concept must be examined briefly.

The Body Image, Ideal Type, and Group Values

Everyone has some sort of conception of what his body is like. This
"image" is built up from different sources; not only from what we
can see and feel of the body, but also from cultural traditions about
the body and from how other people regard us and treat us. One's
body image may be at variance with the physical facts. A man who
is paralyzed may deny it. An attractive woman may feel ugly. A phys-
iologically normal man may experience a confusion of sexual identification and feel somehow feminine, and a woman may have obsessive, unfounded notions that she gives off an awful odor. A man's
concept of himself as potent or impotent may be shaped by the attitudes of his sexual partner. Thus, a person's body image has social
and cultural sources, as well as physiological ones. The body image
is plastic and undergoes changes with growth and in response to illness, traumatic experiences, and mental disorder.

Clothes may become part of the body image and may supplement
felt deficiencies. This suggests a possible symbolic explanation for a
woman's concern with hats and handbags, or a man's with ties. Seeing
clothes as extensions of the body image lends added interest to cross-
cultural studies of dress, tattooing, and bodily decoration, the use of
masks in primitive rituals, and practices of transvestism in cultures
like the Iatmul.

The pioneer work on the body image is Paul Schilder's *The Image
and Appearance of the Human Body*[23] from which the foregoing

---

[22] Karen Machover, *Personality Projection in the Drawing of a Human Figure*
(Springfield, Ill.: Charles C Thomas, 1949), p. 29.

[23] Paul Schilder, *The Image and Appearance of the Human Body* (New York:
International Universities Press, 1950).

ideas have been drawn. A more recent contribution to this field, which summarizes earlier studies, is *Body Image and Personality* by Seymour Fisher and Sidney E. Cleveland.[24]

What evidence is there that a subject tends to project his own body image when he makes a drawing of a person?

Kotkov and Goodman compared drawings made by obese women with those of an ideal-weight control group and found that the horizontal area covered by the obese female drawings was greater than that of the ideal weight female drawings. Head areas were larger and shoulders more square in the obese female drawings. These contrasts appeared in the drawings of the female, not of the male figure.[25] Berman and Leffel found a general correlation between the somatotypes of 39 male subjects and the body build of the figures drawn.[26] In a study of World War II leg amputees, S. Levy found that the lower parts of the body were often omitted.[27] Lauretta Bender claims that children with severe body defects, such as a shortened leg, often depict them in their drawings.[28]

While these citations provide some evidence for the idea that an individual's drawing of a person may reflect his body image, it should be evident that such correlations are not invariable. Fat women sometimes draw thin female figures; husky men may draw weak ones, and subjects who have had legs amputated may draw men with legs.

Silverstein and Robinson collected drawings from 22 children who had suffered from poliomyelitis, together with drawings from 44 children in normal health; but judges were unable to distinguish between these two groups of drawings. The authors concluded that one cannot assume that the physical body, the body image, and the drawn person are in isomorphic relation.[29]

Wayne Dennis, who has made a large collection of children's

---

[24] Seymour Fisher and Sidney E. Cleveland, *Body Image and Personality* (Princeton, N.J.: D. Van Nostrand Co., 1958). One cross-cultural application of this concept appears in G. Morris Carstairs, *The Twice-Born. A Study of a Community of High-Caste Hindus* (Bloomington, Ind.: Indiana University Press, 1958), in which there is a chapter on "The Hindu Body-Image."

[25] Benjamin Kotkov and Morris Goodman, "The Draw-a-Person Tests of Obese Women," *Journal of Clinical Psychology,* Vol. 9 (1953), pp. 362–64.

[26] S. Berman and J. Leffel, "Body Type and Figure Drawing," *Journal of Clinical Psychology,* Vol. (1953), pp. 368–70.

[27] Sidney Levy, "Figure Drawing as a Projective Test," in L. E. Abt and L. Bellak, *Projective Psychology* (New York: Grove Press, 1959), p. 276.

[28] Lauretta Bender, *Child Psychiatric Techniques* (Springfield, Ill.: Charles C. Thomas, 1952).

[29] A. B. Silverstein and H. A. Robinson, "The Representation of Orthopedic Disability in Children's Figure Drawings," *Journal of Consulting Psychology,* Vol. 20 (1956), p. 340.

drawings from different parts of the world, states that most boys, when asked to draw a man—a whole man, not just the head and shoulders—draw men who are young or middle aged, not old men; and they draw men in good health, not deformed or crippled men. Only five drawings in Dennis's cross-cultural collection of 2,550 drawings had mouth corners turned down. No crippled man was drawn, and only three fat men. Negative, cartoonlike figures are seldom drawn by children under 14 years of age. Dennis's assumption is that children get their values from adults and that what the children draw expresses *group* values.[30]

An alternative to both the body image hypothesis and Dennis' value hypothesis is that children draw what they are familiar with. However, Dennis points to some data which are inconsistent with this view. In Sudan, traditional clothes—long, unbelted cotton gowns—are worn by the majority, but 85 percent of the urban children drew people in Western clothing. In San Cristobal, Chiapas, Mexico, where dominant Ladinos and the more submissive lower class Chamula Indians live in proximity (like the Mixtecans of Juxtlahuaca, Mexico, and Gillin's Ladinos and Indians of San Carlos, Guatemala), no Indians were drawn in 400 Ladinos' drawings, while the Chamula Indian boys, though wearing Indian dress, drew 70 percent Ladinos and only 30 percent Indians.

None of the white American children in Dennis's sample drew a Negro, while few Negroes drew Negroes; they drew whites.[31] Similar findings have been made in South Africa.

In a large group of 2,300 African children, aged 6 to 13, who took the Goodenough Draw-a-Man Test, only six subjects drew figures identifiable as native. The most typical figures drawn by the African children were: (1) a Wild West hero, with spurs, boots, and sombrero, and (2) a Man-about-town, idle, well-dressed, and smoking a cigarette.[32]

These findings suggest that ideal types and values are expressed in these drawings more than body image or what is familiar to the drawer. In the case of children's drawings, at least, it seems that children tend to draw what they admire, envy, or would like to be.

---

[30] Wayne Dennis, *Group Values through Children's Drawings* (New York: John Wiley & Sons, 1966).

[31] Ibid.

[32] V. Hunkin, "Validation of the Goodenough Draw-A-Man Test for African Children," *Journal for Social Research* (Pretoria, S. Africa, Vol. I, No. I [July 1950]), pp. 52–63.

Some poignant illustrations of this principle are given by Robert Coles. Coles used drawing analysis as one way of learning about the feelings and attitudes of Negro children in the South during the time when schools were first being integrated and hostile white crowds were howling murderous threats at the few Negro children who came to the school. One of these children was a six-year-old girl named Ruby. Coles noted that during a four-month period, Ruby never used brown or black crayons, except to indicate soil on the ground, which she covered with green grass. "She did, however, distinguish between white and Negro people. She drew white people larger and more lifelike. Negroes were smaller, their bodies less intact. A white girl we both knew to be her own size appeared several times taller."[33] When drawing herself or other Negro children, Ruby might leave out an eye, fingers, or toes, or even a mouth, but none of these features were omitted in her drawings of white people. It may be that the tendency for Negro children to draw white rather than Negro persons is changing or will change with more political and social involvement in black power and allied movements.

Not only do people sometimes draw persons of another race in the DAP test; they may also draw someone of the opposite sex in the first drawing, although it is more common for subjects to make same-sex drawings.

Sidney Levy has asserted that of a group of 5,500 adult subjects 89 percent drew their own sex first. The subjects in question included college and high school students, clinic and hospitalized patients, and patients undergoing therapy.

If the 280 drawings secured from patients in clinics and hospitals are treated separately, the percentage of those who draw their own sex first is reduced to 72 per cent of the latter group. Most of the research reported in the literature verifies that: (1) the great majority of people draw their own sex first; (2) the incidence of deviation from the rule is greater among individuals who request or require psychotherapy. There has been some variation in the actual percentages reported.[34]

Machover has suggested that if the subject first draws a member of the opposite sex, this may be an indication of homosexuality.[35] There are at least three studies, however, which tend to disprove this

---

[33] Robert Coles, *Children of Crisis. A Study of Courage and Fear* (Boston, Mass.: Little, Brown and Co., 1967), p. 47.

[34] Sidney Levy, "Projective Figure Drawing," in E. F. Hammer, *The Clinical Application of Projective Drawings*, pp. 91–92.

[35] Machover, *Personality Projection in the Drawing of a Human Figure*, p. 101.

assumption. In a group of 50 male homosexual soldiers in the Army, 46 drew the male figure first.[36] From a study of drawings by Sing Sing prisoners, E. F. Hammer has concluded that there is not much support for the idea that the sex of the first figure drawn can "serve as an index of the subject's sexual identification or indicate the presence of psychosexual conflicts or sexual inversion."[37] Florence R. Mainord presents evidence that women tend to draw the opposite sex first more than men do (43.4 percent of women did so in a college psychology class containing 175 females). She also points out that Levy does not state the proportion of male and female subjects in his group. Mainord concludes: "It is not surprising that in our society, which is predominantly androcentric, that a large proportion of females might draw the male figure first and thereby reflect recognition that the role of the male has many advantages not afforded the female."[38]

Hammer suggests that the person drawing may reflect any of the following: (1) a self-portrait, depicting what the subject feels himself to be, (2) an ego-ideal or ideal self, and (3) the depiction of a significant person in the subject's life.[39] The drawing may represent a kind of blend of all three. A difficulty here is in detecting which of the selves is more significant in the drawing.[40]

These qualifications make the task of drawing analysis seem very complicated. It would therefore seem advisable to combine drawing analysis with other data on the subject, such as the Rorschach, TAT, and biographical information.

Aspects of DAP Interpretation

There are many approaches to the interpretation of DAP drawings, such as: consideration of the size and placement of the drawn figures, a comparison of the male and female figures with respect to

---

[36] Alman J. Barker, Jerry K. Mathis, and Clair A. Powers, "Drawings Characteristic of Male Homosexuals," *Journal of Clinical Psychology,* Vol. 9 (1953), pp. 185–88.

[37] Emanuel F. Hammer, "Relationship between Diagnosis of Psychosexual Pathology and the Sex of the First Drawn Person," *Journal of Clinical Psychology,* Vol. 10 (1954), pp. 168–70.

[38] Florence S. Mainord, "A Note on the Use of Figure Drawings in the Diagnosis of Sexual Inversion," *Journal of Clinical Psychology,* Vol. 9 (1953), p. 189.

[39] E. F. Hammer, *The Clinical Application of Projective Drawings,* p. 197.

[40] Bernard I. Murstein (ed.), *Handbook of Projective Techniques* (New York: Basic Books, 1965), p. 655.

size and treatment. Formal characteristics may be interpreted in the manner of Elkisch, Schmidl-Waehner, and others who pay attention to such features as line pressure, size and placement of the drawn figure, rigidity of forms, and so forth.[41]

Machover and Levy cite examples of possible diagnostic indicators. They note that an emphasis on the mouth may reflect an "oral" dependent tendency. If the nose is made unduly large, this may represent compensatory efforts on the part of a man who has feelings of impotence. Enlargements or distortions of the ear may express sensitivity to social criticism or paranoid tendencies. A subject's treatment of the neck is significant because it represents a link between the head (rational control) and the body (impulse life). (A similar "link" is the waist.) Omission of the neck may indicate immaturity or regression, while a very long, extended neck may be an indication of a schizoid or schizophrenic personality. The manner of portraying arms and hands may reflect the nature of the subject's ego development, social adaptation, and mastery of the environment, and from their treatment one may get clues to the sense of confidence, efficiency, ambition, or aggression of the subject. Emphasis on rounded hips in a male subject is said to be a possible indication of homosexuality. Sexually disturbed subjects sometimes refuse to complete the drawing below the waistline or sketch it in only vaguely. Omission of feet may be an expression of insecurity. Treatment of clothing may also be significant for personality clues. Machover and Levy agree in various symbolic interpretations, some of which seem a bit *a priori*.

Buttons are usually indicators of a dependent, infantile, inadequate personality. If buttons are drawn along the mid-line, the subject may have somatic preoccupations. If buttons are drawn on cuffs and other equally inconspicuous areas, the subject is probably an obsessive-compulsive individual. The latter will also draw shoelaces, wrinkles, etc.[42]

Ties are interpreted as phallic symbols. Pockets are held to indi-

---

[41] Paula Elkisch, *Children's Drawings in a Projective Technique*, Psychology Monographs, 1, 58 (1945); Trude Schmidl-Waehner, "Formal Criteria for the Analysis of Children's Drawings," *American Journal of Orthopsychiatry*, Vol. 12 (1942), pp. 95–103; and *Interpretation of Spontaneous Drawings and Paintings*, Genetic Psychology Monographs 33 (1946), pp. 3–72; Rose H. Alschuler and La Berta Weiss Hattwick, *Painting and Personality. A Study of Young Children* (Chicago: University of Chicago Press, 1947); Louis H. Stewart, *The Expression of Personality in Drawings and Paintings*, Genetic Psychology Monographs, 51 (1955), pp. 45–103.

[42] S. Levy in *Projective Psychology*, p. 281.

cate dependency, oral and affectional deprivation. For further illustrations of this approach, the reader should consult the works of Machover and Levy.

The question is sometimes raised as to whether or not drawing ability or art training may not distort the results of a DAP Test. Walter A. Woods and William E. Cook have argued that hands and feet are more difficult to draw than other body parts, and that the manner of representing hands is a function of the subject's level of proficiency in drawing. In that case "symbolic" interpretations of hands hidden behind the body, or of an inadequate treatment of hands may be invalid.[43]

Hammer does not believe that art training distorts the results of a DAP Test. He points out that those who learn to write in school by the Palmer handwriting method soon develop a characteristic and idiosyncratic style of handwriting.

Art training, by its nature, favors free expression more than does handwriting training, and as such it probably contaminates projective drawing interpretation even less than handwriting training does handwriting analysis.

In fact, it has frequently been observed that one's skill as an artist serves to enhance the capacity for expressing one's self graphically in the projective media rather than to interfere with it.[44]

In regard to the degree of success with which drawings were interpreted, Schmidl-Waehner found no difference between the art products of students with and those without art training.[45]

Some Adult Chippewa Drawings

In the summer of 1944, I collected Draw-a-Person drawings from Tom Badger and his wife, Julia. After my return to New York I asked Dr. Werner Wolff of Bard College if he would assay a "blind" interpretation of these drawings, and he consented.

It may be of interest here to supplement Lowenfels' analysis of children's drawings with Dr. Wolff's interpretation of drawings

---

[43] Walter A. Woods and William E. Cook, "Proficiency in Drawing and Placement of Hands in Drawings of the Human Figure," *Journal of Consulting Psychology*, Vol. 18 (1954), pp. 119–21.

[44] E. F. Hammer, *The Clinical Application of Projective Drawings*, p. 50.

[45] Trude Schmidl-Walhner, *Interpretations of Spontaneous Drawings and Paintings*, Genetic Psychology Monographs, No. 33 (1946), pp. 3–70.

made by two adults: (1) Tom Badger, a conservative old-timer, priest of the Medicine Dance religion, in his seventies, and (2) Julia Badger, his wife, whose fantasies were discussed in Chapter 12.[46] The drawings appear in Figures 14–1, 14–2, and 14–3. It may be noted that Julia drew a woman and a man together on one page at the top left-hand corner. Tom first drew a man, then was asked to draw a woman on a separate sheet of paper.

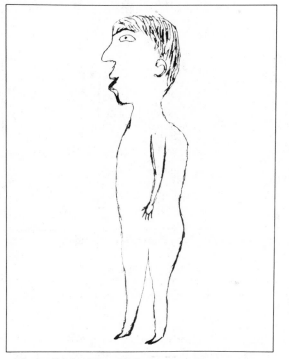

Figure 14–1. Tom Badger's Drawing of a Man

Dr. Wolff pointed out the continuous interruption in Tom Badger's line and said:

He stutters in his drawing. There is also an absence of pressure. The man's head is very large compared with the rest of the body, and there is a strong emphasis on the mouth. Although the man is naked, he has no sex organs.

[46] Julia's autobiography appears in the Appendix to my *Acculturation and Personality among the Wisconsin Chippewa;* Tom's autobiography may be found in my "Reminiscences of a Chippewa Mide Priest," *The Wisconsin Archeologist,* Vol. 35, No. 4 (1954), pp. 83–112.

Figure 14–2. Tom Badger's Drawing of a Woman

In Tom's drawing of the woman there is an emphasis on the breasts. She is dressed; he covers her sex organs. Both figures have very weak arms and legs.

The emphasis on the head would indicate a stress on matters of the intellect over things of the body. This is supported by the weak arms and legs. He is probably a passive person, always dreaming, thinking, and not acting.

The woman is given more importance than the man through more detail, more realistic observation, more perseverance, more strokes. The woman is bigger in both horizontal and vertical size; she has attributes, such as clothing.

His strokes indicate strong inhibition, which is supported by the sexual frustration implied in his omission of the man's sexual organs.

The entire picture is very primitive. If we used a Freudian interpretation in explaining his emphasis on the mouth, we might say that frustration in the sexual sphere has resulted in a transfer to the oral region. All of the interest is centered in the upper half of the body, not below.[47]

From my personal impressions of Tom Badger, I would not have described him as being so passive and ineffectual. Tom struck me as being rather practical and quite competent in manual crafts.

---

[47] Dictated to me by Dr. Werner Wolff.

When I knew him, he was still making serviceable birchbark canoes. He had some ability in carpentry. However, he may well have been an emotionally dependent person, for similar impressions along these lines appear in some analytic remarks made by Dr. Pauline Vorhaus about Tom Badger's Rorschach record at a Rorschach Workshop at Crafts, New York, in 1946:

Human relationships are smooth enough. There is no underlying hostility (*Fc, FC, M*). But there is some confusion about sex. His form level is good, except for the sexual responses. He has a great deal of sensitivity and tact and gives the impression of being a conformer (*P%*). His *M*'s have a passive, holding-on quality, indicating his dependency.

Figure 14–3.   Julia Badger's Drawing of a Woman and Man (drawn in the upper left-hand corner of a page)

Here are Dr. Wolff's comments on Julia Badger's drawing:

She is younger. On the whole, however, she is in an even more childish level than her husband, although she has much more artistic ability and a greater "life of the soul" than he. He might have a greater intellectual life. She sees more details, ornaments, more individualized expression. Tom's approach is schematic. Hers is individual.

She has a high feeling for proportion, distributions in space. For instance, the distance from the head line on the woman to the breast line is equal to the distance from the breast line to the line of the feet. Her drawing is very symmetrical. The feet are right in the center of the woman's skirt. The two figures are mirroring and complementary. Notice the two bands which go to the left and the right. The woman's left foot is big, her right foot small. The man's left foot is small, his right foot big.

She shows more inner shape, patterning, and order than he; but this may be either positive or negative. Many neurotics and psychotics have a high degree of order in their drawings. They may be striving for order, because they really have none.

She shapes the woman more than the man. He has no real face, no neck, no hands. The thing the man holds is smaller than the one the woman holds. The man has no hair, but she has. She is conscious of her leading role and of her dominance over him. But she has the feeling of belonging to him—a motherly attitude, perhaps—although we can't tell from the drawings. She tries to emphasize that the woman and the man belong to each other. This is indicated by the feather on both of the heads.[48]

Much of this analysis seems valid and in agreement with data from other sources.[49] While some of Dr. Wolff's deductions are hard to assess, there is nothing in these interpretive comments which is in contradition to the known facts about Tom and Julia Badger. With the knowledge of hindsight, I feel that some aspects of Julia's drawings might have given a cue to her rather schizoid nature. The placement of the figures high on the page would be interpreted by John N. Buck as a tendency to involvement in fantasy. It is of interest in this connection to note that in Kotkov and Goodman's study of obese women's drawings, the female drawing was found to be more often in the top left-hand third of the page than in the case of the ideal weight control group.[50]

The stunted, flipperlike limbs suggest Mrs. Badger's passivity. The narrowness of the woman's neck is a bit exaggerated, and the conventional turned-up smile has a stereotyped, childish character, Dr. Wolff did not label Julia "schizoid," but he did point out that she is a dreamy person.

---

[48] Dictated to me by Dr. Werner Wolff.

[49] See Julia Badger's fantasies, Chapter 12.

[50] Kotkov and Goodman, "The Draw-a-Person Tests of Obese Women," p. 363.

THE HOUSE-TREE-PERSON TEST

Buck's House-Tree-Person (H-T-P) Test[51] can incorporate, and add to, Machover's DAP Test, particularly if a chromatic series of drawings is added to the pencil drawings. A four-page form sheet, with pages smaller ($7 \times 8\frac{1}{2}$ inches) than those used in the Machover test is given to the subject. One surface is exposed at a time, at first with the long axis of the page placed horizontally before him. (Later, for the tree and person drawings, this axis is vertical.) The subject is asked to draw as good a house (and later, as good a tree and person) as he can. He may erase as much as he wishes and take as much time as he wants.

While the subject is drawing, the tester makes observations on his behavior and times his performance. After the drawings are completed, the subject is given a rather lengthy interrogation incorporating 64 questions.

It is believed that a subject is apt to feel less self-conscious about drawing a house or tree than a person, and is less aware that he may be giving himself away. The house and tree were selected for this test because of their symbolic associations, their universal familiarity, and because they form among the earliest subject matter of children's drawings.

Interpretation of the test is based partly on stylistic features (for instance, shading is believed to indicate anxiety), placement on the page (use of the upper half of the page, for example, is held to indicate a preoccupation with fantasy), and symbolic interpretations of the content.

The latter have been particularly developed by Buck. Some of his symbolic equations seem aprioristic and subject to many qualifications. However, Buck's individual H-T-P analyses carry a good deal of conviction.

A subject's drawing of a house may involve many different things. The drawing may reflect such things as (1) his present home situation, (2) his past home situation, (3) his "dream house" of the fu-

---

[51] John N. Buck, "The H-T-P Technique, A Qualitative and Quantitative Scoring Manual," *Journal of Clinical Psychology,* Part I, Vol. 4 (1948), pp. 317–96; Part II, Vol. 5 (1949), pp. 37–74.

ture, (4) a symbolization of the mother, or (5) a symbolization of the self.[52]

Emphasis on chimneys—if they are detailed or lofty—is believed to indicate sexual inadequacy, with a compensatory assertion of virility, comparable to the drawing of a large nose or tie on the male person drawing. Abundant smoke may indicate anxiety.

The tree drawing is considered to be often the subject's most revealing self-portrait, since it involves less awareness of self-revelation than the person drawing. It is believed to express a "deeper" level of personality than the person drawing. According to Hammer, it is less susceptible than the latter to change on re-testing.[53]

Some of the symbolic meanings attached to the tree and its parts in H-T-P literature are as follows: The choice of tree is considered significant—whether a depressed weeping willow, sturdy oak, or heavily laden apple tree. The trunk is said to represent ego strength. The branches represent reaching out toward the environment. The roots indicate the nature of contact with reality. Reinforcement of the trunk lines may suggest a striving to maintain one's personality intact, while very sketchy trunk lines may indicate a sense of impending personality collapse.[54]

Holes in the tree may be expressive of traumatic experiences, and it has been suggested that their height from the ground may give a clue to the age of the trauma.[55] Children frequently draw apple trees and seem to sometimes identify themselves with the apples. Mothers may also draw apple trees, but identify their children with the apples and themselves with the tree. A dead tree is considered a bad sign, with a poor prognosis. So is a "split" tree, in which the two sidelines of the trunk form no connection at top or bottom; this is considered to indicate schizophrenia. Many more features of the tree drawing are interpreted in symbolic fashion; these examples will have to suffice.

After the subject has completed the four drawings—house, tree, person, and person of sex opposite to the one already drawn—he may be given the same test once more, but this time with colored crayons. This series is believed to tap a "deeper" layer of personality than the pencil drawings. The subject's reactions to color may be

---

[52] E. F. Hammer, Lecture at Workshop on Projective Drawings, New York, Summer 1961.

[53] E. F. Hammer, *The Clinical Application of Projective Drawings*, p. 172.

[54] Ibid., p. 184.

[55] M. Levine and E. Galanter, "A Note on the 'Tree-and-Trauma' Interpretation in the H-T-P," *Journal of Consulting Psychology*, Vol. 17 (1953), pp. 74–75.

studied, as in the Rorschach Test. The selection of colors may be of diagnostic significance—whether depressive browns and blacks are used, explosive reds, or inhibited cool colors. It has been suggested that the association of crayons with childhood may lead to the tapping of deeper personality levels. With crayons, erasing is not possible. This factor, together with the requirement to do the test all over again, may lead to a more emotional self-expression on the subject's part. Hammer has presented some case histories which support these assumptions rather well.[56]

A possible drawback of the H-T-P Test for ethnological field workers is the length of the inquiry following the test. In this inquiry Buck asks questions such as these: How many stories does that house have? Is that your own house? Whose house were you thinking about while you were drawing? Would you like to own that house? Why? Is that a happy, friendly, sort of house? Do you feel that way about most houses? Why? What kind of tree is that? About how old is that tree? Is that tree alive? Is any part of the tree dead? What part? Is that tree by itself or is it in a group of trees? What is the weather like in this picture? What does that tree make you think of? Is it a healthy tree? What is there about it that gives you that impression? Is it a strong tree?

For the person drawing, Buck asks for the age, sex, and identity of the person, what he is doing, thinking, and feeling. Is he well? Is he happy? How do you feel about that person? Do you feel that way about most people? Why?

Buck also asks what the house, tree, and person need most, and many other such questions.[57]

I have made use of a modified form of the H-T-P technique in two cross-cultural studies, and it seems to me to be a promising technique. My two studies involved: (1) comparisons of H-T-Ps of Japanese, Indian, and American college students, and (2) an experiment designed to gauge the psychological effects of voluntary sterilization among married men in rural Maharashtra, India. Each of these experiments will be briefly described.

Japanese, Indian, and American H-T-Ps

The H-T-Ps were administered on a group basis to introductory psychology classes in Tokyo, Japan, and Poona, India, and to an

---

[56] Hammer, *The Clinical Application of Projective Drawings,* pp. 208–35.

[57] J. N. Buck, "The H-T-P Technique . . . ," pp. 328–41.

introductory anthropology class in Milwaukee, U.S. Most of the students in all three groups were freshmen, 18–19 years of age. There were 84 females and 28 males in each sample.[58] The students were asked to write their age and sex but not their names. Two person drawings were asked for in the manner described above. Students were allowed about 10 minutes for each drawing.

After the drawings were completed, the students were asked the following questions:

1. How old is the house? How old is the tree? How old are each of the two persons?
2. What is the best part of the house? What is the best part of the tree? What is the best part of each of the two persons?
3. What is the worst part of the house? (Same question asked for the tree and each of the two persons).
4. What does the house (the tree, each of the two persons) need most?
5. Is the tree alive or dead?
6. Write a description of each of the two persons.

The Indian students were also asked to write a description of the house.

These questions, suggested by Emanuel F. Hammer, were designed as a substitute for Buck's postdrawing interrogation.

The instructions and questions were given in both English and Marathi in Poona, and in Japanese in Tokyo by the instructors of the class. Answers were generally written in the native language, later translated into English by interpreters.

It was my impression that in each H-T-P administration the students enjoyed taking the test, a welcome break in the academic routine.

No particular hypotheses were established beforehand. The aim was to see whether there were any characteristic differences in the drawings of these three groups of students, and, if so, whether they seemed to reflect differences in cultural traditions, personality patterns, or some combination of the two.

---

[58] For an explanation of this sample and details on range of ages, see Victor Barnouw, "Cross-Cultural Research with the House-Tree-Person Test," in John N. Buck and Emanuel F. Hammer (eds.), *Advances in the House-Tree-Person Technique: Variations and Applications* (Los Angeles, Calif.: Western Psychological Services, 1969), p. 420. The two studies described below are discussed in more detail in this publication, from which tables 14–1 and 14–2 have been drawn.

There turned out to be various characteristic differences in the three collections of drawings. Profiles and back views were more common among the Poona students than in the other two groups. Nine Indian girls drew a woman as seen from behind; three Tokyo girls drew rearview female figures, while no Milwaukee girls did so. According to Buck, profile and back views indicate a reluctance of the subject to face his environment, a desire to withdraw and hide his inner self. But the frequency of Indian female back views may be influenced by the fact that all three groups of girls emphasized the hair, and an Indian girl's hair, either rolled up at the back of the head or hanging down in a pigtail, is best seen from a rear view perspective.

Partial figures, showing only head and shoulders, were rare among the Japanese drawings but common in both the American and Indian samples. American heads tended to be larger than the Indian ones. Nine Milwaukee students drew large heads, filling up most of the page. This was not done by any Japanese or Indian students.

The groups of students differed in the age of the person drawn. Twenty of the Poona girls drew girls below the age of 12 years; only 11 Tokyo girls and 8 Milwaukee girls did so. Eighteen Poona students drew children playing (e.g., skipping rope) ; only 6 Tokyo and 5 Milwaukee students did so. The Poona students also tended to give lower ages for the tree in the tree drawing than did the Japanese or American students. Forty Indians gave an age below 16, as against 21 Japanese and 23 Americans. One gets an impression that in this sample of Indian girls there was some clinging to childhood or nostalgia for it. The Poona girls did not draw persons of their own age as often as did Tokyo and Milwaukee girls; nor did they draw as many "glamorous" pretty girl drawings, which may be related to the greater stress on romantic love in the United States and Japan. The Indian girls come from a conservative (mostly Brahman) section of Poona, where marriages are generally arranged and where dating does not usually take place.

References to religion appeared more frequently in the Indian girls' H-T-P descriptions (16), than in the Japanese (4), or American (1).

The Tokyo students tended to draw larger figures than did the Indian or American students, and they drew fewer small figures. This gave me the impression that there is a sense of self-confidence among the Japanese students; on the other hand, it may be related to the art instruction they receive, for according to Wayne Dennis, "The Japanese child is taught that whatever the size of his paper his drawing should occupy most of the space available."[59] However, the Japanese drew more small houses than did the other groups. Fifteen Tokyo students drew a house about two inches long or less, as opposed to only one Poona student and three in Milwaukee.

In writing descriptions of the house, the Indian students often wrote in a euphoric vein, not at all characteristic of the American students.

In their descriptions of the persons drawn, the Japanese often referred to the pressures of school work and a drive for achievement. The Milwaukee girls often described the female person drawn as being popular, well-liked by others, fun to be with, intelligent, well-balanced, and warmhearted, evidently a wish-image or ideal type.

While the data are not self-explanatory, we seem to have material here which can be compared cross-culturally. There clearly are group differences in these H-T-Ps. Some of the most interesting information to be derived from them comes not from the drawings themselves but from the written descriptions of the persons drawn.

The Sterilization Project

A second experiment with the H-T-P concerned the psychological effects of voluntary sterilization among married men in rural Maharashtra, India. Thousands of men have been sterilized by vasectomy in the state of Maharashtra in recent years in the effort to check population growth. Although interviews have been conducted with vasectomized men to assess their reactions to the operation, no "depth" techniques had been used to gauge whether or not there might be any harmful psychological consequences. That was the purpose of my own research, which had the cooperation of the Office of Family Planning in Poona.

In 1963, I gave the Rorschach Test and the House-Tree-Person Test to 100 men from three rural villages near Poona. Fifty of these men had been sterilized; 50 had not. The subjects were selected by officials of the Office of Family Planning. I was not told which men had been sterilized and which had not. They were all married men,

---

[59] Dennis, *Group Values through Children's Drawings*, p. 71.

generally with two or three children or more; most were poor farmers with little education. Data were collected from each subject as to his age, number of children, occupation, approximate income, caste, religion, and number of years of school attendance. I had an excellent interpreter. The tests and interviews were given in the villages where the men lived.

In the modified H-T-P our subjects were asked to draw a house, a tree, and the persons in the usual manner. The interpreter and I went over the drawings with each subject, asking for clarification of ambiguous features. We asked for the sex and ages of the persons drawn, the age of the tree, what type of tree it was, and what the persons were doing.

Two sorting experiments were undertaken with the data. The first experiment was to determine to what extent I and two of my colleagues, Emanuel F. Hammer and Blanche G. Watrous, could guess from the projective data which of the men had been sterilized. Hammer was chosen for this project because of his work with eugenically sterilized patients in the United States, to whom he gave the H-T-P Test. Hammer showed that castration anxiety appears in symbolic form in the H-T-P drawings of a group of subjects about to undergo eugenic sterilization. Their drawings were contrasted with those of a control group, and some rather consistent differences were found in the treatment of chimneys, branches, tree trunks, arms, legs, feet, and other items which may be seen, in traditional Freudian fashion, as having a phallic significance.[60]

A correct list of the sterilized men was kept on file at the Office of Family Planning in Poona. Our guesses as to which 50 men had been sterilized were sent in to the Office of Family Planning. Then we received the correct list.

A second experiment involved our drawing up a list of the 50 men whom we judged to be better adjusted and a list of 50 less well-adjusted men. On reception of the correct list of sterilized men, we were able to see what correlation there might be between the experience of sterilization and the degree of adjustment, as measured by our tests. Details of the procedures involved in the construction of our lists will not be given here; they are set forth in the article cited. Suffice it to say that our guesses for the list of the 50 men who

---

[60] Emanuel F. Hammer, "An Investigation of Sexual Symbolism: A Study of H-T-P's of Eugenically Sterilized Subjects," *Journal of Projective Techniques,* Vol. 17 (1953), pp. 401–13.

had been sterilized were poorer than chance. We had 22 correct hits, while 25 would have been chance. But this does not mean that our experiment can be written off as a failure, for an interesting association was found between our list of better adjusted men and the sterilized list. This association is shown in Table 14–1.

Table 14–1. ASSOCIATION BETWEEN STERILIZATION AND ADJUSTMENT RATINGS

	Sterilized Men	*Unsterilized Men*	*Total*
Better adjusted	33	17	50
Less well-Adjusted	17	33	50
Total	50	50	100

Here it will be seen that 33 of the men whom we rated as better adjusted fell in the sterilized group. This figure exceeds chance expectations and is significant at the level of 1 percent.

Two interpretations of these data suggest themselves. One is that it was only the better adjusted men who were able to decide upon and to go through with the sterilization operation. Perhaps it was the men with *less* castration anxiety who elected to be sterilized. This explanation has the virtue of accounting for our inability to correctly guess which men had been sterilized. We may have been looking for castration anxiety in the wrong group of men.

Table 14–2 shows that the unsterilized men seemed to show more body preoccupation in giving anatomical and sexual responses than did the sterilized men. Some of the unsterilized men, indeed, gave what we considered to be classic castration responses. One man, in responding to Rorschach Card I, said "Sterilization. Something is cut there." (A Whole response.) Another saw a broken penis in both cards I and VI; the one seen in Card VI (upper central detail) was "broken from an operation." Still another man saw a "penis which may be cut in two" in the bottom central detail of Card V. We guessed that these men had been sterilized, but they actually had not.

Body preoccupation seems to be a widespread characteristic among these Maharashtrian peasants. According to Carstairs, anxiety about loss of semen is the "commonest expression of anxiety neurosis among the Hindu communities of Rajasthan, and perhaps elsewhere as well."[61] This kind of anxiety may therefore be common among both the sterilized and unsterilized men in our sample.

A second possible interpretation of the association between better adjustment and sterilization shown in Table 14–1 is that sterilization removes the fear of further pregnancies. Such men might have

Table 14–2. ANATOMICAL AND SEXUAL RESPONSES IN THE RORSCHACH TEST

	Sterilized Men	*Unsterilized Men*	*Total*
Anatomical	18	34	52
Sexual	8	20	28
Total	26	54	80

less fear of economic disaster, and thus have a more relaxed view of life. Both interpretations may have some validity. They are not conflicting.

If further work is done with projective tests in exploring the psychological consequences of sterilization, it is suggested that the men be tested both before and after the operation. Ideally, three tests should be made: (1) shortly before the operation, (2) shortly after the operation, and (3) after the lapse of several months.

To conclude, the H-T-P seems to me to be a useful research technique whose potentialities deserve further exploration in cross-cultural studies in culture-and-personality. It is easy to employ, requires little equipment, and the drawings provide a permanent record of a subject's expression of personality. Allowances must be made for cultural factors, such as the differences in house types and trees present in different parts of the world. But rich material seems to be available in the employment of the H-T-P technique, as well as in other procedures in drawing analysis, such as those used by Wayne Dennis, Trude Schmidl-Waehner, and others.

SUGGESTIONS FOR FURTHER READING

I recommend the books by Machover, Dennis, Buck, Hammer, and Alschuler and Hattwick mentioned above, and the articles by Schmidl-Waehner and Elkisch which have been cited. For another potential device

---

[61] Carstairs, *The Twice-Born,* p. 87.

in drawing analysis, see Robert C. Burns and S. H. Kaufman, *Kinetic Family Drawings* *(K-F-D)* (New York: Brunner/Mazel, 1971).

Film: A beautiful film about a class of Japanese elementary school students and the drawings they make is *Children Who Draw Pictures,* Brandon Films, black and white and color (38 minutes).

chapter 15

The Analysis of Folklore
and Art

THREE APPROACHES TO FOLKLORE

One may distinguish three general kinds of studies which concern folklore in relation to personality. First, there are explorations by such pioneer psychoanalysts as Freud, Jung, Abraham, Rank, Reik, and Roheim, which sometimes range over the field of mythology and folklore at large. The aim of such studies has generally been to demonstrate the occurrence of Oedipal motifs and other Freudian features in the folklore of various societies and to provide evidence for the universality of Freudian symbolism, or, in Jung's case, archaic archetypes.[1]

A second, very different approach to folklore involves cross-cultural surveys, with scoring systems and statistical correlations. There are three studies which make use of the Human Relations Area Files and attempt to relate certain emphases in folklore to certain patterns in child training. McClelland and Friedman have studied Coyote stories taken from eight American Indian groups and scored them for the need for achievement evidenced in the tales. Their next step was to see how these findings correlated with child training patterns in the different groups.[2] A study along simi-

[1] For a bibliography of such literature, see Weston La Barre, "Art and Mythology," in Bert Kaplan (ed.), *Studying Personality Cross-Culturally* (Evanston, Ill.: Row, Peterson & Co., 1961), pp. 394–403.

[2] David C. McClelland and G. A. Friedman, "A Cross-Cultural Study of the Relationship between Child Training Practices and Achievement Motivation Appearing

lar lines was undertaken by Child, Storm, and Veroff, who obtained a sample of 12 tales from each of 46 cultures. The stories were scored for *n*-Achievement; the socialization practices of the groups in question were then analyzed in relation to achievement-oriented behavior.[3] In another study, George O. Wright scored 12 folktales for each of 33 societies—drawn from Oceania, Asia, Africa, North and South America—for aggressive and nonaggressive acts. Again, an effort was made to relate the presence of aggressive themes in folklore to patterns of child training.[4]

A third approach to folklore and its relation to personality is one which involves a more or less intensive analysis of the folklore of a particular society. Such an approach generally rests, at least implicitly, on two assumptions: first, that there is a basic or modal personality structure characteristic of the society in question; second, that cultural integration tends to develop a certain consistency in folklore. Contrasts may be made between the folklore of this group with that of other societies, to highlight its characteristic patterns. Parallel features may be noted in other aspects of the culture, or in the Rorschach or TAT protocols of members of the group. One example of such a study is Virginia Heyer's analysis of the relations between men and women in 60 Chinese stories.[5] Another is Margaret Lantis' analysis of Nunivak Eskimo mythology.[6] In this case, however, Lantis explicitly states that she is *not* trying to derive the basic personality structure of the Nunivak Eskimos from their folklore, although she *is* trying to find some "major central tendencies in emotion, attitude, and behavior and to give a 'personality construct.' "[7]

In any event, the present chapter will be devoted to the third

in Folk Tales," in Guy E. Swanson, Theodore M. Newcomb, and Eugene L. Hartley (eds.), *Readings in Social Psychology* (rev. ed.; New York: Henry Holt & Co., 1952), pp. 243–49.

[3] Irvin L. Child, Thomas Storm, and Joseph Veroff, "Achievement Themes in Folk Tales Related to Socialization Practice," in John W. Atkinson (ed.), *Motives in Fantasy, Action, and Society* (Princeton, N.J.: D. Van Nostrand Co., 1958), pp. 479–92.

[4] George O. Wright, "Projection and Displacement: A Cross-Cultural Study of Folk-Tale Aggression," *Journal of Abnormal and Social Psychology*, Vol. 49 (1954), pp. 523–28.

[5] Virginia Heyer, "Relations between Men and Women in Chinese Stories," in Margaret Mead and Rhoda Metraux (eds.), *The Study of Culture at a Distance* (Chicago: University of Chicago Press, 1953), pp. 221–34; see also John Hast Weakland, "An Analysis of Seven Cantonese Films," ibid., pp. 292–95.

[6] Margaret Lantis, "Nunivak Eskimo Personality as Revealed in the Mythology," *Anthropological Papers of the University of Alaska*, Vol. 2, No. 1 (1953), pp. 109–74.

[7] Ibid., p. 162.

approach, the one just mentioned. It does not seem necessary at this point to review the exhaustive surveys of the pioneer psychoanalysts. Nor will the second approach be dealt with here. This is largely because these cross-cultural studies seem rather inconclusive. The Child, Storm, and Veroff study does not confirm the previous study by McClelland and Friedman. Moreover Child and his coworkers confess that their analysis of *n*-Achievement in folktales has led to no very conclusive results.

Wright is more confident and claims that "Enough consistency of trends has been found in the present study to suggest that the relationships of child-training practices and the expression of aggression in folk tales are real and not accidental or spurious."[8] Be that as it may, the focus of this chapter will be on the third approach, the analysis of the folklore of a particular society.

PERSONALITY CLUES IN FOLKLORE

Our primary question, then, is: Can one learn something about the personality tendencies in a particular society from a study of its folklore? Certainly, the values and attitudes prevalent in a society are often clearly expressed in its folklore. Kwakiutl folktales, for example, reflect the great concern with rank and prestige described by Benedict, Boas, and others. As Boas has written: "There are tales that consist of nothing else than the enumeration of crests and privileges obtained by marriage or war, and in other tales also names, crests and privileges occupy an inordinate amount of space."[9]

The Ifugao of the Philippines are similarly concerned with status and with the payment of debts—concerns which are, again, manifest in their folklore. "The only emotional situations to be found in any myths are those connected with the increase of the pigs, the chickens and the rice, the collection of debts (or the reverse—escape from the clutches of creditors), the overcoming of enemies, the shunting aside of sorceries, evil spirits, and sickness."[10] It would

---

[8] Wright, "Projection and Displacement," p. 528.

[9] Franz Boas, *Kwakiutl Culture as Reflected in the Mythology*, Memoirs of the American Folklore Society, Vol. 28 (1935), p. 176. The Northwest Coast emphasis on status is also reflected in "Cinderella" themes of a rags-to-riches type. See Betty Uchitelle Randall, "The Cinderella Theme in Northwest Coast Folklore," in Marian W. Smith (ed.), *Indians of the Urban Northwest* (New York: Columbia University Press, 1949), pp. 243–85.

[10] Roy F. Barton, *The Mythology of the Ifugaos,* Memoirs of the American Folklore Society, Vol. 46 (1955), p. 17.

seem likely, therefore, that the analysis of a people's folklore would provide insights into their personality tendencies.

However, three objections may be raised against such analyses. First is the argument that the folklore may reflect culture-and-personality patterns of an earlier stage in the society's history and not those of the present. Old folktales, like those of Grimm, may persist as a kind of cultural lag and may not be particularly relevant to the current scene. Conservatism of folklore appears in Zuñi folklore, as well as in our own. In Zuñi tales, as Benedict tells us, ". . . entrance to the house is by means of a ladder to the roof and down another ladder from the hatchway, yet doors have been common in Zuñi since 1888 and are today universal except in the kivas."[11] In the same way, archaic stone knives figure in the stories, rather than the store-bought knives known to the present-day Indians. We will come back to this problem presently.

A second objection to the psychological analysis of a society's folklore is that folktales diffuse widely from one society to another. For example, many stories, like the Magic Flight, and various trickster episodes, were told widely throughout aboriginal North America.

A third objection is that we cannot tell, from the presence of particular folklore motifs, whether these directly express a characteristic pattern in the society, or whether they represent wish fulfillment or reaction formations. Eskimo folklore, to cite an illustration, is full of tales expressing tension between husband and wife; aggressive women seem to be feared. Can we assume from this that male-female relations were less satisfactory among the Eskimo than in societies where such folklore motifs are less prominent? Love stories with happy endings, on the other hand, are a notable feature of our own culture. But does this mean that our marriages are happier than marriages in societies where such themes are not stressed? (There are, of course, stories of contrasting type in our culture.)

Our problem, then, is: Does a particular theme express actual relationships, wishful fantasies, fears, or reaction formations? And how can one determine which is the case?

In answer to the first of the objections mentioned, one might say that stories will not continue to be told if they are too much at variance with the prevailing values and attitudes of the society. David Riesman has shown that present-day children's stories have assumed quite a different complexion from those of our more inner-

---

[11] Ruth Benedict, *Zuñi Mythology,* Columbia University Contributions to Anthropology, Vol. XXI (1935), p. xiv.

directed forebears,[12] and Martha Wolfenstein has pointed out differences between a modern American version of "Jack and the Beanstalk" and the earlier English one.[13] This point, reminiscent of Spengler's and Benedict's demonstrations of selectivity in the borrowing of cultural items, would apply to the second objection as well. A folktale may be borrowed but subtly transformed in the process. Such distortions and changes of emphasis should provide clues to the dominant attitudes and values of the group.

The Tlingit, Tsimshian and Kwakiutl of the Northwest Coast are neighboring tribes which share a host of folktales in common. Nevertheless, these bodies of folklore have different emphases, as Franz Boas has pointed out. For instance: "In the tales of marriages with supernatural being or animals, the theme of the offended animal seems to belong primarily to the Tlingit, while the theme of the helpful animal is much more frequent among the Tsimshian."[14] (Boas did not try to account for this difference; he simply pointed it out.) In the same way, Boas drew attention to a number of contrasts between Kwakiutl and Tsimshian mythology. The Tsimshian have tales in which a father turns down all of his daughter's suitors; daughters are most carefully guarded. There are, however, stories of girls who marry against their father's wishes. Such themes do not form the foundation of Kwakiutl plots. Moreover: "The love between husband and wife, between brothers and other members of the family is dwelt upon in Tsimshian tales and forms one of the motives used to develop the plot. This is rarely the case among the Kwakiutl."[15]

Neighboring tribes, then, may share folktales in common, and much diffusion may take place between them. But characteristic patterns and emphases may still be found in the folklore of such groups. This point has been made for other culture areas than that of the Northwest Coast—for instance, by Haeberlin in his contrast of the Pueblo and Navaho tribes.[16]

The third objection to analyzing folklore for clues to personality

---

[12] David Riesman, with Nathan Glazer and Reuel Denney, *The Lonely Crowd, A Study of the Changing American Character* (Abridged; New York: Doubleday, Anchor Books, 1953), pp. 120–31.

[13] Martha Wolfenstein, "'Jack and the Beanstalk': An American Version," in Margaret Mead and Martha Wolfenstein (eds.), *Childhood in Contemporary Cultures* (Chicago: University of Chicago Press, 1955), pp. 243–45.

[14] Franz Boas, *Tsimshian Mythology*, Bureau of American Ethnology Annual Report, No. 31 (Washington, D.C., 1916), p. 874.

[15] Franz Boas, *Kwakiutl Culture as Reflected in the Mythology*, p. 174.

[16] H. K. Haeberlin, *The Idea of Fertilization in the Culture of the Pueblo Indians,* American Anthropological Association Memoirs, Vol. III, No. 1 (1916).

tendencies is that one cannot tell whether certain themes or motifs reflect existent patterns, or whether they express reaction formations or wish elements. The main answer to this must lie in familiarity with the culture and with the members of the society. Some further considerations may be added, however. The folklore of a society does not express all aspects of its people's life; and it is interesting to note which aspects of it form the focus of stories and which aspects are ignored. For example, one might expect the Eskimo to emphasize cold weather, snow, and ice, but weather is not an important feature of most of their stories. Instead, there is an emphasis on interpersonal relationships.[17] Sheepherding, at the present time, occupies an important part of Zuñi life, but there is no mention of it in Zuñi tales.[18] In the Northwest Coast area where the Clackamas Chinook Indians lived there was a widespread interest in seasonal rituals, girls' puberty ceremonials, marriage negotiations and rituals. Despite the interest, however, Clackamas Chinook folklore does not touch upon these matters. Their culture was also characterized by fears of sorcery and an interest in shamanistic cures, but there were few stories dealing with such concerns. Melville Jacobs explains this by saying that the society "had long since devised the daily means for airing feelings about these things," and goes on to conclude:

The point, then, is that the literature served needs for which the society had not provided public outlets. That which the culture truly repressed was the tension about women, grandparents, some other relatives, and in-laws. Here is the area of tensions where the screen of culture served. This is why poisoning, shamanism, rituals, and girls' puberty rites are so conspicuously absent from the stories. Stresses which were comparatively conscious, incessantly verbalized, and resolved in such completely public and institutionalized procedures as shamanistic curing, winter spirit-power performances, seasonal rituals, girls' puberty initiations, and marriage rites did not need to be projected onto the screen of a Myth Era. It was the suppressed tensions which found their way as if by subterranean streams, out into the light of literature and which thereupon dominated its expressive content. I think that psychoanalytic writers are essentially right in their conviction that myths are the screen for projecting that which is overtly denied and repressed and, one should add, for whose handling few or no cultural institutions exist.[19]

----

[17] Lantis, "Nunivak Eskimo Personality . . . ," p. 15. However, see also p. 113.

[18] Benedict, *Zuñi Mythology*, p. xiv.

[19] Melville Jacobs, *The Content and Style of an Oral Literature. Clackamas Chinook Myths and Tales*, Viking Fund Publications in Anthropology, No. 26 (New York, 1959), p. 130.

This is a useful hypothesis, which may help to explain the presence or absence of certain areas of life in the folklore of a group.

I have tried to answer three objections to the analysis of folklore for clues to personality tendencies in a particular society. (There may, of course, be other possible objections.) I have also stated two assumptions upon which such analyses depend: (1) that the society in question is characterized by a more or less distinctive basic (or modal) personality type, and (2) that cultural integration develops some consistency in the folklore material, thus imbuing it with characteristic features which may offer contrasts with folklore patterns in other societies.

Folklore from two hunting-gathering cultures will now be discussed to illustrate this approach: (1) the Eskimo of Nunivak Island, and (2) the Chippewa. Let us start with Margaret Lantis' analysis of Nunivak Eskimo mythology.

ESKIMO FOLKLORE: NUNIVAK ISLAND

Margaret Lantis collected folklore at Nunivak Island, off the Alaskan coast, where she also administered the Rorschach Test to 32 Eskimo subjects. The Rorschachs were interpreted independently by two analysts, Eugenia Hanfmann and Alice Joseph. We will turn to their Rorschach analyses later. First a few general comments on the folktales.

Lantis says that the stories show a good orientation to reality. A strong ego-ideal is presented in them. Lantis deduces that Nunivakers have a clear picture of their own goals and work toward them realistically.[20] "This is not a morbid mythology in which most of the characters die, overcome by the inherent conflict of their situation. Almost always, destructive forces are combated successfully."[21] Nevertheless, there is a good deal of aggression and bloodshed in the folklore. Lantis presents a "Table of Physical Dangers in Nunivak Mythology," in which the most frequently mentioned dangers are cutting or stabbing (usually both), and biting or eating. There are many tales of decapitation and dismemberment of bodies. When supernaturals are involved, it is the spirits who cut and bite the protagonist, not vice versa. Lantis points out that there are remarkably few cases of trickery and deceit, in contrast to Plains

---

[20] Lantis, "Nunivak Eskimo Personality . . . ," pp. 122–23.
[21] Ibid., p. 139.

mythology.[22] This contrast applies to Chippewa mythology as well, as will be apparent in the discussion of Chippewa folklore below.

A common theme in Eskimo folklore is that of a hero who overcomes obstacles. In an unpublished Ph.D. thesis by Frank J. Essene, cited by Lantis, it is stated that roughly one third of all Eskimo folklore falls under this heading. About half of these tales are about a poor orphan boy who ultimately triumphs over his enemies. He usually lives with a female relative—a grandmother or sister.[23] Individual achievement is stressed in Eskimo stories, rather than group cooperative effort, which may, however, appear in war narratives. There are not many parent-child tales.

An important theme is that of the haughty girl, who rejects her suitors or leaves her husband and insists on living alone. A husband, on the other hand, is rarely shown as leaving his wife.[24] Mother and grandmother figures are always depicted as good, but wives are often shown to be arrogant or aggressive. Lantis accounts for this negative picture of the wife by reference to some features of the old Nunivak culture. Men and boys of five years and over spent almost no time in the family home, but lived in a ceremonial house. At the age of 11 to 13 years a girl was usually married to a strange man of between 20 and 30 years. Such marriages, according to Lantis, were difficult and full of tension. Not only were the girls reluctant, but the men were apt to be disappointed in marriage, due to the early loss of the mother (through removal to the ceremonial house) and due to their frustrated hopes for a cherishing maternal wife.

This explanation may apply to the Nunivak Eskimo, but it should be noted that aggressive and dangerous women are also depicted in the folklore of the Central Eskimo, who do not have the institution of the men's ceremonial house.

A motif singled out for discussion by Lantis is that of oral aggression. She notes that Eskimo frequently use their lips and teeth in moistening and working skins, chewing boots, and eating meat. Thus, "the people always have before themselves images of both men and women cutting and biting some part of the animal. The cannibal women cutting off human heads and boiling them is not hard for a Nunivaker to imagine even though he has never known

---

[22] Ibid., pp. 131, 135.
[23] Ibid., p. 156.
[24] Ibid., pp. 116, 126.

a case of cannibalism."[25] Moreover, the Eskimo seem to have some sense of guilt for killing animals in order to live.[26]

Lantis deduces from Nunivak mythology that the "id-needs" of these people are not repressed. Sex and other bodily functions are presented naturally. There are strong restraints, however, on aggression. The Eskimo like to be with other people, but wish to maintain their individuality. Lantis finds that the most common defenses are wish-fulfillment, altering of reality, avoidance or flight, projection, reaction formation, and repression.[27]

Turning now to the Rorschach analysis, Dr. Hanfmann and Dr. Joseph scored each subject on a personality rating sheet. Lantis also scored them on the basis of her personal acquaintaince. These ratings did not agree very well, but there was good agreement on the summaries, according to Lantis. She does, however, point to some areas of disagreement in the Rorschach generalizations made by Hanfmann and Joseph. While some of these may be of minor importance, others seem hard to reconcile. For example, Joseph says that the Rorschach records indicate a free expression of emotion and great spontaneity, while Hanfmann finds a high degree of constriction. Joseph sees more aggression and anxiety and describes the anxiety as "focused," while Hanfmann labels it "diffuse."

However, there are also areas of agreement. The level of intelligence is declared to be "high average"; energy is rated high, and socialization is good. The Nunivak Islanders are declared to be prevailingly extroverted and conforming, but not submissive. There is evidence of preoccupation with sex, but no conflict or guilt about it, and an indication of dependency, associated with oral aggression. Although some features, like oral aggression, were noted both by Lantis in the folklore and by the Rorschach specialists in the protocols, the Rorschach analyses do not seem to throw much light on the folklore, or vice versa. The fact that some serious differences of opinion appear in the Rorschach analyses further complicates matters.

CHIPPEWA FOLKLORE

In contrast to the Eskimo, Chippewa tales do not stress achievement, and there are many stories of trickery and deception. This is

---

[25] Ibid., p. 135.
[26] Ibid., p. 136.
[27] Ibid., p. 164.

illustrated in a long Chippewa origin legend which I collected from Tom Badger in the summer of 1944.[28] This story tells of the experiences of Wenebojo, the Chippewa trickster culture hero. Many of the themes in this origin legend have their parallels in the trickster stories of other American Indian tribes, for example the flood and earth-diver episodes. But there are some characteristic features in the Chippewa cycle. If, for example, we compare this Chippewa origin legend with a Navaho one,[29] a number of contrasting features emerge.

Social Relations

There is much more collective action in the Navaho myth. The legend describes the experiences of classes of animals and human groups, while the Chippewa legend describes the adventures of a lone individual, Wenebojo.

Wenebojo's mother and grandmother disappear from the story after the opening section, while the father (the sun) plays no role beyond that of impregnation. Wenebojo calls all of the animals "brother," but he trades upon alleged kinship ties for purely selfish exploitative purposes. Wenebojo seems to be happiest when he is all alone. In this version of the Wenebojo cycle he never marries. William Jones presents a story in which the culture hero (here called Nanabushu) gets married,[30] and the Wisconsin Chippewa tell a story, which had a wide distribution in aboriginal America, of how Wenebojo "married" his two daughters through a ruse. But in most of the Chippewa tales about him, Wenebojo either lives alone or is described as living with his grandmother. In the origin legend I collected, the grandmother and mother soon drop out of the story.

The Navaho origin legend represents a marked contrast in these respects. Women figure as prominently as men in the Navaho myth, and the relationship between them is one of the main motifs. Men and women have their differences; at one point they attempt a sep-

[28] Victor Barnouw, "A Psychological Interpretation of a Chippewa Origin Legend," *Journal of American Folklore,* Vol. 68, No. 267 (1955), pp. 73–85; No. 268, pp. 211–23; No. 269, pp. 341–55.

[29] Aileen O'Bryan, *The Diné: Origin Myths of the Navaho Indians,* Smithsonian Institution, Bureau of American Ethnology, Bulletin 163 (Washington, D.C., 1956). In order to have the lengths of the two narratives roughly comparable, my remarks about the Navaho legend will be confined to its first 34 pages.

[30] William Jones, *Ojibwa Texts,* Publications of the American Ethnological Society, Vol. VII, Part I (New York, 1917), pp. 423–29.

aration, but soon find that they can't live without each other and make up again ". . . First Woman came and threw her right arm around her husband. She spoke to the others and said that she could see her mistakes, but with her husband's help she would henceforth lead a good life. Then all the male and female beings came and lived with each other again."[31] Later, yucca is rubbed over the woman's heart and the man's heart. "This was done so they would love each other; but at the same time there arose jealousy between the man and the woman, his wife."[32]

In the Chippewa cycle mother figures appear in the first and last episodes. In the first, Wenebojo and his two brothers are conceived when the sun causes a wind to blow up a girl's skirt and make her pregnant. In the last episode, the spirits give Wenebojo a set of "parents," who become the first members of the human race. Apart from these two episodes and the murder of a "grandmother" figure in another, women play no role in the myth whatever. The closest emotional bond in the Chippewa legend is that between Wenebojo and his adopted "nephew," a young wolf. Apart from this relationship, themes of close friendship and loyalty are absent.

Consider Wenebojo's relationships with his two brothers. The youngest brother is a stone, so he can't hunt with the other two and stays at home all the time. This begins to annoy Wenebojo, since their range of travel is limited. They must return to camp every day. Wenebojo tells his other brother that he would like to kill the stone. The brother remains noncommittal. The stone-brother has magically heard what Wenebojo said and asks, "Why don't you do what you were talking about? If you can do it, go ahead and start right now." Wenebojo accordingly tries to kill his brother.

Wenebojo beats the stone with a poleax but can't even scratch him. The stone says that he won't succeed that way. He instructs Wenebojo to build a fire and put the stone in it, and then, when the fire is red-hot, to throw water over it. Wenebojo does this; the stone cracks and dies.

This is the first death, the first murder. Now the two boys are free to travel wherever they wish. However, Wenebojo's brother walks more slowly than Wenebojo and easily gets tired. Wenebojo always has to wait for him to catch up. Finally he suggests to his brother that they dig a hole in the ground for the brother to stay in. After

---

[31] O'Bryan, *The Diné*, p. 8.
[32] Ibid., p. 33.

four days Wenebojo will come back and dig him up again. The brother agrees to this. Wenebojo digs the hole, the brother gets in, and Wenebojo covers him up. He sets up a stone to identify the place and goes off. More than four days go by, however. Wenebojo has forgotten all about his brother. When he finally remembers, he returns to the place, but his brother has gone by then and has made a road to the other world, over which Indians in the future will have to travel when they die.

Three times in this cycle irritation is expressed at being held back by others, and at one point an implicit regret is voiced that children take so long to mature and reach independence, whereas animals can walk shortly after birth.

Aggression and Duplicity

There are very few themes of aggression in the Navaho origin legend, while murders abound in the Chippewa narrative, the victims including Wenebojo's two brothers, his "nephew," two kings of the underwater spirits, the "grandmother" figure previously referred to, and various animals. Wenebojo is himself killed, but he revives.

In addition to these sadistic motifs there are also masochistic themes. The stone gives Wenebojo instructions as to how to kill him. In one episode Wenebojo pulls out his own intestines; in another he roasts his behind over a fire; in a third he chops off his own calf muscles.

Themes of duplicity, which are rare in the Navaho myth and in Eskimo folklore, are common in the Chippewa cycle. To give one example: Wenebojo meets a collection of water birds and tells them that he is going to make a place where they can dance. Wenebojo makes a sturdy wigwam, with only one entrance and covers all the holes in the structure. Then he tells the birds that he wants them to dance with their eyes closed. Anyone who opens them will have red eyes forever. While the birds dance with their eyes shut, Wenebojo goes about wringing their necks.

However, although it is never explicitly stated, there seems to be some notion of retribution in these stories, some conception that crime does not pay. At least, Wenebojo usually suffers punishment in these trickster episodes. On two occasions, after killing animals through trickery (one involving the birds just mentioned), Wenebojo is deprived of his meat, and someone else eats it all. The expression of hostile impulses seem to be attended by danger and some expectation of retribution.

In reading a collection of Chippewa folktales, like that of William Jones, one is struck by the recurrence of aggressive themes. A particularly cruel story, for example, concerns Wenebojo's revenge against his grandmother for making him fast. He comes home to find his grandmother enjoying sexual relations with his grandfather. Wenebojo then applies a burning stick to his grandfather's buttocks. The old man runs away. Wenebojo hopes to get something to eat, but his grandmother gives him nothing, and the next morning she says that he must fast for another day and go out hunting. Wenebojo goes to find his grandfather, kills him, cuts him up, and takes home some of the meat, which he asks his grandmother to cook. After they have eaten, he suggests that they go and bring home the rest of the meat. At the scene of the murder, the grandmother recognizes her husband's remains. Wenebojo makes her carry home some of the meat, and when they get home he tells her to cook it and to dance about the fire while the kettle is boiling. Then Wenebojo makes her eat some of the meat and tells her that she is eating her husband's penis.[33]

This story might be labeled an Oedipal legend. Elsewhere I have described two Chippewa stories of father-son conflicts which seem to be more directly Oedipal.[34]

Oral Themes

The importance of corn to the Navaho is suggested by reference to it on the first two pages of their origin legend and elsewhere. Some vegetables are referred to, and there are some themes of hunger, and a mention of bread cake.[35] But oral themes do not seem to be prominent, especially when comparison is made with the Chippewa origin legend. In the latter there are references to the mouth and to food or tobacco in various sections. As I mentioned, there are themes of oral frustration, in which food is cooked and

---

[33] Jones, *Ojibwa Texts*, p. 465.

[34] Barnouw, *Acculturation and Personality among the Wisconsin Chippewa*, pp. 49–50. The presence of such themes may be significant, for Stephens reports that for nearly all societies father-son conflict motifs in folklore are rare. See William N. Stephens, *The Oedipus Complex. Cross-Cultural Evidence* (Glencoe, Ill.: Free Press of Glencoe, 1962), p. 159.

[35] O'Bryan, *The Diné*, pp. 6, 7, 8, 16, 18.

ready to eat, but someone else enjoys the meal. Seemingly unpleasant food substances are referred to in some places, such as intestines and vomited food. In two episodes feces float around Wenebojo's mouth.

Anal Themes

There are no anal motifs in the Navaho origin legend. The presence of such themes is a striking aspect of the Chippewa narrative. There are many examples.

A bird indicates to Wenebojo that he would defecate if he ate a certain type of grass. Wenebojo is skeptical but eats some of it. Soon he begins to defecate and can't stop. He jumps into a deep hole, which fills up with feces, in which Wenebojo floats, with the feces around his mouth and nose. Later, Wenebojo is frightened by an unfamiliar sound; he is breaking wind—something he'd never heard before.

Wenebojo envies a fox who makes a nice tinkling noise. He begs the fox to make him the way he is, so that he can make a noise like that. The fox is reluctant, but at last he agrees. He makes Wenebojo find a round stone for him and asks Wenebojo to bend over. The fox then cuts around Wenebojo's rectum and ties the end of his intestines to the stone. When Wenebojo moves, it sounds like bells ringing. Wenebojo likes that. After he has walked a little way, however, the sound becomes fainter. He turns and sees that his intestines now stretch into the distance behind him. When he grabs them, they break off in his hands. Wenebojo then hauls in his guts and throws them over an elm tree, saying, "My aunts will have the benefit of eating this stuff when they are hungry." (When Wenebojo speaks of his "aunts" and later of his "uncles," he is thinking of the future race of Indians.) Wenebojo does this a second time, throwing his guts over another tree and says, "This kind will taste sweet. That's what they'll eat as long as the earth lasts."

While waiting for some birds to cook, Wenebojo becomes sleepy and decides to have a nap. He asks his rear end to keep watch and to warn him if the South Wind men approach. After Wenebojo has gone to sleep, the South Wind men come around a bend. Wenebojo's rear end breaks wind to warn him. Wenebojo wakes up, but the South Wind men hide. Since Wenebojo can't see anything, he goes back to sleep. The South Wind men again approach. This time they have some red dye, with which they plug up Wenebojo's rectum, so that it can't make a sound. They eat all the birds and then leave.

When Wenebojo wakes up, he finds that all the birds have been eaten. He feels the red dye in his rectum and pushes it in as far as it will go, saying, "All right, you can have this, if you want it so badly. You can keep it."

Angered at his rear end and determined to punish it, Wenebojo builds a fire and roasts his rear end over it. Then he walks through some brush, leaving a trail of scabs and blood. This is the origin of tobacco. Wenebojo walks through different kinds of brush in this way, creating different types of tobacco, one kind of which tastes "very good and sweet." He also slides down a mountain, leaving a trail of scabs, and says, "My aunts will cook these when they are hungry," thus creating another type of food.

It is striking that tobacco, the Indians' sacred link with the supernatural world, has its origin in the bloody scabs trailing from Wenebojo's rectum. Note that in two of the episodes just cited products of the anal region are labeled "sweet"—a type of tobacco, and the intestines which Wenebojo throws over the tree.

The anus appears in association with the mouth in many Chippewa stories. One character believes that he is feeding his brother in the dark, while in reality he is pushing food into a woman's anus. In another story Wenebojo makes his grandmother swallow some of her own fecal matter.[36] Again, in Jones' folklore collection Painted-Turtle feeds Bear his own feces, telling him that they're blueberries; and Bald-Eagle suckles her children at her buttocks.[37] In an anecdote told at Court Oreilles, Coon tricks Wolf into eating his own feces. In a recent Chippewa story, which bears various marks of acculturation, the villain is punished by being thrown head first into a toilet at the order of the "king" (*ógima*).

Some Chippewa stories stress the theme of punishment or penetration of the rectum. This is notable in the episode above where Wenebojo roasts his rear end until it bleeds. Other Chippewa folktales have similar features. In one anecdote Wenebojo kills a *windigo* (cannibal giant) by telling a weasel to run up the giant's anus. Reference has already been made to the story in which Wenebojo applies a burning stick to his grandfather's buttocks.

In a story told in northern Wisconsin, Wenebojo captures a buzzard by pretending that he is a dead moose. All the birds flock down

---

[36] Jones, *Ojibwa Texts*, p. 447.

[37] Ibid., Part II (1919), pp. 699, 455. 767

to eat his body. When the buzzard comes to eat the flesh around the rectum and pushes his head inside, Wenebojo tightens his sphincter muscles and clamps the bird's head, so that he can't escape. This story accounts for the bad smell and the scabby neck which the buzzard has.

Anal motifs seem to be lacking in the Navaho mythology I have read and also, as far as I can find, in Dakota, Iroquois, and Eskimo folklore. However, Chippewa folklore is not unique in this respect. The Menomini share many of the same anal themes, and so do the Winnebago.[38] These are neighboring tribes. It came as a surprise to me, however, to find some of the same, or very similar, themes in the folklore of the distant Gros Ventre, Arapaho, and Blackfoot. After the bird-killing episode, the Gros Ventre trickster awakens, finds that the food has been eaten, and punishes his rear end for failing to warn him.[39] The same sequence appears among the Arapaho and, in somewhat different form (lacking the closed-eye dance) among the Blackfoot.[40] The punishment, in most of these cases, is effected not by standing over a fire but by thrusting a stick or firebrand into the rectum, a pattern which also appears in a Fox version.[41] In a Cree story the trickster punishes his rear end for breaking wind when he is hunting, thus warning away game. In this case the trickster performs the punishment by sitting on a hot stone; later he eats one of his scabs, thinking it meat.[42]

The distribution of these tales suggests that the sequence of themes involving the bird dance with closed eyes, failure of anus to give warning, and the subsequent punishment, must be of northern Algonkian origin. The Winnebago, who appeared relatively late in Wisconsin, ultimately taking on a Woodland culture, must

---

[38] For the Menomini, see Alanson Skinner and John V. Satterlee, *Folklore of the Menomini Indians,* Anthropological Papers of the American Museum of Natural History, Vol. 13 (1915), pp. 258, 271, 293, 297, 303. For the Winnebago, see Paul Radin, *The Trickster, A Study in American Indian Mythology* (New York: Philosophical Library, 1956), pp. 16, 17, 18, 25, 26, 27.

[39] A. L. Kroeber, *Gros Ventre Myths and Tales,* Anthropological Papers of the American Museum of Natural History, Vol. 1, Part 3 (1907), p. 71.

[40] G. A. Dorsey and A. L. Kroeber, *Traditions of the Arapaho,* Field Columbian Museum Publications, No. 81, Vol. 5 (1903), p. 60 fn; Clark Wissler and D. C. Duvall, *Mythology of the Blackfoot Indians,* Anthropological Papers of the American Museum of Natural History, Vol. 2 (1908), part 1, pp. 26, 38–39.

[41] William Jones, *Fox Texts,* Publications of the American Ethnological Society (Leyden: E. J. Brill, 1907), Vol. I, pp. 279–89.

[42] Alanson Skinner, "Plains Cree Tales," *Journal of American Folklore,* Vol. 29 (1916), p. 351. See also Alanson Skinner, *Notes on the Eastern Cree and the Northern Saulteaux,* Anthropological Papers, American Museum of Natural History, Vol. 9 (1911), part 1, pp. 88–92, 114–15.

have borrowed these stories from their neighbors, probably the Menomini.

Does the fact that other tribes, with quite different cultures, tell some of the same or similar "anal" stories negate the psychological significance of these themes in Chippewa folklore? For reasons given above (pp. 374–77), I don't think so. I feel that their retention and elaboration in Chippewa folklore is significant. Hallowell has noted the prevalence of anal humor among the Lac du Flambeau Indians. "We were not long on the reservation before all of us were struck by the fondness of these Indians for dirty stories embodying an anal type of humor. The men told them to us with evident relish, and often repeated the same story on different occasions."[43] Landes has noted anal humor among the Ontario Chippewa.[44] This seems to be an old and persistent pattern. Moreover, "anal" motifs appear in other connections, as will be noted further on. Finally, there is the quantitative factor. There simply seem to be more such stories in Chippewa folklore than in most of the other bodies of folklore that have been cited.[45]

Colors, Darkness, and Light

Colors play a prominent role in the Navaho origin legend, but not in the Chippewa myth. Black, white, blue, and yellow are mentioned on the first page of the Navaho legend; blue, yellow, white, and turquoise on page two; these colors continue to be mentioned with frequency in succeeding pages. Colors are associated with different directions and with different worlds or layers. The second world, for example, is a blue world, containing blue jays, blue herons, and other blue birds, while the third world is a yellow world.

Only three colors are mentioned in the Chippewa origin legend: black, white, and red. Of these red is mentioned the most frequently. Wenebojo's brother becomes a "red-hot coal"; red bark is used for anklebands and headbands in one episode, red dye is stuffed into Wenebojo's anus, and his red scabs become tobacco.

---

[43] A. I. Hallowell, "Myth, Culture, and Personality," *American Anthropologist,* Vol. 49 (1947), p. 554.

[44] Ruth Landes, *Ojibwa Sociology,* Columbia University Contributions to Anthropology, Vol. XXIX (New York: Columbia University Press, 1937), p. 24.

[45] Shoshone folklore also stresses anal themes, although different ones, while also emphasizing aggressive sexual themes. See Robert H. Lowie, *The Northern Shoshone,* Anthropological Papers of the American Museum of Natural History, Vol. 2, part 2 (1909).

Darkness and light are referred to in symbolic fashion. To enter the other world one must cross a log (which is really a snake) over a river. On the right hand of the snake-log the water is clear; on the left-hand side the water is black. We also learn that at the topmost layer of sky (which has four layers) it is "always day," while at the lowest layer of the earth (which also has four layers) it is always night. Navaho color symbolism is much more elaborate and more frequently involved in the narrative.

Locality

Various specific landmarks in the regional environment are mentioned in the course of the Navaho origin legend. These cover a broad territory: Mount Baldy near Alamos, Colorado; Mount Taylor, New Mexico; San Francisco Mountain, Arizona; El Huerfanito Peak, New Mexico; Shiprock, and various other mountains and mesas.[46]

The Chippewa origin legend, in contrast, is lacking in such references except for a few allusions to the Lake Superior region. Indeed, the narrative is very expressive of a wandering nomadic way of life. "Wenebojo traveled here and there in every direction, and traveled and traveled and traveled. He didn't know which way he was going. He was just traveling." "The wolves had no place they could call home. They traveled just like Wenebojo did." This restless and rootless spirit is characteristic of the narrative.

The Character of Wenebojo

Wenebojo is clearly not the Western Promethean type of hero who struggles against evil for the good of mankind. When he creates something for the future race of human beings, it is usually done as a capricious afterthought, as in his creation of food for his future "aunts," and in the making of tobacco.

Apart from his murder of the two kings of the underwater spirits Wenebojo possesses no long-range goals or purposes. He assumes various forms and manifestations in an apparent (but haphazard) quest for some sort of personal fulfillment or identification, asking animals whom he happens to encounter if they will make him look

---

[46] O'Bryan, *The Diné*, p. 4, fn; p. 26.

or sound the way they do. One is tempted to observe that Wenebojo is not "emotionally mature." At one point he engages in a sort of temper tantrum. This episode, and its outcome, are worth a brief summary.

In his travels Wenebojo suddenly remembers how the underwater spirits killed his "nephew," the wolf with whom he lived and who hunted for him. Wenebojo has killed the kings of the underwater spirits in revenge, but now the recollection makes him unhappy again. He sits down by the beach with his feet nearly in the water and cries and cries. He speaks to the earth and says, "Whoever is underneath the earth down there, I will pull them out and bring them up on top here. I can play with them and do whatever I want with them, because I own this earth where I am now." (Wenebojo created the world we live in.) Wenebojo then speaks to the sky: "Whoever is up there, those *mánidog* [spirits] up there, I will get them and pull them down. I will play with them here and do just as I please with them. I will even knock down the sky." Wenebojo sniffs from crying, and the sky makes a loud noise like the cracking of ice.

The two chief spirits of the universe are alarmed by these threats. They send a series of messengers to Wenebojo, asking him to attend a council of the spirits, but Wenebojo ignores them all. Finally, a white otter addresses Wenebojo as "cousin" and asks him to come to the meeting. This is one case in which Wenebojo responds sincerely to kinship relations, for he agrees, since they are related. At the subsequent meeting of all the spirits Wenebojo is given a set of "parents," the founders of the human race.

Interpretation

The outstanding features of this origin legend are: (1) the isolation of the hero, the absence of close social bonds; (2) the recurrence of oral and anal themes; and (3) themes of aggression and duplicity.

What may be deduced from these themes? We get the impression that Chippewa culture and social life fostered an emotionally isolated kind of personality. Social ties were weak and uncertain. Relationships between men and women were probably lacking in warmth and affection.

The themes of aggression against brothers in this narrative suggest that in the often isolated family groups there may have been strong feelings of hostility. Oedipal motifs also occur in Chippewa folklore, with stories of father-son conflict, although according to Stephens such motifs are rare in the world's folklore.[47]

The themes of oral frustration may have some relation to the former scarcity of food in the Chippewa region. In John Tanner's early 19th-century narrative about his life among these Indians, there are at least 25 references to hunger and starvation.[48] Most early accounts of the Chippewa contain comments on the dangers of famine. *Windigo* stories were an expression of this concern, for people were said to turn into *windigog* (greedy cannibal giants) as the result of prolonged hunger.

The Wisconsin Chippewa were relatively rich in food resources compared with their Canadian brothers. However, many informants spoke about experiencing hunger in childhood. In the chapter on the TAT, mention was made of the recurrence of oral themes in children's stories.

The stress on anal themes cannot be traced to early severe toilet training in aboriginal Chippewa culture. *A priori* one would not expect undue insistence on cleanliness in a seminomadic culture such as this. In the first year of life the Chippewa baby spent most of its time in the cradleboard, surrounded by dried padded moss which absorbed its urine and feces. The moss was thrown away and replaced when necessary.

A possible clue to the stress on anal themes appears in the work of Alexander and Menninger. These authors have demonstrated a relationship between constipation, depression, and delusions of persecution.

The frequent constipation of patients suffering from persecutory delusions is mainly conditioned by their conflict about anal sadistic tendencies which they deny and project. Their frequent deprecatory attitude and delusions about their food is another manifestation of the projection of their anal sadistic impulses.

A statistical study of 40 patients suffering from depression corroborated the clinical observation regarding the frequent coincidence of depression and constipation.[49]

---

[47] Stephens, *The Oedipus Complex*, p. 159.

[48] John Tanner, *A Narrative of the Captivity of John Tanner,* Edwin James (ed.), (London; 1830).

[49] Franz Alexander and William Menninger, "The Relation of Persecutory Delusions to the Functioning of the Gastro-Intestinal Tract," *Journal of Nervous and Mental Diseases,* Vol. 84 (1936), pp. 541–54.

Kardiner has written that "one often sees in patients prolonged periods of constipation when the dominant emotion is an anxiety of losing support or protection."[50]

Concerning delusions of persecution Fenichel writes: "It is interesting that among the organs projected onto the persecutor, feces and buttocks play a prominent role." He refers to Bibring's case of a woman who believed that she was persecuted by a man named "Behind." "She attributed to this man a number of characteristics which were in fact true of her own gluteal region.[51] This personification is reminiscent of the episode mentioned earlier in which Wenebojo talks to his "rear end" as if it were another person, and then punishes it for its lack of cooperation. The theme of penetration of the rectum may also be related to paranoid fears or unconscious desires.[52]

Did the Chippewa suffer from constipation? Some Chippewa informants referred to constipation, but it would be hard to say whether this complaint was more prevalent among them than among other people. It is interesting, however, that one section of the origin legend is devoted to the discovery of an herbal physic. It is also striking that these Indians, in aboriginal times, independently invented the enema syringe.[53] Syringes are still used nowadays to relieve constipation.[54]

What are we to make of the relationship between mouth and anus in some of the Chippewa stories? The answer may seem fanciful, but it could be interpreted as due to an unconscious desire to reincorporate what has been lost. As Fenichel puts it:

The impulse to coprophagia which certainly has an erogenous source (representing the attempt to stimulate the erogenous zone of the mouth with the same pleasurable substance that previously stimulated the eroge-

---

[50] Abram Kardiner, *The Individual and His Society. The Psychodynamics of Primitive Social Organization* (New York: Columbia University Press, 1939), p. 302 fn.

[51] Otto Fenichel, *The Psychoanalytic Theory of Neurosis* (New York: W. W. Norton, 1945), p. 429.

[52] Ibid., p. 275.

[53] See A. I. Hallowell, "The Bulbed Enema Syringe in North America," *American Anthropologist,* Vol. 37 (1935), pp. 708–10; and R. F. Heizer, "The Bulbed Enema Syringe and Enema Tube in the New World," *Primitive Man,* Vol. 12 (1939), pp. 85–93.

[54] One northern Wisconsin female informant said, "When the children get feverish, and I know they're constipated, I syringe them and make them sit right on the pot. They can't go out after that. I even syringed my husband like that. He only went to the toilet about once or twice a week. I often wondered how he could stand it. He never used anything except when he got sick." (Ernestine Friedl, field notes).

nous zone of the rectum) simultaneously represents an attempt to re-establish the threatened narcissistic equilibrium; that which has been eliminated must be reintrojected.[55]

Oral frustration seems to have been anticipated by the Chippewa (as well as the frustration of needs for dependency and affection). In reaction to this state of affairs a character might develop which seeks to hang on to what it has, to resist being deprived of anything, and, if need be, to reincorporate what has been lost. This is comparable to the "anal" personality described by Freud, Jones, and Abraham, although the Chippewa "anal" traits seem to have a somewhat different character and a different etiology from the European ones.

The general picture, then, is one of emotional isolation, with somewhat "paranoid" tendencies. The absence of color references in the origin legend may be a parallel to the characteristic color avoidance by Chippewa subjects in the Rorschach Tests and by Chippewa children in the drawings analyzed by Lowenfels. It will be seen that this analysis of the origin legend agrees in many ways with the findings of Hallowell, Landes, Watrous, Caudill, and others who have worked with the Chippewa.

CHIPEWYAN FOLKLORE MOTIFS

The Chipewyan Indians are not to be confused with the Chippewa; they are an Athapaskan-speaking subarctic north Indian hunting gathering tribe whose culture had much in common with that of the Chippewa. An analysis of the relative emphasis on dependency and on self-sufficiency in the themes of Chipewyan stories has been made by Ronald Cohen and James W. Van Stone, involving a comparison between characteristic themes in European Grimm's fairy tales and Chipewyan motifs. One of the authors' conclusions is that "Chipewyan tales seem to lack almost any reference to power over others, or a desire not to affiliate with others, while both of these motivations are expressed in the Grimm's tales."[56] The authors suggest a linkage between the emphasis on self-sufficiency in the Grimm stories with the Protestant ethic of western European culture, with its stress on achievement. There is also an

---

[55] Fenichel, *The Psychoanalytic Theory of Neurosis,* p. 67.

[56] Ronald Cohen and James W. Van Stone, "Dependency and Self-Sufficiency in Chipewyan Stories," *National Museum of Canada, Bulletin No. 194, Contributions to Anthropology,* 1961–62; Part II, 1963, pp. 43–44.

emphasis on self-sufficiency in the Chipewyan stories, but this is nearly matched by an almost equal emphasis on themes of dependency.

STYLE

An aspect of folklore which will only be touched on here but which deserves at least brief mention is the question of style. Frank J. Essene refers to the Eskimo style of narration as being "terse and stiff."[57] Boas has vividly described the method of telling narratives in the Central area:

Old traditions are always related in a highly ceremonious manner. The narrator takes off his outer jacket, pulls the hood over his head, and sits down in the rear part of the hut, turning his face to the wall, and then tells the story slowly and solemnly. All the stories are related in a very abridged form, the substance being supposed to be known. The form is always the same, and should the narrator happen to say one word otherwise than is customary, he will be corrected by his listeners.[58]

The "terse and stiff" style of Eskimo folklore may be contrasted with the prolix style of Ifugao folklore which, as Barton tells us, is hampered by the inclusion of "an enormous number of tiresome details."

If the myth relates the setting forth of a character on a journey, it has him pound his rice, winnow it twice, put water in a pot, sift in the rice, fire the pot, force the fire, boil the rice, take off the pot, set it by the fire to roast ("dry"), paddle the rice out onto a basket or wooden bowl, eat, put the utensils away, untuck his hip bag, take out betels, lime them, place the quid between his teeth, crunch it, turn the spittle red and thick and then spit it out. After that the character packs up what he wants to carry on his journey, tucks on his hipbag, "follows" this act by belting on his scabbard, takes his spear in hand, descends from his house, crosses the outskirts of his village, and the reader will thank God that his hero is at last on his way and will hope for something interesting. But his hope will die a-borning, for the journey itself will be described in like detail—uphill, downhill, around the hill, up and down, along the rice dikes, across streams, the naming of many places—and the character will sit down once or twice to chew betels in equal detail and perhaps even cook and eat again. And when he returns by the same route it is all to do over again. The same overloading with detail enters into descriptions of rituals and techniques.[59]

---

[57] Quoted in Lantis, "Nunivak Eskimo Personality . . . ," p. 157.

[58] Franz Boas, *The Central Eskimo,* Bureau of American Ethnology Report No. 6 (1888), p. 564.

[59] Barton, *The Mythology of the Ifugaos,* p. 18.

This recalls Huizinga's description of stylistic features in the late Middle Ages:

Art and letters in the fifteenth century share the general and essential tendency of the spirit of the expiring Middle Ages: that of accentuating every detail, of developing every thought and every image to the end, of giving concrete form to every concept of the mind. [Huizinga gives the example of a series of sermons, described by Erasmus, to which a preacher devoted all of Lent. The sermons concerned the Prodigal Son.] He described his journeys on his setting out and on his return, the bill of fare of his meals at the inns, the mills he passed, his dicing, etc.[60]

Huizinga sees this tendency to elaboration as a symptom of decadence. It would be interesting to compare and contrast bodies of folklore from this standpoint and to see what features, if any, are shared by those which have a terse Eskimo-like style of narration and those which have an Ifugao-medieval prolixity.

It would seem that the analysis of folklore is a promising field for culture-and-personality investigations. Obviously, it must be supplemented by techniques which more directly gauge the personality characteristics of members of the society. Moreover, the culture in question should be well known; otherwise, interpretations may be wide of the mark.

THE INTERPRETATION OF ART

Can one learn something about the modal personality tendencies of a particular society from an analysis of that society's art? Some anthropologists have thought so and have attempted interpretations of art—of both style and content—from this point of view. In these efforts anthropologists have been preceded by culture historians and art historians, whose writings often verge on the field of culture-and-personality. We have just noted Huizinga's interpretation of the elaborate style of narration characteristic of the late Middle Ages in France and the Netherlands. Huizinga found the same tendency in the painting of this period, notably in the work of Jan van Eyck, who paid the most extraordinary attention to detail. Huizinga also noted analogous features in the architecture and sculpture, in the costumes and festivals of the time.

---

[60] J. Huizinga, *The Waning of the Middle Ages. A Study of the Forms of Life, Thought, and Art in France and the Netherlands in the XIVth and XVth Centuries* (London: Edward Arnold, 1924), p. 255.

Burgundo-French culture of the expiring Middle Ages tends to oust beauty by magnificence. The art of this period exactly reflects this spirit. All that we cited above as characteristic of the mental processes of the epoch: the craving to give a definite form to every idea, and the over-crowding of the mind with figures and forms systematically arranged— all this reappears in art. There, too, we find the tendency to leave nothing without form, without figure, without ornament. The flamboyant style of architecture is like the postlude of an organist who cannot conclude. It decomposes all the formal elements endlessly, it interlaces all the details; there is not a line which has not its counter-line. The form develops at the expense of the idea, the ornament grows rank, hiding all the lines and all the surfaces. A *horror vacui* reigns, always a symptom of artistic decline.[61]

Curt Sachs has made similar generalizations about corresponding tendencies in the arts of 14th-century Europe, including the music of that time.[62]

A parallel may perhaps be pointed out in the arts of Bali. Here sculpture has an elaborate and flamboyant quality.

The gates of a North Balinese temple are tall and slender, with a flaming, ascendant tendency as if trying to liberate themselves from the smothering maze of sculptured leaves and flowers, out of which peer, here and there, grotesque faces and blazing demons, their shape almost lost in the flames that emanate from their bodies.[63]

Balinese painters of the conservative style take pains to fill all of the available space covered by a design, even to the spaces between groups of figures. As offerings to the gods, women make very intricate structures of fruit, flowers, cakes, meat, stomach tissue, and so forth which seem to present a "baroque" appearance.[64] Balinese music is very complex, a "delicious confusion," as it seemed at first to Colin McPhee, who later began to discover "a feeling of form and elaborate architecture" in the music.[65] Perhaps we can say that there is a kind of *horror vacui* in Bali, both in music and the visual arts.

Now, *horror vacui* is said to be often found in the art of schizophrenics.[66] Perhaps in cultures having *horror vacui* tendencies in art

---

[61] Ibid., pp. 227–28.

[62] Curt Sachs, *The Commonwealth of Art. Style in the Fine Arts, Music, and the Dance* (New York: W. W. Norton, 1946), pp. 93, 274.

[63] Miguel Covarrubias, *Island of Bali* (New York: Alfred A. Knopf, 1937), p. 185.

[64] Ibid., pp. 189–90, 161.

[65] Colin McPhee, *A House in Bali* (New York: John Day, 1946), p. 37.

[66] Ernst Kris, *Psychoanalytic Explorations in Art* (New York: International Universities Press, 1951), pp. 107, 152.

there may be common features in the upbringing of children which tend toward a schizoid adult personality.

Herbert Barry III has made a cross-cultural survey, examining the pictorial art of 30 nonliterate societies for which Whiting and Child have data on socialization; 549 works of art were rated on 18 criteria of art style on a seven-point scale. Eleven art variables were considered to be measures of complexity of art style. Barry found a correlation between severity of socialization and complexity of design in art works.

> In the majority of cultures with complex art style . . . the typical individual learns self-reliant behavior to a high degree and is punished or frustrated for overt expression of dependence . . . . The correlation of complex art style with severe socialization . . . apparently applies primarily to severe socialization pressures toward independent behavior rather than toward obedient behavior.[67]

Among the cultures rated as having complexity of design above median we find both the Kwakiutl and the Balinese. It seems to me, however, that Kwakiutl art does not have the same degree of *horror vacui* that one finds in Bali and in the Lowland Maya area. There is some *horror vacui* in Northwest Coast art, as manifest in slate carvings, shaman's rattles, and Chilkat blankets, but much Northwest Coast art is powerful and stately, without any fussiness.[68]

Among the societies whose art is rated as complex we also find both the Alorese and the Arapesh. In view of Barry's hypothesis, this is rather paradoxical, since the Alorese are described as being unmaternal and the Arapesh as very maternal and cherishing. Besides, the Alorese are said to have little interest in the arts.[69]

Correspondences in stylistic features of the different arts of a culture or of a particular period have preoccupied many writers on the arts, like Curt Sachs and Wylie Sypher. For Sypher there is a mannerist drama and mannerist poetry, as well as mannerist painting. His book, *Four Stages of Renaissance Style,* traces the development of the arts from 1400 to 1700, showing that analogous features appear in the literature, architecture, and painting of a particular

---

[67] Herbert Barry III, "Relationships between Child Training and the Pictorial Arts," *Journal of Abnormal and Social Psychology,* Vol. 54 (1957) , p. 382.

[68] However, Drucker states *horror vacui* to be a characteristic of Northwest Coast art. See Philip Drucker, *Indians of the Northwest Coast* (New York: McGraw-Hill Book Co., 1955) , p. 170.

[69] Abram Kardiner, with the collaboration of Ralph Linton, Cora Du Bois, and James West, *The Psychological Frontiers of Society* (New York: Columbia University Press, 1945) , p. 127.

period. "Not all kinds of styles are available at any given time, since a style is modified by the artist's own vision, and his vision, in turn, by the world he inhabits. Vision has its own history. There are 'period' styles, period techniques, period angles of approach, periods of history."[70]

The same assumptions underlie Egon Friedell's three-volume work, *A Cultural History of the Modern Age*. See, for example, Friedell's perceptive description of the rococo period, with observations about the different arts of the age: costume, furniture, porcelain, *chinoiserie*, style of conversation, and so forth.[71]

An approach similar to those just noted has been followed by the anthropologist Francis L. K. Hsu, in illustrating some contrasts between Western (particularly American) and Chinese ways of life. However, Hsu places more emphasis on content than on style. He points out that human subjects are prominent in Western paintings but relatively scarce in Chinese. When figures do appear in Chinese paintings, they are submerged in and dominated by the landscape. Moreover, these figures express no emotion; their faces are blank. Western paintings, on the other hand, are full of emotion and the depiction of human feelings. There is a great deal of suggestive sexuality, which is generally absent in Chinese formal art, although present in pornography.

Hsu believes that Western culture is "individual-centered," with an emphasis on the predilections of the individual, while Chinese culture is "situation-centered," with a stress upon the individual's awareness of his proper place and behavior in relation to others. Thus, "In Western art the focus is on man or woman as an individual. In Chinese art the important thing is the individual's place in the external scheme of things. In addition, American art often reflects the inner tension of the individual; this concern is practically absent from Chinese art."[72]

The diverse attitudes toward sex in relation to art are explained in terms of this contrast. In America sex is regulated more by internal restraints; in China it is regulated more by external barriers. There is more guilt in the Western world, but the tabooed

---

[70] Wylie Sypher, *Four Stages of Renaissance Style. Transformations in Arts and Literature 1400–1700* (New York: Doubleday, Anchor *Books,* 1955) , p. 13.

[71] Egon Friedell, *A Cultural History of the Modern Age. The Crisis of the European Soul from the Black Death to the World War,* trans. from the German by Charles Francis Atkinson (New York: Alfred A. Knopf, 1931) , Vol. II, chap. III.

[72] Francis L. K. Hsu, *Americans and Chinese* (New York: Doubleday Natural History, Press, 1972) , p. 18.

material exerts a force which leads to its sublimated expression and enjoyment in art.

Hsu finds the same contrasting patterns evident in the literature of the two cultures. Chinese novels describe external behavior, while American novels are more concerned with what the characters think and feel. Western literature is more introspective. The union of hero and heroine is the climax of an American love story. Many obstacles may have to be surmounted to reach that point and a great deal of emotion generated in the process. Chinese novels, however, treat sex more casually.

Sexual union usually occurs early in the narrative; it is never the climax of the story. The balance of the novel is concerned with how the hero goes about marrying the heroine properly, with the rectifying wedding ceremony tediously described to the last detail. Mutual attraction between an individual man and woman is not enough. Their personal feelings are never more important than the sanctions and assistance of the family and the society.[73]

Hsu's method, like that of Spengler, Huizinga, Friedell, and Sypher, lies in finding parallel expressions of a particular "world view" in the different arts of a society.

The same approach is also followed, although not, to my mind, with so much success, in Nikolaus Pevsner's book, *The Englishness of English Art.*[74] Pevsner finds certain "English" tendencies reflected not only in the work of some selected painters—Hogarth, Reynolds, Blake, and Constable—but also in the Perpendicular style in architecture. This general method, then, is one that has been widely followed by culture historians and art historians who wish to characterize the salient characteristics of a nation, a culture, or an age.

Meyer Schapiro has pointed out some difficulties in this approach. There are cultures which have two or more styles at the same time. Men and women may practice different arts having different traditional styles. There may be class or regional variations within a culture, and the religious art may differ from the secular. Moreover, one of the arts may serve as an important avenue of expression, while others are relatively neglected.

We look in vain in England for a style of painting that corresponds to Elizabethan poetry and drama; just as in Russia in the nineteenth century there was no true parallel in painting to the great movement of

---

[73] Ibid., p. 25.

[74] Nikolaus Pevsner, *The Englishness of English Art* (New York: Frederick A. Praeger, 1956).

literature. In these instances we recognize that the various arts have different roles in the culture and social life of a time and express in their content as well as style different interests and values. The dominant outlook of a time—if it can be isolated—does not affect all the arts in the same degree, nor are all the arts equally capable of expressing the same outlook.[75]

This may be granted. But most art historians have dealt with the changing styles of Western Europe, which has undergone tremendous cultural changes since the Middle Ages. We may expect to find more homogeneity in the arts of non-Western cultures which have had enough stability to achieve some cultural integration. And if there is such a thing as basic or modal personality, it should find some expression in the different arts of a society.

Very little has been done in the psychological interpretation of non-Western art, but some explorations in this field may be singled out. Douglas Fraser, for example, has contrasted Mundugumor and Tchambuli sculpture in ways that seem to accord with Mead's generalizations in *Sex and Temperament.* (See Chapter 6.) Fraser speaks of Mundugumor art as having "an overpowering emphasis on aggressive qualities," while of Tchambuli art he writes:

> The forms and their expression, in comparison with those of the Mundugamor [*sic*], are markedly less aggressive; they are more lucid in their internal relationships, more languid in their quality. But Tchambuli art is limited in projection and range. . . . The Tchambuli, while not exactly all sweetness and light, is graceful and sensuous. Essentially it is self-involved. The Mundugamor, on the other hand, is filled with double images, positive-negative relationships, and uneasy juxtapositions. Its formal structure is difficult to grasp; its total effect is completely disturbing.[76]

Influence of the Arts on Thought and Behavior

In this chapter we have considered ways in which folklore and art express personality patterns, but these arts must also be seen as influencing thought and behavior. The Balinese drama of Rangda and Barong, while perhaps expressing projections of parental figures, as suggested above (p. 257), also seems to reinforce these identifications in the minds of the audience, which includes young children. This is a field which needs more investigation. A pioneer

---

[75] Meyer Schapiro, "Style," in A. L. Kroeber (ed.), *Anthropology Today. An Encyclopedic Inventory* (Chicago: University of Chicago Press, 1953), p. 295. Copyright 1953, University of Chicago Press.

[76] Douglas Fraser, "Mundugamor Sculpture: Comments on the Art of a New Guinea Tribe," *Man,* Vol. 55 (1955), pp. 19–20.

effort in this direction is an analysis of Indonesian proletarian drama (*ludruk*) by James L. Peacock. The author shows that some of the plots in these dramas glorify proletarian young men who rise in status without their parents' help. In various ways the plots encourage modernization and the judging of people in terms of what they can do instead of class origin. The dynamic nature of this drama is contrasted with the escapist ritual drama of Bali.[77] "By encouraging people to break with parents, speak Indonesian, be egalitarian, join national groups, go to school, follow youth-ways, ludruk fosters the flowering of friendship as an institution."[78] Peacock's adventuresome analysis of *ludruk* should encourage others to explore the influence of the arts on thought and behavior in other sociocultural contexts.

SUGGESTIONS FOR FURTHER READING

On oral literature in general, see Alan Dundes, "Oral Literature," in James A. Clifton (ed.), *Introduction to Cultural Anthropology. Essays in the Scope and Methods of the Science of Man* (Boston: Houghton Mifflin Co., 1969), pp. 117–29; Alan Dundes (ed.), *The Study of Folklore* (Englewood Cliffs, N.J.: Prentice-Hall, 1965), and Stith Thompson, *The Folktale* (New York: Dryden Press, 1951). For sociopyschological emphasis, see J. L. Fischer, "The Sociopsychological Analysis of Folktales," *Current Anthropology*, Vol. 4 (1963), pp. 235–95. I have discussed recurrent themes in Central Eskimo folklore in Victor Barnouw, *An Introduction to Anthropology, Volume II: Ethnology* (Homewood, Ill.: The Dorsey Press, 1971), pp. 280–84. A good source of Central Eskimo folklore is Knud Rasmussen, *Intellectual Culture of the Iglulik Eskimos*, Report of the Fifth Thule Expedition, 1921–24, Vol. VII, No. 1 (Copenhagen, 1929). There are many published collections of Chippewa folklore, perhaps the best of which is William Jones' *Ojibwa Texts*. See also J. P. B. de Josselin de Jong, *Original Odžibwe Texts* (Baessler-Archiv, V) (Leipzig and Berlin, 1913), pp. 5–30, for a version of the Wenebojo cycle. Recurrent themes in Aymara folklore are presented in Weston La Barre, "The Aymara: History and Worldview," in Melville Jacobs and John Greenway (eds.), *The Anthropologist Looks at Myth* (Austin, Texas: University of Texas Press, 1961), pp. 130–44.

A classic of art history which approaches the border of culture-and-personality is Heinrich Wölfflin, *Principles of Art History. The Problem of the Development of Style in Later Art*, trans., M. D. Hottinger (New York: Dover Publications; first published in 1915). See also Arnold

---

[77] James L. Peacock, *Rites of Modernization. Symbolic and Social Aspects of Indonesian Proletarian Drama* (Chicago: University of Chicago Press, 1968), pp. 222–23, fn. 6.

[78] *Ibid.*, p. 228.

Hauser, *The Social History of Art* (New York: Vintage Books; 4 volumes, 1957–61).

For an imaginative paper on art styles which, like that of Herbert Barry III, makes use of the cross-cultural files, see J. L. Fischer, "Art Styles as Cultural Cognitive Maps," *American Anthropologist,* Vol. 63 (1961), pp. 79–93.

The 1963 edition of this book contained an exposition and criticism of Anthony F. C. Wallace's psychological analysis of Maya art. This is omitted in the present edition. For Wallace's interpretation, see Anthony F. C. Wallace, "A Possible Technique for Recognizing Psychological Characteristics of the Ancient Maya from an Analysis of Their Art," *American Imago,* Vol. 7 (1950), pp. 239–58.

part **V**

SOME APPLICATIONS

Part V illustrates a point touched on previously in this book, that culture-and-personality research can make contributions to our understanding of some of the practical issues and problems of contemporary life.

Chapter 16 deals with the cross-cultural study of mental disorders and considers such questions as the nature of mental disorder, the cultural patterning of such disorders, and whether there is more mental breakdown in some societies than in others.

One of the problems discussed in Chapter 17 is why some societies have undergone rapid economic development, while others have experienced great difficulty in that respect. This can no longer be seen as a purely economic problem; questions of values, attitudes, and motivation are involved, as economists like Everett E. Hagen recognize. Similarly, a political scientist, Richard H. Solomon, has applied a culture-and-personality approach to the understanding of Mao Tse-tung's cultural revolution.

Child-rearing methods in an Israeli kibbutz are also examined in Chapter 17. They contrast markedly with those in a European or American nuclear family. What are the effects of these methods on the personalities of kibbutz children and adolescents?

Clearly, these are all serious, eminently practical issues; culture-and-personality research can throw some light on them.

chapter 16

Culture and Mental Disorders

In the *Milwaukee Journal* for April 24, 1972, a psychologist from the National Institute of Mental Health was quoted as saying that "almost no family in the nation is entirely free of mental disorders." The psychologist, David Rosenthal, stated that possibly 60 million Americans are borderline schizophrenics; there are more than 1.75 million schizophrenic or potentially schizophrenic persons walking the streets and at least 500,000 in hospitals, while psychoneurosis—emotional illness short of insanity—is "so prevalent in the population that it is almost impossible to estimate."

At the same time, there are some writers who assert that there is no such thing as mental illness. In saying this, they do not deny the seriousness of the picture just presented; rather, they wish to remove the stigma of sickness from those so characterized. Thomas S. Szasz has argued that the model of organic ailment is a false analogy. Sharing this view, Thomas J. Scheff has argued that the application of a diagnostic label to a patient, who may be in a confused suggestible state, may reinforce his acceptance of the role of a mentally ill patient.[1] From the viewpoint of a traditional psychiatrist, diagnosis is the first step leading to a cure. From Scheff's point of view, diagnosis may confirm the patient in his "abnormality."

In support of the "no sickness" model is the fact that many cases of mental disorder seem to have no organic impairment; they are

---

[1] Thomas J. Scheff, *Being Mentally Ill. A Sociological Theory* (Chicago: Aldine Publishing Company, 1966), chap. 3.

"functional," psychogenic in origin. But not all psychiatrists or psychologists would agree to that. Bernard Rimland, for one, believes that most mental disorders probably do have an organic basis, but our present limited knowledge does not allow us to identify the organic defects in many cases.[2]

Related to these issues is the question of cultural relativity. Ruth Benedict pointed out that some behavior (trance, possession, visionary experience, homosexuality) which is considered abnormal in our society is held to be normal in others, while some behavior considered normal in our society is seen as abnormal in others. For example, a man with strong achievement motivation and initiative might be branded as a witch by the Zuñi.[3] Today we have movements like the Gay Liberation Front which aims to remove the "sick" label which society has affixed to homosexuality and to promote a more relativistic view of deviant behavior. Taking drugs for unusual psychedelic experiences has become popular in some segments of our population. Should those who do so be characterized as "abnormal"? Should we adopt a statistical view of abnormality, counting those who deviate from a norm as "sick" persons? Benedict counseled against such an approach. Erich Fromm even argued that the majority of persons in a society may suffer from "culturally patterned defects" associated with behavior which is culturally approved but which may be emotionally crippling.[4] Fromm, then, would tend to have an absolute view of emotional health, transcending cultural differences, in keeping with a fulfillment model of personality. Fromm has made use of multiple criteria to gauge the relative sanity of societies: not just hospital admission rates (which might only reflect increasing care), but also rates for suicide, homicide, and alcoholism.[5]

In claiming that 80 percent of New Yorkers suffer from some "emotional disability," Marvin K. Opler, like Fromm, takes an absolute view of mental health.[6] His figure is based on a large-scale

---

[2] Bernard Rimland, "Psychogenesis versus Biogenesis. The Issues and the Evidence," in Stanley C. Plog and Robert B. Edgerton (eds.), *Changing Perspectives in Mental Illness* (New York: Holt, Rinehart & Winston, 1969), pp. 702–35.

[3] Ruth Fulton Benedict, "Anthropology and the Abnormal," *The Journal of General Psychology*, Vol. 10 (1934), pp. 59–80.

[4] Erich Fromm, "Individual and Social Origins of Neurosis," *American Sociological Review*, Vol. 9 (1944), pp. 380–84.

[5] Erich Fromm, *The Sane Society* (New York: Rinehart and Co., 1955), pp. 7–10.

[6] Marvin K. Opler, *Culture and Social Psychiatry* (New York: Atherton Press, 1967), p. 265.

survey, the Midtown Manhattan study of 1962, which has revealed a serious mental health impairment rate of 23.4 percent of the population as compared with a "well" frequency of 18.5 percent and a combined "mild-moderate" representation of 58.1 percent.[7] In another recent study, a large-scale investigation of a rural area in Canada, a similarly high incidence of mental disorder has been reported; 18 percent of the population were classified as significantly impaired psychiatric cases. If a second group of persons with psychophysiological or sociopathic symptoms is added, the percentage of impaired becomes 26 percent, while the asymptomatic group constitutes only 19 percent of the total sample.[8]

Opler states "In New York City, we found people who had never been known to psychiatry or psychological medicine who were as utterly incapacitated as any I have seen in chronic wards."[9] Oddly enough, opposed to this remark is a comment by Braginsky, Braginsky, and Ring, who found schizophrenic patients on chronic wards to be quite normal; ". . . they did not appear to us to be the disoriented, dependent, and socially inept creatures that the textbooks described."[10]

The sickness model of mental health has been associated with a taxonomy of disorders, like those for organic ailments. We have terms like manic-depression, schizophrenia, hebephrenia, catatonia, hysteria, neurosis, and many others. The putative advantage of such classifications is that a differential diagnosis should lead to a specific course of treatment. A drawback, however, is that different psychiatrists often apply different labels to the same patient. Walter Mischel observes that although it is possible to get reasonable agreement among raters for very broad categories of deviant behavior, such as "organic," "psychotic," or "characterological," less gross psychiatric classifications cannot reliably be made.[11]

---

[7] Leo Srole et al., *Mental Health in the Metropolis, the Midtown Manhattan Study* (New York: McGraw-Hill Book Co., 1962) .

[8] Alexander H. Leighton, "The Stirling County Study: Some Notes on Concepts and Methods," in Paul H. Hoch and Joseph Zubin (eds.) , *Comparative Epidemiology of the Mental Disorders* (New York: Grune and Stratton, 1961) , pp. 29–31.

[9] Opler, *Culture and Social Psychiatry*, pp. 266–67.

[10] Benjamin M. Braginsky, Dorothea D. Bragisnky, and Kenneth Ring, *Methods of Madness. The Mental Hospital as a Last Resort* (New York: Holt, Rinehart & Winston, 1969) , p. 29.

[11] Walter Mischel, *Personality and Assessment* (New York: John Wiley & Sons, Inc., 1968) , p. 194. For some references to surveys of diagnostic ratings by different psychiatrists, see Robert B. Edgerton, "On the 'Recognition' of Mental Illness," in Plog and Edgerton, *Changing Perspectives in Mental Illness*, p. 68.

Karl Menninger, who has campaigned for nearly 50 years against the psychiatrists' urge to classify mental disorders, argues that the best way of conceiving of mental illness and health is as a continuum with the sicker persons ranged at one end and the "weller" ones at the other. All persons, in his opinion, have mental illness of different degrees at different times.[12]

The present chapter is based on the assumption that there are, after all, such things as mental or psychiatric disorders, which may be defined as "patterns of behavior and feeling that are out of keeping with cultural expectations and that bother the person who acts and feels them, or bother others around him, or both."[13]

Opler's figures on the high rate of emotional disability in New York City lead one to ask some questions: Is mental disorder on the increase? Is there more mental disorder in modern, complex civilizations? Are there lower rates of mental disorder in simpler, nonliterate cultures? Are some societies harder to live in or adjust to than others, and is this reflected in comparative rates of mental breakdown? Are different cultures characterized by different types of mental or emotional disturbance?

These questions, unfortunately, are not easy to answer. Some writers have claimed that psychoses are rare or absent in primitive societies,[14] but there is not much evidence to support such claims. In a review of cross-cultural literature, Paul K. Benedict and Irving Jacks tentatively conclude that the major functional psychoses occur in all human populations.[15] There may, of course, be different rates of incidence in different societies, both at "primitive" and "civilized" levels; but it is difficult to make cross-cultural comparisons.

Most studies of incidence in the Western world are based on hospital admissions rates, which cannot be used for truly "primitive" groups. Some studies in Africa have made use of hospital sta-

---

[12] Karl Menninger, with Martin Mayman and Paul Pruyser, *The Vital Balance. The Life Process in Mental Health and Illness* (New York: The Viking Press, 1963), p. 32.

[13] Alexander H. Leighton, "A Comparative Study of Psychiatric Disorder in Nigeria and Rural North America," in Plog and Edgerton, *Changing Perspectives in Mental Illness,* p. 180.

[14] C. G. Seligman, "Temperament, Conflict and Psychosis in a Stone-Age Population," *British Journal of Medical Psychology,* Vol. 9 (1929), pp. 187–202; George Devereux, "A Sociological Theory of Schizophrenia," *Psychoanalytic Review,* Vol. 26 (1934), pp. 315–42.

[15] Paul K. Benedict and Irving Jacks, "Mental Illness in Primitive Societies," *Psychiatry,* Vol. 17 (1954), p. 377.

tistics, but mentally disturbed persons in Africa, unless they are particularly violent, are often kept at home with their families and never reach a hospital. Hospital facilities are often inadequate in such underdeveloped countries, and diagnoses may be unreliable. It is therefore difficult to get adequate figures for the incidence of different types of mental disorders.

For example, a number of authorities have stated that very few cases of depression appear in Africa.[16] Both Carothers and Tooth explain this rarity by saying that there is a relative absence of self-blame and guilt among Africans. M. J. Field, however, found depression to be the most common mental illness among women in rural Ghana. Field did not work in a hospital but attended shrines where anxious persons came for help. She interviewed such individuals and accumulated abundant case material. It is Field's belief that African women suffering from depression would not be apt to go to a European hospital; hence the rarity of reported cases.[17]

But when we make cross-cultural comparisons, may we impose on other cultures our own conceptions of normality and abnormality? Or should we consider as abnormal only those persons who are so regarded in the communities where they live?

It would be easy to make errors either way. Let us take a particular example. W. Lloyd Warner has described a man called Laindjura, a member of the truly "primitive" Murngin tribe in northeastern Arnhem Land in Australia. Laindjura is famous in the southeastern Murngin country as a killer and sorcerer. He described many of his murders to Warner. These murders could not possibly have taken place as the man describes them. Laindjura tells of tomahawking a young girl between the eyes, after which he pushed his arm up through her vagina, pulled out some of her intestines, and grasped her heart. Laindjura collected some of her heart's blood and sprinkled ants on the girl's intestines, which stood out several feet. Then he pushed the intestines back into her body and fixed up the wounds so that nothing untoward was visible. After

---

[16] B. J. F. Laubscher, *Sex, Custom, and Psychopathology. A Study of South African Pagan Natives* (New York: Robert M. McBride & Co., 1938), p. 300; J. C. Carothers, "A Study of Mental Derangement in Africans, and an Attempt to Explain its Peculiarities, More Especially in Relation to the African Attitude to Life," *Psychiatry*, Vol. 11 (1948), pp. 80–81; Geoffrey Tooth, *Studies in Mental Illness in the Gold Coast* (London: His Majesty's Stationery Office, 1950), Colonial Research Publications, p. 25.

[17] M. J. Field, *Search for Security. An Ethno-Psychiatric Study of Rural Ghana* (Evanston, Ill.: Northwestern University Press, 1960), p. 149. There may, of course, be regional differences involved in these contradictory findings, although Tooth worked in the same general area as Field.

this, the girl got up. Laindjura told her that she would live for two days and then die. She went off to gather lilies with some other women, and Laindjura heard them laughing. Two days later she died.

This is only one of several such stories told by Laindjura, each of which is full of similar ghoulish detail. Warner is certain that Laindjura believed a great part of these stories. If that is so, isn't Laindjura insane? The mere fact that the alleged murders follow traditional cultural patterns does not make Laindjura a normal man. Yet, his fellow Murngin tribesmen do not regard him as peculiar, and Warner says that he was not very different from the ordinary man in the tribe, although perhaps a bit more alert. "He was a good hunter as well as an excellent wood carver, and had several wives and a number of children. There was nothing sinister, peculiar, or psychopathic about him; he was perfectly normal in all of his behavior."[18] This seems hard to credit, in view of his stories.

Let us take another example. The Saora of Orissa in central eastern India are hill people who feel themselves to be much inferior to Hindus. They believe that after death they go to a vague sort of place where life is much the same as on earth, although the quality of the palm wine is not as good. Hindus, on the other hand, go to a more splendid afterworld, where they live in palaces and fly about in airplanes. It sometimes happens, however, that a Hindu in the other world takes a fancy to a living Saora girl and appears to her, asking her hand in marriage. Verrier Elwin collected many autobiographical accounts of such courtship, telling of exciting rides through the air with Hindu suitors on horseback or by airplane, and other dramatic episodes.

Perhaps we may shrug off these accounts as the erotic dreams and fantasies of shy young girls. (One also thinks of the imaginary playmates of lonely children.) But the important point about these fantasies is that for many Saora they persist for a lifetime. If the girl continues to refuse her suitor's hand in marriage, she falls ill. Her parents therefore arrange a wedding with the invisible groom. This makes the girl a shaman. Henceforth she has contacts with the other world through her husband's mediation. She may become possessed; then he and other spirits speak through her. The same applies to men who become shamans by marrying Hindu women in the other world. The shaman, whether male or female, may marry a

---

[18] W. Lloyd Warner, *A Black Civilization. A Social Study of an Australian Tribe* (rev. ed.; New York: Harper, 1958), p. 198.

living Saora and have children. But they also have children by their spouses in the other world. The Saora women suckle them at night. They keep track of the progress of their children in the other world as they grow older and tell stories about them.

Doesn't there seem to be something abnormal about this lifetime involvement in fantasy—a fantasy which becomes extraordinarily complicated and elaborate, as Elwin's pages testify? Yet neither the Saora nor Elwin himself consider the shamans to be abnormal. According to Elwin the Saora are, in general, a happy people, devoted to their children. One seldom hears crying in a Saora village. The people sing as they work. They have few repressions or inhibitions, and their attitudes toward sex are frank and simple.[19] As for the shamans, they are "almost always very good people, by any standards. They are kind and affectionate, hard-working and unselfish . . ."[20] Shaman girls are described as being very self-possessed, dignified, and motivated by ideals of charity.

We are faced here with the same problem as in evaluating the behavior of the Murngin socerer. Both the people themselves and the ethnographer in each case judge the individuals in question to be normal.

Perhaps this is the right approach, since in each case the behavior is culturally patterned, and, in contrast to such culturally patterned disorders as *windigo, latah, imu, saka,* and *pibloktoq* which are discussed below, they are not held to be pathological by members of the society. This view would be in keeping with Ludwig van Bertalanffy's notion that soundness of mentality is determined by whether or not the individual has an integrated universe consistent within a given cultural framework. The Murngin cultural framework may contain ideas which are bizarre from our point of view, but Laindjura's "integrated universe" is consistent with it; so perhaps he should not be regarded as mentally ill.[21] Laindjura's crazy notions are culturally patterned; there are other men who have the same delusions. Since ideas of this kind are rather widespread in Australia, they must be rather old. Is it possible that there have been men in

---

[19] Verrier Elwin, *The Religion of an Indian Tribe* (London: Oxford University Press, 1955), pp. 57, 567.

[20] Ibid., p. 568. In evaluating Elwin's observations, it must be said that he is an excellent ethnographer but that he has a tendency to champion and perhaps idealize the hill peoples of India.

[21] Ludwig von Bertalanffy, "System, Symbol, and the Image of Man (Man's Immediate Socio-Ecological World)," in Iago Galdston (ed.), *The Interface between Psychiatry and Anthropology* (New York: Brunner/Mazel, 1971), p. 109.

every generation with the same delusions for a thousand years or more? The delusions, in their patterned form, have to be kept alive by being experienced in each generation by men like Laindjura. This is a selective kind of cultural transmission. Only some men in each generation have such delusions, just as only some men become shamans.[22]

The Murngin and Saora cases illustrate the difficulties of assessing normality and abnormality in non-Western cultures. But in the Western world there are also ambiguous cases. Many Nazi officials who were well adjusted to the Germany of the Hitler regime might be regarded as emotionally disturbed.[23] For reasons such as these it is hard to say whether there is more mental disorder in one non-literate society than in another.[24]

It seems likely that some cultures bear down more heavily on the individual than do others and cause more stress. One thinks of the Egyptian town of Silwa and of the Aymara discussed in Chapter 2. By contrast there are the Okinawans of Taira, described in Chapter 9, who give an impression of being happier people. But we have no comparative figures on the incidence of mental disorders in these communities.

Marvin K. Opler believes that there is proportionately much more mental disorder in our modern civilization than in simpler primitive cultures.[25] The implication is that as civilization advances and tensions increase, the rates of mental disorder go up. This notion would be in keeping with some of the studies cited in earlier chapters, such as Malinowski's picture of the well-adjusted Trobriand Islanders and Margaret Mead's contrast of carefree Samoan adolescence with the storm-and-stress of European and American youth.

---

[22] Some similarities may be noted between Laindjura's "murders" and the experiences of Arunta men in central Australia who seek to become shamans. Some such men lie down before a cave and go to sleep. It is believed that during the night a spirit comes out from the cave, "kills" the man, removes his entrails, replaces them with a new set, and then brings the man back to life. The Arunta shaman's fantasy is passive; he is the victim. Laindjura's fantasy is active; he is the aggressor who does the killing and disemboweling.

[23] See Douglas M. Kelley, *22 Cells in Nuremberg* (New York: Chilton Co., 1947).

[24] On the question of defining normality and abnormality, the interested reader should consult Henry J. Wegrocki, "A Critique of Cultural and Statistical Concepts of Abnormality," in Clyde Kluckhohn and Henry A. Murray, *Personality in Nature, Society, and Culture* (New York: Alfred & Knopf, 1948), pp. 551–61; John J. Honigmann, *Culture and Personality* (New York: Harper, 1954), pp. 369–423; Donald A. Kennedy, "Key Issues in the Cross-Cultural Study of Mental Disorders," in Bert Kaplan (ed.), *Studying Personality Cross-Culturally* (Evanston, Ill.: Row, Peterson and Co., 1961), pp. 405–25.

[25] Opler, *Culture and Social Psychiatry*, p. 271.

As noted in Chapter 1, the idea is also in keeping with a conflict model of personality like Freud's. If culture is repressive, an individual should be better off in a simpler culture with fewer restrictions. In *Totem and Taboo,* Freud interpreted fear of ghosts of the recently dead among primitive peoples in terms of emotional ambivalence and projection or displacement of the survivor's hostility onto the ghost. Freud noted that such fear of the dead has practically disappeared among ourselves and suggested that perhaps this was because primitive peoples were more ambivalent than we are. This interpretation would imply that we are less neurotic than our primitive ancestors were. But in a later work, *Civilization and Its Discontents,* Freud expressed a different view, claiming that primitive man was better off than we in lacking restrictions on his instincts. Thus, as civilization has increased, so has sexual repression. And with an increase in such repression, one would expect an increase in mental disorder.[26] However, it was noted in Chapter 11 that in the large-scale cross-cultural examination by Leighton and his associates of psychiatric disorders among the Yoruba of Nigeria on the one hand and in Stirling County in Canada on the other, the similarities in the findings for the two culture areas were more striking than the differences, despite the great differences in the two cultures. Moreover, Bernard Rimland claims that rates of hospitalization for mental disorder in the United States have recently been going down, not up, largely due to the use of biochemical antipsychotic drugs. At the end of 1965 there were 83,000 fewer hospitalized patients than in 1955, in spite of a considerable increase in total U.S. population during the decade.[27]

CULTURALLY PATTERNED DISORDERS

One of the questions raised earlier was whether different cultures tend to bring about different types of mental disturbance. It is evident that there must be some cultural patterning in at least the *content* of delusions and hallucinations. A person must have some familiarity with European history, however slight, if he is to arrive at the notion that he is Napoleon. An unacculturated Eskimo who

---

[26] Sigmund Freud, *Civilization and Its Discontents,* in James Strachey (ed.), *The Standard Edition of the Complete Psychological Works of Sigmund Freud,* Vol. XXI (1927–31) (London: The Hogarth Press, 1961), p. 115. As early as 1897 Freud wrote in a letter to a friend, ". . . incest is anti-social and civilization consists in a progressive renunciation of it." (Editor's Introduction, Ibid., p. 60).

[27] Rimland, "Psychogenesis versus Biogenesis," p. 729.

develops paranoia will have to be mad in a somewhat different way, although the underlying structure of his ailment may be the same as in Europe.

A common delusion among the insane in the Western world is that of being controlled or influenced by rays or electricity. This notion will be absent among people with no knowledge of electricity, as among unacculturated African Negroes. However, among more acculturated African Negroes this pattern does occur.[28] The same contrast appears between lower class and better educated middle-class Bahian patients in Brazil, among whom the latter, but not the former, entertain notions about being influenced by electricity.[29] Culture thus influences the *content* of delusions and hallucinations.

In studying mental disorders in non-Western societies one can either look for manifestations of the traditional neuroses and psychoses of the Western world and so classify mentally disturbed individuals, or else one can approach the subject from the indigenous viewpoint. In most societies there are terms for mental disorders; one can learn what these terms are and then find to which persons they are applied. The Berndts used this approach in a study of Australian aboriginal concepts of abnormality.[30] But the most elaborate application of this method is in a work by George Devereux.

Devereux presents Mohave terms for different types of sickness and the traditional symptoms associated with them. He points out that the patient's knowledge of what disease he is suffering from may lead to a kind of unconscious "malingering," so that the appropriate symptoms appear in due course. That such processes are at work is suggested by the fact that the shamans who specialize in certain cures are frequently most effective in removing the symptoms.[31]

This suggests one way in which culturally patterned disorders may come to characterize certain societies. Among disorders which appear to be culturally patterned are *windigo, latah, imu, saka,* and *pibloktoq.* These ailments appear to be sufficiently distinct, so that the native terms for them have been retained when they are discussed

---

[28] Tooth, *Studies in Mental Illness in the Gold Coast,* p. 52.

[29] E. Stainbrook, "Some Characteristics of the Psychopathology of Schizophrenic Behavior in Bahian Soceity," *American Journal of Psychiatry,* Vol. 109 (1952), p. 333.

[30] Ronald M. Berndt and Catherine H. Berndt, "The Concept of Abnormality in an Australian Aboriginal Society," in George B. Wilbur and Warner Muensterberger (eds.), *Psychoanalysis and Culture. Essays in Honor of Géza Roheim* (New York: International Universities Press, 1951), pp. 75–89.

[31] George Devereux, *Mohave Ethnopsychiatry and Suicide: The Psychiatric Knowledge and the Psychic Disturbances of an Indian Tribe,* Smithsonian Institution, Bureau of American Ethnology, Bulletin 175 (Washington, D.C., 1961), pp. 19, 20.

in the literature. A justification for once again dealing with these often described syndromes is that some new points of view about these disorders have been expressed in recent years, and these deserve to be examined.

Windigo

The *windigo* or *wiitiko* psychosis is a form of disorder formerly found among Chippewa, Cree, and Montagnais-Naskapi Indians in Canada, characterized by cannibalistic impulses and delusions. In these cases the affected individual, who is usually deeply depressed, may believe that he has been possessed by the spirit of a *windigo,* or cannibal giant with a heart or entrails of ice. He may also have symptoms of nausea, anorexia, and insomnia, and may see the people around him turning into beavers or other edible animals (like Charlie Chaplin's famished companion in "The Gold Rush"). Indeed, the disorder has been attributed to the experience of starvation and isolation in wintertime.[32]

Seymour Parker is skeptical of this explanation for two reasons. First, those who suffer from the psychosis are not always threatened by starvation. Secondly, there are peoples, like the Eskimo, among whom starvation is a frequent danger but where no analogue of the *windigo* psychosis has developed. Hence Parker suggests a psychoanalytic interpretation, influenced by Abram Kardiner's views, in which the pattern is ultimately traced to frustrated dependency needs in childhood. The prototype of the cannibal giant is seen to be the frustrating mother. Parker accepts a statement by Landes to the effect that women rarely succumb to this ailment; it particularly affects men who have had repeated failures in hunting. Parker sug-

---

[32] Ruth Landes, "The Abnormal among the Ojibwa," *Journal of Abnormal and Social Psychology,* Vol. 33 (1938), pp. 14–33; John M. Cooper, "The Cree Witiko Psychosis," *Primitive Man,* Vol. 6 (1933), pp. 20–24.

Vivian J. Rohrl has suggested the possibility that biological factors, particularly vitamin deficiency, contribute to *windigo* psychosis. Rohrl notes that a traditional "cure" of *windigo* symptoms was to feed the victim fatty meat, and she suggests that the Indians somehow acquired a half-conscious "knowledge" of the relationship between dietary deficiency and psychosis, as this custom implies. (Vivian J. Rohrl, "A Nutritional Factor in Windigo Psychosis," *American Anthropologist,* Vol. 72 [1970], pp. 97–101.) Jennifer Brown, however, has taken issue with this suggestion, pointing out that fatty meat eating is seldom mentioned as a *windigo* cure. Moreover, in the two such cases which are cited its main purpose was not to give nourishment but to induce the vomiting up of the cannibal's "heart of ice." (Jennifer Brown, "The Cure and Feeding of Windigos. A Critique," *American Anthropologist,* Vol. 73 [1971], pp. 19–22.)

gests that such men feel abandoned and worthless, not only because they have no food, but because they feel bereft of their power.

Under these conditions, the dam (constituted by ego defenses) is shattered and the repressed cravings for the expression of dependency and aggressive needs bursts forth. The depressive conflict between the rebellious rage and the submissive fear is resolved. If this interpretation is correct, then the psychotic symptoms serve, at the same time, to allay dependency cravings (by becoming one with the object of dependency) and to aggress against this frustrating object (by killing and eating it). The psychotic aspect of this behavior consists not of the dependent and aggressive feelings in themselves, but in the failure of the normal personality and institutionalized defenses and the resultant overt expression of hitherto repressed or socially channelized impulses.[33]

In criticism of Parker, both Raymond D. Fogelson and Thomas H. Hay (discussed below) point out that most American Indians have been described as having strong "oral" dependency needs, but they do not all have the *windigo* syndrome. Hence, an explanation of the *windigo* psychosis in terms of Ojibwa modal personality would not seem to be sufficient. However, there seems to be some support for a psychoanalytic interpretation of *windigo* psychosis in William M. Bolman's account of a 37-year-old single white female patient, a secretary whose symptoms had some similarities to *windigo* cases. The patient obsessively bought and hoarded hamburgers. For the first two years of this behavior she bought from 2 to 5 pounds of raw hamburger a day, but this steadily increased to huge quantities of about 60 pounds a day. The patient was acutely anxious. Indeed, Bolman states that "anxiety" is too mild a word, "stark terror" being more appropriate. After nearly three years of treatment, the patient began to express some ideas about herself. She had had a fantasy that she was a dangerous, murderous person, who killed people as they slept and ate them. Her mother, her dead father, and her younger sister were all associated with the hamburgers. Fear of separation or loss of these ambivalently regarded persons seems to have contributed to the obsessive hamburger hoarding. The patient did not, however, eat the hamburgers but kept the raw meat until after it became rotten. An interesting parallel with the *windigo* syndrome is that the patient said that when she was out at night looking for places where she could buy hamburgers, she was like ice inside. The cannibalistic impulse seems to have been mainly unconsicous,

---

[33] Seymour Parker, "The Wiitiko Psychosis in the Context of Ojibwa Personality and Culture," *American Anthropologist,* Vol. 62 (1960), p. 620.

although expressed in fantasy and enacted symbolically in her rituals with hamburgers.[34]

Raymond D. Fogelson holds that the *windigo* "psychosis" is not a unitary phenomenon. He has tried to break down the reported *windigo* cases into five basic types, with some subtypes. Fogelson believes that these variants represent different forms of mental disorder ranging from mild and severe episodes of anxiety neurosis to full-blown psychoses.[35]

Morton Teicher has canvassed the available literature on the *windigo* psychosis and has identified 70 cases, of which 45 were Chippewa (or, following Teicher, Ojibwa with 30 cases and Saulteaux with 15). The others were Montagnais-Naskapi (11 cases), Cree (9), Beaver (1), Tête de Boule (1) and 3 of unknown source. Most of the cases were from northeastern Canada and occurred in the 19th century. In 44 of the episodes cannibalism actually took place; it was a real threat in the others as well. About half of the *windigo* sufferers were killed by members of the community. Of the 44 cases involving cannibalism, members of the immediate family were eaten in 36 cases. Teicher believes that this is because of the nature of the social order, with small isolated families often living alone. Forty of the 70 cases were males; 29 were females, and in one case the sex was not specified.[36] (The relatively high number of female *windigo* sufferers does not argue well for Parker's theory.) Teicher estimates that, at most, 25 of the 70 cases were associated with famine conditions. In these cases the term "psychosis" seems to be inappropriate, for Teicher points out that these individuals killed from hunger and sometimes had the support of others in violating the taboo on cannibalism. It was only in their later behavior that members of this group showed mental disturbances,[37] which would suggest a different psychodynamic picture for the development of the disorder in these cases.

Teicher thinks that *windigo* cases must have been rare. The number must have been much greater than the 70 cases he records,

---

[34] William M. Bolman, "Hamburger Hoarding. A Case of Symbolic Cannibalism Resembling Whitico Psychosis," *The Journal of Nervous and Mental Disease,* Vol. 142 (1966), pp. 424–28.

[35] Raymond D. Fogelson, "Psychological Theories of *Windigo* 'Psychosis' and a Preliminary Application of a Models Approach," in Melford E. Spiro (ed.), *Context and Meaning in Cultural Anthropology* (New York: The Free Press, 1965), pp. 74–99.

[36] Morton I. Teicher, *Windigo Psychosis. A Study of the Relationships between Belief and Behavior among the Indians of Northeastern Canada,* Proceedings of the American Ethnological Society (Seattle, 1960), pp. 44, 107–9.

[37] Ibid., p. 110.

since these depended on "the fortuitous presence of a white re-corder."[38] Even so, Teicher is struck by the rarity of reported cases.

Thomas H. Hay writes that "Since cannibalistic impulses are fre-quent among psychotic people in all societies, *windigo* cannibalism is not to be explained by peculiarities of the psychodynamics com-mon to the Northern Algonkians."[39] As mentioned earlier, Hay re-jects Parker's psychoanalytic interpretation. At the same time, he gives some weight to psychodynamic considerations, such as Freud's idea that by introjecting (eating) a lost love object, a bereaved per-son may have the feeling that he is bringing him or her back to life. Hay cites Fenichel's suggestion that cannibalism may have the un-conscious significance of preserving a relationship. In many cultures ritual cannibalism has this connotation, and there seems to be a manifestation of this notion in the strange behavior of the ham-burger hoarder described above. Cannibalism was regarded with horror, at least on a conscious level, by the northern Algonkians, and patterns of ritual cannibalism were not available. But an opening wedge for *windigo* behavior, which Hay cites as a contributory factor, was the Algonkian emphasis on individual acceptance of un-conscious promptings, as reflected in dreams.

Latah, Imu, Saka, and Pibloktoq

These disorders are grouped together (although they are reported for different geographical areas), since they have a number of fea-tures in common and are generally considered to be forms of hysteria, primarily affecting women. *Latah,* found in Southeast Asia and Indonesia, involves a startle reaction; the subject is easily frightened and may cry out. She then engages in compulsive imita-tive behavior, repeating actions she has observed (echopraxia) or phrases she has heard (echolalia).[40]

David F. Aberle has described *latah* behavior in Mongolia, which is similar except that here men seem to be often the victims.

He may put his hand in the fire when the investigator merely gestures toward it, or undress completely when some one takes off an outer gar-ment, or jump in the river when some one pretends to start to jump. . . .

---

[38] Ibid., p. 107.

[39] Thomas H. Hay, "The Windigo Psychosis: Psychodynamic, Cultural, and Social Factors in Aberrant Behavior," *American Anthropologist,* Vol. 73 (1971), p. 17.

[40] F. H. G. van Loon, "Amok and Lattah," *Journal of Abnormal and Social Psy-chology,* Vol. 21 (1926), pp. 434–44.

A severe latah may react imitatively in any novel or disturbing situation, such as meeting a stranger or a superordinate, even when the other person has no wish to provoke imitation. The latah may imitate natural objects or animals, in the absence of any human audience.[41]

Aberle says that a man who has been frightened may shout obscene exclamations (coprolalia), especially words for male and female genitalia.

Imu is a somewhat similar condition found among the Ainu of northern Japan. It particularly affects older women, although it is sometimes found among young girls. Winiarz and Wielawski report that its incidence is frequent. In three Ainu villages of 1,000 there were 12 *imu* cases. In five of these the symptoms developed right after the woman had been bitten by a snake. Other cases were also related to snakes, either through seeing or dreaming about one. The attack may be started if someone pronounces the word for snake or any loud sharp sound. The woman affected may then curse and engage in excited aggressive behavior or else run away in panic. Echopraxia and echolalia also appear. As in Indonesia and Mongolia, the victim is aware of the incongruity of her behavior but cannot stop herself, and she continues with her compulsive mimicry until worn out. Women often claim to feel better after an attack.[42]

Although it is not known why, there has been a dramatic decrease in the incidence of *imu* in recent years, dropping from 111 cases in 1934 to only 1 case in 1958.[43]

Not all writers agree in classing *latah* and *imu* as forms of hysteria. Tadeusz Grygier says that the symptoms of *imu* correspond roughly to the Western standard of catatonia and not of hysteria.[44] Benedict and Jacks take the same view of *latah*, and, with some qualifications, of *pibloktoq*.[45]

Marvin K. Opler classifies *latah, imu, pibloktoq,* and *amok* as "nuclear forms of schizophrenias" (distinguishable from chronic and paranoid types) which are open to spontaneous remission or

---

[41] David F. Aberle, "'Arctic Hysteria' and Latah in Mongolia," in Yehudi A. Cohen (ed.), *Social Structure and Personality. A Casebook* (New York: Holt, Rinehart, & Winston, 1961), p. 471.

[42] W. Winiarz and J. Wielawski, "Imu—A Psychoneurosis Occurring among Ainus," *Psychoanalytic Review,* Vol. 23 (1936), pp. 181–86.

[43] Y. Kumasaka, "A Culturally Determined Mental Reaction among the Ainu," *Psychiatric Quarterly,* Vol. 38 (1964), pp. 733–39.

[44] Tadeusz Grygier, "Psychiatric Observations in the Arctic," *British Journal of Psychology,* Vol. 39 (1948), p. 92.

[45] Benedict and Jacks, "Mental Illness in Primitive Societies," p. 386.

curable by shamanism or other techniques.[46] They could also be called forms of "hysterical psychosis," which are characterized by "a sudden and dramatic onset temporally related to a profoundly upsetting event or circumstance. Its manifestations include hallucinations, delusions, depersonalization and grossly unusual behavior."[47]

Saka is described as a form of hysteria found among women of the Wataita tribe in Kenya. Grace Harris gives the following picture:

> Women beginning to have attacks of saka sometimes show evident signs of a generalized restlessness and of anxiety. However, sometimes without any obvious warning a woman begins the characteristic convulsive movements. The upper part of the body trembles but often the head and shoulders are more affected so that, while the shoulders shake rapidly, the head is moved rhythmically from side to side. As the attack continues the eyes may close and the face becomes expressionless. Some women perform certain simple acts in monotonous repetition, or they repeat strange sounds which are supposed to be foreign words. If there is singing or drumming or other music, the woman in saka may move about as in a trance. There sometimes appears to be a loss of consciousness, and at such times the woman becomes rigid, her teeth are clenched, and she must either be supported or gently helped to lie down.
>
> Susceptibility to saka attacks is so common among married women that in some localities as many as half the married women are subject to them at least occasionally. Some women claim and are acknowledged by others to have saka very severely; others are subject to much milder attacks. . . . The immediate events which bring on an attack vary, for each woman has her own sensitivities, though all of these fall into a pattern. Sometimes a particular sight, smell or sound is responsible: the sight of a motor car, the sound of a train whistle, the sight or smell of a cigarette, the sound of a match being struck, the sight of a bright piece of cloth, the smell, sight, or taste of bananas.[48]

One form of cure for *saka* is to have the woman drink water in which a man's lower garment has been washed. A woman may also ask to suck some of her husband's blood. There is also a public form of therapy, a *saka* dance, in which the women wear bright cloth garments saved for such occasions, a red fez or a man's felt hat, bandoliers, and perhaps a man's belt around the waist. The purpose of the dance is to get the women "all danced out," so that they won't have more attacks.

Pibloktoq is a disorder found among Polar Eskimo in northern

---

[46] Opler, *Culture and Social Psychiatry*, pp. xix, 279–80.

[47] Marc H. Hollender and Steven J. Hirsch, "Hysterical Psychosis," *American Journal of Psychiatry*, Vol. 120 (1964), p. 1073.

[48] Grace Harris, "Possession 'Hysteria' in a Kenya Tribe," *American Anthropologist*, Vol. 59 (1957), pp. 1047–48.

Greenland. It may affect both sexes, but more commonly women. The subject is at first irritable or withdrawn, then engages in a burst of violent excitement. He may shout, tear off his clothes, break things, and then run out across the ice. Friends and relatives chase after him and try to keep him from harming himself. After this period of excitement the subject sometimes has convulsive seizures and then may fall asleep. Upon awakening he may be perfectly normal and have no memory of the attack. In this respect there seems to be a contrast with *latah* and *imu,* also in the lack of emphasis on echolalia and echopraxia. *Pibloktoq* sometimes has a high incidence, especially in winter, and a number of persons living in a small community may be afflicted in the course of a season.[49]

Somewhat similar disorders have been described for the Ona and Yahgan of Tierra del Fuego, but the information is scanty.[50]

Some Interpretations

A number of theories have been put forth to account for the manifestations of *latah, imu, saka,* and *pibloktoq,* either separately or as a group. Some have attributed *latah*-like reactions to racial factors (since they often appear among Mongoloids) or to climatic extremes. P. M. Yap observes that both of these theories are rendered unlikely by the fact that similar disorders have been reported for Caucasoids in Maine—the "jumping Frenchmen."[51] The similarity of *saka* in Kenya to *latah* has also been noted. Yap points out, as Van Loon has also done, that most cases of *latah* are middle-aged women. These women, moreover, tend to come from the lower social strata of their communities and to be uneducated. Yap remarks that those subject to *latah* do not have strongly integrated personalities, and are passive, submissive individuals. He also claims that a low level of technological development is characteristic of all cultures where *latah*-like behavior appears.[52]

David F. Aberle suggests that *latah* behavior is a form of defense

[49] Anthony F. C. Wallace, "Mental Illness, Biology, and Culture," in Francis L. K. Hsu (ed.), *Psychological Anthropology* (Cambridge, Mass.: Schenkman Publishing Co., 1972), pp. 370–72.

[50] Isador H. Coriat, "Psychoneuroses among Primitive Tribes," *The Journal of Abnormal Psychology,* Vol. 10 (1915–16), pp. 201–8.

[51] P. M. Yap, "Mental Diseases Peculiar to Certain Cultures: A Survey of Comparative Psychiatry," *Journal of Mental Science,* Vol. 97 (1951), pp. 313–27.

[52] P. M. Yap, "The Latah Reaction: Its Pathodynamics and Nosological Position," *Journal of Mental Science,* Vol. 98 (1952), pp. 515–64.

against the fear of being overwhelmed. This defense consists partly in identifying with the aggressor—through imitation.

They "go over to" (identify with) the stimulus, flee from it, destroy it —or stifle the unconscious material with a cry. . . . My present guess (and it is only that) is that the latah's problem is one of disturbance and ambivalence with respect to submissive behavior, that this disturbance is based on an unconscious connection between submission and a dreaded and desired passive sexual experience akin to being attacked, and on the idea that the world stands ready to "overwhelm" the victim in this double sense.[53]

Grace Harris presents an ingenious analysis of *saka*. She points out that the things which bring on attacks in susceptible women, and which may also appear in the therapeutic measures used to cure them, have some features in common. They fall into three over-lapping categories: (1) things which are the concern of men, nor-mally forbidden to women, such as cigarettes, male attire, bananas (which are planted by men) , and water in which a man or his clothes have been washed; (2) purchased goods such as clothing, sugar, and cloth; (3) foreign items, such as automobiles, a fez, a train whistle, foreign words.

The second category consists of "women's things," bought mainly with money earned by the men. The third category consists of things outside of the usual experience of women, but with which the men have more contact through their wage work away from home. "Thus all the objects and acts which, in the context of saka, seem to excite strong fear and desire in women and which also appear to relieve the symptoms accompanying these emotions, have to do with the differ-ences between men and women with respect to goods and activities."[54]

Harris explains that in this Kenya society men are the owners of land and livestock, which women cannot inherit. Women earn very little money, the trading and wage work being done mainly by men. Women are in a dependent and relatively inferior position in rela-tion to men. Harris suggests as one possible interpretation for *saka* behavior that the symptoms reflect envy of the men and ambivalence about the female role.

Here one would note the obviously Freudian symbolism of cigarettes, bananas, dirty water, blood, and dancing staves, as well as the appearance of both fear and desire accompanying the convulsive movements. Giving women the objects they desire, protecting them from what they fear, and

---

[53] Aberle, " 'Arctic Hysteria' and Latah in Mongolia," pp. 474–75.

[54] Harris, "Possession 'Hysteria' in a Kenya Tribe," p. 1051.

giving them an opportunity to be the center of attention might then be thought compensatory or even therapeutic.[55]

The author's analysis is more extensive than this and cannot be dealt with in full. Harris does not refer to *latah* or *imu* in her paper, but as we shall consider presently, there may be similar relationships between men and women in other cultures where *latah*-like behavior appears.

Turning to *pibloktoq*, a psychoanalytic interpretation of this disorder has been made by A. A. Brill, who considered it to be a form of hysteria in which the seizures express frustration at lack of love.[56] Zachary Gussow has elaborated on this theme and interpreted the flight of the victim as an invitation to be pursued, an infantile attention-getting maneuver to gain love and reassurance.[57]

Seymour Parker believes that hysteria is relatively common among the Eskimo. He cites a condition known as "kayak fright" and other hysterical manifestations in this area. Parker makes the suggestion that hysterical behavior tends to prevail in societies:

a) Where early socialization experiences are not severe and involve minimal repression of dependency needs and sexual drives. In such societies, where there is relatively high gratification of dependency needs, the modal super-ego structure will not be severe or rigid.

b) Where there is an emphasis on communalistic values, a relatively great amount of face-to-face cooperative patterns, and high expectations of mutual aid.

c) Where the female role involves considerable disadvantages and lower self-esteem compared to the role of the male.

d) Where the religious system involves beliefs in supernatural possession, and where "hysterical-like" behavior models are provided in the institutionalized religious practices.[58]

Parker then proceeds to show that these patterns prevail among the Eskimo. They also seem to apply to the Kenya tribe described by Harris, where the female role seems to be subject to various disadvantages. The position of Ainu women is also said to be very low; belief in possesion, moreover, is related to the *imu* syndrome, for

---

[55] Ibid., pp. 1054–55.

[56] A. A. Brill, "Pibloktoq or Hysteria among Perry's Eskimos," *Journal of Nervous and Mental Diseases*, Vol. 40 (1913), pp. 514–20.

[57] Zachary Gussow, "Pibloktoq (Hysteria) among the Polar Eskimo. An Ethnopsychiatric Study," in Warner Muensterberger and Sidney Axelrad (eds.), *The Psychoanalytic Study of Society* (New York: International University Press, 1960), Vol. I, pp. 218–36.

[58] Seymour Parker, "Eskimo Psychopathology in the Context of Eskimo Personality and Culture," *American Anthropologist*, Vol. 64 (1962), p. 81.

"imu" means "possessed" in the Ainu language.[59] Parker's thesis seems to be plausible and consistent.

However, the problem of interpreting hysterical manifestations has been placed in a new light with the appearance of a paper by Anthony F. C. Wallace. Wallace points to the necessity of considering possible biological factors in the etiology of hysteria. It appears that calcium deficiency may produce symptoms like those of *pibloktoq*.

> Observation and testing in the field would be required to confirm the hypocalcemic hypothesis and to rule out alternative diagnoses (hypoglycemic shock, hysteria, food poisoning, virus, encephalitis, etc.). It is also possible that a tendency toward epilepsy may have been genetically determined by inbreeding in this small isolated group; this is suggested by reports that epilepsy is more common in northern Greenland than elsewhere on the island. The hypocalcemia and epilepsy theories are not mutually exclusive, however, since hypocalcemia probably would tend to precipitate a latent seizure in persons prone to epilepsy.[60]

Wallace provides some evidence for the existence of low calcium resources in this arctic area. He also suggests that the apparent decline in cases of hysteria in the Western world since the 19th century may have been due to changes in dress, diet, and other factors which have provided for better calcium intake in the population of Europe since 1900; and he notes that the discovery of the values of sunlight, milk, foods containing vitamin D, and the improvement of living conditions in the 20th century was accompanied by a great decrease in the frequency of rickets, tetany, and hysteria.[61] If calcium was not sufficiently available to many 19th-century Europeans, the same state of affairs was very likely present in many areas where *latah*-like behavior has been found. Biological factors (of which, as Wallace indicates, calcium deficiency may be only one) are therefore possible causative agents in the development of such behavior. Nevertheless, cultural factors are still operative, since these disorders seem to have culturally patterned manifestations. Whether calcium deficiency is present or not, the theories of Harris and Parker may still have their relevance.

Incidentally, although Wallace accepts the view that cases of hysteria have declined in the Western world, some psychiatrists

---

[59] Winiarz and Wielawski, "Imu—A Psychoneurosis Occurring among Ainus," p. 182.

[60] Anthony F. C. Wallace, "Mental Illness, Biology, and Culture," in F. L. K. Hsu (ed.), *Psychological Anthropology*, p. 374.

[61] Ibid.

would disagree. Thomas Szasz claims that hysteria is still prevalent in America and Europe, mainly among lower class, relatively uneducated persons, who do not go to psychiatrists but consult physicians. The latter generally refer them to neurologists and other *medical* specialists.[62] Hollender and Hirsch also believe that there has been no decline in cases of hysterical psychosis in the past half century.[63]

"Wild Man" Behavior in New Guinea

Two authors, Philip L. Newman and Lewis L. Langness, have written articles about what Newman has termed "wild man" behavior and what Langness has classified as "hysterical psychosis" in the highlands of New Guinea. There are both similarities and differences in these two accounts. The seizures described by the authors affect only young males, roughly between the ages of 22 and 35.

A kind of "running amok" pattern characterized by hyperactivity, running and jigging up and down was described for the Bena Bena case reported on by Langness. Some break with reality is suggested by the glazed eyes of the young man at a high point in his excitement and by the fact that he did not react to loud shouts in his ear. The young man gave panting gasps, and his skin was cold to the touch. It is believed by the Bena Bena that this behavior is brought about by malevolent ghosts of the same clan as the young man, who has evidently offended one or more of them. Langness reports that this disturbance is rarer among acculturated men, who have more mobility and may be less hemmed in by the social world, the pressures of which weigh heavily on young newly married men who are often lectured to and scolded by older men.[64]

A somewhat similar picture is given by Newman of an episode affecting a man of the Gururumba tribe. In this case the man asked various people to give him certain objects, which he placed in a stolen net bag. These demands were accompanied by aggressive, threatening gestures and sometimes blows. Newman's "wild man" was hyperactive and sometimes seemed to be not in full control of

[62] Thomas Szasz, *The Myth of Mental Illness. Foundations of a Theory of Personal Conduct* (New York: Harper and Row, 1961) , pp. 76–77.

[63] Hollender and Hirsch, "Hysterical Psychosis," p. 1066.

[64] Lewis L. Langness, "Hysterical Psychosis in the New Guinea Highlands: A Bena Bena Example," *Psychiatry,* Vol. 28 (1965) , pp. 258–77.

his body. In such cases there is said to be an increase in respiratory and circulatory rates, sweating, and a drop in skin temperature. The "wild man" sometimes appears not to hear what is said to him, and there seems to be some reduction in his ability to speak.

On the evening of the third day of "wild man" behavior, the Gururumba man described by Newman ran into the forest. He reappeared briefly the next day, without his bag of stolen loot, and said that he was going off to collect pandanus nuts. The man was gone for 13 days; on his return to the community he was accepted by the villagers and resumed normal life.

Like Langness, Newman draws attention to the social stresses which affect young married men in highland New Guinea tribes. Marriages are arranged by kinsmen and village-mates, not by the parties involved, and the betrothal periods are long, so that men are often in their mid-twenties before they begin to lead an active married life. The establishment of a family entails economic obligations and payment of debts, which place the young men under considerable pressure, to which may be added the problems of having a dissatisfied young wife. Wives often run away, and tensions then develop between a man and his in-laws and between the respective kin groups. Newman believes that the economic pressures that beset young Gururumba males is related to some aspects of the "wild man" behavior. "The accumulation and destruction of objects becomes an understandable outlet for a man beset by difficulties arising from his inability to effectively control objects."[65]

FURTHER EXAMPLES OF CULTURAL PATTERNING IN MENTAL DISORDERS

In the preceding pages some culturally patterned mental disorders have been discussed. There are other such disorders; for instance, the fear of sorcery which can lead, not only to sickness, but even to death.[66] There is the condition of *amok,* found in Indonesia and elsewhere, in which a brooding depression succeeds to a dangerous explosion of violence. There is the anxiety state known as *koro,* found in Southeast Asia, in which the patient is afraid that his penis

---

[65] Philip L. Newman, "'Wild Man' Behavior in a New Guinea Highlands Community," *American Anthropologist,* Vol. 66 (1964), p. 13.

[66] Walter B. Cannon, "'Voodoo' Death," *American Anthropologist,* Vol. 44 (1942), pp. 169–81.

will withdraw into his abdomen and cause his death.[67] There is also the condition known as *susto,* or magic fright, sometimes found in peasant communities in Latin America, and the trancelike state reported for Formosa, known as *Hsieh-ping.*[68]

There is the phenomenon of tarantism which has a recorded history of 600 years in Europe and is still to be found in some peasant communities in south Italy. Here there is a notion that a kind of madness is inflicted by the bite of a spider or tarantula, which can be alleviated by dancing until exhaustion, to the music of an orchestra. That the toxic effects of an actual spider bite are not crucial in this syndrome is shown by the fact that the dancing delirium is for many persons an annual event, occurring shortly before the festal day of St. Peter and St. Paul at Galatina in south Italy. Victims of such seizures are generally women, beginning in adolescence or early adult life, but often continuing until old age. Somehow the figure of St. Paul has become identified with the tarantula. Those who have recently been affected by tarantism and have recovered go to the chapel to give thanks to the saint.[69]

Even when we have a category of mental disorder, such as schizophrenia, under which patients may be classified in different countries, there may still be variations in behavior and characteristic symptoms from one cultural group to another. It has been noted, for example, that hospitalized schizophrenic patients are less violent and aggressive in India, Africa, and Japan than in the Western world,[70] and William Caudill has observed that reports from some non-Western countries, like Japan, indicate that schizophrenic patients manifest less withdrawal than they do in the United States.[71] An African psychiatrist reports that delusions of grandeur are rare among Yoruba paranoiacs, and he explains this by saying that Yoruba culture demands total allegiance and submission to ancestral cults

---

[67] Ralph Linton, *Culture and Mental Disorders* (Springfield, Ill.: Charles C Thomas, 1956), pp. 67–69. See also P. M. Yap, "Koro—a Culture-bound Depersonalization Syndrome," *The British Journal of Psychiatry,* Vol. 3 (1965).

[68] Eric Wittkower and J. Fried, "A Cross-Cultural Approach to Mental Health Problems," *American Journal of Psychiatry,* Vol. 116 (1959), p. 425.

[69] "Tarantism. St. Paul and the Spider," *The Times Literary Supplement,* London, Eng., April 27, 1967, pp. 345–47. (No author's name is given.)

[70] Wittkower and Fried, "A Cross-Cultural Approach to Mental Health Problems," p. 424.

[71] William Caudill, "Observations on the Cultural Context of Japanese Psychiatry," in Marvin K. Opler (ed.), *Culture and Mental Health, Cross Cultural Studies* (New York: The Macmillan Co., 1959), p. 233.

and deities. In such a cultural climate, delusions of persecution may develop, but not those of grandeur.[72]

Within the Western world there may also be variations in behavior and symptomatology among schizophrenic patients from different ethnic or national groups. Marvin K. Opler has reported differences between Italian and Irish schizophrenic patients. He found that Irish patients had preoccupations with sin and guilt related to sex; this was not true of the Italians.

The Italian patients did not have the elaborate systematized delusions often found among the Irish patients; instead they were given to hypochondriacal complaints and body preoccupation. There was more open rejection of authority among the Italians.

[The Italians] had more prominent problems of overflow (schizo-affective features) which took the form of elated overtalkativeness, curious mannerisms, grinning and laughing hyperactivity, or even assaultiveness. . . . While Italian patients might oscillate between hyperactivity and underactivity, or show an inability to time their activities, thoughts, or emotions effectively, the Irish, with no such difficulties in estimating time or guarding their emotions, showed an inversely large proportion of rich and extensive fantasy.[73]

Fantl and Schiro discovered similar contrasting patterns among Irish and Italian female schizophrenics. They found, for example, a higher degree of sex guilt in a small group of Irish patients and more impulsive, unruly behavior and conflicts with authority figures in a corresponding group of Italians.[74]

Anne Parsons, who givs a good description of the schizophrenic episode of a young girl in Naples,[75] has compared the behavior of southern Italian schizophrenic patients with American schizophenics. In south Italy psychotic delusions concern the family or neighborhood, while in the United States delusions often relate to large-scale institutions, such as the hospital, the Communist movement, or an advertising agency. American delusions, according to

---

[72] T. Adeoye Lambo, "The Role of Cultural Factors in Paranoid Psychosis among the Yoruba Tribe," *Journal of Mental Science,* Vol. 101 (1955), p. 251.

[73] Marvin K. Opler, "Cultural Differences in Mental Disorders: An Italian and Irish Contrast in the Schizophrenias—U.S.A.," in Marvin K. Opler (ed.), *Culture and Mental Health,* pp. 437–38. Published originally under the title "Cultural Perspectives in Research on Schizophrenias: a History with Examples," *The Psychiatric Quarterly,* Vol. 33 (1959), pp. 519–20.

[74] Berta Fantl and Joseph Schiro, "Cultural Variables in the Behavior Patterns and Symptom Formation of 15 Irish and 15 Italian Female Schizophrenics," *International Journal of Social Psychiatry,* Vol. 4 (1959), pp. 245–53.

[75] Anne Parsons, "A Schizophrenic Episode in a Neapolitan Slum," in Anne Parsons, *Belief, Magic, and Anomie* (New York: The Free Press, 1969), pp. 212–34.

Parsons, tend toward abstraction, while south Italian delusions are more concrete.[76]

Despite these differences, related to different cultural or social backgrounds, there are some common features of schizophrenia which seem to be present in all cultural settings, such as "social and emotional withdrawal, auditory hallucinations, delusions, and flatness of affect."[77] The coexistence of both common transcultural patterns and local cultural differences in psychiatric syndromes is indicated in a survey by Robert B. Edgerton of conceptions about psychosis in four East African tribes: the Sebei, the Pokot, the Kamba, and the Hehe, who were discussed earlier in Chapter 3. Over 500 persons were questioned, chosen by probability sampling techniques, excluding highly Europeanized subjects. All males included were heads of households; the females were their wives. The interviews were held in private under standardized conditions.

A striking finding of this survey is that there was considerable agreement among the four tribes in their conceptions of psychosis, and also much agreement on the part of all four tribes with conceptions of psychosis in the Western world. There were also some differences, however. "Going naked" was often mentioned as an aspect of psychotic behavior. Murder, attempted murder, or serious assault were also cited, to a degree which would exceed Western-based expectations. On the other hand, hallucinations were seldom mentioned as aspects of psychotic behavior, although the author states that they do occur in East African mental hospitals.

Edgerton does not claim that his survey supports either the view that psychoses are essentially the same transculturally or the view that they differ according to the nature of the culture. Support for either position could be derived from the results of his survey.[78]

We have now reviewed a wide variety of culturally patterned disorders. The existence of such variety seems to show that most cultures have some traditional form or forms of aberrant behavior. They are maintained over the generations by folklore, memory, and gossip. People who display aberrant behavior may be typed, let us say, as being *windigo,* even though this category may include a wide range of deviant behavior. The existence of such a category and label

---

[76] Anne Parsons, "Abstract and Concrete Images in Paranoid Delusions: A Comparison of American and South Italian Patients," in Parsons, ibid., pp. 204–11.

[77] Ari Kiev, "Transcultural Psychiatry: Research Problems and Perspectives," in Plog and Edgerton, *Changing Perspectives in Mental Illness,* p. 116.

[78] Robert B. Edgerton, "Conceptions of Psychosis in Four East African Societies," *American Anthropologist,* Vol. 68 (1966), pp. 408–25.

may induce deviants to behave in ways that accord with the stereotype, especially when the deviant is in a confused suggestible state.
As Thomas J. Scheff has put it: "In a crisis, when the deviance of an
individual becomes a public issue, the traditional stereotype of
insanity becomes the guiding imagery for action, both for those
reacting to the deviant and, at times, for the deviant himself."[79]
This view is in keeping with George Devereux's suggestion, mentioned earlier in this chapter, that a Mohave patient's knowledge of
what ailment he is suffering from may lead to a kind of unconscious
"malingering" and adoption of the appropriate symptoms.

CLASS AND MENTAL DISORDER

In an often-cited study Faris and Dunham showed that rates for
schizophrenia in Chicago were highest in the central part of the city,
in the "hobohemia," rooming house area where many migrants, Negroes, and foreign-born lived. Rates for schizophrenia were much
lower in the better class residential sections of the city. Manic-depression showed no such clustering but seemed to have a random distribution.[80] This indicated that schizophrenia was influenced by
socioeconomic factors. In 1941 Tietze, Lemkau, and Cooper reported findings along similar lines—that there was more schizophrenia in lower class groups and relatively more manic-depressive
psychosis in higher classes.[81]

It is interesting that a similar state of affairs has been claimed for
Chinese communities in Taiwan, where T. Y. Lin found a high
rate of schizophrenia in the lower class and more manic-depression
in the upper. He even found the tendency, reported by Faris and
Dunham, for schizophrenia to occur more frequently in the central
zone of each area than in the peripheries. This zonal distribution of
schizophrenia has now appeared in nine studies of American cities,
although some other investigations have found somewhat different
distributions.[82] A high incidence of suicide has also been found in

---

[79] Scheff, *Being Mentally Ill*, p. 82.

[80] Robert E. L. Faris and H. Warren Dunham, *Mental Disorders in Urban Areas*
(Chicago: University of Chicago Press, 1939).

[81] Christopher Tietze, Paul V. Lemkau, and Marcia Cooper, "Schizophrenia, Manic-
Depressive Psychosis, and Socio-Economic Status," *American Journal of Sociology*, Vol.
47 (1941), pp. 167–75.

[82] H. Warren Dunham, *Sociological Theory and Mental Disorder* (Detroit: Wayne
State University Press, 1959), pp. 141–45; T. Y. Lin, "A Study of the Incidence of Mental
Disorders in Chinese and Other Cultures," *Psychiatry*, Vol. 16 (1953), pp. 313–36.

central, socially disorganized rooming house areas of some large American cities.[83]

In 1953 a paper was published by Robert M. Frumkin which showed that there was a high incidence of mental illness among low-income, low-prestige, and low socioeconomic status groups in first-admissions cases in Ohio state mental hospitals.[84]

Two studies of New Haven have demonstrated that the lower the socioeconomic class, the greater the proportion of mentally disturbed patients in the population. The incidence of psychoses in the lowest class (Class V) is almost three times greater than in the two highest socioeconomic groups (Classes I and II) and twice the rate for Class IV.[85] Hollingshead and Redlich were able to rule out the hypothesis of "downward drift" which some critics have invoked to explain the Faris and Dunham findings—that is, the idea that persons drift toward the slums as they become affected by schizophrenia. Indeed, Myers and Roberts showed that a majority of schizophrenics had been *upwardly* mobile—more so than their siblings.[86] The upward mobility of schizophrenics has also been discussed by E. Ellis.[87]

A possible contributory factor to the class differences in rates for schizophrenia is the availability of treatment in psychotherapy. Those who are better off are more apt to be accepted by psychiatrists or clinics for treatment. Moreover, cultural differences may make communication more difficult between lower class patients and therapists.[88]

Still another way of looking at these matters has been provided by Braginsky, Braginsky, and Ring. Lower class patients whose life is difficult in the outer world and who are not deterred by the social stigma of institutionalization may—at least in some of the better mental hospitals—find many advantages in the "last resort" of the

---

[83] Andrew F. Henry and James F. Short, Jr., *Suicide and Homicide. Some Economic, Sociological, and Psychological Aspects of Aggression* (Glencoe, Ill.: The Free Press, 1954), p. 135.

[84] Robert M. Frumkin, "Occupation and Major Mental Disorders," in Arnold M. Rose (ed.), *Mental Health and Mental Disorder. A Sociological Approach* (New York: W. W. Norton, 1955), pp. 136–60.

[85] August B. Hollingshead and Fredrick C. Redlich, *Social Class and Mental Illness, A Community Study,* (New York: John Wiley & Sons, 1958), pp. 235–36. See also Jerome K. Myers and Bertram H. Roberts, *Family and Class Dynamics in Mental Illness* (New York: John Wiley & Sons, Inc., 1959).

[86] Myers and Roberts, Ibid., pp. 130–33.

[87] E. Ellis, "Social Psychological Correlates of upward Social Mobility among Unmarried Career Women," *American Sociological Review,* Vol. 17 (1952), pp. 558–63.

[88] Jerome K. Myers and Leslie Schaffer, "Social Stratification and Psychiatric Practice," *American Sociological Review,* Vol. 19 (1954), pp. 307–10.

mental hospital and may make the quite "rational" choice of trying to prolong their time in the hospital under the diagnosis of chronic schizophrenia.[89] If this should be so, an understandable correlation between lower class membership and hospital diagnosis of schizophrenia could be brought about.

In reviewing epidemiological studies, H. Warren Dunham concludes that schizophrenia is found in every social class, and that its prevalence in lower class groups is due to the extreme competitiveness of American life, for which the preschizophrenic personality is poorly equipped.[90] It would be interesting to have comparative data on the incidence of schizophrenia in socialist or communist societies in which the nature or extent of competitiveness might differ.

Since there is so much consistency in the reports cited, the alleged relationship between economic class and rate of mental disorder seems to be rather well established. There have, however, been some contradictory findings. Jaco found that while incidence rates were highest among the unemployed in Texas, the highest standardized rates for those employed at the time of becoming psychotic were found among professionals and semiprofessionals. Jaco points out that studies in Singapore and Norway have likewise found high incidence rates among professional groups.[91]

MIGRATION AND MENTAL DISORDERS

There is evidence from various parts of the world for a connection between migration and mental disorder. Needless to say, this association is not invariable; many migrants are free of mental ailments and many stay-at-homes succumb to them. But there seems to be some connection, all the same, either because mentally disturbed persons are driven to leave home and try their chances elsewhere, or because of the stresses involved in adjusting to a new environment.

Ødegaard made a study of Norwegian-born immigrants in Minnesota and found that over a period of four decades their rate of hospital admissions for mental disorders was much higher than those for either native Americans or Norwegians in Norway. Interestingly enough, a still higher rate of mental disorder was found among emi-

---

[89] Braginsky, Braginsky, and Ring, *Methods of Madness*, pp. 166–73.

[90] H. Warren Dunham, *Community and Schizophrenia. An Epidemiological Analysis* (Detroit, Mich.: Wayne State University Press, 1965), p. 256.

[91] E. Gartly Jaco, *The Social Epidemiology of Mental Disorders* (New York: Russell Sage Foundation, 1960), pp. 141, 178.

grants to the United States who later returned to Norway. There seemed to be more schizophrenia and fewer affective psychoses among the Norwegian-born of Minnesota than in Norway.[92]

Another interesting finding is that internal migration within Norway was not accompanied by increased mental disorder; on the contrary, migrants have lower admission rates than those who remain in their natal communities. Oslo constitutes an exception, either because the migrants represent a less favorable selection, or because they meet with more difficulties there. Ødegaard concludes that migration within Norway is not so drastic a move as emigration to the United States and does not involve so marked a break with the family, friends, home community, and traditional customs. Thus, it is less traumatic in its effects.[93]

In a study of New York State admissions, Malzberg and Lee found that, over a three-year period, migrants greatly exceeded nonmigrants, both for schizophrenia and manic-depression, as well as for other psychoses. The rates were much higher for recent than for earlier migrants.[94] Foreign-born patients with mental disorders have also been shown to have higher admission rates than native-born in practically all age groups from 1917 to 1933 in Massachusetts.[95]

Isaac Frost found that psychoses often develop among foreign domestic servants in Britain, usually within 18 months of their arrival. Reporting on a study of 40 Austrian and German domestic servants, Frost notes that acute confusional and schizophrenic disturbances associated with bodily signs of toxemia usually occur, and that about 60 percent of the victims recover within about a year.[96]

Libuse Tyhurst made a study of European displaced persons in Montreal who, like Frost's subjects, were working at domestic or unskilled labor. Among those newly arrived, the author noted a sense of well-being, for the first two months or so, with an increased psy-

---

[92] Ørnulv Ødegaard, "Emigration and Insanity. A Study of Mental Disease among the Norwegianborn Population of Minnesota," *Acta Psychiatrica et Neurologica,* Suppl. 4; Oslo: 1932, pp. 80–83, 103, 176.

[93] Ørnulv Ødegaard, "The Distribution of Mental Diseases in Norway, A Contribution to the Ecology of Mental Disorder," *Acta Psychiatrica et Neurologica,* Vol. 20 (1945), pp. 270–76.

[94] Benjamin Malzberg and Everett S. Lee, *Migration and Mental Disease. A Study of First Admissions to Hospitals for Mental Disease 1939–1941* (New York: Social Science Research Council, 1956), pp. 119–22.

[95] Neil A. Dayton, *New Facts on Mental Disorders* (Springfield, Ill.: Charles C. Thomas, 1940), p. 104.

[96] Isaac Frost, "Home-sickness and Immigrant Psychoses. Austrian and German Domestic Servants the Basis of Study," *Journal of Mental Science,* Vol. 84 (1938), p. 801.

chomotor activity which served to release tension. This phase was followed by a sense of strain with a greater awareness of the social situation, difficulties encountered with the language, and unfamiliar customs. Nostalgic fantasies of a happy past provided escape from these realities. About six months after arrival various symptoms were noted: suspiciousness and paranoid tendencies, anxiety and depression, and a variety of somatic and psychosomatic complaints.[97]

Migration has been related to mental disorder in other parts of the world beside Europe and the United States. Laubscher interpreted the higher rate of male over female admissions for mental disorders among South African natives in terms of the fact that the men were more migratory.[98]

Carothers, who found the rate of mental disorder among Kenya Africans to be very low, also found that the rates were higher among men who were not living in their native villages. Among Africans living at home, the certification rate was about 2.3 per 100,000, while for those employed or living away from home the rate was 13.3 per 100,000.[99]

Okinawans are well known for their low rate of mental disorder, but Okinawans who have migrated to Hawaii have a very high rate of psychosis, significantly higher than that for any other major group in Hawaii, and two and a half times as high as that for the total population.[100]

Patterns similar to those found by Tyhurst in the Montreal study have been observed among Andean highland migrants to lowland Peru. Here, however, the picture is complicatd by the change in altitude, which brings about various physiological consequences. Seguin found that young migrants, aged 15 to 25, often develop what he calls a psychosomatic maladjustment syndrome, which may appear from within a week or two after arrival in Lima, to a year later. Upsetting experiences of various kinds may be the precipitating factors. Homesickness is associated with this picture, as among the

[97] Libuse Tyhurst, "Psychosomatic and Allied Disorders," in H. B. M. Murphy (ed.), *Flight and Resettlement* (Paris: UNESCO, 1955), pp. 202–13.

[98] B. J. F. Laubscher, *Sex, Custom, and Psychopathology, A Study of South African Pagan Natives* (New York: Robert M. McBride & Co., 1938), p. 256.

[99] J. C. Carothers, "A Study of Mental Derangement in Africans, and an Attempt to Explain its Peculiarities, More Especially in Relation to the African Attitude to Life," *Psychiatry*, Vol. 11 (1948), p. 57.

[100] B. M. Wedge, "Occurrence of Psychosis among Okinawans in Hawaii," *American Journal of Psychiatry*, Vol. 109 (1952), pp. 255–58; for a discussion of the mental health of Okinawans in Okinawa, see James Clark Moloney, "Psychiatric Observations on Okinawa Shima," *Psychiatry*, Vol. 8 (1945), pp. 391–99.

immigrants in Montreal. The symptoms are varied and include cardiovascular failures, gastritis, peptic ulcer, constipation, colitis, hemorrhoids, bronchitis, pseudotuberculosis, neuritis neuralgias, headaches and migraines.[101]

Jacob Fried, who has discussed the problems facing migrants to Lima, sent a questionnaire to psychiatrists in a number of countries to see if similar patterns appear elsewhere in connection with migration. From the replies he received there seems to be evidence for psychosomatic disorders being associated with migration in other regions. A doctor in Taiwan, for example, writes:

> The outstanding characteristic of the clinical picture of both neurotics and psychotics among the group of migrated patients [i.e., Mainland Chinese] as compared with the group of Formosan born [is the] . . . great tendency to utilize somatic symptoms in neurotic patients of the migrated group.[102]

One is reminded here of De Vos' Rorschach studies of Algerians who had left their native communities and moved to the Casbah, and of Japanese living in the United States. In both groups he found more body-preoccupation content in the Rorschach responses than for comparable rural samples in Algeria and Japan. De Vos remarks, "These results suggest that there may be a turning in of hostility and/or an emotional withdrawal from difficult object relationships within a social context into an unhealthy self-preoccupation."[103]

Distinctions should probably be made between different kinds of migration and migrants—voluntary migrants, overseas students, indentured workmen or servants, displaced persons, refugees, and so forth. Different types of stress are no doubt associated with different sorts of migration. H. B. M. Murphy has pointed out that in Israel and Singapore immigrants are reported to have less mental hospitalization than the natives, and he suggests that the large main cities of a country, like Oslo, Paris, and New York, may attract different types of migrants than do other communities.[104]

---

[101] Alberto Seguin, "Migration and Psychosomatic Disadaptation," *Psychosomatic Medicine,* Vol. 18 (1956), pp. 404–9.

[102] Jacob Fried, "Acculturation and Mental Health among Indian Migrants in Peru," in Marvin K. Opler (ed.), *Culture and Mental Health,* p. 120.

[103] George De Vos, "Symbolic Analysis in the Cross-Cultural Study of Personality," in Bert Kaplan (ed.), *Studying Personality Cross-Culturally* (Evanston, Ill.: Row, Peterson & Co., 1961), p. 608.

[104] H. B. M. Murphy, "Social Change and Mental Health," in *Causes of Mental Disorders: A Review of Epidemiological Knowledge, 1959* (New York: Milbank Memorial Fund, 1961), pp. 286–90, 304.

Miriam L. Gaertner has made a comparison between the adjustments of European refugees and Puerto Rican immigrants to New York soon after World War II. She found that the former were much more successful in making a place for themselves. They were better equipped culturally for assimilation and for getting jobs and were financially better off than the Puerto Ricans. The latter could return home whenever they wished, but the Europeans were forced to make good in their country of adoption and made a more aggressive effort to do so. The Puerto Ricans tended to fail to learn English, which further handicapped them. The European refugees, moreover, met with a more favorable reception in the new country. The nature of the migration and the assets and resources of the migrants must therefore be taken into consideration.[105]

The age of migrants should also be considered, for, as Murphy has noted, rates of hospitalization for migrants are generally highest in youth and old age. Children do not seem to be much affected by displacement, as long as they remain with their parents; persons of middle age also seem to be less affected by the stress of migration.[106]

ACCULTURATION AND CULTURE CHANGE

Acculturation and culture change are closely related to migration, although culture change may take place without either migration or acculturation, and migration may take place without either acculturation or culture change. High rates of mental disorder have often been attributed to rapid acculturation in formerly colonial, underdeveloped countries.[107]

But, again, it is necessary to qualify. Margaret Mead has described the dramatically swift transformation of Manus culture which has taken place within a generation, but which has not, as far as one can gather from her book, been accompanied by any increase in mental disorders—unless the Cargo Cult in which many Manus participated be taken as a manifestation of such disorder. One gets the impression

---

105 Miriam L. Gaertner, "A Comparison of Refugee and Non-Refugee Immigrants to New York City," in H. B. M. Murphy (ed.), *Flight and Resettlement* (Paris: UNESCO, 1955), pp. 99–112.

106 Ibid., pp. 310–11. For two recent reviews of studies on the relationship between migration and mental illness, see Mildred B. Kantor, "Internal Migration and Mental Illness," in Plog and Edgerton, *Changing Perspectives in Mental Illness*, pp. 364–94; and Benjamin Malzberg, "Are Immigrants Psychologically Doomed?" Ibid., pp. 395–421.

107 H. B. M. Murphy, *Flight and Resettlement*, p. 309.

that, if anything, the Manus are happier now than they were in the old days.[108]

To cite another example, Eric Berne reports that acculturation processes do not seem to have increased rates of mental disorder in the Fiji Islands. Citing census figures since 1911, Berne claims that such disorders were actually more frequent in the preindustrial, prewar era than in the recent period.[109] There may, then, be exceptions to the stressful nature of acculturation and culture change.

What are some of the consequences common to the experiences of migration, acculturation, and rapid culture change? One may be a kind of confusion and disorientation, sharpened by a sense of emotional isolation. Murphy has listed some types of situations which may provoke acute confusional states—for example, students in their first year at college, immigrants arriving off a ship, soldiers recently inducted.[110] An abrupt change in cultural context may have effects similar to the emotional isolation of rooming house life noted by Faris and Dunham and others, as among young Africans who go to Britain to study and who often have mental breakdowns there.[111]

METHODS OF THERAPY

Related to the topic of mental disorder is that of therapeutic techniques. As Ari Kiev has pointed out, "As cultures produce characteristic tensions, they also provide mechanisms for the release of tensions.[112] Anthropologists did not formerly pay much attention to such mechanisms. Some interest was, of course, taken in the performances of shamans, diviners, and priests, but usually without considering the possibility that their actions might actually have some therapeutic value. More attention is now being given to this subject, partly because of a growing skepticism about the efficacy of our own techniques for dealing with mental illness. There are dif-

[108] Margaret Mead, *New Lives for Old. Cultural Transformation—Manus, 1928–1953* (New York: William Morrow & Co., 1956).

[109] Eric Berne, "Difficulties of Comparative Psychiatry: The Fiji Islands," *American Journal of Psychiatry*, Vol. 116 (1959), pp. 104–9.

[110] H. B. M. Murphy, *Flight and Resettlement*, p. 321.

[111] M. J. Field, p. 318. See also John C. Lilly, "Mental Effects of Reduction of Ordinary Levels of Physical Stimuli on Intact, Healthy Persons," *Psychiatric Research Reports of the American Psychiatric Association*, Vol. 5 (1956), p. 7; and Arthur J. Prange, Jr., "An Interpretation of Cultural Isolation and Alien's Paranoid Reaction," *International Journal of Social Psychiatry*, Vol. 4 (1959), pp. 254–63.

[112] Ari Kiev, "The Study of Folk Psychiatry," in Ari Kiev (ed.), *Magic, Faith, and Healing. Studies in Primitive Psychiatry Today* (London: The Free Press of Glencoe, 1964), p. 25.

ferent schools of psychiatry with different basic assumptions and therapeutic techniques. One would think that some practitioners or schools of though would be closer to the basic truths about the human personality than others and would consequently have a higher incidence of cures. But it seems that the various schools and methods of treatment do not vary much in their rates of cure. "Most statistical studies show that 65–70% of neurotic patients and 35% of schizophrenic patients improve after treatment regardless of the type of treatment received."[113] Since many mentally disturbed persons make a spontaneous recovery without any treatment at all, the role of the physician in such recoveries is obscure. A combination of confession by the patient and suggestion and reassurance by the physician may often be enough to bring about a cure. These services are also performed by shamans and priests, perhaps as successfully as by psychiatrists in many cases, or even more successfully. Thus we might as well give some serious attention to how practitioners in non-Western societies go about their cures.

The book edited by Ari Kiev, cited above, is addressed to this subject. It includes an article by Weston La Barre on the use of confession as cathartic therapy in American Indian tribes; an article by Jane B. Murphy on the therapeutic aspects of shamanism among the St. Lawrence Island Eskimos; and other essays on "folk psychiatry" among the Yoruba, Ndembu, Temne, Shona, and Luo of Africa, the Balahis of Central India, the Cochiti, Apache, and Navaho Indians, Australian aborigines, Yemenite Mori, Turkish villages, and natives of south Texas.

Commenting on the therapeutic methods used in these various societies, Kiev points to the fact that they generally serve to allay fear and anxiety on the part of the patient and mobilize a sense of hope, features which are often more important for recovery than a correct diagnosis.[114] While there may be some mumbo jumbo in a particular shamanistic performance, the mumbo jumbo plays a part in giving the patient the feeling that he is in good hands.

As another aspect of non-Western therapeutic methods, William Sargant has drawn attention to the role of abreaction in the curing practices of some nonliterate peoples. If a mentally disturbed patient is worked up to a state of excitement, followed by collapse, his

---

[113] Ibid., p. 5.
[114] Ibid., p. 461.

symptoms may disappear on his recovery, in a manner similar to the experience of a person who has undergone electric shock therapy.[115]

SUMMARY

It is hard to decide whether there are fewer mental disorders in simpler non-Western cultures than in our own, partly because adequate figures are not available, but also because of the fact that behavior considered normal in our society may be regarded as queer in others, while behavior considered abnormal in our society (trance, possession, visionary experience, transvestism) is perfectly acceptable in many cultures. Assessment of the rate of mental disorder is complicated by the "pathology of normalcy" or by what Erich Fromm has called "culturally patterned defects" associated with behavior which is culturally approved but which may be emotionally crippling.

There is evidence that mental disorders may be culturally patterned, and some examples have been discussed—the *windigo* psychosis, *latah, imu, saka,* and *pibloktoq*. There is also evidence that schizophrenia may follow somewhat different courses in various countries, involving different symptoms and behavior patterns, as, for example, among Irish and Italian patients.

It may be concluded that most cultures have some traditional form or forms of aberrant behavior which are maintained over the generations by folklore, memory, and gossip. People who display aberrant behavior may be typed by the rest of the group as belonging to the traditional deviant category, which may induce suggestible deviants to act in ways that accord with the stereotype.

While there are contradictory findings in some surveys, many studies have provided convincing evidence for a relationship between mental disorder and socioeconomic class, with the lower classes having a much higher rate of serious mental illness (such as schizophrenia) than the upper classes. There also seems to be convincing evidence for a relationship between migration and mental disorder, as well as for rapid acculturation and mental disorder, although these are not invariable associations.

---

[115] William Sargant, *Battle for the Mind* (New York: Doubleday & Co., 1957), pp. 65–80.

SUGGESTIONS FOR FURTHER READING

On the question of defining normality and abnormality, see the references in footnote 24 in this chapter.

For studies of mental disorders in non-Western cultures, see especially Opler's volume, *Culture and Mental Health*, M. J. Field's *Search for Security*, and Devereux's *Mohave Ethnopsychiatry*, also cited in this chapter.

For a recent collection of papers, see Iago Galdston (ed.), *The Interface between Psychiatry and Anthropology* (New York: Brunner/Mazel, 1971).

A problem not discussed in this chapter concerns the relative rates of mental disorder in rural and urban areas. This was omitted because the findings are so often conflicting. Some studies claim that urban rates, in certain areas, are much higher than rural rates: for instance in Benjamin Malzberg, *Social and Biological Aspects of Mental Disease* (Utica, N.Y.: State Hospitals Press, 1940), p. 350; and "Important Statistical Data about Mental Illness," in Silvano Arieti (ed.), *American Handbook of Psychiatry* (New York: Basic Books, Inc., 1959), Vol. I, p. 171.

Some urban-rural comparisons in various parts of the world, however, have shown no particular differences in rates of hospitalization for mental disorders. Ødegaard found about the same admission rates in Norwegian cities and rural areas. The main exception was Oslo, the only large city in Norway, where the higher incidence was partially attributed to the unusually good hospital facilities there. (Ørnulv Ødegaard, "The Distribution of Mental Diseases in Norway. A Contribution to the Ecology of Mental Disorder," *Acta Psychiatrica et Neurologica*, Vol. 20 (1945), p. 283). Beaglehole reports that the number of psychotics from urban and rural areas in Hawaii is about the same. (Ernest Beaglehole, *Some Modern Hawaiians*, University of Hawaii Research Publications, No. 19 [1937], p. 162). Eleanor Leacock has drawn attention to some other investigations in Sweden, Finland, Ohio, and Michigan, in which the urban rates for mental disorder do not exceed the rural. In fact, in Ohio the rural rates appear to be somewhat higher. Leacock concludes that the significant question is not the extent of urbanization, but the degree of social integration represented in an area. She points out that there are many stable community groups in northeastern urban areas and also many anomic migrant farm populations. (Eleanor Leacock, "Three Social Variables and the Occurrence of Mental Disorder," in Alexander H. Leighton, John A. Clausen, and Robert N. Wilson (eds.), *Explorations in Social Psychiatry* (New York: Basic Books, 1957), pp. 314, 321.

Some writers have assumed that rural populations are mentally healthier than urban ones, exposed to less conflict and tension. The reason studies have been made of mental health among the Hutterites is that these religious farming people have gained a wide reputation for their alleged "peace of mind." In a study of the Hutterites, Eaton and Weil found that paranoid and manic symptoms were uncommon and that there was a "virtual absence of severe personality disorders, obsessive-compulsive neuroses, psychopathology, and psychoses associated with syphilis, alcoholism, and drug addiction." (Joseph W. Eaton and Robert J. Weil, *Culture and Mental Disorders. A Comparative Study of the Hutterites and Other Populations* [Glencoe, Ill.: The Free Press, 1955], p. 215). However, in a succeeding study, based largely on the analysis of Thematic Apperception Tests and Sentence Completion Tests, Kaplan and Plaut concluded that some forms of psychopathology were widespread and that the Hutterites "are considerably worse off mental healthwise than they appear to be." (Bert Kaplan and Thomas F. A. Plaut, *Personality in a Communal Society. An Analysis of the Mental Health of the Hutterites,* University of Kansas Publications, Social Science Studies [Lawrence, Kan., 1956] p. 102.) Leacock's point about the rural-urban controversy seems important—that there are different types of rural areas having different degrees of social integration.

There are also differences among cities. Austin, Texas, which Belknap and Jaco have characterized as a "political-type city," has a relatively low rate of hospitalization for mental disorders, while industrial cities tend to have relatively high ones. (Ivan Belknap and E. Gartly Jaco, "The Epidemiology of Mental Disorders in a Political-Type City, 1946–1952," in *Interrelations between the Social Environment and Psychiatric Disorders,* Milbank Memorial Fund, 1953, pp. 235–43.)

Another question not raised in this chapter, since the findings seem ambiguous, is whether or not mental disorders are on the increase. Malzberg alleges that there has been a real increase of such disorders in New York State, as indicated by rates of first admissions to state hospitals from 1913 to 1950. (Benjamin Malzberg, "Important Statistical Data about Mental Illness," pp. 164–65). Goldhamer and Marshall, focusing only on psychoses and not concerning themselves with the incidence of neuroses and character disorders, have covered a longer time period—a century of first admissions rates in mental hospitals in Massachusetts. Their findings are at variance with Malzberg's and may be summarized by saying that there has been no increase in the incidence of psychoses during the past century. This applies, however, to the psychoses of early and middle life; there has been an increase in admission rates for older persons. (Herbert Goldhamer and Andrew W. Marshall, *Psychosis and Civilization. Two Studies in the Frequency of Mental Disease,* [Glencoe, Ill.: The Free Press, 1949], pp. 91–92).

In conclusion, another interpretation of the etiology of schizophrenia may be referred to; this is the "double-bind" hypothesis. In this approach, schizophrenia is seen as resulting from a confusion in communication—principally between mother and child, although the "double-bind" is not limited to this relationship. A "double-bind" takes place when an individual is involved in an intense relationship with another person, a relationship from which he cannot escape. The person with whom he is involved conveys two mutually contradictory messages, and he is unable to respond adequately, in view of the inherent contradictions. For an elaboration of this concept, see Gregory Bateson, Don D. Jackson, Jay Haley, and John H. Weakland, "Toward a Theory of Schizophrenia," *Behavioral Science,* Vol. 1 [1956], pp. 251–64, and John H. Weakland,

"The 'Double-Bind' Hypothesis of Schizophrenia and Three-Party Interaction," in Don D. Jackson (ed.), *The Etiology of Schizophrenia* (New York: Basic Books, 1960), pp. 373–88.

Some other studies of recurrent patterns in the families of schizophrenic patients have noted similar mechanisms, without making use of the same terminology. See, for example, Murray Bowen, "A Family Concept of Schizophrenia," in D. D. Jackson (ed.), *The Etiology of Schizophrenia,* pp. 346–72.

chapter 17

Culture, Personality, and Culture Change

When the culture of a society changes and it develops new institutions, the members of the society must adapt themselves to the new conditions. Such adaptation may involve changes in personality which may, in turn, lead to further changes in culture. For example, a number of writers have discussed the changes in values and attitudes that developed in Europe as the feudal system broke down and as mercantile capitalism increased in importance.

BURCKHARDT ON THE RENAISSANCE

A pioneer in the analysis of such topics was Jacob Burckhardt, whose book, *The Civilization of the Renaissance in Italy,* was published in 1860. Burckhardt argued that there was a great growth of individualism in 14th-century Italy, in contrast to conditions in earlier medieval times. According to Burckhardt, there were not even any prevailing fashions in men's attire in Florence in 1390.[1] Burckhardt was struck by the number of "complete," or many-sided men, appearing in Italy at this time, culminating in such figures as Leon Battista Alberti and Leonardo da Vinci. There was a concern with personal glory and achievement. Cults surrounded the birthplaces and graves of famous men. And there was a new development of biography and autobiography (for instance, those of

---

[1] Jacob Burckhardt, *The Civilization of the Renaissance in Italy* (Oxford: Phaidon Press, 1945), p. 82.

Cellini and Girolamo Cardano) with a keen interest in the distinctive characteristics of individuals. Burckhardt also cited the lawlessness of the times, for individualism was expressed in acts of aggression and crime as well.[2] To support these generalizations, Burckhardt drew contrasts between the earlier Middle Ages and the Renaissance, between northern Europe and Italy. The key to these developments was seen in the political situation in Italy, with its competing states and petty despots. In the courts of such men, individualistic self-expression was encouraged, at least in some spheres. In this respect Italy was in the forefront of Europe, for the stress on individualism was to become one of the emphases in Western culture.

Burckhardt's interpretation seems convincing, although J. Huizinga pointed out that "individualistic" behavior was exalted in earlier Norse sagas, that a thirst for personal glory was present in the ideals of medieval chivalry, and that there is some difficulty in locating clear boundary lines between the Middle Ages and the Renaissance.[3]

FROMM ON WESTERN MAN

Erich Fromm is another writer who has dealt with these themes.[4] Fromm has been influenced not only by Burckhardt but by the writings of Max Weber and Richard H. Tawney as well as by those of Freud and Marx. From Fromm's point of view, the new freedom of the Renaissance had ambivalent connotations for men of the time. For those with wealth and power it provided opportunities for self-fulfillment and intellectual and aesthetic discoveries and was congenial to well-placed persons who had an exploitative orientation. But for many persons of the lower classes the breaking up of medieval society led to a feeling of isolation. The individual no longer had a secure and recognized position in society. Commerce and competition grew rapidly in the 14th and 15th centuries, and the condition of the peasantry and small tradesmen deteriorated.

---

[2] Ibid., pp. 84–92, 119 f., 275 f.

[3] J. Huizinga, *Men and Ideas. History, the Middle Ages, the Renaissance*, trans. James S. Holmes and Hans van Marle (New York: Meridian Books, 1959), pp. 260–61.

J. Huizinga, *The Waning of the Middle Ages. A Study of the Forms of Life, Thought, and Art in France and the Netherlands in the XIVth and XVth Centuries* (London: Edward Arnold, 1924), p. 59.

[4] The following is a brief summary of Chapter III in Erich Fromm, *Escape from Freedom* (New York: Rinehart & Company, 1941.)

The individual was now on his own, free but alone and powerless.

Fromm sees Lutheranism and Calvinism as religions which appealed to the urban middle class, the urban poor, and the peasants because they gave expression not only to the new sense of freedom but also to the feelings of anxiety and powerlessness felt by these classes. The value of effort was stressed by Calvinism, referring at first to moral effort but later being increasingly concerned with hard work in one's occupation, success in which came to be regarded as a sign of God's grace. Fromm believes that the new ethic of hard work had a compulsive quality related to the sense of anxiety and powerlessness, which the individual sought to overcome through hectic activity. Thus, man became his own slave driver. European man's voluntary application of energy to work resulted in the rapid expansion of the new economy. But men had to pay a price for their compulsive devotion to work. Being thwarted in the areas of emotional and sensual expression, the lower and middle classes developed strong feelings of resentment and hostility.

A hoarding orientation was fostered by conditions in the 18th and 19th centuries. This involved both the positive aspects of being practical, reserved, cautious, tenacious, orderly, and methodical, but also the negative aspects of being stingy, suspicious, cold, anxious, stubborn, obsessional, and possessive.[5] The exploitative orientation also found channels of expression in the 18th and 19th centuries. But, according to Fromm, conditions have changed in the capitalism of the 20th century. "Instead of the exploitative and hoarding orientation we find the receptive and marketing orientation. Instead of competitiveness we find an increasing tendency toward 'teamwork'; instead of a striving for ever-increasing profit, a wish for a steady and secure income. . . ."[6]

"Marketing orientation" refers to a man's sense of himself as a marketable commodity, his conception of his own value depending upon how well he can sell himself and succeed in the business world. If he succeeds, he has a good opinion of himself; if not, he feels that he is a failure. Fromm believes that this kind of personality, characteristic of our time, is marked by a sense of alienation from the self and from others.[7]

Fromm writes as a moralist; he is a preacher but a good one. Yet, stimulating though his insights are, they suffer from the draw-

---

[5] Erich Fromm, *The Sane Society* (New York: Rinehart & Company, 1955), p. 91.

[6] Ibid., p. 99.

[7] Ibid., pp. 120, 142.

back that such broad scale reconstructions are hard to adequately document with supporting evidence. Besides, the material which Fromm covers is susceptible to other historical and psychological generalizations. For example, while Fromm writes that Lutheranism and Calvinism were religions of the urban middle class, the poor in the cities, and the peasants, Abram Kardiner in a chapter on "Basic Personality and History," writes that the Reformation was not a movement of the oppressed lower classes or of the peasants but of the new burgher class which was trying to establish a secular state. Calvinism would not seem to appeal to the poor, from Kardiner's viewpoint, since the idea that success is proof of virtue easily leads to contempt for the poor and the unsuccessful.[8] Questions of fact as well as of interpretation are involved here. Fromm's generalizations (and Kardiner's too) need much more documentation to carry conviction. In this respect the study of a Mexican village by Erich Fromm and Michael Maccoby, to which we will return later in this chapter, is much more satisfactory.

RIESMAN ON THE CHANGING AMERICAN CHARACTER

Another writer who presents a wide-ranging picture of changing personality patterns in different stages of history is David Riesman, who together with Nathan Glazer and Reuel Denney, wrote *The Lonely Crowd. A Study of the Changing American Character*. David Riesman, a professor of social relations at Harvard University, is interested in determining the characteristic way in which a society ensures the conformity of its members. In *The Lonely Crowd* he argues that there have been different modes of ensuring conformity at different periods of history, related to the nature of the population curve. In the Western world there has been an S-shaped population curve. "The bottom horizontal line of the S represents a situation where the total population does not increase or does so very slowly, for the number of births equals roughly the number of deaths, and both are very high."[9] This is a condition of "high growth potential," for a population boom could result from a drop in the

---

[8] Abram Kardiner, with the collaboration of Ralph Linton, Cora Du Bois, and James West, *The Psychological Frontiers of Society* (New York: Columbia University Press, 1945) , pp. 438, 440.

[9] David Riesman, with Nathan Glazer and Reuel Denney, *The Lonely Crowd. A Study of the Changing American Character*, abridged by the authors (New York: Doubleday and Co., 1953) , p. 21.

death rate. When such a spurt occurs (represented by the climbing bar of the S), a society is said to be in a stage of "transitional growth." Then, when the rate of population growth slows down, at the top bar of the S, the society is in a stage of "incipient population decline."

Riesman suggested that each of these three stages is associated with a characteristic mode of ensuring conformity. Societies of high growth potential are dependent on *tradition*-direction; in societies of transitional growth, conformity is achieved through *inner*-direction, while societies of incipient population decline depend upon *other*-direction.

In conservative underdeveloped countries such as India and Egypt and among nonliterate tribal peoples and "folk societies," one finds the first of these methods of ensuring conformity, tradition-direction. In such societies there is a rather rigid etiquette regarding kinship relations, clan or caste membership, and age and sex groups. Not much effort is devoted to finding new solutions to old problems. A quasi-automatic acceptance of traditional culture is instilled in the child, who is not apt to become aware of cultural alternatives.

Inner-direction is associated with transitional growth societies which are experiencing expansion and economic development, such as occurred in Europe from the time of the Renaissance. As Burckhardt suggested, there is greater individualism and personal mobility and more accumulation of capital. It is a period of opening frontiers. More choices and alternatives confront the individual; the weight of tradition is lighter, and the circumstances favor persons who, early in life, have internalized a set of values which will enable them to cope successfully with all kinds of new challenges and situations. Instead of rigid traditions, a rather rigid personality is required. Goals such as wealth, fame, or achievement are pursued by the individual.

The hard work of several inner-directed generations finally brings about an advanced industrialized economy which now requires different virtues of its participants. There is a decline in the numbers and proportion of persons engaged in industrial production and agriculture and an increase in white-collar and service trades. What this system demands is harmonious working within an established organization. An other-directed personality is in keeping with this need, a personality which is sensitive to the moods and feelings of others and adaptable to external influences. Riesman finds this type to be American rather than European, appearing especially in the upper middle class of our larger cities.[10]

In application to the American scene, Riesman's picture of the inner-directed character of the transitional growth period is reminiscent of Frederick Jackson Turner's thesis that American national character was decisively shaped by the experience of frontier life, leading to the development of such traits as independence, resourcefulness, and self-reliance. With the closing of the frontier, there was presumably less need for these qualities.[11]

Some articles by Leo Lowenthal and by De Charms and Moeller give support to Riesman's views. In a review of the kinds of persons who served as topics of popular magazine biographies between 1901 and 1941, Leo Lowenthal found that the more recent publications emphasized "idols of consumption," such as film stars, baseball players, and night club entertainers, rather than "idols of production," such as the business tycoons written about in earlier years.[12] In a study of 150 years of children's readers, Richard de Charms and Gerald H. Moeller found a consistent decline in achievement imagery after the 1880s.[13] But this is indirect evidence; it tells us what was being published and offered to the public, which might not necessarily reflect the attitudes of the readers. A more direct reflection has been provided by Fred I. Greenstein in an analysis of a "forgotten body of survey data," consisting of a number of studies giving questionnaire findings about children's expressed ideals between 1902 and 1958. In these investigations children were asked what person they would most like to resemble. Greenstein's analysis of this material showed that although identifications with business and political leaders are rare today, they were also rare at the turn

---

[10] Ibid., pp. 21–38. A similar analysis, although couched in different terminology, appears in *The Organization Man* by William H. Whyte, Jr. (New York: Simon and Schuster, 1956). Whyte believes that the Protestant ethic of orderliness, thrift and hard work is being replaced in our time by a social ethic which emphasizes the virtue of belonging in a group, which is seen as the source of creativity. An essay on changing American values by the anthropologist Clyde Kluckhohn is in general agreement with the views of Riesman and Whyte. Clyde Kluckhohn, "Have There Been Discernible Shifts in American Values during the Past Generation?" in Elting E. Morison (ed.), *The American Style: Essays in Value and Performance* (New York: Harper & Bros., 1958), pp. 145–217.

[11] Frederick Jackson Turner, *The Frontier in American History* (New York: Henry Holt and Co., 1920).

[12] Leo Lowenthal, "Biographies in Popular Magazines," in Paul F. Lazarsfeld and Frank N. Stanton (eds.), *Radio Research 1942–43* (New York: Duell, Sloan and Pearce, 1944), pp. 507–48.

[13] Richard de Charms and Gerald H. Moeller, "Values Expressed in American Children's Readers: 1800–1950," *Journal of Abnormal and Social Psychology*, Vol. 64 (1962), pp. 136–42.

of the century. Greenstein found little evidence for a change in values along the lines suggested by Riesman.[14]

Riesman's writing, like Fromm's, is persuasive, but when examined critically in detail, it shows various weaknesses, which have been noted by such critics as David M. Potter, Carl N. Degler, Seymour M. Lipset, and David Riesman himself. The role of incipient population decline in bringing about other-direction has been questioned by David M. Potter, professor of history at Stanford University. Potter points out that incipient population decline is characteristic of England and France, but he doubts that typical Englishmen or Frenchmen could be said to be other-directed.[15] Seymour M. Lipset, professor of sociology at Harvard, notes that in 1961 the United States had one of the highest rates of population growth in the Western world, which should presage a return to inner-direction, if the correlation is valid.[16]

In a new preface to *The Lonely Crowd* in 1961, Riesman conceded that the use of the population cycle was probably less effective than would have been a discussion of economic development, urbanization, and the spread of education.[17]

Carl N. Degler observes that Riesman's analysis of American character deals only with the middle class, not with the lower class, and only with city people, not rural people, while David M. Potter has pointed out that Riesman's generalizations, like those of Frederick Jackson Turner, apply mainly to men and not to women. According to Potter, women have always been dependent, other-directed, and sensitive to the moods and interests of others, but at present, with growing economic opportunities, many women now seem to be becoming less other-directed.[18]

Both Degler and Lipset agree that other-direction is an important aspect of American national character, but they do not believe that it is a recent phenomenon related to our advanced economy and incipient population decline. Instead, both Degler and Lipset

---

[14] Fred I. Greenstein, "New Light on Changing American Values: A Forgotten Body of Survey Data," *Social Forces,* Vol. 42 (1964), pp. 441–50.

[15] David M. Potter, *People of Plenty, Economic Abundance and the American Character* (Chicago: University of Chicago Press, 1954), p. 61.

[16] Seymour M. Lipset, "A Changing American Character?" in Seymour Martin Lipset and Leo Lowenthal (eds.), *Culture and Social Character. The Work of David Riesman Reviewed* (New York: The Free Press of Glencoe, Inc., 1961), p. 157.

[17] David Riesman, *The Lonely Crowd. A Study of the Changing American Character* (New Haven, Conn.: Yale University Press, 1961), pp. xxx, xxxi.

[18] David M. Potter, "American Women and the American Character," *Stetson University Bulletin,* Vol. 62 (1962), pp. 1–22.

trace other-direction back as far as the early 19th century, relating it to early American egalitarian democratic traditions, and citing in evidence such early commentators on American character as Alexis de Tocqueville and Harriet Martineau.[19]

Some documentation for Riesman's views is provided by interview and life history material in *Faces in the Crowd. Individual Studies in Character and Politics* by David Riesman in collaboration with Nathan Glazer.[20] But Riesman's claims for this documentation are very modest: ". . . there is, it should be clear, no proof offered here for the generalizations in that book [*The Lonely Crowd*] . . . reasonably conclusive judgements concerning large-scale historical hypotheses, especially perhaps in typological form, cannot be made on this kind of evidence alone."[21] He also says that we are a long way from relating other-direction to modern urban America, or tradition-direction to any particular preliterate society. Besides, the three types overlap one another; they are not discrete.[22] Thus, we are left with some rather blurry generalizations, the validity of which have not been demonstrated.

It is interesting to note, however, that there is some correspondence between Riesman's views about the shift from tradition-direction to inner-direction and the contrasts made by Whiting and Whiting between the Type A and Type B cultures of the Six Cultures project described in Chapter 9. The Type A cultures, you will recall, are characterized by subsistence farming with little economic specialization, while the Type B cultures have more cultural complexity, a cash economy, class or caste stratification, and a centralized political and legal system. There are more chores for children and more emphasis on obedience in the Type A cultures, more individualism and competitiveness in the Type B cultures. Robert A. LeVine's comment about folk and peasant societies is worth repeating in this context. LeVine suggested that the severe aggression training in such groups ". . . may be part of a larger tendency to make children orderly, obedient, and pacific, producing an inhibitedness that manifests itself in performance on cogni-

---

[19] Carl N. Degler, "The Sociologist as Historian: Riesman's *The Lonely Crowd*," *American Quarterly*, Vol. 15 (1963), pp. 483–97; Lipset, "A Changing American Character?" pp. 302–30.

[20] David Riesman, in collaboration with Nathan Glazer, *Faces in the Crowd. Individual Studies in Character and Politics* (New Haven, Conn.: Yale University Press, 1952).

[21] Ibid., p. vi.

[22] Ibid., p. 7.

tive tasks."[23] This might be a way of characterizing tradition-direction.

THE GAP BETWEEN GENERATIONS

A number of commentators on the American scene, including Margaret Mead, Geoffrey Gorer, and Urie Bronfenbrenner, among others, have written about the break between generations and the consequently dominant role of the peer group in this country. This is an old theme. In 1933 an American mother complained about the loss of parental influence on children: "Their standards and their ideals are formed in the school atmosphere, and more by their companions than their teachers."[24]

Mead and Gorer both explain the break between generations in terms of the experience of immigration to the New World. The children of immigrants became ashamed of their parents, with their Old World ways, and tried to become more American than they, which they could learn better from their peers than from their parents. American parents expect their children to be different from them and to surpass them. More likely than not, the son will take up a profession different from his father's and move away from home.[25] According to Gorer, the Old World immigrant father lacked the authority of the European father and was rejected by his son. This established a new pattern for father-son relations in the New World. But the mother, being associated with food, love, and care, retained an important emotional role and assumed a dominant position in the family, disciplining the children and becoming their source of moral conduct.[26]

Bronfenbrenner on American Children

A more recent analyst of the changing American scene is Urie Bronfenbrenner, a professor of psychology at Cornell University.

[23] Robert A. LeVine, "Cross-Cultural Study in Child Psychology," in Paul H. Mussen (ed.), *Carmichael's Manual of Child Psychology* (3d ed.; New York: John Wiley & Sons, 1970), p. 594.

[24] L. P. Jacks, *My American Friends, 1933,* quoted in Richard L. Rapson, "The American Child as Seen by British Travelers, 1845–1935," *American Quarterly,* Vol. 17 (1965), p. 522.

[25] Margaret Mead, *And Keep Your Powder Dry. An Anthropologist Looks at America* (New expanded edition; New York: William Morrow, 1965; first published in 1943).

[26] Geoffrey Gorer, *The American People. A Study in National Character* (New York: W. W. Norton and Co., 1948), chaps. I and II.

Bronfenbrenner has made studies of children in both the United States and the Soviet Union, and he makes comparisons between the two national groups, mostly to the advantage of the U.S.S.R. This is suggested by the fact that Part I of his book has the heading "The Making of the New Soviet Man," while Chapter 4 is entitled "The Unmaking of the American Child."

What is unmaking the American child? Largely, according to Bronfenbrenner, it is the decreasing contact which a child has with its parents and other adults. By default, children spend most of their time with their peers, so that our society is becoming segregated not only by race and class, but also by age. Families are smaller, and a child has fewer meaningful contacts with adults than formerly. In one study, 766 sixth-grade children reported spending, during the weekend, an average of two to three hours a day with their parents, slightly more time with groups of friends, and an additional two or three hours per day with a single friend. An analysis of their data led Bronfenbrenner and his colleagues to conclude that the peer-oriented children are more influenced by lack of attention at home than by the attractiveness of the peer group.

The vacuum left by parental withdrawal is also filled by the television set. According to one study, the average viewing time for children between 6 and 17 years of age is 22 hours per week. In another study TV viewing time was said to range from 17 hours per week at second grade to 28 hours per week at sixth grade.

Bronfenbrenner cites some studies which indicate that the watching of violent TV films leads to increased aggressiveness. At the same time, decrease in parental concern contributes to a decrease in qualities of responsibility and leadership and to lowered self-esteem.

The peer group also plays a large role in the Soviet Union but in a more constructive way, being directly influenced by adults, while the American peer group is more autonomous, having little contact with the adult world. If these current trends persist, Bronfenbrenner predicts increasing alienation among American children and adolescents, more indifference, antagonism, and violence.[27]

The Hippie Scene

A highly visible manifestation of the generation gap today is the difference in appearance of the older and many of the younger

[27] Urie Bronfenbrenner, with the assistance of John C. Condry, Jr., *Two Worlds of Childhood. U.S. and U.S.S.R.* (New York: Russell Sage Foundation, 1970), pp. 95–119.

generation, who (as of 1972) often have long hair, faded, patched blue jeans, and such features as beads and Indian headbands. Not all who dress in this style are hippies, and some members of the younger generation claim that the hippie period is now over, already passé. Be that as it may, there was a period in the 1960s when the hippie cult was a recognized phenomenon and when hippies were proud to claim the title.

Lewis Yablonsky, a professor of sociology at San Fernando Valley State College, California, who conducted interviews with many hippies in New York and California in 1967, estimated that there were then about 200,000 identifiable hippie dropouts in the United States, another 200,000 teeny-boppers (teen-age part-time hippies), several hundred thousand "Clark Kent" hippies who used drugs and interacted with hippies but who kept regular jobs or attended college, and millions of hippie "fellow travelers," many of whom were in the academic community.[28]

Yablonsky gave over 700 questionaires to hippies. According to his data, over 70 percent came from middle- and upper-class families; 77.6 percent had graduated from high school, and 50.6 percent had attended some college. There were more male (75.5 percent) than female (24.5 percent) hippies. Most hippies smoked marijuana; some took LSD, methedrine, or amphetamines. About half had been locked up at some time, either in a prison or mental hospital.[29]

Evidently this is (or was) a new way of life or subculture in the United States which rejects the dominant life-style and the traditional goals and values of middle-class America. Like militant blacks, white hippies are against the system, but the blacks seem to want to get out of the ghetto and share the opportunities and advantages enjoyed by middle-class whites, while many hippies have left comfortable middle-class homes to live in the ghetto.

How Much of a Gap?

To what extent does this movement signalize a real generation gap? Some writers consider the generation gap to be profound. According to Margaret Mead the gap is a worldwide phenomenon, not limited to the United States. The generation born after World War II, she tells us, has spent its whole life with a knowledge of the existence of the atom bomb. Members of the older generation are

---

[28] Lewis Yablonsky, *The Hippie Trip* (New York: Pegasus, 1968), p. 36.
[29] Ibid., pp. 340–48.

now immigrants, not in space but in time, strangers in a postwar world which may be better understood by the young. Indeed, Mead states that none of the young ". . . is untouched by the sense that there are no adults anywhere in the world from whom they can learn what the next steps should be."[30] A similar view is set forth in the optimistic best seller, *The Greening of America* by Charles A. Reich. Reich, who teaches law at Yale University Law School, believes that members of the younger generation are acquiring a consciousness different from that of their parents; he calls it Consciousness III. Reich's sentimental faith in the young is expressed in this quotation: ". . . the young people of Consciousness III see effortlessly what is phony or dishonest in politics, or what is ugly or meretricious in architecture and city planning, whereas an older person has to go through years of education to make himself equally aware."[31] Reich predicts that Consciousness III will bring about a bloodless revolution which will change our country's political system as its final act.

The impressionistic views of Mead and Reich about differences in the generations are based upon their reading and conversations, not on any organized interviews or questionnaires. A more balanced view, to my mind, is provided in an essay by Joseph Adelson, "What Generation Gap?"[32] Adelson points out that it is common for writers on this subject to generalize about the young on the basis of only a segment of the younger generation, usually those in college rather than noncollege workers, and usually left-wing activists rather than more conservative students. Adelson considers some different criteria for the generation gap. One is conflict or lack of understanding between parents and children. Four studies on this topic are cited, including one by Adelson and Elizabeth Douvan of 3,000 young people aged 12 to 18. All four studies give similar findings: most interviewees report good relationships with their parents. One study estimates that about 10 percent of the students interviewed were seriously at odds with their parents.

Another criterion for the generation gap is differences of opinion about politics, with the young being assumed to be more radical

[30] Margaret Mead, *Culture and Commitment. A Study of the Generation Gap* (New York: Natural History Press, 1970) , p. 68.

[31] Charles A. Reich, *The Greening of America* (New York: Bantam Books, Inc., 1971) , p. 283.

[32] *The New York Times Magazine,* Jan. 18, 1970, reprinted in Michael McGiffert, *The Character of Americans, A Book of Readings* (Rev. ed.; Homewood, Ill.: The Dorsey Press, 1970) , pp. 378–88.

than their parents. This, too, is open to question. An analysis of voting patterns in the 1968 election showed that the under-30 voter was overrepresented in the Wallace constituency and that outside the South, Wallace got proportionately more support from younger than from older voters. Adelson points out that in most cases (about 75 percent) children vote for the same party as their parents. Adelson also cites a *Fortune* poll of 18 to 24 year olds, in which more than 80 percent reported that they do not think that there are any great differences in values between themselves and their parents. Two other investigations give similar findings.[33]

There is no doubt that the hippies represented a break with the dominant culture and that many young people share some hippie beliefs and values, but in general there does not seem to be as marked a cleavage between today's generations as some writers have claimed.

ECONOMIC DEVELOPMENT AND PERSONALITY

Related to the works by Fromm and Riesman discussed earlier in this chapter is the question of the relationships between economic development and personality. Why have some nations, such as those of western Europe, experienced a surge of economic advance within a relatively short time, while other less developed nations have struggled along slowly, having great difficulty in raising living standards and increasing industrial production? Max Weber was a pioneer in examining this problem cross-culturally and in suggesting that it was not a question of economic factors alone. Weber noted that the great economic advance in Europe was associated with Protestant rather than Catholic countries. He concluded that the new independence and autonomy of Protestantism and its emphasis on asceticism and hard work led to a new breed of men, ". . . men who had grown up in the hard school of life, calculating and daring at the same time, above all temperate and reliable, shrewd and completely devoted to their business, with strictly bourgeois opinions and principles."[34]

This is a personality characterization, a personality associated with a particular religious movement. As we have seen, Fromm

---

[33] This passage was written before announcement of the results of the 1972 presidential election, which would seem to support these conservative conclusions.

[34] Max Weber, *The Protestant Ethic and the Spirit of Capitalism,* trans. by Talcott Parsons (New York: Charles Scribner's Sons, 1952), p. 39. (First published in German in 1904–5.)

carried this analysis further by arguing that the lower and middle classes of Europe were drawn toward Protestantism because they experienced anxiety and powerlessness with the collapse of the feudal social system, while Riesman related these developments to the transitional growth phase of the population cycle.

In 1961 two books were published which made further contributions to the study of the relationship between economic development and personality. One was by a psychologist from Harvard, David C. McClelland, who concerned himself with economics; the other was by an economist from M.I.T., Everett E. Hagen, who became involved in studying personality. Both authors echoed Weber's point that development is not understandable in solely economic terms, with McClelland citing G. M. Meier and R. E. Baldwin to the effect that "economic development is much too serious a topic to be left to economists."[35] At the same time, both McClelland and Hagen criticized Weber's stress on the Protestant ethic as the source for economic advance in Europe. For McClelland, the emphasis on work connected with the Protestant ethic is only a special case of a more general phenomenon, for there has been a similar emphasis on hard work in other societies which are not Protestant, such as modern Japan and the Soviet Union. McClelland saw the key psychological factor as being the need for achievement (*n*-Achievement).[36]

Achievement Motivation

The strength of the achievement motive varies among individuals and among societies; it has been more in evidence at some time periods than in others. How can one gauge its relative strength at different times in the past? McClelland found an index of *n*-Achievement in children's readers. He and his colleagues collected 1,300 children's stories from 23 countries, all translated into English. The stories came from readers used in the second to fourth grades in two time periods: around 1925 and around 1950. Codes were used on proper names, so that scorers would not guess the story's country of origin. The tales were mixed up and coded for *n*-Achievement.

McClelland also needed an index for a country's degree of economic development. The one he selected was the amount of

---

[35] G. M. Meier and R. E. Baldwin, *Economic Development* (New York: John Wiley & Sons, Inc., 1957), p. 119.

[36] See above, pp. 282–83, 372.

electricity produced in kilowatt-hours per capita. "The correlation between the n-Achievement level in the children's readers in 1925 and the growth in electrical output between 1925 and 1950, as compared with expectation, is a quite substantial .53, which is highly significant statistically."[37] A concern for achievement, as expressed in the children's stories, was thus related to a more rapid rate of economic development, as measured by increase in use of electricity. This generalization applied not only to such Western democracies as England and the United States but also to Communist countries such as Russia, Bulgaria, and Hungary.[38] McClelland pointed out that the 1950 n-Achievement level was not correlated with *prior* economic growth between 1925 and 1950. Evidence for high n-Achievement *precedes* economic growth, suggesting that the achievement motive is a causative factor, not an epiphenomenon, in opposition to the assumptions of economic determinism.

A study of Spanish economic development by Juan B. Cortés is based on this same psychological determinism. Cortés predicted that a rise in the level of achievement motivation would directly precede a rise in Spanish economic growth. This was tested by scoring Spanish literary material from three time periods: 1200–1492, a period of economic growth; 1492–1610, a period of economic climax; and 1610–1730, a period of economic decline. Various indices were used to measure economic production, such as the number of sheep (important in the woolen trade) and the amount of shipping from various key ports. Achievement motivation was judged to be highest in the early period; it had dropped by the time of economic climax.[39]

A similar study has been made of English industrial growth from around 1400 to around 1830.[40]

What conditions favor the development of n-Achievement? A number of studies indicate that parental attitudes in childhood are important: a setting of high standards combined with the granting of autonomy to the child, so that he can learn to work things out for

---

[37] David C. McClelland, "The Achievement Motive in Economic Growth," in Bert F. Hoselitz and Wilbert E. Moore (eds.), *Industrialization and Society* (The Hague: Mouton and UNESCO, 1966), p. 81.

[38] David C. McClelland, *The Achieving Society* (Princeton, N.J.: D. Van Nostrand Company, 1961), p. 105.

[39] Juan B. Cortés, "The Achievement Motive in the Spanish Economy between the 13th and 18th Centuries," *Economic Development and Cultural Change*, Vol. 9 (1960), pp. 144–63.

[40] Norman M. Bradburn and David E. Berlew, "Need for Achievement and English Industrial Growth," *Economic Development and Cultural Change*, Vol. 10 (1960), pp. 8–20.

himself and enjoy doing so. A favorable combination seems to be a somewhat dominating mother with high standards and a father who allows his children considerable autonomy. An authoritarian father-dominated family is less likely to foster need for achievement.[41]

Group Status and Economic Development

In the course of his discussion of the Protestant ethic, Max Weber pointed out that national or religious minority groups, excluded from positions of political influence, often turn to economic activities as a way of gaining recognition for their abilities. Weber cited as examples the Jews, the Poles in Russia, the Huguenots in France under Louis XIV, and nonconformists and Quakers in England.[42] A similar theme has been pursued by Everett E. Hagen, who argues that leaders in the transition to economic growth are apt to come from groups which have lost some of their former status and are looked down upon by the leading social group. In a traditional society the leading elite lacks the interest in innovation required for economic development. Elite members believe themselves to be essentially different from what Hagen calls "the simple folk," a category which includes peasants, artisans, craftsmen, shopkeepers, and menials. Since one general distinctive trait of the simple folk is that they work with their hands and become dirty in the process, members of the elite pride themselves on not doing such work. A "Protestant ethic" is not for them. The elite members have an authoritarian, as opposed to an innovational, character. An authoritarian individual, according to Hagen, does not see the world as forming an orderly system, capable of analysis. Hence he is a dependent, rather anxious person. The authoritarian person sees power as stemming from ascribed status, rather than from achievement. The innovational person, in contrast, conceives of the phenomena of the world as being susceptible of analysis, and he sees the world as valuing him. He is high in the needs for autonomy, achievement, and order.

In a traditional society adults discourage initiative, exploration, and innovation among children. The superior authority of the

---

[41] See Bernard C. Rosen, "Socialization and Achievement Motivation in Brazil," *American Sociological Review*, Vol. 27 (1962), pp. 612–24; Norman M. Bradburn, "N Achievement and Father Dominance in Turkey," *Journal of Abnormal and Social Psychology*, Vol. 67 (1963), pp. 464–68.

[42] Weber, *The Protestant Ethic and the Spirit of Capitalism*, p. 39.

father is insisted upon, especially during the "Oedipal period" in a boy's development. The son's consequently submissive attitude becomes generalized to other persons in authority. In such societies, according to Hagen, repressed feelings find an outlet in sexual conquests, occasional outbursts of aggression, and attitudes of *machismo,* or emphasis on masculinity. The pain and frustration experienced by the individual find an explanation in the hierarchy of the unseen supernatural realm which rules the world.

Because of this general picture of traditional society, says Hagen, rapid economic development is not likely to occur. But disturbing events may affect some groups in the society which have lost status and seek to regain it. Their first reaction to the shock of lowered status is apt to be *retreatism,* an increasing abandonment of traditional cultural goals and institutionalized norms of behavior. But this creates new conditions of home life which affect children in a different way than in the traditional upbringing, making possible a more innovational personality. Hagen suggests the following characteristic sequence: authoritarianism, withdrawal of status respect, retreatism, creativity.[43] Hagen's generalizations are illustrated by accounts of economic development in England, Japan, Colombia, Indonesia, and Burma. His observations on Burma will be discussed later in this chapter.

Achievement Motivation in Nigeria

It is useful to generalize on a broad scale, as both McClelland and Hagen have done. But it is also necessary to investigate particular areas where economic growth is occurring. In the following pages, accordingly, we will deal with some more restricted studies dealing with (*a*) Nigeria, (*b*) a Mexican village, (*c*) India, and (*d*) Japan. First, let us briefly consider Robert A. LeVine's analysis of three Nigerian ethnic groups: Hausa, Yoruba, and Ibo.[44]

LeVine's work seems to give support to the theories of both McClelland and Hagen, but perhaps particularly to the latter, since LeVine notes that the Ibo, much more than either the Hausa

---

[43] Everett E. Hagen, *On the Theory of Social Change. How Economic Growth Begins* (Homewood, Ill.: The Dorsey Press, 1962), p. 217.

[44] LeVine's work was discussed earlier in the chapter on life history and dream material; it will be recalled that he sought evidence for the strength of *n*-Achievement in the dream reports of Nigerian male students. The research methods used by LeVine, and his findings, are set forth in Chapter 12.

or Yoruba, suffered from withdrawal of status respect. The Ibo
have also been the greatest innovators. The Hausa, who scored
lowest on *n*-Achievement, was the group which suffered least in
social disparagement under colonial rule.

The accomplishments of the Ibo were not limited to economic
advancement but involved most branches of education, in which
there has been a steady increase since the early 1920s. As one example: in the early 1920s there were 12 Nigerian physicians, of which
8 were Yoruba and none Ibo. By the early 1950s, however, there
were 160 Nigerian physicians, of which 76 were Yoruba and 49
Ibo, a remarkable increase from zero to more than 30 percent of
the nation's physicians.[45]

Economic Change in a Mexican Village

A careful and detailed study of the relationship between community development and social personality is Fromm and Maccoby's study of a Mexican village in the state of Morelos. The interview methods used in this study were discussed in Chapter 11. On
the basis of an interpretative questionnaire, supported by findings
from the Rorschach and TAT, the authors concluded that most of
the villagers have a helpless, receptive orientation, particularly
landowners who raise sugar cane, while a minority group of
productive exploitative entrepreneurs are able to take the initiative
in capitalistic ventures. Since these entrepreneurs are agents of
change, it might seem, at first glance, that productive-exploitative
tendencies should be encouraged. But Fromm and Maccoby warn
that not all psychological traits which spur economic development
are desirable from a human standpoint. They would rather see the
development of a strong cooperative movement which would restrain the development of class stratification and the exploitation of
the peasants by entrepreneurs. Fromm and Maccoby visualize something like an Israeli kibbutz or progressive Mexican *ejido*. But they
realize that such a goal would be difficult for peasants who are individualistic and suspicious of one another—traits summed up in
Banfield's phrase "amoral familism," which refers to the peasant's
focus on his own particular family to the exclusion of all other en-

---

[45] Robert A. LeVine with the assistance of Eugene Shankman and Leonard Unterberger, *Dreams and Deeds: Achievement Motivation in Nigeria* (Chicago: University
of Chicago Press, 1966), p. 74.

tanglements.[46] This tendency occurs in the Mexican village. Mutual suspicion, a "hoarding orientation," and strong sense of private property militate against the development of cooperatives. Nevertheless, Fromm and Maccoby are able to cite some successful efforts in that direction.[47] However, their final conclusions are not optimistic. Fromm and Maccoby point out that industrialism is destroying traditional values in Mexico, with nothing to replace them except for longings for the good life of the city. Movies have taken the place of fiestas, and radio has replaced the local band. The peasant "not only is materially poor, but is made to feel humanly backward, 'under-developed.' He dreams of the good life for his children, yet only very few of them can ever attain it. And if they attain it, is it the good life?"[48]

Most studies of economic growth and the need for achievement have assumed that economic development is desirable. Particularly in the work of Hagen, there is a tendency to see the creative innovators with their high *n*-Achievement as the Good Guys and the authoritarian traditionalists as Bad Guys. From this perspective economic development would seem to be a self-evident boon. But in Fromm and Maccoby's study we find that assumption questioned.

Economic Development in India

India seems to exemplify Hagen's description of a traditional society. The caste system, with its hierarchical structure and notions of pollution stemming from contacts with members of lower castes, confirms in the elite the notion of their own essential superiority. The dislike for practical and menial work and the reluctance to get one's hands dirty is certainly present in the higher ranks of society.

In a review of the possible reasons for the relatively slow pace of India's economic advance, N. V. Sovani, an Indian economist, found part of the explanation in two culture-and-personality studies of Indian life. One is by William Stephens Taylor, an article

---

[46] Edward C. Banfield, *The Moral Basis of a Backward Society* (Glencoe, Ill.: The Free Press, 1958). This is a pessimistic account of an isolated Italian peasant community, in which the author expresses doubt of the possibility of making any changes in the peasants' outlook and behavior.

[47] Erich Fromm and Michael Maccoby, *Social Character in a Mexican Village. A Sociopsychological Study* (Englewood Cliffs, N.J.: Prentice-Hall, Inc., 1970), pp. 203–25.

[48] Ibid., pp. 237–38.

entitled "Basic Personality in Orthodox Hindu Culture Patterns";[49] the other is G. Morris Carstairs' *The Twice-Born. A Study of a Community of High-Caste Hindus.* Sovani concludes, after citing these works, that the slow pace of progress in India must be partly attributable to the presence of "a widely common personality pattern devoid of personal initiative, purposefulness, involvement, etc."[50]

Let us briefly consider the works by Taylor and Carstairs to see what the source of such alleged patterns might be. Taylor points out that traditional Hindu culture limits an individual's opportunities for making significant decisions. In many parts of rural India there is a system of economic exchange of goods and services which has come to be known as the *"jajmani* system." Under the usual operation of this system, a person's occupation is determined by birth—through membership in a particular caste. What is more, the individual's clientele—if he belongs to one of the service castes— is also determined by birth, since there are hereditary ties linking particular families; a barber serves the families formerly served by his father, and so on. While this system is now breaking down in many parts of India, with the growing incursion of a money economy and an increasing involvement of India's villages in the larger national economy, a person's choice of occupation is still limited, to a considerable extent, by the caste into which he was born.

Another area in which decision making is limited is marriage. Marriages are generally arranged by parents, almost always within the same caste. With regard to choice of occupation, clientele, and marriage, therefore, the individual in much of traditional village India has little to say. It is consonant with this system that the individual is brought up to be relatively passive and compliant. He is rewarded for his submission by the assurance of support from family and caste and by his recognized position in the social order.

According to Taylor, Hindu society is thus able "to create a basic personality pattern in which personal initiative is replaced by the sense of conformity, in which responsibility is exercised without personal authority, in which security is associated with a sense of helplessness, and in which opportunities for frustration and acute anxiety are minimized."[51]

---

[49] William Stephens Taylor, "Basic Personality in Orthodox Hindu Culture Patterns," *Journal of Abnormal and Social Psychology,* Vol. 43 (1948), pp. 3–12.

[50] N. V. Sovani, "Non-Economic Aspects of India's Economic Development," *Administration and Economic Development in India,* Duke University Commonwealth Studies Center, 1962.

[51] Taylor, p. 123.

Carstairs' work is limited to the study of a community of high-caste Hindus in Rajasthan and is not meant to apply to all of India. However, his picture has much in common with that of Taylor. He points out that in a joint family household a man or woman may not fondle their children in the presence of the man's parents, and that a man "so long as he remains under his own father's roof, must keep up the fiction of denying that he leads an active sexual life of his own. Not to do so is to be disrespectful."[52] Carstairs emphasizes the stress on submission, resignation, and obedience in family life and in religion.[53]

These generalizations seem to apply to modern Indian intellectuals as well as to less educated persons. Shils has written that "The center of gravity of the internal life of the family is almost always determined by the more traditional members, and especially the women of the family, who in nearly all cases are more traditional than the men in the same family."[54] And Bradford Smith has observed:

The educated Indian lives in two worlds—the world of government administration and schools and cinemas, which is primarily Western; and the family home, which is Indian. Even when he is grown up and married, he still has to leave every major family decision to his father. At the office his word is a command—at least to those below him in a very rigid hierarchy. But at home, he is still a child. . . . His father will decide where the children should go to school, and how the family income should be spent.[55]

India is a large, complex, and diverse country. Needless to say, there must be many exceptions to the foregoing generalizations, some of which apply particularly to higher caste urban middle-class groups. As S. C. Dube has pointed out, joint families are more commonly found in cities and small towns than in villages, where they are often rare. Joint families are considered the ideal, but they tend to break up in the South Indian villages studied by Dube. In a study of 125 families he found that 34 percent of the sons had separated from their parents within two years of marriage and 36 percent

[52] Carstairs, *The Twice-Born. A Study of a Community of High-Caste Hindus* (Bloomington: Indiana University Press, 1958) , p. 67.

[53] Ibid., p. 147. For a critical review of Carstairs' book, see Morris E. Opler's review, *American Anthropologist*, Vol. 61 (1959) , pp. 140–42; see also *American Anthropologist*, Vol. 62 (1960) , pp. 504–11.

[54] Edward Shils, *The Intellectual between Tradition and Modernity: The Indian Situation*, Comparative Studies in Society and History. Supplement I (The Hague, Neth.: Mouton & Co., 1961) , pp. 62–63.

[55] Bradford Smith, *Portrait of India* (Philadelphia: J. B. Lippincott Co., 1962) , p. 180.

between two and three years of marriage. Only 22 percent of the sons were still found living with their parents five years after their marriage.[56]

Dube has discussed different patterns of behavior at three socio-economic levels studied in the village of Shamirpet, near Hyderabad on the Deccan plateau. He states that all three levels value family solidarity, respect old age and social position, and recognize the superiority of the male. But these patterns are adhered to most successfully by the highest level. In the lowest, frequent division of property makes family solidarity hard to maintain. Women have more freedom and mobility; there is more open quarreling and more divorce and remarriage.[57]

Class, caste, and regional differences must therefore be considered in any attempt to delineate Indian modal personality tendencies. But it is significant that an economist like Sovani should draw attention to personality variables in a discussion of India's economic development.

The same has been done by Kusum Nair in a recent book on India's village development program.[58] Mrs. Nair cites the case of a peasant in Mysore who had an irrigated channel passing through his property but who let the water flow by without tapping it; and she quotes a government official associated with the project:

> We carry manures and improved seeds in a trailer and offer to deliver them right at the door-step to induce these cultivators to use them. We offer them loans to buy the seeds and manures. We go to the fields and offer to let in the water for them. We request them to try it out first in two acres only if they are not convinced. They could quadruple their yields if they would only take our advice and at least experiment. Still they are not coming forward.[59]

Mrs. Nair notes that community attitudes toward work vary greatly in different regions, and she believes that such attitudes may be more decisive for raising agricultural productivity than material or technological resources. "Unless a man feels the desire to have more material wealth *sufficiently to strive for it,* he cannot be expected to have much interest in new techniques; there will be little attempt on his part to innovate."

---

[56] S. C. Dube, *Indian Village* (Ithaca, N.Y.: Cornell University Press, 1955), p. 135.

[57] Ibid., pp. 138–41.

[58] Kusum Nair, *Blossoms in the Dust, The Human Factor in Indian Development* (New York: Frederick A. Praeger, 1962).

[59] Ibid., p. 48.

Recognition of the importance of these culture-and-personality variables leads Mrs. Nair to recommend that they be taken into account in future development programs.

> . . . when a development scheme is projected, the relevant social and psychological attributes of each community will need to be studied and examined in the same intensive manner as an inventory of the physical resources is made at present. On the basis of such studies means will have to be found for bringing about the necessary changes in people's attitudes and behavior and the beliefs underlying them. These means and methods will have to be within the framework and in keeping with the general policy and the principles of democratic planning.[60]

It is evidently difficult to assess the direction of events in India. A new perspective on India's economic development is provided by Milton Singer's investigation of beliefs and attitudes among a group of industrial leaders in Madras. Judging from Singer's report, these men do not seem to fit the passive, dependent picture described by Taylor, Carstairs, and Smith. Singer describes them as being shrewd, hardworking, and enterprising. The Madras industrialists believe that their work is in the best interests of India, in accord with their *dharma,* or religious duty, and that tremendous progress has been made in India's industrialization, in which they are proud to have played a part.[61] Although the generalizations made by Taylor and Carstairs may be true enough for many Hindus, Singer's work shows that hard-driving, enterprising leaders are also produced by the social system.

This calls for a kind of applied culture-and-personality. Something approaching this has been attempted in a series of projects in India designed to stimulate achievement motivation in Indian businessmen.[62] McClelland and his associates in this undertaking judge their program to have been successful; but since it was discontinued, it cannot be called an unqualified success. An Indian writer, J. B. P. Sinha, has questioned the merit of trying to increase competitiveness in India. He cites the view of C. Wright Mills that a competitive spirit can flourish only when there is consciousness of unlimited opportunity; competitiveness becomes antisocial under conditions of scarcity. In a laboratory experiment, Sinha found that

---

[60] Ibid., p. 195.

[61] Milton Singer, "Industrial Leadership, the Hindu Ethic, and the Spirit of Socialism," in Milton Singer, *When a Great Tradition Modernizes. An Anthropological Approach to Indian Civilization* (New York: Praeger Publishers, 1972) , pp. 272–366.

[62] David C. McClelland and David G. Winter et al., *Motivating Economic Achievement* (New York: The Free Press, 1969) , pp. 94–95.

if competitiveness is increased under conditions of limited resources, the group's output is less than it would be if cooperation is stressed. Sinha thinks that efforts to increase achievement motivation in India may be dangerous under present conditions of scarcity. These cautionary qualifications are like those of Fromm and Maccoby cited earlier and show the complexity of the issues involved. McClelland takes issue with some of Sinha's conclusions, pointing out that competition cannot be equated with n-Achievement, which involves "competition with a standard of excellence," trying to do better than one has done before.

Economic and Political Development in Burma

Two members of the Center for International Studies at Massachusetts Institute of Technology have done research on economic and political development in Burma and have written books in which they draw attention to culture-and-personality factors affecting such matters. The first writer is Everett E. Hagen, whose theories were presented earlier in this chapter; two chapters of his book are about Burma. The second author is Lucian W. Pye, who has also written about Chinese "political culture" in psychocultural terms, a topic to be discussed later in this chapter. Both authors believe that the Burmese socialization process and the formation of personality in childhood have an important influence on the economic and political behavior of Burmese in adult life. Both Hagen and Pye refer to studies of Burmese child-rearing and personality by Lucien M. Hanks, Hazel Marie Hitson, and Geoffrey Gorer.[63] Both authors draw attention to the seeming contradiction of mild, carefree, happy-go-lucky behavior among Burmese on the one hand and a high rate of violence and homicide on the other. Hagen is struck by the sluggishness of Burma's economic development, while Pye is concerned with the psychological obstacles to "nation building" in Burma.

Since the two authors draw from the same sources, they give similar pictures of the Burmese socialization process. Infancy is described as characterized by indulgence, demand feeding, and

---

[63] Lucien M. Hanks, "The Quest for Individual Autonomy in Burmese Personality with Particular Reference to the Arakan," *Psychiatry*, Vol. 12 (1949), pp. 285–300; Hazel Marie Hitson, "Family Patterns and Paranoidal Personality Structure in Boston and Burma," Ph.D. dissertation, Radcliffe College, 1959; Geoffrey Gorer, "Burmese Personality," (New York: Institute of Inter-Cultural Studies, 1943), mimeographed.

soothing of the child to keep him from crying. But in later child-hood the mother alternates between warm and cold behavior; she may be teasingly cruel to her child. Children are deliberately frightened with threats of being carried away, given to strangers, or attacked by evil spirits. Most Burmese adults are said to believe in the existence of evil spirits and to see the world as being full of dangers.[64]

Burmese consider children to be thoughtless and unable to learn by themselves. In contrast to the Rajputs and Mixtecans (see above, pp. 203–4), and the Chinese to be discussed later in this chapter, a child is not scolded or punished for aggression against neighboring children, unless it gets the parents into trouble. Deference to elders and loyalty to the family are emphasized. The discipline of boys is reinforced when they go to a Buddhist monastery at about eight years of age, where they are drilled in rote learning and given severe punishments. The outcome of this childhood gamut of ex-periences is an outwardly disciplined, submissive person, who, at the same time, is full of fear and repressed hostility. According to Hagen, there is self-doubt and often an escape into celibacy. One of every 30 or 35 adult men in Burma is a monk.[65] The happy-go-lucky behavior of Burmese is interpreted by Hagen as a defense against repressed rage.[66]

Pye considers the manifest level of Burmese politics to be char-acterized by friendliness and the latent level by tension. Hatred and violence may flare up without warning.[67] Political power is highly valued by Burmese. At the same time, a power seeker is held back by the need to show deference and respect for others, a conflict which brings about feelings of paralysis and resentment.[68] Burmese politicians realize that open debate about issues is essential in a democracy, but they find it hard to prevent such debates from turn-ing into personal aggression.[69] There is an individualistic stress in this society. According to Pye, the idea of improving the national economy has little meaning for Burmese. People are oriented to the

---

[64] Melford E. Spiro, *Burmese Supernaturalism. A Study in the Explanation and Reduction of Suffering* (Englewood Cliffs, N.J.: Prentice-Hall, Inc., 1967), p. 73.

[65] Hagen, *On the Theory of Social Change,* p. 170.

[66] Ibid., p. 174.

[67] Lucian W. Pye, *Politics, Personality, and Nation Building: Burma's Search for Identity* (New Haven, Conn.: Yale University Press, 1962), p. 141.

[68] Ibid., pp. 146–49.

[69] Ibid., p. 163.

present and have little sense of history or concern with planning for the future.[70]

Hagen states that Burmese politicians often express enthusiastic interest in economic development, but actual undertakings to that end are generally unsuccessful, often marked by irresponsibility and poor planning. Hagen cites several examples of failures in leadership and management. He does not think that corruption is a sufficient explanation for such failures, although corruption exists. Nor is it enough to say that the Burmese have "traditional" personalities, resistant to change. Rather, Hagen suggests that the Burmese find it difficult to focus on actual problems of economic development, not because of lack of intelligence but because of certain personality tendencies accentuated by the experience of colonial rule. British administration led to a destruction of the traditional Burmese community life. Burmese administrators had somehow to identify with the aggressor and become like him, an experience that must have been uncomfortable and conflicting but at the same time valued for the enjoyment of power.

After independence, Burmese political leaders knew that it was necessary to industrialize and build factories, and so they launched such projects but without carefully considering what they were doing. ". . . their behavior was compulsive; the common sense of a normal traditional individual would not have permitted him to behave so irresponsibly as they have done."[71] Elsewhere Hagen observes: "They acted, so it seemed to observers, as though the substance of those problems had at best only a shadowy significance to them."[72] In a way, such administrators were continuing in the tradition of British colonial officialdom, which did not have much interest in the technical details of projects. ". . . the concept of government office involved rote administrative paper work, correct attitude, and pride of position rather than effective entrepreneurship."[73]

The insights and speculations of Hagen and Pye are stimulating, but it still is not clear just how Burmese socialization practices have influenced economic development and "nation building" in Burma.

---

[70] Ibid., pp. 202–3.
[71] Hagen, *On the Theory of Social Change*, p. 467.
[72] Ibid., p. 461.
[73] Ibid., p. 467.

Economic Development in Japan

In contrast to India and Burma, Japan has seen remarkably rapid economic development. In 1965 John Whitney Hall wrote, "A century ago Japan was a land bound by a traditional technology, meager resources, and a policy of national isolation. Today Japan ranks fifth in production among the advanced industrial nations. . . ."[74] By 1971, only six years after this was written, Japan's economy had moved to third place after those of the United States and the Soviet Union.

A Weberian interpretation of this signal 100 years' accomplishment is suggested by Robert N. Bellah's analysis of the religion of the Tokugawa period (1600–1867) and the early development of Japan's polity and economy. The concepts of *on* and *giri* discussed in Chapter 10 were emphasized in both Buddhist and Confucian teachings. These teachings were particularly stressed in the warrior class of samurai. Tokugawa Mitsukuni (1628–1700) wrote that the samurai's only business was to maintain *giri*. ". . . if there were no *samurai*, right (*giri*) would disappear from human society, the sense of shame would be lost, and wrong and injustice would prevail."[75] Duty to one's parents and one's feudal lord were emphasized, as in this quotation from the Budò Shoshinshu, dating from the 17th century:

For he who is born brave will be loyal and filial to his lord and parents, and whenever he has any leisure, he will use it for study, neither will he be negligent in practicing the military arts. He will be strictly on his guard against indolence and will be very careful how he spends every penny. . . . And so, ever obedient to his lord and parents he preserves his life in the hope some day of doing a deed of outstanding merit, moderating his appetite for eating and drinking and avoiding over-indulgence in sex, which is the greatest delusion of mankind, so that he may preserve his body in health and strength.[76]

Bellah notes that there was a clear-cut distinction between upper and lower samurai, with little mobility between them. The upper samurai received sufficient stipends to support them; the lower did not but had to supplement their income by spinning, handicrafts, and surreptitious trade. Bellah states that the lower

---

[74] John Whitney Hall, "Aspects of Japanese Economic Development," in John Whitney Hall and Richard K. Beardsley, *Twelve Doors to Japan* (New York: McGraw-Hill Book Co., 1965), pp. 538–39.

[75] Robert N. Bellah, *Tokugawa Religion. The Values of Pre-Industrial Japan* (Glencoe, Ill.: The Free Press, 1957), p. 90.

[76] Ibid., pp. 96–97.

samurai, more than any group, was responsible for the Restoration of 1868; the new Meiji government was largely formed from their ranks, and they became the leaders in new political and economic enterprises.[77] The notions about *on* and *giri* emphasized in the samurai code of conduct may have provided part of the impetus to hard work and saving in the manner of the Protestant ethic in Europe.

Everett E. Hagen has applied his theoretical approach, outlined earlier in this chapter, to the case of Japan.[78] Hagen notes that during the Tokugawa period the merchant class advanced economically but still held an inferior status. At the same time, the economic position of the *daimyo* or feudal lords was worsening, leading them to reduce their samurais' stipends. Merchants, samurai, and peasants all experienced withdrawal of status respect. According to Hagen's scheme, this should lead to retreatism, and he claims that it did, but he does not provide much evidence to support that view. Some of the developments cited under the heading "Manifestations of Retreatism" seem to be more indicative of creativity than retreatism: the development of new forms of drama, such as *kabuki,* and the new wood-block prints of scenes of everyday life. However, Hagen claims that this was a period of frivolity and dissipation. Following this "retreatism," many samurai and merchants found new meaning in Confucian and Zen Buddhist tenets and the inspiration needed for a regimen of hard work and capital accumulation.[79]

George De Vos has also applied a culture-and-personality approach to the understanding of Japanese economic development. He stresses the importance of the Japanese family, whose characteristics were discussed in Chapter 10. "This adventure in modernization was peopled by participants in government, in education, and in newly founded enterprises that were guided and organized by a quasi-religious paternalistic familism that united more than it divided into economic classes, created more harmony than dissension, more morale than alienation."[80] De Vos contrasts this familism with the "amoral familism" of the south Italian community described by Banfield.[81] The individual Japanese does not mistrust his

---

[77] Ibid., p. 45.

[78] Hagen, *On the Theory of Social Change,* chapter 14.

[79] *Ibid.,* pp. 336–43.

[80] George A. De Vos, "Achievement Orientation, Social Self-Identity, and Japanese Economic Growth," *Asian Survey,* Vol. 5 (1965) , p. 578.

[81] See above, footnote 46.

fellowman, does not feel defeated by the environment, and is not pessimistic, but sustains himself with hard work, not just for individual gain but from a sense of self-realization and devotion to family and nation. The importance of the family in relation to economic development was pointed out by Bellah, who noted that the vast majority of Tokugawa businesses were small family enterprises. "It was these small businesses with the help of electrical equipment later on, which produced the bulk of Japanese light goods, always the main export and the basis of the economy."[82]

But even in the large industrial companies which developed later, the individual employee has a somewhat familistic attitude, which is fostered by the paternalism of such companies. "The company president, in the fantasy of many Japanese, has replaced the *daimyo* or feudal lord. Individuals are still motivated by feelings of loyalty to the organization."[83] De Vos concludes that "Psychological factors contribute both in respect to achievement motivation and in respect to the effectiveness of the social organization in bringing about commonly accepted new goals."[84]

These generalizations should be considered in connection with the discussion of Japanese national character in Chapter 10.

To conclude this section on economic development and personality, it seems to me that the studies of Nigeria, the Mexican village described by Fromm and Maccoby, and the studies of India, Burma, and Japan, all provide good evidence for the importance of culture-and-personality factors in economic development.

CHINESE "POLITICAL CULTURE" AND PERSONALITY

Two works on Chinese "political culture" seek to apply a "psychocultural" approach to the understanding of recent events in China. The first, a speculative essay by Lucian W. Pye, need not be discussed at length, since the author does not supply much evidence to support his hypotheses.[85] The book will serve, however, to introduce a weightier work along similar lines by Richard H. Solomon, a professor of political science at the University of Michigan.[86] Pye

---

[82] Bellah, *Tokugawa Religion,* p. 187.

[83] De Vos, "Achievement Orientation, Social Self-Identity, and Japanese Economic Growth," p. 588.

[84] Ibid., p. 589.

[85] Lucian W. Pye, *The Spirit of Chinese Politics. A Psychocultural Study of the Authority Crisis in Political Development* (Cambridge, Mass.: The M.I.T. Press, 1968).

[86] Richard H. Solomon, *Mao's Revolution and the Chinese Political Culture* (Berkeley, Calif.: University of California Press, 1971).

and Solomon make references to each other's work and seem to have influenced one another. One of the ideas which they have in common is that the traditional Chinese socialization process strongly restricts the expression of aggression, leaving the individual with a fund of repressed hostility, which political leaders like Mao have known how to manipulate and direct in the process of attaining and maintaining political control. According to Pye, the strict Chinese restraint of aggression is related to the hierarchical nature of the Chinese family and society in general and to the stress on ritual and etiquette. Pye thinks it significant that many Chinese Communist leaders had violent confrontations with their fathers, a topic also discussed by Solomon, particularly in connection with the life history of Mao Tse-tung.

Solomon believes that the surprising developments of Mao's Cultural Revolution indicate the value of a culture-and-personality approach to an understanding of Chinese politics. Solomon has made use of traditional culture-and-personality techniques in research with Chinese refugees in Taiwan and Hong Kong, in a way reminiscent of the Harvard study of Russian national character.[87] Solomon and his associates administered a questionnaire on social attitudes and life experiences, a biographical schedule, an attitude survey, the Rorschach Test, and a modified Thematic Apperception Test. The sample of subjects interviewed was 91. Although the Rorschach Test was given, no reference to the results is made in the book; the author notes in a footnote that the Rorschach Test will be dealt with in a future publication. However, considerable use is made of the modified TAT, the nine plates of which are reproduced in the Appendix of Solomon's book. More material on the TAT and questionnaire findings appear in a separate article by Solomon.[88] The TAT drawings are of excellent quality.

The culture-and-personality sections of Solomon's work, however, are open to criticism; but before finding fault, let us first see what some of his conclusions are.

Solomon believes that to understand China's "political culture" one must have an understanding of the Chinese socialization process. The attitudes toward persons in authority formed within

---

[87] See above, pp. 218–19.

[88] Richard H. Solomon, "Mao's Effort to Reintegrate the Chinese Polity: Problems of Authority and Conflict in Chinese Social Processes," in A. Doak Barnett (ed.), *Chinese Communist Politics in Action* (Seattle, Wash.: University of Washington Press, 1969), pp. 271–361.

the family later become extended to authority figures elsewhere. Since the Chinese tend to go through the same general socialization process and share the same culture, their characteristic values and attitudes toward authority should be widely shared.

The period of infancy and early childhood is described as being one of great indulgence and oral gratification, which Solomon believes sets the stage for the frequent use of oral metaphors in Chinese conversation.[89] But a great change occurs between five and seven years of age, when the father, in particular, drops his playful indulgent manner and becomes remote, strict, and severe. This is in agreement with a study of child training made by Margery Wolf in Taiwan. According to Wolf, Chinese fathers say that you cannot be a son's friend and at the same time correct his behavior; it is necessary to be aloof and strict if you want to encourage the behavior required of an adult.[90]

A child's inquisitive, exploratory tendencies are discouraged; such activities as swimming and tree climbing are considered dangerous and are often punished. Of Solomon's interviewed subjects who gave information on childhood punishments, 79 percent recalled receiving frequent physical punishments such as beatings with boards, whips, or rulers.[91] Strict controls reinforce the dependency needs established in the happier days of infancy. The threat of isolation from the family is also used as a parental sanction. Ambivalent attitudes toward parents and other authority figures develop in such a setting. As one of Solomon's interviewees remarked, "When you saw him [his father] you would both fear him and want to get near him."[92]

At the beginning of this strict period in childhood, children often respond by throwing temper tantrums, but adults neither comfort nor scold them for this behavior, and the children eventually give it up. Henceforth there is an emphasis on reserve and emotional control.

One reason for the parents' switch from indulgence to strictness

---

[89] A Freudian essay which pursues themes very similar to Solomon's, emphasizing dependence and orality is Warner Muensterberger, "Orality and Dependence: Characteristics of Southern Chinese," in Warner Muensterberger (ed.), *Man and His Culture. Psychoanalytic Anthropology after 'Totem and Taboo'* (London: Rapp and Whiting, 1969), pp. 295–329.

[90] Margery Wolf, "Child Training and the Chinese Family," in Maurice Freedman (ed.), *Family and Kinship in Chinese Society* (Stanford, Calif.: Stanford University Press, 1970), p. 41.

[91] Solomon, *Mao's Revolution and the Chinese Political Culture*, p. 51.

[92] Ibid., p. 60.

is that they expect their children to take care of them in old age, and they do not want the child to become too self-indulgent.

Punishment for any aggression, even in self-defense, is particularly swift. One of Solomon's informants said, "We hold things in our hearts, *in our stomachs*. . . . We hold hatred in . . . ," an "oral" statement of the repression of hostility. Another remarked, *"I swallow my anger, put it in my stomach."*[93] One of Mao's techniques in political action, according to Solomon, is to try to make peasants conscious of their repressed hostility and to direct their rage against exploitation toward the enemies of the revolution. A means to that end is the *su-k'u* or "speak bitterness meeting," at which peasants are encouraged to "vomit the bitter water" of injustices suffered from the local gentry.[94]

Mao wants peasants to be active and to overcome the passivity brought about by fear of authority. Dependency must be replaced by aggressive action. We find an echo of Mao's thought in the writings of another revolutionary activist, Frantz Fanon, who viewed resort to violence as a cleansing force for the repressed masses, freeing them from despair, inaction, and the sense of inferiority. "Violence alone, violence committed by the people, violence organized and educated by its leaders, makes it possible for the masses to understand social truths and gives the key to them.[95] We have noted before that many peasant societies are characterized by apathy, passivity, and repressed hostility.[96] In line with Solomon's analysis, such societies should be amenable to revolutionary uprisings through Mao's techniques of promoting consciousness of repressed hostility.

Solomon's analysis on the whole is plausible and internally consistent, so it may seem almost pedantic to raise questions about it. The criticisms that follow concern not the conclusions but the evidence on which they are based—the interviews, questionnaires, and TATs. Since the questionnaires required literacy, Solomon's 91 subjects (all males) were all literate and mostly from middle- or upper-class families. In a footnote on page 82, Solomon tells us that the literate segment of China's population between 1600 and 1900 was

---

[93] Ibid., p. 70. Italics as in the original.

[94] A striking example of such a session is given in Solomon, *Mao's Revolution and the Chinese Political Culture*, pp. 198–99.

[95] Frantz Fanon, *The Wretched of the Earth*, Constance Farrington trans. from the French (New York: Grove Press, 1966), p. 117.

[96] See p. 52.

between 1 and 2 percent of the total. According to J. L. Buck's *Land Utilization in China* (1937), a survey of 46,601 rural families in different parts of China in the 1930s showed that 69.3 percent of the men and 98.7 percent of the women were illiterate.[97] Solomon's subjects were thus from a minority group; none of them were peasants, who formed the target of Mao's propaganda efforts, and who make up the vast majority of China's population. Solomon gives thumbnail biographies of his 91 subjects in an Appendix; it is clear from these sketches that many of these men came from wealthy families.

The TAT pictures to which the subjects responded generally show well-dressed men in Western-style clothing in middle- or upper-class settings, not farmers in rural peasant environments.

Solomon frankly admits that his subjects were not peasants, but he thinks that this does not matter, since China's traditional culture is so uniform that class and rural-urban differences have no great significance. But this is a convenient assumption, not something which can be taken for granted.

Part of Solomon's analysis of Chinese socialization has to do with the parents' expectation that they will live with their children in their old age and that their children will take care of them. This expectation assumes the existence of a joint family household consisting of grandparents, their children and grandchildren, the kind of family we are apt to think of as being characteristic of China. But even before the Communist period, the joint family was not the normal type of Chinese family. In 1946, Olga Lang presented statistics which showed that the joint family predominated only among landlords.[98] In a broad scale survey of Chinese farming families, Irene B. Taueber reported that more than 60 percent were nuclear, including only father, mother, and children.[99]

We find, then, that Solomon has made deductions about illiterate Chinese peasants' attitudes toward authority largely based upon questionnaire and TAT responses given by literate, considerably urbanized middle- and upper- class refugees, of whom about one

---

[97] Cited in Olga Lang, *Chinese Family and Society* (New Haven, Conn.: Yale University Press, 1946), pp. 72–73.

[98] Ibid., p. 137.

[99] Irene B. Taueber, "The Families of Chinese Farmers," in Freedman (ed.), *Family and Kinship in Chinese Society*, p. 81. During the present period of Communist rule, the sanctity of the joint family and the importance of the age hierarchy have been under considerable attack. The traditional joint family system is even weaker today than formerly. See C. K. Yang, *The Chinese Family in the Communist Revolution* (Boston, Mass.: The Technology Press, 1959) chap. V, "Crumbling of the Age Hierarchy."

third had formerly been associated with Chiang K'ai-shek's National-ist government.[100] The author's conclusions thus seem to rest on a shaky foundation. The only way to get around this difficulty would be to emphasize, as the author does, the uniformity of Chinese culture. "Our data reveal no significant variation in concern with social conflict or differences in conception of authority associated with socioeconomic class or educational level. Direct observations of peasant life by anthropologists support this [*sic*] data."[101]

Solomon does not at this point cite any anthropologist in par-ticular. A leading figure in this field, however, is Francis L. K. Hsu, who has the advantages of being Chinese and an anthropologist who has done fieldwork in China; moreover, Hsu's main focus of interest is culture-and-personality.[102] Some of Hsu's generalizations about the small village community which he studied in southwestern China are at variance with Solomon's picture. In various ways Hsu con-trasts the life-styles and attitudes of the rich and poor. He also makes a point which does not jibe well with Solomon's analysis: although, like Solomon, Hsu emphasizes the submissive attitude toward authority in the Chinese villager, he mentions as a second outstanding quality a strong drive for success and a competitive spirit.[103] A strong drive for success would seem to be at odds with the passive dependency depicted by Solomon. While both rich and poor are described by Hsu as being competitive, their goals are said to be different. The poor compete to keep going and to stay alive, while the rich compete to outshine others in conspicuous con-sumption and display. To reach their objectives, the poor must be frugal, the rich extravagant.[104] Thus, one would assume that TAT stories and questionnaire answers given by Solomon's refugees would reflect many differences from the protocols of poor peasants in mainland China. These considerations seem to be damaging to Solomon's thesis. It is, however, a well-done work in many ways.

REVITALIZATION MOVEMENTS

In the anthropological literature there are accounts of many kinds of religious movements, variously labeled nativistic, messianic,

---

[100] Solomon, *Mao's Revolution and the Chinese Political Culture*, p. 16.

[101] Ibid., p. 93.

[102] See above, p. 220.

[103] Francis L. K. Hsu, *Under the Ancestor's Shadow. Kinship, Personality, and Social Mobility in Village China* (Rev. ed.; New York: The Natural History Library, 1967), p. 265.

[104] Ibid., pp. 8–9, 210–12.

millennarian, or utopian movements. Examples include the Seneca Handsome Lake religion, the Ghost Dance of the Plains, and the cargo cults of Melanesia. Some writers have tried to make distinctions between different types of such movements; Ralph Linton, for example, provided a typology of "nativistic movements."[105] Anthony F. C. Wallace, however, has grouped them all under the single rubric of "revitalization movement," by which he means a deliberate concerted effort by members of a society to create a more satisfying culture. Wallace would even include the Russian Communist Revolution of 1917 under this heading. The idea of revitalization depends upon an organismic analogy; a society is compared with a living organism, as suggested by Wallace's title, *The Death and Rebirth of the Seneca.*[106] If a society is threatened by some traumatic experience, such as defeat in war or disorganization brought about by acculturation, the old way of life is disrupted. A revitalization movement may then seek to bring about a new order of things, which may also bring about changes in social character.

The key agent in such a movement is a charismatic leader who usually experiences hallucinations in which a supernatural being appears and explains what has gone wrong with the society and what should be done about it. Such a visionary experience may cause personality changes in the recipient, who now becomes a prophet, seeks converts, and launches the movement. Revitalization movements, then, are seen as responses to stress and disappointment, initially on the part of a single person, and later among other disaffected persons who rally to his cause and find satisfaction of their dependency needs in so doing.[107]

Similar analyses have been provided by David F. Aberle and Weston La Barre, among others. Aberle uses the term "relative deprivation" for the feeling among members of a traumatized group that their current lot is not as good as it used to be or might be, or not as good as that of members of some other group.[108] Weston La Barre writes that charismatic leaders come to the rescue in stress situations by providing crisis cults, "the response of society to prob-

---

[105] Ralph Linton, "Nativistic Movements," *American Anthropologist,* Vol. 45 (1943), pp. 230–40.

[106] Anthony F. C. Wallace, *The Death and Rebirth of the Seneca* (New York: Alfred A. Knopf, 1970).

[107] Anthony F. C. Wallace, "Revitalization Movements," *American Anthropologist,* Vol. 58 (1956), pp. 264–81.

[108] David F. Aberle, "A Note on Relative Deprivation Theory as Applied to Millennarian and Other Cult Movements," in Sylvia L. Thrupp (ed.), *Millennial Dreams in Action. Essays in Comparative Study,* Comparative Studies in Society and History, Supplement II (The Hague, Neth.: Mouton & Co., 1962), pp. 209–14.

lems the contemporary culture failed to solve. . . . Each religion is the Ghost Dance of a traumatized society."[109]

Thus, in the Melanesian cargo cults the natives felt a sense of relative deprivation by seeing that the whites had all kinds of fancy equipment, such as refrigerators, electric ranges, and other goods. There was no way of knowing how these things were made; they come by ship or airplane. The advantages shared by the whites must be due to some special relationship with spirits, perhaps connected with the flagpoles and marching rituals performed by the whites. Various charismatic Melanesian leaders have appeared from time to time, announcing that a cargo will soon be coming in, destined, this time, for the natives themselves. These prophetic cults have sometimes involved imitative features such as marching, drilling, and flagpole ceremonies. Sometimes the cultists have been urged to throw away their old belongings so that the new cargo will come. A cult of this kind flourished among the Manus of New Guinea and may have contributed to the rapid culture change which has occurred there.

CHILD-REARING IN AN ISRAELI KIBBUTZ

The Israeli kibbutz movement represents a remarkable effort not only to establish a progressive, collective egalitarian society but also to achieve a new kind of social character through collective child-rearing practices which involve rejection of the traditional nuclear family. According to Bruno Bettelheim, this rejection was influenced by the German *Wandervogel* (migratory bird) movement, a revolt on the part of middle-class youth against their authoritarian families and the strict German education of the early 20th century.[110] (There seems to be a parallel here to the recent development of hippie cults and the formation of communes in the United States.) In the eastern European *shtetl* communities from which the Israeli kibbutz founders migrated, the family was a particularly exclusive unit. The mother was mainly occupied with rearing and feeding her children. In describing his mother, a man from a *shtetl* expressed the ideal: "She was a perfect Jewish woman, clean, patient, hardworking, and silent, submissive to God and to her husband,

---

[109] Weston La Barre, *The Ghost Dance. Origins of Religion* (New York: Doubleday and Co., 1970), p. 44.

[110] Bruno Bettelheim, *The Children of the Dream* (New York: Avon Books, 1969), p. 35.

devoted to her children . . . her own well-being was unimportant. . . . I don't remember my mother sitting at the table when we ate, except for Friday night and Saturdays."[111] The family meal not only bound the family together but had religious functions.

In rebelling against what seemed to them a stifling ingrown family system, the kibbutz founders removed the tasks of child rearing and food preparation from the mother. In some kibbutzim (not all) children sleep with their peers from infancy on in a separate children's house. There are no family meals. Husband and wife have quarters of their own and eat with other kibbutzniks in a communal dining room, while children eat separately with their peers. Freed from the demands of cooking and child rearing, women now take part in the collective work of the kibbutz as the equals of men.

The kibbutz founders were influenced not only by the Communist teachings of Marx, but also by the doctrines of Freud. As they saw it, the ingrown family breeds mother fixation, Oedipus complex, and neurosis. These features should be obviated by collective child rearing, leading to the formation of a healthier, sturdier, and more cooperative personality.

The first kibbutz was founded in 1909. There are now over 230 settlements with a total population of nearly 100,000, the typical kibbtuz having about 500 members. The history of this collective movement has thus been quite different from those of most Utopian communal settlements, such as those of the United States, which generally lasted only a short time. The latter were aberrant islands within a larger society which regarded them with hostility or indifference, while the kibbutz in Israel is a valued, accepted institution. The kibbutz also contrasts with the collective units of the Soviet Union, in that membership is voluntary and not determined by the central government. One may leave a kibbutz if one wishes.[112]

Let us now consider some features of the collective child-rearing system, keeping in mind that not all kibbutzim have such features as separate children's houses, for some let children sleep in their parents' quarters. The picture presented here is based mainly on Rabin's report and secondarily on those by Melford E. Spiro, Gerald Caplan, and Bruno Bettelheim, each of whom has tried to assess

[111] Mark Zborowski and Elizabeth Herzog, *Life Is with People. The Culture of the Shtetl* (New York: Schocken Books 1962), p. 130.

[112] A. I. Rabin, *Growing Up in the Kibbutz* (New York: Springer Publishing Co., 1965), pp. 1–9.

how the collective child-rearing system influences the personalities of those involved in it.

After a child is born, it is taken to an infant house, where there may be five or six babies in a room. Although the child does not sleep with the mother, she breast-feeds it and for the first six weeks is always available for demand feeding during the day; about five times a day after that. She also changes diapers, carries, and plays with the child. The mother returns to part-time work after six weeks and to full-time work after four months. The child is weaned by about six months.

The nurse in charge of an infant house is called a metapelet. Between six and nine months a group of about five children is assigned a permanent metapelet who stays with the group for the next four or five years, until they enter kindergarten. She accompanies them when they move to a Toddler's House, where they stay for about three years. The metapelet is the main person involved in feeding, dressing, and toilet training the children. Parents continue to visit their children daily and put them to bed at night. Children may also visit their parents' quarters, where some toys may be kept for them.

Children leave kindergarten and enter elementary school at seven, which involves moving to a new building and acquiring a new metapelet and teacher-counselor who stay with the group until they enter the Mosad, a kind of high school, at the age of 12. There is no grading system in this school. Everyone gets promoted from one grade to the next; there are no dropouts.

The solidarity of age mates in a peer group is said to be very strong. But the kibbutz authorities also want children of different ages to interact and work with one another. Hence there is a Children's Society for grades two to six, to foster contacts between older and younger children. This takes such forms as working on a newspaper, sports, and farm work.

Between the ages of 16 and 18, young people are expected to put in about three hours of work a day for the kibbutz. This is an apprenticeship period, during which the youngsters are exposed to the various sectors of the kibbutz economy, learning shopwork, agriculture, and animal husbandry. As adolescents spend more time at these tasks, they also spend less time visiting their parents.

Equality of the sexes is the ideal. There is no separation of sexes in dormitories or showers, but there is much modesy and a somewhat puritanical attitude. Boys and girls of the same kibbutz tend to think of one another as brothers and sisters and rarely marry a member of the same kibbutz. Although there is no formal regulation about this, a kind of incest taboo or rule of group exogamy seems to have developed.[113]

The reader will remember that in Chapter 1 there was a discussion of the psychological consequences of maternal deprivation and institutionalization. There does not seem to be maternal deprivation in the kibbutz, since the child continues to see his mother daily, although he does not sleep in his parents' quarters. There also seems to be no lack of stimulation, and there is a high ratio of caretakers to children. Nevertheless, some investigators have found evidence of a relative lack of maturity among young kibbutzniks, although this is apparently counteracted and overcome at a later stage of development.

In one study Gerald Caplan reported that there was much more thumbsucking, enuresis, temper tantrums and lack of control over aggression among communally raised children below six years of age than among children of the same age reared in families. But signs of emotional disturbance generally disappeared by 10 or 11 years of age, and young adult kibbutzniks were seen to be remarkably nonneurotic.[114] On the other hand, Melford E. Spiro did not consider kibbutz adolescents to be so well adjusted; he described them as being shy, introverted, hostile, and seldom forming close friendships.[115] It should be remembered that life in a kibbutz may be hard and exacting. Before entering high school, children have six hours of classes; then, after an hour of rest, they have three hours of work; then homework and visits with parents and various social activities. The schedule becomes still more demanding in high school, with even less free time.[116] Tensions during adolescence may thus stem from current situational conditions rather than being carry-overs from early childhood frustrations.

The most detailed study of the effects of early childhood experiences on personality in the kibbutz is that of A. I. Rabin. Rabin divided his subjects into four groups: (1) infants (10–18 months),

---

[113] Ibid., pp. 10–34. See also Melford E. Spiro, "Is the Family Universal?" *American Anthropologist*, Vol. 56 (1954), p. 846.

[114] Gerald Caplan, "Clinical Observations on the Emotional Life of Children in the Communal Settlements of Israel," in Milton J. E. Senn (ed.), *Problems of Infancy and Childhood* (New York: Josiah Macy Jr. Foundation, 1954.)

[115] Melford E. Spiro, *Children of the Kibbutz* (Cambridge, Mass.: Harvard University Press, 1958), p. 424.

[116] Bettelheim, *The Children of the Dream*, p. 251.

(2) 10 years olds, (3) adolescents (17–18 years old), and (4) army young men (19–20). The subjects came from six kibbutzim. A control group was provided by a moshav or moshavim (plural). A moshav is a cooperative, primarily agricultural settlement, much like the kibbutz but with the traditional family structure unchanged. Members of both the kibbutzim and the moshavim came from similar countries of origin, had about the same educational level, and shared the same general ideals and values. Among the psychological tests given to these groups were a Mental Development Scale and a Social Maturity Scale (for the infants); Draw-a-Person (DAP), Sentence Completion, Rorschach, and Blacky Pictures (for the 10 year olds); and Thematic Apperception Test (for the adolescents and army young men, who were also given a Sentence Completion Test).

When the two infant groups (kibbutz and moshav) were tested, the moshav children were found to be superior to those of the kibbutz both in general development and social maturity. Rabin suggests that perhaps the experience of multiple mothering is frustrating to the kibbutz child, who withdraws from interpersonal relationships, which reduces identification and retards learning.[117]

Spiro has pointed out that kibbutz children are left alone at night and that the departure of parents and nurses at night may be a threatening experience for young children. This may be one source of anxiety. Another may be the fact that their caretakers are often changed.[118]

In defense of their sytem, the kibbutzim have argued that it protects the child from bad mothering. If there are many caretakers, it does not matter much if some of them do a poor job, since there will also be some good ones to make up for it, whereas a child with only one mother is at her mercy, if she is a bad mother.

Although Rabin's control group of moshav infants performed more successfully than the kibbutz children, the discrepancy between the two groups is apparently overcome by age 10. Rabin found that the intellectual development of the 10-year-old kibbutz children equaled or surpassed that of the control group. The kibbutz children were better in ego strength and overall maturity, although they showed more anxiety. There was more guilt manifest in the nonkibbutz children and more signs of Oedipal attachments. The kibbutz children showed more positive attitudes toward the family

---

[117] Rabin, *Growing Up in the Kibbutz,* pp. 66–111.
[118] Spiro, *Children of the Kibbutz,* pp. 431–33.

and less intense sibling rivalry, while the nonkibbutz children showed more indications of having long-range personal goals. Among the kibbutz children there was less clear-cut identification with a parent of the same sex and less superego development. Contrary to Spiro's impressions, however, Rabin did not find more hostility in kibbutz children than in the control group.

Apparently, judging from Caplan's and Rabin's findings, there are some negative aspects of infancy in the kibbutz child-rearing system which retard mental development and social maturity to some extent; but there are enough positive countervailing tendencies after the first year of life to overcome the initial setback. The goals of the kibbutz system seem to be furthered through their child-rearing methods, producing a personality which is in keeping with the collective social order.

RESTUDIES

We may conclude this discussion of culture, personality, and culture change, by noting that anthropologists are in a good position to study culture change through the medium of restudies. Writers such as Fromm, McClelland, and Riesman have made inferences about personality patterns in past times from historical accounts. In their ethnographic work anthropologists are able to observe such processes more directly.

The anthropologist who writes an ethnographic account is also writing history; he preserves for later generations an account of the customs and behavior of a given society at a particular moment in time. If he is a culture-and-personality researcher he also records something of what the people were like as individuals—their degree of reserve or emotionality, passivity, or aggression. From such information we may be able to understand more clearly why members of that society responded as they did when faced with alternative courses of action.

In a restudy a community which has formerly been described is visited again, either by the same ethnographer or by another.

While various purposes may be served by restudies, one is the investigation of culture change, in which the first study serves as a base line.

One example of such an investigation is Margaret Mead's restudy of Manus, which she first visited in 1928 and described in *Growing Up in New Guinea* and other publications. Twenty-five years later, in 1953, Mead returned to Manus and found this culture transformed to an almost unbelievable extent. In 1928 the Manus lived in pile dwellings in a lagoon; the women wore aprons of sago leaves, while the men had barkcloth G-strings. Today the Manus live on shore and wear Western-style clothing. In 1928 their religion involved a cult of the recently deceased family head in each household; diviners and mediums were consulted to learn the disposition of these and other spirits. This religion has been completely abandoned, and the Manus are now churchgoing Christians. Mead's description of a Sunday service sounds like something out of the Middle West, with the congregation in their Sunday best and the Manus children wearing ready-made clothes which are imported from Australia in cellophane packages.[119]

Anthropologists have often emphasized the resistance to culture change found in various parts of the world, even in cases where potential changes would bring tangible benefits to the people. Benjamin Paul's volume, *Health, Culture, and Community,* provides a number of examples of such resistance—persistent efforts to induce Peruvian villagers to boil their water have met with little success; an inexpensive medical clinic fails to attract patients in a Mexican town; and so on.[120] Since resistance of this type is such a common experience, the Manus receptivity to change is all the more remarkable.

In *Growing Up in New Guinea,* Mead provided a possible key to understanding this receptivity. She described the Manus as having a sort of Protestant ethic; the men were traders, bent on making profits and valuing hard work, thrift, and prudence. Perhaps it is not surprising, then, that the Manus were able to identify with and to emulate the American soldiers stationed in their islands during World War II. In *New Lives for Old,* however, Mead offers another kind of interpretation. She believes that the old culture implanted feelings of dissatisfaction and restlessness in the Manus child, and that new ways of living were eagerly received because of this underlying discontent.[121] Whatever the reason, the Manus seem to have had the makings of what McClelland calls an "achieving society."

Henceforth it will be possible to check on many communities in

---

[119] Margaret Mead, *New Lives for Old. Cultural Transformations—Manus—1928–1953* (New York: William Morrow & Co., 1956), p. 266.

[120] Benjamin D. Paul (ed.), with the Collaboration of Walter B. Miller *Health, Culture, and Community. Case Studies of Public Reactions to Health Programs* (New York: Russell Sage Foundation, 1955).

[121] Mead, *New Lives for Old.,* pp. 158, 365.

different parts of the world at recurrent time intervals. Since the cultures studied by anthropologists are often in the throes of sweeping culture change—or soon will be—we are now able to observe the psychological concomitants of acculturation in a variety of settings.

SUGGESTIONS FOR FURTHER READING

The writings of Fromm, Riesman, Hagen, McClelland, and Bronfenbrenner cited in this chapter are recommended. See also the collected articles in Michael McGiffert (ed.), *The Character of Americans. A Book of Readings* (Homewood, Ill.: The Dorsey Press, 1964); a revised edition issued in 1970 contains articles by Potter, Greenstein, Lipset, and Adelson cited in this chapter.

For the Indian scene, see S. C. Dube, *India's Changing Villages. Human Factors in Community Development* (Ithaca, N.Y.: Cornell University Press, 1958). *For Japan:* Richard K. Beardsley, John W. Hall, and Robert E. Ward, *Village Japan* (Chicago: University of Chicago Press, 1959).

On revitalization movements, see William A. Lessa and Evon Z. Vogt, *Reader in Comparative Religion. An Anthropological Approach* (New York: Harper and Row, 1965), pp. 499–541; Anthony F. C. Wallace, *Religion: An Anthropological View* (New York: Random House, 1966), and Peter Worsley, *The Trumpet Shall Sound: A Study of Cargo Cults in Melanesia* (London: MacGibbon and Kee, 1957).

On restudies: For some examples of restudies and a brief discussion, see Oscar Lewis, "Controls and Experiments in Field Work," in A. L. Kroeber (ed.), *Anthropology Today, An Encyclopedic Inventory* (Chicago: University of Chicago Press, 1953), pp. 466–72. Lewis is the author of one of the best known restudies, *Life in a Mexican Village: Tepoztlán Restudied* (Urbana, Ill.: University of Illinois Press, 1951) which contains culture-and-personality data, among other matters.

chapter 18

Retrospect, Prospects, Criticisms and Justifications

Culture-and-personality research was initiated with the pioneer studies of Malinowski, Benedict, and Mead discussed in Part II of this book. A clinical approach, influenced by psychoanalytic theory, was later introduced by the school of Linton, Kardiner, and Du Bois, which drew attention to the importance of early childhood experiences and the need for getting life history material and projective test data. There was a high level of confidence and enthusiasm in work along these lines in the 1940s.

The first serious criticism of culture-and-personality research came in reaction to the sweeping childhood determinist generalizations about national character made by Geoffrey Gorer and others during and shortly after World War II. It had been asserted that Japanese national character was derived from strict early toilet training; Russian national character was brought about by the swaddling of infants. Although this simplistic determinism was denied by some of its exponents, such as Gorer and Mead, the impression remained that this was, in effect, what they had stated.[1]

A critical review of childhood determinist writings in general was made by Harold Orlansky, who questioned the adequacy of the

---

[1] For disclaimers, see Geoffrey Gorer and John Rickman, *The People of Great Russia. A Psychological Study* (London: The Cresset Press, 1949), pp. 128–29; Margaret Mead, "The Swaddling Hypothesis: Its Reception," *American Anthropologist*, Vol. 56 (1954), pp. 395–409.

basic Freudian assumptions underlying such work.[2] In an article published in 1950, the field of culture-and-personality was subjected to a probing analysis by Alfred R. Lindesmith and Anselm A. Strauss. These authors did not limit their criticism to the childhood determinists, but included as well configurationists like Ruth Benedict and others. Among their criticisms were: that investigators in this field do not describe very clearly or in detail how their characterizations are arrived at; that oversimplification and selectivity are in evidence, with neglect of inconsistent data; and that while the results of projective tests are sometimes offered as confirmatory evidence, the test results are not self-explanatory but must be interpreted like other data and may, like them, be subject to bias. The critics also charged culture-and-personality researchers with a lack of attention to alternative hypotheses and cited Orlansky's criticisms of the childhood determinist school.[3]

A general commentary on culture-and-personality research appears in the 1948 edition of A. L. Kroeber's encyclopedic work, *Anthropology*. Because of the author's commanding position in his field, Kroeber's views deserve our attention. Here are some of his observations:

> It seems possible, theoretically, for two peoples to show much the same psychological character or temperament and yet to have different cultures. The reverse seems also to hold: namely, that culture can be nearly uniform while national character differs. Western Europe, for instance, has basically much the same civilization all over, yet the temperaments of its peoples are sharply distinguishable. . . . the normal or typical personalities of these several nations appear often to be more distinct than the cultures of these same nations. Or at least, to put it with less assumption, the psychologies seem in part to vary independently of the cultures.
>
> If this is correct, then recent attempts to assign each culture a strict counterpart in a "basic personality structure" or "modal personality" type go too far. There can be little doubt that some kind of personality corresponds to each kind of culture; but evidently the correspondence is not one-to-one; it is partial.[4]

Thus, by the 1950s there was some disillusionment about the field of culture-and-personality, and anthropology graduate students began to be attracted to other kinds of research, such as the renewed interest in cultural evolution engendered by Julian H. Steward and

---

[2] Harold Orlansky, "Infant Care and Personality," *Psychological Bulletin,* Vol. 46 (1949), pp. 1–48.

[3] Alfred R. Lindesmith and Anselm A. Strauss, "A Critique of Culture-Personality Writings," *American Sociological Review,* Vol. 15 (1950), pp. 587–600.

[4] A. L. Kroeber, *Anthropology* (New York: Harcourt, Brace, 1948), pp. 587–88.

Leslie A. White. There continued to be a great interest in culture-and-personality, however, as is indicated by the number of readers and texts published in the 1950s and 1960s.[5]

It seems likely that one reason why fewer anthropology graduate students have been specializing in culture-and-personality is that, as our understanding of the problems in culture-and-personality has increased, there has been a correspondingly greater reluctance to enter a field where there is so much ambiguity, where it is so difficult to demonstrate anything conclusively. A graduate student would have to think twice before committing himself to writing a doctoral dissertation on a culture-and-personality topic, when there are simpler, more manageable subjects available.

One salutory result of the criticisms and skepticism about culture-and-personality research is that those who have done work in the field since the 1950s have shown greater attention to problems of methodology, sampling, and research design than did their predecessors. This may be seen, for example, in the studies by William Caudill, Robert A. LeVine, and Robert B. Edgerton. Some of the best recent work has involved rather large-scale group enterprises with many participants: the Six Cultures project, the Harvard values project at Rimrock, the Cornell-Aro project, the Culture and Ecology in East Africa Project, and the Fromm-Maccoby study of social character in a Mexican town. All these projects have been characterized by careful planning and coordination. The vitality of these undertakings is sufficient to show that culture-and-personality is not dying or dead, as is sometimes alleged. However, there are some serious problems which researchers in the field will have to come to terms with in one way or another.

One of these is the selection of a workable model or conception of personality. Many of the early writers in culture-and-personality were influenced by Freudian psychoanalytic theory, although only a few, such as Weston La Barre and George Devereux, have been

---

[5] Clyde Kluckhohn, Henry A. Murray, and David M. Schneider (eds.), *Personality in Nature, Society, and Culture* (2d rev. ed.; New York: Alfred A. Knopf, 1953); John Honigmann, *Culture and Personality* (New York: Harper & Bros., 1954); Douglas G. Haring (ed.), *Personal Character and Cultural Milieu* (3d rev. ed.; Syracuse, N.Y.: Syracuse University Press, 1956); Francis L. K. Hsu (ed.), *Psychological Anthropology. Approaches to Culture and Personality* (Homewood, Ill.: The Dorsey Press, 1961); Bert Kaplan (ed.), *Studying Personality Cross-Culturally* (Evanston, Ill.: Row, Peterson and Co., 1961); Anthony F. C. Wallace, *Culture and Personality* (New York: Random House, 1961, 1970); Victor Barnouw, *Culture and Personality* (Homewood, Ill.: The Dorsey Press, 1963); John Honigmann, *Personality in Culture* (New York: Harper and Row, 1967).

consistent advocates and exponents of it. Like projective testing, Freudian theory continues to be assailed by academic psychologists and seems to be losing ground in psychiatry. To keep some alternatives in mind, I presented in Chapter 1 the three models of personality distinguished by Salvatore Maddi: the conflict model, the fulfillment model, and the consistency model. Reference to these alternatives has been made from time to time in this book. There would be no reason for culture-and-personality to collapse as a field of research, if one of these models should prove to be unworkable.

Related to the issue of what model of personality to accept is the question of what sort of terminology should be used by culture-and-personality researchers. The use of terms like "id" and "superego" of course implies acceptance of the Freudian scheme. But there is also the question of employing diagnostic clinical terms such as paranoid, hysteria, megalomania, and whatnot, which anthropologists have often used. If you are going to characterize the personality of an individual or group, some adjectives are necessary. But, as pointed out in Chapter 16, critics like Walter Mischel, Karl Menninger, and Thomas Szasz object to clinical classifications of individuals and the use of such terms. If the practice is of doubtful validity when applied to individuals, its application to whole groups of people should be even less justified.

If, when using clinical terms to characterize a group, an anthropologist presents a negative picture of the people he has studied (and more reports seem to stress negative rather than positive features), he opens himself to the charge of stereotyping and prejudice.[6] If the anthropologist wants to avoid such criticisms (and who would not?), he would have to write only favorable descriptions or else decide not to publish descriptions which have negative features. This dilemma could lead to the end of culture-and-personality research. The world is smaller now, literacy greater, and the writings of anthropologists are beginning to find their way back to the communities which they have described. This dilemma is further compounded by the fact that culture-and-personality research

---

[6] See, for example, the blast of criticism by Harold Hickerson against anthropologists, including the author, who have made unflattering analyses of the Chippewa or Ojibwa: Harold Hickerson, "Some Implications of the Theory of Particularity or 'Atomism' of Northern Algonkians," *Current Anthropology*, Vol. 8 (1967), pp. 313–43. For other charges of stereotyping and prejudice, see Jessie Bernard, "Sociological Mirror for Cultural Anthropologists," *American Anthropologist*, Vol. 51 (1949), p. 676; Géza Roheim, *Psychoanalysis and Anthropology. Culture, Personality, and the Unconscious* (New York: International Universities Press, 1950), p. 394; and C. W. M. Hart, "The Sons of Turimpi," *American Anthropologist*, Vol. 56 (1954), p. 260.

has been largely an American enterprise. Hardly any work in this field has been done in Europe.[7] It would thus be easy for critics to link culture-and-personality research with charges of American imperialism and prejudice. This poses a problem for anyone contemplating culture-and-personality as a field for research.

Where the use of projective tests is involved, this may also raise ethical problems. Apart from the issue of invasion of privacy, projective tests are often administered with some deceptive explanation, such as that the TAT pictures are a test of the imagination. In this connection Louise H. Kidder and Donald T. Campbell have referred to the "deceptive-deprecatory-exploitative attitude toward 'subjects'" on the part of some social psychologists, a potential danger in culture-and-personality research.[8] If some people studied by an anthropologist subsequently learn that they have been given personality tests without realizing what they were, they may very well feel resentment.

This raises the question of whether such projective tests should be used and whether the information to be gained from them is worth the deception. As noted in Chapter 13, there has been a barrage of criticism of projective techniques, and there has been a decline in their use, especially the Rorschach, in culture-and-personality research in recent years. At the same time, some of the best culture-and-personality studies, such as those of Alor and Truk, have made productive use of projective tests. Cora Du Bois' use of the Rorschach, together with ethnographic and life history material and children's drawings, with the projective tests and life histories being independently analyzed "blind" by different specialists, seemed an excellent way to get around the problem of an ethnographer's subjective impressionism. If such supplementary devices as the Rorschach Test are not used, we will have nothing against which to check the anthropologist's fallible judgments about the personalities of the people he has studied. To abandon projective testing without some substitute would take us back to the kind of early ethnographic reports by Ruth Benedict and Margaret Mead, in which everything depended on the anthropologist's observation

---

[7] Robert Heine-Geldern, "Recent Developments in Ethnological Theory in Europe," in Anthony F. C. Wallace (ed.), *Men and Cultures,* Selected Papers of the Fifth International Congress of Anthropological and Ethnological Sciences (Philadelphia: University of Pennsylvania Press, 1960), p. 51.

[8] Louise H. Kidder and Donald T. Campbell, "The Indirect Testing of Social Attitudes," in Gene F. Summers (ed.), *Attitude Measurement* (Chicago, Ill.: Rand McNally and Co., 1970), p. 334.

of behavior and interviews and on the anthropologist's deductions and intuitions from such information. There are those, like Jules Henry, who consider this method to be still the best. A person who now sets out to do research in culture-and-personality must choose between two alternatives: (1) abandon the use of projective tests, or (2) make such productive use of projective tests that criticism will be ineffectual. The second would seem to be the happier outcome, but it depends upon a gamble; success cannot be guaranteed.

It seems that, at the present time, there is some opposition to analyses of social character. This has a counterpart in clinical psychology's growing use of behavior modification therapy, in which particular isolated traits of an individual are changed through conditioning processes. No attempt is made to analyze the personality of the patient; that is not considered necessary. This movement away from diagnosis, classification, and analysis may also have some influence on anthropologists contemplating work in culture-and-personality.

Much of the work in culture-and-personality has been devoted to finding aspects of personality common to a particular group of people, as in the concepts of social character, basic personality structure, and national character. If more attention were given to individual personalities, the charge of stereotyping might be obviated. There seems to be a current tendency among some anthropologists to focus more on the individual. Both Mary Ellen Goodman and Robert B. Edgerton, for example, have emphasized the independence and autonomy of individuals at all levels of cultural development.[9]

If culture-and-personality research is so full of difficulties and open to charges of stereotyping and bias, there would have to be some very good reasons for persisting in such research. What justification, then, can it have? On behalf of culture-and-personality research, I suggest the following three main reasons:

1. As mentioned in Chapter 1, culture-and-personality research provides an alternative way of learning about human personality which can check and supplement the findings of psychology and psychiatry. The anthropologist studies man in his natural sphere of

---

[9] Mary Ellen Goodman, *The Individual and Culture* (Homewood, Ill.: The Dorsey Press, 1967) ; Robert B. Edgerton, "Anthropology, Psychiatry, and Man's Nature," in Iago Galdston (ed.) , *The Interface between Psychiatry and Anthropology* (New York: Brunner/Mazel, 1971) , pp. 28–54.

action, neither as a patient nor as the subject of a laboratory experiment.

This has been valuable in showing the great range of variation in human behavior. Such variation may be illustrated graphically to an audience by showing two films: *The Feast* about the Yanomamö Indians of southern Venezuela in South America, and *The Hunters* about the Bushman of the Kalahari Desert in South Africa. These peoples seem to differ not only in culture and social organization but also in temperament or personality. The Yanomamö think of themselves as "fierce people." "That is how they conceive themselves to be, and that is how they would like others to think of them."[10] The Kung Bushman, on the other hand, call themselves "the harmless people."[11] These contrasts in self-image, ideal type, and temperament are well reflected in the two films. Contrasts like these were documented by the pioneers in culture-and-personality research, with Ruth Benedict contrasting the Apollonian Pueblo Indians and the more Dionysian Indians of the Northwest Coast, and Margaret Mead contrasting the gentle Arapesh and the aggressive Mundugumor. It is valuable to have descriptive ethnographic accounts of the everyday lives of people in such societies and to see how personality tendencies are directed in one direction or another. Without such documentation we would have a much more limited conception of the range of possibilities in human behavior.

2. Related to the foregoing point is the consideration that culture-and-personality research contributes to an understanding of the relationship between culture and mental disorders, as discussed in Chapter 16. Anthropologists have shown that some patterns of behavior which we would consider abnormal in our society, such as trance, possession states, or transvestism, are accepted without stigma in other societies and may even be a source of prestige. This knowledge should contribute to a more relativistic and tolerant view of forms of deviant behavior to which we are often quick to assign pejorative clinical labels. Some psychiatrists such as Thomas S. Szasz, R. D. Laing, and A. Esterson, and some sociologists such as Erving Goffman and Thomas J. Scheff, have argued against the use of a medical or sickness model of mental disorders and have tried to understand the deviant's behavior in terms of the social setting in

---

[10] Napoleon A. Chagnon, *Yanomamö. The Fierce People* (New York: Holt, Rinehart, & Winston, 1968) , p. 1.

[11] Elizabeth Marshall Thomas, *The Harmless People* (New York: Alfred A. Knopf, 1959) , p. 24.

which he lives.[12] Cross-cultural research should help us to learn what factors are commonly at work in such cases. Learning to think in new ways about what it means to be "mentally ill" may be facilitated by culture-and-personality research.

3. Culture-and-personality research may contribute to an understanding of historical events, of why particular human groups responded as they did to particular challenges. We cannot make sense of history only in terms of economic and political factors, holding human nature constant.

In much historical writing one finds an economic determinism which does hold human nature constant. To give an example, here is a statement by George T. Hunt in his book *The Wars of the Iroquois:*

If Indians of other nations or institutions had lived in the country in which the Iroquois lived, they would have been subject to the same pressure of circumstance; the trade of other nations would have been desirable and even necessary to them; and they would, presumably, have taken about the same steps to obtain it as did the Iroquois. Had the position of the Hurons and the Ottawa been exchanged for that of the Iroquois, it is scarcely a mere conjecture that the Iroquois would then have used the Ottawa River highway and that the tribes living in New York would have blockaded it and attempted to destroy them.[13]

In an earlier publication, I contrasted this passage with one by Abram Kardiner: "We can assume with complete confidence that the history of the Alorese would be different from the Comanche even if both were subjected to the same external vicissitudes, because each culture is characterized by different life goals and values."[14]

I commented as follows:

It is evident that the imaginary experiment of substitution suggested by Hunt, of placing one society in the shoes of another, is an impossible one.

---

[12] Thomas S. Szasz, *The Myth of Mental Illness. Foundations of a Theory of Personal Conduct* (New York: Harper and Row, 1961); R. D. Laing and A. Esterson, *Sanity, Madness and the Family. Families of Schizophrenics* (Harmondsworth, Eng.: Penguin Books, 1969); Erving Goffman, *Asylums. Essays on the Social Situation of Mental Patients and Other Inmates* (New York: Anchor Books, Doubleday & Co., 1961); Thomas J. Scheff, *Being Mentally Ill. A Sociological Theory* (Chicago, Ill.: Aldine Publishing Co., 1966).

[13] George Hunt, *The Wars of the Iroquois* (Madison, Wis.: University of Wisconsin Press, 1940), p. 159.

[14] Abram Kardiner with the collaboration of Ralph Linton, Cora Du Bois, and James West, *The Psychological Frontiers of Society* (New York: Columbia University Press, 1945), p. 414.

No two societies having different historical traditions and patterns of culture can ever be said to be in the "same" situation, or be exposed, as Kardiner suggests, to the "same" external vicissitudes. But since the problems of group personality and history call for some sort of comparative approach, a reasonable approximation to a controlled experiment may be found in cases where two or more adjoining cultures have been affected by the same general sweep of historical events, by equivalent pressures and social dislocations.[15]

As an example, consider the adjoining Hausa, Yoruba, and Ibo tribes of Nigeria discussed earlier in Chapters 12 and 17. Although all three tribes have been affected by acculturation, the Ibo seem to have manifested the most enterprise and achievement motivation. It is clear that the three groups did not respond in the same way to the new challenges and opportunities. This suggests that human nature should not be held constant and that group differences in personality, in attitudes, values, and ethos partly determine how different peoples respond to the "same" situation.

In the Rimrock area of the Southwest, five groups live in close proximity: Spanish-Americans, Texans, Mormons, Navaho, and Zuñi. They share the same geographical environment but have different cultural traditions. As the studies discussed in Chapter 3 indicate, these groups have different value orientations. People act in terms of their dominant values, beliefs, and assumptions about reality; so the members of these five groups probably respond to the "same" situations and challenges in characteristically different ways. Hence, in order to understand how a particular group of people behave in a particular historical situation, we should have knowledge of their culture, their values and attitudes. That is why I claim that culture-and-personality research may contribute to an understanding of historical events.

In Chapter 17 we saw that different societies have shown differences in achievement motivation. Social cooperation is more easily secured in some societies than in others. There is more art, more individualism and freedom of self-expression in some societies than in others. Researchers in the field of culture-and-personality try to learn what factors bring about such differences. If it is true that character is destiny, some knowledge of the social character of a group may contribute to an understanding of its history.

This book has provided a review of accomplishments in the field

---

[15] Victor Barnouw, *Acculturation and Personality among the Wisconsin Chippewa,* Memoir No. 72, American Anthropological Association, 1950, p. 7.

of culture-and-personality, the main contributions and criticisms thereof, the advantages and drawbacks of the research methods used, and the dilemmas which confront further work in this field. We cannot predict the future of such research, but at least it can be said that something of substantial value has been accomplished so far. Within about half a century there has appeared a considerable body of literature in culture-and-personality, whose best works will surely serve as permanent contributions to man's long effort to understand himself.

index

Index